A NEW HANDBOOK
OF CHRISTIAN
THEOLOGY

P9-DHB-634

A NEW HANDBOOK OF CHRISTIAN THEOLOGY

Donald W. Musser
AND
Joseph L. Price,
EDITORS

ABINGDON PRESS
Nashville

A NEW HANDBOOK OF CHRISTIAN THEOLOGY

Copyright © 1992 by Abingdon Press

All rights reserved.
No part of this work may be reproduced or transmitted in any form or by any means, electronic or mechanical, including photocopying and recording, or by any information storage or retrieval system, except as may be expressly permitted by the 1976 Copyright Act or in writing from the publisher. Requests for permission should be addressed in writing to Abingdon Press, 201 Eighth Avenue South, Nashville, TN 37203.

This book is printed on recycled, acid-free paper.

Library of Congress Cataloging-in-Publication Data

A new handbook of Christian theology / edited by Donald W. Musser and
Joseph L. Price.
    p. cm.
  ISBN 0-687-27802-3 (alk. paper)
   1. Theology—Handbooks, manuals, etc. I. Musser, Donald W.,
1942–   . II. Price, Joseph L., 1949– .
BR95.N393 1992
230—dc20   91-44847
                                          CIP

Grateful acknowledgment is made for use of excerpts from the following:

From the Revised Standard Version of the Bible (RSV), copyright © 1946, 1952, 1971 by the Division of Christian Education of the National Council of Churches of Christ in the USA. Used by permission.

From the New Revised Standard Version of the Bible (NRSV), copyright © 1989, by the Division of Christian Education of the National Council of Churches of Christ in the United States of America. Used by permission.

From the Revised English Bible, © Oxford University Press and Cambridge University Press 1989.

MANUFACTURED IN THE UNITED STATES OF AMERICA

To
the Memory of
Our Fathers
CLARENCE W. MUSSER (1904–1983)
G. NORMAN PRICE (1912–1980)

ACKNOWLEDGMENTS

The experience of editing an earlier volume of fourteen theological essays provided us with the awareness and enthusiasm to undertake the more challenging task of co-editing the 148 articles that constitute *A New Handbook of Christian Theology*. The linchpin to bringing our project into print was the timely performance of the 137 authors who accepted our invitation to write. Our fear of the horror story that other editors had told us to expect in undertaking a project of this kind was made all but groundless by these contributors. Our deepest gratitude goes to them.

A volume of this size and complexity required the additional cooperation of a diverse body of people. We wish to acknowledge our thanks to them. Administrators at Whittier College and Stetson University provided financial support that enabled us to rendezvous on several occasions with briefcases bulging with manuscripts for editing and that prevented us from being nickeled and dimed to death with petty expenses. Ulrike Guthrie, our editor at Abingdon Press, caught the vision of our efforts and exuded dogged determination and professional efficiency to bring our book into print. Our spouses, Bonnie Price and Ruth Musser, gave us the freedom and emotional support indispensable for our project. Subtly, but most assuredly, we must recognize the continuing inspiration of the enigmatic Franz Bibfeldt, around whom our earliest scholarly collaboration buzzed while we were but would-be theologians in graduate school.

We appreciate the contribution of Stetson University by granting Don a year's sabbatical to edit the book while he was a Fellow of the Southeastern Consortium Humanities Program, partially funded by the Dana Foundation and directed by Professor Robert Detweiler at the pleasant environs of Emory University. We also express appreciation to Whittier College for providing a Faculty Research Grant to Joe, which enabled him to complete much of his editorial work.

In addition we thank a number of persons who have participated in our editorial tasks: Daniel Bell, Jr., Carl Dury, Darrell Fasching, Darcie Gaare, Brenda Halbrooks, John Hewett, Pam Hill, J. R. Hope, Martin E. Marty, Robert Olsabeck, Luis Pedraja, Elizabeth C. Pippio, James R. Price III, Tyler Shely, and D. Dixon Sutherland. Our editorial efforts are dedicated to the memories of our fathers, from whom we learned patience and perseverance, perhaps the two most essential requirements for editing a multi-authored volume of this magnitude.

PREFACE

In 1958 Marvin Halverson and Arthur A. Cohen jointly edited *A Handbook of Christian Theology,* a volume of 101 essays that has served admirably to introduce students and interested laity to a basic understanding of theological terms, concepts, and trends.

The volume went through more than twenty printings and helped four generations of students, including the co-editors and many of the contributors to the present work, to become fluent in the field. But because the cultural and religious situation has changed dramatically since the 1950s, the time has come for *A New Handbook of Christian Theology,* a compendium of 148 fresh articles to map the contours of a changed theological terrain.

The earlier *Handbook* appeared in a cultural and religious situation defined in the wake of World War II and the Korean War and in the initial gusts of the chilling winds of the cold war. Distinctly Protestant in focus, it bore the imprint of the neoorthodox (or neo-Reformation) theology and existential philosophy that characterized that era. Its bibliographies make frequent reference to the European giants of neoorthodox thought (Karl Barth, Donald and John Baillie, Emil Brunner, Rudolf Bultmann, Martin Buber, and Nicholas Berdyaev) and the progenitor of modern existentialism, Søren Kierkegaard. The voices of Roman Catholics, women, and minorities are barely audible in its pages.

More than three decades have passed since the initial publication of Cohen and Halverson's *Handbook,* and theology has entered a revolutionary period in light of a new cultural situation. Theologians now work in the wake of the knowledge of the Holocaust, which has called for reappraisal of the doctrines of God and human being and suffering; the civil rights movement, which raised issues about the theological meaning of economics and justice and led to black theology; the Vietnam War, which brought fresh thought about peace and idolatry; the Second Vatican Council, which engaged Roman Catholicism with modern thought; the dialogue between the principal religious traditions in the world, which made pluralism a household word; the rise of feminism, which engendered alternative readings of the Bible and the history of doctrine and has led to proposals to rethink radically the content of the principal doctrines; and ecological threats to the future of the planet, which brought issues about science into the mainstream of theology. Classic theological topics in method and ethics boldly came to the forefront; new subjects such as the liberation theologies burst into view.

Although Catholic and Protestant theologians now collaborate more than ever because of the influence of the ecumenical movement, theology today claims no established method, no unified doctrine of revelation, and no common approach to appropriate the history of theology. Consequently, theologies have proliferated in a cultural situation dominated by multiple emphases and cascading streams of thought, each of the new theological movements often having a unique method and focus that lead to content that has new contours. For example, *A New Handbook of Christian Theology* contains articles on theologies that have been born since the 1950s; namely, black, confessional, death of God, deconstructionist, feminist, liberation, marxist, narrative, political, postmodern, process, and womanist theologies.

Theologians, students, and laity respond variously to the present theological situation. Some dive deeply into one of the new methodologies and become immersed in radically venturous thought. Others, more conservative in nature, retain allegiance to older approaches, attempting to reform and refine established paradigms of theological thought. Still others, who become more like spectators than participants, view the situation as a revolution in theology that awaits the outcome of the debate and the rise of new, normative approaches. Another group, hearing a cacophony of dissident voices, retreats from theological reflection altogether in anger or despair.

Believing that the present theological situation is diffuse (because no globally recognized figures or methods dominate) but not chaotic (because clearly defined theological options and promising thinkers are emerging), we have included a pluralism of perspectives in selecting topics and authors. A faint outline of a vaguely defined theological future gestates within the essays in this volume.

We initiated conversations about editing *A New Handbook of Christian Theology* in 1987. First, we determined to include only articles on subjects of current interest, not articles of strictly historical significance. We culled possible topics from the initial *Handbook,* other reference works, but most significantly from our joint understanding of today's theology. Early on, we recognized that we are not only describing the field; in some sense we are defining the field. We therefore proceeded cautiously and in collaboration with other scholars in the subfields of theology to chart the relevant theological topics that represent the variegated terrain of Christian theological studies. In the several years that we have worked on the project, we have added a couple of topics to our original list (Space and Womanist Theology, for example) because the emerging and communal character of Christian theology has continued to touch new concerns, express new voices, and inspire new visions.

Because we perceived the current theological scene not to be dominated by any one powerful movement or dominant voice, we ranged across the theological spectrum and the globe to pinpoint writers appropriate for our topics. In some cases we chose established experts with a magisterial command of a topic; in others we tapped younger scholars whose work is known so far only in the proceedings of the theological professional societies and articles tucked away in journals, but whom we judged to have promising futures. Only four of the authors of articles in the earlier *Handbook,* all of whom were just starting their careers at the time, have been retained to write for *A New Handbook of Christian Theology*. Fresh voices, including those of women and minorities, are heard in these pages. The authors represent diverse geographical regions and assorted confessional traditions; in fact, some stand outside any explicit version of the Christian tradition. Our aim is to present a set of perspectives that adequately and comprehensively records the situation in theology at the end of the twentieth century.

Donald W. Musser
Joseph L. Price
June 1991

ROUTES FOR READING

Biblical Theology—Authority, Biblical Criticism, Biblical Theology, Canon, Christology, Covenant, Death and Eternal Life, God, Holy Spirit, Inerrancy, Inspiration, Kingdom of God, Miracles, Resurrection, Soul/Body, Structuralism

Christ—Atonement, Christology, God, Incarnation, Kingdom of God, Soteriology, Trinity

Churches—Confessional Theology, Eastern Orthodox Christianity, Ecclesiology, Ecumenism, Evangelicalism, Missiology, Pentecostalism, Pluralism, Protestantism, Roman Catholicism, Tradition, Vatican II

Conservative Protestantism—Creation Science, Dispensationalism, Evangelicalism, Fundamentalism, Inerrancy, Pentecostalism, Protestantism

Human Being—Alienation, Ambiguity, Anthropology, Autonomy, Freedom, God, Health, Humanism, Imagination, Sanctification, Secularity, Sexuality, Sin, Soul/Body, Suffering

Liberation Theologies—Basic Christian Communities, Black Theology, CELAM II, Economics, Feminist Theology, Liberation Theology, Marxist Theology, Praxis, Womanist Theology

Philosophical Theology—Agnosticism, Alienation, Apologetics, Atheism, Being/Becoming, Cosmology, Deconstructionism, Epistemology, Evil, Existential Philosophy, Heresy, Language–Religious, Metaphysics, Miracles, Mysticism, Natural Theology, Panentheism, Paradox, Phenomenology, Philosophical Theology, Postmodern Theology, Space, Theism, Time, Transcendence

Religion—Civil Religion, Experience–Religious, Faith, Pluralism, Popular Religion, Religion

Roman Catholicism—CELAM II, Celibacy, Insight, Moral Theology, Papacy, Priesthood, Roman Catholicism, Vatican II

Systematic Theology—Anthropology, Atonement, Christology, Creation, Death and Eternal Life, Dogmatic Theology, Ecclesiology, Election, Eschatology, Evil, Faith, God, Grace, Holy Spirit, Incarnation, Justification, Providence, Resurrection, Revelation, Sanctification, Sin, Soteriology, Systematic Theology, Trinity

Theological Ethics—Ecology, Ethics–Christian, Freedom, Holocaust, Hope, Idolatry, Justice, Love, Moral Theology, Peace/Peacemaking, Sexuality, Social Gospel, Society, Space, Virtue

Theological Method—Authority, Correlation, Deconstructionism, Experience–Religious, Hermeneutics, Language–Religious, Paradigm, Postmodern Theology, Revelation, Structuralism, Theological Method

Theological Movements—Black Theology, Death of God Theology, Dispensationalism, Empirical Theology, Feminist Theology, The Hartford Appeal, Liberalism, Liberation Theology, Marxist Theology, Narrative Theology, Neoorthodoxy, Political Theology, Postmodern Theology, Process Theology, Social Gospel, Womanist Theology

Theology and the Arts—Aesthetics, Comedy, Culture, Hermeneutics, Imagination, Metaphor, Myth, Narrative Theology, Symbol, Tragedy

Theology and the Natural Sciences—Cosmology, Creation, Creation Science, Ecology, Miracles, Naturalism, Science and Christianity, Space, Technology, Time

Theology and the Social Sciences—Civil Religion, Economics, Liminality, Marxist Theology, Political Theology, Practical Theology, Praxis, Science and Christianity, Society

Worship—Homiletics, Laity, Liturgical Movement, Ordination, Priesthood, Ritual, Sacraments/Sacramental Theology, Silence, Worship

A NEW HANDBOOK
OF CHRISTIAN
THEOLOGY

AESTHETICS

Seldom do concerns that we think of as aesthetic occupy the center of attention in Christian life and thought. Whereas one can talk about the ethics of Jesus or the eschatology of Paul, one cannot sensibly talk about Jesus' aesthetics or Paul's theory of taste. Although Christian theologians have reflected on beauty as well as on goodness, truth, and holiness, it is in fact beauty that they have most often slighted. The church, for its part, has made extensive use of the arts without making any consistent effort to understand what is distinctive about artistic contributions to worship and the Christian life.

It would nevertheless be a mistake to assume that aesthetics must be inconsequential for Christian piety and theology simply because aesthetic factors often receive minimal attention in themselves. Liturgies invariably reflect (for good or ill) the exercise of aesthetic as well as theological judgment. Furthermore, as Hans Urs von Balthasar has shown, aesthetic categories such as beauty, harmony, integrity, and radiance of form are employed again and again in theological interpretations of Christian doctrines. Indeed a number of Christian thinkers today believe that aesthetic theory can contribute significantly to a theological understanding both of Christian faith in its multiple dimensions and of culture as a whole.

One's conception of the relevance of aesthetics to theology depends, however, on one's conception of aesthetics in general. It was not until the eighteenth century that the term "aesthetics" gained currency. Coined by Alexander Baumgarten (who had in mind the Greek *aisthetika,* meaning "perceptibles"), the word was picked up by Kant, who both modified its meaning and gave the term wider circulation. Although aesthetics was initially tied to the notion of a science of sensory knowledge and taste, it soon came to be understood more broadly as theoretical reflection on matters pertaining to the arts, beauty, and whatever else attracts attention by virtue of formal, sensory, and expressive qualities.

Aesthetics borders on a number of other fields, into which it regularly crosses. When aesthetics aims to shed light on traits evident in specific works of art, it contributes to practical criticism. When it focuses on features of a given art form such as literature or painting, it merges with such disciplines as literary theory and art theory. When it concentrates on questions of representation, meaning, structure, and interpretation, it converges with hermeneutics, linguistics, and semiotics. Studies of relationships between taste and class establish links between aesthetics and sociology. Inquiries into conditions of creativity, expression, and response join aesthetics with psychology. Aesthetic analyses of gesture and stylized action are pertinent to ritual studies and liturgics, while attempts to discern the moral import of artworks are obviously tied in with ethics. Studies that contemplate the ways in which artworks and other aesthetic phenomena can embody insight or reveal truth are allied with epistemology, often via theories of metaphor, symbol, and narrative. Finally, when thinkers try to discover how aesthetic factors play a role in relationships between self, others, world, and God, aesthetics becomes explicitly theological.

Regardless of these cross-disciplinary connections, modern theorists (as contrasted with postmodern ones) have by and large emphasized that aesthetics proper has a realm to itself. Pure beauty, they have affirmed, is valued simply for its own sake. Formalist theories of the sort embraced by certain "New Critics" in the mid–twentieth century go so far as to argue that genuinely aesthetic perception and judgment exclude moral, religious, pragmatic, and cognitive considerations. The "aesthetic attitude," formalism claims, is attentive to sensory and formal qualities alone. An aesthetic response to the Parthenon will delight in its harmony, symmetry, and grace while ignoring its religious and political associations. Correspondingly, a poem or a painting allegedly represents, in the end, nothing so much as itself.

The purism of such an approach to aesthetics has been shared even by some theorists who regard expression or meaning rather than form per se as central to aesthetics. According to theorists such as Benedetto Croce, R. G. Collingwood, and Susanne Langer, feelings and intuitions expressed or symbolized aesthetically are quite different in kind from the desires, commitments, ideas, and understandings vital to theology and ethics. While aesthetic expressions or meanings may form a preconceptual basis for non-aesthetic ideas and acts, they have no direct commerce with the larger concerns of religion and life. Even a thinker like Nelson Goodman, who speaks of world-making as a principal function of art, thinks of the worlds of art as quite distinct from worlds made and inhabited by other means.

Such purist theorizing, though recently challenged, has in various guises been prevalent in aesthetics since the time of Kant (though influenced by only one side of Kant's own complex aesthetics). While purism supports the important insight that aesthetics cannot be reduced to something else—whether science or religion or morality—it fails to do justice to the equally important insight that aesthetic response normally affects and reflects ideas and feelings that are not immediately aesthetic and that may in fact be religious and moral. Purism is powerless to account for the fact that if we were to exclude all "non-aesthetic" awareness from our experience of Mt. Fuji or of Tolstoy's "The Death of Ivan Ilych" or of Rembrandt's *The Return of the Prodigal Son,* we would find these things much less impressive even aesthetically. At the same time, purism fails to explain why religious, civic, and personal life is so deeply indebted to aesthetic media: songs, stories, celebrations, monuments, pictures. Thus the dominant varieties of modern aesthetics largely treat as irrelevant the actual uses and enjoyments of aesthetic objects, including their function in religious life.

Because of this inadequacy in mainstream modernist aesthetics, rival theories have now appeared that argue in favor of "anti-aesthetics," "paraesthetics," or "neo-aesthetics." Whether or not they choose to label themselves "postmodern,'' all of these theories attempt to rethink (and in some cases to discard) the sharp modernist distinction between aesthetic and non-aesthetic, between judgments of taste and judgments of other kinds—social, moral, intellectual. Thus the newer theories emphasize the intrinsic impurity of aesthetic production and response. Uncovering the often intricate and hidden ways in which aesthetic acts and artifacts function within cultural systems, they show how artistic judgments and products can either underwrite or undercut values associated with class, gender, race, and religion. Simultaneously, many recent theories call attention to the fictive element in all our images of self, society, and reality. They depict the arts as conspicuous examples of modes of imagination, fabrication, figuration, and emplotment that are at work in virtually every sphere of life and thought, from the activity of dreaming to the writing of history.

Various emphases and possibilities within modern and postmodern philosophical aesthetics extend into the theological sphere. In the first place it can be said that even formalist aesthetics, which reacts partly against the perennial impulse to impose religious and moral criteria onto aesthetic creation and evaluation, is nonetheless compatible with some kinds of theological aesthetics. Since beauty has over the centuries been taken to be one of the transcendental names of God, a beautiful sensuous form per se can be looked on as at once intrinsically good and a shadow or imprint of divinity. Even Kant declares that the beautiful, precisely as a good in itself, is a symbol of the morally good. Analogously, Karl Barth sees the beautiful as a symbol of the religiously good. The music of Mozart in particular seems to him to constitute a perfect world unto itself—harmoniously ordered, blessedly comic, and hence also a veritable parable of the kingdom of God. Again, Hans Küng has observed that the intrinsic aesthetic rightness of an artistic landscape provides a foretaste of eschatological fulfillment. In a related vein Nicholas Wolterstorff has argued that aesthetic delight is part of the *shalom,* or peaceable flourishing, that faith looks for in seeking the kingdom of God. In the same spirit liberation theologians such as Dorothee Soelle maintain that a desirable social order necessarily includes the freedom of aesthetic creation and the joy of aesthetic response, which are part of knowing and loving God.

The idea that beauty has a kind of divine right to exist has in point of fact been held by Christian thinkers as diverse as Augustine, Pseudo-Dionysius, Jonathan Edwards, and Étienne Gilson. In this regard what is innovative about postmodern theologies is the degree to which the beauty they celebrate is of a kind that is perceptible to the senses. Whereas the whole neo-Platonic tradition within Christian thought has viewed our delight in sensory beauty as but an inferior though necessary step toward appreciating the higher realm of intellectual and spiritual beauty, the tendency in postmodern theology is to interpret the doctrines of creation and Incarnation as affirming the holy communion of the spiritual and the material.

In view of the relative autonomy and freedom of aesthetic creation, modern and postmodern theologians often look on aesthetic creativity as an important feature of humanity's having been made in the image of God. Jacques Maritain, for example, holds that creative intuition and production continues in its fashion the work of divine creation. And Nicholas Berdyaev stresses how the artist exercises freedom in such a way as to go beyond all mere imitation to strive after beauty that is as yet unseen, and unforeseen even by God.

Related to theologies of beauty and creativity are theologies of artistic expression and revelation. For instance, the influential theology of culture devised by Paul Tillich finds implicit religious significance even in art that is overtly secular. According to Tillich, works such as Picasso's *Guernica* can express, through tensions that shatter complacency, a radical concern for what is ultimate—for the inexhaustible ground of being and meaningful existence, which traditionally is called God. Theologians influenced by Heidegger and Gadamer likewise look to art and poetry as a special unveiling (and mysterious concealing) of otherwise inarticulate truth. Alternatively, they may view art as potentially sacramental in its sensuous embodiment of what transcends intellectual sense.

More recently, theologians of art have come to see that some art is much more ironic or genuinely playful than is suggested by talk of ultimate concern, revelation, and truth. Moreover, even in the creation and experience of art at its most serious level, it seems possible that selves and communities are typically rather fragmented and unstable, characterized as much by penultimate concerns as by a concern for what is ultimate. Particularly when theologians are attentive to deconstructionist ideas, they may suspect that art can be errant and incoherent in ways far more subtle and pervasive than thinkers since the time of Plato have recognized (or feared). Do beauty and unity really encompass the goals and effects of art? Is the self really capable of integrity? Is religion? In raising such questions, theological aesthetics has begun to take more extensive account of formal fragmentation and expressive negation in both art and religion. For some theologians this also means taking seriously the possibility of a tragic or at least tragicomic theology for which redemption is literally incomprehensible (though perhaps still affirmable).

There is, in any event, a growing theological recognition that aesthetic experience and insight—whether positive or negative—cannot fully be absorbed or contained in the medium of theological concepts. That is to say, the meaning and insight embodied in (or evoked by) artistic expressions and representations are never entirely separable from the style and medium of expression. Art does not merely mirror. It reconfigures and reconstructs in ways not strictly replicated by other modes of making and meaning.

Yet, as theologians have realized more and more, the language of art (in the broadest sense) is native to religion and so requires theological attention. Christian ideas and practices are unavoidably rooted in aesthetically rich forms: myth, metaphor, parable, song, ritual, image, edifice. With regard to scriptures, moreover, it is now clearer than ever that literary strategies are intrinsic to the biblical texts and their religious import.

Biblical scholars today thus join forces with scholars of religion and literature, who for some decades have argued that religious reflection depends on the artistic cultivation of language and imagination, just as literary art in turn taps religious experience and thought. Meanwhile, scholars in related areas have taken pains to demonstrate the religious involvements of such arts as drama, dance, music, painting, architecture, and film.

Because many such inquiries have dealt with modern culture, they have been able to show that in our own time religious questions and affirmations continue to be interwoven in, and reinterpreted by, the work of artists—from Stravinsky and Messiaen to Philip Glass and Arvo Pärt; from Kandinski and Mondrian to Barnett Newman and Anselm Kiefer; from T. S. Eliot and W. H. Auden to Walker Percy and Alice Walker. Furthermore, several interpreters of art and religion have analyzed popular film and television, detecting a resurgence and reshaping of religious themes, whether in horror movies, science fiction, or more realistic genres. Thus on many levels one observes the continuing interanimation of art and religion, or aesthetics and theology.

What all of this suggests is not, of course, that everything aesthetic is especially religious or that everything religious is especially aesthetic. It suggests, rather, that religion lives and thrives partly by means of aesthetic forms and that any reflection on Christian belief and practice in particular must therefore take aesthetic media into consideration. Such is the testimony, certainly, of Hans Urs von Balthasar's multi-volume work *The Glory of the Lord: A Theological Aesthetics,* and it is a basic assumption of most theologians now engaged in aesthetics.

It may be that aesthetics as a theological enterprise has just begun to come into its own. It seems probable that theologians will increasingly care about the constructive and subversive powers of artistry, about popular arts as well as elite, about styles of life and thought as well as styles of art, about the role of "tastes" in the formation and evaluation of religious identities and differences, and about the aesthetic values of the natural world as well as those of human culture. Finally, with the renewal of studies in spirituality, theology is likely to ponder anew the ways in which aesthetic disciplines and sensitivities contribute to spiritual life and an awareness of God.

FRANK BURCH BROWN

Bibliography

Hans Urs von Balthasar, *The Glory of the Lord: A Theological Aesthetics.*
Frank Burch Brown, *Religious Aesthetics: A Theological Study of Making and Meaning.*

21

Gerardus van der Leeuw, *Sacred and Profane Beauty: The Holy in Art.*
James Alfred Martin, Jr., *Beauty and Holiness: The Dialogue Between Aesthetics and Religion.*
Nicholas Wolterstorff, *Art in Action: Toward a Christian Aesthetic.*

Cross Reference: Comedy, Culture, Deconstructionism, Humanism, Imagination, Language–Religious, Ritual, Spirituality, Tragedy, Transcendence.

AGNOSTICISM

Agnosticism is the intellectual disinclination to assert or deny truth claims without compelling evidence. More narrowly defined, it is the disinclination to assert or deny statements regarding the existence and nature of God. The adoption of agnosticism as a general intellectual orientation is motivated by the conviction that there is insufficient evidence for steadfast cognitive commitments. Like philosophical skepticism, agnosticism is less a doctrine than a refusal to be doctrinaire. As regards the existence of God, agnosticism is the position that shuns both the theistic claim that God exists and the atheistic claim that there is no God.

The word 'agnosticism' was coined in 1869 by the English biologist Thomas Henry Huxley. A staunch defender of Darwinism, Huxley made agnosticism central to his conception of scientific rationality. In an 1889 essay, ''Agnosticism and Christianity,'' he wrote: ''It is wrong for a man to say he is certain of the objective truth of a proposition unless he can produce evidence which logically justifies that certainty. This is what agnosticism asserts and, in my opinion, is all that is essential to agnosticism.'' Clearly Huxley's conception of agnosticism was of the broader sort, because he identified it closely with a general prescription governing rational beliefs; this maxim is now commonly called 'the evidentialist principle' and is associated especially with the empiricist philosophy of John Locke. Huxley inferred from his prescription that belief in God's existence is not rationally assertible. Another Darwinian, Herbert Spencer, expressly associated agnosticism with the unknowability of basic facts about God.

The Greek root of 'agnosticism' may mean either ''unknown'' or ''unknowable.'' Similarly, an agnostic may admit to lacking knowledge about God because he or she has, in fact, failed to secure such knowledge or because he or she is convinced that, in principle, this sort of knowledge is not attainable by even the most persistent and proficient human inquirer. Protagoras and David Hume were philosophers who exemplified a sort of ironic humility toward theological matters, while Plato and Immanuel Kant confessed to a principled nescience about God's nature and existence. Kant argued that belief in God arises as a postulate of practical reason rather than from a proof of theoretical reason. The wide influence of his view made agnosticism an ironic and polite form of atheism that led some philosophers to accentuate the immanent character of God and prompted some theologians to acknowledge the confessional character of faith.

Broader social forces also have effected the diminished prominence of agnosticism as a category for describing basic beliefs about the world. Secularism, as the social legitimation of nonreligious values and behaviors, makes unqualified atheism less shocking, while at the same time making systematic indifference to religion more feasible. Also, historicism, as the acknowledgment that one's beliefs are historically conditioned—often in unconscious ways—makes a professed suspension of judgment regarding religious matters less credible. Thus in its specific meaning as disbelief in God based on methodological grounds, agnosticism has lost its original status as a prime alternative to theism or atheism. It may just as easily be understood today as a critical moment within theism or as an undisguised adjunct to atheism.

In the sense that nineteenth-century agnostics not only eschewed belief in God but likewise eschewed theism and atheism as classical doctrines regarding God, they presaged twentieth-century thinkers who are not convinced of the value or necessity of foundational discussions about God's existence and nature. Having rejected philosophy's function of arbitrating between competing truth claims, Richard Rorty practices a more conversational variety of philosophy and feels no obligation or inclination to continue traditional theological disputations. Upon the assumption that beliefs are epistemologically innocent until proven guilty, Alvin Plantinga says that God's existence is in no greater need of demonstration than the existence of other minds or past historical events. Among theologians, Karl Barth excluded epistemological concerns from the task of theology, and Gustavo Gutiérrez has urged theologians to reorient their attention from nonbelievers to the poor and oppressed. Many philosophers and theologians no longer consider agnosticism itself an important topic of discussion.

PETER VAN NESS

Bibliography

R. A. Armstrong, *Agnosticism and Theism in the Nineteenth Century.*
David Hume, *An Enquiry Concerning Human Understanding.*
Thomas H. Huxley, *Collected Essays: Volume V: Science and Christian Tradition.*
Herbert Spencer, *First Principles,* 1862; 6th ed.

Cross Reference: Atheism, Theism.

ALIENATION

Alienation is one of the virtually undefinable terms that distinguishes the spirit of its time. Two distinctions, however, help to establish clarity from the chaos of its various uses. The first distinction emerges out of the contrast between alienation and estrangement. Works like Dostoevski's *Notes from the Underground* or Camus's *The Stranger* have engraved the image of the modern anti-hero in current thought. Out of the dark and irrational depths of the anti-hero arises estrangement from the self and the loss of a worldly anchorage. Although the individual experience of alienation may be as profoundly irrational as that of estrangement, alienation more properly derives from a social malformation.

Second, alienation is not adequately defined as a secularized version of the concept of sin. More adequately, it is understood as a strikingly modern way of defining evil as it infects the entire social order. As such, it inevitably has religious implications. Alienation takes its place beside the concepts of shame and guilt as an alternative expression of the way a society experiences and symbolizes evil.

Although the term in its verb form is of Latin origin and has been used since ancient times, G. W. F. Hegel established the paradigm for the modern understanding of alienation in his *Phenomenology of the Spirit*. Hegel presents alienation as a necessary and recurrent moment in the self-realization of both finite and Absolute spirit. Freedom is empty self-assertion unless it embodies itself in the objective structures of reality. Yet initially the self confronts the world as something that stands over against it. Alienation derives from the inability of self-conscious, self-determining realities to find themselves reflected in the objective structures of the historical world. The *Phenomenology* traces the stages of the becoming of Absolute spirit through the human struggle to achieve freedom in the mutual recognition of self and other.

At least five traits are common to virtually all theories of alienation after Hegel:

1. Alienation is a product of history. All theories assume that alienation takes many forms and that each form is rooted in its historical setting. These malformations are a product of human action and can, therefore, be transformed. Theories of alienation are always accompanied by a theory of liberation that overcomes alienation.

2. Alienation is the antithesis to self-determination. A theory of alienation and liberation presupposes some vision of the truly human. Given the historical character of alienation, these visions commonly stress agency and self-determination as central to human life. The substance of our vision of the truly human is, therefore, historically relative. Numerous African American and feminist theologians, in particular, have insisted upon the situated character of all theological reflection.

3. Alienation is a systemic, structural deformation of the social world. Evil is present not as a social problem that can be compartmentalized but as a malignancy of the whole. To devise a systemic theory of alienation the theologian draws upon some critical social theory. Various theories trace the genesis of alienation to a single root, such as racism, sexism, or classism. Others reject monocausal theories as unhistorical and inadequate to the complexity of evil. These theories examine what Rosemary Ruether calls the "interstructuring" of different forms of alienation. Cornel West, among others, argues that theologians must devise criteria, including theological criteria, for selecting an adequate social theory.

4. *Alienation manifests itself in some form of false consciousness.* Marx's famous criticism of religion in his *Critique of Hegel's Philosophy of Right* stressed the role of self-deception in the loss of self that occurs in an alienated condition. For Karl Marx, religious ideas were the quintessential expression of false consciousness, the flowers entwined in the economic and political chains that imprison us. Subsequent to Marx, Walter Rauschenbusch, Reinhold Niebuhr, and Paul Tillich stressed a similar theme in their theories of the idealization of evil, pretentiousness, and the demonic. Current thinkers argue that theology must devise a critique of ideology if it is to respond to alienation effectively.

5. *A theory of alienation implies critical reflection on praxis.* The immediate followers of Hegel, the "Young Hegelians" who included Ludwig Feuerbach and Marx, did add one important element to the modern concept of alienation. They took Hegel's concept and transformed it into a theory of the crisis of the age designed to alter the course of history. A theory of alienation became critical reflection on praxis, that is, a model composed of the above four elements that discerns within the present crisis the possibilities for world-transforming action.

Like any paradigm of evil, the concept of alienation and liberation has its limits. Theories of alienation tend to obscure issues of personal guilt and traditional questions of theodicy. According to thinkers like Hannah Arendt, the concept of freedom as creation of and participation in a constitutional order is clouded in the close linkage of alienation and liberation. Yet these concepts, developed in a multitude of competing models, remain an indispensable vantage point for addressing modern embodiments of evil.

CHARLES R. STRAIN

Bibliography

Gregory Baum, *Religion and Alienation.*

Rosemary Radford Ruether, *New Woman/New Earth: Sexist Ideologies and Human Liberation.*

Richard Schacht, *Alienation.*

Charles R. Strain, "Ideology and Alienation: Theses on the Interpretation and Evaluation of Theologies of Liberation," *Journal of the American Academy of Religion* 45 (1977): 473-90.

Cornel West, *Prophesy Deliverance: An Afro-American Revolutionary Christianity.*

Cross Reference: Autonomy, Black Theology, Evil, Feminist Theology, Liberation Theology, Marxist Theology, Sin.

ALLEGORY (*See* HERMENEUTICS, METAPHOR.)

AMBIGUITY

Ambiguity is a general term that expresses the irreducible pluralism and uneven change in the world, especially as these affect theology. Experience in the modern world can be one of bewildering complexity and a baffling encounter with multiple values and points of view. This aspect of experience produces diverse interpretations that resist human simplification. The experience of change often has unforeseen effects: having to choose among imperfect courses, having to accept the consequences of decision, experiencing competing interests, and facing explanations that yield different interpretations.

Absolute ethical norms and unambiguous truth claims are elusive. For example, the concepts of "good" and "bad" are relative terms because the same thing, event, or person may be simultaneously good for some and bad for others, or good in some respects and bad in others to the same persons at the same time, or may change in character as good or evil over time. Apparently unambiguous truths are also relative over time. Change, diversity, and polyvalence characterize experience, although experience also includes times of stability, continuity, and consensus. Such an ambiguous world is capable of many value systems and multiple interpretations at any one time or through time.

Order is necessary in the world, but it is achieved temporarily, and it is never discovered as the world's underlying characteristic, because change overturns all attempts at finality of order. This world is not chaotic in the sense of lacking all order, but it is continually changing because it is "orderable" rather than ordered, capable of being shaped and reshaped by whatever or whoever can make a difference. Thus, cyclones may reorder part of the world physically, or military dictators may reorder it socially. Even then, further change is always a possibility.

The ambiguity that is true of every feature of experience is also true for religion in general and Christianity in particular. Every religion has had varieties of interpretations of its fundamental beliefs, texts, and practices. Christian theology throughout history has used a variety of philosophical systems in order to interpret the biblical revelation in changing cultural circumstances. Change and diversity in Christian theology can be seen in the earliest texts, for example in the different portrayals of Jesus in the Four Gospels. Yet, theologians have been resistant to acknowledge the existence of ambiguity. In the first account of creation in Genesis, God is described as bringing about order and calling that order "good." Order has therefore been closely identified with God, and change and diversity have been interpreted as disorder, which is consequently understood as destructive and impious. Moreover, the platonic philosophy that influenced early Christian theology supported the notion of one unchanging truth. Therefore, unwelcome changes in belief were labeled heresy.

Theologians not only resisted ambiguity caused by change, they also denied

26

diversity. Vincent of Lerins in the fifth century propounded the Vincentian canon, which became an orthodox maxim for the Catholic faith: The church proclaimed what has been believed everywhere, always, and by everyone. It is difficult today to see what *content* that canon could hold when one observes the multiple understandings of God and Jesus Christ through the centuries. Another unambiguous emphasis, moreover, remains embedded in some theology: God has given one true order to the world, however much the world has been disrupted by sin. This oversimplified understanding is still visible, for instance, in theological accounts of biological evolution. When evolution was finally accepted by many churches, after widespread attempts at rejection, it was interpreted as God's manner of creating in an orderly way over a long period of time. Theology has scarcely acknowledged the existence of evolutionary dead ends or the impact of climatic change, both of which challenge the notion of an orderly creative process.

One way to give theological value to ambiguity is to believe that what God freely gave (and continues to give) creation is the possibility to act freely rather than a world already ordered. Whatever results from our actions is ultimately a response to the divine gift, although at the same time it is a finite and contingent becoming. Thus through evolution and history the possibilities giving rise to the continuing orderability of the world have been actualized, changed, and refashioned in multiple ways, producing the ambiguity described above.

In terms of chaos theory, God-given possibility gives an instability to any status quo such that new orderings are possible. But if God's only action were granting the free use of possibility, there would be nothing to create belief in divine love. To include divine love one must affirm divine creation in freedom and God's loving companionship through the ambiguity of the world. If God had created order, there would be nothing more relational to do than to monitor its working; but if God has given possibility, then God is involved in all the processes of actualization—encouraging, provoking, confronting, comforting. If God's action is characterized by freedom and love (and the same may be said of Jesus Christ), then the freedom given to reflective humanity carries with it the responsibility of using that freedom with love, even within and among the ambiguities of the world.

Ambiguity is a concept of the first importance. Nothing escapes the problems and possibilities of a diverse and changing world. Therefore, theologians who take the concept seriously find that it implies fundamental changes to the content of theology and to the claims made for theology. Everything has to be rethought to incorporate the changed perception of how the world is.

RUTH PAGE

Bibliography

Ruth Page, *Ambiguity and the Presence of God.*
I. Prigogine and I. Stengers, *Order Out of Chaos.*

27

Stewart R. Sutherland, *Faith and Ambiguity*.
David Tracy, *Plurality and Ambiguity*.

Cross Reference: Experience–Religious, Language–Religious, Process Theology.

ANALOGY (*See* LANGUAGE–RELIGIOUS.)

ANTHROPOLOGY

Formulated by Christian traditions and reflections, Christian anthropology is a set of beliefs about human being in the world. These beliefs provide a particular orienting vision of human being and are crafted from the mythologies, narratives, creeds, and doctrines distinctive of Christianity. At the same time, however, these beliefs variously engage the cultural matrices within which the beliefs are developed.

As beliefs embedded in cultural matrices, Christian anthropology is thus a region of theology where interchange between theological and extra-theological disciplines is especially intense. Christian beliefs about human being in the world require collaboration not only with philosophy but also increasingly with the natural sciences, social sciences (political science, economics, anthropology, sociology, psychology), history, and literature. Christian anthropology is also a rapidly changing dimension of theology, because of the ever-changing interaction between beliefs theologians forge from their distinctive traditions, on the one hand, and these beliefs as they are shaped by or in tension with other cultural and disciplinary viewpoints on humankind, on the other.

Three recurring themes usually pervade the belief structure of Christian anthropologies. These can be presented as constituting the orienting vision of human being in the world usually affirmed by Christian traditions, while also enabling analysis of how that vision is related to diverse cultural issues. These three themes are humankind's origins in God, "the Fall," and a new humanity and earth.

Origins in God. Christian anthropologies initially emphasize the origin of human being, the world, and the cosmos in the creating activity of God. Some Christian thinkers read the creation accounts of the Hebrew scriptures as descriptions of *how* humans came to be, thus rivaling or (as some say) supporting, evolutionary viewpoints. Most theologians, however, have eschewed viewing the Genesis creation accounts as descriptive of how the natural mechanisms of creation came to be, and instead they stress the connection of human creaturely presence with the originating activity of God. Whatever be the first dynamics of creation, what matters in Christian anthropology is the belief that those dynamics have their source in, and continuing relation to, God.

28

This view of the origins of the human is reflected in the crucial notion of humans as created "in the image of God." Humans are understood to be image-bearers of God, thus distinguishing them from the rest of creation. In this there is an original relatedness to God. For some theologians, humans' physical uprightness was the mark of the good human who bore God's image. For most theologians, however, the Genesis accounts suggest that humans are image-bearers by reason of more complex traits.

Among members of the latter category, one group has taken the view that humans are distinguished by their *rationality*. Aristotle argued that "the animals other than [hu]man, live by appearances and memories . . . but the human race lives by art and reasonings." Patristic and medieval theologians, including Augustine and Thomas Aquinas, stressed that the human soul as rational and intellectual was the seat of the image of God in people.

For a second group, humans display the image of God in their being given *responsibility for the earth*. As God creates and sustains, so humans exercise their creativity on earth and care for it, and in this are image-bearers of God.

A third group has stressed the human *conscience*, a moral awareness of good and evil, as the mark of the image of God in humankind. As God is a God of justice, humans reflect that God in their consciences' sense of the just and the good. Even a disturbance of conscience, the "uneasy conscience," could be seen as testimony to humans' God-likeness.

For a fourth group, the image is sometimes founded in the human capacity for *self-transcendence*. Again, humans' ability to reason can be emphasized here, not as the mark of God's image but as a means to transcending self and apprehending God. The experience of self-transcendence becomes the seat of the image of God. As God is transcendent, somehow greater than, more than, or beyond creation, so humans have potential to transcend themselves in various ways. This view is evident in the works of Augustine, Thomas Aquinas, and some Protestant thinkers. For Paul Tillich, for example, humans possess the image of God in having a structure of freedom that "implies potential infinity." Humans themselves are never infinite, but there is "a drive toward the infinite" that enables them to experience self-transcendence in their finitude. Similarly, Wolfhart Pannenberg proposes self-transcendence—for him, openness to the future and anticipation of God—as establishing a "broad consensus for a contemporary anthropology seeking the uniqueness of humankind."

Pannenberg, however, as well as others, also utilizes a fifth understanding of the image of God. This fifth view stresses that humans are bearers of God's image in their *relationality*, their being with and for others. The others to whom humans relate are other humans, with whom a "co-humanity" (Karl Barth), nature, and the world more generally (Pannenberg) is shared. As Jürgen Moltmann put it forcefully, we must not think of humans as made in the *imago Dei* without also knowing humans as made in the *imago mundi*. Still other theologians (e.g., R. R.

29

Ruether) working with this fifth perspective also stress that this relationality should be "authentic," liberating, egalitarian—avoiding, for example, tendencies to construct itself in a dominative mode that favors male, Caucasian, or other aspects of privilege.

The Fall. A second pervasive theme of Christian anthropologies in the West is evident in the fact that theologians have traditionally interpreted humans as "fallen," "deformed," or variously failing to manifest and realize the good that they are created in God's image to be.

Whether theologians presume a first "fall" in history (a first sin of some sort that historically inaugurates the more widespread departure of later peoples from their created goodness) or whether they take the scriptural and doctrinal notions of "the fall" more symbolically (as representing the recalcitrant and pervasive reality of human evil), the perduring theme in Christian anthropology is that humans exist in a condition that is against that which is good in and for them. This condition is described in different terms: as "condemnation," "lostness," "depravity," "radical deformity," "estrangement," "alienation," or "oppression." A Christian thinker's view of human "fallenness" is distinctively shaped by which of these terms are selected. In whatever way the condition of fallenness is characterized and in whatever terms, several related key controversies rage around this theme.

A first set of controversies concerns *the extent of the distortion.* How radical is human evil? To what degree is the goodness of humans as created in the *imago Dei* destroyed? Conceivably, a spectrum of responses to these questions could range from one side asserting that the fallenness is complete, such that there are no vestiges of goodness in humans, to another side taking the fallenness as a disruption that, however extensive and painful, still leaves human goodness as capable of redressing the evil. Traditionally, however, even the widest extremes among positions in classical Western theologies resist easy correspondence with the two ends of this conceivable spectrum.

Neither Augustine nor Calvin—both of whom stress the radical deformity of humans through the fall—denies the persistence in human creation of the good gifts of God. The radicality of the fall, for both thinkers, signifies not that human creaturely life has lost every vestige of goodness, but that humans are so hampered they cannot themselves redress what ails them; the radicality of the fall also means that every domain of human life—affections, thoughts, actions—is distorted even if there remains the occasional good affect, good thought, or good action.

Similarly, theologians who see the extent of the distortion as less drastic rarely claim that the remaining goodness of humanity is in itself capable of redressing the fallenness. Friedrich Schleiermacher, for example, who wrote that human consciousness involves not just original sinfulness but also an "original righteousness," still taught that some further transformation was necessary if that perduring "righteousness" was to redress the pain and suffering in human life.

A second set of controversies concerns *the locus of the distortion.* Where in human life is the distortion seen primarily at work? One approach identifies certain "faculties" of the human soul (affections, body sensations, mind, and will). A given theologian may privilege one of these as the primary locus of human fault, but usually when this is done, the other "faculties" play contributing or correlative roles. So Augustine, for example, may focus primarily on the will as problematic—its bondage and its refusal or inability to will the good. But the will is stimulated by its bondage; it steers the whole being wrongly because of the appetites of the body and related affections, and in consequence turns the mind wrongly away from contemplating the things of God, toward contemplating things of earth and body.

The controversy here has reached new levels of intensity in late-twentieth-century discussions, especially when Christian feminist theologians challenge the dominant anthropology, as exemplified by Augustine, which would accuse the body and its appetites and affections for humanity's evil will. Feminists do not simply reverse the Augustinian stance, thereby praising body and faulting mind; rather, they see the locus of the distortion in precisely the dichotomizing, fragmenting opposition of body and mind. Further, they point out that this dualism's devaluation of the body also devalues woman and nature, both of which are perceived as dangerous bodily domains that are distorting and in need of control. The locus of the distortion is, then, according to these critiques, to be found in what Rosemary Radford Ruether has termed a dualist "distorted relationality" rather than in some single faculty of human being.

The question of the locus of the fall, again, however it is conceived of (e.g., as estrangement or lostness), can also be focused individually or communally. In the classical theologies, especially in Western societies, the focus has largely been on what individuals do and have—their guilty consciences, their wills, their bodily desires, their false thoughts, and their idolatries. It is true that Augustine could speak of "original sin" as a great "train of evil"—a legacy, if you will, by which individuals were conditioned; this does tend to shift the locus toward domains and circumstances larger than any individual. But the sin or fallenness showed its real force in the way it entered the individual's bodily life, especially his or her sexuality, and affected the individual being.

In contrast, especially by the nineteenth century, theologians began articulating human fault and distortion as a communal or social problem, in part because of interaction with emerging cultural and social theory. Paradigmatic here is Schleiermacher, for whom sin is elaborated as "corporate sin." For him sin pertains not severally to each individual, but "in each the work of all, and in all the work of each; and only in this corporate character, indeed, can it be properly and fully understood." More recently this issue has arisen again, especially in Latin American liberation theology, wherein, without denying the personal or

31

individual locus of sin, the liberation theologians stress regions of "institutionalized violence" as the locus of the distortion that needs primary theological address.

A third set of controversies concerns *human responsibility* for the fall. Debate has been intense and occurs frequently between those who take a "moral" view of human evil and those who emphasize a "tragic" view. Reinhold Niebuhr and Paul Tillich focused this debate keenly at mid–twentieth century. Niebuhr stressed the moral responsibility for human evil, primarily human sin as pride that is continually enacted in history. Tillich, while also attending to humans' moral responsibility for evil, tended to place this moral view within a tragic view—one that stresses the universality and unavoidability of the fall, hence suggesting that it is too much to make humans alone responsible for the distortion. How theologians navigate the tensions between the moral and tragic view of human fallenness and evil has in many ways intensified in difficulty as late-twentieth-century humanity wrestles not only with the persistent issues of guilt, suffering, and death, but also with the particular forms these take in struggle with addictions, the loss of ecological habitat, the threat of nuclear holocaust, gender injustice, and the growing gap between rich and poor.

In whatever way Christian anthropologists settle the relationship between the tragic and the moral, other debates also occur concerning the nature of human moral responsibility. What is the nature of sin? Classical traditions have fused the notions of being "curved in on oneself" and of "pride." The predominant failure, then, is one of a self's turning in upon itself and then exercising the will to power and self-aggrandizement. This notion of sin has worked strongly to identify and name the "sin" of powerful leaders and groups who exploit others for their own purposes. Human failing then is "sinful" in the human's defense of self-interest and desire for power.

On the other hand, for exploited groups—whose lives are routines of self-doubt and reluctance to exercise power—sin as pride has not sufficed to articulate their human failing. Both African American and feminist theologians have stressed, in contrast, that self-abnegation or the refusal to seek empowerment of oneself and one's people is just as serious a failure to exercise moral responsibility, just as viable a notion of "sin." In other words, the self can be alienated from itself through both pride and sloth, through will to power and failure to exercise power.

A New Humanity and a New Earth. A third theme of Christian anthropologies has been emphasis on the promise and potential for a new humanity and a new earth. Because humans and their world are suspended and held in the originating and sustaining nexus—the creative and providential activity of God—humans are believed to be transformable, restorable, healable creatures. Christian doctrines of human being, in this respect, are not exhausted by their discourse about "origins" or "fallenness" but include narratives and symbols of release into wholeness.

Here, then, anthropology opens out into soteriology—into discussion of humans' need for salvation (from *salvus*, healed), for "healing."

The focus on a new, healed humanity also opens anthropology into Christology because the healing and healed *humanum* has traditionally been represented by Jesus Christ. In Pauline language, Christ is "the second Adam" (Rom. 5:12-21). Christ is humanity as originally created to be. In Christ, thus, is the completion of humanity in the *imago Dei*. Of course, as the meaning of the *imago Dei* differs, so also will the meanings of Christ as one in whom this *imago* is fulfilled. There is remarkable consonance, however, among Christian anthropologies as various as those of Thomas Aquinas, John Calvin, Schleiermacher, and Rosemary Radford Ruether that the divine act of creation is not complete until the redemptive (or restorative or healing) work is experienced by humanity. The notion of Christ as "second Adam" presents the Christian redeemer figure as the one in whom the creation of humankind finds fulfillment.

The notion of an individual Christ as "second Adam," however, is not a sufficient symbol for representing the newness needed by a "fallen" humanity. More collective or communal symbols have therefore been employed to symbolize the needed transformation and to facilitate doctrinal reflection: kingdom of God, city of God, corporate grace, new earth. These symbols have often been restricted by theologians to ecclesiology, eschatology, and pneumatology, but they also function as symbols of a new, healed humanity and hence are not separable from Christian anthropologies.

These communal symbols of human wholeness and completion of creation place at the heart of Christian anthropology two tensions that are still being debated as the twenty-first century draws near. These tensions can be expressed in two questions.

First, is the new, reconstituted humanity to be found primarily in the renewal of dynamics of *individual* faith and practice or primarily in the emergence of new *collectivities*—new ways of relating human to human, human to nature, and human to cosmos? In the last decades of the twentieth century, one finds numerous and strong Christian communities throughout countries of the North Atlantic that give primacy to the proclamation of human renewal through individual spiritual experience and growth. On the other hand, within these same countries and throughout third-world regions of the Southern Hemisphere, experiences of ethnic strife, political repression and oppression, and loss of the environmental world have granted to many a new sense of urgency in proclaiming a *telos* (goal or end) for humans in the world that is communal, celebrating the differences between particular groups but seeking new connections and alliances that are restorative for all.

Second, the more communal symbols prompt renewed inquiry in Christian anthropology on another tension, one long intrinsic to the Christian tradition. Will the reconstitution of humans in the world, hence the fulfillment of their

33

createdness, be articulated theologically as renewal of *this* earth and *this* cosmos or as emergence of some new "transcendent" order articulated as replacement for this earth and cosmos? Amid late-twentieth-century despair and resignation—in the face of threats to ecostructure, from nuclear holocaust, and from intransigent economic and political structures—the tendency is strong among many Christian thinkers to turn away from this order of things and to articulate a kind of hope that does not restore creation, but looks for a complete rupture (dramatized for some by a "rapture" of Christians from this troubled world) and toward completely new order.

In tension with this vision are other Christian thinkers who recall that biblical visions of a "new heaven" are regularly related to, or are affirmed alongside, the vision of a "new earth." On this view, there cannot be and must not be any resignation to the loss of created earth, but there must be instead an experience of renewal that sets humans laboring with all of creation for the construction of the new earth which is the new heaven. From the vantage point of such a Christian anthropology, not only is the survival of humans in the world at stake, but so also are the fulfillment and thriving of humankind and all of creation.

MARK KLINE TAYLOR

Bibliography

José Comblin, *Retrieving the Human: A Christian Anthropology.*
Edward Farley, *Good and Evil.*
Catherine Keller, *From a Broken Web: Separation, Sexism, and Self.*
James Nelson, *Embodiment.*
Wolfhart Pannenberg, *Anthropology in Theological Perspective.*

Cross Reference: Christology, Creation, Eschatology, Freedom, Institutionalized Violence, Kingdom of God, Liberation Theology, Sin, Society, Soteriology.

APOCALYPSE (*See* ESCHATOLOGY, FUNDAMENTALISM.)

APOLOGETICS

From time to time a representative of a given religion is invited (and occasionally required) to speak as an advocate or defender of the representative's faith in a public forum. The occasion may arise as a result of a clash of religious options that a particular group wishes to resolve or as a result of a new philosophical insight that seems at odds with an earlier religious consensus. In recent times, the occasion has often been the result of a new scientific theory or a sociological change that calls into question the prevailing religious view. And postmodern critics, who sense the failure of various modern nontheistic world views, have fostered a reexamination of religion as a part of a more comprehensive world view.

Whatever the case, the rational advocate or defender of the faith is called an "apologist." Apologetics is the field of study that examines the methods employed by the apologist. The following historical and modern examples illustrate apologetic methods that have been used.

In the New Testament, Hebrews is an early example of an apology that addresses the problem of choosing between religious options. It seems to be addressed to persons being forced to choose between Christianity and Judaism although the first Christians understood themselves to be both Jews and Christians. The writer maintains that the essential truth of Judaism has found its fulfillment in Christianity, so the best way to be a true Jew is to choose Christianity and depart from Judaism.

When they encountered the thought world of Greek philosophy, early Christian theologians learned to use Greek concepts in order to interpret the faith for an audience familiar with Greek terminology. The practice of appropriating philosophical language in defense of the faith reached a climax in the works of Thomas Aquinas (1225–1274). Using Aristotelian logic to advocate an ultimate cause of all existing things, he then identified God as this ultimate cause and used the imagery of the Christian religion to give definition to the God thus identified.

The ascendancy of the theory of evolution in the nineteenth century provides a prime example of a scientific theory that caused a crisis of faith. The discovery of a developmental potential within nature itself made the hypothesis of God as the source of nature's apparent organization seem unnecessary. The first response of a number of Christians was to question the credibility of science in ways that often undermined their own credibility. Some theologians embraced the theory of evolution creatively. Teilhard de Chardin celebrated the developing structure of nature and saw the love of God as the dynamic source that makes evolution possible. Others devised similar views of God as guiding evolution.

The emergence of psychology as a field of scientific study exemplifies another crisis for faith. Freud (1856–1939) devised an explanation of religion as a human invention that addresses deep psychological needs for security. Paul Tillich, on the other hand, building on Freudian insights, discovered in psychology the existential need to be committed to an ultimate concern. He argued that the courage of faith was necessary to make an authentic (and thus salvific) commitment to the only "true" ultimate, which is God.

Another great theologian of the twentieth century, Karl Barth avoided apologetics altogether. He regarded faith as pre-rational in the sense that one could not reason to a position of faith. Rather one must be moved to such a position by the power of the Word of God through the medium of Scripture or preaching. Therefore, any effort of human logic or argumentation was of no value in promoting authentic faith. Generally Barth's approach seems dogmatic and arrogant, for the modern world citizen experiences too many competing world views and sociological shifts to embrace any one option precritically.

Sociological changes also give rise to apologetic reflection. Changing male and female roles in modern society are one example of this phenomenon. The organizational structures of many religions are decidedly paternalistic. The feminist movement reflects a sensitivity to social structures that limit women to secondary roles and incomplete fulfillment of potential. Feminists urge a reformation of such structures in order to provide equality for women; and if such reform is not possible, they often advocate rejection of traditional religion in favor of alternative religions. The apologist seeks to emphasize a liberating heritage within religious structures as a basis for advocating new opportunities for women or runs the risk of alienating increasing numbers of women.

Advocates of a postmodern view indicate that modern world views that looked to science and technology to solve all human problems have become bankrupt because science and technology have generated as many problems as they have solved and have given rise to some particularly threatening realities such as nuclear weapons and ecological disasters. In this milieu there is a call for a more comprehensive world view. One element of the emerging new world view is the desire to recognize a transcendent or spiritual dimension to reality. This desire has prompted a renewed interest in religious dialogue and a new chapter in the history of apologetics.

F. WILLIAM RATLIFF

Bibliography

Diogenes Allen, *Christian Belief in a Postmodern World.*
Avery Dulles, *A History of Apologetics.*
Jerry H. Gill, *Faith in Dialogue.*
C. S. Lewis, *Mere Christianity.*
D. Elton Trueblood, *A Place to Stand.*

Cross Reference: Culture, Epistemology, Hermeneutics, Philosophical Theology, Postmodern Theology.

APOSTASY (*See* HERESY.)

ASCETICISM (*See* CELIBACY.)

ATHEISM

The term "atheism" is as slippery to define as it is fraught with emotion. Doubtless, these two facts are intimately entwined. In part the problem in defining atheism rises from its relativity—as a negative term—to the denial of varying positive religious frameworks in which God or the gods are differently understood. This makes atheism dependent on historical setting and community belief. In part, the problem of definition also rises from emotions stirred against a perceived challenge to deeply felt community beliefs: "Atheist" has often been used as a term of abuse.

Xenophanes of Colophon (c. 570–500 B.C.E.) was widely reviled as an atheist for poking fun at the anthropomorphic foibles of the Olympian deities accepted by the orthodox in his day. It did not alter his classification as an atheist that he affirmed a single, motionless, non-anthropomorphic god, cited approvingly by Aristotle two centuries later. Anaxagoras of Clazomenae (c. 500–428 B.C.E.) was prosecuted and condemned to exile for atheism because he denied the divinity of the heavenly bodies and, instead, insisted that the sun and moon were glowing stones, the sun even larger than the Peloponnesus. Socrates (470–399 B.C.E.), too, was condemned and was executed as an impious atheist despite his acknowledgment of personal spiritual guidance from a divine agent.

Other examples of the protean character of atheism abound. Baruch Spinoza (1632–1677), though the "God-intoxicated philosopher," was excommunicated as a Jewish heretic by his synagogue (1656) and was denounced by Moses Mendelssohn for his "atheism." Paul Tillich, though a Christian theologian, was considered an atheist by some for his rejection of any belief in God as "a being over against other beings," but he was not so considered by others, because of his affirmations of the "God beyond the god of theism."

Recognizing the inescapable dependence of the term on historical setting and circumstances and avoiding any abusive overtones, our definition will be explicitly relative to what might be called "minimal Judeo-Christian theism." Atheism in this sense is defined as rejection of belief in the existence of a cosmic reality—whether literally infinite or merely vast beyond human conception—of whom religiously important personal attributes like knowledge, purpose, action, goodness, or love can be at least analogically or symbolically affirmed. This rejection can be of two sorts: first, rejection as *disbelief,* in which arguments may be given for the logical impossibility, empirical improbability, or theoretical implausibility of belief in such a cosmic reality; or, second, rejection as *dismissal,* in which theistic utterances are held to be cognitively meaningless, not qualifying for belief or disbelief and thus not a fit basis for ordering policies of life or for worship.

Arguments for Disbelief. 1. Arguments for the logical impossibility of the existence of God depend, like any a priori argumentation (that is, arguments from the necessity of ideas rather than from evidence of experience), on a careful definition of the God-idea that is held to lead to the logical contradiction or necessary incoherence that rules out belief. The dual task of a priori atheist arguments of this sort is to show that the definition offered is legitimately derived from genuine religious theism and, at the same time, fatally flawed.

Jean-Paul Sartre, for example, observes that the God of theism must be believed both to possess a maximum of secure reality, that is, a maximum of "being" of the strongest conceivable sort, and simultaneously to possess a maximum of interiority—of freedom, thought, love, and self-awareness to an eminent degree. If God were lacking in either of these aspects, God would not be the God that theists adore. But, Sartre points out, the two aspects are mutually incompatible. Secure being is the sort of phenomenon that can be "in itself" only by being entirely solid, ponderous, closed to possibilities of being in any way other than it is. Self-awareness, on the other hand, is the sort of phenomenon that can be "for itself" only by being a sort of nothingness, pure possibility, radical freedom. But to try to combine them constitutes a contradiction! What we want in a God is a projection of our own thirst to link impossibly the two aspects of ourselves between which we are torn. We are dangerously free, like it or not, and we wish—passionately—that we could at the same time be something solid. We attribute such an ideal, unreachable unity to God, but this projected God of our existential anguish is a "useless passion." Sartre's atheism, in consequence, is theoretically necessary. If the underlying Sartrian categories of "being" and "nothingness" can be shown not to be compelling, however, then the impossibility of belief in God on this ground vanishes.

Another example of an a priori argument less dependent on special background assumptions for the logical impossibility of belief in God is John Findlay's ontological disproof. He points to the religious requirement that God—to be worthy of worship—be absolutely perfect in all ways, including the way in which God exists: God must not exist merely contingently (the possibility of God's not being would be a terrible imperfection), but necessarily, as Anselm recognized and made the basis of his ontological argument. But, Findlay asserts, modern logic has shown that since all existential statements are contingent, "necessary existence" is an oxymoron. God must be conceived as enjoying necessary existence, but necessary existence is ruled out in principle. Atheism is required, therefore, since any God worthy of worship turns out to be impossible. This a priori argument for disbelief in God, like the first, rests on a theoretical framework, though an even wider one than Sartre's. Its key theoretical assumptions are that all existential propositions are included within the class of empirical propositions and that all empirical propositions are contingently true. This fundamental framework is no less open to rejection than the first if, for example, synthetic a priori propositions can be defended or if some existential propositions simply do not share the logic of empirical ones.

2. Arguments for disbelief in God may, in addition, be grounded in a posteriori modes of reasoning (that is, arguments from the evidence of experience). Assuming the inconclusiveness of the so-called theistic proofs, the atheist position

pushes beyond indecision toward a negative judgment. In the foregoing section we saw how the traditional ontological argument can be reversed in an attempted a priori disproof of the existence of the allegedly Necessary Being. Likewise, but in an a posteriori mode, the traditional cosmological argument, arguing for the existence of a First Mover, can be counterattacked with an appeal to modern empirical science in which motion is no less self-explanatory than rest and in which cosmological theory has come to depict the universe's origins in an impersonal Big Bang rather than in divine purpose. The traditional argument from design, from an atheist's perspective, is even more vulnerable to counterattack. Not only does evolutionary science offer an alternative, impersonal explanation for orderliness and mutual adaptation within the biological world, but also close observation reveals maladaptations, extinctions, and vast domains of suffering.

The problem of evil, raised in one of its sharpest forms by this counterattack against the argument from design, is a mainstay in the atheist's arsenal against the probability of an all-powerful and all-benevolent God. Given the evidence as a whole, containing not only adaptation and beauty but also plague and earthquake, birth defects and innocent suffering among both humans and animals, how could any rational mind infer a perfectly well-intentioned intelligence in full control? As David Hume allowed, it may be possible by sophisticated argument to "square" these empirical findings with the hypothesis of theism, but surely no reasonable inference directly from our mixed data to an unmixed, perfect God is possible. Therefore, barring a priori information about a hidden God purposely veiling divine perfection behind a most imperfect creation, atheism would appear to hold the balance.

3. Even if a strong probable case for atheism is difficult to work out, because of the vastness of the range of relevant evidence as well as conceptual problems in quantifying relative likelihoods in this domain, suspension of judgment (such as is advocated by agnosticism) would not be warranted as long as the theoretical plausibility of belief in God is weaker than the plausibility of disbelief. A belief becomes implausible when it is gratuitous or redundant or arbitrary, even if probabilities cannot be exactly counted. In the spirit of Laplace's retort to Napoleon, that he had "no need for the hypothesis" of God, modern atheists find no need compelling them to introduce references to the divine in their accounts of reality. Jacques Monod, for example, argues that a complete story of living things can be told with reference only to molecules operating according to chance and necessity. Paul Edwards asks why we should be asked to suspend a negative judgment in connection with gratuitous claims about the Judeo-Christian form of theism any more than we should continue to suspend such judgment about similarly gratuitous claims concerning the gods of Mount Olympus or about the devil or witches.

Arguments for Dismissal. The most radical form of atheistic argument in the twentieth century has been the dismissal of theistic language as empty of possible belief-content. The characterization of this position as atheistic is sometimes rejected on the ground that, if theism cannot be affirmed, then neither can its contradictory. But this objection is somewhat mischievous, at best, since if the logical dismissal of theism succeeds, then what is left is a world devoid of God-talk and full of science-talk—which is exactly the outcome sought by more traditional atheistic arguments.

The classic statement of the argument for dismissal was made by A. J. Ayer as part of his general condemnation of metaphysical discourse on behalf of logical positivism. The key doctrine of logical positivism is the equation of factual meaning with actual or possible verifying experience. Mere tautologies do not carry factual significance, since they are true under all factual circumstances; all true sentences in logic and mathematics can be classified as more or less elaborate tautologies. Likewise, mere emotional outbursts do not carry factual significance, since they simply express the feelings of the utterer. Non-emotive, non-tautological language will have to carry any factual significance, and this will turn out to be exhaustively expressible in terms of the sorts of experience that would tend to verify the assertion of a fact if it is true. This can be expressed in a principle: namely, that the meaning of a factual proposition is equivalent to the method of its verification.

But it is clear that language about God has no ready method of verification. If anything is verified, it will be by mundane human experience. "God"—if more is intended by the term than such actual or possible experiences as the regularity of seasons, or the orderliness of the astronomical bodies, or the feeling of satisfaction upon performing certain actions mandated by ecclesiastical organizations—is never verified as God. Anything that could be so verified would be indignantly denied as truly God by theists; thus, by making God transcendent in principle, theists remove all factual meaning from God-language. And if it is impossible to assert truths about God in a philosophical tone of voice, it is equally impossible to "believe" them "by faith." According to this doctrine of meaning, there is literally nothing to be believed.

This verificational analysis of meaning fell onto hard times in the later part of the twentieth century, since (among other problems) it could not account for its own non-tautological, non-emotive, apparently assertive (but not empirically verifiable) meaning. But a closely related challenge to the unfalsifiability of theistic claims forced careful rethinking by theists. If, as Antony Flew demanded, every possible state of affairs is compatible with theistic belief—if, that is, nothing could conceivably falsify such claims—then is anything definite being claimed at all? What is the "bottom line" difference between a theist and an atheist? Has theism died the "death of a thousand qualifications"?

A remarkable episode in twentieth-century Christian theology occurred when certain theologians took all these criticisms to heart and embraced the "death of God" within their theological work. The movement, extending mainly through the decade of the 1960s, was highly diverse in method and content. Gabriel Vahanian was misunderstood if considered an atheist at all; Paul M. Van Buren blended dismissive elements from logical positivism with Barthian neoorthodoxy; Thomas Altizer affirmed genuine atheism of a most unusual sort, holding that God had in fact died at a point in history in order to set human history free and to save it; Bishop John A. T. Robinson spoke of the absence of God "out there" but retained an impenetrable Tillichian ambiguity about what might be real "deep down" at reaches of being accessible only by subjectivity.

Atheism, though mainly a minority opinion, has flourished in different forms since the rise of critical thought in human history. Various atheisms abound in our own time. It is wise to remember that by the standard that condemned Anaxagoras to exile we would all be declared atheists. That the moon is made of rock is not, after all, religiously shocking in the setting of theism today.

The circumstances of theistic belief are constantly changing, though the changes are often too slow or complex for a living generation to notice. One of the agents of this change within any historical setting is the atheism of its time. Atheism, as primarily a counterattacking position, is the critical voice that constantly opens new possibilities for thought about the ultimately real. When this voice is heard with care, new possibilities of theism may be suggested. What shall 'God' mean in the future? Every meaning of 'God' presupposes a theoretical framework of some sort, old or new, familiar or alien. Within these frameworks, whether derived from A. N. Whitehead, Charles Hartshorne, Teilhard de Chardin, or some other source, God-talk is provided its function and is related to other domains of thought and life. Atheism is the rejection of some specific sort of God-talk, whether by disbelief or dismissal. As long as such rejection is encouraged to be clearly articulated, theological dross is subjected to cleansing fires of criticism, and the human project of relating cognitively and practically to the most high and the most real is advanced.

FREDERICK FERRÉ

Bibliography

Thomas J. J. Altizer, *The Gospel of Christian Atheism.*
A. J. Ayer, *Language, Truth, and Logic.*
Paul Edwards, "Atheism," *The Encyclopedia of Philosophy*, vol. 1.
Antony Flew and Alasdair MacIntyre, eds., *New Essays in Philosophical Theology.*
Jean-Paul Sartre, *Being and Nothingness: An Essay on Phenomenological Ontology.*

Cross Reference: Agnosticism, Death of God Theology, Evil, God, Language–Religious, Theism.

ATONEMENT

Atonement ("at-onement," a sixteenth-century coinage) is the reconciliation of sinners with God, especially through the cross, as communicated through the gospel and the sacraments. The cross is proclaimed as somehow resolving the

41

human predicament; but the predicament and its resolution can be understood in quite different ways. Is the problem in humans' relation to the powers of evil, in their relation to God, or within themselves?

1. The patristic emphasis was on the first of these, *the powers of evil*. If human beings are in bondage to the devil (collectively the "powers of evil"), then they must be redeemed by paying a "ransom." But how? to whom? by what? In using the metaphor of the devil's being lured by the bait of Christ's humanity, patristic writers suggested that the powers of evil overstepped their authority and discredited themselves. Although the powers of evil may have had a legitimate claim over sinners, who had yielded to temptation and were bound by guilt, they did *not* have the same claim over Christ, who, after identifying himself with sinners and captives, and being accused and executed as though he were a sinner, was vindicated by God in his resurrection. Thus, all those who attach themselves to Christ through faith and baptism are freed from the devil. In this way patristic theologians considered that Christ provided a ransom for humans' sins and bondage to evil.

Although this "ransom" motif is often despised as crass and mythological, it manifests some of the processes of scapegoating and victimization of which liberation movements have made us newly aware. Liberation theology concerns domination by the powers of evil, whose claim is expressed in "structures of evil" and enforced through a combination of guilt and fear. In liberation the framework of legalism (which can be "just" as well as oppressive) is not simply abolished; rather, it is brought to defeat itself in its very administration. Through undeserved suffering the powers of domination are unmasked and discredited, losing moral authority in the forum of public opinion. The captives are not only freed from moral and psychological bondage but are empowered for a new mode of life.

2. Atonement as a change in *the human relationship to God* is present in New Testament and patristic thought, especially in the motif of sacrifice, either as "expiating" human sins or as "propitiating" God's anger, but it was not developed into a theory until the medieval and Reformation periods.

Anselm's *Cur Deus Homo* set the stage by thinking of God on the model of the feudal overlord whose honor is offended by sinful humanity. God's justice requires either punishment (involuntary suffering and damnation) or satisfaction (making up for the offense through voluntary suffering, a model for which was at hand in the practice of penance). In keeping with the second possibility, satisfaction is offered by Christ as God-human, whose acts are not only sinless but of infinite merit.

The Reformers shifted the focus from God's honor, which can be satisfied through penitential sacrifice, to God's wrath, which seems rather to demand punishment. Thus Christ is viewed as the "substitute" for sinful humanity, bearing the full force of God's wrath and rejection on the cross.

42

Because this theory involves an "exchange" between a sinful humanity, which deserves God's condemnation, and the sinless Christ, who enacts God's love, it seems to introduce a division, or at least a tension, into God. Salvation, to be sure, is initiated by God, in order to accomplish God's initial purposes for creation; but it is presented as resolving a problem "within God," as though the Son must satisfy the conditions of divine justice, or even propitiate the Father's wrath, in order that sinners be forgiven or justified.

All theories of this type, furthermore, view suffering, and even punishment, as salvific—an assumption that has been questioned on moral and psychological grounds, most recently by liberation and feminist theologians who see it as a reinforcement of domination and abuse. And yet in today's theology the cross is often linked with a wider divine suffering and identification with those who suffer in order to overcome evil. Which kind of suffering must be rejected, and which can be accepted?

3. Atonement as a change *within human being* is linked with Peter Abelard in the eleventh century and with modern liberal theology. Here the cross is viewed as the expression of God's forgiving love for sinful humanity, even in the face of human rebellion and violence toward its bearer. Because the goal is understood to be a change in human attitude and mode of life, this theory is called the "moral influence" theory—a term often misunderstood, for it means not "merely" moral or exemplary, but influencing the inmost affections through an appeal that is consciously apprehended. The emphasis is upon the dynamics of human subjectivity, human possibilities for growth, and the transforming role of interpersonal relations.

If there is a current trend, it is away from insistence upon a single metaphor for atonement and the conceptual framework that seems to grow from it, and toward appreciation of the variety of images, each of which suggests something important about divine initiative, human response, and continuing obstacles to the renewal of life.

EUGENE TESELLE

Bibliography

Joanne Carlson Brown and Carole R. Bohn, eds., *Christianity, Patriarchy, and Abuse: A Feminist Critique.*
Dennis Edwards, *What Are They Saying About Salvation?*
Paul S. Fiddes, *Past Event and Present Salvation: The Christian Idea of Atonement.*
Robert S. Franks, *The Work of Christ: A Historical Study of Christian Doctrine.*
Colin E. Gunton, *The Actuality of Atonement: A Study of Metaphor, Rationality, and the Christian Tradition.*

Cross Reference: Anthropology, Christology, Evil, Justification, Sin, Soteriology.

43

AUTHORITY

The issue of authority is central for Christian theology. Most broadly, authority deals with the sources of legitimation for theological assertions. Given the plurality of theological positions within the Christian orb today and the many theological methods and styles on the scene, it is apparent that sources of authority are quite varied. Most basically, Christian theology deals with the living God who is the source of all. This includes the recognition that it is God who "authorizes" theological claims. Yet recognizing this point raises the further issue of how humans can discern and understand the means God uses to disclose God's truth. How are theological truth claims authorized?

Avenues of Authority. Current approaches to the issue of authority have their roots in the history of Christian theology. An appreciation of today's discussions can be enhanced by looking at the sources from which these approaches emerge.

Since the earliest days of the church, theologians have wrestled with the question of how God's "authority" is to be understood and the avenues by which it comes to us. Since this is such a basic question, other theological issues and doctrines have taken their trajectories from the various viewpoints established. Several avenues of authority have functioned in normative ways for Christian theology.

1. Church. After the death of the apostles of Jesus, the emerging Christian community faced the question of how God's authority would be maintained. Through Jesus and his immediate disciples, the community had experienced what it considered to be God's authoritative word and presence. As the early centuries went on, however, three important new sources of authority emerged in the church: the canon of Scripture (Old and New Testaments); the creeds of the church and church councils; and the advancing authority ascribed to church leaders, such as bishops, elders, and deacons. The Middle Ages saw the growth of the papacy and the structured authority of the Roman Catholic Church as the chief expression of Christianity in the Western world. Within the Roman church, the sources of Scripture and tradition vied for a place as the ultimate authority for the church's life. Persons who appealed to the tradition of the church as having its roots in the church's oral traditions and ultimately with the apostles themselves argued that these ecclesiastical traditions are the arbiters of validity. The Scriptures gain the authority conferred to them by the church, and the Christian community is the adjudicator of Christian doctrine.

2. Scripture. The Protestant Reformers challenged this conception of the church's authority by rejecting the primacy of the papacy and the magisterium as the foremost interpreters of Christian doctrine. Martin Luther contended that Scripture interprets itself through the work of the Holy Spirit. John Calvin, agreeing with this stance, went on to argue that the church is built on the Word of

God, "the teaching of apostles and prophets" (Eph. 2:20), now found for the church in the writings of Holy Scripture (*Institutes of the Christian Religion* 4.2.4). For Calvin, Scripture is the "Word of God" (*Institutes* 1.7.1), superior to all human wisdom since it originates with God. God used human writers, accommodating the divine wisdom to human capacities for understanding and thus communicating God's divine message through human thought forms. Scripture authenticates itself as the Word of God by the testimony of the Holy Spirit, which is "more excellent than all reason" (*Institutes* 1.7.4) and which seals the conviction that Scripture is God's Word in the experience of believers. This concentration on Scripture as the primary authority for Christian theology and for the church led to the Reformation slogan, "sola scriptura."

3. Spirit. Within Protestantism, the Anabaptist movement was marked by a rejection of Lutheran and Reformed teachings on several doctrines (most notably, baptism) and by a differing emphasis on the source of authority. Among these believers, "God's Spirit, which the Anabaptists believed themselves to possess, is the ultimate authority which first gives authority to the written word of the Bible" (Reventlow, 53). Anabaptists stressed the "outer word" (Scripture) and the "inner word" (the legitimation by the Holy Spirit). A biblical text without the penetration and testing of the Spirit was a "dead letter." Spiritual authority—of whatever kind—was grounded in the promptings of the Holy Spirit in an individual's heart. The "authority" of church and Scripture must yield to this "inner light" (Quakerism) of immediate revelation as the ultimate and final authority for Christian theology and the Christian life as well.

Another factor has been active in these three avenues of authority. The place of human reason also must be considered. Although opinions differ on the extent to which "reason" is a "theological" as opposed to a "natural" factor, reason is a means by which theological systems are judged and theological claims assessed (the historic controversies on the relation between reason and revelation point to the necessity to consider reason as an important factor). Appropriation of the church's tradition, the interpretation of Scripture, and the discernment of individual revelation are all filtered (as Immanuel Kant showed) through the eye of "reason." Today, theorists recognize that in the interpretations of texts, the interpreter as well as the text itself must be interpreted: One's own cultural milieu and setting in life actively influence interpretation. In the broadest sense of "reason" as the agent by which we understand and articulate what we perceive as church tradition, Scripture, or the Spirit, this dimension of human involvement and the human community is always present.

In the post-Reformation period, the principal avenues of authority were broadened further by various theological movements. The authority of the church and its traditions was fortified through the Council of Trent (1545 63), in which the Roman Catholic Church asserted that church teachings could be drawn "from Sacred Scripture, the apostolic traditions, the holy and approved councils, the

45

constitutions and authorities of the supreme pontiffs and holy fathers, and the consensus of the Catholic Church.'' The authority of the Pope as the interpreter of the Roman Catholic tradition was confirmed by the First Vatican Council, which gave official status to the dogma of papal infallibility in 1870. This gave the Pope's pronouncements binding authority in the church when he spoke in an official capacity *(ex cathedra)* under prescribed conditions. The Pope was said to be ''the true vicar of Christ, the head of the whole Church, the father and teacher of all Christians.''

Against Counter-Reformation attempts at Trent to establish the authority of the church, Protestant theology in both its Lutheran and its Reformed expressions sought to prove the authority of the Bible as the inspired Word of God that must be obeyed and that would take precedence over even the authority of the church. In the elaborate theological systems constructed by Protestant ''scholastic'' or ''orthodox'' theologians, Scripture functioned as the formal principle on which a scientific theology could be constructed. Crucial to this treatment of the Bible was detailed attention to the inspiration of Scripture and, in some writings, to what became known as Scripture's ''inerrancy.'' The Helvetic Consensus Formula (1675), a Reformed confession, pronounced that the Bible was inspired ''not only in its matter, but in its words.'' This inspiration was found ''not only in its consonants, but in its vowels—either the vowel points themselves, or at least the power of the points.'' This view accompanied the corollary of Scripture's inerrancy—that, because Scripture was inspired by God, it could exhibit no ''errors'' of any kind, including all statements of fact in areas such as geography, science, and history.

In reaction to the interconfessional disputes among continental orthodox churches, the Pietist movement arose in the eighteenth century. It sought a revival of religious fervor and emphasized the religious renewal of individuals through the ''new Birth.'' The work of the Holy Spirit was a primary source of authority for Pietism and the proof of the Spirit's work was in the works of ''piety'' performed. This emphasis stood in contrast to what the Pietists regarded as the formalism of orthodoxy, which was thought to be so heavily influenced by technical theology and the established church structures that lively spiritual experience was virtually lost. In a European culture where the prospects of maintaining a ''Christian civilization'' were being questioned, the Spirit's work in individuals became Pietism's focus.

Attacks on Authority. The period from the seventeenth to the nineteenth century saw massive attacks on these traditional sources of Christian authority. Rapid changes in the European intellectual and social climate spurred by new currents in the studies of the natural sciences, philosophy, and literature put authority on all planes on the defensive. The formulations of Isaac Newton for mathematical physics presented nature as a rational, unified order where there were no ''hidden purposes'' (of God) to discover. As a result of Newton's work, ''God'' was no longer needed as the hypothesis to authorize the world; ''God'' became a projection of nature. The scientific method of Francis Bacon, who emphasized the inductive approach to knowledge, allowed science to pursue truth on its own terms, thus freeing it from having to seek theological warrants as authority. This shift led to a heightened stress on reason as a primary authority for interpreting all human experience. It meant as well that traditions (as promoted by the church) or supernatural appeals to the ''Spirit'' were suspect. The Cartesian method that led to the ''I think'' *(cogito)*—the human being's existence as a thinking being as the primary datum for reflection—became the starting point for authority. The emphasis of John Locke on reason as a ''natural revelation'' made reason alone the arbiter of the correctness of any claims to revelation. For English Deism, reason was the supreme reality. Authority was rooted in human perception in ''the Age of Reason.''

Similar movements in literary fields brought about the beginnings of biblical criticism. The rise of historical consciousness in which it was realized that people in the ancient biblical cultures perceived reality and asked questions in ways different from those of Europeans of the nineteenth century was an important factor. So too were developments from archaeological explorations that enabled history to be reconstructed apart from the biblical data. Biblical texts themselves were being examined in ways that questioned or negated earlier orthodox assumptions. Thus attacks on the Bible as ''infallible'' or ''inerrant'' became commonplace.

Traditional authority was also questioned by David Hume and Immanuel Kant. Hume attacked causality, and with it the validity of making any empirically demonstrable statement about God. In Kant's analysis of reason and the possibility of metaphysics, he concluded that ''the only theology of reason which is possible is that which is based upon moral laws or seeks guidance from them.'' Thus in the Enlightenment period, the metaphysical structure of reality, on which traditional models of authority (and Christian revelation) were based, was apparently destroyed.

Alternatives. Christian theologians in the nineteenth and twentieth centuries responded to the Enlightenment attacks by shifting the grounds on which authority is based. Friedrich Schleiermacher turned to the realm of religious experience as the foundation for faith. The feeling of ''absolute dependence'' and the Christian experience of redemption provided the framework by which he believed theology could be possible. Albrecht Ritschl focused on the historical Jesus as the object of faith and revelation of God's will. Ritschl saw Jesus as the intersection of the religious and ethical foci of theology and as the model for the value judgments that religion makes, particularly as Jesus symbolized the moral ideal of the kingdom of God. Thus Ritschl sought to emphasize the ethical implications of Christian faith.

47

The challenge of the Enlightenment was met differently by Karl Barth. Instead of seeking an authority grounded in religious experience or history as his liberal teachers had done, Barth turned to God's self-revelation and disclosure in Jesus Christ as the foundation for all authority. Jesus Christ is the Word of God, God's address to the world, and the ground and basis for all knowledge of God and language about God. God's incarnate Word is mediated to humanity through the Bible as the written Word and through preaching as the Word proclaimed. Scripture has authority as God uses it to witness to God's revelation in Jesus Christ. The Bible must be approached in faith (given by the Holy Spirit)—not by "external proofs"—for its authority to be recognized. Barth's christological approach sought to give authority a divine basis not dependent on the specifics of human experience or rational or historical standards used to judge Scripture.

Paul Tillich's approach to authority is characterized by his emphasis on the "method of correlation"—correlating culture's existential questions with the religious symbols of Christianity. The primary symbol is Jesus as the Christ, who is the "new being." In the living encounter with this symbol (facilitated by the Scriptures), humans receive God's revelation and their salvation. Thus Tillich found the emergence of authority in the mediation of power and the new awareness of the self enabled by one's encounter with the divine (the "ground of being"). Tillich's whole theological approach was concerned to unite sacred and secular since all being is grounded in the divine reality of God.

A number of other views of authority have emerged from current theological movements and theologians. The Second Vatican Council (1962–65) led Roman Catholicism to ecclesiastical reforms and to a view that church tradition helps ensure the correct interpretation of Scripture. The Council also taught that tradition does not contain any truth not also revealed in Scripture.

In the later 1970s some conservative Protestants formed the International Council on Biblical Inerrancy (ICBI), which tried to reestablish and interpret the inerrancy of Scripture as the prime authority for today. Other conservative Protestants have preferred the term "infallibility" to designate Scripture's authority for salvation and the life of faith.

Liberation theology emphasizes the priority of *praxis,* the practical situation, or beginning "where the pain is," for engaging in theology. This means that human experience—whether that of the poor, blacks, women, or others oppressed—has a decisive role as authority for theology. Experience is also central in process theology, where one is involved in the evolution of God and the world into future possibilities.

Authority Today. Today's scene presents a wide array of sources appealed to as authority for theology. The traditional bases—church and tradition, Scripture, Holy Spirit and experience, and reason—reemerge in varying ways as norms and criteria for theological discourse. Use of these sources is not drawn along specific ecclesiastical lines. In the pluralistic world of theology now, all appear with differing accents and emphases, thus pointing to the importance of the concept of authority for the full range of theological work.

DONALD K. McKIM

Bibliography

Avery Dulles, *Models of Revelation*.
David H. Kelsey, *The Uses of Scripture in Recent Theology*.
Donald K. McKim, *What Christians Believe About the Bible*.
Henning Graf Reventlow, *The Authority of the Bible and the Rise of the Modern World*, trans. John Bowden.
Jack B. Rogers and Donald K. McKim, *The Authority and Interpretation of the Bible: An Historical Approach*.

Cross Reference: Ecclesiology, Inerrancy, Inspiration.

AUTONOMY

In Greek antiquity, the concept of autonomy (*autonomia*, self-determination or self-regulation, from *autos* [self] and *nomos* [law]) was used, with rare exceptions, in a political frame of reference. It referred to the political independence that was the aim of the Greek city-states. In the ancient Latin world, the concept was absent, but its sense was approximated in such phrasings as "the power to live according to one's own laws"; except for one appearance of the Greek word itself in Cicero, the word *autonomia* was not used. In the Latin Middle Ages, too, the concept was absent, but it was revived and played an important role in connection with the political and religious controversies of the seventeenth and eighteenth centuries. Only with Kant and post-Kantian idealism does the concept acquire philosophical and theological meanings. This development provides the immediate background of its use, in conjunction with the concepts of heteronomy and theonomy, in the twentieth century. Its most prominent role emerges in the philosophical theology of Paul Tillich.

Early Usage. As a political concept, autonomy signified the right to arrange a political entity's own affairs independently of outside powers. Herodotus in the fifth century B.C.E. contrasts autonomy both with external dependence on foreign domination and also with internal tyranny. The word's rare nonpolitical sense is illustrated by Sophocles' Antigone when she is described as heading toward death not as a victim of disease or the sword but "autonomous, living, alone" (*Antigone*, line 821). At the beginning of the modern period, the concept becomes important in jurisprudence. Thus, it was invoked to interpret the Peace of Augsburg (1555), which recognized the legitimacy of Lutheran and Catholic

49

confessions by providing an arrangement, lasting until the Treaty of Westphalia (1648), for subjects in each land to follow the religion of their ruler *(cuius regio eius religio)*. In an effort to find a designation for the Protestant demand for religious freedom, Franciscus Burgcardus, author of the important treatise *De Autonomia, das ist von Freystellung mehrerlay Religion und Glauben* (1586), had recourse to the Greek word *autonomia;* for, unlike the Latin terms for liberty *(libertas)* and freedom of religion *(licentia credendi)*, it had political as well as religious connotations. Burgcardus, however, still associated the concept with the medieval theory of social orders rather than with personal subjectivity. In the period following, the term had both a religio-political sense, when referring to the Catholic princes' loss of their privileges upon converting to Protestantism or to the "establishment of freedom of religion, freedom of conscience" (Peace of Westphalia), and also a more general sense, when referring to having one's own right and being one's own master instead of being subject to imperial power.

The Concept in Kant. More important for present-day use of the term in religion and philosophy than the developments in the juridical concept (including the distinction between private autonomy and civic autonomy) is Kant's embracing philosophical concept of autonomy as expressed in the remark, "All philosophy . . . is autonomy." Here it means no longer a right to institutional self-determination but the possibility of human beings to be self-determining according to the form of reason. The concept of autonomy is thus set over against the concepts of nature and of social form; to act freely is synonymous with acting autonomously and in an ethically good way. Autonomy is the capacity of the rational will to determine itself rather than be determined from the outside, that is, by empirical intuitions and natural drives or inclinations (even those leading to self-love and arrogance), hypothetical imperatives (instead of categorical imperatives), and natural causes. If, for example, one furthers the happiness of others because one is moved by sympathy with fellow human beings, the will is determined by an object rather than by a rational form produced by reason; that is a state of heteronomy. If, however, one furthers the happiness of others because reason gives to the self-loving inclinations the form of universality, extending to all rational beings and independent of feelings, then the action is determined by the rational form; and that is autonomy *(Critique of Practical Reason,* A 59). Along with autonomy and heteronomy, Kant mentions, although only in passing, "heautonomy" as the reflexive power of judgment to prescribe a law not to nature (as it does in autonomy) but to itself *(Critique of Judgment,* Introduction A xxxv/B xxxvii). Kant regarded the Christian principle of morality itself as autonomous, in contrast to certain theological elements with which it was connected and which made it heteronomous.

Against this Kantian notion of autonomy, made more radical through J. Fichte and F. W. J. Schelling, early opponents raised the objection that it denied the essential human obligation to God. In an essay from 1801, K. L. Reinhold called autonomy the "basic error" that was taken for the "basic truth." F. H. Jacobi called Kant's and Fichte's autonomous form of morality a "self-deification." F. von Baader called Kantian critique blind to God for not recognizing that conscience is a co-knowledge, a knowing of oneself as being known by God, and that the spontaneity of the will rests on the indwelling of God in the will and not on an impersonal moral law of reason; and to the autonomous self of Descartes's *cogito ergo sum* (I think, therefore I am) he contraposed the formula *cogitor ergo cogitans sum* (I am thought, therefore I am a thinking someone). Indeed, Baader regarded as antimoral, antireligious, and revolutionistic all moral doctrines based upon an absolute autonomy.

Neo-Kantianism and After. Kant had developed the concept chiefly by reference to the rational will (practical reason), while also indicating its more comprehensive sense. With Neo-Kantianism this universal sense, which had been obscured by the ethical framework of the discussion, returns. Thus, H. Cohen, in his *Ethik des reinen Willens* (1907), declares that the concept of autonomy must be drawn from logic as well as from ethics and that what constitutes heteronomy is fundamentally the mistrust of theoretical reason. On this basis, several concrete, autonomous spheres can be defined: the autonomy of science, religion, the social, and the aesthetic. An important variation of ethical autonomy is found in the ethics of material values associated with N. Hartmann and M. Scheler, the latter of whom emphasized that the act of obedience to what is given to reason as a norm is itself an autonomous act of the will. Here the theory of the autonomy of values means that norms of action are pregiven to the individual agent as objective, material values, which the agent needs to appropriate and master, not to produce, through ethical activity. Personal autonomy presupposes the prior existence of such material values. In this case, heteronomous validity is "introcepted" (W. Stern) into an autonomous obligation.

The discussion of autonomy in religious thought today is complicated by the addition of a third concept, theonomy, which emerges briefly in the post-Kantian discussion but does not stand out until Tillich develops it in connection with his theology of culture and of history. Tillich's discussion of autonomy has the double distinction of working out the dynamics of autonomy and of conceiving the relation between the autonomous and theonomous by reference to what he calls "form" and "depth."

Autonomous reason is reason that actualizes its structure without regard to its depth; heteronomous reason is a structure of reason that is imposed upon reason as the depth of reason; and theonomous reason is autonomous reason when, as autonomous, it is simultaneously transparent to its depth, or to what in his early works Tillich called *Gehalt*. "Autonomy does not mean the freedom of the individual to be a law to himself [but] the obedience of the individual to the law of

51

reason, which he finds in himself as a rational being" (*Systematic Theology*, 1:83f.); the "problem of heteronomy is the problem of an authority which claims to represent reason, namely, the depth of reason, against its autonomous actualization" (1:84); and theonomy means "autonomous reason united with its own depth" (1:85). This concept of autonomy differs from the Kantian conception, according to which empirical knowledge is heteronomous, because it is dependent upon sense-intuition, in contrast to the moral law, which is immanent in reason. For, in contrast to Kant, Tillich conceives autonomy as the self-determination of a structure that is already a bipolar structure of subject and object (in epistemological terms) or self and world (in ontological terms). "The *nomos* ('law') of *autos* ('self') . . . is the law of subjective-objective reason" (1:84). Hence, autonomy is not the self-determination of the subject over against the object but the state in which the subject-object structure determines and is determined by itself; and genuine empirical knowledge is, consequently, not heteronomous, as in Kant, but autonomous (1:64). The question of autonomy in Tillich is not whether the subject is determined by itself or by an object in the world but whether the self-world structure determines and is determined by itself, that is, whether it is free to be the structure it is. Heteronomy has, therefore, a negative connotation in Tillich that it does not have in Kant; it refers to a state of affairs in which one element of the whole structure of reason is equated with the depth of reason and placed over against the structure of reason.

The dynamics of reason are related to the way in which, under the conditions of existence, autonomous reason is in conflict with heteronomous reason as the result of losing its transparency to depth. Heteronomy is the imposition of a law on reason from outside reason; but the outside of reason is in fact an element of reason. "Heteronomy is . . . authority which claims to represent reason . . . against its autonomous actualization" (1:84). Such heteronomy arises as a reaction against an autonomy that has lost its depth. But the reaction is destructive, and the conflict between the two leads to the quest for a new theonomy, that is, a reunion of depth and rational form.

Autonomous reason, the structure of the self in relation to its other, is theonomous when its own rational structure is transparent to the depth of the structure, when "depth" means the transrational that, because it exceeds rational grasp, is neither subject (in opposition to object) nor object (in opposition to subject) but equally beyond as well as apparent in both subject and object—"the absolute Nothing and the absolute Something" that is neither a being nor the substance or totality of beings but "above all being" ("Theology of Culture," 162). Similarly, autonomous being is theonomous when it is transparent to the depth of being, which is neither the self nor the world but apparent in both of them.

A typology of current usages of the concept of autonomy can be drawn from Tillich's concept. If Tillich represents one type, then a second type, represented by

Karl Barth, sees autonomy and heteronomy as constituting the alternative, the one referring to human self-determination and the other referring to determination by something or someone other than one's own self, whether the other be worldly objects or other persons. Theonomy, in turn, is not an alternative to autonomy or heteronomy; it belongs to a different frame of reference. Thus, Barth contrasted the theonomy of his dogmatics with the autonomy of a philosophical system by the difference in the center. At the spot where a system of thought has a "basic intuition" as its organizing center, dogmatics has an opening (like, Barth said, the open ring in the center of a wheel) for the self-showing of God (*Kirchliche Dogmatik*, 1/2:969). This open place is only provisionally filled and always subject to change. The presupposition, made in Barth's dogmatics, that God shows himself in the word of God, is the concrete representation of this theonomous element, which is as different from autonomy as it is from heteronomy. "Autonomy should not be understood, any more than heteronomy, as in opposition to theonomy but as in correspondence and correlation to theonomy" (1/2:958). All other presuppositions are at best provisional and can be corrected as warranted. Barth's use of autonomy, heteronomy, and theonomy differs from the type represented by Tillich in two ways. Unlike Tillich, but like Kant, Barth's type includes in the legitimate structure of being or reason both an autonomous and a heteronomous element—so that both autonomy and heteronomy can answer to and be related to theonomy. Thus, the assertion of the self-revealing of God in the word of God as an absolute presupposition is intended to be neither autonomous nor heteronomous. In Tillich's type, such an absolute presupposition would have to be regarded as heteronomous because it is a rational assertion—an assertion about something by someone—but it is treated as though it cannot be rationally judged.

The third type, placed somewhere between Tillich and Barth, is represented by Bultmann, in whose view there is no intermediate position between autonomy and theonomy. Theonomy is either autonomy or heteronomy; but if autonomy is understood in a genuine sense, then autonomy is theonomy. This resembles the Barthian type in seeing autonomy and heteronomy as the alternative, but it differs from Barth in allying theonomy with autonomy and not with heteronomy. It differs from Tillich because it operates with a polarity of self and other (self-world, subject-object) but not with a polarity of structure and depth (or form and *Gehalt*).

As the typology of uses indicates, the concept of autonomy cannot be understood in isolation from its related terms. When understood in relation to them, its valuation changes depending on whether theonomy is compatible with heteronomy as well as with autonomy or only with autonomy or only with heteronomy.

ROBERT P. SCHARLEMANN

Bibliography

Karl Barth, *Kirchliche Dogmatik* (Church Dogmatics).
Rudolf Bultmann, "Humanism and Christianity," *Journal of Religion* 32 (1952): 77-86.
R. Pohlmann, "Autonomie," in *Historisches Wörterbuch der Philosophie,* vol. 1.
Paul Tillich, "On the Idea of a Theology of Culture [1919]," in *What Is Religion?*
Paul Tillich, *Systematic Theology,* vol. 1, 83-86, 147-50; vol. 3, 249-68.

Cross Reference: Alienation, Freedom, Ultimate Concern.

BAPTISM (*See* SACRAMENTS/SACRAMENTAL THEOLOGY, WORSHIP.)

BASIC CHRISTIAN COMMUNITIES

Basic Christian communities (*communidades eclesiales de base,* "basic ecclesial communities") are small lay Catholic communities that are transforming the face of Catholicism in Latin America. They are found primarily among the poor and marginal in urban slums and isolated rural areas. Since their appearance in the mid-1960s, they have grown to an estimated 150,000 communities with concentrations in Brazil and Central America. One reason for their rapid growth is the severe shortage of priests in Latin America, where there is now less than 1 priest for every 5,000 Catholics. Without the base communities, large numbers of the faithful, particularly in isolated areas, would have to do completely without study, worship, and the Eucharist. Base communities are closely associated with liberation theology and its emphasis on ending the oppression of the poor. Just as liberation theology is the theological expression of the base communities, the base communities are the social expression of liberation theology. This is reflected in their twofold purpose: evangelization and social action.

In a typical meeting of a base community, the people gather together, with or without clergy, to read and discuss the Bible in light of their own situation, to celebrate the Eucharist, to pray, to talk politics, and to plan for action. (Several such dialogues and Bible studies from one base community in Nicaragua are collected in *The Gospel in Solentiname.*) The base communities share many features with the Protestant pietist practice of home Bible study and prayer groups. What is different about the basic communities is directly related to the specific historical situation of Latin American Roman Catholicism.

Beyond the simple need to revitalize the church and to cope with the shortage of priests, the base communities clearly have a social and political agenda. Because the Roman Catholic Church came to Latin America by conquest, its hierarchy have had historic ties with conservative wealth and political power. Consequently, it has been largely distant from the numerous poor, which has contributed to a highly passive approach to religion among the laity. The basic communities are an attempt to overcome this hierarchical and passive past. They seek to empower the laity, especially the poor and, more recently, women, over against the established social order and the hierarchy. They work on local political and social action programs, such as improving the water supply, supporting a literacy campaign, or gaining access to health care. They challenge the exclusive right of the clergy to teach and interpret the Bible, and even allow laity to celebrate the Eucharist. With the increased role that women have taken in many communities, they also press the question of women's participation in the mass and women's ordination. They thus constitute a revolutionary challenge to established Catholic understandings of the church; in the words of the Brazilian theologian Leonardo Boff, they are "reinventing the Church."

The basic Christian communities raise important questions that the Catholic church will need to confront in the twenty-first century. They offer a way to involve the laity, to respond to the shortage of priests, and to curb losses of members to conservative evangelical Protestant churches. Yet many in the church hierarchy, both in Latin America and in Rome, fear that the communities endanger the unity of the church and the office of the priesthood. Among their concerns, they ask: How will authority and power in the communities be distributed in the absence of a priest? Do training and education count for nothing in interpreting the Scripture? How are conflicting interpretations to be resolved? The base communities, like the liberation theology they embody, employ Marxist analysis and categories. How will they respond to the drastic changes sweeping over the Marxist and formerly Marxist states of Europe? To be sure, the end of one form of Marxism does not mean the end of all forms, and there is much more to liberation theology than Marxism; but the issue will need to be addressed.

By no means are these questions limited to Latin America or even to Catholicism. Some have suggested that the base community model can be transferred or adapted to North American and European situations. North American Catholicism also faces a shortage of priests, and most mainline Protestant churches may soon face a similar shortage of clergy. At the same time, laypersons are more educated and literate (at least in general, if not about religion) than ever before in history, and they are increasingly unwilling to be told what to believe. These trends are linked to the growth of universal literacy and the spread of mass communications, which are not likely to be reversed. All these developments will require a reconsideration of what it means to be the church, and the base communities will play an important part in this task.

GARRETT E. PAUL

55

Bibliography

Leonardo Boff, *Ecclesiogenesis: The Base Communities Reinvent the Church.*
Ernesto Cardenal, ed., *The Gospel in Solentiname,* 3 vols.
Sergio Torres and John Eagleson, eds., *The Challenge of Basic Christian Communities.*

Cross Reference: Ecclesiology, Laity, Liberation Theology, Praxis.

BEING/BECOMING

Alfred North Whitehead contended that the hymn lines "Abide with me; fast falls the eventide" set forth "the complete problem of metaphysics." "Abide" speaks for constancy and "falls" for change. The question of the relative weight to be given these testimonies is the problem of Being and Becoming: whether being is more basic than becoming, or becoming more basic than being. The answer hinges on how God, history, human nature, and non–human nature are characterized.

People who argue that being is more basic affirm that constancy gets at the heart of things more than change, while people who argue that becoming is more basic affirm just the opposite. If being is more basic, then what is truly divine, historical, human, or natural must be unchanging and, it is usually added, universally the same; but if becoming is more basic, then what is truly divine, historical, human, or natural must be changing and, it is usually added, different in different situations.

The issue is historic. The pre-Socratic Parmenides of Elea argued that what is "simply is—now altogether, one, continuous," while the pre-Socratic Heraclitus of Ephesus argued that "everything flows and nothing abides." It is safe to say that Parmenides' bias toward being prevailed in Western philosophy and theology until the twentieth century, when modern physics (particularly quantum physics) argued that events are most basic and that these events in some respects are indeterminate, perhaps even innovative. Nevertheless, determinisms in natural science (e.g., the chance-free world of relativity physics) and in social science (e.g., the predictable world of sociobiology) remain strong, and place greatest emphasis on being-like continuities.

All general thinkers, whatever their tendency, must have some way of accounting for the side they de-emphasize. Accordingly, Plato, a philosopher of being, will account for becoming, locating it in the "less real" world of ordinary events. Equally, Hegel, a philosopher of becoming, will account for being, locating it in the Absolute to the extent that it provides the rational impetus for all that happens. While some—for example, Charles Hartshorne—aspire to give equal weight to being and becoming, it can be argued that coherence requires, finally, that an implicit if not an explicit preference be given to one side or the other.

Equally, theologians may favor either being or becoming, but they must account for the side they de-emphasize. Those who emphasize being are heavily affected by ancient Greek philosophies of being; those who emphasize becoming are heavily affected by ancient Hebrew notions. In the former tradition God is closely associated with ahistorical being, human souls participate in that being, and both are everlasting; but this tradition usually allows, even if unwittingly, that God changes enough to absorb effects of the world and that souls change enough to be subject to corruption. In the latter tradition God is closely associated with historical becoming and people are formed largely by historical circumstance; yet even amid historical flux these theologies find in God a consistent influence and in people a personal identity through time.

Today's theologians of being find the deepest threat to life's worth in the moral, spiritual, or intellectual incompleteness that comes from falling away from being, so that fulfillment lies in the communion with being, which gives eternal life, forgiveness, or meaning. Today's theologians of becoming find the deepest threat to life's worth in the loss of an aesthetic sense of becoming, so that fulfillment lies in the communion with becoming, which overcomes what William James called *tedium vitae*.

In recent theology of being, reality is found beyond history; followers of Karl Barth, narrative theologians, and fundamentalists look to continuous traditions while followers of Paul Tillich look to ontological absolutes. These theologians must explain how a theology based on what is eternal and, usually, universal can be credible in a world where change seems so basic. In recent theology of becoming, reality is found within history; empirical theologians or postmodern theologians ranging from neopragmatists, to deconstructionists, to new historicists look to the changing testimony of nature, language, or culture. These theologians must explain how a theology that places trust in what is transitory and, usually, local can remain appropriate to a continuing religious tradition. In recent anti-metaphysical theologies, both being and becoming are treated in principle as meaningless metaphysical abstractions; linguistic theologians, for example, make this anti-metaphysical move. These theologians must explain how it happens that in practice they favor being-like constancy or becoming-like change.

WILLIAM DEAN

Bibliography

Charles Hartshorne and William L. Reese, *Philosophers Speak of God.*
Paul Tillich, *Systematic Theology,* vol. 1.
Henry Nelson Wieman, *Religious Experience and Scientific Method.*

Cross Reference: Metaphysics, Panentheism, Philosophical Theology, Process Theology.

BELIEF (*See* FAITH.)

BIBLICAL CRITICISM

Biblical criticism uses a wide range of methods; all of them involve reading the biblical text "from a distance." It can be put this way: "Reading" the Bible means entering into the text directly, letting it open its own world to the reader, while "criticism" means looking at the text in order to understand it according to standards that come (at least in part) from a different world and not directly from the text itself. There is no pure "reading" without some form of critical distance (even if unreflective) to enrich it, and all forms of criticism also imply some direct appreciation of the text.

The Historical Critical Method. Most modern biblical criticism has been strongly historical, so much so that the "historical critical method" has often been called the only critical way to read the Bible. Historical study usually moves "behind" the text, to reconstruct the events, people, and religious and social practices from which the written books emerged. The historical critical method emphasizes the movement of history in time but not necessarily as an evolutionary movement from the simple or primitive to the more developed. Also basic to the historical method is comparison between the biblical tradition and the cultures of the environment.

Often historical study of the Bible has been rigidly convinced that the criteria for interpretation should be taken wholly from modern experience, so that anything foreign to the historian's experience would be explained by modern criteria of reasonableness. Thus, how to interpret miracles was a classic question raised by historical study of the Bible, since most modern people do not experience miracles directly. But historical study can also allow the different world of the past to open new possibilities for the present that would not have seemed reasonable apart from the biblical text.

Historically oriented study of the Bible also raises the question of the canon; that is, what makes the biblical books distinctive, for historical study often points out the similarities between what is found in the Bible and other customs and faith. Modern discoveries of Jewish and early Christian books closely related to parts of the Bible have made the canon an urgent question for modern study of the Bible. What if such a work as the Gospel of Thomas (discovered in Egypt in the twentieth century) were to give a picture of Jesus somehow on a par with that of the Gospels?

Historical study of the Bible runs the danger of being interested only in the distant past. Hence other forms of criticism supplement or replace it. Most of them look at the formal patterns of the biblical literature (*see* below).

Canonical Criticism. Canonical criticism bridges the gap between critical historical study and the tradition of faith. Historical criticism has often looked "behind" the text to reconstruct a history or an earlier form of the biblical literature, but canonical criticism focuses on the biblical books themselves, usually in their completed present form, since these are the books the church has revered. It affirms that the meaning of the Bible is found in the believing community, yet that this meaning has not been constant, but was always discovered in concrete situations at particular times. Thus the history of the community and its interaction with the biblical texts gives access to the meaning of the Bible today. For example, the repeated effort in the Bible to discover and express a single loyalty to the one God (i.e., the many and varied rejections of idolatry) can be taken, in canonical criticism, to disclose a theme that will be central for interpreting the Bible now.

Sociological Criticism. Sociological criticism is a type of historical study that inquires about the social conditions in which a biblical work originally functioned. It shifts attention away from the individual believer to the group, and it reminds the reader that what was originally written for a very different social situation is misunderstood if it is simply applied to a modern individual reader.

Textual Criticism. Printing made a standard text possible. The collection, ordering, and evaluation of the myriad variations in the several thousand manuscript copies of the Bible (or parts of it) is the task of textual criticism. The careful, word-for-word comparison of biblical manuscripts with some standard text and the recording of all the variations is a task that is far from complete today. Recent discoveries of texts both of the Hebrew Bible (especially those among the Dead Sea Scrolls or Qumran discoveries) and of the New Testament (especially among the papyri found in Egypt), have added far older witnesses to the biblical text than were available until this century.

The task of sifting these variations in the text and deciding on the best text is the second phase of textual criticism. It involves the weighing of the age of the variation in question, and also the weighing of the probabilities of how this "reading" fits the thought of the book as otherwise known and how effectively it explains other variations of the same verse or section. For example, in Matthew 5:22, "Every one who is angry with his brother *without cause* shall be liable to judgment," the phrase "without cause" has been rejected from modern texts and translations on both counts: It is not found in many early copies of Matthew, and it is not consistent with the sharp challenge that the Sermon on the Mount offers elsewhere.

Philology and Linguistics. The Hebrew, Aramaic, and Greek languages of the Bible have been studied with the goal of determining, as accurately as possible, the particular meanings of words and sentence structures. The splendid grammars and dictionaries of biblical languages now available are the fruit of this philological

59

study. Philology sees language "diachronically," as it develops in time; it has also shown how the languages of the Bible are related to those of neighboring cultures.

Modern linguistics focuses sharply on the structures of language as a "synchronic" system, as it functions as a self-regulating system at a particular time, without regard to its historical development. Negatively, linguistics makes relative the dictionary approach to language by showing that words do not have constant, self-contained meanings, but that they always function in relationships, in a context within which meaning is created.

Linguistics distinguishes between "language," the whole system that makes possible the production of any particular sentence, and "speech," the concrete acts of speaking or writing, and it shows how specific acts or statements in language are made possible by the more general structures. In biblical studies linguistics has been especially fruitful in the work of translation. Since words and sentence structures do not correspond exactly from language to language, a careful attention to functional equivalents is important.

Form Criticism. Many passages in the Bible functioned in the life of the community before they were included in the books where we now find them. Psalms, hymns, and parables are clear examples, but others, such as laws, required historical study before the existence of the form prior to the written text could be recognized. Form criticism is the study of formal patterns that functioned in particular sociological ways. First used in the study of the Hebrew Bible, it was able to offer new classifications of the psalms (praise, lament, etc.) and to show patterns of legal, prophetic, and wisdom speech.

Also important for form criticism is the boundary between oral and written language, for many of the forms discerned were originally oral ones. The extent of the influence of oral speech—with its pattern of repetition and its creative reformulation as a story is retold—on biblical literature is a hotly debated topic. Unfortunately, the original setting of many forms can be reconstructed only hypothetically. In New Testament studies, form criticism has been especially useful in classifying the forms of the sayings and narratives in the Synoptic Gospels. Form-critical analysis, by showing the general pattern of a parable or miracle story, for instance, is able to make much clearer the force of a particular parable by showing how it both uses and creatively distorts the basic form.

Redaction Criticism. Redaction criticism studies the changes that an author made in the traditions incorporated into a finished work. It aims to understand how Jews and Christians responded to new situations by creatively reworking their traditions. Form criticism presupposes sufficient stability in tradition so that earlier (often originally oral) forms can be recognized in a later work. Redaction critics agree, but they look at the often slight changes in a section of the Bible and in the introductory and concluding settings of a passage to interpret how the final author related the tradition to a later community and a later pattern of faith.

Redaction criticism is on firm ground when both earlier and later stages of the tradition are available. A clear case is the use of Mark by Matthew and Luke, according to the "two document theory" (*see* below). Changes that Matthew and Luke made in Mark's formulation of the tradition about Jesus indicate the special interests of the later writers and their churches. Redaction criticism can also be very successful even when the earlier form of the tradition is present only in its later setting. The editing of earlier forms of the Hebrew story by the writer or writers of Judges and I and II Kings, for instance, tells us a great deal about the faith of these authors (*see* Judg. 2:19).

Redaction criticism thus assumes that the writers of the biblical books were not mere collectors (as has sometimes been thought by form critics) but were authors who expressed distinct points of view. Yet its clues to the meaning of a work are found in specific parts; it is left to literary criticism to look at the overall pattern of a book.

Literary Criticism. Literary criticism may be focused in various ways, but in biblical studies most literary criticism has dealt either with literary history or with literary form.

Literary criticism as literary history led to the discovery that many biblical books were not written as unified wholes by single authors but were collections that used earlier sources. The classic "Documentary theory" of the writing of the first five books of the Bible and the "two document theory" of the writing of the first three Gospels in the New Testament are primary examples of historical literary criticism. The Documentary theory of the Pentateuch or first five books of the Hebrew Scriptures holds that these books were compiled from a number of previously written "documents," two of which, "J" and "E," were narratives of the Hebrew past, and two of which, "D" (the deuteronomic source) and "P" (the Priestly document), were collections of laws. The clue that led to the discovery of this hypothesis is a shift between two names of God, "Yahweh" ("J" in German) and "Elohim" ("E"), in the narrative parts of the books in question. Since an unreflective reading of these books suggests that they were all written by a single author, Moses, the Documentary theory was exceedingly controversial when it was first advanced. Current study, for the most part, accepts the view that these books were compilations, but it is much more flexible about the details, since today oral tradition is recognized as playing a large part in the transmission of the traditions that we now find in these books.

A similar study of the first three Gospels of the New Testament led to the "two document theory," which is now very widely held, though not universally accepted. It holds that Matthew and Luke both used Mark as a source, and also used a lost document, "Q," which was a collection of the words of Jesus.

61

Essential though it is, historical literary criticism, like all forms of historical study, risks leaving the Bible in the distant past if it is the only method employed. Literary criticism that looks at the form of the passage or book in question is more open to present-day appropriation.

Literary criticism directed to form is quite varied. From the time of Aristotle's *Poetics* to the New Critics of the twentieth century, formal literary criticism has studied how the form of a work (or shorter passage) is related to the effects the work produces. Attention is shifted away both from the history of the work and from its ideas as abstracted from their role in the work itself. Instead, criticism is turned to how the work appeals to the imagination and to feelings. Such formal criticism thus includes both a rigorous attention to the interrelation of the parts of the work—how plot, characters, setting, and language are related, for instance—and a sensitivity to the work's symbolic, imaginative, and aesthetic aspects.

Narrative is a prominent literary form in the Bible, and formal literary criticism has been exceptionally fruitful in interpreting biblical narrative. Narrative criticism illuminates how the subtle characterization of figures like Joseph is achieved and how the actually narrated story of the Gospels is related both to the figure of Jesus and to the expected events that lie beyond the scope of the Gospel narrative. Study of biblical narrative has also emphasized the contrast between narratives such as the Gospels, which help the reader find a place, and narratives such as the parables, which often dislocate or displace the reader.

Structural criticism has its roots in the formal criticism briefly described above. It attempts to achieve greater rigor, and thus to depend less on intuition, by analyzing a passage into constituent units of meaning, showing how they are related step-by-step as one moves through the work, and how they derive their dynamic from deeper, more general or abstract forces that lie beneath the surface interactions that are studied in traditional formal criticism. Structural criticism is an extension of linguistics to units larger than the sentence. It attempts to show how the deeper structures, such as the fundamental existential tension between life and death, and the fundamental ethical tension between good and evil, provide the energy or dynamic for the production of meaning.

A specific type of literary criticism is genre criticism, which seeks to identify the larger forms of biblical literature and relate them to their functions in the life of the community. An example is the genre of the Gospels, which has been the focus of intense study. How appropriate is the description of the Gospels as biographies? It was long held that their lack of interest in Jesus' inner life made it wrong to class the Gospels as biographies, but more recent study of Hellenistic biographies has shown that the Gospels are close enough to some ancient biographies that this is an appropriate way to think of them. Yet the apocalyptic element in the Gospels has led some students to think of them as a modification of the form of the apocalypse, while others point to the element of *kerygma* or proclamation and see the Gospels as a unique genre, created to proclaim the Christian message. The diversity of views is a reminder that important writings may not fit established patterns of genre.

Audience criticism considers how a work makes its impact on its audience. It may deal with the original audience, or with a modern one. In either case, such criticism notes how the reader or hearer must make a creative contribution to what the work becomes as it is understood, so that the meaning of a work is not fixed, but is changed or enriched as people with different backgrounds and questions encounter it.

Conclusion. The specialization that marks academic work has tended to separate biblical criticism from theology, but these two studies always interact and deeply need each other. Historical biblical study contributed enormously to theology when an important task of theology was to show how the biblical narratives or biblical figures such as Jesus were functioning in a world in many respects like the present world. This is still an important contribution, but at the present time another contribution of biblical criticism, especially in its various literary modes, takes precedence. This involves showing how faith is communicated not simply through the intellect, but by narrative or story, metaphor, and imagination. Biblical literary criticism is challenging theology to deal less with ideas and doctrines, important though these are, and to reflect on how God's presence and purpose are communicated in imaginative ways.

WILLIAM A. BEARDSLEE

Bibliography

Eldon Jay Epp and George W. MacRae, eds., *The New Testament and Its Modern Interpreters.*
John H. Hayes and Carl R. Holladay, *Biblical Exegesis: A Beginner's Handbook.*
Douglas A. Knight and Gene M. Tucker, eds., *The Hebrew Bible and Its Modern Interpreters.*

Cross Reference: Biblical Theology, Canon, Hermeneutics, Structuralism.

BIBLICAL THEOLOGY

Biblical theology in its simplest form is the effort to state what is the theology of the Bible or the theology found within the Bible. Although that may be understood narrowly as referring to what the Bible says about God, more often biblical theology is concerned with a broader range of theological concerns, seeking to give an account of Scripture's statements about numerous topics. It differs from systematic and constructive theology in that it does not turn to other sources such as experience or tradition to construct theology, although such sources may have some implicit role to play (and indeed the discussion today is raising various questions about the place of such aspects of the theological enterprise in the formulation of biblical theology). Rather, biblical theology seeks theological formulation in some constructive, holistic, and unified manner of what one finds in the Bible.

Background. The twentieth century has seen the discipline of biblical theology go through various swings and changes, increasing and decreasing in popularity. The earlier tendency to articulate a biblical theology much as if it were a history of Israelite religion (a tendency that grew out of the origins of biblical theology in the Enlightenment as a *historical* discipline), shifted in the post–World War II period under the impact of the theologians Karl Barth and Rudolf Bultmann. In the United States and Europe, vigorous endeavors to set forth the theology of the Bible or of one of the Testaments or of some particular biblical topic multiplied. The emphasis on history did not disappear, but it no longer determined the structure of any particular formulation. The developmental notions that were earlier present and tended to bring forth a reading of the Old Testament pointing to its archaic, primitive character gave way to readings of the theology of the Bible that assumed and sought to demonstrate the Bible's immediacy and accessibility for modern faith and the forms that theology takes in preaching, personal piety, and social action.

Within the last quarter-century, however, the broad sway of biblical theology and the consensus about its character have broken down for reasons from within the field of biblical study, well described by Brevard Childs in his *Biblical Theology in Crisis* (1969), and from within the broader fields of systematic theology, suggested, for example, in a now famous essay by Langdon Gilkey, "Cosmology, Ontology, and the Travail of Biblical Language" (*Journal of Religion* 41 [July 1961]: 194-205). Gilkey challenged the intelligibility of fundamental axioms of contemporary biblical theology, particularly its effort to build faith upon historical events that are accepted as the revelation and activity of God. Childs pointed to the many ways in which widely accepted assumptions that undergirded the broad emphasis upon biblical theology had come under severe question. These assumptions included an overemphasis upon history as the category of divine revelation and uncertainty about what that history consisted of; an insistence upon the unity of the Bible at a time when much biblical study was sharpening up the sense of its diversity and its multiple, if not contradictory, voices; a claim for a distinctive way of "biblical" thinking that rested upon poor linguistic procedures; and an apologetic claim for the uniqueness of biblical religion in the ancient world that could not be sustained in the face of the increasing knowledge of that world and its impact upon the Bible. Childs described a growing sense that the broad sway of biblical theology, within American biblical studies particularly, had had its day and was now gone. His own analysis reinforced that fact even though he desired to chart a new way for biblical theology.

The dominance of biblical theology that was apparent in the 1940s and 1950s in the United States indeed disappeared in the succeeding decades. New modes of analysis, such as literary criticism and social history, that were less interested in the theological dimensions of the Bible—if not hostile to them in some respects—came into currency and still command much attention. History of religion studies, which had been eclipsed in the movement toward biblical theology, came back to the forefront. Despite all of this, however, the sense that the Bible, with God and Jesus as its central subject matter, is in very basic respects a theological document and one that shapes the theology of the communities of faith that adhere to it, has meant that the effort to formulate a theological understanding of Scripture has continued to occupy the attention of interpreters of the Bible.

Some Approaches. A look at some of the more comprehensive efforts at biblical theology and the options they suggest identifies possibilities and issues that confront the biblical theologian. In several works, history provides the fundamental datum or framework for biblical theology. Although he never wrote a biblical theology and his views changed in the course of his lifetime, G. Ernest Wright wrote a seminal volume, *God Who Acts: Biblical Theology as Recital,* in which he argued that "the primary and irreducible assumption of biblical theology is that history is the revelation of God." Wright means that biblical theology is "first and foremost a theology of recital," a confession of faith in which the redemptive and formative events are recited. The task of biblical theology is to lay out and interpret those events and to make the appropriate inferences from them, such as the election of Israel, the covenant relationship, and the unity and meaningfulness of universal history. Wright's exclusive focus on history, to the neglect of nature as well as the wisdom literature, has been criticized frequently, yet the historical emphasis has been carried forward in a quite different fashion in the work of Gerhard von Rad. His two-volume *Old Testament Theology* is built around a historical framework, but that framework is not the event-determined history of which Wright spoke. It is the *history of Israel's traditions,* of the various *testimonies* to the power and activity of God, that are the subject matter of biblical, or in this case, Old Testament theology. The actual history is often inaccessible, but theology is built upon the interpretation or understanding of that history, not the history itself. The result is a biblical theology that is, in effect, a sequence of testimonies, often radically different. The diversity of the Scriptures is lifted up. One does not seek to blend all these testimonies into a single unified perspective, even though they often hold much in common.

Von Rad's approach has some similarities to Rudolf Bultmann's epochal New Testament theology. He also assumed both that the actuality behind the texts was often inaccessible, or even nonexistent, and that the subject matter of New Testament theology is the interpretation of the Christ event as that takes place in the different New Testament writings. In his case also, the theology of the New Testament is self-consciously set forth in relation to an analysis of being that is provided by existentialist philosophy. The center of New Testament theology is Paul, both because he is the primary interpreter of the meaning of the Christ event, which was the subject matter of the kerygmatic preaching of the early church, and because his theology is susceptible to an anthropological emphasis. More recent efforts at New Testament theology, including the work of Bultmann's own student Hans Conzelmann, have pressed the theological significance of the close connection between the risen Christ and Jesus of Nazareth in the early Christian community as well as in the New Testament.

Relating more directly to the work of von Rad and contributing significantly to the post-Bultmannian directions in New Testament theology have been the efforts of the Old Testament scholar Hartmut Gese and the New Testament scholar Peter Stuhlmacher, working independently but in conversation with each other, to uncover connections between both Testaments out of the stream of *history of traditions*. Growth of the biblical traditions begins in the Old Testament and continues into the New Testament. The two Testaments make up a unified, organic whole, according to Gese. Indeed, the history of biblical traditions in the Old Testament is not complete until it reaches the New Testament. This process of tradition history is, in effect, a process of revelation history (Gese).

One way of trying to hold together the diverse theological voices of Scripture is to search for a *center* around which everything revolves. The most notable and ambitious effort at this approach was that of Walther Eichrodt, in whose theology the covenant is the center and organizing framework of the Old Testament and thus of its theology. Ludwig Koehler's Old Testament theology sought to center the whole around the concept of God as Lord. In some fashion, most such proposals have claimed that the center of Old Testament theology has to do with God, whether it takes the form of the First Commandment requiring exclusive worship of the Lord; or the self-presentation formula, I am the Lord; or the covenantal formula, Yahweh (the Lord) the God of Israel and Israel the people of Yahweh. From the New Testament side, Peter Stuhlmacher and others have suggested that the Christ of the gospel provides the center of the whole of Scripture, Old Testament and New Testament. The fundamental character of such assertions of the centrality of God, or of God at work in Jesus Christ, as the subject matter can hardly be denied. Less clear is the question about whether such a center really holds together the diverse voices and subject matter of the Testaments.

Somewhat in reaction to that problem, some scholars have proposed to organize the biblical material theologically around certain *polarities* or *tensions* that are more comprehensive than a single center and that allow for diversity and tension. Samuel Terrien's *The Elusive Presence* constructs a biblical theology around the tension between the presence and absence of God and sees reflections of that tension in the relationship of ethics and aesthetics, word and vision, ear and eye, name and glory. In this effort, he seeks to hold together the historical and covenantal dimensions with the wisdom literature and psalms, avoiding the one-sided theological formulations of earlier efforts. A dialectical approach to the theology of the Bible is apparent also in the various works of Paul Hanson on apocalyptic, providence, the unity and diversity of scripture, and the notion of community, as well as in Claus Westermann's orienting much of his Old Testament theology around the two polarities of petition and praise, salvation and blessing. Although he has not as yet produced an Old Testament theology, Walter Brueggemann has taken a similar approach in devising a proposal for shaping such a theology around a dialectic that can be expressed in several ways: structure legitimation in tension with the embrace of pain, contractual and critical theology, cultural embrace and cultural criticism, creation theology and covenantal theology.

This line of approach seems more open to holding together some of the strains and the diversity of Scripture. Although it is primarily found among Old Testament scholars, they seek to demonstrate its applicability to biblical theology as a whole and not simply to the first of the Testaments.

One of the most fruitful theological studies of the New Testament in recent times has been the work of J. Christiaan Beker on the theology of Paul *(Paul the Apostle* and *The Triumph of God: The Essence of Paul's Thought)*. The subtitle of the second volume is somewhat misleading. For while Beker insists on the fundamentally apocalyptic framework of Paul's gospel (i.e., Paul's interpretation of the Christian message), his primary approach to the theology of the apostle is in working out "the dialectic of coherence and contingency" in Paul's thought. By coherence he means "the unchanging components of Paul's gospel," and by contingency he means "the changing situational part of the gospel, that is, the diversity and particularity of sociological, economic, and psychological factors that confront Paul in his churches" (15-16). Beker's dialectic is shaped differently from that of the Old Testament theologians cited above and risks the possibility that the coherence becomes a center and the dialectic disappears. The dangers generally present in such an approach rest primarily in the tendency to reduce diversity and plurality to duality—or in Beker's case, to a single essence or core—and the concomitant possibility that one pole becomes de facto a kind of ruling or normative one.

Perennial Issues. This brief survey of approaches to biblical theology has amplified the ways in which the *shape and structure* of a biblical theology is crucial to its presentation. Is it formed around a center, a polarity, a dialectic? Does it take its structure from innerbiblical categories, for example, covenant and election (as in Wright and Eichrodt), from the shape and order of the canon, from the sequence of biblical witnesses (as in von Rad), or, as was customary in an earlier time and still merits more attention than is usually given it by biblical theologians, from the categories of dogmatic theology?

The way in which the *unity* of Scripture is discerned in the midst of the *diversity* of voices is a continuing theological issue that has been approached in different ways: from Eichrodt, who seeks to establish a unitary principle in the form of the covenant, to the proponents of a dialectic or polarity, who claim a kind of middle ground between the awareness of the great diversity of the material and a sense that it holds together but only with tension, to von Rad, who relinquishes the search for a unity on the grounds that it is inappropriate and ultimately to be frustrated because the material is self-consciously a cluster of witnesses from different times and circumstances.

Less apparent than the problem of perceiving unity within diversity is the hotly debated question about whether a biblical theology should be *descriptive,* not requiring any position vis-à-vis the material, or *normative,* implicitly making claims about the nature of reality and the will of God. In a well-known article on biblical theology in *The Interpreter's Dictionary of the Bible,* Krister Stendahl argued that the task of biblical theology is descriptive, responsible for determining what the texts meant in their original setting, a possibility open to historical critical study and not presupposing anything about their continuing or present meaning. That concern belongs to hermeneutics and systematic theology. His formulation brought forth an unresolved debate. In some cases, positions have been taken in principle; in other cases, the presentation functions in an implicitly normative fashion (as in Brueggemann). That the latter is often the case is suggested by the reticence to engage in biblical theology on the part of Jewish biblical scholars because of a perception from the literature that normative and confessional stances are both implicitly and explicitly characteristic of biblical theology. That issue is pressed in a somewhat different fashion when one encounters a forthright claim that biblical theology is and ought to be located in communities of reference and faith, a claim found in the work of such theologians as Hanson and Brueggemann.

Present Challenges. Finally, the biblical theologian is aware of currents in biblical studies today that pose some challenges to the theological enterprise. One of these is the question of whether or not feminist and liberationist readings of Scripture can contribute to biblical theology. The focus of these approaches—on social location, the authoritative or normative character of women's experience, the resistance to the male domination within the content of the Bible and over the process of transmission and interpretation, and the centrality of outside voices in the theological task—means that biblical theology will have to devise some different ways of working to take account of this challenge.

It further remains to be seen to what extent the various literary approaches to biblical interpretation and the attention that is being given to the social history and analysis of biblical texts and their location will contribute to the work of biblical theology. Although the domination of historical critical exegesis over theology has been moderated, if not broken, such exegesis was understood by many biblical theologians in the past to work closely with biblical theology, and it indeed contributed to the strong historical thrust that was present among them. At least some literary approaches are resistant to a theological reading of biblical texts, seeing it as extrapolating theological content in a way that is unfaithful to a text's presentation of itself. Finally, the effort of the social historians and scientists—or those who use their methods—to read the texts through the lens of social history is a priori not conducive to a theological interpretation.

PATRICK D. MILLER

Bibliography

Gerhard Hasel, *Old Testament Theology: Basic Issues in the Current Debate.*
John H. Hayes and Frederick Prussner, *Old Testament Theology: Its History and Development.*
Henning Graf Reventlow, *Problems of Biblical Theology in the Twentieth Century.*
_____, *Problems of Old Testament Theology in the Twentieth Century.*

Cross Reference: Biblical Criticism, Covenant, Dogmatic Theology, Election, Incarnation, Justification, Kingdom of God, Miracles, Resurrection.

BLACK THEOLOGY

During the 1960s, in the midst of the outward progress made by the civil rights movement—and perhaps because of it—the face of America was changed. Much like the sinister vision of William Butler Yeats, some "rough beast, its hour come round at last, slouched toward Bethlehem to be born." In the 1960s, this event was the rise of black power. The term "black power," as we now understand it, was first given currency by Adam Clayton Powell, Jr., at a rally in Chicago in May 1965.

The term "black power" was and remains charged with tremendous emotive energy. It became the rallying cry for black nationalist groups, political radicals, and cultural revolutionaries; as such, it was the hallmark of the break between the black radical movement and the more accommodationist civil rights movement. The central intent of the black power movement was the empowerment of black people.

The need for black power was sharpened by the presence of oppression and racism. Black people historically found themselves the victims of scorn, rebuke, violence, rape, and death because of the color of their skin. This victimization, most sharply felt in slavery and continuing in subtle forms of racism and discrimination, which afflict black people today, denies the humanity of black people as equally endowed creations of God. "Black power" was the call to black people to shed those ideas of inferiority, which racial oppression fosters, and to engage in a struggle to liberate their bodies, minds, and spirits.

The cry for black power was not limited to the streets of urban America or to the "secular" radicals in the black community. It was also heard in the black churches. Many black clergy heard and responded to the anguished cry of the oppressed. For them black power posed a radical challenge to the normative notions of theology and ministry in the black community. Many of these clergy articulated the need for a theology with its focus, content, and method firmly rooted in the struggle for liberation of black people. European and American theology had never taken the suffering of black people as a serious theological issue and therefore was incapable of speaking prophetically in the midst of their oppression. Out of this vacuum, black theology in its present form emerged.

Black power was the political source of black theology, but black theology had a spiritual source as well—black religion drawn from the remnants of African traditional religions and slave religion. Although one can speak about these sources as distinct entities, they are inseparable. The traditional Western separation of the physical and the spiritual, the sacred and the secular, is foreign to the African American sensibility. Black religion provides black theology with a world view and a metaphysical base from which to view the physical world and the social order. It has historically affirmed the inherent worth of black people, their dignity as creations of God even in inhumane situations, and God's special providential care for them.

Under the circumstances of slavery and oppression in the United States, this slave religion carried with it an inescapable dimension of black radicalism. This radical religion manifested itself in a number of ways. It always sought independence from white control. The growth of slave religion itself was a spiritual form of rebellion and autonomy. The founding of the independent black churches in America was an instance of the seizure of institutional freedom. The emergence of black theology in the 1960s was a continuation of this radical tradition in the form of intellectual freedom from the canons of white theological thought. This radicalism was not limited to the black church but was seen in a variety of social and political expressions in the black community. However, because the black community did not divide the world into the sacred and the secular, the presence of the spirit of freedom in settings other than the ecclesiastical was quite consistent with the African American religious sensibility.

Black religion, especially its creative use of symbolism, gave black theology a distinct language with which to express the deepest convictions and longings of an oppressed people. Its prayers, poetry, sermons, songs, and litanies provided the context for the telling of the black story. The folklore of black people contains stories that are more than entertainment. These stories embody, in narrative form, the historical hope and eschatological confidence of black people. Black theology has always been expressed in the language of black religion and folklore. Because it emerged from the experience of black people, black theology expressed the deepest religious commitments of black people in a language they created. Therefore, black theology could not remain true to its identity and adopt the language of Europe and North America. It had to be expressed as a folk theology.

Black theology is also a biblical theology. A great deal of the religious self-understanding of black people is expressed in biblical language. This biblical language is not simply the result of black people reading and reiterating the Bible. Rather, this language has become an integral part of black self-expression. One must not underestimate the role the Bible played in the formation of the folklore of black people. Biblical images became so interwoven into the fabric of black experience that now it is almost impossible to appreciate black folklore fully without attention to the Bible. The Bible is a text that is not simply the possession of the black church; rather, it is part of the language of the black community as a whole. The Bible became so important for black people in America because in it they saw their own experiences reflected. Therefore, they understood themselves to be a part of the tradition of the faithful of history for whom the Bible was the standard by which fidelity was measured.

Black theology was nurtured in the soil of black religion and blossomed, in its present form, with the black power movement. Until its emergence virtually no attention was given to the effect that a particular social context had on the method, structure, and content of American theology. (A kind of contextual theology that focused on the ideological dimensions of theological thought was fairly well established in Europe in the 1940s and 1950s.) It was assumed that theology existed outside the tensions of society, supposedly unaffected by the unjust distribution of wealth and power within society. American theologians had no real interest in the concrete issues of the creation of a more just society. American theologians did not take as their point of departure the most significant social tension in American society—racial oppression. One wonders—in light of DuBois' prophetic statement that the problem of the twentieth century would be the problem of the color-line—how these theologians could overlook it in their work. This omission could be accounted for by examining the social origins of their theologies. Because most American professional theologians were heirs to the privileges of being white and male in American society, the race issue or the issue of gender would not enter naturally into their theological consciousness.

Black theology, however, has always been intrinsic to the struggle for black liberation. It has always been expressed in the idiom of the black community. Thus, black theology is inseparable from its social context or surroundings. This does not mean that black theology is reducible to sociology, ideology, or culture. Rather, it means that black theology is always concrete, applied in a particular situation, by a particular people, and in a particular way. Black theology addresses

71

the question, What does the gospel of Jesus Christ have to do with the struggle of black people for liberation from white oppression?

Black theology is a theology that equates liberation with salvation. It proclaims that the gospel affirms the black quest for freedom because the gospel of Jesus Christ is freedom. The relation between Jesus and the freedom of the oppressed means that God is revealed as the One who delivered Israel out of the house of bondage, the God who the slaves believed would liberate them, and the God who sides with the oppressed today. Christ in black theology is not the blond-haired, blue-eyed, white-skinned man who appears in European-American culture and art. Christ was poor, oppressed, despised, and persecuted. Christ died the death of a slave and rose again to witness the power of God over the forces of oppression. This is the Christ of black theology. The Holy Spirit in black theology is not simply that force which compels us to lead pious lives. The Holy Spirit is the presence of God in the world. The Holy Spirit is the spirit of freedom. Black theology, in essence, is the spiritual expression of the black power movement and the political expression of African American faith.

Black theology is a church theology and a folk theology. It did not come from seminaries or divinity schools. As such it is not just an "intellectual" enterprise. This does not mean that there is no place for black theology in the academic setting; rather, it means that the criteria for its authenticity must be rooted in the black religious community. Black theology also represents the prophetic strand in African American religious thought. There are other strands within the tradition. More conservative black religionists tend to eschew the radicalism of black theology; others adopt a kind of agnosticism that sees the religion of black folk as a crutch for the weak. Both of these strands are subordinate within the tradition of black theology and almost always submit to canons of evaluation that are not drawn from the black community. Thus, for virtually all black theologians, prophetic black Christianity alone is authentic.

Black theologians acknowledge their debt to the life and work of Martin Luther King, Jr., as well as to the black power movement. While King had reservations about the black power movement and its strategies for liberation, he embodied a radicalism of his own that was fully consistent with the African American religious tradition of resistance. King's work, like that of David Walker, Sojourner Truth, and Henry McNeal Turner, is a progenitor of today's black theology.

Although black theology is noted for its concentrated focus on the meaning of the gospel for black people, it is not monolithic. Black theology has always been a corporate enterprise. The first anguished utterances of black theology were not issued in a book-lined study but among a group of black clergy trying to make sense of the senseless suffering their people were experiencing. One of the dangers that black theologians face today is isolation from one another and from the black community. This can easily happen when a black clergyman or clergywoman finds himself or herself the lone black faculty member on an otherwise all-white faculty or when an assignment takes him or her to some remote academic enclave. To counter this danger, black theologians must insist on creating opportunities for collegial work and communal witness. This is especially important because black theology is still developing. It is vital and alive. It is not a body of doctrine that has been set into stone but is a way of believing that has been set in flesh. The study of black theology, then, is inquiry not into dead tradition but into living history.

In spite of the pain and alienation caused by racial oppression, black theologians, like black people in general, remain open to the possibility of God's redemption of the oppressors. This means that black theologians are willing to engage in dialogue with other theological perspectives that seek to confront the challenge of the message of liberation in the gospel. Process theologians and theologians of hope have been among the first white theologians to engage in this dialogue. Dialogue and even coalition are possible, given prior commitment to the liberation of the oppressed.

Black theology is also applicable to the didactic or teaching ministry of the church. Black theologians have something to say to Christian educators in their churches, to college and university students in their quest for an accurate reading of black religion, and to graduate theological students. Without this applicability, black theology would be a mere pastime for seminary professors and their students.

Finally, black theology continues to define the doctrinal affirmations of African Americans. What a people confess and believe says a great deal about who they are. Without the theological attempt at self-definition, the black church would be doomed to wander without a self-identity.

Black theology is a third-world theology. It is the theological reflection of a third-world people living in a first-world nation. Black theology shares with other third-world theologies a focus on liberation as the content of the Christian gospel. Historically, black theology in the United States and Latin American liberation theology arose at about the same time. Independently of each other, these two expressions came to the conclusion that the Christian gospel was consistent with the struggle of the oppressed for their liberation. Thus, black theology is related to the majority of Latin American liberation theologies by virtue of its emphasis on praxis, concrete theological formulations, and liberation as salvation. Black theology is also the product of an African people and therefore shares with other theological expressions from the African continent and from Asian peoples a distinctive attitude toward history and religion. This perspective on the power of indigenous religion is apparent in the black folk religion, which is the religio-cultural basis of black theology.

Black theology in the United States, Latin American liberation theology, and black theology in South Africa are political theologies in the sense that they are concerned about the ordering of the world in a more just fashion. God's righteousness is seen as the demand to bring about right relationships between

73

members of and groups within the human family. The main obstacle to justice and peace is the continued oppression of the poor by the rich. Wealth and poverty are both actual and symbolic conditions of human life. They are the primary divisions within the human family. The term ''poor'' has become a political designation for those in Latin America who actually suffer the lack of material resources, as well as for those who have entered into solidarity with the poor and thereby experience, albeit in a derivative fashion, powerlessness. In black theology in South Africa, blackness and whiteness have become political designations for those who are actually classified by the government as black, as well as for those who see their destinies intertwined with their black brothers and sisters and thereby experience the effects of racial humiliation.

Black theology, African theology, and Asian theology are cultural theologies in the sense that they are concerned with the recovery and preservation of their indigenous traditions and history. The pre-Christian and non-Christian elements in both black religion and Asian religions are not seen as impediments to the full presence of Christian faith; nor arè these ancient religions seen as only preparatory stages for the advent of the higher religion of Christianity. African traditional religions, their remnants in the black folk religions of the African diaspora, and the great Asian religions are vital traditions that still anchor their adherents in a positive sense of belonging to a sympathetic universe. As an African-Asian theology, black theology in the United States embodies certain tendencies and predispositions that are not traceable to any Western or European influence. This element of otherness distinguishes it from other Western theologies. In these African-Asian theologies, important topics include the nature of the primary social unit (i.e., family, clan, tribe), the social responsibilities of members of the community to care for one another, and the expansion of the concept of community to include those who are no longer living. In these theologies, culture is the basis for assessing the identity of the human group. By turning inward, so to speak, and rediscovering the inner resources in its ritual, worship, and communal life, the community may resist the deadening effects of political, economic, and social oppression. In this instance God is affirmed as One who is present in the culture of the oppressed and who is made manifest in the symbols of holiness within that culture. Because the God is an immanent God rather than a God who shuns the particularity of culture, the theology that results is cultural discourse. That is, black theology, African theology, and Asian theology focus on their cultural and religious uniqueness as a sign of God's presence.

Theology as cultural discourse has flourished in those situations where the oppressed have suffered the religio-cultural domination of Western nations. In these instances, missionary endeavor often became the advance guard of colonial exploitation. The Western Christian churches have presented themselves as institutions that devalue the culture of the indigenous people and in many ways equate Christianity with its Western garb. It is this ecclesiastical conquest that liberation theologians oppose. The solution to this problem is for indigenous peoples to find God among themselves.

Black theology in the United States is both a global and a cultural discourse. Although it shares with Latin American liberation theology and South African black theology the conviction that there is a relation between Christian faith and political praxis, black theologians also recognize the rich resources of black religion and black culture. Although black theologians share with Asian theology the conviction that there are tremendous resources for survival present in indigenous culture and religion, black theologians also recognize that culture is not synonymous with God's revelation. At times, God acts in history to redeem and transform culture as well as society. In sum, black theology embodies within itself the dimensions of cultural discourse and global discourse. It is truly an African American theology in the sense that it struggles with the dilemma described by DuBois: participating in two communities with its identity fully grasped by neither.

JAMES H. EVANS, JR.

Bibliography

James H. Cone, *A Black Theology of Liberation.*
Gayraud S. Wilmore, *Black Religion and Black Radicalism.*
Gayraud S. Wilmore and James H. Cone, *Black Theology: A Documentary History.*

Cross Reference: Justice, Liberation Theology, Political Theology, Praxis, Suffering.

BODY (*See* SOUL/BODY.)

CANON

"Canon" comes from Greek *kanon* and Hebrew *qaneh:* "stalk" or "reed." Since this plant was uncommonly straight, the term acquired a derived meaning of "standard" or "rule" (cf. Ezek. 40:5). In the early Christian centuries, canon denoted the church's "rule of faith" or accepted doctrinal teaching. By the fourth century, canon referred to writings that the church viewed as in basic agreement with its rule of faith. Eventually, canon meant that corpus of writings that the church recognized as holy scripture. Although it is a specialized concept in theology and biblical studies, canon also signifies any requisite body of written materials, even in a secular setting.

Canon is closely associated with Christian tradition; but Judaism is fundamentally responsible for developing the *concept* that central to the faith and life of a religious community is a particular body of authoritative writings. Expressed negatively, "external books" *(separim hisonim)* were uncanonical; expressed positively, documents that "rendered the hands unclean" *(mettame't ha-yadayim)* were holy and canonical. The refinement of this idea over time eventuated in Judaism's becoming a "people of the book." Nascent Christianity shared Judaism's understanding of canon, except that Christianity viewed the teaching and apostolic interpretation of Jesus as ultimately superior. For the most part, the early Christians read Jewish scriptures to justify their claims about Jesus. Christianity in the end accommodated its view of Judaism's scriptures to the documents that were to become the New Testament.

Most scholars concur that Judaism and Christianity are *biblical* religions in the sense that certain writings played crucial roles in their development. But the respective communities took centuries to view canon as a hermetically sealed group of inspired texts. Before this, canon or scripture was conceived of in rather fluid and dynamic terms. This explains why subsets of Judaism and Christianity saw no difficulty in making use of an array of scriptures. Even today strictly speaking, Christianity has yet to agree on what scriptures are canonical. For example, the books accepted as canonical by Protestants are not exactly the same as those accepted by the Roman Catholic Church.

Notwithstanding, most scholars still contend that one can legitimately regard canon as a property of ancient Judaism and Christianity as long as the word is properly defined and the enscripturation process carefully described. The elements of this consensus are roughly as follows: (1) "Canon" and "scripture" should be distinguished; the former refers to a fixed corpus of authoritative documents, the latter to any text of which the community of faith made use; (2) "canon" in the strict sense was a relatively late development in both Judaism and Christianity; (3) no understanding of canon in either Judaism or Christianity prevented the parallel growth of highly influential interpretative traditions (e.g., the Talmud for Judaism; ecumenical creeds for Christianity); (4) the process of canonization should be seen primarily as a function of the community of faith rather than of leaders or councils; (5) the criteria for canonization doubtless included antiquity, authorship, apostolicity, orthodoxy, perceived inspiration, and even socio-political factors, but in the final analysis the writings that the community saw as most expressive of its deepest religious and theological convictions were deemed canonical; (6) neither Judaism nor Christianity should be seen exclusively as a function of their respective canons; both were and remain complex religio-historical phenomena that cannot be reduced to communities completely defined by a set of sacred texts.

These data have led many scholars to regard the emergence of the concept of canon as largely unfortunate in that it tends to obscure the rich theological pluralism and complex socio-historical situations that existed in ancient Judaism and Christianity, not to mention Israel. Granted, studying the process of canonization is essential for determining the role of canon in these important religious communities. But as the key to understanding them, canon as such should be given no priority; to the contrary, one must be careful not to allow the canon to undercut proper historical analysis.

To counter this trend, James Sanders advocates "canonical criticism," which aims to ascertain how communities of faith initially read and subsequently resignified in differing settings the "texts" (any tradition) that were believed quintessential for their religious identity and practice. Canonical criticism combines the full range of standard historical-critical tools and a theological orientation that takes seriously the Bible's role as the canon of synagogue and church.

In spite of many impressive insights, Sanders's understanding of canon does not seem to accord with the more usual meaning of canon as an authoritative body of texts. The canonical texts have no more claim to theological validity than any other. For Sanders, the value of canon does not lie in its being either an exclusive or a primary religious authority, but in the information it provides on how texts function in believing communities. Canon provides a hermeneutical guide for theological discourse. Thus, contemporary theological reflection is *analogous to* rather than *derivative of* canon. What Sanders calls "canonical criticism" seems actually to be a version of the "history of traditions" *(Traditionsgeschichte)*. Such a discipline is justifiable on its own terms, but whether it should finally fall under the rubric of "canon" is arguable.

Brevard Childs approaches canon along more classical lines. He criticizes modern scholarship for failing to take seriously either the importance of canonical process in the founding communities of Judaism and Christianity or the production of the final canon as a proper context for theological reflection. Childs does not reject standard critical treatments of scripture per se, but he insists that they should be placed in the service of a canonical reading; the critical tools are actually indispensable because they highlight how the text has been shaped as the community's canon. He merely rejects the exclusive goal of criticism: to locate the precanonical text in its original historical setting. Likewise, he rejects the anti-critical stance of conservative scholarship because its view of biblical inspiration is too narrowly conceived and because its understanding of the canon's development is historically naive.

Childs argues that the canon does not simply represent a "frozen moment" in the history of the community of faith. The canon did not result from the arbitrary selections of a victorious party that succeeded in imposing its will on everyone. Rather, from the very beginning the community selected and shaped the traditions that it believed mediated God's self-disclosure in human affairs. From the outset the community was aware that "canonical" traditions were foundational. Regardless of the date of its actual "completion," canon is the result of thousands of theologically constitutive decisions that the community had been making all along. The growth of greatly revered and influential interpretative traditions alongside the canon does not obviate the fact that Judaism and Christianity never accorded these traditions equivalent status. Although much mainstream critical scholarship bypasses canon to get at the community's historical claims, Childs believes canonical formation, rightly conceived, affords the best opportunity for uncovering precisely what those claims were. According to Childs, the existence of neither a plurality of texts nor of different canonical collections should divert attention from the decisive canonical impulse that was present in the community of faith from its inception.

Historically, even biblical religions have worked out their faith and life by appealing not only to canon, but also to tradition, experience, and reason. Certainly, this is the case for the Christian church, although the exact relationship between each of these important sources of authority has yet to be spelled out satisfactorily. Nevertheless, the spirited debate about canon that has taken place over the last quarter century has given prominence to issues once dismissed as irrelevant. But if biblical authority in particular and religious authority in general are concepts still worthy of serious consideration, then the continuing debate over the nature and function of canon can only be salutary.

FRANK ANTHONY SPINA

Bibliography

James Barr, *Holy Scripture: Canon, Authority, Criticism.*
Brevard S. Childs, *Introduction to the Old Testament as Scripture.*
_____, *The New Testament as Canon: An Introduction.*
L. M. McDonald, *The Formation of the Christian Biblical Canon.*
James A. Sanders, *Canon and Community: A Guide to Canonical Criticism.*

Cross Reference: Authority, Biblical Theology, Inspiration, Tradition.

CELAM II

In 1968 the second general *ConferencE* of *Latin AM*erican Bishops (CELAM II) met in Medellin, Colombia; the first conference had been held in Rio de Janeiro in 1955. Although the title of the conference, "The Church in the Present-Day Transformation of Latin America in the Light of the Council," implied that the bishops were applying Vatican II to the particular circumstances of their continent, "Medellin," as the meeting and its final document were generally called, became an important reference point for pastoral work and theology during the next two decades, and it was arguably the moment when Latin American Catholicism moved from being an extension of a European church and took on its own identity.

Methodologically, Medellin reversed the traditional doctrine-to-application model of Roman Catholic theology by first focusing on the reality of the social, economic, and political situation of Latin American society before proceeding to theological reflection and pastoral commitment. This new approach is evident in each of the sixteen final documents and in the presentation of the conclusions as a whole. First, the documents deal with the current situation, focusing on peace, justice, education, and family; a second set of documents takes up various aspects of pastoral work, such as catechetics and liturgy; and the last set deals with the structures of the church (e.g., priests, religious life, and laity), operating on the assumption that these should function to serve the church's mission within the current situation. In their pastoral reflection and planning, church workers were quick to invoke the "Medellin method," following a similar procedure in order to set their pastoral activity within an overall economic, political, and social framework.

The bishops several times used the language of liberation. God's action in salvation history, for example, is one of "integral liberation." Human development is viewed as a kind of exodus, in which there is a continuity between human efforts to create more humane living conditions in a material sense, through the building of communities, and ultimate union in God. The church is called to be committed boldly to the "liberation of every human being and all human beings."

Medellin's denunciation of "institutionalized violence" and "structures of sin" were frequently cited thereafter. With regard to approaches to development, the bishops questioned "conservative" and "developmentalist" mindsets, and they spoke positively of a "revolutionary" framework, which they identified not with violence but with an emphasis on structural change and a conviction that people should be "agents of their own development," rather than objects of planning by technocrats. In their call for liberating education not only in schools but also in the church's own education work, the bishops implicitly endorsed the ideas of Paulo Freire, author of *Pedagogy of the Oppressed*, and indeed several times they spoke of "consciousness-raising" as part of pastoral work. They also urged the formation of Christian base communities and provided both a theological and a sociological rationale for such a pastoral strategy. An important theme was poverty: the stark reality of the living conditions of most Latin Americans, the gospel ideal of poverty, and voluntary poverty as a symbol of solidarity with the poor. Although several Protestant observers were present at Medellin, ecumenical issues were a relatively small concern in the 1960s when Latin America was still regarded as Catholic.

The Medellin conference reflected the turbulence of the 1960s. Latin American social scientists were developing the consequences of "dependency theory" not only in economics but also in other spheres. Vatican II had unleashed a great deal of questioning among priests, sisters, and active laypeople, and numerous groups issued manifestos questioning inherited pastoral practices and theology. Not accidentally, Peruvian theologian Gustavo Gutiérrez provided the first sketch of a

Latin American theology of liberation in a talk to clergy about a month before Medellin.

The 130 bishops assembled at Medellin representing the Latin American episcopacy were aided by about 100 advisors, including Gutiérrez, who may have seen more than the bishops themselves saw as the implications of the texts. For a brief period the various pastoral institutes run by CELAM in Colombia and elsewhere were centers for the diffusion of the new liberation theology. By the early 1970s, however, a backlash set in as conservatives under Colombian Archbishop Alfonso Lopez Trujillo took over the CELAM administration. CELAM III, held at Puebla, Mexico, in 1979, was far more tightly controlled, and although it did not reverse Medellin, its conclusions were more of an admixture of many elements. Under Pope John Paul II (1978–), the Vatican itself vigorously endorsed the more conservative approach represented by Lopez.

PHILIP BERRYMAN

Bibliography

Edward L. Cleary, *Crisis and Change: The Church in Latin America Today.*
Second General Conference of Latin American Bishops, *The Church in the Present-Day Transformation of Latin America in the Light of the Council;* vol. 1, *Position Papers,* vol. 2, *Conclusions.*

Cross Reference: Basic Christian Communities, Institutionalized Violence, Liberation Theology, Praxis, Sin, Vatican II.

CELIBACY

Narrowly defined, celibacy means the renunciation of genital sexuality. Some devout Christians choose freely to practice such celibacy as an aid to contemplation, for the sake of apostolic ministry, or for the sake of both. Eastern rite churches currently require celibacy of bishops. The Roman Catholic Church currently requires celibacy of both bishops and priests. More broadly defined, celibacy means the cultivation of religious chastity and its attendant virtues.

Biblical scholarship suggests that Jesus of Nazareth lived a celibate life. If he did, he probably had to choose it, since, with the exception of ascetics like the Essenes, voluntary celibacy did not ordinarily count as a virtue for Jewish males of the first century.

The apostle Paul (who may have been a widower) espoused celibacy in order to have more freedom to devote both to religious matters and to spreading the gospel (I Cor. 7:7, 25-40). The first Christians esteemed unmarried widows who devoted themselves to pious works (I Tim. 5:3-16). Ordinarily, however, those in positions of leadership in the apostolic church married (I Tim. 3:4).

Celibacy became more widespread in the fourth century through the eremitic movement when Christian ascetics, who ordinarily espoused celibacy even if previously married, retired to wilderness areas on the outskirts of cities in the pursuit of religious contemplation, virtue, and simple living. With time these Christian hermits gathered in contemplative cenobitic communities partly because the demands of Christian love made life in solitude anomalous and partly because solitary living bred eccentricities that the discipline of community life tempered. These communities of hermits evolved into monastic communities usually in a rural setting. With the growth of cities in the Middle Ages and afterward, monasticism eventually evolved into separate, apostolically mobile communities of men and women vowed to lives of Christian poverty, chastity, and obedience.

In its origins, religious chastity encouraged contemplation and longing for fulfillment in a life beyond this one; but as religious spirituality took a more active, apostolic turn, religious chastity also promoted pastoral availability.

During the patristic period, other cultural forces besides Christianity shaped attitudes toward religious chastity and celibacy. The dualistic distinction between spirit and matter that characterized both middle Platonism and Neoplatonism and that surfaced in a more extreme form in the Gnostic religions suffused late Greco-Roman culture with a suspicion of the body and of sexuality. These cultural influences certainly colored the original Christian practice of celibacy, even though Christian asceticism today tends to judge such anti-physical attitudes unacceptable.

Religious chastity offers one way of cultivating Christian charity. Charity exhibits at least four descriptive traits: concreteness, reciprocity, gratuity, and universality. The concreteness of Christian love results from the fact that it always terminates at living persons. Its reciprocity binds one to mutual love in community. Its gratuity imitates the gift of divine love revealed in Christ. Its universality excludes no one in principle from concern and reaches out especially to those in greatest need, whoever they may be.

The love that religious chastity encourages bears witness in a special way to the gratuity and universality of Christian charity. Religious chastity bears enhanced witness to the gratuity of Christian love, because it commits the vowed person to love others in Jesus' image without assurance of the response of love that marriage promises. The vow of chastity bears witness to the universality of Christian love when those who cultivate the virtue of chastity in fact reach out to those in greatest need.

Christian charity also blends three fundamental kinds of love: the love born of need, atoning love, and contemplative love. Christian charity includes the love born of need because it always remains a human love that enables one in times of strength to minister to the needs of others and in times of need to accept gratefully being ministered to by others. Christian charity includes atoning love because it imitates the forgiving love of Christ; and it includes contemplative love because it springs from faith and from the prayerful response of the human heart to the divine beauty incarnate in Jesus and in those whose lives resemble him. Some Christians like the Carmelites or the Trappists take the vow of chastity in order to grow in contemplative love. The renunciation of genital sex and of the family that normally results from sexual activity brings with it more leisure for prayer and growth in a contemplative relationship with God.

Natural human love takes four fundamental forms: The love of need, affection, friendship, and romance. The love of very small children best exemplifies the love born of need. The family trains the growing child in the love of affection. Peer socialization introduces children to the experience of friendship. And sexual maturation brings with it the possibility for romantic love.

Although commitment to a life of celibacy entails the renunciation of the genital expression of romantic love, it has the ability to enhance the love of affection and friendship, particularly when it introduces one into a religious community committed to ministering in love to the needs of its members and of those whom the community serves. In such communities affection and friendship can mature into the love of companionship, which commits friends to live together in the service of a common enterprise and binds them together for the long haul.

The impulse to require celibacy of the Christian clergy emerged at the beginning of the fourth century and resulted in the canonical requirement of celibacy of bishops. In 325 C.E., however, the Council of Nicea refused to require the celibacy of presbyters or priests. When in the twelfth century Roman Catholicism imposed celibacy by canon law on priests, it did so largely for financial reasons: in order to prevent the loss of priestly benefices to the church through inheritance. The practice of the early church and the experience of Christian communions other than the Roman Catholic make clear the compatibility of the two vocations of marriage and ordained ministry. Today, a growing number of Catholic theologians want to make clerical celibacy optional. Presumably, those who would opt for clerical celibacy would do so in order to cultivate its religious virtues.

DONALD L. GELPI

Bibliography

Joseph Blenkinsopp, *Celibacy, Ministry, Church.*
George H. Frein, ed., *Celibacy: The Necessary Option.*
John Paul II, *The Theology of Marriage and Celibacy: Catechesis on Marriage and Celibacy in the Light of the Resurrection of the Body.*
Marc Oraison, *The Celibate Condition and Sex.*
Edward Schillebeeckx, *Celibacy.*

Cross Reference: Priesthood, Spirituality.

CHARISMATIC (*See* PENTECOSTALISM.)

CHRISTOLOGY

At the center of the Christian faith is the person of Jesus of Nazareth, and Christology is essentially the explanation for this. Christology deals with questions about who Jesus is and about why he makes the decisive difference in human destiny. There are some christological issues about which all Christian traditions and denominations are agreed, and others that divide the various churches.

Positions on which there is agreement among all Christian traditions are these: Jesus of Nazareth was a real human being, a first-century Palestinian Jew, who was reared in Nazareth of Galilee in a devout family, and trained to be a carpenter. He left home as a young man to take up a wandering life as a preacher and healer, and came into conflict with the religious authorities and under suspicion of the Roman colonial occupation. Knowingly risking arrest and execution for the sake of his message and mission, he was arrested, tried, and cruelly executed, but raised from the dead to a new life that has provided enlightenment and empowerment for his followers ever since. Jesus is savior; he stands in a unique relationship to the transcendent God.

Some important questions are not answered uniformly by all Christian traditions: What is meant by the claim that Jesus is divine? Did he himself make that claim before his death and resurrection? Does any divinity claim apply to his whole life from the first moment of his human existence, or does it refer to the time after his resurrection from the dead? Does the divinity claim begin with his baptism by John in the Jordan, or is it in some sense progressively realized? Is he the savior of all who are in good faith or only of those who explicitly acknowledge him as savior? And finally, in quite recent times, is he the definitive and only savior given for all peoples at all times, or might there be other saviors for other peoples and cultures?

The claim that Jesus saves is basic to the whole structure of Christology, and it assumes that there is something very wrong from which all human beings need to be saved. The Hebrew scriptures (beginning with Genesis 3) describe what is wrong as an estrangement from God that causes confusion in all aspects of human life and relationships, requiring new intervention of God the creator to restore the balance and focus. The New Testament, particularly in the letters of Paul, makes the claim that moral law and religious observances have never been enough to accomplish this restoration, but that in the person, life, teaching, death, and resurrection of Jesus there has been a radical reversal of the fate of the human community. Those who first proclaimed this did so on the grounds of their own experience of radical change for the better in their lives as individuals and as communities. For all subsequent Christians, who were brought to faith in Jesus

83

Christ by the testimony of others, it has been important to ask why Jesus makes this radical difference.

One approach is through the theme of Adam in the Genesis story of creation and sin: Jesus is the "new Adam" who by the provident will of God assumes the corporate identity of the human race, and in that identity reverses the disobedience of Adam by his own perfect obedience to the will of the heavenly Father and creator of all. This approach describes the identity of Jesus with reference to the human race and its history, acknowledges the full humanity of Jesus, and simply does not need to address the divinity claim. Another approach is through the theme of Messiah, the anointed of God, promised as savior and champion in God's name to redeem God's people as promised in the Hebrew scriptures. This is the origin of the name "Christ," from the Greek term meaning anointed. Christians have given the concept of messiah a more specific and univocal meaning than it had in Hebrew tradition. However, by using this term, Christian preaching was able to suggest both a mediating function for Jesus between God and the human community and a mysterious identity for Jesus, placing him above the ordinary human sphere and calling for reverence and worship. This approach defines the identity of Jesus in a dynamic way in relation to human history as seen by the Hebrew tradition, and it avoids an ontological or essential definition of his identity. It casts a certain aura of divinity about him without having to define exactly what that means.

A third approach, one that has caused great arguments and divisions among Christians, defines Jesus as uniquely and essentially the Son of God, one with God from eternity, sent from the Father into the world and its history to assume a human life. This approach is found in a poetic, suggestive way in the New Testament in the writings of John, especially in the prologue to John's Gospel. Jesus is identified in John as having an existence prior to his human life—a preexistence as the Word, the speaking or uttered thought by which God created in the beginning. That speaking or thought is something that is always with God and is God, but that speaking has now been realized, made concrete, enfleshed in a particular human being. The letters of John suggest a parallel in the thought that God is essentially love, that Jesus is wholly love in his attitude to the Father and in his relationship to other human beings, and that Jesus is therefore an incarnation or personification of the love of God. Sooner or later, however, this approach is bound to raise questions about what exactly is meant by equating Jesus with the Word, Wisdom, Image, or Love of God, and by adding that Word, Wisdom, Image, and Love of God *are* God and not other realities outside God. That, in turn, raises the question how there can be two who are the one God, which led historically not only to a highly developed Christology, but also to the inclusion of the Holy Spirit or Breath of God, and to the development of a trinitarian theology.

Some Christians regard the divinity terms used in relation to Jesus as courtesy titles, not intended to be taken literally. The Arian controversy that was settled at the Council of Nicea in 325 c.e. left the majority of the churches with a commitment to take the divinity of Jesus literally; those who did not agree were labeled Arian heretics. The majority, however, faced further questions about how one individual could be at the same time divine and human. One obvious possibility is that we are speaking not exactly of a double personal identity, but of a very close union of another sort. For instance, we might think of Jesus as essentially a human person, so wholly attuned to God's will in everything that his presence is in effect the presence of God, and his impact on the world in effect the Word or utterance of God. Again, however, representatives of the then existing churches (local rather than denominational in definition) met in council at Ephesus in 431 c.e. to discuss a proposal to this effect, and vehemently rejected it, forcing those who still held this explanation into schism from the other churches, and designating them Nestorians. Most Christian churches today accept the authority of that council and therefore are committed to the explanation that Jesus is personally and literally divine.

Of course, anyone who thinks about the matter carefully has to probe further: If Jesus is personally and literally divine, is he really a human being like the rest of us, or is he really a divine being appearing to us as a man so that we might see him and relate to him? Or is he perhaps a divine being somehow expressing himself in a human body but not really subject to our limitations? For instance, did Jesus really suffer? Were there things he did not know? Did he have to consider situations, think about them, pray about them, and struggle to come to a decision? Or did the divine fullness of being, omnipotence, and omniscience preclude all this? That certainly is a very important set of questions because these issues relate immediately to what we understand by redemption and how we see our own role in accepting and responding to the divine initiative in redemption. Here again, Christians today are heirs of an answer given long ago. In 451 c.e., representatives of the churches still in communion with one another gathered at Chalcedon and hammered out a formula that was supposed to answer these persistent questions: There is one person, Jesus, who is truly of the same being as God the Father and creator in his divine aspect and truly of the same being as we are in his human aspect; when Jesus acts it is always God acting and man acting. Almost all the Christian churches still consider this the orthodox formula of Christian faith.

Nevertheless, many ordinary believers, preachers, and theologians wonder whether the Chalcedonian formula is adequate to describe the nature of Jesus. For example: If Jesus acts simultaneously as God and man, and invariably does the Father's will, can he seriously be said to have a human will at all? If as God he knows everything, does he really have a human mind that learns things progressively? And so on. To all such questions the considered answer of the churches after debate and reflection has always been: Whatever is integral to being human must also be predicated of Jesus. Contemporary Christian scholars have pointed out that the formula of Chalcedon with its subsequently agreed corollaries is not so much an answer that rationally explains the nature of Jesus, but rather is an answer that suggests a way of accommodating a mystery that we can know in some sense but never fully comprehend.

A good question, of course, is why there should need to be such concern and endless debate on this topic. Over the centuries various authors have given answers to the question of Jesus' dual nature that still hold today, and others that we find quite strange. From Athanasius of the fourth century, we get the answer, gathered from many voices in the earlier tradition, that what we see in Jesus is a kind of exchange whereby the divine enters into our experience and our problems, providing a point of entry at which we might in turn come to share the clarity and power of the divine life, which offers the resolution of our problems. If Jesus were not truly divine and truly human at the same time then this exchange would not be open to us. From Anselm, around the year 1100, we get a different answer that has been very influential in the past, although it does not appeal to most Christians today: Jesus had to be divine to be truly the savior because what we needed to be redeemed from was the wrath of God, who in infinite majesty had been infinitely offended by sin and therefore could only be appropriately compensated by obedience and worship of infinite value, such as could be offered only by one who was truly divine and truly human.

In twentieth-century Christian theology, there has been a strong tendency to return to the Gospels and other early testimonies. The exclusively "descending" style of Christology (beginning with dogmatic formulations declaring the divinity of Jesus and then fitting his humanity and the facts of his earthly life into the picture) has come under heavy criticism, first of all because it moves from the unknown (the being of God) to the known, which is bad method, and second, because it takes a later stage of development in Christian doctrine as the starting point, and tends to read those later positions back into the earlier sources, which is also bad method. Today's Christology has insisted on ascending approaches (those which begin with our knowledge of what it is to be human and with the available testimonies about the human life of Jesus and then consider what it might mean to speak of this man as divine), because biblical, historical, and patristic scholarship offers us much better access to the historical Jesus and his society, culture, and religious circumstances than was available for most of the Christian centuries, and also because recent philosophies such as existentialism, phenomenology, and process thought have opened up methods of reflection better suited to an ascending approach than were the classical philosophies. Since these possibilities have been opened up, attention in Christology has turned to some questions that did not really come into focus before. One of these is how the death of Jesus is the outcome of the choices and decisions he made in his life, and what that tells us about his own understanding of salvation and of the process of redemption in the history of the world. In a descending Christology it was easy to assume that the death of Jesus was redemptive because the Father had decreed it in eternity and therefore it constituted the infinitely valuable radical act of obedience that turned the scales. An ascending Christology does not claim to know what the Father decrees in eternity, but painstakingly looks for clues in the recorded sayings and doings of Jesus in the framework of the known hopes and convictions of the Jewish people at that time in order to try to understand why Jesus concluded that he had to pursue a path that would provoke his early arrest.

Along the same lines, present approaches to Christology question whether Jesus really intended to found a new religion—Christianity—or actually intended to uncover the core of Judaism. A related question asks why a ministry that was in Jesus' lifetime entirely confined to Israel is expanded with the mandate at the end of Matthew's Gospel to evangelize all nations. In the traditional descending Christology it was not necessary to ask this question, because the fact that it happened later was assumed to mean that it was in the divine plan decreed from eternity. Moreover, in descending Christology the fact that Jesus was a Jew was not treated as being in itself significant; it was only mentioned with reference to the fulfillment of prophecies cited to substantiate the messianic claims made for him.

Perhaps the most important question that has arisen in a new way within Christology is the question of who Jesus is, and where he stands, in relation to the social, political, and economic issues of human history. Among the various "liberation theologies," the question of where Jesus stands in relation to the suffering and hopes of the vast masses of oppressed and destitute peoples is central to Christology. This approach to Christology goes to the roots of the term: It asks what is meant by calling Jesus the anointed (messiah, christ) of God, noting that sin is not an abstraction but consists of violence, injustices, prejudices, greed, and so forth, from which real people suffer progressive hardship, degradation, and dehumanization.

A new interest in the meaning of the miracles of the gospel and of the resurrection has also unfolded. In current thought, these no longer appear simply as proofs of the claims made for Jesus, but as representative actions and events interpreting our world in the light of God's presence and power. Similarly, Jesus is seen not only as the presence and revelation of the divine, but also as the presence and revelation of the truly and fully human. The task of Christology is to ask not only what we learn about God from Jesus, but also what we learn about our own being and its possibilities and true destiny. Moreover, this is not merely a question about after-life, but centrally and extensively a question about the life we know in world, history, and society.

Finally, in today's world where many traditions and cultures mix in daily life, we cannot avoid the question about the uniqueness of Jesus as savior and divine incarnation. Some theologians resolve the issue by turning to traditional claims that Jesus is the one and only savior, but allowing the possibility of his saving grace reaching those who do not explicitly confess faith in him. How to preserve Christian faith but also remain open to the evidences of saving grace in non Christian faith communities has become a central question in Christology. It goes back to the original issue: Who is Jesus, and what difference does he make in the destiny of the human community?

MONIKA K. HELLWIG

Bibliography

Donald M. Baillie, *God Was in Christ.*
Leonardo Boff, *Jesus Christ, Liberator.*
John B. Cobb, Jr., *Christ in a Pluralistic Age.*
Monika K. Hellwig, *Jesus, the Compassion of God.*
Wolfhart Pannenberg, *Jesus: God and Man.*
John T. Pawlikowski, *Christ in the Light of the Christian-Jewish Dialogue.*

Cross Reference: Atonement, Incarnation, Liberation Theology, Soteriology, Trinity.

CHURCH (*See* CONFESSIONAL THEOLOGY, ECCLESIOLOGY.)

CIVIL RELIGION

In the mid-nineteenth and early twentieth centuries, two European visitors to the United States observed an unfamiliar relationship between American religion and its cultural and political surroundings. Alexis de Tocqueville wrote in *Democracy in America* (1846),

> Religion in America takes no direct part in the government of society, but it must nevertheless be regarded as the foremost of the political institutions of that country. . . . I am certain that [all Americans] hold it to be indispensable to the maintenance of republican institutions.

Later G. K. Chesterton noted in *What I Saw in America* (1922) that

> America is the only nation in the world that is founded on a creed. That creed is set forth with dogmatic and even theological lucidity in the Declaration of Independence. . . . Nor do I say that they apply consistently this conception of a nation with the soul of a church . . . [but] that the Americans are doing something heroic or doing something insane.

Because religion was dissimilarly related to both nineteenth-century French society and twentieth-century British life, both Tocqueville and Chesterton had little immediate precedent for evaluating the American "civil religion." Although civil religion predates both of them, it is hardly a consistent cultural universal, and both French Catholicism and British Anglicanism precluded the strange admixture of American religion and culture now recognized as civil religion.

88

Among modern intellectuals, however, the French seem most sensitive to the possibility of a nation's history and traditions or a culture's significant symbols and values being elevated to a level of theological meaning and explanation. Thus Jean Jacques Rousseau in *The Social Contract* (1762) was the first to use the term "civil religion" in a sense not inconsistent with its modern application. To Rousseau, religious diversity and pluralism threatened to undermine the likelihood of a civil peace and commitment to society. What was needed, therefore, was a civil faith that would alleviate religious differences and also form the basis of a civil solidarity. Following the French Revolution, visionaries such as Auguste Comte contemplated the cultural utility of a "New Religion of Humanity," stripped of the substance of orthodox Christian beliefs, and built around a new thirteen-month calendar that highlighted secular holidays. Rousseau and Comte's countryman Emile Durkheim, author of *The Elementary Forms of the Religious Life* (1912), later implied that civil religions are nearly inevitable because of the interrelatedness of religion and society. For Durkheim, all social institutions derive from religion, while religion is little other than a society worshiping itself—exalting its beliefs and normative order to a transcendent significance. When a people gather and reaffirm their beliefs and traditions, their ritual acts and shared creed are intrinsically religious. In this sense civil religion provides a nonsectarian pattern of symbols, myths, and practices acting as a sort of cultural glue that binds together a people and provides them with a shared vision of their place in the world.

Although one might trace the origins of civil religious thinking back to Plato *(The Republic)* and the practices of citizens of the Greek city-states, and although the basis for conceiving of modern civil religion has mostly French influence, the links to what most Americans now embody as civil religious tenets and practices probably come through England and the seventeenth-century Puritans. As much as the Puritans were guided by evangelical religion, they also shared a common civil purpose of building "God's new Israel" in America.

John Winthrop, the first governor of Massachusetts Bay, the main Puritan colony, was representative of civil religious thinking among the early Puritans. With America as the "Promised Land" and with the prospect of building a "City on a Hill," the Puritans sought to apply the principal tenets of the Hebrew scriptures to the new society of Massachusetts Bay. Winthrop quoted frequently from Moses' farewell address in Deuteronomy 30 in support of his understanding of the divine covenant that God was making with the chosen people in establishing the kingdom of God in the new world. God was providing them a second opportunity to bring the Reformation to its political fulfillment.

Because they saw themselves as God's people with a special calling, the Puritans sought to expand their spiritual responsibilities beyond church life. If all of life including one's work is a sacred trust, then Sacvan Bercovitch is also correct in his assessment in *The Puritan Origins of the American Self* (1975) that Puritan themes, tensions, and literary strategies had a persisting influence on "the American self as the embodiment of a prophetic universal design."

That the more narrow Puritan vision of America as God's covenanted "Promised Land" was not realized as they had wished was obvious 150 years later when the writers of the Declaration of Independence sought to express a less sectarian and more diffused version of the Puritan ideal. Their vision also was permeated with rational, Enlightenment notions of the place of God, so that civil religious rhetoric took a Deistic turn that still holds today. Thomas Jefferson and James Madison in particular articulated the revised, syncretistic civil religion.

The result of the Revolutionary War also validated the civil religious assumptions of many. With George Washington as a Moses figure who separated the young nation from the Egypt of Europe and established it securely as a "Promised Land," future presidents would incorporate civil religious rhetoric into their pronouncements, especially their Inaugural Addresses, so that they functioned as the high priests of this religion that effectively combined popularly understood theology, history, and political theory. Clearly, by the time of the Civil War, the outline of a civil religion was in place and included five components identified by Richard Pierard and Robert Linder (*Civil Religion and the Presidency*, 1988): (1) the "chosen nation" theme devised by the Puritans; (2) a civil millennialism that secularized ideas resulting from the First Great Awakening; (3) a broad national religious consensus that merged evangelical Protestantism with democratic ideals; (4) the rational Deistic influence, especially in matters political and intellectual; and (5) the self-authenticating history of the American experience.

Civil religious rhetoric and understanding ebbed and flowed in the decades after the Civil War, becoming particularly visible in times of national conflict and duress. In the modern era, its themes reemerged in the 1940s and 1950s in the setting of World War II and the resulting cold war against godless international communism. One oft-quoted (and misquoted) statement came from President-elect Dwight Eisenhower in an address to the Freedoms Foundation prior to Christmas, 1952. Eisenhower said, "Our form of government has no sense unless it is founded in a deeply felt religious faith, and I don't care what it is." Eisenhower's invocation of a deeply felt religion of apparently little substance inadvertently captured what for many is the intrinsically elusive nature of the idea of civil religion when contrasted with more orthodox religious expressions.

About the same time, anthropologist W. Lloyd Warner was in the midst of research for his famous "Yankee City" series of ethnographic studies. One of these included an examination of an "American sacred ceremony," that of Memorial Day observance. Warner's brilliant description, making use of a Durkheimian interpretation of the functional significance of such ceremonies, still stands as a successful early effort at a systematic analysis of how civil religion works. In *American Life: Dream and Reality* (1953), he concluded,

The Memorial Day rite is a cult . . . not just of the dead as such, since by symbolically elaborating sacrifice of human life for the country through, or identifying it with, the Christian church's sacred sacrifice of their god, the deaths of such men also become powerful sacred symbols which organize, direct, and constantly revive the collective ideals of the community and the nation.

With the advantage of hindsight, one can now understand Eisenhower and Warner as providing the basis of popular and academic reflection for what culminated in Robert Bellah's provocative essay "Civil Religion in America" *(Daedalus)* in 1967. Although Bellah puzzled in a footnote, "why something so obvious should have escaped serious analytical attention," Martin Marty would later demonstrate in *A Nation of Behavers* (1976) that, in fact, between the late 1940s and the mid-1960s, numerous scholarly attempts had appeared. Some, such as Will Herberg's explanation of the religion of "the American way of life" in *Protestant, Catholic, Jew* (1955) and J. Paul Williams's encouragement of democracy as religion in *What Americans Believe and How They Worship* (1952), even received serious scrutiny among scholars. Bellah's essay provided the focal point around which all subsequent discussion of civil religion would be conducted.

First, Bellah's choice of the term "civil religion" seems to have captured the fancy of academics. Civil religion has never been discussed widely by "persons in the street," but as a label, it has communicated a reality to intellectuals that earlier terms such as "American Shinto" or "religion in general" did not. Although the "reality" of civil religion was not new, Bellah was correct in insisting that as a social construction, it "existed from the moment the winter 1967 issue of *Daedalus* was printed."

Second, civil religion captured the attention of intellectuals from a broad spectrum of academic life. Initially, sociologists and anthropologists and then historians, rhetoricians, theologians, and political theorists responded to the term and its underlying reality from discipline-specific perspectives in a way that earlier terms had not elicited. Perhaps intellectual historians were most perplexed, for they knew "something" like civil religion had been a topic of discussion for longer than Bellah conceded.

Third, Bellah himself remained a part of the discussion for nearly fifteen years (see *Varieties of Civil Religion,* 1980), and his own rhetoric contributed to debate over both the descriptive validity and normative significance of what he sought to explain. The responses to Bellah's *The Broken Covenant* (1975), which revised and elaborated several of his earlier views, were then heightened by America's excitement with the 1976 Bicentennial celebration.

Finally, by his linking civil religion to a "third time of trial," that of the Vietnam War, Bellah stirred the imagination of those seeking a normative understanding of the public debate over the war, while he also offered a fascinating case study by which to contrast the American experience of the foregoing twenty years. Thus he provided a selective context in which Americans would locate a collective understanding of themselves.

Bellah's definition of civil religion seemed simple enough: "a collection of beliefs, symbols, and rituals with respect to sacred things and institutionalized in a collectivity" and "an understanding of the American experience in the light of ultimate and universal reality." He buttressed his descriptive explanation with conceptual and historical examples not unlike those cited above, but he focused upon the role of the president and the place of the rhetoric in presidential inaugural addresses. For Bellah, John Kennedy's 1961 Inaugural Address was merely the latest to state the "obligation, both collective and individual, to carry out God's will on earth." Both Kennedy's "New Frontier" and Lyndon Johnson's "Great Society" were restatements of the "American Israel" theme. Bellah also picked up on Warner's use of Memorial Day to provide further examples constituting an annual calendar for civil religion—the birthdays of Lincoln and Washington, the Fourth of July, Veterans Day, and Thanksgiving. And he specified several symbols, both rhetorical and historical, including Exodus, New Jerusalem, and Arlington National Cemetery.

Two important contributions to the debate about civil religion that sought to clarify the descriptive utility of Bellah's article came from Donald Jones and Russell Richey and from Martin Marty in *American Civil Religion* (1974), still the best secondary source.

Jones and Richey argue that civil religion has five interrelated meanings, or five "sub-types," with Bellah's own explanation being only one of them. The five are: (1) folk religion—a common religion emerging from the ethos and history of all Americans; Herberg's "American way of life" fits here; (2) transcendent universal religion of the nation—historian Sidney Mead had offered "religion of the Republic" as a cosmopolitan faith, and Bellah also fits here; (3) religious nationalism—the nation becomes an object of adoration and takes on a sovereign character; (4) democratic faith—Williams's democracy as religion fits here, as various humane ideals are elevated to become a national faith; and (5) Protestant civic piety—a fusion of Protestantism and nationalism that pervades the national ethos.

Configuring the map of civil religion somewhat differently, Marty wrote of "two kinds of two kinds of civil religion," and he constructed a conceptual 2 × 2 matrix. One variable is that of transcendence. Here the choices are between including a transcendent deity, so that the nation is "under God," or making references to an "other" God minimal, with the nation itself possibly assuming godlike qualities. The second variable is that of style or approach, either prophetic or priestly. Prophetic religion afflicts the comforted, and priestly religion comforts the afflicted. In Marty's scheme, Bellah's description fits into the prophetic, nation-as-transcendent cell of the matrix.

The importance of the analytical schemes of Jones and Richey and of Marty is their sensing of the pluralistic tendencies inherent in the interaction between religion and culture. Bellah spent a great deal of time and energy, as did other commentators, in explaining the similarities and differences among versions of civil religion. Both Jones and Richey and Marty alert all to the difficulties, both in definition and also in comparison of civil religions, partly arising from different assumptions and functional criteria employed by different scholars.

Similar differences arose when critics explored the normative implications of Bellah's work. In the original essay, he used the example of the Vietnam War to posit the possibility of transcending a nationalistic civil religion. He asked: Could American civil religion become merely one part of a new civil religion of the world that Americans could accept as a fulfillment of the eschatological hope of American civil religion? Bellah also pointed out the divisive aspects, alongside the functionally integrative qualities, of any civil religion. Others would emphasize that civil religion existed as the vision of the establishment, while minority and marginal views tended not to be incorporated. Still others questioned Bellah's basic assumption that civil religion had ever become institutionalized to the degree that he assumed, particularly in a society characterized by religious sectarianism and committed to the ideal of the separation of church and state.

One of the best responses to Bellah and a recent evaluation of civil religion has come from Robert Wuthnow, *The Restructuring of American Religion* (1988). Just as Bellah had allowed that civil religion does have differing relationships to the republican and liberal civil heritages in America, and as Marty distinguished priestly from prophetic civil religion, so Wuthnow notes that two visions of civil religion exist—"one conservative, one liberal, [which] have, by virtue of their very tendency to dispute one another, become less capable of providing the broad, consensual underpinnings of societal legitimation that have usually been associated with the idea of civil religion."

For most of American life, the conservative, priestly version of civil religion has dominated, especially during episodes seeking American solidarity. But the possibility of interpreting that understanding prophetically, especially for an international community, is a persisting reality. Whether the various visions within civil religion can ever be joined is not likely, but in the meantime, civil religion is a powerful reality offering differing meanings to its adherents.

JAMES A. MATHISEN

Bibliography

Robert N. Bellah, "Civil Religion in America," *Daedalus* 96 (1967).

James A. Mathisen, "Twenty Years After Bellah: Whatever Happened to American Civil Religion?" *Sociological Analysis* 50 (1989).

Richard V. Pierard and Robert D. Linder, *Civil Religion and the Presidency*.

Russell E. Richey and Donald Jones, eds., *American Civil Religion*.
John F. Wilson, *Public Religion in American Culture*.

Cross Reference: Covenant, God, Popular Religion, Religion, Secularity, Society.

COMEDY

The association of the term "comedy" with theology is, in one sense, a distinctively modern phenomenon. Since the 1960s, the study of the relationships between religion and comedy has become a subfield of religious studies, pioneered by works such as Harvey Cox, *The Feast of Fools*, William Lynch, *Christ and Apollo*, Dan O. Via, Jr., *Kerygma and Comedy in the New Testament*, and Conrad Hyers, *The Comic Vision and the Christian Faith*.

In another sense, however, the connections between comedy and theology have long been recognized; otherwise, the claims now made are the fabrication of a modernity without roots in tradition. In the nineteenth century, Søren Kierkegaard drew heavily upon comedy, satire, and irony in criticizing what he saw as the pretensions of Hegelian theology and the State Church of Denmark. In the fourteenth century Dante boldly entitled his religious masterpiece *Commedia*, by which he meant that he had couched the drama of salvation in the humble, ordinary language of home, street, and tavern (Italian) rather than in the elite, classical language of the day for church, scholarship, and scripture (Latin). Dante also meant that this work proceeded from *Inferno* to *Paradiso* and therefore followed the pattern of many comedies in moving from difficult straits to a light and happy ending. Hell is the least comic place—a point pursued in the mid–twentieth century by C. S. Lewis in *The Screwtape Letters*—for it is the natural conclusion of self-love and thus of pride, greed, jealousy, lust, gluttony, and hatred. Each descending level of hell is smaller than the foregoing one, while heaven is the most comic place, for those who are there are the most open and free. As Dante exclaimed on approaching the eighth level of *Paradiso:* "I seemed to see the Universe alight with a single smile." Discussions today also draw upon suggestions made by Paul in characterizing the Gospel as *moira*—a term whose associations in Greco-Roman culture were with comic characters, clowns, and fools. The preaching of the cross is foolishness, God's work in the world is foolishness, and the people through whom God works are noted for their foolishness (I Cor. 1:14-31). In making such associations, Paul is seen as offering a summation of themes that are common to biblical theology and ancient comedies. The comic motifs of confounding human wisdom, exposing self-righteousness, thwarting pride, overturning social hierarchies, exposing hypocracies, and coming to the defense of the lowly and oppressed, are common to both comedy and the Bible. "Those that exalt themselves shall be humbled, and those that humble themselves shall be exalted'' is a comedic as well as Christian text.

The fact that the corollary of the word ''comedy'' is tragedy has suggested further connections for recent discussion. Early in the twentieth century the classicist F. M. Cornford advanced the thesis that the origins of both tragedy and comedy are to be found in the ancient Greek spring rites, with tragic action rooted in the first movement of the rites, upon the death of the king and the old year, and the winter return to chaos and infertility. Comic action was rooted in the second movement of the rites, with the resurrection or replacement of the dead king, a royal marriage, and a wedding feast. In these terms, as Wylie Sypher has proposed, the Christian celebration of the Eucharist and the Jewish Passover from which it was derived share in a movement from the tragic to the comic.

Another important connection has been pointed to by Northrop Frye. Tragedies, from ancient Greek to Shakespearean, concern themselves with the noble deeds of divine and royal families *(Oedipus Rex, King Lear)*, while comedies belong more to ordinary people and everyday affairs *(Lysistrata, Much Ado About Nothing)*. In these terms, a biblical anthropology shares in the largely ''proletarian'' and ''egalitarian'' character of comedy, with its suspicion of human might and greatness and elevation of the weak, the powerless, and the despised.

Frye has also noted that, whereas tragedies tend to be *exclusive,* separating people into opposing factions and sorting people out into hierarchies of importance and worth, comedies tend to be *inclusive,* embracing the whole of the human spectrum, and aiming toward reconciliation, reunification, and celebration: hence the dictum that tragedies often end in funerals, while comedies end in feasts and weddings. The implications of this have been extended further by Conrad Hyers in his observation that tragedies espouse heroic deeds and military values—honor, duty, loyalty, pride, courage, unwillingness to compromise—whereas comedies espouse the simple joys of everyday life and the virtues of mediation: humility, flexibility, give-and-take, confession of weakness, playfulness, good humor. As a result, while tragedies are willing to sacrifice any number of persons to principles, comedies are inclined to sacrifice principles to persons. Hungry disciples and human suffering take precedence over sabbath laws; forgiveness and mercy transcend judgment and condemnation.

The related subject of religion and humor also has gained considerable attention in recent decades, sparked by Elton Trueblood's *The Humor of Christ* (1964). While humor is an element in comedy, and may be equated with the comic spirit that inspires and directs comedy, humor has a wider range of vehicles for its expression: puns, quips, anecdotes, stories, jokes, clowning, and so forth. The main lines of recent discussion have been: (1) the presence of humor in biblical literature, its types and implications; (2) the relevance of humor for doctrine and the theological enterprise; (3) the place and importance of humor in spiritual development, worship, preaching, healing, and the religious life; (4) connections between the role of biblical figures and comic figures: clown, jester, fool, trickster.

The common thread of these various inquiries has been the affirmation that, when the positive forms of the comic spirit are missing, the result is a fall into a variety of evils: absolutism, dogmatism, pride, rigidity, intolerance, fanaticism, idolatry. Without a developed sense of humor and of the human comedy, human affairs easily become tragic, while the noblest attempts at proclaiming a message of love, joy, peace, faith, and hope are easily subverted and turned into their opposites.

CONRAD HYERS

Bibliography

George Aichele, Jr., *Theology As Comedy*, 1980.
Harvey Cox, *The Feast of Fools*, 1969.
J. Cheryl Exum, *Tragedy and Comedy in the Bible*, 1984.
Conrad Hyers, *The Comic Vision*, rev. ed., 1992.
_____, *And God Created Laughter: The Bible As Divine Comedy*, 1987.
Cal Samra, *The Joyful Christ*, 1986.
Elton Trueblood, *The Humor of Christ*, 1964.

COMMUNION (See SACRAMENTS/SACRAMENTAL THEOLOGY, WORSHIP.)

CONFESSIONAL THEOLOGY

The term *confessio* originally referred to the testimony of faith offered by a martyr. From this meaning, the term was extended to refer to the shrines or tombs of martyrs. It eventually came to take on the sense of a clear and definite statement of religious conviction. Confessional theology, therefore, means theology that takes its point of departure within the framework of faith and a given faith community.

The term "confessional theology" is used in two senses. The first refers to a kind of Protestant theology, predominantly of the Lutheran and Reformed churches. These traditions devised carefully written statements of their convictions in the sixteenth and seventeenth centuries: in the Lutheran tradition—the Augsburg Confession and *The Book of Concord;* and in the Reformed (Calvinist) tradition—the Westminster Confession and Catechism (for example).

These documents are understood by their confessing communities not to be creeds like the Apostles' Creed and the Nicene Creed, but documents that provide interpretative guides to scripture and earlier creedal traditions. To a lesser degree, the Thirty-nine Articles of the Church of England serve a similar function for the

Anglican (in the United States, the Episcopal) communion, and the Schleitheim Confession for the Mennonites.

Within these traditions, some theologians engage in confessional theology. They discuss theological topics in modern terms and in ways consonant with these confessional documents. Such theologians defer to confessional documents as authoritative and fundamental statements of the core of Christian conviction, or at least as clear statements of the distinctive features of the understanding of Christian faith according to their particular tradition.

Since the confessional documents provide a framework of shared theological perspective, they enable their communities to engage in focused and lively debate, often in contrast to the diffuse character of much modern theology. Intellectually rigorous theological discussion can often be found most clearly in those communities which share such a confessional heritage.

On the other hand, all classical confessions antedate the historical critical study of the Bible and the deep appreciation of historical and cultural relativity of every particular place and time that characterizes modern consciousness. Confessionalism therefore can be highly parochial and make claims to certainty and clarity regarding revelation that are difficult to sustain. Also, a theological idea that is firmly entrenched in a particular confessional tradition (e.g., "law and gospel" for Lutherans) may be difficult to challenge or question from within that tradition in cases where, in light of historical experience, it becomes dated or ethically problematic.

The second sense of the phrase "confessional theology" is distinctively modern, and derives from H. Richard Niebuhr's *The Meaning of Revelation*. In that work, he employs the term "confessional theology" to articulate a theological method that accepts the cultural and historical relativism of modern social sciences and yet affirms a distinctive Christian "revelation." According to that understanding, theology does its proper work when it articulates the language and view of the world that characterizes the Christian faith in all its particularity. Niebuhr's confessional method, however, recognizes that "self-defense is the most prevalent error in all thinking and perhaps especially in theology and ethics." Therefore, Niebuhr advocates a theology which concerns itself with finding the *communally shared affirmations* of Christians. As Niebuhr concisely summarizes his method, "[W]e can proceed only by stating in simple, confessional form what has happened to us in our community, how we came to believe, how we reason about things and what we see from our point of view." Although this use of the term "confessional theology" is Niebuhr's, there are in this respect clear lines of affinity between Niebuhr's method and Friedrich Schleiermacher's.

Though not always labeled confessional theology, Niebuhr's perspective has wide influence in current theology. Many of Niebuhr's students (James M. Gustafson and Gordon Kaufmann are two clear examples) approach theological reflection in ways that have deep continuities with Niebuhr. The current emphasis

97

on unapologetic particularity in Christian ethics (e.g., Stanley Hauerwas) stands in a direct line of descent from Niebuhr. "Theologies of story" often find at least part of their inspiration in Niebuhr. Not all, of course, would meet equally with Niebuhr's approval, but they do share fundamental impulses that are in common with his.

More broadly, the question of relativism and particularity so clearly stated by Niebuhr lives on in discussions of foundationalism and non-foundationalism, relativism and objectivism, and postmodernism and theology.

MARTIN L. COOK

Bibliography

Willard Dow Allbeck, *Studies in the Lutheran Confessions.*
Nestor Beck, *The Doctrine of Faith.*
Arthur C. Cochrane, ed., *Reformed Confessions of the Sixteenth Century.*
Martin L. Cook, *The Open Circle: Confessional Method in Theology.*
H. Richard Niebuhr, *The Meaning of Revelation.*
Douglas Ottati, *Meaning and Method in H. Richard Niebuhr's Theology.*

Cross Reference: Ecclesiology, Law and Gospel, Narrative Theology.

CONVERSION (*See* SOTERIOLOGY.)

CORRELATION

Theological methods of correlation represent one set of options available within modern Christian thought to meet the permanent obligation upon all theologians to express for their own particular time and place the contemporary meaning of Christian faith.

Distinctive to theologies of correlation are the recognition that Christian tradition and contemporary culture are theologically co-determinative, and the insistence that the two must somehow be made to stand in a relationship that preserves their independence as well as their interdependence. There are, therefore, two conditions that must be satisfied by any theologically adequate method of correlating the claims of historical Christianity and the shared experience of contemporary culture; namely, the autonomy condition and the reciprocity condition.

Theologians of correlation are inclined to seek their theologically legitimating antecedent in the attempts by Friedrich Schleiermacher (1768–1834) to repair the fracture in modern culture that resulted from the unresolved conflict between defenders of the older orthodox "supranaturalism," whose theology had become increasingly anachronistic, and champions of the newer autonomous critical reasoning, who were effectively left with no option but to embrace an increasingly anti-Christian "naturalism."

In response to this stalemate, which he feared would lead both to the intellectual starvation of Christian faith and to the impoverishment of spiritual values within the wider culture, Schleiermacher called for a permanent alliance between historical Christianity and modern learning. According to the terms of this treaty, the interdependence of faith and learning was to be established, but not at the expense of their individual autonomy, so that "faith does not hinder learning, nor learning exclude faith." Just how to effect the terms of such an accord was Schleiermacher's dilemma.

In twentieth-century religious thought, the use of correlation as a methodological strategy is preeminently associated with the name of Protestant theologian Paul Tillich and, to a lesser extent, with that of Roman Catholic theologian David Tracy.

Despite differences in detail, their methods of correlation can be described as examples of a postliberal strategy that aims to meet the challenges of modernity, while steering a course between the modernist temptation to identify the Christian message with the dominant ideologies of the day and the counter-modernist temptation to evade the demands of the present, either by retreating to some idealized Christian past or by surrendering to some authoritarian version of Christianity.

Paul Tillich characteristically spoke of Christian theology as a correlation between certain "questions" implied in an analysis of human existence and the "answers" implied in an analysis of the symbols in which the Christian message is expressed. This question-answer schema defines the structure of his *Systematic Theology:* the question implied in the concept of "reason" is correlated with the answer implied in the symbol "revelation"; the question of "being," with the answer "God"; the question of "existence," with the answer "the Christ"; the question of "life," with the answer "the Spirit"; and the question of "history" with the answer "the Kingdom of God."

Tillich's account of his method has been subjected to exhaustive critical discussion, much of which has concentrated on the adequacy of the question-answer schema. On the one hand, some critics have doubted whether a question from one realm of discourse can ever be appropriately answered from a different realm. A specifically philosophical question can be answered, if at all, only in properly philosophical terms, such that a specifically theological answer could never be correctly correlated with a philosophical question without violating "the autonomy condition" of an adequate correlative relation.

Despite the impression that he himself sometimes left, Tillich's method of correlation was not intended as a general theory of relations between philosophy and theology. His question-answer schema was instead meant to apply only to certain sorts of theologically significant philosophical questions; namely, to those questions that push up against the limits of human reason and experience, questions that Tillich called "ultimate questions." Among such questions could be counted the Leibnizian puzzle, "Why is there something and not nothing?" Even if these questions should originate within philosophy, they are not capable of being answered within purely philosophical terms. Although some philosophers would hold that they are consequentially improper questions, Tillich defends their philosophical propriety while insisting that their "answer" necessarily lies beyond the reach of philosophy.

On the other hand, critics of a different kind have complained that Tillich's account of philosophical questions and theological answers is so rigidly constructed that there is an entirely one-way relationship between philosophy and theology. Such an objection, though not simply mistaken, reflects the propensity of critics to concentrate too much upon what Tillich said about his method of correlation and to neglect what he did with it in practice. In operation, Tillich's method was always more subtle than were his accounts of it, which tended to be wooden in outline and misleading in detail.

David Tracy is among those theologians who have concentrated their criticism of Tillich on the allegedly non-dialectical nature of relations between "questions" and "answers" in the method of correlation. In effect, Tracy charges that Tillich's methodology fails to satisfy the reciprocity condition: Tillich merely juxtaposes, rather than actually correlates, the two poles of the theological enterprise.

Having described himself as committed both to "the modern experiment" and to "the Christian vision of human possibilities," Tracy sets out to revise Tillich's method so that it will allow for full reciprocity between the two poles. Such reciprocity, which Tracy names "mutually critical correlation," requires the theologian to treat both commitments as subject to modification by means of their mutual critique. Tracy emphasizes that the exact character of such correlations cannot be determined beforehand and that his method of mutually critical correlation can be tested only by its actual use in the constructive work of fundamental, dogmatic, and practical theology. Like Tillich before him, Tracy too recognizes that the adequacy of one's theological method must be measured by its results.

JOHN CLAYTON

Bibliography

John Clayton, *The Concept of Correlation*.
Paul Tillich, *Systematic Theology*, 3 vols.
———, *Main Writings/Hauptwerke*, 6 vols.
David Tracy, *Blessed Rage for Order*.
———, *The Analogical Imagination*.

Cross Reference: Systematic Theology, Theological Method.

COSMOGONY (See CREATION.)

COSMOLOGY

The term "cosmology" can be defined in a variety of ways: as the scientific study of the structure and history of the universe (related to astronomy and astrophysics); as the philosophical inquiry into the most adequate and applicable categories for interpreting the universe; and as the theological study of the origin, purpose, value, and meaning of the universe as the creation of God. Clearly, theology in every age has been influenced to some extent by prevailing cosmologies, from the period of the ancient Yahwist community to the New Testament evangelists and throughout the diverse interpretations of the biblical witness in Christian history.

Initially the focus here is on scientific cosmology, turning specifically to the twentieth-century discovery of the expansion of the universe; then the emphasis moves to several philosophical implications that can be drawn from the scientific results and their potential relevance for Christian theology today.

A Description of the Scientific Data. On a clear night with a dark sky, away from city lights, one can probably see around 3,000 stars along with the broad mottled-white streak of the Milky Way. All these stars, including those that constitute the "streak," are actually part of our galaxy of over one hundred billion stars. What we familiarly call the Milky Way is just the region in the sky of the galactic plane, where the density and great distance of stars give the appearance of a continuous flow. The rest of the stars we see are also part of the galaxy, appearing like a veil as we look away from the galactic plane.

An important exception is what appears to the naked eye as a small smudge of light near the constellation Pegasus. This object is not a part of our galaxy but is another galaxy, the Great Spiral Galaxy in Andromeda, lying several million light years away. To look farther we need modern telescopic instruments. With these instruments—both ground-based and in Earth orbit—astronomers have made staggering discoveries about the universe.

We now know that our galaxy floats amid a cluster of galaxies, which is, in turn, part of a supercluster approximately 75 million light years in diameter. Recent evidence suggests that the distribution of clusters and superclusters forms enormous strings and filaments in space.

But the most remarkable discovery of this century, first reported by Edwin Hubble in the mid-1920s and now confirmed over enormous scales, is that these superclusters are moving apart from one another with speeds proportional to their separation distance. We have discovered the expanding universe, arguably the greatest scientific achievement of this century! But if the universe is expanding, it must mean that far back in time it was arbitrarily small and dense. Was this the "creation" of the universe? And will its expansion ever end? In order to address these questions we must turn from observation to theory.

Theoretical Cosmology. In 1905 Albert Einstein published his Theory of Special Relativity (SR) in which space and time are united into four-dimensional geometry—spacetime. Einstein extended this work in 1916 with his Theory of General Relativity (GR). In it, gravity, the only force in nature of significance at cosmological scales, is interpreted as a manifestation of the curvature of spacetime. In the late 1920s, G. Lemaitre, working closely with Hubble's observational program, provided three theoretical models of an expanding universe. In the "closed" model, the universe is like the surface of a three-dimensional sphere, with a finite size and a finite age. After expanding to a maximum size (perhaps one hundred billion years from now), the universe recollapses upon itself. In the "open" model, the universe is like the surface of a three-dimensional saddle, with a finite age but an infinite size. Here the universe will expand forever. A third model is called "flat" since it has zero curvature, neither positive (closed, finite) nor negative (open, infinite). It is infinite in all directions and is expanding, just as the other models are.

Today astronomers are still undecided about which model best describes the universe we live in. However, current evidence seems to favor the flat model. In any case, the universe has a finite age, probably 15 to 20 billion years. If standard GR is the correct theory of gravity, then such a universe must have arisen out of a "singularity" at $t = 0$ (where t is the parameter time). As we approach this event temperatures soar, the universe shrinks to below the size of an atom, densities climb to infinity, and the laws of physics as we know them begin to fail us.

Alternative models have been studied that obviate the $t = 0$ problem, most notably the "steady-state cosmology" of H. Bondi, T. Gold, and F. Hoyle (1948). Hoyle's model was eventually eliminated by factors including the discovery of universal microwave background radiation by A. A. Penzias and R. W. Wilson (1965). Still, the standard Big Bang model has serious problems. Why is there, apparently, more matter than anti-matter in the universe? What produced the clumping of matter into galaxies in a symmetric universe? What could have caused the very early universe to be in thermal equilibrium, before there had been sufficient time for all of its parts to interact? Finally, why of all possible scenarios is the universe flat (i.e., why is its curvature *precisely* zero)?

Underlying these problems is the need to bring together a theory of gravity with quantum physics. If the universe were once arbitrarily small, then the correct cosmological theory will have to be consistent with quantum mechanics, the standard theory for subatomic processes. Hence the current task is to formulate a *quantum* theory of gravity and to apply it to the problem of the very early universe.

Inflationary models of the early universe as devised by A. Guth and others could solve several of the problems left over by standard Big Bang cosmology. Very recent work by J. B. Hartle and S. Hawking suggests that quantum gravity would lead to a universe with a finite past but *no* beginning. R. Penrose has proposed a model in which the universe emerges spontaneously out of a background field. Highly complex and extremely hard to test, these models underscore the staggering difficulty scientists have in accounting for the early universe and the fundamental problem of its origin at $t=0$.

Philosophical Problems. Underlying the technical difficulties in current scientific cosmology are profound philosophical issues. These involve assumptions lying behind the working theories in cosmology as well as concepts and testing procedures employed in cosmology. B. Stoeger suggests that they include: (1) The "cosmological principle"—that we do not occupy a privileged position in the universe; (2) the assumption of the universal validity of physical laws and natural constants; (3) the choice of a theory of gravity, Einstein's or a competitor's; and (4) the assumption that we can scientifically study a unique object (presumably the universe is "all there is") with a unique, unrepeatable history, which includes the community of inquiry (scientists) and its methods as part of the phenomenon.

Are there limits *in principle* to verification in cosmology? G. Ellis has pointed to the unobservability of the early universe and its final state. There are highly restrictive limits *in practice* as well. Even observational data on the universe collected over thousands of years would disclose only a tiny fraction of the entire history and scope of the universe.

A different set of questions arises when we attempt to use our scientific models in constructing a new philosophy of nature as a prelude to a theology of nature. Given the relativity of theories, we must consider which features should be taken seriously and which ones will turn out to be historically contingent and replaceable in future theories. For example, is the initial singularity ($t=0$) a fact about nature or a revisable characteristic of our current theory? Does the lack of an "arrow of time" in physics undermine the human experience of the difference between past and future, or will a future theory incorporate time's arrow into fundamental physics?

How pervasive is the contingency of the universe? For example, could all logically possible universes be actual, as in the so-called "many-worlds theories," or is our universe truly unique? If our universe is the only actual universe, why is it that the only actual universe is consistent with the highly restrictive properties necessary for life to evolve? Why is the actual universe orderly and intelligible, given that one can imagine both an intelligible universe that is highly disorderly and an orderly universe that is unintelligible in detail? Ultimately the issue of contingency becomes the question of why the universe exists *per se*.

Theological Issues. When considering the theological significance of cosmology, one should first ask how cosmology and theology might be related in general.

Following the typology of Ian Barbour for relating science and religion, some believe that (1) there are conflicts between science and religion (as in scientific materialism or creation science); (2) science and religion should be kept separate in principle, with nothing in common (as in Protestant neoorthodoxy and existentialist theology); (3) there can be dialogue regarding the philosophical, methodological, and boundary questions; or (4) there might be a more direct interaction between science and religion, including a renewal of natural theology, a reformulation of theological doctrine in light of science, and even a synthesis among the fields in which science too could be fruitfully reexamined. Theological issues raised by writers who take positions three and four include:

1. Does "$t = 0$" bear on the doctrine of creation? For example, how might it relate to *creatio ex nihilo* understood as an initial act of creation, the origin of time, the finitude of time (in the past), and the contingency of the universe?

2. Does the fundamental role of chaos in quantum cosmology (as well as in quantum physics, thermo-dynamics, chaos theory, and biological evolution) bear on the doctrine of God's *continuous creation* in and through natural processes?

3. What is the theological significance of the (possible) infinitude, intelligibility, and contingency of the universe? For example, in what ways would an infinite universe undercut the distinction between God and nature? Does either the intelligibility of the universe (evidenced by the explanatory and predictive "success" of science) or the global contingency of the universe (why it is as it is, why it is at all, and why the laws of science take on their specific forms) affect the doctrine of creation or the doctrine of God (particularly God's transcendence of and God's immanence in the universe)?

4. Does current cosmology strengthen the philosopher of religion's theistic arguments? For example, can one convincingly argue that the best possible explanation of the universe as known through current cosmology is the theistic hypothesis? Does the universe suggest a cosmic teleology? If so, how does the now scientifically informed philosopher's God relate to the biblical God?

5. What is the role of humankind in the universe? Is life an anomaly in a vast, uncaring universe or a special and valued product of an enormous and still-functioning cosmic experiment? Is our role in nature one of steward or possibly of created co-creator? How do we relate the Spirit as the source of life to biological evolution and cosmological expansion? Are the physical and biological laws of the universe a manifestation of the divine Logos?

6. How can one relate the Resurrection to the contingency of natural laws and the significance of space, time, and causality? Can the Resurrection narratives be interpreted in a consistent fashion that respects both the New Testament kerygma and historical and natural scientific perspectives? In what way could an event in human history have truly cosmological significance?

7. What is the eschatological significance of the far future of the universe? Is the future open to divine action? How does one understand the relation of unending cosmic time and divine eternity? What is the destiny and religious significance of life in the universe, the ultimate grounds for hope and victory, in the face not just of personal death or species extinction but eventually of the end of the earth, sun, and even the universe?

8. On a different note, are there implicit philosophical and theological elements *in cosmology* that could bear closer examination and possible alteration to the benefit of cosmology?

In sum, then, how might scientific discoveries about the universe—including space, time, matter, and causality—relate to the entire spectrum of Christian theology? In particular, can God be understood as acting in and through the processes of nature as well as history, and how might this understanding be shaped fruitfully by today's cosmology?

These and other questions are now being pursued in theological research.

ROBERT JOHN RUSSELL

Bibliography

Ian G. Barbour, *Issues in Science and Religion.*
————, *Religion in an Age of Science.*
Timothy Ferris, *Coming of Age in the Milky Way.*
Arthur Peacocke, *Creation and the World of Science.*
Ted Peters, ed., *Cosmos as Creation.*
Robert John Russell, William R. Stoeger, and George V. Coyne, eds., *Physics, Philosophy, and Theology: A Common Quest for Understanding.*
James S. Trefil, *The Moment of Creation.*

Cross Reference: Creation, Creation Science, Ecology, Philosophical Theology, Science and Christianity, Space, Time.

COVENANT

A covenant ordinarily refers to an agreement that is arranged between two or more parties: It states their relationship and stipulates their future rights and responsibilities. Such an agreement rests upon the promise, ability, and full faith and credit of the parties consenting to it. Although covenants may recognize natural (e.g., kinship) relations, they do not rest upon them for social power. *Covenant* signifies a preeminently historical relationship, more like a social contract than an organic process.

The term "covenant" enters Christian theology from the biblical world, where it is said that God relates to all creatures, especially to Israel and the church, by a free decision and the gift of life together. In the Hebrew scriptures, covenant is prominent in the Deuteronomic tradition, in which God and Israel establish a moral relation that authorizes ethical relations between persons within Israel. Whether as a social ideology for a premonarchic egalitarian society (Gottwald) or as a theological construct of the preexilic prophets to delegitimate established power (Nicholson), the idea of God's special interest in and concern for justice and peace as the basis for human flourishing and God's promise to see to it that such a condition is realized remains at the heart of the matter. In the stories of Israel, there are covenants with the patriarchs, with Moses and all Israel, with David, and in the prophetic hope for Israel, with all people and the earth itself.

In the Christian scriptures, "covenant" is an important theological concept, especially in the texts concerning the Lord's Supper and in Romans and Hebrews. The promise, "I will be your God and you shall be my people," is fulfilled in the life and destiny of Jesus Christ, anticipated in the Christian community, and ultimately realized in the transfiguration of heaven and earth (Revelation). Paul uses covenant to speak of the economy of grace whereby God ordains salvation, life, and blessedness for us. While he contrasts an old and a new covenant in II Corinthians, it is clear that they represent one saving purpose of God.

Theologically, "covenant" signifies four complementary ideas. As an arrangement created by God who makes covenant, it is a gracious gift. As it stipulates a form of life based on the gift, it is realized in a response of faith and obedience. Because it is based on consent rather than coercion, it establishes a responsible moral relation between people and God; sociality becomes solidarity. And as it envisions a way of life pressing beyond the limits of any particular culture, it establishes a history of seeking a universal community of justice and friendship, "a blessing in the midst of the earth."

The idea of covenant has always been one of the themes of Christian theology. It is present in principle wherever a history of salvation approach is taken, as in Irenaeus (c. 130–200). It was taken up especially in Reformed theology, in which it signified the entire relation of God to creatures and established a history of redemption and creation. Following Calvin (1509–1564), one gracious covenant was held to be the unifying purpose of all God's ways and works, the framework for specific "covenants." Beginning with H. Bullinger (1504–1575), through the seventeenth-century English Puritans, to J. Cocceius (1603–1669) and the "federal theology," the idea served as an organizing principle for systematic theology. Originating with an eternal election and ending with its realization in the final state of creatures, the divine design is woven into the fabric of natural and historical solidarities. The effect of this was to limit the covenant of grace to a select group, however, and to exclude all others on the basis of a covenant of works. A tension existed between the universal and the restrictive understandings of covenant.

In the twentieth century, Karl Barth (1886–1968) used the idea of one covenant of grace to link God's activity in Creation and Redemption, thus situating Christ in a cosmic setting. When so construed, covenant emphasizes the idea of the divine self-limitation as well as the central meaning and purpose of creaturely life and human history. God is the One who makes and keeps covenant, and human beings are those who are to co-exist in responsible relations of praise, love, and justice. In this view, Christ makes actual the divine election that embraces all, establishing the conditions for human partnership with God. The covenant of grace is unrestricted.

Socio-politically, "covenant" belongs to the establishment of a community rather than to its originating events (Bellah). It provides the arrangements within which ordinary life can flourish. It defines the common center of value that holds the community together and creates the conditions for free and responsible interactions. All historical covenants appear to be restrictive (constituting a people over against other people) and broken (subject to the struggle of interests and temptations of power). The theological idea of the covenant of grace is a critical principle that justifies human attempts at solidarity but denies the claim of any to be God's order on the earth, pointing beyond all arrangements of the terrestrial city to the better justice and peace of the city of God (Augustine).

THOMAS D. PARKER

Bibliography

Karl Barth, *Church Dogmatics* 3/1 and 4/1.
Robert Bellah, *The Broken Covenant; American Civil Religion in Time of Trial.*
Norman K. Gottwald, *The Tribes of Yahweh.*
E. W. Nicholson, *God and His People: Covenant Theology in the Old Testament.*

Cross Reference: Basic Christian Communities, Biblical Theology, Ecclesiology.

CREATION

The doctrine or symbol of creation—derived especially from Genesis 1–3, the Psalms, Second Isaiah, and John 1—is rich in religious and existential meaning. It has set the terms for most Christian (and Jewish) world views or metaphysics, and it has provided the essential presuppositions for every other important Christian doctrine or symbol: human dignity and freedom, sin, revelation, Incarnation, redemption, history, and eschatology. Without the assumption of creation, most of the other affirmations of Christian piety and loci of theology would make no sense. Second, creation has been the subject of great Christian controversies, especially in the early church and in the present era, when literal, biblical views of creation find themselves in opposition to most of modern science. Finally, this symbol, as much ignored as it was presupposed in most theology, has now come into sudden prominence because of the present crisis concerning the integrity, even the existence, of nature. In this short essay, each of these three aspects of creation is discussed in turn.

The Religious Meaning of Creation. Every fundamental religious symbol implies, even requires, a certain mode of existing in the world; this is its "religious" meaning. The "religious" meaning of creation refers to the attitude toward reality, life, and its meaning that the symbol expresses—in this case an attitude toward God, the world, and human life in space and time. Religious symbols also manifest metaphysical implications as an attitude toward the larger reality or universe in which we exist; they are thus in the broadest sense cognitive even though they are not "scientific." The Christian view of creation provided important parts of the groundwork for the rise of modern empirical science, for the belief in creation implied a real and an orderly, although contingent, material world and therefore one open for empirical investigation into its pervasive and invariable features. In what follows, emphasis is on the religious rather than the metaphysical implications of creation; the former have been surprisingly consistent throughout Christian history while the latter, however important, have received differing philosophical explication in different epochs; for example, Platonistic, Aristotelian, rationalistic, idealistic, neoclassical, and so on.

To say, as the scriptures do, that God created all things meant to the tradition from the beginning that God is the sole source of all. Quite early, therefore, theology declared that God had not created "out of matter," since then something—matter—would be co-eternal with God and not created by God. Nor was creation thought to be an emanation from God, a "fall" away from God, but the result of God's deliberate and hence free action. Therefore, since God was known to be good, creation is good. To be finite, temporal, bodily, mortal, even dependent and vulnerable—as all creatures are—is therefore good and not evil. If God created all, then there is no essential, ineradicable evil; suffering is neither fated nor necessary, and redemption from it is possible. Similarly, the body, created by God as is mind or spirit, is good, not evil. Life, therefore, in its essential structure of finitude, spatiality, temporality, individuality, and sociality, is thus potentially creative and meaningful.

Creation implies the absoluteness and unconditionedness of God as the source or ground of all, and the relatedness of God as that on which the world is continually dependent. God is therefore transcendent to the world as well as immanent within it. Creation implies the eternity of God as the source of time and yet the temporality and changeability of God as related to a world in process. It even implies the passivity and suffering of God as experiencing, knowing, and caring for a vulnerable, mortal world. These paradoxes about God implied by the religious meaning of creation have puzzled and challenged Christian philosophy since the beginning; they represent a "sign" of the mystery of the divine as creator.

Creation thus both expressed and anchored firmly the monotheistic center of Christian (and Jewish) faith: As the source of all things there was God—alone, unconditioned, and eternal, and yet in continual and essential relation to a changing creation. Central to the implications of creation, therefore, was what it said about human existence, its possibilities, its dilemmas, and its destiny. One implication was that the Christian affirmation that men and women were created by God established the freedom and the dignity, the spiritual constitution, and the value of human life—all of which were represented by the crucial phrase in Genesis that humans had been created "in the image of God." As a consequence of their creation, humans were free and responsible, that is, moral creatures, on the one hand subject to a moral law that obligated them to one another, and on the other hand capable of irresponsible and even evil action. The freedom, responsibility, and potential "fault" of human existence all appear with creation.

A second implication of the symbol of creation was that God created all the essential conditions of human life: its bodily base, its material environment, its spatial and temporal parameters. In principle these parameters of finitude were also established as "good" if humans lived up to their image.

Third, since God created time, ruled the sequences of historical events, and "acted" purposefully in history, history was given a potentiality of meaning unknown in religious and cultural life before. Creation, in other words, established the basis for the glory and the personal intimacy of God, for the value and spiritual dignity of women and men, for the positive assessment of nature and life generally, and for the decisive and hopeful character of temporal existence. As is evident, not only was the religious meaning of the symbol creation central to the religious attitudes of Christians toward God, their world, and themselves in that world, but even more it provided the bases for assumptions about reality that have been central to Western consciousness generally and have continued to define that consciousness long after the latter has become "secular." To many for whom no religious meanings at all are valid, these implications of creation remain nevertheless accurate assessments of reality and of life's possibilities within reality.

Creation and Science. As the summary above shows, the religious meanings of creation are rich and important, even to a secular scientific and technological culture. Like all the other religious affirmations within the Hebrew and Christian scriptures, these attitudes were expressed with and communicated by narratives and images, the "stories" about God and God's actions. With regard to creation, these stories center in the first chapters of Genesis where witness is reverently and poetically given to the great events through which God brought the universe into being and established its main features. Not surprisingly, the story recorded there reflects the understanding of the natural order characteristic of the Hebrews in the seventh or the fifth centuries B.C.E.: of the heavens, of the earth, of the flora and fauna of the earth, and of human history. It is therefore a relatively "archaic" view of the origins and early history of the world, laced with and expressive of these religious meanings. One important task for the modern theologian—in fact, for any modern Christian—is to separate that archaic science and archaic history from these religious meanings and to re-express the latter in terms of the cosmology and the historical consciousness of the modern world. Like the symbol of original sin, therefore, the symbol of creation has represented a fascinating, unavoidable, and yet very difficult challenge to theology to be at once "biblical" and modern.

Most of the principal Christian traditions, Protestant and Catholic alike, have recognized the historical relativity of the literal story, have assented to the authority of science and historical inquiry, and have thus sought to translate the religious meanings of creation into the terms of modern cosmology. All present Christians, however, by no means see it this way. To many the scriptures have been verbally inspired, and hence every proposition is literally as well as religiously or symbolically valid. The "science" of Genesis is as true and as important for them as are the "religious" meanings of Genesis; in fact, for them these two cannot be separated. Thus arises the familiar "warfare" between religion and science over "creation science" or "God's science" and what they term "evolutionary science."

One of the most unexpected novelties of the present epoch has been the appearance of "creation science," an alternative "biblical" cosmology of origins sharply contrasted with that of contemporary evolutionary science. On the one hand, creation science is deliberately modeled on aspects of the Genesis cosmology taken literally (e.g., separate creation of "kinds," especially human beings, a miraculous worldwide Noachic flood, and "sudden creation from nothing" of the entire universe about 10,000 years ago). On the other hand, creation science also claims to represent a genuinely "scientific" model of origins, based, as its adherents put it, on "scientific data" and "inferences from those data."

Although fundamentalism has not accommodated itself to the conclusions either of modern scientific or of modern historical inquiry, nevertheless, in promoting creation science it has sought to co-opt scientific procedure and authority as enthusiastically as it earlier used and in part transformed on its own terms the technological, commercial, capitalistic, and nationalistic culture of modernity. In fact, creation science as a body of theory was authored by Ph.D.s in natural science who are also fundamentalists.

In the creationist-evolution controversy, fundamentalism has taken the literal form of the creation story and insisted on its unchanging authority and "scientific" validity. This strange fusion of fundamentalist content with an ersatz science into creation science has received important political and social help from the alliance of rightwing evangelicalism with conservative Republicanism, the latter probably unconcerned with biblical literalism, but happy to cement their liaison with significant segments of the middle and lower middle classes. As a result, a number of states have proposed laws mandating the teaching of creation science, along with evolution, whenever the question of origins is raised in science classes. To date, the federal courts have struck down these laws as violating the Constitution.

Creation and Nature. In the nineteenth century, when science and religion seemed in temporary conflict, theological reflection concentrated on nature's processes and devised a number of evolutionary theisms. Later, from 1914 through roughly 1960, when European society was in turmoil, theology concentrated its attention on the question of the meaning of history and tended to ignore the role and the relevance of nature. A number of theologies in fact were almost loathe to articulate systematically even the religious meanings outlined above (e.g., Gustav Aulen, *The Christian Faith;* Rudolf Bultmann, *History and Eschatology;* and Oscar Cullmann, *Christ and Time*). In the past two decades, however, the integrity and preservation of nature have posed an absolutely crucial problem for modern civilization. Almost every front—the air and the atmosphere, the seas and lakes, the forests, the waters under the earth, the species on the earth, even the temperature—has shown itself to be endangered by industrial civilization, already perhaps mortally wounded. As has always been known but hardly felt, history is utterly dependent upon nature; yet, as we now realize for the first time, history has the ability not only to exploit nature but also to destroy it—and with that, to destroy itself. A deep sense of the self-destructive possibilities of human creativity and freedom is genuinely "biblical," as it is also Greek. Neither the Christian nor the Greek traditions, however, contemplated the immanent destruction of nature and life through the enlarged powers of high civilization, and yet that is just what is upon us today.

As a consequence, increasingly since the late 1960s theologies of nature have appeared. They represent efforts to articulate anew the meaning for Christian faith of the symbol of creation and, even more, to give that reinterpreted symbol a centrality in systematic theology unknown before. Earlier in the century the relation of theological reflection to philosophy and to the methods of history was predominant in theologies of revelation, Incarnation, and history; now the relations of theology to science, technology, and ecology are very much to the fore. This renewed interest in nature has rekindled Christian theologies of creation; and they have emphasized the goodness and value of nature; of the purposes of God for the natural order and not just for us; and even of the redemption of nature as well as the redemption of men and women. Thus many theologies (including my own) have emphasized that nature was made in God's image as a material order of inherent value, not just for us, but for itself and for God, and hence is in its being and its value also a sign or symbol of God. Such a reappreciation of nature, as opposed to its traditional role as backdrop to history or stage for the human drama, sees nature as itself an object of the divine purpose. The divine care has transformed the theological and religious meaning of creation far from its traditional anthropological bias.

As the above indicates, one of the most important aspects of the ecological crisis is the attitude of men and women toward nature. Is nature there only for us, as the stage for our actions, as raw material for our consumption, as a vacation place? A "pragmatic" view of nature esteems the world only insofar as it is of use to us, as it resolves our problems and dilemmas, and as it adds to our well-being. Correspondingly, a scientific view of nature tends to reduce the richness, variety, and integrity of nature—its mystery—to what empirical science can uncover about our physical environment. Thus in modern culture the reality of nature as an objectified and determined system of "vacuous" entities (to use A. N. Whitehead's phrase) corresponded to our assessment of nature as of value solely to us and so as subject entirely to our use. For this reason, as Herbert Marcuse has said, modern empirical science—if taken as an exhaustive description of the reality of nature—provides the ideological justification for the industrial exploitation of nature; it clears the way for the unimpeded greed of commercial culture. Clearly what is needed is to reawaken human beings to other ways of "knowing" nature's reality than as the system of determined objects of scientific inquiry and as the usable raw material of industrial process.

The effort to reach beyond both scientific positivism and anthropocentric pragmatism is a multifaceted enterprise. Many scientists have initiated and organized this important work, and artists, writers, and responsible moralists have led the way with regard both to the reality and to the value of nature. There is little question, however, that among these healing forces religion is potentially of vast importance. Historically, it has been through religious intuitions of nature and religious symbolism, ritual, and myths that the richness, independence, power, terror, and sublimity of nature have been "known" (these are cognitive relations to nature) and expressed—and that a creative, cooperative relation has been encouraged. These relations need to be reawakened. In the biblical tradition, the symbolism of creation is potentially the locus for a new set of cognitive, emotional, and moral relations to nature. Even the tradition of natural theology—the effort to find in natural experience "signs" of the divine presence—inescapably revives a deeper and richer "knowledge" of nature's reality. In seeking to establish the reality of God through our experiences of nature as God's creation, natural theology may effect as much of a change in our attitude toward nature as it does in our confidence in the divine presence. Suddenly and quite unexpectedly, therefore, the symbol of creation, now in relation to our knowledge of and care for nature, has again moved into prominence. Now human well-being and the meaning of history are inextricably intertwined with the independence and integrity of nature. No longer is creation solely of anthropomorphic importance as merely a storehouse and a playground for human beings. Possibly with the ecology crisis there will be a new Copernican revolution with regard to the value of nature.

LANGDON GILKEY

Bibliography

Langdon Gilkey, *Maker of Heaven and Earth*

Jürgen Moltmann, *God in Creation.*

Howard J. Van Till, et al., *Portraits of Creation: Biblical and Scientific Perspectives on the World's Formation.*

Cross Reference: Creation Science, Fundamentalism, Holy Spirit, Inerrancy, Science and Christianity, Space, Symbol, Time.

CREATION SCIENCE

Creation science ("creationism" or "scientific creationism") is the recent attempt by fundamentalist Christians to establish on scientific grounds that the created order was established suddenly from nothing *(ex nihilo)* in six days about 10,000 years ago, that a catastrophic worldwide Noachic flood accounts for the earth's geological features, and that the theory of evolution is an insufficient account of origins. Creation science is a complex phenomenon that includes (1) a theological component that defends a fundamentalist view of the Bible and its doctrine of creation; (2) a scientific component that claims that creation science is "science" and not religion; and (3) a social and legal component that seeks to disseminate its views to the public and to defend its attempt to mandate the teaching of creation science in science classes in public secondary schools.

As a theological movement, creation science, based on an allegedly "literal" reading of Genesis, holds that the universe was brought into being in six, twenty-four-hour days about 10,000 years ago. Its proponents are all associated with twentieth-century Protestant fundamentalism. Especially prominent supporters of creation science have been the Institute for Creation Research (ICR) and the Creation Research Society (CRS), both based in California. The CRS was established by Henry Morris and Duane Gish in 1963 to pursue scientific research that would show that a "literal" (fundamentalist) understanding of the Genesis accounts of creation is consonant with modern science. The ICR is the chief arm of publication (Creation-Life Publishers) and public relations (e.g., the newsletter *Acts and Facts*) of the movement. Along with promoting creation science, its literature castigates the theory of evolution as an inadequate theory of origins that is aligned with an anti-Christian world view.

Although creation science's supporters have much in common theologically with those who supported the prosecution of John Scopes in 1925 for teaching evolution in the Tennessee public schools, creation science in its present form has devised a new strategy by claiming to be a science. Because it is thought to be a scientific theory of origins, proponents, on the basis of fairness, seek equal time with evolution in classrooms. Despite this claim, in the trials in Arkansas and Louisiana, the courts have concluded that creation science is a veiled attempt by creationists to teach a fundamentalist interpretation of the Christian religion in public schools. Scientists have almost unanimously also denied its scientific validity. Regardless of creationists' rhetoric to the contrary, to date they have not established a recognized research program, have not published in respected scientific journals the results of research that has validated their position, and have not swayed scientists outside their fundamentalist fold that their conclusions have any merit. A creation science research program is not impossible; yet presently no grounds warrant the conclusion that creation science is science.

As a social phenomenon, creation science has caught public attention because of the litigation surrounding the attempts of the states of Arkansas and Louisiana in 1981 to legislate "equal time" in biology classes for its inclusion (with evolution) in the discussion of the origins of the universe and the earth. Despite the results of recent polls that show that 75 percent of the population favors equal time for creationist and evolutionary accounts of origins in the public schools, the laws were struck down because the courts determined that creation science was inherently religious and, therefore, that teaching it in public schools was a violation of the First Amendment of the Constitution. When the Supreme Court in 1987 (in a split vote) rejected the Louisiana law, some tolled the legal death knell of creation science. Legal battles will doubtless continue, however, because of strong public support for creationism and the zeal and organizational genius of its supporters.

Creation science fails to persuade fair-minded inquirers because it has not established its claims about origins on scientific grounds. It fails to sway others because it indulges in reading the Genesis creation accounts as though they are scientific treatises when those texts should be read as theology. Creation science's only success has been to persuade a large portion of the public (many of whom are not well-informed about both science and theology) that it should be given "equal time" with evolution in science classrooms. Despite its apparently groundless claims, creation science will remain a contentious irritant for jurists and theologians alike.

DONALD W. MUSSER

Bibliography

Roland Mushat Frye, ed., *Is God a Creationist? The Religious Case Against Creation-Science*.
Langdon Gilkey, *Creationism on Trial*.
Henry Morris, *History of Modern Creationism*.
Howard J. Van Till, Davis A. Young, and Clarence Menninga, *Science Held Hostage: What's Wrong with Creation-Science AND Evolutionism*.
Howard J. Van Till, et al., *Portraits of Creation: Biblical and Scientific Perspectives on the World's Formation*.

Cross Reference: Creation, Fundamentalism, Science and Christianity.

CREED (*See* CONFESSIONAL THEOLOGY, DOGMATIC THEOLOGY, ECCLESIOLOGY.)

CULTURE

Culture entails every aspect of the social, artistic, and linguistic environment humanity receives from the past and creates for the future. We recognize culture in the most trivial aspects of the human environment and in the loftiest: from fast food and petroleum advertisements, to the folkways and mores of nations and neighborhoods, to achievements in law, the sciences, and the arts that transcend their own times to enter the global commonwealth of ideas, institutions, and values. We speak both of particular cultures and of culture as a universal human condition.

H. Richard Niebuhr defined culture as "the 'artificial, secondary environment' which man superimposes on the natural. It comprises language, habits, ideas, beliefs, customs, social organization, inherited artifacts, technical processes, and values." Anthropologist Clifford Geertz specifies the cognitive implications that "culture" has for many disciplines: "It denotes an historically transmitted pattern of meanings embodied in symbols, a system of inherited conceptions expressed in symbolic forms by means of which men communicate, perpetuate, and develop their knowledge and attitudes toward life."

For Geertz, religion is a "cultural system" of symbols that serves a fundamental human need: to unite a people's vision of what reality is (their "world view") with their vision of how life ought to be lived (their "ethos"). This synthesis of "is" and "ought" serves a basic need for meaning and coherence, and it resists the basic threat of chaos or "bafflement." Religion would be, then, a function within culture, from which it is clearly inseparable. By this view, theologians must acknowledge that their tools—language, ideas, images, texts, and so forth—are themselves products of culture and that their own situations in history are thoroughly cultural. Culture is thus an aspect of the "hermeneutical circle" within which theology and other disciplines must work. Yet theologians usually wish to differentiate culture from religious faith. To do so, their arguments must indeed be *theological,* based on claims about God or some reality "other than" culture. For example, Rudolf Bultmann distinguishes "world view" (i.e., culture, whether mythical or scientific) from the New Testament "kerygma," a message about a relation with God, encountered in faith, and "wholly other" than world view.

In the Bible, culture is evident both as promise and as problem. Culture, for better or worse, is part of the created order; for better, when God allows Adam to name the creatures; for worse, when God scatters the builders of Babel and confuses their tongues. The people of Israel are to be a separate culture among cultures, and they are tempted to forsake their covenant relationship with God for unrighteous accommodations with their neighbors. This ambivalence is heightened in the New Testament, where attitudes toward Hellenistic culture vary from accommodation (e.g., "Render therefore to Caesar the things that are Caesar's, and to God the things that are God's" [Matt. 22:21]) to apocalyptic negation (e.g., "I saw a new heaven and a new earth" [Rev. 21:1]).

Augustine began his theory of scriptural interpretation, which was also a theory of culture, by distinguishing things and signs. Things are good, insofar as they are understood and loved as part of divine creation. Signs are also good, insofar as through them we learn and teach what is understood and loved. Like things, signs can be misused or loved for their own sake (rather than God's). Culture is the milieu for the Christian's difficult pilgrimage toward God. The question is whether this environment is mostly hostile or friendly, deceitful or truthful. In such terms did H. Richard Niebuhr lay out a typology of *moral* relationships between Christ and culture. The problem is that culture is both something for which Christians must take responsibility and something from which they should remain distinct. Niebuhr's five types, along with some of their exemplars, are: *Christ against culture:* First John, Tertullian, the Mennonites, Tolstoy; *Christ of (at one with) culture:* Gnosticism, Abelard, Albrecht Ritschl; *Christ above (fulfilling and transcending) culture:* Thomas Aquinas; *Christ and culture in paradoxical tension:* Paul, Luther, Kierkegaard; *Christ the transformer of culture:* Gospel of John, Augustine, Calvin. The typology is not neutral. Christ as transformer is the paradigm that Niebuhr most cherished, and it is implicitly his norm for assessing the other types.

Were the second type named "Christ disclosed in culture," it might have included Paul Tillich (who may also fit the third, fourth, and fifth types). Tillich's "theology of culture" has roots in German idealism and romanticism and concerns the spiritual "depth" of culture. Tillich offers several axioms: (1) Religion is the substance of culture, culture the form of religion; (2) spiritual substance is disclosed by means of cultural forms whose "style" expresses depth or "ultimate concern"; and (3) the truly ultimate is God, the "ground" and "abyss" of being, or being-itself. Since being-itself is infinite and prior to the divide between subjective experience and objective expression, God for Tillich is indeed "other than" yet disclosed with culture, though ambiguously. The theologian of culture must show where depth is creative in culture and must criticize cultural forms (such as nationalism) where depth is manifestly destructive, demonic, or idolatrous. In his analyses of art and architecture, Tillich greatly appreciated expressionistic styles, in which depth appears to shatter (and hence criticize) form from within.

The lasting import of Tillich's thought is its critical, prophetic imperative, which has counterparts in many modern theologies. Particular cultural expressions (in the arts, philosophy, social sciences, etc.) can identify the idolatries and pretensions of both culture itself and religious traditions; likewise, religious traditions provide symbolic conceptions (e.g., doctrines) that are intrinsically self-critical and can call culture into judgment. The appeals by Christians to symbols of grace, justice, and reconciling love in the midst of social and political change are cases in point. This critical, transformative imperative survives changes in culture and theology now apparent at the close of the twentieth century.

Theology can no longer take for granted a cultural milieu that is predominantly Western, secular, individualistic, and defined by scientific and romantic paradigms. These traits remain evident in the West, but they are inadequate to the pluralism of late-twentieth-century life and thought. Cultural pluralism means that we live within and among diverse cultures and religious traditions within our common local and global spaces. Such pluralism enriches our awareness of creation while boding tragic conflict and confusing babble. Amid many voices and perspectives, the impression of sheer relativism challenges theology to articulate distinctive, clear, and persuasive claims about God and reality. The pluralist must risk the challenges of real dialogue without forgetting his or her own finite limits and commitment to truthfulness. As pluralists seek to learn from the many voices within Christianity itself and from other traditions, religions, and socio-political realities, they will benefit from a variety of methods and fields of knowledge—convinced that no single angle of vision will comprehend the ever-changing intersections among God, ourselves, and others.

LARRY D. BOUCHARD

Bibliography

Rudolf Bultmann, *Jesus Christ and Mythology.*
Clifford Geertz, *The Interpretation of Cultures.*
H. Richard Niebuhr, *Christ and Culture.*
Paul Tillich, *Theology of Culture.*
David Tracy, *The Analogical Imagination: Christian Theology and the Culture of Pluralism.*

Cross Reference: Aesthetics, Civil Religion, Economics, Experience–Religious, Humanism, Language–Religious, Pluralism, Secularity.

DEATH AND ETERNAL LIFE

The question "What is death and its significance for humanity?" lies at the very foundation of Christian theology. From time to time this question grips all persons regardless of their beliefs and in spite of their best efforts to evade it, because the question of death's meaning is bound inextricably to the question of life's meaning. Whether questions about death and future life capture us by means of the only too frequent news account of random tragedy, or by means of the cruel loss of

117

a loved one or friend, or perhaps most directly by our contemplation of our own demise, these questions challenge us to think about extraordinary matters shunned by ordinary disciplines.

Christian thought about death rests upon a rich historical tradition comprising several different views. Customarily this tradition traces its roots from early Hebraic thought, according to which persons are part of a natural order created and maintained by God, as is the death of any person. For centuries the Hebrews described life after death as a shadowlike existence in Sheol following the loss of God's vivifying spirit. By the time of Christ, several views of death had emerged within Judaism. The Sadducees identified death with personal extinction, the Pharisees anticipated a kind of bodily resurrection, and the Essenes believed in the immortality of the soul.

Early Christian thinking about death and eternal life was influenced not only by Jewish traditions but also by Greek culture and Neoplatonism. According to the Platonic world view, soul and body are separable substances joined at birth (dualism). The soul is eternal and changeless, the body temporal and corruptible. Early Christians struggled between understanding life after death to mean the resurrection of the physical body, as did the Pharisees, and the separation of the soul from the body.

Recent theological reflection on these subjects acknowledges traditional concepts but analyzes them in the light of new cultural, historical, and theoretical developments. One of the most significant recent challenges to Christian theology has been the meeting of the world's religions and the interpretation of conflicting truth claims between them. John Hick has worked specifically on the concept of eternal life in a theological exposition that draws from various religious traditions, from Christianity to Buddhism to Hinduism. For Hick, God is first and last a God of love, who created the universe precisely for the salvation of all humanity, regardless of the historical circumstances into which each person is born. In *Death and Eternal Life,* he describes life after death as a process by which persons come increasingly into communion with God, first in a disembodied stage of afterlife, then in embodied stages, until at last they commune directly with God for eternity. Although Hick's work has been criticized for being too heavily dependent on a Western conception of God to succeed as a genuinely interfaith work, it nevertheless represents a substantial step in the direction of a global theology of death and eternal life.

Another recent theological movement that has turned attention to the issue of death and eternal life is process theology. It views God as a partner with nature in creation, assisting in the process of creation but not having absolute control over it. Based primarily on the metaphysical philosophy of Alfred North Whitehead, process theology considers each person not as a single entity through time but as "perpetually perishing" and re-creating the self through a sequence of moments. Process thought does not accept a predetermined end of history in the form of a salvation drama, in which the faithful shall rise to heaven and the damned shall be cast down to hell. Rather, history is an open-ended process of mutual creation by God and by the universe. From a process perspective, philosophical theologian Charles Hartshorne views death as the absolutely final event in the life of an individual and rejects the notion of bodily resurrection or of an immortal soul. For Hartshorne, "eternal life" is God's perfect knowledge and memory of us throughout the entire chain of events that constitutes creation. Other process theologians have argued in varying ways for personal survival of death, and there does not appear to be agreement among process scholars on this important issue at the present time.

Roman Catholic theology has long held that at death the soul separates from the body. For Karl Rahner, one of the creative twentieth-century Roman Catholic theologians, death is the pivotal point in a person's life at which the person's life is fully affirmed. It is not merely the end of personal existence, but the summation and fulfillment of personal existence. At death, the soul separates from the person's body and unites with the natural, universal order. Rahner views the eternal life of the soul as a life of persistent individual identity in close relation with the universe. History and salvation are thus joined together, not torn apart by a cataclysmic event such as the "end of time" foreseen by some Christians as the time when the Christ returns to judge the world. Rahner understands Christ's death to be the fundamental event of God's redemption, in which Christ is unified with the universe as a whole and thus has saved it. Similarly, he believes that each of us at death contributes our life's work to reality when our souls join with the universe.

Finally, today's liberation theologians seek to raise consciousness about the ways in which the promise of "life after death" might undergird oppressive social structures. Among Latin American liberation theologians, J. P. Miranda criticizes the church's view of death and eternal life for shifting Christian focus away from the injustices of this world and for compelling individuals to look toward death as the positive resolution of worldly strife. He argues instead that the right view of death is not "liberation," which can only be achieved within history and which can only be understood as justice for all humanity. Among black theologians, James Cone argues that death and belief in an afterlife must challenge the present historical world order. For Cone, death has meaning when persons risk dying in order to overcome oppression and injustice. Yet he maintains continuity with Christian faith by affirming belief in an afterlife while rejecting the tendency to speculate extensively about its nature.

In these various ways, then, Christian theologians have dealt with the fundamental human experience of death while interpreting the unique Christian affirmation that the resurrection of Christ is the firstfruit of the resurrection of all Christians.

HAROLD HEWITT, JR.

Bibliography

Charles Hartshorne, *The Logic of Perfection*.
John Hick, *Death and Eternal Life*.
Hans Küng, *On Being a Christian*.
Karl Rahner, *On the Theology of Death*.

Cross Reference: Anthropology, Liberation Theology, Pluralism, Process Theology, Resurrection, Suffering.

DEATH OF GOD THEOLOGY

The death of God or radical theology is really two things: a media event and a serious theological movement. The media event began unfolding in October 1965 when the *New York Times* and *Time* magazine reported on the work of three Protestant theologians: Thomas Altizer, Paul Van Buren, and William Hamilton. Although the media event lasted briefly, the radical or death of God theology was a serious scholarly inquiry that began in the Protestant tradition and eventually influenced both Jewish (cf. Richard Rubenstein, *After Auschwitz*) and Catholic (cf. Leslie Dewart, Eugene Fontinell, and the early Michael Novak) traditions.

In many ways the formation of the theological perspectives of Altizer and Hamilton could scarcely have been more different. Altizer was trained in the history of religions under Mircea Eliade at the University of Chicago; Hamilton was a product of Union Theological Seminary's postwar neoorthodoxy, to the left of Karl Barth and to the right of Paul Tillich. In the work of Altizer, Hamilton, and Paul Van Buren, author of the important *The Secular Meaning of the Gospel,* there was a serious and continuing attempt to explore the possibility of the Christian faith and life without the reality or doctrine of God. The essays of the movement's earliest stage can still be profitably studied in Altizer and Hamilton, *Radical Theology and the Death of God* (1966). Altizer's influential *Gospel of Christian Atheism* and chapter 2 of Hamilton's *New Essence of Christianity* (''Belief in the Time of the Death of God'' [1961]) are other early sources.

Indeed, one reason that death of God theology has refused to go away, as other subjects of media events have tended to do, is that it has attached to itself a whole cultural state of affairs. Death of God is not just a parable by Nietzsche, not just an easily ignored newspaper story in mid-twentieth-century America, but a continuing cultural tradition. The death of God, for example, is at the center of the interpretations of modern drama by Martin Esslin and Eric Bentley. J. Hillis Miller similarly has offered a reading of nineteenth-century and twentieth-century poetry in the light of the disappearance and death of God in *The Disappearance of God* and *Poets of Reality*. Politics and the death of God were the shared passion of both Albert Camus in *The Rebel* and Michael Harrington in his remarkable essay *The Politics at God's Funeral.*

In the mid-1960s, death of God theologians perceived that God was newly withdrawing from the American and European soul; this withdrawal needed historical and systematic study and begged for detective work, which is still needed. Today in each of the three great monotheistic faiths of the West—Islam, Judaism, and Christianity—God is reappearing in a variety of dangerous and evil forms. What is there, death of God theology asks, about belief in one God that makes persons and cultures evil? If it is the case that belief in but one God leads to the destruction and dehumanization of those not so believing, is it not the case that Christian justice and love require the elimination of that God as a source of evil?

Toward the end of the twentieth century three of the most fruitful theological movements in Christianity are black theology, feminist theology, and the theology of the East-West dialogue, which raises the vexing problem of Christian uniqueness. Death of God theology is, or should be, a presence in each of these important developments, for it raises the problem of the limits of redefinition of the idea of God. We cannot, the radicals insist, simply redefine the idea of God so that it suits our correct ideological needs, whether of color, gender, or political involvement. Historical Christianity is, probably, incurably sexist and anti-Semitic, and the theology of the death of God may help, at least slightly, in assuaging the damage done by these grievous illnesses.

A number of interesting theological explorations presently continue the work of the death of God theologians. Altizer, always the intense and powerful Hegelian dialectician, continues to write from within the Christian tradition, insisting that Christianity is today only possible in the form of the negation of God. Altizer is currently exploring the relations between death of God theology and deconstructionist literary criticism. Hamilton, less methodologically committed, has worked obliquely on the idea of the death of God through literature and cultural history. Still distinguishing between two kinds of death of God experience (which he calls the murderer and the detective), Hamilton has recently devised an interpretation of Herman Melville as a significant artist of the experience of God's death in *Melville and the Sea* (1985) and *Reading Moby Dick and Other Essays* (1989).

New voices include those of Don Cupitt and Graham Shaw (see his *God in Our Hands* [1987]) in England, Charles Davis in Canada (see the admirable *What Is Living, What Is Dead in Christianity Today* [1986]), and Jens Glebe-Möller in Copenhagen (see his two essays on Christian atheism, *A Political Dogmatic* [1987] and *Jesus and Theology* [1987]). They are plotting the relationships among the political, liberationist, and radical theologies. Death of God theology today is neither victorious nor ubiquitous. But within Christianity it continues to explore that possible space between what used to be called belief and unbelief.

WILLIAM HAMILTON

121

Bibliography

Thomas J. J. Altizer, *The Gospel of Christian Atheism.*
Thomas J. J. Altizer and William Hamilton, *Radical Theology and the Death of God.*
William Hamilton, *The New Essence of Christianity.*
Paul Van Buren, *The Secular Meaning of the Gospel.*

Cross Reference: Black Theology, Deconstructionism, Feminist Theology, Liberation Theology, Political Theology, Silence.

DECONSTRUCTIONISM

"Deconstructionism" (with the "-ism" added) is a term that is rarely used as such in technical philosophical and theological literature, but it has come to refer in more popular parlance to a variety of critical and interpretative methods that deny there is any obvious order of metaphysical truth to which literary, religious, and philosophical texts refer. The term ultimately derives from the works of the French philosopher Jacques Derrida and secondarily from the German thinker Martin Heidegger.

In religious thought the so-called deconstructionists have been identified with a group of philosophical theologians, who have each in his own way introduced Derridean and Heideggerian styles of expression into traditional Christian, or post-Christian, discourse. The leading deconstructionist theologian has been Mark C. Taylor *(Erring, Deconstructing Theology,* and *Altarity).* Other figures include Carl A. Raschke *(The Alchemy of the Word* and *Theological Thinking),* Charles Winquist *(Epiphanes of Darkness),* and Robert Scharlemann *(The Being of God: Theology and the Experience of Truth).*

Taylor's work has been influenced heavily by the ideas of Thomas J. J. Altizer, who sparked the movement known as "death of God" theology in the mid-1960s. In fact, deconstructionism in theology has been called a "hermeneutic of the death of God," or "the death of God put into writing." Such an interpretation, however, belies the richer and more intricate strands of development in late-twentieth-century religious thinking to which earlier philosophical and literary "strategies" of deconstruction have given rise.

For example, although Taylor in *Erring* maps out what he dubs an "a/theology," centering on the loss of selfhood and the final and complete "incarnation" of God's presence in written texts, Raschke in *Theological Thinking* argues that the "method" of deconstruction can actually revive for formal theologians the long-abandoned Barthian emphasis on divine transcendence. Interestingly, Taylor himself has recently veered in this direction. At the same time, Winquist has employed the Derridean view of language itself, which withstands some comparison to Freudian psychoanalysis, to lay the groundwork for a new pastoral interpretation of the deep unconscious, as well as for a concrete mode of social praxis. Scharlemann has adapted the rhetorical rhythms of the deconstructionist literature to rehabilitate in many important respects the older agendas of the theologian Paul Tillich—in particular, Tillich's preoccupation with the negativity of human existence, or what Scharlemann calls "the being of God when God is not being God."

The impact of deconstructionism on theology in the present era has sometimes been compared to the role of existentialism during an earlier period. In one way the parallel is accurate. Deconstructionism in the late twentieth century, like existentialism between the two world wars, has within a relatively brief time greatly transformed the grammar and concerns of theological writers. Like existentialism, it has left its imprint mainly on the curricula of colleges and seminaries while remaining an object of confusion and distrust in local parishes. Finally, deconstructionism has played to many of the same "postmodern" impulses that existentialism did in an earlier generation. It has served as a consistent and metaphorically fertile fund of disclaimers against orthodox theism. It has also rekindled a creative fervor within the theological idiom and redefined a kind of autonomy for the field that seemed to have vanished in the early 1970s, when the trend was toward reducing theology to other forms of intellectual inquiry or cultural expression (e.g., "political theology," "feminist theology," and "theology of play").

Yet the various deconstructionist theologies, or varieties of "theological thinking," have to date proved themselves incapable, as was not the case with existentialism, of making a direct impact on the culture at large. There are, for example, no well-known "deconstructionist" poets or novelists. There are no deconstructionist coffeehouses. The simple explanation may be that deconstructionism per se, as first indicated in such philosophical texts as Heidegger's *What Is Called Thinking?*, Derrida's *Of Grammatology*, and Michel Foucault's *The Archaeology of Knowledge*, has remained above all a *view of language* rather than a philosophy of existence.

The popularity of deconstructionism can be understood on the one hand as a long-overdue revolt in philosophical theology against the sovereignty of logical positivism and linguistic analysis, which left little room for a sense of the mysterious. The deconstructionist slogans "thinking the unthought" and "saying the unsaid"—phrases borrowed from Heidegger—can be construed as the postmodern equivalent of the Barthian encounter with God as "wholly other." In addition, deconstructionism has permitted theological writers a freedom to assimilate other disciplines such as linguistics, literary criticism, philosophical pragmatism, and to a certain extent even scientific theory, in a manner that was denied to them just a decade before. But the gains have been almost entirely academic.

What, then, are some of the general themes marking the deconstructionist program in the theological arena? Although these themes are not necessarily common to all deconstructionist authors, they can be summarized as follows:

1. The End of Theology. Just as Heidegger announced "the end of philosophy" as a continuing *metaphysical* tradition of argument, so deconstructionists proclaim the "end of theology" as a coherent process of inquiry and inference based upon certain claims of experience, or statements of belief. Deconstructionists lean toward either a Sartrean stance, in which the liberty of language discloses the sheer nothingness lowering at the edges of the world, or a Kierkegaardian "leap of faith" by which the incommensurability between discourse and the divine is radically upheld.

2. The Death of God "the Transcendental Signified." Deconstructionists generally agree that the word "God" has no straightforward referent and that the Nietzschean phrase "God is dead" means the dissolution of this referent—or what Derrida terms "the transcendental signified." Deconstructionism is part and parcel of a linguistic paradigm whereby "meaning" stems not from an act of denotation or connotation, but from the displacement of one grammatical element by the next. This displacement in deconstructionist parlance is known as the "moment of difference." If displacement, or "differencing," constitutes the act of meaning, then the word "God" cannot refer to any object, state, or condition, but it must reveal instead a profound absence where language itself in its unfolding had created the illusion of presence. This disclosure of absence encapsulates what is shadowed in the notion of "God's death."

3. The Disseminated Word. For Taylor, "Incarnation is understood as Inscription." In other words, the death of God as "the transcendental signified" brings with it the pure manifestation of the divine word as writing, or as text. Derrida himself rejects every ontology of the "revealed word"—whether that word be divine speech, sacred scripture, or even the Platonic metaphysics of heavenly forms. Instead he advances the supposition that meaning as "presence" is not to be discovered beyond the text, but wholly within the "texture" of the text itself. Such a standpoint has been called "Talmudic," and it does expose the rabbinic backdrop to much of Derrida's philosophy. For certain theological deconstructionists, however, it represents a consummate reading of the Johannine legacy of the "Word made flesh." For Taylor especially, the embodiment of the word as text corresponds to the primeval murder and sacrifice of the Father, which Freud described in *Totem and Taboo.* Textuality is the dismemberment and "dissemination" of the word of the death God.

4. Holy Nomadism. Theology, according to Taylor, is a "wandering," an errancy, a nomadism. "The erring nomad," he says, "neither looks back to an absolute beginning nor ahead to an ultimate end." In other words, a deconstructed theology, or an a/theology, amounts to a kind of vagrant writing, "a tissue woven of threads that are produced by endless spinning." Eschatology becomes what Derrida calls "grammatology"—inscription that endlessly replaces inscription.

The world does not end by fire; it merely hangs on the hook of a semicolon. Raschke, however, in *Theological Thinking* uses the same motif of nomadism to argue that the deconstruction of texts must lead to a radical "faith" in the One who encounters the writer as the "depths of Spirit."

5. *"History as Apocalypse."* Even though Altizer, the originator of the phrase, cannot be identified as a deconstructionist per se, such a thought embraces the underlying "eschatology," or what Taylor dubs "an/eschatology," of the strictly Derridean theologians. Altizer understands deconstruction "as a contemporary expression of demythologizing." This demythologizing, in turn, eventuates in the recognition that past and present are "indistinguishable," and that "God is the name of that center which is everywhere." For deconstructionism, history itself is God's unveiling, which is at the same time God's death.

CARL RASCHKE

Bibliography

Thomas J. J. Altizer, *Total Presence*.
Jacques Derrida, *Of Grammatology*.
Carl Raschke, ed., *Deconstruction and Theology*.
Robert P. Scharlemann, *The Being of God: Theology and the Experience of Truth*.
Mark C. Taylor, *Erring: A Postmodern A/Theology*.

Cross Reference: Death of God Theology, Hermeneutics, Postmodern Theology, Silence.

DESTINY (*See* Freedom.)

DETERMINISM (*See* Freedom.)

DIALECTICAL THEOLOGY (*See* Neoorthodoxy, Paradox.)

DISPENSATIONALISM

Dispensationalism is an approach to theology and the Bible that is based on dividing history into "dispensations" or "economies," which are seen as different phases of God's progressive revelation. The word comes from the Greek *oikonomeo* and its derivatives, which are found about twenty times in the New Testament and refer to the management or regulation of a household. When used of God, the word means God's sovereign plan for the world (*see* Luke 16:1-2; Eph. 1:10, 3:2, 9; and Col. 1:25).

According to C. I. Scofield, a leading spokesperson for dispensationalism in the early twentieth century, a dispensation is a period of time during which man is tested in respect of obedience to some specific revelation of the will of God. . . . These periods are marked off in Scripture by some change in God's method of dealing with mankind, in respect to two questions: of sin, and of man's responsibility. Each of the dispensations may be regarded as a new test of the natural man, and each ends in judgment—marking the utter failure in every dispensation.

Scofield counted seven such economies: innocence (before the Fall), conscience (the Fall to Noah), human government (Noah to Abraham), promise (Abraham to Moses), law (Moses to Christ), grace or the church age (the period between Christ's two comings), and the millennial kingdom (after Christ's return).

John Nelson Darby (1800–1882), an early leader of the Plymouth Brethren in Great Britain, was the first to articulate a complete dispensational theological system. Darby's dispensationalism grew out of his eschatological views. As a premillennialist, Darby believed that the biblical prophecies of the "last days" were still to be fulfilled and that Christ's second coming will occur *before* the beginning of the millennium. Using a strict literalistic hermeneutic, Darby detected in the Bible two distinctly different programs operating in history: one for an earthly people (Israel) and the other for a heavenly people (the church). The key to Darby's system was keeping these two plans and their respective prophecies completely separate.

In Darby's view God's plan for Israel became clear through a series of covenants (with, in sequence, Adam, Noah, Abraham, Moses, and David) that promised redemption through a messiah and the establishment of God's kingdom on earth. When Jesus was claimed as Messiah, however, the Jews' rejection of him forced God to postpone the kingdom, turn away from Israel, and raise up a new people from the Gentiles, the church. According to this "postponement theory," God will not deal again with the Jews until the church is complete and Jesus takes it to heaven in the "rapture" (the "catching up" of believers described in I Thess. 4:17). When this occurs, the "great parenthesis" in prophetic time will end and events of the "last days" will unfold: the great tribulation, the rise of Antichrist, the battle of Armageddon, the second coming, the binding of Satan, and the establishment of the millennial kingdom. This scenario comes from a complicated interpretation of certain apocalyptic prophecies in Ezekiel 37–39, Daniel 7–9, Matthew 24, Mark 13, Luke 21, I Thessalonians 4, II Thessalonians 2, and Revelation. Characteristics of dispensational theology include a firm commitment to biblical inerrancy, a speculative interest in the "signs of the end-time," and a deep concern for the Jews, who are expected to play an important role in end-time events.

During a number of visits to America in the 1870s, Darby persuaded some prominent evangelical pastors and teachers (including James H. Brookes, William

E. Blackstone, James M. Gray, and Scofield) to affirm his theology. Dispensational views spread quickly in conservative evangelicalism through Bible and prophetic conferences, Bible institutes, influential religious journals, and the *Scofield Reference Bible* (1909, rev 1967), whose notes explained the biblical texts from a dispensational perspective. Ironically, at the same time that higher critics began to undercut traditional confidence in the Bible, dispensationalists managed to maintain older views of biblical inspiration while arguing that the Bible was incomprehensible apart from a dispensational perspective. By the late 1920s and 1930s, thanks to teachers like Harry Ironside, Arno Gaebelein, and Lewis Sperry Chafer—the movement's most influential theologian—dispensationalism became almost synonymous with fundamentalism. In the 1970s dispensationalism reached a new audience with Hal Lindsey's *The Late Great Planet Earth,* which was the best-selling book of the decade.

Since the mid-1960s dispensationalists have debated the limits of doctrinal development within their system, and they have discussed which elements are nonnegotiable. In *Dispensationalism Today* (1965), Charles Ryrie argued that the *sine qua non* of dispensationalism had three aspects: the distinction between Israel and the church, the commitment to the "normal or plain" interpretation of the Bible, and the belief that there was an underlying doxological purpose in all God's dealings with humanity. But other dispensationalists have challenged his position. It is not unusual now for dispensational theologians to question the complete separation of Israel and the church, the necessity to interpret the Bible literally, and the suitability of using the notion of dispensations as the organizing principle for theology. In short, if the current revisionism continues, dispensationalists will find it difficult to distinguish themselves from other kinds of conservative and evangelical theologians.

TIMOTHY P. WEBER

Bibliography

Craig Blaising, "Development of Dispensationalism by Contemporary Dispensationalists," *Bibliotheca Sacra* 145 (July-September 1988): 254-80.
Lewis Sperry Chafer, *Systematic Theology,* 4 vols.
D. P. Fuller, *Gospel and Law.*
C. N. Kraus, *Dispensationalism in America.*
C. C. Ryrie, *Dispensationalism Today.*

Cross Reference: Eschatology, Fundamentalism.

DOGMATIC THEOLOGY

Traditionally described as "faith seeking understanding," dogmatic theology explores reflective insights and generates understanding regarding the dogmas of the

Christian church. Dogmas are "the normative statements of Christian belief adopted by various ecclesiastical authorities and enforced as the official teaching of the church" (Jaroslav Pelikan). Dogmatic theology differs from fundamental theology (which argues to the truth claims of faith), from systematic theology (which uses insights and tools from culture), and from practical theology (which considers the ethical stance of responsibility and commitment on social and political problems). Although the term is often expanded today to include the reflective-interpretative enterprise of all the principal world religions, for example Hindu theology or Jewish theology, we are restricting its use here to the Christian tradition.

Dogmatic theology studies the beliefs of the Christian community as they are expressed primarily, but not entirely, in their creeds or confessions of faith. These beliefs constellate around God (Father, Son, and Spirit), the world (creation, providence, and eschaton), humans (image of God, sin, and salvation), and Christian life (the church, sacraments, discipleship, and faith). Christian usage applies the word "creed" to the Apostles' Creed, the Nicene Creed, and the Athanasian Creed, which are intended for general use in rituals and religious education. "Confession of faith" refers to the comprehensive declarations of the Protestant and Anglican churches, including the Augsburg Confession, the Formula of Concord, the Westminster Confession, and the Thirty-nine Articles.

Some dogmas are common to almost all Christian churches, stemming from biblical confession, the creeds, and early ecumenical councils (e.g., Nicea, Chalcedon, and Constantinople). Roman Catholic dogmatic theology also includes the study of beliefs defined after the historical divisions from the Orthodox and Protestant traditions. These include the dogmas of the seven sacraments (at Trent), papal infallibility (at Vatican I), and the two Marian dogmas of the Immaculate Conception and the Assumption (in the nineteenth and twentieth centuries).

Some Protestant theologians claim that there cannot be a development of doctrine, but only a history of theology since the time of scripture. The point is debated among Roman Catholic theologians today, however, with many of them arguing that the concepts and propositions expressing their faith must be constantly updated to keep pace with the growth of human consciousness under the impact of successive historical experiences. They claim they are following generations of theologians—including the biblical authors, Greek and Latin fathers, and Scholastics—who rethought and reformulated their faith in the light of the most pressing problems of their day. The discussion boils down to a tension between truth as fixed and truth as growing, between a position that regards dogmas as final, petrified conclusions and one that considers them means that open the way to ever greater truth.

Dogmatic theology is sometimes considered the enemy of freedom from two different perspectives: teaching authority and personal faith. First, in Christian groups where dogmatic theology depends on an ecclesial teaching authority (e.g.,

Roman Catholicism), the authority has sometimes been rigorous, abstract, absolute, and backward-looking. When this occurs, dogmatic theology progressively alienates itself from modern secular society, which is self-critical, concrete, relativist, and future-oriented. Because dogmatic theology lacks a decision-making process in this situation, it becomes the enemy of freedom. Second, dogmatic theology often results in traditional formulations that call for submission. The venerable and interesting ideas contained in the dogmas are sometimes couched in language and principles that are so abstract they hinder and conceal faith rather than facilitate and reveal it. Although the source of dogmas—the gospel—connotes Spirit, freedom, and life, the language of dogmas sometimes suggests the institution, law, and fixed belief. When this happens, it does violence to human freedom and all but rules out personal faith in the person of Jesus Christ.

At the end of the twentieth century, dogmatic theology is often criticized because it has become largely a matter for professional schools, and its education pertinent to priestly training or ministerial leadership of churches. For dogmatic theology to thrive, it has to serve several audiences simultaneously: the scholarly academy, the church, and the wider society (David Tracy). Dogmatic theologians of the future will be compelled to relocate God and faith within this world and this life, if for no other reasons than the pervasive process of secularization and the sheer magnitude and absurdity of human suffering. In order to rethink the symbolic experiences and expressions of faith they will have to follow the lead of systematic theologians in using different root metaphors: process, liberation, creativity, play, storytelling, revolution, technology, and so forth. They will have to analyze dogmatic formulations critically in terms of historical conditioning and socio-cultural factors. Dogmas are the result of particular and contingent events in which believers struggled to express divine truth through inadequate human concepts. The theologians have the task of expressing in current form what earlier generations believed, without falling into the trap of keeping the old words but substituting new meanings.

Global, ecumenical gatherings of dogmatic theologians, such as the Faith and Order Conferences, have contributed many well-informed reflections to dialogue, especially regarding the sacraments. Because they do not all share the same dogmas, however, the theologians find it much easier to pray and witness together than to formulate common dogmatic statements (E. Schlink). Perhaps in our age of global world civilization, in the inevitable encounters with other principal world religions, they will find a way beyond this impasse. In the future they can no longer be content to try to find common statements for the basic substance of faith: They will have to transpose this lasting faith into new and pluralistic horizons of understanding.

Dogmatic theology always retains two basic tasks: It has to lead people to genuine religious experience and it has to explicate God's self-communication in

129

Jesus. These are not easy tasks. First, whereas real faith sets people on the side of peace, social justice, and responsible use of world resources, dogmatic theology has too often caused them to stand for divisiveness, destruction, and oppression. The fierceness with which dogmas have been defended has often surpassed the zeal spent on inciting believers to right living. Theologians have to establish a correlation between dogmas and the social problems of the day, between the ultimate questions raised by human beings and the ever new challenge of the word of God (Paul Tillich). Second, whereas real faith directs people toward the personal center of its life, namely Jesus Christ, dogmatic theology has too often succeeded in scattering people in their faith. Dogmas are never ends in themselves, however, and theologians have to make them function as an expression of the church's understanding of the Christian mystery, as given to it by the Holy Spirit.

LEONARD J. BIALLAS

Bibliography

Avery Dulles, *The Survival of Dogma.*
George Lindbeck, *Nature of Doctrine: Religion and Theology in a Postliberal Age.*
Gerald O'Collins, *The Case Against Dogma.*
Schubert Ogden, *On Theology.*
David Tracy, *The Analogical Imagination: Christian Theology and the Culture of Pluralism.*

Cross Reference: Ambiguity, Apologetics, Authority, Confessional Theology, Ecclesiology, Ecumenism, Freedom, Systematic Theology.

DOUBT (*See* AGNOSTICISM, FAITH.)

EASTERN ORTHODOX CHRISTIANITY

As "church" the Eastern Orthodox Church attributes its origins to the apostolic witness of Jesus' disciples and the missionary work of Paul. Historically the religious conversion of the Roman emperor Constantine and his subsequent decision to make Christianity the empire's religion placed an indelible stamp on the character of Eastern Orthodoxy.

The armies of Constantine and his imperial successors carried the faith of the Greek-speaking church to every corner of the eastern branch of the Roman Empire. From 400 to 800, when the Western, Latin-speaking church was struggling against invasions from Germanic tribesmen, the Eastern church was enjoying a flourishing expression of monasticism, theology, liturgy, and iconography. The Arab Muslim conquest of the Middle East in the seventh century stripped the Orthodox churches of the Middle East of their political and financial powers and confined them to strictly liturgical and pastoral functions. The Turkish capture of the Byzantine capital Constantinople in 1453 marked the end of the Eastern Christian empire itself. Thereafter the ancient Patriarchal sees (ecclesiastical jurisdictions) of Constantinople, Alexandria, Antioch, and Jerusalem became largely administrative centers for a church of millions who lived for centuries under a succession of Muslim caliphs and sultans.

The influence of the Eastern Orthodox Church was greatly expanded in the eleventh century with the missionary work of saints Cyril and Methodius among the slavs of Rumania, Moldavia, and Serbia. In 988 the peoples of Kiev and all the Russians were converted to the faith of Eastern Orthodoxy. At a time when the Eastern church fell under the control of Arab, Mameluke, and Turkish rulers, slavic expression of Eastern Orthodoxy flourished. When the Turks captured Constantinople, the Orthodox Patriarchate of Moscow began to see itself as the "Third Rome," the true successor of the Byzantine capital. Such dreams were brought to an abrupt halt in 1917 when the Bolshevik revolution curtailed the influence of the Orthodox church in Russian society, as it did for the church generally in Eastern Europe. Today, witnessing the decline of Communist-controlled government in Eastern Europe, we may well expect a corresponding increase of freedom of worship among Orthodox peoples, and also an increase of the church's influence in social and political affairs.

As "orthodox" the Eastern Orthodox Church upholds the decisions of the seven ancient ecumenical councils that defined the essential dogmatic content of Christian faith. The most important truths of faith that united as "orthodox" both the Eastern, Greek-speaking church and the Western, Latin church concerned the Trinity and the person of Christ. The first Council of Nicea (325) determined that the Son, the second person of the Trinity, was "consubstantial" with the Father. Under this norm a contrary theological position known as Arianism (which stressed "similarity" between Son and Father) was branded heterodox or heretical.

The bishops meeting at the Council of Chalcedon (451) further determined that the person of Christ consisted of two natures, divine and human, fully and mysteriously united. On the basis of this norm, the rival christological formulation called "Monophysitism" (that the human nature of Christ was subsumed under the divine nature) was condemned as heresy.

The doctrinal decisions at Chalcedon proved particularly divisive to the Eastern church as a whole. Defending "Monophysitism" as the true teaching on Christ's nature, several regional churches—Coptic, Ethiopian, Syrian Jacobite, and Armenian—declared their independence of the Chalcedonian formulation championed by the churches of Constantinople and Rome. Thus were born a group

131

of national churches whose liturgy is formally identical to the Eastern Orthodoxy, but whose "orthodoxy" is questioned by both Greek and Latin churches.

Other important conciliar decisions shaping the mind of the Eastern Orthodox Church were the official adoption of the Nicene-Constantinopolitan Creed (381) and the acceptance and clarification of icons as constituting authentic expression of worship (787).

Although they shared a common dogmatic basis of faith, the first great rift between Orthodox Christianity and Western Catholicism occurred over a controversial change in the original formulation of the Trinity as expressed in the Nicene-Constantinopolitan Creed. As stated in the original Greek formulation, the Holy Spirit was defined as "proceeding from the Father by the Son." In the sixth century in Spain, a different wording was used by churchmen who spoke of the Spirit proceeding "from the Father and the Son." The insertion of a new and different clause—"and the Son," (*Filioque* in Latin)—had the effect of dividing the Eastern and Western halves of Christendom, a division that had both theological and political consequences. When the Western church eventually adopted the Filioque clause, the Eastern church rejected it as a betrayal of the true orthodox doctrinal faith.

The Filioque controversy might have remained a merely theological dispute if important political developments had not also alienated Orthodox and Roman Catholic churches. The growth of the Roman Catholic Church following the establishment of the Carolingian Empire in 800 caused envy and apprehension among Eastern Orthodox Church leaders, particularly when Emperor Charles the Great became a champion of the Filioque.

Further, the Filioque controversy marked the end of the deference the Patriarchate of Constantinople had paid to the Church of Rome as Peter's See. The Greek church would not tolerate what it considered Rome's deviation from the dogmatic authority of the ancient conciliar decisions. The crack in the wall of Christendom introduced by the Filioque would widen with the centuries and finally produce a decisive break in the eleventh century when the growth of Roman church power antagonized the Greek Orthodox Patriarch of Constantinople. When the Holy Roman Emperor Henry II persuaded Pope Benedict VIII to adopt the Filioque for the Latin mass, a formal break between the churches became inevitable. Forty years later in 1054, Roman Pontiff Leo IX excommunicated the Patriarch of Constantinople Michael Caerularius for not adopting the Filioque and for ordaining married priests (another source of dispute). The Orthodox Patriarch in turn excommunicated the Pope for the heresy of confessing the Filioque.

The Great Schism, as this formal break was called, was widened beyond repair in the Fourth Latin Crusade when Venetians and Franks were diverted from their goal in conquering the Holy Land and invaded Constantinople. The city was plundered and its great collection of saints' relics was carried off and distributed among the churches of Western Europe.

One of the finest chapters in the history of the Eastern Orthodox Church was also one of its most bitterly divisive. In the seventh ecumenical council (787), the church had accepted the use of icons in worship. A careful distinction was drawn between true worship (Greek: *latria*) of God alone, and the act of veneration (Greek: *proskenesis*) expressed through the kissing of icons and the lighting of candles before them. Through veneration of icons, the believer is allowed to focus attention on Christ or the Virgin or any one of the number of saints and thereby express personal love of God. Thus the icon as a natural object fixes human attention on the icon's heavenly prototype.

However, under the influence of the Islamic prohibition against any visual portrayal of the deity, Leo III and later Byzantine emperors of the eighth and ninth centuries supported the "iconoclastic movement" that viewed the liturgical use of icons as idolatrous. Opposing the "iconoclasts" were the vast majority of cloistered monks, whose influence prevailed on the Church of Constantinople to condemn iconoclasm as a heresy in 787. The veneration of icons was officially restored by Empress Theodora in 843. From the point of view of religious art and the aesthetics of worship, the acceptance of icons on the part of the Eastern Orthodox Church was fortunate because the icons of the Eastern church provide one of the most distinctive and moving expressions of religious feeling in the whole of Christian worship.

The theology of the icon in Eastern Orthodoxy is not well understood. According to the analysis of Ernst Benz, the Eastern church icon has an "archaic strangeness" that partly fascinates and partly repels the viewer. This results from the deliberate effort on the part of the iconographic artist to remove any trace of personal creative style from the work; the artist's aim is to separate the work from the genre of creative religious art that one finds, for example, in the Italian Renaissance, as in the work of Raphael. By contrast the Eastern iconographer strives for the creation of an image which in no way reflects the iconographer's thought or talent but which in every way points upward to the holy reality of which it is an object. "Icons," Benz writes, "are often group products, each monk attending to his own specialty. One paints the eyes, another the hair, a third the hands, a fourth the robes, so that even in the productive process itself the factor of creative, artistic individuality is eliminated." Thus the creation of an icon is not attributable to the creative imagination of any one person, enabling one to focus attention not on the icon but on the sacred reality through veneration of the icon. The icon exercises its true function as a "window" through which the earthly glimpses the eternal; the artistic object reproduces the sacred archetype. Reinforcing the sense of the representational is the two-dimensionality of the icon, where, as Benz states, "the celestial figures manifest themselves exclusively upon the mirror surface or window surface of the icon."

The Eastern Orthodox Church also places a high value on monasticism, whose finest religious and architectural embodiments can be found at Mount Athos in

Greece, in the monasteries of the Sinai and Judean deserts, on the Greek islands, and in Russia. The spirit of Orthodox monastic meditation is expressed through a ceaseless, verbally minimal form of prayer known as hesychasm, or "silence." In hesychasm the monk awaits a vision of the "uncreated light." This psycho-spiritual experience is interpreted as a human sharing in the divine light that surrounded Jesus when he was transfigured on Mount Tabor in the presence of Moses and Elijah (Mark 9:2-8). The mystical practice of hesychasm, always a controversial subject in the church, was widely accepted after the approval expressed by the influential theologian Archbishop Gregory Palamas at the Council of Constantinople in 1341.

The Orthodox church, unlike Roman Catholicism, accords no special dogmatic status to the Virgin Mary beyond the definition *theotokos,* or "God-bearer." Mary's origins are regarded as wholly human, and the Roman Catholic conception of her "sinlessness," expressed through the doctrine of the Immaculate Conception, is rejected. Also rejected is the Catholic dogma of Mary's "bodily assumption" into heaven.

As noted earlier, the Orthodox principle of confessional and dogmatic authority is rooted in the decrees of the seven ancient ecumenical councils. Given its conciliarism, the Eastern church rejects the specific Roman Catholic dogma of papal infallibility. Yet the Eastern church makes a distinction between "holy tradition" (unalterable, biblically based, and decreed by the ecumenical councils), and "church tradition," which is revisable with changing times. This distinction parallels the Catholic distinction between "dogma" and "doctrine." For example, where the biblically based practice of a celibate episcopacy is a "holy tradition," recognized in the sixth ecumenical council (692), the acceptance of married clergy is a historically developed, "church tradition."

From the church's beginning until the seventeenth century, Eastern Orthodoxy recognized two sacraments, Eucharist and Baptism, after which, under Western influence, the five other standard sacraments were accepted. Infant baptism is practiced by the Eastern church, and adult baptism only in the case of converts.

The framework of the church's worship is the verbally rich and tonally warm liturgy designed by John Chrysostom. The central theme of the liturgy is Christ's resurrection, the most joyous expression of which occurs at the midnight service on Easter Sunday. Celebration of the Eucharist takes a prominent place in the Eastern Orthodox liturgy, but the church offers no special metaphysical theory, comparable to the Roman Catholic notion of transubstantiation, to explain the conversion of bread and wine into the body and blood of Christ. This conversion is attributed to the answered prayer of the celebrating priest who invokes the Holy Spirit to enter the physical substances and graciously transform them.

The role of the priest is not only to chant the liturgy but also to "protect" it from confusion with or contamination by the secular world. This principle of "protection" of the sacred from the secular, as many observers have noted, helps explain the marked formalism in priest-led Eastern Orthodox liturgical worship. The laity, strictly speaking, does not participate in the liturgy, which is performed in its presence. The conception underlying the liturgy is that of a "terrible mystery of the divine presence in the church" (Meyendorff)—a sacred mystery protected by the priesthood in the conduct of the ritual.

Today Eastern Orthodoxy makes up approximately one-sixth of the world's Christian population and comprises some seventeen independent churches in the ancient sees of Constantinople, Alexandria, Antioch, and Jerusalem, in the Patriarchates of Moscow, Rumania, Serbia, and Bulgaria, in the churches of Greece, Georgia, Albania, Poland, Crete, Finland, Lithuania, and Estonia, and in the monasteries of Patmos and Sinai. The growth, wealth, and influence of Eastern Orthodox Churches in the United States and the Americas have stretched the meaning of "eastern" beyond its normal geographic borders.

THOMAS A. IDINOPULOS

Bibliography

Ernst Benz, *The Eastern Orthodox Church: Its Thought and Life*.
S. Bulgakov, *The Orthodox Church*.
V. Lossky, *The Mystical Theology of the Eastern Church*.
John Meyendorff, *The Orthodox Church: Its Past and Its Role in the World Today*.
Timothy Ware, *The Orthodox Church*.

Cross Reference: Christology, Dogmatic Theology, Historical Theology, Roman Catholicism, Spirituality, Worship.

ECCLESIOLOGY

Ecclesiology, the church's understanding of its own existence, grows out of the history of the church's development and theological reflection on the integrity of its existence in light of the gospel that calls it into being. The diversity of the historical, cultural, and political situations in which the church exists makes any definitive statement of the doctrine of the church very difficult, if not impossible. In whatever ways that the doctrine of the church develops, however, it follows the historical reality of the church.

The New Testament knows nothing of people conceiving the church and then bringing it into existence in the manner that other human institutions have come to be. The first Christians discovered that they were the church, having been created as a community by the impact of the life, death, and resurrection of Jesus Christ and by their receipt of the gift of the Holy Spirit. Consequently, they continually had to improvise to meet unanticipated organizational needs.

The early church was initially a part of Judaism and gradually became a separate community, believing that Jesus was the messiah and conceiving itself as the new Israel. The original leaders of the community were the apostles who qualified for leadership by being witnesses to the resurrection of Jesus Christ. Because of their separate locations and because of the various New Testament traditions that influenced their worship, theology, and life, the New Testament churches were so diverse that no single pattern of church organization prevailed in them. In general, the New Testament identifies the church as the community of Christians in a particular place (I Cor. 1:1-2), and sometimes it refers to the church as the whole body of believers (Eph. 4:4). All New Testament references to the church, however, assume that to confess Jesus Christ as Lord and Savior is to be the church.

The growth of ecclesiology in the ancient Catholic church stemmed from the practical need for defining Christian identity. Moving from the status of an "illegal" Jewish sect (according to the Roman authorities) to a position of governmental favor (first under Constantine and then officially under Emperor Theodosius in 380), the church that had found unity in a common experience and in the power of the Holy Spirit now had to accommodate itself to emerging political structures. Ignatius, for example, could say that wherever Jesus Christ is, there is the church; but in the same sentence he could add that where the bishop is present the church should gather (Letter to the Smyrnaeans 6). Early in the fourth century the church adopted a commonly accepted creed (the Nicene Creed of 325), an approved list of authoritative books (the Old Testament and the New Testament), and the episcopate (an organization that was shaped by the political environment as well as by the faith). These three external authorities were all intended to guarantee the apostolic witness by which the church lives.

In credal terms, the ancient church defined itself as the one, holy, catholic, and apostolic in the Nicene-Constantinopolitan Creed of 381. Ever since, each one of the terms has been continually clarified in debate and controversy. For example, the holiness of the church has been defined variously as the holiness of its members, or the holiness of its ministers or priests, or the holiness of the activity of the Holy Spirit, especially through the sacraments and preaching.

The ancient church also had to determine how the organized membership of the church was related to the body of Christ. Addressing this issue, Augustine introduced the distinction between the visible and the invisible church, a distinction that has continued to play a part in the church's thinking about itself: The church is always visible, but the true reality of the church is an affirmation of faith, and its boundaries cannot be set by human observation.

The thousand years from Augustine to the Protestant Reformation were a time of organizational transition for the church. Eastern churches separated from Western churches, forming autocephalous churches (national churches) that were governed by the consensus of their constituent communities—a process called *sobornost*. In the West bishops of Rome consolidated churches under Roman leadership, a development that was made possible by the absence of strong political powers and by a remarkable missionary activity that brought various peoples of northern Europe into the church. During this period the church defined itself over against political powers and maintained an independence of the state that was never characteristic of Eastern churches. Papal power reached its apogee in the eleventh through the thirteenth centuries, and the development of the sacramental system received its dogmatic statement at the Council of Florence (1438–1445). The church became less a community of faith and more and more an institution that could give or withhold salvation.

While focusing on the theological issue of salvation, the Protestant Reformation in the sixteenth century sought to recover the apostolic focus of the church. Luther emphasized the priesthood of believers, the communal nature of the church, and the hearing of the Word of God. Calvin and the English reformers emphasized organization more than Luther, but many Protestants agreed that the church exists where the Word of God is rightly preached and the sacraments rightly administered. The radical reformers likewise emphasized the communal nature of the church as the gathered church of believers. In so doing, they repudiated the system of the parish church, which identifies the church with a region under the supervision of a bishop.

Since the Reformation, factors that have influenced the development of ecclesiology include the emphasis on personal freedom, the emergence of secularism, the rise of Third World church identities, the spirit of ecumenism, and the documents of Vatican II.

In the seventeenth and eighteenth centuries, church people increasingly recognized that religion itself cannot be forced upon persons but that it remains their free choice. One outgrowth of this Enlightenment emphasis on personal freedom was the development of denominations—Christian communities in secular and pluralistic societies, supported by voluntary contributions, and believing that they are the holy catholic church, but not the only form of it.

More recently, secularism (especially in association with totalitarianism or with pluralism) has challenged the life and form of the church. The parish church no longer exists in Western Europe or in the United States; and in its place there is a voluntary church in a free, pluralistic, secular, mobile, mass-media dominated society.

The emergence of Third World churches also has provided new patterns of church life in the twentieth century. The enormous increase of radical Protestants, including pentecostal and charismatic groups in today's society and especially in the Third World, undermines church structures that arose under the influence of more authoritarian and hierarchical societies.

The ecumenical movement, culminating not only in church mergers but also in councils of churches, especially the World Council of Churches, has been an achievement of the twentieth century. The World Council has continued the work of the Faith and Order movement, regularly issuing statements on the unity of the church.

The spirit of ecclesiological revision has been manifest also within the Roman Catholic Church, which at Vatican II formulated several relevant documents on the church, the role of the church in the modern world, the priesthood, the laity, and the relation of the church to non-Christian religions.

At the end of the twentieth century, the doctrine of the church faces three practical questions: How does the church understand its own unity? How is the church related to the political order? And how is the Christian church related to non-Christian religions? Additionally, ecclesiology has to take seriously the perennial question of how the form of the church is expressive of the hearing of the word of God in Jesus Christ, as attested in scripture by which the church lives.

JOHN H. LEITH

Bibliography

Walter M. Abbott, ed., *The Documents of Vatican II.*
R. Newton Flew, ed., *The Nature of Church.*
John H. Leith, ed., *The Creeds of the Churches,* 3rd ed.
See also the dogmatic theologies of Karl Barth, Emil Brunner, Hans Küng, and Karl Rahner.

Cross Reference: Confessional Theology, Eastern Orthodox Christianity, Ecumenism, Protestantism, Roman Catholicism, Systematic Theology, Vatican II.

ECOLOGY

In 1967 Lynn White published his now famous article, "The Historical Roots of Our Ecologic Crisis," in which he concluded that the Christian understanding of human beings as the *imago Dei* has brought us to the brink of ecological ruin by licensing human domination of nature. For two decades this article set the terms and the tone for thinking theologically about the natural world. Much of theology's reflections, as a result, have been defensive; theologians sought to prove Christianity not as guilty of fostering wanton exploitation as White charged. Recently, however, theologians have begun to explore alternatives that emphasize a more positive approach. These alternatives build on Christian resources, including biblical resources, and they emerge from the methodological, theological, and ethical arenas of Christian theology.

One of the crucial methodological issues involved in theological reflection on the status of the natural world concerns the relationship between theology and the natural sciences. "Ecology," in common usage, is a biological science that seeks to understand the relationships among living beings and between living beings and their environment. Although most of their attention has been focused on nonhuman beings, ecologists have included studies of the effects of human activities on nonhuman life. Ecologists analyze scientifically data about relationships between living beings and their environment, attempting to understand and predict events in the natural world. As a result, ecological studies provide great insights into the workings of nature. These insights are then available as a resource for theological reflection. What theologians must decide is the extent to which they will make use of this important resource. At least two significant questions must be addressed in such a decision: the reliability of data and conclusions provided by ecologists, and the authority of the scientific method. These are clearly methodological questions whose impact reaches well beyond the question of the status of the natural world.

Regardless of the specific answers given to these questions, deliberate inclusion of the natural world in theological reflection affects the development of certain themes and doctrines. The most obvious of these is creation. Awareness of the natural world entails expanding the theological vision to include in a serious way all that was created. Such an expansion comes not only from scientific information but also from biblical and experiential warrants. In addition to the Genesis creation texts, theologians may also turn to passages from Job, Isaiah, and Psalms in the Hebrew scriptures and passages from Colossians and the Gospels in the New Testament. Theologians may also appeal to the experience or feeling of being connected to nature that many feminists and other writers have described.

Expanding the notion of creation leads to a rethinking of other important doctrines. For example, as soon as plants, animals, land, air, and water receive studied attention as creations of God, the focus on the human as the "crown of creation" is not so single-minded. For many theologians, this has led to a conversion from an anthropocentric to a theocentric perspective. In this situation, care is required in deciphering the meaning of dominion over God's nonhuman creatures. Similarly, when the theme of creation is so enriched, so will be the theme of redemption. More fundamentally, attention to the status of the nonhuman world affects how God is understood. Revisions or alterations in the theme of creation and redemption require a reappraisal of the nature of the divine, since it is the divine who is imaged as Creator and Redeemer.

Theological reflection on these methodological and thematic or doctrinal issues has important consequences for ethics. Methodologically, choices concerning the use of science for theology also affect moral reflection. For example, do scientific descriptions of nature become a new "natural law"? Do they affect how the relationship between "what is" and "what ought to be" is described? Furthermore, new theological articulations of doctrines such as creation and redemption shape a different ethical outlook. For example, a doctrine of creation that attends to every created being suggests an ethic that respects the value of each of those beings. Such an ethic cannot condone or justify activities that carelessly destroy nonhuman life. Ethicists who pursue this line of thought are often divided between those who focus on the care of the natural world as a whole and those who focus on the care of specific parts. The care of animals, both as individuals and as species, is the subject of increasing attention.

Theologians and ethicists from various perspectives are including the natural world in their reflections. Feminist theologians, process theologians, and a growing number of others have turned an ear toward what ecologists are offering. Although they do not all come to the same conclusions, they do agree that the natural world ought to be an important ingredient in Christian thought. And they agree that Christianity provides important resources for thinking constructively about the natural world.

LOIS K. DALY

Bibliography

Charles Birch, et al., *Liberating Life: Contemporary Approaches to Ecological Theology.*
Sean Donagh, *The Greening of the Church.*
James M. Gustafson, *Ethics from a Theocentric Perspective,* 2 vols.
Rosemary Radford Ruether, *New Woman—New Earth: Sexist Ideologies and Human Liberation.*
H. Paul Santmire, *The Travail of Nature: The Ambiguous Ecological Promise of Christian Theology.*

Cross Reference: Cosmology, Creation, Holy Spirit, Naturalism, Space.

ECONOMICS

The rise of the capitalist commercial and industrial systems rendered most of the church's traditional economic teaching and practice obsolete. The new system was based on money earning money, whereas since biblical times this had been condemned as usury.

Many Christians simply abandoned the economic sphere to specialists and concentrated on the moral and spiritual aspects of life. In doing so they often produced hard-working and disciplined labor for industry and became prosperous themselves. John Wesley noticed how the disciplines he taught led to an economic prosperity that then undermined spiritual passion.

The free exchange of labor and goods that is the heart of the modern economy is called "the market." The core of modern economic theory is the discovery that when the market is left to itself, it tends to grow, thus bringing greater wealth to the whole community. Nevertheless, the market is ruthless with respect to individuals. It provides no sustenance for those individuals whose labor it does not need.

Christians have, therefore, had a second role to play in relation to the modern economy; that is, to care for those who cannot gain a livelihood in the market: the aged, the infirm, the handicapped. This care is sometimes administered by individual Christians, sometimes by churches, and sometimes by the state.

The market, left to itself, is ruthless with respect to its workers also. It pays as little as possible and extracts as much work as it can. Christians have often protested the resultant conditions among workers. In the United States, these protests were expressed in the Social Gospel movement, which insisted that the Good News was of salvation for human beings in their economic, as well as personal, relationships. Partly due to the work of Christians and partly due to successful organization of the workers, women received some protections, child labor was abolished, the forty-hour work week became standard, and much was done for comfort and safety in the workplace.

Christians have also tried to ameliorate the suffering caused in the poorer countries by the global market. They have supported programs of aid to developing countries and tried to influence the terms of trade so that they will favor the poor nations instead of the rich ones. Christians have engaged in their own development programs in many parts of the world.

A minority of Christians have criticized these approaches to the economy because they accept the free market as basic and then undertake to ameliorate the hardships that result. Some are convinced that the market system is itself inherently immoral and unjust because it is based on greed and encourages exploitation of people. It leads not only to the evils just noted but also to the growing gap between rich and poor. The alternative these Christians favor is social control of the means of production. In short, they oppose capitalism and favor socialism. Such theologians as Karl Barth, Paul Tillich, Jürgen Moltmann, and Dorothee Soelle have supported democratic socialism.

Socialism has received more vigorous and practical meaning in the hands of Latin American liberation theologians. In their countries, the principal liberation movements have been socialist and sometimes communist. Most theologians have maintained critical distance from particular political parties and programs, but many have undertaken to reformulate theology so that it gives support to concrete movements of liberation.

An important achievement of these liberation theologians, together with black and feminist ones, has been to force other theologians to look at their social location. When the gospel speaks so clearly for the poor and oppressed, how can so much Christian theology have ignored slavery, colonialism, the abuse of women, segregation, and genocide? The answer must be that the questions we pose ourselves and the issues that preoccupy us are determined more by our place in the economy than by an objective reading of our biblical sources or a fair appraisal of the most urgent issues of the day.

While one segment of the theological community has become radical by these

141

reflections, another has begun to celebrate the market. Michael Novak has done particularly important work in emphasizing that personal freedom and democratic institutions are correlative with the market economy. If, as he and many Christians believe, freedom and democracy are crucial values, Christians should stop criticizing and restricting the market and, instead, support it and encourage its extension. The real issue is whether to restrict the market now in favor of more equal distribution of its products or to free the market to grow so that there will be more products to distribute. Whereas church pronouncements usually support more equal distribution now, Novak points out that this policy, in the long run, is self-defeating, since there will be less to distribute in the future.

Beginning in the late 1960s, some Christians began relating these debates to a concern for the physical environment. Both socialists and capitalists were committed to economic growth, and most Christian thinking had assumed that only by great increase of gross national product, especially in developing countries, could the needs of the poor be met. But in the ensuing decades it has become clear that continuing industrial growth of the sort we have known is not sustainable. Even the present level of pressure on the environment is seriously disruptive of natural systems on which life depends.

In the mid-1970s, the World Council of Churches asserted that we need a just, participatory, and sustainable society. Since then the need for sustainable agriculture, sustainable development, and a sustainable economy has been more and more widely acknowledged. Whereas most Christian reflection about the economy has accepted modern economic theory as a given, the goal of a sustainable economy requires reconsideration of the fundamental concepts of economic theory, including growth, from a Christian point of view.

JOHN B. COBB, JR.

Bibliography

Herman E. Daly and John B. Cobb, Jr., *For the Common Good: Redirecting the Economy Toward Community, the Environment, and a Sustainable Future.*
M. Douglas Meeks, *God the Economist: The Doctrine of God and Political Economy.*
Michael Novak, *The Spirit of Democratic Capitalism.*
Prentiss L. Pemberton and Daniel Rush Finn, *Toward a Christian Economic Ethic: Stewardship and Social Power.*

Cross Reference: Ethics–Christian, Justice, Liberation Theology, Political Theology, Social Gospel.

ECUMENISM

The noun "ecumenism" and the adjective "ecumenical" are derived from the Greek word *oikoumene,* which is used in the New Testament to mean the Roman

Empire or, more generally, the whole inhabited world. Gradually, the term came to refer to the whole church (as opposed to that which is divisive) or to the whole faith of the church (as opposed to that which is partial or defective).

It is not surprising, therefore, that the word would be used to designate a modern Christian movement concerned with the unity, renewal, and universal mission of the church. Specifically, the ecumenical movement has used the term with reference to (1) the unity and renewal of the entire Christian community (i.e., the growing relationship among the now-separated churches and their common effort to be the one, holy, catholic, and apostolic church), (2) the worldwide mission of the church (i.e., the work of the church throughout the *oikoumene*), and (3) the unity of all humankind—indeed, of all creation—and the relationship of such unity to the church.

These different meanings also reflect different priorities within the ecumenical movement: (1) *Common fellowship*. This concern for church unity found early expression in the Faith and Order movement, whose first world conference was held in Lausanne, Switzerland, in 1927. Faith and Order efforts have generally been directed at overcoming barriers to the mutual recognition of members and ministers of the various churches, at overcoming barriers to shared celebration of Holy Communion, at helping the churches to express more thoroughly the apostolic faith and to recognize various expressions of that faith in their ecumenical partners, and at discovering ways of making decisions together. (2) *Common service*. This concern for addressing those things that disrupt the human community found early expression in the Life and Work movement, whose first world conference was held in Stockholm, Sweden, in 1925. Life and Work has sought to foster inter-church aid, to enable shared Christian response to the victims of war, poverty, oppression, and natural disaster, and (particularly in recent decades) to call the churches to oppose economic and social injustice, including racism and sexism. (3) *Common witness*. This concern for cooperative mission and evangelism found early expression in the International Missionary Council, whose roots, like those of Faith and Order and Life and Work, go back to the Edinburgh World Missionary Conference of 1910.

Despite the fact that these three priorities are now officially embodied in the World Council of Churches (founded in 1948), their work has at times been regarded as more competitive than complementary. At its best, however, the ecumenical movement has articulated a vision of the church and the gospel that powerfully integrates these various definitions and priorities.

That vision rests on a scripturally based understanding of the one church as a gift of God in which former enemies are now united in one interdependent body as a result of their common experience of grace through faith in Jesus Christ (cf. Eph. 2:11-22, 4:4-6; Rom. 12:4-8). Through the ecumenical movement, Christians have come to see more clearly that the church is by very definition (if not in actual fact) not

143

provincial, embracing persons from every nation and culture (cf. Acts 10:34-35). The church is by very definition (if not in actual fact) inclusive, embracing women and men, persons of all races and ethnic groups, persons of every "class" and vocation, persons with different abilities and disabilities (cf. Gal. 3:27-29). The church is by very definition (if not in actual fact) a community of diverse theological perspectives, embracing Jews and Gentiles, "liberals" and "conservatives," those who describe themselves with such terms as "orthodox," "catholic," "protestant," and "pentecostal" (cf. Rom. 14:1–15:7; I Cor. 1:10-13). Even more, the church is by definition a community of mutuality in which one part cannot say to another "I have no need of you" and in which each part suffers and rejoices with the rest (cf. I Cor. 12:12-26).

Such a vision, if it is to achieve visible expression, requires the renewal and transformation of the church as it now exists. Thus, ecumenism is misunderstood if equated with attitudes of democratic tolerance or reduced to matters of inter-church cooperation. The ecumenical vision insists not merely that Christians learn to coexist, but that they need one another and the gifts that each can bring if they are to live more faithfully as the one body of Christ.

This vision also requires that Christians think and live beyond the church to the world as a whole—that unity and mission be held together (John 17:20-23). A familiar theme of recent years is that the church is called to be a sign, instrument, and foretaste of the reconciliation that God gives and wills for all creation. Thus, to take but one example, the church betrays its calling if it tolerates racial barriers within its fellowship or fails to oppose them in the wider society.

A crucial method for promoting ecumenical growth is "dialogue," a form of conversation that requires a willingness to seek common ground and an openness to learn how God is speaking through one's faith partners. This attitude is beautifully captured in the following passage from the single most influential document on ecumenism written in the twentieth century, *The Decree on Ecumenism* (1964) of the Roman Catholic Church's Second Vatican Council:

> There can be no ecumenism worthy of the name without a change of heart. For it is from newness of attitudes, from self-denial and unstinted love, that yearnings for unity take their rise and grow towards maturity. We should, therefore, pray to the divine Spirit for the grace to be genuinely self-denying, humble, gentle in the service of others, and to have an attitude of brotherly generosity towards them.

As an area of theological inquiry, ecumenism involves the study of such things as the nature of Christian unity and universality, the faith, order, and mission of the now-separated churches and their relations with one another, the means through which the churches may arrive at a more comprehensive manifestation of their unity and universality, and the work of the church in overcoming divisions within the whole human family. It also involves the study of the various instruments or expressions of the ecumenical movement, including local, national, and international councils of churches, united churches (e.g., the Church of South India and the United Church of Christ [USA]) and current church union negotiations (e.g., the Consultation on Church Union), bilateral conversations between Christian communions (e.g., the Anglican-Roman Catholic International Commission), and forms of "spiritual ecumenism" (e.g., the Week of Prayer for Christian Unity).

The modern ecumenical movement has been concerned from its inception with the relationship of the Christian community to people of other living faiths; but inter-faith questions have generally been a subtheme in discussions of mission or social development. In recent years, however, dialogue with other religious communities has assumed a larger share of the ecumenical agenda. Whether the ecumenism of the future will place a concern for inter-faith reconciliation alongside its historic concern for the unity, renewal, and mission of the church remains to be seen.

MICHAEL KINNAMON

Bibliography

Robert McAfee Brown, *The Ecumenical Revolution.*
"The Decree on Ecumenism" in *Documents of Vatican II*, ed. Walter M. Abbott.
W. A. Visser 't Hooft, *The Pressure of Our Common Calling.*
World Council of Churches, *Baptism, Eucharist, and Ministry.*

Cross Reference: Ecclesiology, Vatican II.

ELECTION

Election is that act of grace by which God chooses a companion with whom to live in an intimate relationship of love and responsibility. This companion is identified in the scriptures variously as humankind, Abraham, the people Israel, David, Jesus Christ, and the community called church. Election has been and remains one of the more disputed doctrines in Christian theology. In the classical and Reformation periods the debate centered on the question, How is God's electing grace related to free will? Augustine, Luther, and Calvin devised a pastoral view of election that emphasized God's grace as free (devoid of consideration of merit) and prevenient (preceding human acts). This was hardened and narrowed by some theologians into a deterministic, metaphysical view of predestination that denied all human freedom. Others (e.g., Aquinas) attempted to reconcile God's electing grace with human freedom. Still others attacked the doctrine as incompatible with human responsibility.

In the modern period two different questions concerning election came to the fore, particularly among Reformed theologians: What is the unit of divine care? and, Does God choose to save all persons or only some? Friedrich Schleiermacher answered the first question by rejecting the classical assumption that God singles out individuals for this special relationship and argued that communities or the totality of the world were the focus of divine care. Karl Barth answered the second question by criticizing the traditional, dualistic view that God chooses some and rejects others and by affirming the election of all persons in Jesus Christ.

Today election is attracting attention from theologians because of the growing recognition that the notion of divine favor or preferential love is problematic. Although some still defend election in terms of the doctrine of prevenient grace, most choose not to talk about it directly (preferring covenant language). Increasingly, theologians are raising fundamental questions about this teaching. The first and most radical question comes out of the dialogue between theology and science: Is divine preference *in any sense* tenable in a world that no longer has humankind as its value center? James Gustafson argues that the belief that God specially values individuals, communities, or the human species or that God guarantees their benefit is incompatible with both modern science (which has overthrown the anthropocentric paradigm) and theocentric piety. Gustafson's argument has profound implications for all talk of God choosing or favoring any one element of creation over others. The second question comes out of the dialogue between Christianity and other religions: Is the concept of chosenness an obstacle to genuine pluralism? Rosemary Radford Ruether criticizes Christianity's use of election to denigrate Judaism as a particularistic, exclusivist community and to elevate itself as a universal community. She claims that its "universalism" is but a religious version of Greco-Roman imperialism. Paul Van Buren also criticizes Christianity for using election to bolster supersessionism and anti-Judaism, and he offers as an alternative the idea of a single eternal covenant with the Jews into which Christians are grafted (through the renewed covenant in Jesus Christ). He speaks of the "derivative election" of the Gentiles as "recruitment for [the] task" of serving the covenant with Israel. Walbert Buehlmann sees God's choice of Israel as the revelation of "God's affections for all peoples" and recommends interpreting election in terms of the inclusive vision of God. Theologians concerned with Christianity's relationship with African or Native American religions also have denounced Christianity's imperialistic use of election. They have suggested instead that the One God of the universe has made several distinct and equally valid covenants with different peoples.

The third question comes out of the dialogue between Christianity and feminism: Is election inherently hierarchical and sexist? No Christian feminist theologian has pursued this with the care that Judith Plaskow has taken within Judaism. She argues that the notion of uniqueness (the definitive characteristic of election for centuries) usually implies hierarchical exclusion. Election is thus linked to the "stubborn implication of privilege" and superiority in the community's relations with others outside and to the subordination of others inside (women). She proposes that we reject the concept of election, retain the notion of distinctiveness, and devise a theory of part-whole that will allow us to value differences positively. To this criticism from a feminist perspective we may add the following: As traditionally understood and used (i.e., to stress God's free grace over against human work or worth), election may operate as an impediment to women's spiritual maturation and their full participation in Christian communities. Understood uncritically, it may reinforce women's socialization toward being chosen rather than choosing and thus contribute to our passivity and oppression.

All talk of election must be approached with suspicion. The fact that it usually and perhaps inevitably implies antinomianism, anthropocentrism, imperialism, and sexism must be taken very seriously. But these do not constitute a sufficient condition for discarding election. In spite of these problems, the teaching of election lies at the heart of Christian piety and must be reappropriated in a liberating way. For it bears witness to our profound need for and conflicted experience of God—the Power-that-makes-for-belonging-in-the-world. Belonging is that complex, entangling, and freeing experience of simultaneous choosing and being chosen that lovers, committed members of marginalized groups, members of religious communities, and others know. Belonging is the way human beings find a home for themselves in a universe not centered in or on them.

With the concept of belonging it is possible to interpret election (and its cognate teaching, covenant) in a theocentric *and* feminist way, that is, in a way that emphasizes our dependence on God as the center of value without sacrificing the integrity of individual selves or communities. A radical reconstruction of election in this direction would not simply avoid the dangers mentioned above but would offer fruitful possibilities for countering some of the harmful tendencies in current thought and practice. For example, radical reconstruction could help refine existing feminist and process arguments against individualism by further specifying and analyzing our fundamentally relational existence. For belonging, as a just and intimate relationship that involves God, self, and others, includes: a commitment to the other as other in dynamic tension with an attentiveness to the self as individual, trust, fierce loyalty, and a nondefensive stance that allows one to respond to change and difference in creative ways.

Radical reconstruction could also help counter the prevailing tendency toward denial of moral and social responsibility; for belonging brings with it not greater privilege, but wider and deeper joy, obligations to others, and suffering. It could help counter tendencies toward Western Christian imperialism, androcentrism, and anthropocentrism, all of which assume a privileged status for a limited group or make absolute what is a finite and relative viewpoint; for belonging brings with it the acknowledgment that one is a participant rather than a ruler. Finally, the

147

teaching of election reconstructed as belonging could help to counter the tendency toward spiritualism (the devaluing of embodied life); for each of us belongs only in and through the stubbornly concrete and particular experience that is ours.

MARY POTTER ENGEL

Bibliography

Walbert Buehlmann, *God's Chosen Peoples.*
James M. Gustafson, *Ethics from a Theocentric Perspective,* vol. 1.
Judith Plaskow, *Standing Again at Sinai: Judaism from a Feminist Perspective.*
Rosemary Radford Ruether, "Feminism and Jewish Christian Dialogue," in John Hick and Paul F. Knitter, eds., *The Myth of Christian Uniqueness: Toward a Pluralistic Theology of Religions.*
Paul Van Buren, *A Theology of the Jewish-Christian Reality.* 3 vols.

Cross Reference: Covenant, Feminist Theology, Kingdom of God.

EMPIRICAL THEOLOGY

Empirical theology is American in origin and development, beginning as early as Jonathan Edwards's aesthetic baptism of John Locke's empiricism or as late as Henry Nelson Wieman's functionalist baptism of John Dewey's naturalism. In the late twentieth century, empirical theology has evolved, both through consulting writings more recent than the classic empiricist texts and through critically examining its own modernist assumptions.

Empirical theologians are said to treat experience as the primary source of religious knowledge. But for empirical theologians, "experience" has been always a central and contentious term, easily confused with the use of "experience" by other theologians. It is clear that any theology treating experience as the primary authority for religious knowledge denies that scripture, institutional tradition, and reason are the highest authorities. Beyond this, however, there are enormous differences among experiential theologies. Empirical theologians take the category of experience from eighteenth-century British empiricism, adding to the five senses of that empiricism a kind of sixth sense—a nonsensuous perception of what may be called the moral, aesthetic, or religious value of the organic whole. William James, John Dewey, and Alfred North Whitehead refer to this empiricism by such terms as, respectively, "radical empiricism," "immediate empiricism," and "causal efficacy"; empirical theologians Henry Nelson Wieman and Bernard Meland refer to empiricism by such terms as, respectively, "mysticism" and "appreciative awareness." This empiricism regards the raw, unrefined, usually unconscious early stages in the moment of experience as a primary source for religious truth. Following a quite different and Continental tradition, Schleiermacher and Tillich see experience as a historical window to ahistorical realities. Following an equally different and positivist tradition, fundamentalist theologians and some philosophers of religion see experience as a sign of external objects. Experience for the empirical theologians refers not to ahistorical realities, but to natural, societal, and personal events; not to external objects, but to vague, indistinct, and bodily relations with the past.

Empirical theology in its current setting may be better defined not by reference to the priority of experience but by reference to the priority of the concrete particular. This not only distinguishes empirical theology from other experiential theologies but separates it from those theologies that seek general truths. For empirical theology does not seek general truths, simply substituting process for substance, pluralism for monism, immanence for transcendence, naturalism for supernaturalism, and pragmatic tests of truths for correspondence tests of truth. Rather, empirical theology begins by regarding a particular, problematic situation, so that it is that situation and its resolution rather than general truth itself that is at issue. Empirical theology begins as a practical theology, a religious dodge around an unavoidable predicament. Only later are the method (the empiricist theory of knowledge and the pragmatic test) and the naturalistic world view made explicit and formal. By this reading, empirical theology is concrete, and it protests the disappearance of the particular amid philosophical and theological abstractions.

Although empirical theology may have begun with Jonathan Edwards's decision to add to John Locke's five senses a sense of beauty, it attained its full expression only in the twentieth century at The University of Chicago. It was anticipated from 1900 to 1946 by the "socio-historical" method of the "Chicago School" theologians (principally, George Burman Foster, Gerald Birney Smith, Shailer Mathews, and Shirley Jackson Case), as they made religious knowledge largely a function of social history. It was brought to flower from the 1920s to the 1960s by Henry Nelson Wieman and Bernard E. Meland, as they used philosophy (especially the philosophy of science) in addition to social history as a basis for both method and world view in empirical theology. It entered a revisionist phase with the last writings of Bernard M. Loomer, as he argued that empirical theology is practical and that it should give to aesthetics and ambiguity a central role.

In the 1970s and 1980s, empirical theology underwent a renaissance, with the founding of *The American Journal of Theology and Philosophy,* the Highlands Institute for American Religious Thought, and the Group on Empiricism in American Religious Thought within the American Academy of Religion. However, empirical theology faces new criticisms, this time not so much from the moral skepticism of its original neoorthodox critics, but from the epistemological skepticism of postmodern relativists, pluralists, and historicists. These latter groups challenge empirical theology's past efforts to define religious experience inductively and generically and to define God universally and realistically. The future of empirical theology may depend on its ability to answer these challenges.

WILLIAM DEAN

Bibliography

Nancy Frankenberry, *Religion and Radical Empiricism.*
Bernard E. Meland, ed., *The Future of Empirical Theology.*
Randolph Crump Miller, *The American Spirit in Theology.*
Wayne Proudfoot, *Religious Experience.*

Cross Reference: Experience–Religious, Philosophical Theology, Postmodern Theology, Practical Theology, Process Theology, Social Gospel.

EPISTEMOLOGY

Epistemology is the philosophical term for the theory of knowledge. It attempts to understand how knowing occurs and to discover its grounds, its limitations, its validity and trustworthiness, and its relation to truth.

In theology, the concerns of epistemology are most directly related to the doctrine of revelation. But since all the symbols and doctrines of Christian faith represent at least in part a claim to knowledge, some position on epistemological questions is directly or indirectly involved in every important theological topic. For example, any attempt to state the meaning and authority of religious experience and faith, the authority of scripture and tradition, or the teaching authority of the church will involve the theologian's view of knowledge. If truth is somehow revealed in scripture and tradition, we nevertheless recognize that we must *interpret* documents and events in order to discover that truth; since all interpretation aims at establishing what we can know about the meaning of the text or the event being interpreted, some theory of knowledge underlies all biblical and historical interpretation. The theologian's epistemological views will also influence how the theologian understands God's relation to and action within the world and consequently how he or she interprets every symbol and doctrine of the faith. In short, both the content of theological analysis and the understanding of how theology ought to operate (theological method) are deeply influenced by the theologian's epistemological position.

In order to understand why theology operates as it does, we must have some appreciation of the historical background. Traditionally, Western Christianity argued that the truth of the Christian faith and the certainty of religious knowledge were based in (1) the authority of divine revelation, as expressed in scripture and tradition; (2) the teaching authority of the institutional church, guided by the continuing presence of the Spirit; (3) the occurrence of miracles, especially the resurrection of Jesus Christ, which proved the truth of faith through direct divine action in the world; and (4) reason reflecting on our experience of the world, which could establish by rational arguments such basic claims as the existence of God and the goodness of God's design and providential governance of the world (natural theology). All of these traditional grounds for the certainty of religious knowledge were challenged and undercut by the Enlightenment and the growth of modern science.

The combined effects of developments in philosophy, the empirical sciences, and the study of history led the Enlightenment to views of knowledge markedly different from those of the past, views that characterize the whole of the modern period. The success of the empirical method of science and the shift to concentration on the experience of the human subject in philosophy (beginning with Descartes [1596–1650]) led to the view that all knowledge must be based in experience. The only useful concepts are those derived from experience, and the only trustworthy ideas are those that have been tested against experience. Only the rational, responsible subject can determine to what extent our ideas give us knowledge of the truth; no external authority can establish truth independent of experience and reason.

Modern science gradually removed appeals to God and God's action from scientific explanations of the physical world. In a development that culminated with Charles Darwin (1809–1882) and his theory of evolution, modern science produced a view of the world radically different from the traditional Christian view. Features of the world that were formerly used as evidences supporting arguments for God's existence and providential action in the world could now be given completely natural explanations. Since science appeared to be able to explain everything in nature without needing to appeal to God, all of the traditional grounds for reasoning our way to God from examining the world around us appeared to dissolve. The growth of modern science created a continuing problem for theology: How are the claims of religion related to what we know of the world and its history through the discoveries of science?

The development of historical consciousness revealed the historical relativity of all human institutions and claims to authority. Scripture was now seen as a collection of ancient documents produced by and embedded within a particular historical and cultural world view. Instead of providing us with divinely revealed universal truths, it communicated the views of people quite remote from us in time, place, and culture. The truth of such views was, at best, relative. As Lessing (1729–1781) argued, no universal truth could be established by reference to some particular historical event.

These developments in philosophical reasoning, scientific explanations, and historical consciousness are involved in the Enlightenment critique of religion. In thinkers such as David Hume (1711–1776), we find a radical empiricism that restricts the notion of experience to sense experience. Hume's philosophy leads to a thorough skepticism and includes a complete rejection of all of religion's claims to knowledge. In Hume's analysis of experience there is no ground for any rational argument proving God's existence, for belief in the occurrence of miracles, or for any claim that we possess divinely revealed knowledge.

Immanuel Kant (1724–1804) tried to overcome the skepticism of Hume's philosophy and to rescue religion from Hume's attack by focusing on the limitations of reason. Kant agreed that religion can find no ground in "pure reason," which deals with our sense experience. But he stressed that we also experience a sense of moral obligation, which is a distinct and separate kind of experience with its own type of knowledge. "Practical reason" addresses this area of our experience; and here, Kant argued, religion finds its ground in the postulates that can be reasonably assumed as the necessary foundations of our sense of moral obligation. Religion, then, is a kind of knowledge, resulting from "practical reason," and it does not conflict with the knowledge resulting from "pure reason." Kant's solution has influenced many theologians, but it seems to make religion secondary to and dependent on ethics and offers no way of understanding how the knowledge resulting from "practical reason" is related to the knowledge based on "pure reason."

Formulating the chief theological response to the Enlightenment critique of religion, Friedrich Schleiermacher (1768–1834) argued that religion is grounded neither in sense experience and "pure" reason nor in moral experience and "practical" reason. Instead, religion originates and has its ground in its own distinctive kind of experience, the feeling of absolute dependence. Christianity is distinguished by its own unique religious experience of Jesus Christ as redeemer, which is foundational for Christian life and thought. Theology is the continuing attempt to express and interpret this religious experience in relation to the human experience of life in the world. Schleiermacher thus advanced on Kant's solution by recognizing that religious knowing and acting flow from a distinctive type of experience that is inherently related to our human experience of life in the world.

Schleiermacher's response to the Enlightenment challenge has greatly influenced nineteenth-century and twentieth-century theology. Whatever their differences, most modern theologians would agree that religion is based in a "special" religious experience that provides the clues to understanding our "ordinary" human experience and the guidance for living in the world. This tendency can be detected even in the "neoorthodox" theology of Karl Barth, which reacted against the "liberal" theology derived from Schleiermacher.

Neoorthodoxy, which dominated Protestant theology through the first half of the twentieth century and still influences numerous theologians (especially in the Evangelical traditions), argues that all religious knowledge is grounded in the self-manifestation or revelation of God. Religious knowledge is a gift that comes to persons through faith in Jesus Christ. It thus has a fundamentally different character from that of all other kinds of human knowledge, which result from human inquiry and effort, and is entirely independent of other ways of knowing. But neoorthodoxy in the end must admit that revelation occurs, is effective, and constitutes "knowledge" only if someone experiences and acknowledges it. The ground of revelation and faith is not some external, objective event; it is the inward, subjective experience of the person who has faith. Thus, despite its effort to found religious knowledge in God and God's actions, neoorthodoxy is driven back to locating the ground of religious knowledge in a "special" form of human experience. This is essentially the position of Schleiermacher.

Most theologians today hold that religious knowledge is the product of our interpretative response to our experience, not some absolutely certain grasp of divinely revealed truth. As such, religious knowledge is partial, historically and culturally conditioned, and open to revision and development. Theology seeks to interpret the meaning of religious experience in relation to our experience of life in the world. Thus theology has two main sources of data: the "special" religious experience at the base of Christian faith and its expressions in scripture and tradition; and the "general" or ordinary experience of human life in the world today. By means of historical, hermeneutical, and philosophical analysis, theology interprets its "special" religious data in order to establish the meaning of Christian symbols and doctrines and to maintain continuity with their intent. But the meaningfulness and value of these symbols and doctrines to our life can be established only by filling them with content relevant to our circumstances. Thus theology must also analyze ordinary experience and must converse with other interpretations of experience, such as science, philosophy, psychology, and social and political theory. The clues to the interpretation of the whole of life arise from what is "special" in experience, but they establish their significance and value by interaction with what is "general" or commonly shared in human experience. In this way, Christian theology seeks to be in fundamental continuity with Christian tradition while addressing new situations and problems and producing novel interpretations of Christian faith.

Most theologians today operate with some version of this very general form of the theological method, but contemporary theology is amazingly diverse in its concrete manifestations. This pluralism in theology makes it at once exciting and confusing. Some of the confusion can be eliminated by recognizing that the pluralism is largely due to (1) the different types of experience or aspects of experience theologians choose to analyze; (2) the different philosophical tools theologians employ in the analysis and interpretation; (3) the different hermeneutical, epistemological, and metaphysical convictions of various interpreters; and (4) the different purposes motivating and governing the interpretations. Types of theology that originated in very different environments also tend to converge around common concerns and purposes. A few examples of different types of theology illustrate these observations.

Existentialist theology focuses primarily on the human experience of existence in the world, and it employs the analyses of the great existentialist philosophers, such as Kierkegaard, Marcel, Heidegger, and Jaspers. Because of its focus, existentialist theology grounds religion and theology in philosophical and theological anthropology. Theologians such as Rudolf Bultmann, Paul Tillich, and John Macquarrie have systematically used existentialist analyses to uncover the "problem-situations" of human existence and the meaning of Christian symbols and doctrines. By interpreting both human experience and religious symbols and claims using existentialist categories, these theologians have attempted to establish the meaningfulness of religion in relation to human existence and to show its value as a guide to authentic selfhood.

Transcendental Thomism is an important type of Roman Catholic theology in Europe, North America, and Australia. It focuses on the human experience of questioning and knowing and aims to produce a critically realist metaphysics in terms of which both human experience in the modern world and a fundamentally Thomist interpretation of Christian faith can be coherently expressed. Karl Rahner worked out his influential theology using an anthropology derived from Heidegger and Aquinas, a "transcendental method" derived from Kant, and a metaphysics influenced by Aquinas and Hegel. Bernard Lonergan grounded his important work on theological method in a profoundly original study of the structure and process of human knowing. His articulation and appropriation of "transcendental method" enabled him to show the relationships among scientific, philosophical, and religious knowing as forms of knowing; to argue for a critically realist metaphysics in which science, philosophy, and religion are coherently related; and to lay the groundwork for a theological method solidly rooted in the structure of the knowing subject.

Process theology is an important school of American theology that has also been convinced of the necessity of metaphysics in the interpretation of Christian faith. Although it has been open to insights drawn from existentialist theology and other theological movements, it has focused more than any other form of theology on responding to the challenges posed by modern science. Process theology uses the "process" philosophies of Alfred North Whitehead and Charles Hartshorne, who consciously worked out metaphysical interpretations of reality in order to synthesize the claims of science, the humanities, and religion into a consistent, coherent world view. Process theology aims at producing an interpretation of Christian faith that is compatible with the modern scientific world view and with contemporary human experience. Its present interaction with liberation theologies and its dialogue with Buddhism indicate that it will continue to make creative contributions to theology.

Hermeneutical theology focuses on the act of interpretation itself. It examines the experience of interpretation and studies how meaning and truth are perceived and created in the interaction between "reader" and "text" and in the conversation between competing and conflicting interpretations. It addresses the plurality of interpretations that emerges within any tradition and the ambiguity that results from the fact that all interpretations are deeply influenced by their historical and cultural circumstances and consequently tend to be the witting or unwitting servants of various ideologies. Hermeneutical theology aims at criticizing and purifying the act of interpretation itself in order to contribute to the healing of society today. It has strong connections to the various kinds of "liberation" theology.

Liberation theology holds that to know the truth is not enough; the purpose of religion and theology is to *do* the truth, that is, to undergird and motivate action for the transformation and healing of society. The term "liberation theology" is a category including types of theology that had independent origins. South American liberation theology arose in a situation of social and political oppression and focuses on the experience of the poor and oppressed in society. It employs various types of critical theory and social and political analysis (especially Marxist analysis) in order to uncover the structures and causes of oppression in society, and it interprets the Christian faith as addressing, urging, and grounding the needed transformation of church and society. Political theology arose in Europe but has similar methods, concerns, and goals. By using critical analysis to make an "ideology critique," it presents Christian faith as demanding a transformation of church and society. Feminist theology, another type of liberation theology, arose by focusing on the experience of women in a society and a church dominated by patriarchal structures and assumptions. Thus the experience of women as an oppressed "class" is the basis for critical analyses of society, church, scripture, and tradition. The aim is to create social and religious forms and structures free of sexual injustice and domination. Black theology, another manifestation of liberation theology, arose from the experience of racial injustice and oppression and uses that experience as the basis for critical analysis of society and church. It aims to transform society, freeing it from racial injustice and domination. Each of these types of liberation theology takes its start in the experience of some oppressed group, critically analyzes society and church, and interprets the Christian faith as demanding action for the transformation of society.

There are three main issues around which most types of Christian theology are now converging: (1) the transformation of human society to remove all forms of economic, political, sexual, and racial injustice; (2) the transformation of society so that the nuclear and environmental threats to the planet and all its life are reduced and eventually eliminated (which represents an ecological extension of the concerns of liberation theology); and (3) the dialogue with other religions. The dialogue with other religions will certainly affect our views of religious knowledge in yet unforeseen ways. But the continuing importance of the first two issues illustrates the widespread conviction that the ultimate purpose of religious knowledge is to affect living—to motivate the active transformation of human life

155

and the world under the guidance of the values and ideals revealed in and through the person of Jesus Christ.

THOMAS E. HOSINSKI

Bibliography

Langdon Gilkey, *Message and Existence: An Introduction to Christian Theology.*
Peter C. Hodgson and Robert H. King, eds., *Christian Theology: An Introduction to Its Traditions and Tasks,* 2nd ed.
Bernard J. F. Lonergan, *Method in Theology,* 2nd ed.
John Macquarrie, *Principles of Christian Theology,* 2nd ed.
David Tracy, *Blessed Rage for Order: The New Pluralism in Theology.*

Cross Reference: Ambiguity, Existential Philosophy, Feminist Theology, Hermeneutics, Liberation Theology, Neoorthodoxy, Process Theology, Revelation, Theological Method.

ESCHATOLOGY

Broadly speaking, "eschatology" means the doctrine of the last things and includes all concepts associated with life beyond death—heaven and hell, paradise and immortality, resurrection and transmigration of souls, rebirth and reincarnation, last judgment and doomsday, and so on. Eschatology is consequently related to our understanding of humanity, value systems, and world views and differs according to whether one's understanding of humanity is naturalistic, spiritualistic, or dualistic.

Eschatology always influences and determines the conduct of life. Individual eschatology connects one's conduct in this life with personal destiny in the hereafter, whereas collective eschatology considers the destiny of all humanity. A cosmic eschatology goes even farther to include the destiny of the earth or of the whole cosmos. Cosmic eschatology often includes a sequence of world periods—first a Golden Age, then a decline accompanied by a period of crises, and finally a return to the conditions of the Golden Age in a period of cleansing and renewal. A cyclical concept of time is thus presupposed.

The basic components of eschatology are embedded in the motifs of the whole religious and cultic life of a people. For instance, in the Canaanite religion of Israel's neighbors, belief in the two seasonal gods Baal and Mot determined religious life while reflecting a cyclical view of the movement of time. In the beginning of summer, the people lamented the death of the fertility god Baal and the triumph of the death god Mot, because the summer drought decimated all vegetation. Half a year later, the people celebrated the death of Mot and the "resurrection" of Baal when the winter rain returned and promised a good crop.

A cultic motif is also expressed through funeral, burial, and mourning customs. For instance, the Christian concept of burial emphasizes symbolically the unity of the person in expectation of a "bodily" resurrection as opposed to the immortality of the soul.

Biblical Foundation. Although the eschatological outlook of the New Testament cannot be adequately explained without reference to the Hebrew scriptures, it has distinctive differences. The individual and communal hope in the future depicted in the Hebrew scriptures is largely focused on this life, characterized by a good and long life as the goal of the individual who hopes to live on through the next generation. In this future orientation of Hebrew thought, the exclusive dominance of the cyclical view of history was broken and replaced by a linear view into which moments of cyclical thought were occasionally incorporated. Communally, the hope awaited the establishment of the Davidic kingdom. Yahweh's judgment was often understood as occurring in this world and was frequently envisioned optimistically in nationalistic and political terms. Yet finally it was understood as the day of the Lord occurring for the whole world. Although in the Hebraic understanding, death was never considered the end of a human being, a clear hope in the resurrection can be discovered only at the end of pre-Christian times.

In the Jewish apocalyptic literature that flourished from approximately 200 B.C.E. to 200 C.E., a distinction was made between the present aeon of turmoil and the future end of history with the coming of the savior. Although Jesus understood his mission, message, and person in eschatological terms and made claims that could be interpreted messianically, he rejected nationalistic and apocalyptic expectations that tended to view salvation narrowly as the liberation of Israel from foreign occupation. These popular expectations also led to questions concerning the delay of his parousia, since even members of the Christian community expected that Jesus as the Christ would visibly assume his heavenly power at the conclusion of his earthly activity.

For the New Testament authors the Hebrew scriptures' history of promise found its complete fulfillment in Jesus. In contrast to Israelite promissory history and its continual reinterpretation, no promises remain outstanding in the New Testament. The New Testament authors attempted to address the possible disappointment over the delay of the parousia and the yet unfulfilled completion of the Kingdom. They argued dialectically that Christ has already assumed his divine power, although empirically speaking, the old aeon is still present. For instance, in Paul's letters Christ is seen as the new Adam, and the new creation is understood in contrast to the first creation. We live in the old creation, but we already anticipate the new creation in Christ's resurrection, which is appropriated to us in the present through baptism. Other writers emphasized the present as a time of testing of the faithful and an occasion for mission in preparation for the final fulfillment.

Basic Trends of Interpretation. The rediscovery of the eschatological proclamation of Jesus marks the beginning of modern, biblically oriented theology and is largely connected with the name of Albert Schweitzer. Schweitzer posed the alternative that Jesus could be understood either eschatologically or noneschatologically, but not both. He then attacked traditional liberalism, which had accepted Jesus as a moral teacher but had rejected as outdated his eschatological claims of the nearness of the Kingdom and the immediate coming of the end. Schweitzer advanced a thoroughgoing eschatological interpretation of Jesus and declared Jesus' ethics as interim ethics aimed at preparation for the Kingdom. Since the Kingdom had not come when Jesus expected it, our ethics cannot be derived from Jesus' ethics. Yet his demand of world denial and perfection of personality remains valid. This approach, often called consistent or consequent eschatology, sees Jesus strictly in the light of a Jewish apocalyptic world view and has dominated twentieth-century theology.

Another approach is associated with Rudolf Bultmann and emphasizes eschatology's existential impact. According to Bultmann the mythical eschatology of the New Testament is untenable since the parousia of Christ never took place as the New Testament expected. But we no longer need this mythical framework, since the parousia should be interpreted not in strictly cosmological terms but in anthropological or existential ones. Bultmann relied especially on the Pauline letters and the Gospel of John, in which eschatology deals with the goal of the individual in existential terms, not with the goal of history in cosmological terms. The individual encounters the eschaton in the immediate present, permitting the believer to exist truly eschatologically in radical openness for the future.

A variation of this present-oriented approach assumes that the decisive event has already happened. The Kingdom has come with Jesus; therefore, waiting for a future eschaton is unnecessary. C. H. Dodd coined the phrase "realized eschatology" for this approach, which attempts to show that Christians gradually understood that, since the decisive event (Christ's coming) had already happened, what is still to come is simply his coming beyond history when all history will be taken up into God's larger eternal purpose.

A third approach tries to maintain the future-directedness of eschatology, and it is advocated by more conservative scholars such as Anthony A. Hoekema. According to this interpretation Jesus never set a date for his parousia, and therefore the idea of a delay of his return is contrary to the New Testament. Since nobody knows the exact date of the parousia, preparedness is the appropriate attitude. Jesus' resurrection is both prelude and guarantee for the parousia, which will come in its own time.

Recently, Jürgen Moltmann has pointed out that eschatology cannot be confined to the so-called last things to happen at the end but that the whole course of history driving toward this end must also be considered. Eschatology is the doctrine of Christian hope that embraces both the object hoped for and the hope it inspires. Similarly, Wolfhart Pannenberg emphasizes the anticipatory aspect of eschatology since in Christ's resurrection the expected end has already occurred in proleptic anticipation, meaning that the end has been realized in a unique way without precluding its final and universal realization. The individual therefore experiences already some of that which is expected at the end, such as the Kingdom or the new life in Christ. Liberation theology, reminiscent of the Hebrew scripture prophets who announced the Kingdom of peace as no mere transcendent reality but as something to be established on earth, goes another step and emphasizes that the eschatological promises are to be partially fulfilled in historical events that project themselves into the future, creating a permanent historical mobility.

Current Issues in Eschatology. Christian eschatology is grounded in the Christ event, especially in his resurrection. This event, however, does not simply direct attention to the future. The first Christian community did not experience the resurrection only as the ground of hope for the future or as the stimulus to spread the gospel. Paul, especially, reminded his readers that the dying and rising of Christ have immense implications for our present life. "We were buried therefore with him [Christ] by baptism into death, so that as Christ was raised from the dead by the glory of the Father, we too might walk in newness of life" (Rom. 6:4).

Baptism enables Christians to participate in Christ's death and resurrection, making them members both of the Christian community and of the body of Christ and therefore new creatures who participate in the benefits attained through Christ's death and resurrection. Their relationship with God in Christ has become new and is reflected in the way they relate to others. A connection between eschatology and ethics is thus established. As Christians live according to the Spirit imparted in baptism, they walk in new life. But the present life is an interim state that will not continue forever. Through life in Christ Christians already see the goal of the all-inclusiveness of the new creation.

Since the New Testament is confident that nothing can separate a person from the love of God and the eschatological promise that God's love entails, Christians are to give witness to their present participation in this new creation. Individually and collectively through the church, Christians are a living witness to the hope that is within them. With its acts of charity and in the struggle for justice, human rights, and access to the necessities of life, the church foreshadows a world free from anguish, suffering, and despair. It radiates a sign of the new world order in which there will be justice and peace for all creation.

The proleptic aspect of the Christian existence is nowhere better exhibited than in the church's liturgical actions. When the community gathers for the eucharistic meal, all distinctions of rank and class disappear. Distinctions exist only with regard to different functions in the church, but no ontological distinction exists between higher and lower ranks. The intimate communion of believers with their Lord foreshadows their new state in the heavenly city. Correspondingly, the

159

twofold assertion in the words of institution, "Do this in remembrance of me," means not only that Christians should remember Christ's sacrifice, but also appeals to God to remember the sacrifice of God's son and realize the completion of the Kingdom. Each time the Eucharist is celebrated, the community prays for the coming of the Lord, proclaims the beginning of the time of salvation, and anticipates the blessing of the parousia.

This interim situation between Christ's resurrection and the final fulfillment of the Kingdom has often tempted Christians to set a date for the coming of the Kingdom or to visualize an eschatological progression through millennial theories. Already in Jesus' time, some of his followers were convinced that they could accurately predict the beginning of the eschaton and the return of Christ, despite such admonitions as, "Of that day and hour no one knows, not even the angels of heaven, nor the Son, but the Father only" (Matt. 24:36). The eschaton is the God-provided goal that will emerge at a certain God-provided point toward which all life should be directed. Yet determining the date of the coming of the eschaton has remained amazingly attractive. At times Hebrew prophecies have been examined for clues of their fulfillment in the present. But these prophecies, Christians believe, have found their fulfillment already in the Christ event, upon which all further events are contingent as the culmination of God's history with the world.

HANS SCHWARZ

Bibliography

Anthony A. Hoekema, *The Bible and the Future*.
Jürgen Moltmann, *Theology of Hope: On the Grounds and the Implications of a Christian Eschatology*.
Hans Schwarz, *On the Way to the Future: A Christian View of Eschatology in the Light of Current Trends in Religion, Philosophy, and Science*. Rev. ed.
Albert Schweitzer, *The Mystery of the Kingdom of God: The Secret of Jesus' Messiahship and Passion*.

Cross Reference: Dispensationalism, Hope, Kingdom of God.

ETERNITY (*See* Death and Eternal Life, Eschatology, Time.)

ETHICS–CHRISTIAN

What is Christian ethics? Christianity itself is an essentially contested concept. Adding "ethics" to it results in even more befuddlement. That may seem odd to persons unacquainted with the literature of Christian ethics, for so often, especially in modernity, Christianity is popularly identified with a clear set of ethical guidelines. Such an identification is highly misleading. In the history of Christianity and even today, widely divergent notions about the moral life have been held.

Before the eighteenth century no literary works fit within the genre "Christian ethics." Rather the moral existence of Christians was simply treated along with more determinative theological and pastoral themes. This meant that discussion on the moral life of Christians was set forth within ecclesiological forms—sermons, the liturgy, pamphlets, and standard theological treatises. The development of confessional practices contributed to the rise of books in moral theology, the earliest examples of which, dating from the fifth century, are the Celtic Penitentials. Known as "casuistical manuals," these books contain lists of sins, lexically arranged, with the appropriate penance. Though often criticized as "minimalistic and legalistic," the casuistical tradition presumed an ecclesial setting suffused with substantial theological and moral conviction.

The Lutheran reformation, with its call "justification by faith alone," challenged the appropriateness of "ethics" in the Christian life. For Luther, ethics was the attempt to avoid the fundamental reality of sin and the requisite trust in God that alone was sufficient. Calvinism did not build as thoroughly a negative response toward the development of Christian ethics; yet even here one does not find a specifiable discipline called "Christian ethics" separate from theological concerns.

The mixed history of moral reflection throughout Christian tradition reveals the difficulty of providing a systematic account of it, let alone providing a coherent account of the discipline of Christian ethics. The development of the "discipline" of Christian ethics, especially in the United States, stems from the nineteenth-century Social Gospel movement and the introduction of a new field in seminary education called "Applied Christianity." Walter Rauschenbusch's *Christianizing the Social Order* was perhaps the first work applicable to this new field. In it, Rauschenbusch claimed that the family, the church (thanks to the Reformation), the educational system, and political life had been successfully Christianized. All that was left to make Christian was the economic order.

Although Rauschenbusch assumed that the task of Christian ethics was nothing less than the transformation of society to correspond more nearly to the kingdom of God, a much later influential work written by James Gustafson even asks the question, Can ethics be Christian? The shift in mood (from Rauschenbusch's optimism at the beginning of this century to Gustafson's questioning anything distinctive that Christianity offers ethics) reflects a shift from an ebullience which was to make this century the "Christian Century" to the reality of a post-Christian society.

This shift in mood also suggests that the development of Christian ethics as a distinct academic discipline is related to the dominance and then the demise of Protestant Christianity as a legitimating force for Western European society and particularly for the United States. As the title "Applied Christianity" suggests, the new field desired to make the Christian witness "relevant" to society by using social-scientific and historical-critical methods that were seen as superior to the old creeds, confessions, and dogma. But the name of this new field is also suggestive of another development. The increasing pluralism in the United States meant that the hegemony of Protestant Christianity was threatened. Christianity now needed to be *applied* through the use of modern methods, including ethical analysis, for it could no longer be assumed that Christianity, particularly in its Protestant mode, was characteristic of the majority of society.

In view of the changed political situation, a methodology was needed that would appear "non-particular" and objective. As a result persons working in Christian ethics have been attracted to the highly formal accounts of ethics generated by the presupposition of liberal political theory. One way this has been expressed is the preoccupation with choosing responses to difficult situations—that is, "situation ethics."

Joseph Fletcher's *Situation Ethics* was the fruit of such debates within the discipline. Christian ethics was reduced to doing the loving thing within the situation. Yet the situational ethics movement ignored moral agents, who were assumed to be individuals who faced "situations" without any constancy of self. Against Fletcher, some argued that Christian moral reflection should be concerned not so much with "decisions," but with *being* a particular kind of person.

Too often accounts of a Christian ethic, both by liberals, such as Fletcher, and conservatives, who claim to find in the Bible a clear "ethic," assume far too readily they know what "ethics" means. Particularly under the influence of Kant, this endeavor takes the form of finding a general principle capable of being translated into a maxim that can then be willed universally, apart from any theological convictions about the nature of God as found in Jesus Christ. The Ten Commandments and the Sermon on the Mount can thus be turned into categorical imperatives.

This way of devising a Christian ethic is doubtful at best, and at worst it is positively destructive for what Christians ought to be about. Indeed the very notion of Christian ethics is a mistake if it presumes that one can articulate the nature of the Christian moral life abstracted from Christians' most fundamental convictions. Cardinal Suhard says, "To be a witness means to live in such a way that one's life would make no sense if God did not exist." Any account of Christian ethics that does not directly entail the existence of the kind of God found in Jesus Christ is surely wrong. Christian ethics cannot be written separate from Christian convictions that in the life, death, and resurrection of Jesus of Nazareth God has decisively determined the destiny of human existence. In this respect, as Karl Barth proposed, any ethic pretending to be autonomous is sin masked as human pretension.

The attempt to devise an autonomous ethic capable of being realized by anyone apart from theological convictions neglects the concern for the habituation of a people who allow the production and sustenance of that ethic in the first place. Thus, a crucial concern for any Christian ethic is the question of audience. As John Howard Yoder has argued, Christian ethics cannot be written for anyone, but it is first and foremost written within and for the Christian community. Christian ethics is unintelligible without a separated community called church embodying practices that make Christian speech intelligible. This claim is not unlike the recent emphasis of Alasdair MacIntyre, who insists that any ethic depends on a continuing tradition and thus is intrinsically historical.

This view of Christian ethics is not widely shared by most working within the discipline. The discipline's *magnum opus* was Ernst Troeltsch's *Social Teaching of the Christian Churches*. Troeltsch argued that the early church had no Christian social ethic, but by ethic he meant a comprehensive guide necessary to form all aspects of the common life of a civilization. He concludes the *Social Teaching* with his synopsis of the social task of the Church: "All we can do is learn to control the world situation in its successive phases just as the earlier Christian ethic did in its own way." That the task of any Christian ethic, even "in its own way," has been to control the world situation is what we dispute. Only a Christian ethic shorn of Jesus' eschatological claims and parasitic upon the Constantinian settlement could imagine this to be the social task of the church.

The Constantinian settlement represents one of the great watersheds of Christian history. Until Constantine everyone in the church was expected to live righteously, even if that expectation was honored often by disobedience. After Constantine, gradations in the ethical life of Christians became accepted as normative. Constantinian Christianity, which identifies church with world through the category of "responsibility," does not speak for the entirety of Christian thinking about the moral life, even though as an academic discipline Christian ethicists often convey the idea that it does.

Troeltsch's attempt to determine the social teaching of the Christian churches through elucidating from them a responsible civilizational ethic resulted in the claim that two primary social options could be derived from Christian tradition. Developing Weber's ideal types and varying somewhat from his distinction between an ethics of conviction and an ethics of responsibility, Troeltsch suggested that the two primary options were those of church and sect. The church accepts the inevitable compromise involved in controlling a cultural ethos. The sect, while laudable for its uncompromising stance, pays the price of political irrelevance.

Troeltsch's typology was later refined by H. Richard Niebuhr in his well-known work *Christ and Culture*. Rather than simply using two alternatives, Niebuhr suggested five primary forms of Christian relationship to culture. He first devised two extreme types: Christ against culture, and Christ of culture. The former he identified with Tertullian and Tolstoy, and it corresponded exactly to Troeltsch's "sect." The latter tended to be closer to Troeltsch's "church." Between these he located "Christ above culture," which he identified with medieval Catholicism, and then "Christ and culture in paradox," which he associated with Lutheranism. The fifth form, which Niebuhr clearly preferred, was called "Christ transforming culture," which he thought was characteristic of Augustine, Calvin, and John Wesley.

The characterization of Christian ethics by Troeltsch and Niebuhr has the great virtue of making clear that Christian ethics cannot be separated from the sociological status of the church. Such an account helps us see why the explicit ethics of Christians at any one time may belie a more fundamental orientation due to their social position than they are often able to articulate. Unfortunately the ideal types that Troeltsch devised have had a more enduring impact than his emphasis on social analysis. Thus, in spite of its great heuristic value, the work of Troeltsch and Niebuhr has greatly distorted the understanding of Christian ethics. Their typologies basically derive from their own church type commitments. As a result, the more radical forms of Christian ethics (such as those found in the New Testament, monasticism, and the leftwing of the Reformation) fail to be appreciated as earnest social and political challenges. Any movement that refuses to speak in the language of the dominant church type is seen as sectarian and as propagating a "ghetto" language.

Troeltsch and Niebuhr's analysis does stand, however, in continuity with some interpreters of the tradition of a natural law ethic that has played a prominent part in Christian moral reflection. Of course, the concept of "natural law" is deeply controverted. Little agreement exists about its justification or content. Moreover, it served radically different functions in different times and thinkers. For example, Aquinas used it primarily as an exegetical principle to help distinguish the aspects of the Old Testament that Christians as Christians need not obey—that is, the juridical and ceremonial prescriptions that apply primarily to Jews and not to Christians. As MacIntyre notes in *Whose Justice? Which Rationality?* for Aquinas natural law suggested that we are sinners. That is why for Aquinas no account of the natural law could be autonomous, for any intelligible account of it presupposed a teleological account of our relationship with God.

However, the natural law ethic under the requirement of the Constantinian settlement was used to devise universal standards for anyone. There is no question that an ideological distortion of Christian ethics occurred at that point as Christians, in the name of natural law, sought to control everyone in their purview. This distortion resulted in accounts of natural law being divorced from their theological rationale—a separation that cannot be blamed on Augustine or Aquinas, since the former emphasized, in particular, the importance of will for the moral life. Augustine recognized you could know the good and still not do it. Therefore, any well-lived life would need grace. As MacIntyre observes, two social options—Gregory VII's attempt to create a Christian civilization and monasticism—gave expression to that systematic point. Ironically, Augustine was the source of these two great social options within Christianity.

Paul Ramsey, a central figure in the discipline of Christian ethics in this century, recognized that natural law or natural justice alone was insufficient. Thus he worked with the concept of "love-transforming natural law." As a formula his concept was more in line with Aquinas, Augustine, and the Christian tradition than the ideas of ethicists who work with the assumption, whether they call it natural law or not, that the controlling force of rationality allows them to devise universal standards accessible to anyone apart from the Christian narrative. "Love-transforming natural law" says that natural justice, if there is such a thing, must first be set within the framework of God's faithful love, *chesed,* or *agape,* found in God's covenantal relationship with a particular, historical people. Thus, rationality itself does not provide normative claims, but only rationality set within this narrative framework does.

It is significant that Ramsey wrote as a Protestant, for a part of Luther's reformation was a challenge to any natural law ethic that neglected the sinfulness of human existence. But Luther's assumption of *simul justus et peccator* also had dire consequences for Christian ethics. If sin prevented the realization of obligations through law by people's use of reason, then how could the church expect to govern temporal political affairs? Luther's answer to this problem was the *congregatio fidelium*—the real church, a faithful congregation that was journeying in a foreign land but unable to be visibly identified. This view of the church was popular to German and Italian princes who were challenging the temporal power of the papacy in their jurisdictions, and it resulted in a distinction between individual and public morality.

Luther emphasized two orders to our moral existence—the order of preservation and the order of redemption. The ethics of the former was basically different from the ethics of the latter. Even though Christians might be required to forgive seventy times seven, in the interest of the order of society they could be called to be "hangmen for Christ." Christians were to obey magistrates or the ethos on which they drew. (The Christian implication in as well as support of the rise of Naziism can at least partly be attributed to the assumption that the ethics of the gospel as identified with the person and work of Jesus is simply not applicable to the wider social sphere.)

Many theologians have challenged this removal of Christian ethics from temporal political affairs. Counter-Reformation theologians, such as the Dominicans Bellarmine, Suarez, and Vittoria, invoked the natural law argument to challenge the notion that political society was only an order of preservation to which the gospel was inapplicable. According to their interpretation of the natural law argument, all people were created in God's image, and therefore the potential to follow God's laws was inherent in each person. The thrust of this argument was not to provide a universal normative stance that all people could follow. Rather it was to limit the exploitation of people outside the faith: One could not indiscriminately kill persons outside the faith under the pretense that they were incapable of following God's will and therefore incapable of obeying the law.

But it would be wrong to assume that the only two positions for a Christian social ethic are the irrelevance of the gospel for political life and the relevance of it through translation into natural norms available to all. This assumption perpetuates the idea that the only two options are the "responsibility" of creating and controlling a Christian civilization, similar to Troeltsch's "church," and the acceptance of the political irrelevance, albeit the integrity, of a monastic, "sectarian" withdrawal ethic. Theologians such as Karl Barth and Dietrich Bonhoeffer challenged the Lutheran distinction between orders of preservation and creation and orders of redemption. Barth emphasized the centrality of God's command for Christian ethics and the inseparability for any account of morality from radical demands found in the gospel. Still, Barth's work has by no means been widely approved by Christians, as many fear that to follow him will result in irrelevance in social orders that are now fundamentally secular. This is a terrible irony since it was Barth who, more than perhaps but a few theologians, challenged the church's implication in Hitler's Germany. "For the sake of the freedom of the Gospel," he called on Christians to stand against Hitler's movement.

It is a sad irony indeed that this witness is lost because of fears that it will be socially irrelevant. In fact, it is precisely the category of "irony," as it was devised by Reinhold Niebuhr, that has caused such a witness by the church to be overlooked. Niebuhr's *Moral Man and Immoral Society* challenged the easy optimism of the Social Gospel movement by reestablishing the significance of sin for Christian theology. But he also accepted a distinction between private and public morality whereby the ethic of Jesus was thought to be applicable only with respect to the life of the individual Christian, but not to society at large. The irony of our existence was that, as creatures who were both finite and who also transcended finiteness, we were caught in the inevitable flux of the relativity of history. Christian love, then, was the "impossible possibility"—the ideal that remained at the edge of history but was yet inappropriate for political society. In the wake of the wide acceptance of Niebuhr's ethics, it is not unfair to say that Protestant theological ethics continues trying to explain why Christians must act in their societies in ways that are incompatible with the ethics of Jesus.

Mennonite theologian John Howard Yoder offers a way out of the church-sect discourse by distinguishing between two aeons—that of the church and that of the world. To be in the church is to live within the eschaton that is not ruled by violence, but to live according to the "war of the lamb" and to place oneself within the "revolutionary subordination" of the eschatologically constituted community—an alternative community whose very existence is a witness to the world that order through force and violence is contrary to an ecclesiological ethic centered on Jesus.

The private-public distinction is also being challenged by the revival by many Methodist theologians of an ethics of sanctification. Wesley understood sanctification as the immediate fruit of justification that results in "holy tempers" in the lives of Christians. Through ecclesiological practices, such as waiting upon all the means of grace—private and public prayer, searching the scriptures, fasting, baptism, the Holy Eucharist, and Christian Conference—the Holy Spirit produces such holy tempers, or virtues, in the lives of followers. Such "holy living" is an alternative social reality.

Parallel developments to those already discussed have arisen in Catholic moral theology since Vatican II. Catholic moral theology was purged to become more scriptural in its orientation and was coupled with a general sense of the need for reform away from what was considered a more authoritarian pattern of the past. The other great development in Catholic moral theology has been the rise of liberation theology, which is no monolithic movement but takes on a variety of shapes. The most serious attempt to expound this position conceptually has been Clodovis Boff's *Theology and Praxis.*

For secular thinkers the issues discussed in this article may not even appear to be ethics. For them, "ethics" is about modes of reasoning to let us determine the right or wrong of in-vitro fertilization, abortion, euthanasia, sexual intercourse before marriage, and so on. Certainly Christian thinkers in modernity have dealt with these issues, which have even been the subject of official pronouncements of church bodies. However, the attempt here has been to show how judgments about these issues presuppose more determinative ecclesial and theological commitments that are too easily forgotten in modernity. Remembering who we are in the call of God in Jesus, rather than searching for justification for what we are to do, is fundamental to *Christian* ethics.

STANLEY HAUERWAS
D. STEPHEN LONG

Bibliography

James Gustafson, *Can Ethics Be Christian?*
_____, *Theocentric Ethics.*
Stanley Hauerwas, *Character and the Christian Life.*
_____, *A Community of Character.*
_____, *The Peaceable Kingdom.*
Alasdair MacIntyre, *After Virtue.*
_____, *Whose Justice? Which Rationality?*
H. Richard Niebuhr, *The Responsible Self.*
_____, *The Meaning of Revelation.*
Ernst Troeltsch, *The Social Teaching of the Christian Churches.*

Cross Reference: Justice, Kingdom of God, Moral Theology, Natural Theology, Peace/Peacemaking, Sanctification, Sexuality, Sin, Social Gospel.

EUCHARIST (*See* SACRAMENTS/SACRAMENTAL THEOLOGY, WORSHIP.)

EVANGELICALISM

The term "evangelicalism" has theological, historical, and even ideological connotations. Here it refers to a movement of spiritual renewal dedicated to the proclamation of the gospel—the Good News of salvation by free grace, mediated through the atoning sacrifice of Christ, received by faith alone, and made manifest in a life of discipleship and holiness. This gospel, moreover, is considered the essential content of scripture, which has primacy over church tradition as well as religious experience. Evangelicals seek both spiritual revival and church reform in accordance with the gospel.

"Evangelical" is wider and narrower than "Protestant"—wider because it embraces similar concerns in Roman Catholicism and Eastern Orthodoxy, narrower because a large segment of Protestantism is no longer oriented toward the revealed truth of the gospel, finding the source of authority in ordinary religious experience, conscience, or speculative reason.

Movements in History. The conflict between Augustine and Pelagius in the fifth century sparked a renewal of the Pauline motif of salvation by grace. Augustine stood firmly for God's initiative in the salvific process, whereas Pelagius stressed the power of the human will to do good apart from divine grace. The church's official condemnation of Pelagianism did not prevent the rise of semi-Pelagianism, which conceived of salvation as partly by grace and partly by works. This compromise position was rejected at the Second Council of Orange in 529, but it has been a continuing source of temptation for Roman Catholic as well as Protestant and Orthodox Christians through the centuries. The distinctive Augustinian motifs were reaffirmed by the Jansenists (a Catholic renewal movement mainly in France and the Low Countries in the seventeenth and eighteenth centuries), but the Catholic church took pains to distance itself from what it regarded as an exaggerated form of Augustinianism.

Evangelical theology was the formative influence in the Protestant Reformation of the sixteenth century. Among the doctrines given special emphasis by Luther, Calvin, Zwingli, and other mainline Reformers were salvation by grace *(sola gratia)*, justification by faith alone *(sola fide)*, the authority of scripture over both church tradition and religious experience *(sola scriptura)*, and the glory of God as the chief motivation in the Christian life *(soli Deo Gloria)*. The Anabaptist side of the Reformation also affirmed the priority of grace and the primacy of scripture, but it sought to balance the emphasis on grace with the call to discipleship.

The salient thrusts of the Protestant Reformation were preserved and defended by the movement of Protestant orthodoxy (from the sixteenth to eighteenth centuries). At the same time, new emphases served to blur the impact of the

Reformation. Assent to sound doctrine was considered almost as important as trust in Jesus Christ as Lord and Savior. Revelation was identified more and more with the propositional content of the Bible; mystery and paradox in revelation were increasingly downplayed in the interest of perfecting a comprehensive, rational system of truth. The Reformation criterion of Word and Spirit, in which knowledge of scriptural truth was made dependent on interior illumination, was overshadowed by an emphasis on the Word alone, and the role of the Spirit was reduced to empowering the will to assent to truth that was generally available to human reason. Early Protestant orthodoxy remained faithful to the claims and concerns of the mainline Reformation, but later, under the rationalizing influence of Descartes and Leibniz, clarity and coherence came to be the criteria by which truth was assessed.

The spiritual movements of purification subsequent to the Reformation—Pietism (Philip Spener, August Francke, Count Nicolaus von Zinzendorf), Puritanism (John Owen, William Perkins, John Bunyan), and British Evangelicalism (John Wesley, George Whitefield, Howell Harris)—pressed for the fulfillment of the Reformation in a reformation of life and character. Genuine theology, it was said, could be engaged in only by regenerate theologians. The experience of conversion, which was increasingly linked with confirmation, was considered just as crucial as baptism, if not more so. The Puritans emphasized purity in worship as well as in life, and this was often accompanied by an iconoclastic protest against ceremonialism and symbolism.

The Holiness movement, which arose out of Methodism in the nineteenth century, sounded the call to personal holiness, holding out the possibility of entire sanctification in this life, sometimes described as "sinless perfection." The Christian life is not so much a continuing struggle against the forces of sin, death, and hell (an emphasis we find in the Reformers) as it is victory over these forces. The state of perfection is regarded not as an achievement but as a gift and is often referred to as a second work of grace or second blessing. In Pentecostalism, which came out of the Holiness revival, this added blessing in the Christian life is linked to power in ministry more than to Christian perfection; the cardinal evidence for this new work of the Spirit (commonly called in both Holiness and Pentecostal circles "the baptism with the Holy Spirit") is held to be speaking in other tongues (glossolalia).

Fundamentalism, which emerged in the latter half of the nineteenth century, represented a hardening of conservative Protestantism in the face of the challenges of historical criticism of Scripture, the theory of evolution, and a scientism that denied the reality of the supernatural. The plenary and verbal inspiration of scripture and its total inerrancy came to be the distinctive marks of the fundamentalist movement. Other doctrines accorded special prominence were the virgin birth of Christ, his deity, his bodily resurrection from the grave, and his premillennial return to reign on a purified earth. Fundamentalism signified the

169

wedding of late Protestant orthodoxy and dispensationalism, the theology enunciated by John Nelson Darby (d. 1882) and C. I. Scofield (d. 1921), which divided world history into seven dispensations, drawing sharp distinctions between the dispensation of law and the dispensation of grace, in which we now live.

Evangelicalism Today. Evangelicalism as a spiritual and ideological movement today is marked by surprising and fascinating diversity. The fundamentalist mentality with its penchant for separatism still reigns in many circles, though many groups and churches that come out of fundamentalism are becoming more ecumenically focused and socially oriented. Protestant denominations that continue to uphold the hermeneutics of biblical literalism and inerrancy include the Plymouth Brethren, the Evangelical Free Church, the Independent Fundamental Churches of America, the Southern Baptist Convention, the Fundamental Baptist Fellowship, the General Association of Regular Baptists, the Conservative Baptist Association of America, the Baptist Bible Fellowship, the Bible Presbyterian Church, and independent Bible churches. Many of these churches are premillennial as well. Paraparochial fellowships that belong to the fundamentalist ethos include Campus Crusade for Christ, Youth for Christ, the Navigators, and Word of Life Fellowship.

Confessional orthodoxy, which is distinguished by strict adherence to the creeds and confessions of the Reformation, embraces the Lutheran Church, Missouri Synod; the Lutheran Churches of the Reformation; the Wisconsin Evangelical Lutheran Synod; the Church of the Lutheran Confession; the Christian Reformed Church; the Orthodox Presbyterian Church; the Associate Reformed Presbyterian Church; the Presbyterian Church in America; and the Protestant Reformed Churches of America. Some of these churches are also fundamentalist in their view of the Bible.

Churches coming out of evangelical Pietism that continue to maintain a Pietistic thrust are the Evangelical Covenant Church, the Moravian Church, the Unity of the Brethren, the Baptist General Conference, the Brethren in Christ, the Evangelical Congregational Church, the Salvation Army, the Church of the Nazarene, the Evangelical Friends Alliance, the independent Christian Churches, the Christian and Missionary Alliance, the Lutheran Brethren of America, the North American Association of Free Lutheran Congregations, the Churches of God in North America, the Church of God (Anderson, Indiana), and the Reformed Church in America.

The rise of a neo-evangelical theology that combines a high view of scriptural authority with the willingness to accept the principle of historical criticism of the scriptures has left its mark on a number of denominations and paraparochial Christian fellowships, including the American Baptist Churches in the U.S.A., the Evangelical Presbyterian Church, the United Wesleyan Church (which can also be listed with the Pietists, above), InterVarsity Christian Fellowship, and Young Life. The neo-evangelical thrust is also evident in the Presbyterian Church, USA; the United Methodist Church; and the Episcopal Church, though it represents only a minority within these largely liberal denominations. Theologians commonly identified with a reformed or refurbished evangelicalism include James Packer, Clark Pinnock, Richard Lovelace, David Wells, Robert Johnston, Bernard Ramm, John R. W. Stott, Bruce Waltke, and Donald Bloesch.

Charismatic evangelicalism, noted for its emphasis on the gifts of the Spirit, especially healing, prophecy, and glossolalia, embraces a wide array of churches that constitute the growing edge of Protestantism—not only in the United States but even more in the developing nations. Among these bodies are the Assemblies of God, the Church of God in Christ, the Church of God (Cleveland, Tenn.), the International Church of the Foursquare Gospel, the Open Bible Standard Churches, the Elim Pentecostal Churches in Britain, the Pentecostal Assemblies of Canada, the Evangelical Pentecostal Church in Brazil, the Methodist Pentecostal Church in Chile, the Apostolic Faith Mission in South Africa, the Muhlheim Christian Alliance in Germany, and the Pentecostal Revival Movement in Sweden.

Neoorthodoxy, associated with the names of Karl Barth, Emil Brunner, and Dietrich Bonhoeffer, marked a resurgence of biblical, evangelical theology in the mainline Protestant denominations, but its influence has waned considerably. It was distinguished by its stress on the uniqueness of the Christ revelation, the unity of the witness of the Bible, the priority and sovereignty of divine grace, and the universal lordship of Christ. Its impact has been felt in Presbyterian, Congregational, Evangelical and Reformed, Lutheran, and Methodist churches.

A catholic evangelicalism intent on maintaining evangelical distinctives within the limits of catholic tradition has now and again come to the fore, especially within Lutheran, Reformed, and Episcopal churches. In addition to the message of grace, there is a corresponding emphasis on the means of grace, especially the sacraments. In addition to the church as the communion of saints, there is a readiness to acknowledge the exemplary role of great saints who inspire all believers to follow Christ in costly discipleship. Theologians who have sought to rediscover the reality of the holy catholic church within all churches and to build bridges between various church traditions without compromising biblical fidelity include Philip Schaff and John Nevin in the old German Reformed Church in this country; Nathan Soderblom of the Church of Sweden; P. T. Forsyth, a Congregational theologian in early-twentieth-century England; Robert Jenson and Carl Braaten in today's American Lutheranism; Robert Webber in the Episcopal Church; T. F. Torrance in the Church of Scotland; Robert Paul and Daniel Jenkins in the United Reformed Church in England; Thomas Oden in the United Methodist Church; and Donald Bloesch in the United Church of Christ. Karl Barth too, particularly in his last years, endeavored to make a case for evangelical catholicity.

171

Key Doctrines. Despite its wide diversity, both sociologically and theologically, the evangelical movement is united around some salient themes and doctrines. The first is its high view of holy scripture. Evangelicals affirm the divine authority of scripture—the source of revelation is the living God; the primacy of scripture—over experience, reason, and church tradition; and the veracity of scripture—the truthfulness of its teaching and doctrine. In the best evangelical theology, scripture is not sundered from the Spirit who inspired it and speaks through it, but is affirmed in its paradoxical unity with the Spirit.

Another distinguishing mark of evangelical theology is its adherence to *sola gratia*—salvation by grace alone. Our deliverance lies not in human power or ingenuity but in the salvific act of God in Jesus Christ, which satisfied the penalty for sin and released a lost and sinful humanity from the stranglehold of the powers of darkness. Our very response in faith to God's salvific work in Jesus Christ is dependent on the prior action of the Holy Spirit, who frees our will to grasp the hand outstretched to save us. Faith is the means by which God's justifying grace is appropriated, but faith in itself is an empty vessel that needs to be filled, not a virtue that wins grace for the recipient.

Christ is upheld as the preexistent Son of God who incarnated himself in human flesh in order to become the substitutionary sacrifice for human sin. He is a divine Savior who voluntarily humbled himself and identified with our plight and misery so that we might be pardoned and redeemed. His perfect righteousness is imputed to us by faith, and our sin is imputed to him through divine substitution. Evangelicals following Luther and Calvin insist that what makes us acceptable before a holy God is the alien righteousness of Christ, which covers our sinfulness, not personal holiness, which, though not without value, is forever deficient on the scales of divine justice.

Evangelical theology also holds to the cruciality of conversion. Although the experience of conversion (or being "born again") cannot be stereotyped, it will always include conviction and confession of sin and joyous assurance of salvation. The salvific experience is not the source or ground of our salvation but is its sign and fruit.

Evangelicals further insist on the pursuit of holiness in thought and life, often appealing to Hebrews 12:14 and I Peter 1:15-16. Although our striving for holiness does not merit salvation, it carries forward the process of sanctification through the inner working of the Holy Spirit. Only Christ's righteousness entitles us to heaven but personal holiness qualifies us for it (Wesley).

Other important tenets of evangelical faith are the ontological Trinity, the sovereignty of God, the church as the believing people of God as opposed to a hierarchical institution, the cruciality of preaching, the priesthood of all believers, the universal call to sanctity, and the urgency of mission.

A number of issues constitute sources of tension within evangelicalism today: the inerrancy and infallibility of the Bible, women in ministry, the gifts of the Holy

Spirit, divine election and reprobation, the role of the sacraments in effecting salvation, the importance of the millennium in eschatology, and the doctrine of an eternal hell. The intrusion of ideology (such as socialism, conservatism, nationalism, and feminism) into the life of the church is also creating problems for the evangelical community, for this means that the gospel is brought into the service of a particular social cause. A growing consensus among evangelicals urges that Christians rise above ideological alignments of both left and right and reaffirm the gospel and the law of God in all their power and purity to a world desperate for truth and meaning in a time of encroaching nihilism.

DONALD G. BLOESCH

Bibliography

Donald G. Bloesch, *The Future of Evangelical Christianity.*
Donald W. Dayton and Robert K. Johnston, eds., *The Variety of American Evangelicalism.*
Mark Ellingsen, *The Evangelical Movement.*
George M. Marsden, *Understanding Fundamentalism and Evangelicalism.*
Bernard Ramm, *The Evangelical Heritage*

Cross Reference: Dispensationalism, Fundamentalism, Inerrancy, Neoorthodoxy, Pentecostalism, Protestantism.

EVIL

"This is an evil in all that happens under the sun," says Qoheleth, "that the same fate comes to everyone. Moreover, the hearts of all are full of evil; madness is in their hearts while they live, and after that they go to the dead" (Eccles. 9:3). This pronouncement by the Preacher rings as true today as it did when it was written, although the current discussion of the perennial problem of evil adds some specifically modern features and is characterized by a wide diversity of approaches and positions. As the antonym of "good," "evil" conveys a negative value judgment. Evil may be most simply defined as that which causes significant harm, usually to human beings. Like philosophy, theology employs a distinction between two main kinds of evil: moral and natural (or physical). Moral evil refers to actions of human agents (whose "hearts are full of evil") whose intent is to harm; examples include murder, theft, and lying. Natural evil refers to natural occurrences that are considered evil because of their harmful consequences; examples include earthquakes, droughts, disease, and death (Qoheleth's "same fate"). Theological discussion of evil focuses on the theodicy question (literally, "the justification of God" in the face of moral and natural evil). The theodicy problem is constituted by the difficulty of reconciling three separate propositions, all of which traditional Christianity has affirmed: (1) God, the creator, is omnipotent (i.e., all-powerful); (2) God is benevolent (i.e., all-good); and (3) evil exists. Another way to state the dilemma is this: If God is able to prevent evil (as #1 implies) and does not, then #2 must be false. If God wants to prevent evil (as #2 implies) and cannot, then #1 must be false. If God is able and willing and does, in fact, prevent evil, then #3 must be false.

Approaches to this problem can be put into three categories, one for each of the three propositions. Each category focuses on the central term of one proposition—rejecting, redefining, or modifying it (by adding a qualifying corollary). The following summary provides a typology of the many diverse options pursued in modern theodicies: Arguments range from traditional (which attempt to preserve full divine omnipotence and benevolence) to radical (which scarcely seem to be justifying God at all). Often a given thinker will combine elements from several of these groups; always she or he will argue them with much more precision and sophistication than is possible here.

The first category of arguments focuses on divine omnipotence. Some thinkers straightforwardly reject omnipotence and state that God's power is limited by other beings. Others argue that divine omnipotence is self-limited; God decided to restrict God's power in love to allow creatures to have free will. Still others contend that creaturely free will does not inhibit divine omnipotence in any way, for something logically nonsensical (e.g., giving creatures free will while also determining that they always choose only good actions) places no limitation on omnipotence. In the preceding understandings of power, God's power (whether limited or unlimited) is viewed as domination. Other definitions, however, are also proposed. Process theologians redefine God's power as persuasive rather than coercive; because of creaturely freedom, God can only attempt to persuade creatures to the good. Feminist and liberation approaches begin with still another, but related, understanding of power: power as enabling, as empowering, as compassionate.

One quite new approach (but with roots as old as the book of Job) is to question outright the complete goodness of God. These impassioned "theodicies of protest" refuse to argue for God's justification (and so are only theodicies in an extended sense) because to do so would profane the memories of those who have endured radical suffering, paradigmatically represented by the Holocaust. Other, less radical, options in this second category protect God's goodness by claiming that it is compatible with God's allowing evil if that evil is understood as a punishment for sin or a trial necessary for growth. Still others argue that God suffers with us in this tragically marred world; whatever responsibility God might bear for human suffering, God's choosing to share in it establishes the divine goodness.

Although the reality of evil seems to be beyond doubt, some thinkers attempt to modify the third proposition. Some argue that, viewed from an ultimate

174

perspective, evil can be seen to contribute to a more extensive, more harmonious whole. Others, often those holding the "growth" position, appeal to a heavenly reward as recompense for any necessary sufferings undergone on earth, sufferings that in the light of heavenly glory will appear to have been insignificant.

The entire modern discussion of theodicy provides much-needed clarification of a complex issue but to date has achieved no consensus. And all too often, these highly theoretical theodicies appear unconnected to and unconcerned about the very real suffering and pain affecting real people. A full theological treatment of the problem of evil must engage more than the intellect; other, more holistic approaches attempt to rectify this state of affairs by enlisting action, emotion, and imagination.

Discussions of a more practical and concrete sort, often having a liberation emphasis, focus on what God is doing to combat evil (e.g., suffering with, sparking resistance, and bringing resurrection out of death); what people should be doing to combat evil (e.g., making the option for the poor, struggling against structural injustice, eschewing masochism, and being with those who suffer); and how humanity can relate to God in the meantime (e.g., expressing anger at God in the manner of the Hebrew psalms of lament, practicing contemplation, and celebrating liturgy and sacraments with others in the community of faith).

Another family of approaches, equally holistic but not so practically oriented, explores the imaginative expressions of the human experience of evil (e.g., in symbol, myth, and classical and current narrative texts). Such studies provide a depth and richness to the understanding of evil (in both its moral and natural forms) that can benefit the more theoretical and practical discussions.

Underlying the diversity of approaches to the problem of evil in theology is a fundamental agreement on the centrality and relevance of the problem. As long as human suffering and belief in a loving God coexist, people will continue to wrestle with the problem of evil, and Christian theology will, at its best, employ its reflective resources to help them live with the question.

PATRICIA L. WISMER

Bibliography

Stephen T. Davis, ed., *Encountering Evil: Live Options in Theodicy.*
Wendy Farley, *Tragic Vision and Divine Compassion: A Contemporary Theodicy.*
Gustavo Gutiérrez, *On Job: God-Talk and the Suffering of the Innocent.*
Paul Ricoeur, *The Symbolism of Evil.*
Richard F. Vieth, *Holy Power, Human Pain.*

Cross Reference: God, Holocaust, Suffering.

EVOLUTION (*See* CREATION, CREATION SCIENCE, SCIENCE AND CHRISTIANITY.)

EXISTENCE (*See* BEING/BECOMING.)

EXISTENTIAL PHILOSOPHY

Existential philosophy is an oxymoron in the sense that it designates a protest against the ideal of rational objectivity that has characterized the mainstream of Western philosophy since Plato. Although one finds "existentialist" motifs in earlier writers such as Paul, Augustine, and Pascal, existential philosophy is a peculiarly modern phenomenon, beginning in the nineteenth century with Søren Kierkegaard (1813–1855) and Friedrich Nietzsche (1844–1900) and reaching its zenith in the mid–twentieth century with Martin Heidegger (1889–1976) and Jean-Paul Sartre (1905–1980). A strong influence on the last generation of Christian theologians—most notably Rudolf Bultmann, Reinhold Niebuhr, Paul Tillich, and the early Karl Barth—existentialism has left an enduring legacy on Christian theology.

The term "existentialism" emphasizes the uniqueness of human existence, a concern tidily expressed in Sartre's famous aphorism, "Existence precedes essence." Human beings, in other words, are in some measure self-created. Unlike other entities or things that have their essences or natures already given, human beings make choices and act on the world in such a way as to create their own essences. Their unique individualities are determined by their choosing some possibilities and not others. The existentialist therefore assumes a substantial measure of freedom for human beings and champions that freedom as a primary value.

The ultimate truth about human beings, then, can be known only through the human subject, the inner life of a concretely existing individual. As Kierkegaard put it, "Truth is subjectivity." Existentialists are willing to grant a limited legitimacy to the mapping of human nature in rational, objective, and universal categories by the natural and social sciences. The most important truths of human life, however, are not those that can be known externally or conceptually by a detached observer, but those that demand commitment and participation. A crucial difference exists, for example, between "knowing" about friendship cognitively (say, from having read an essay by Aristotle on the subject) and "knowing" another person as a friend in a committed relationship. Ultimate truth is not something to be pondered with detached objectivity but to be inwardly appropriated in such a way that one's whole life is transformed. Not surprisingly, many existentialists have spurned the traditional philosophical essay or systematic treatise for novels, stories, poems, and visual arts as their primary media of communication.

Contrary to much popular rhetoric about the joys of freedom, the existentialists emphasize the dread or anxiety that is the inevitable companion of freedom. Freedom, of course, is never absolute, for human life is finite, bounded by a whole series of "givens." The tension between freedom and finitude generates dread or anxiety, for one can never be sure where the limits are. Further, choosing always involves risks, for some choices lead to unintended and unforeseen results, for which the individual must assume responsibility and bear the burden of possible guilt. One can never be certain that one has chosen rightly. Such anxiety creates a powerful tendency to escape from the responsibility of freedom by simply conforming to some external authority (for example, the expectations of one's family or peers, cultural mores, an ethical code, or an authoritative figure). This renunciation of one's freedom is what many existentialists have labeled "inauthentic existence." Existentialism is a challenge to human individuals to become "authentic," that is, to exercise their freedom with awareness of their limits and to accept full responsibility for the choices they make.

Many existentialists have given substantial attention to the inevitability of death (e.g., Albert Camus in *The Plague* and *The Stranger* and Heidegger in *Being and Time*). The emphasis is not due to some morbid fascination, but is rather an effort to free the individual to experience the fullness of the present moment. Awareness that death could come at any moment helps one to distinguish what is ultimately important from what has only relative significance.

Some existentialists like Nietzsche and Sartre have insisted that human freedom can be protected only within an atheistic framework. Others, however, have found intimate connections between existentialism and Christian faith. Kierkegaard, for example, revitalized the notion of faith in terms of "truth as subjectivity." One becomes a Christian, he contended, not by being born into a Christian culture or by giving intellectual assent to a series of metaphysical or historical propositions about God or Jesus, but through a passionate, inward commitment to the way of Christ. Bultmann found in Heidegger's analysis of human existence a framework for demythologizing the New Testament, thereby freeing the radical demands of the gospel from the incrustations of history, myth, and dogma, and enabling them to confront the hearer in the present moment. For Tillich, existentialism provided insight into the fundamental questions of human life, and his theology of correlation sought to show how the Christian gospel provided authentic answers to those questions. Reinhold Niebuhr seized upon the dialectic of freedom and finitude to articulate an analysis of sin as both pride and sensuality. Existentialism has also elicited a searching critique of traditional language about God, most of which appears incompatible with serious claims about human freedom. The result has been a shift away from such metaphysical concepts as omnipotence and omniscience and toward images that focus upon God's love and vulnerability.

Recent theologians have criticized existentialism for its individualistic bias and for its exaggerated distinction between human existence and the natural order. Political and liberation theologians have charged that existentialism has difficulty addressing the social, political, and economic dimensions of human life. Some thinkers contend that existentialism lacks an adequate appreciation of nature and actually undermines concern for the natural environment. Even so, existential philosophy has left a legacy in Christian theology that is apparent in many places: the understanding of faith as commitment to a way of life, the focus on the radical features of the gospel that demand a personal response in the present moment, the new appreciation for the role of narrative and metaphor in theology, and the renewed emphasis on God's love and vulnerability.

JOHN C. SHELLEY

Bibliography

William Barrett, *Irrational Man: A Study in Existential Philosophy.*
Rudolf Bultmann, *Existence and Faith.*
Carl Michalson, ed., *Christianity and the Existentialists.*
Dorothee Soelle, *Political Theology.*
Paul Tillich, *The Courage to Be.*

Cross Reference: Correlation, Epistemology, Freedom, Paradox, Ultimate Concern.

EXPERIENCE–RELIGIOUS

Virtually every theological tradition invokes religious experience as a crucial resource and measure of theological reflection. The word "experience" is typically defined in dictionaries as "a particular instance of encountering or undergoing something" or as "the sum total of the conscious events that make up the life of a person or a community." Thus broadly defined, *religious* experience includes all those times and ways that individuals and groups become aware of things or events that are sacred. As historian of religion Joachim Wach puts it, religious experience "may be characterized as the total response of a man's total being to what he experiences as ultimate reality" (*Types of Religious Experience,* 43).

Christian theological traditions divide over what relative weight to give to the religious experiences of the past and the present. Some theologies appeal to the religious experiences reported in the Bible as their definitive source and standard of all subsequent religious experience and theological reflection. Other theologies make current religious experience the final arbiter in appropriating the religious experiences of the past and formulating the theological affirmations of the present. Even more significant, theological traditions differ among themselves over which dimensions of religious experience they emphasize and over what types of religious experience they recognize as normatively Christian. But every theological tradition seeks to clarify, confirm, and commend a distinctive pattern of religious experiences.

Dimensions of Religious Experience. Any description of religious experience within the Christian heritage is complicated by the mere fact that different religious groups and theological traditions stress different modalities of human experience in matters religious. Although the whole person is engaged in religious experience, priority is usually given to one or another of the characteristic faculties or dimensions of human experience generally. Either the mind, the will, or the heart is often singled out as the seat of religious experience in its constitutive formation and expression.

The *cognitive* dimension of religious experience involves believing and knowing. The transcendent elements and ideal demands of religious experience can never be captured in the language of common sense and literal description. But such ordinary discourse can communicate information and generate insight analogically by finding similarities amid differences between the ordinary world and ultimate reality. The Christian faith conveys its central beliefs primarily through the vehicle of spoken and written stories. Myth, parable, testimony, and history constitute the primary languages of religious experience. But religious experience also gives rise to reflective and analytical statements of belief and knowledge. Homilies, catechisms, credal summaries, and theological systems serve to clarify the concepts and apply the meaning of the narrative expressions of religious understanding. Believing is a crucial part, but it is not the whole of religious experience.

The *volitional* dimension of religious experience involves choosing and interacting. Ritual performance and moral endeavor are the active expressions of religious experience. A religious ritual can be defined as a formal pattern of ceremonial acts and oral expressions carried out in a sacred setting. Religious rituals, which range from simple pious gestures to elaborate liturgical dramas, both represent and evoke the transcendent elements and ideal demands of religious experience. Rituals of passage, including baptism and burial, transfigure the crises of life. Rituals of discipline such as prayer and giving alms strengthen the commitment of faith. As for moral striving, a call to righteousness and a concern for justice are inevitable correlates of authentic worship. Active devotion to God cannot be separated from active compassion for others. Volition is an important dimension, but it is not the whole of religious experience.

The *emotional* dimension of religious experience involves trusting and loving. Of course, the whole range of human feelings enters into religious experiences. Joy and sorrow, bliss and despair, calmness and anger, guilt and purity, fear and courage are tonal qualities of the religious life. But the affective depths of religious experience are essentially positive in form and force. The heart of religious experience is often described as a peace that passes all understanding—as a feeling of absolute dependence, or as moments in which we accept ourselves because we feel that we have been accepted by something greater than ourselves. For the Christian faith, these inner feelings of liberation and affirmation usually carry the

179

presumption that they are bestowed from beyond rather than manufactured from within. They are the very impress of the divine on the human heart. Feeling is an important aspect, but it is not the whole of religious experience.

Religious experience within the Christian heritage involves the interplay of intellect, volition, and feeling. At any time or place in personal or social history, one or another of these distinctive modalities of human experience may enjoy preeminence as the dominant expression of religious experience within the Christian faith. But ideally these distinct dimensions of religious experience are held in some kind of dialectical tension: Beliefs shape acts and frame feelings. Acts confirm beliefs and express feelings. Feelings influence beliefs and trigger acts.

Types of Religious Experience. Any attempt to describe religious experience in the Christian heritage is further complicated by theological disagreements over the distinctive character of religious experience. According to many Christian thinkers, religious experience differs from ordinary experience by virtue of the extraordinary object and extraordinary demand encountered in that experience. Religious experience is an encounter with ultimate reality and ideality, and as such it is *sui generis.* Although Christian thinkers have difficulty describing this unique experience, theological characterizations tend to fall into one of three types of religious experience.

The predominant type of religious experience in the Christian tradition is the experience of *sacred power.* For this approach, God cannot be reduced to an abstract principle or a metaphysical structure. God is an active power who is at once terrifying and uplifting. Rudolph Otto has described this primal experience of sacred power with penetrating insight in his classical study, *The Idea of the Holy.* Otto regards the experience of the holy as the root of all religious beliefs and practices. Although this numinous experience is unique, its subjective characteristics can be described. Otto describes it as the emotional response of a creature being "overwhelmed by its own nothingness in contrast to that which is supreme" (10). He further describes this distinctive feeling by the Latin terms *mysterium tremendum* and *mysterium fascinans.* The ultimate mystery of the universe both terrifies and intrigues us. The encounter with God both repels and attracts, filling us with feelings of profound dread and joy. Like the prophet Isaiah in the temple (Isa. 6:1-9), we are both overpowered and undergirded by an experience of power unlike any other power on earth.

A second type of religious experience in the Christian tradition is the experience of *ultimate concern.* For this approach, God is encountered in and through the active concerns of daily living. Paul Tillich has given the definitive analysis of this approach to religious experience in *The Dynamics of Faith.* Tillich defines faith both functionally and substantively as "ultimate concern." Human beings are concerned about many things. They are concerned about physical survival, psychological enjoyment, and mental development. But they also have spiritual concerns that transcend these creaturely needs. These ultimate concerns raise life to the highest pitch of human possibility and fulfillment. Considered subjectively, an experience is religious only if it "is a total and centered act of the personal self, the act of unconditional, infinite and ultimate concern" (8). Viewed objectively, a religious experience is authentic only if it is directed toward the ultimate itself—toward the unconditional ground and integrating center of everything that exists.

A third type of religious experience found in the Christian tradition is the experience of *mystical union*. Unlike the preceding types of religious experience, the mystic's experience of God is radically discontinuous with normal human experience. William James has summarized the form and the content of these unique experiences in his classic study, *The Varieties of Religious Experience*. Mystical experiences are ineffable (they defy description), noetic (they illuminate reality), transient (they occur episodically), and passive (they remain gratuitous). Despite their ineffability and elusiveness, these mystical experiences have been described in a vast and fascinating literature. Christian mystics generally agree that their experience reveals the ultimate unity and perfection of all things. Whatever the being and value of the material world, the soul is of the same stuff as God. The mystical experience itself is interpreted as a foretaste of the heavenly state where believers will enjoy the direct vision and unbroken union with God forever.

In conclusion, the Christian faith exhibits a complex pattern of religious experience. Different theological and liturgical traditions give different weight to the cognitive, performative, and affective modalities of religious experience. These differences, in turn, are often elaborated into distinct types of religious experience. The emotional exuberance of the charismatics, the moral earnestness of the social activists, and the serene discipline of the contemplatives all can be found in the language and literature, the institutions and individuals that make up the church. Indeed, the findings of the Religious Experience Research Unit at Oxford University, which are based on thousands of written accounts of religious experiences by ordinary laypersons, are broken down into at least *ninety-two* categories. Religious experience is a "many-splendored thing," both within as well as beyond the Christian faith.

LONNIE D. KLIEVER

Bibliography

William James, *The Varieties of Religious Experience*.
H. Richard Niebuhr, *Radical Monotheism and Western Culture*.
Rudolph Otto, *The Idea of the Holy*.

Ninian Smart, *The Religious Experience of Mankind,* 3rd ed.
Paul Tillich, *The Dynamics of Faith.*

Cross Reference: Faith, Language–Religious, Mysticism, Popular Religion, Religion, Ritual, Theological Method, Ultimate Concern.

FAITH

In Christian theology, the term "faith" refers to the dynamic and vital stance of the believer's dependence on God. Hence, the term touches the center of Christian life and thought. Naturally, then, expressions such as "the Christian faith" or the "faith of the Church" are used synonymously with that of "faith." But in order to give form to that which is so central and has implications for all facets of life and thought, first it is necessary to provide a succinct definition of faith and then to characterize its relation to other facets of Christian experience.

Fundamentally, faith is a living confidence and trust in God in the experience of knowing God's gracious presence as manifest in Christ. That which has become known has the character of a gift, namely, a reality that one would not have unearthed by oneself but that has come to be present as a sort of miracle, a happening that encompasses but does not seem to be dependent either on one's seeking or on fleeing the divine.

The gift of faith has been variously defined. In the orthodox theologies of the seventeenth century, faith was affirmed by emphasizing the initiative of God apart from the reception of God; that is, God was the all-determining One, and a person's appropriation of God's initiative was secondary. In Protestant liberalism and sometimes in Pietist traditions, the other side of the equation was emphasized. In contrast to faith as a gift, liberals emphasized faith as an individual act of will or as a decision of moral reason. Roman Catholicism, in a more mediational vein, defined faith as the ability to accept the grace or gift by which one is redeemed. Frequently the ability to make the decision was itself declared to be by grace.

These formulations occurred in polemical settings. As is usually the case in such settings, one side is expressed at the expense of the other, or two facets are combined in a "both-and" fashion that does justice to neither. More adequately stated, faith is the gift of God that reflects the believer's confession that in the depths of one's being one knows the foundation and source of one's decision to be of God. Such a decision is authentic because it validates the self precisely as knowing that its source lies somewhere other than in the self. Hence, the priority of God can never be defined apart from the reception or experience of God. The nature of that which has been experienced always points to a source other than the self.

Faith, then, is neither objective nor subjective; it is an interrelation of both, with priority lying on the objective side in God's activity. Once that foundation is affirmed, the experiential or more subjective aspect of faith can be properly focused. The experiential aspect of the faith relation, however, is not identical with general religious experience or with various elaborations of religious experience. In the last two decades, religious experience as a category of living and understanding has gained a new prominence. With the new interest in spirituality and in meditation, both the strengths and the dangers of such an inner orientation are evident. Hence, careful distinctions and qualifications are necessary.

Emotion, reason, and will also converge in religious experience and faith. In various degrees an emotional element is included in religious experience, which cannot be understood only in emotional terms. Facets of reason also are present in religious experience, but the dynamics of faith cannot be understood simply as an exercise of reason. When reason is narrowly defined, faith and reason stand in opposition; when reason is broadly understood, it belongs to the matrix of faith. There also are aspects of decision, sometimes described in terms of the will, in faith. Hence, the mystery that underlies faith does not mean the cancellation of the self, but its redirection; faith is appropriated neither by an act of will nor without the affirmation of the will.

When faith is defined as the movement of the will by which one assents to the church's dogmatic declarations concerning revelation, too great a stress is placed on human capacities. Moreover, that viewpoint removes the vibrant center of faith and substitutes propositional truth as the center. Both Catholic and Protestant theologies of the seventeenth century suffered from such an approach. Nevertheless, there are aspects of knowledge in faith, though they are not adequately described in terms of faith as "true statements." If God encounters one in faith, cognitive elements are included. Just as emotion and will are included in faith, so too is knowledge. The form of knowledge, however, is neither that of objective statements of truth nor that of verifiable, empirical propositions. Nevertheless, one can speak of a "knowledge" that is appropriate in talk about God.

The instinct of liberal theology that reigned in the early decades of the twentieth century was correct in identifying faith with trust. Liberal theology was on dubious grounds when it defined the relation of faith and trust in such a self-evident fashion that it did violence to the mysterious but gracious activity of God, on the basis of which the possibility of trust is predicated. In Christian thought generally, the mystery and miracle of God's love in Christ, confirmed in the heart of the believer by the Holy Spirit, was the basis of trust and confidence that constituted the disposition of the believer who had known and continued to live by the redemptive reality and promise of God, even when it seemed that God did not always appear to be present.

The crux of faith as trust is expressed in the Pauline formulation "justification by faith," a term forcefully recovered by the Reformers, particularly Martin

Luther. For Paul, justification or righteousness (which meant, according to the legal thinking of the time, "put or made right") is the inexplicable mystery of a justice by which God is faithful and merciful in spite of the continuing sin of human beings. To be justified by faith, therefore, is to be considered as having that justice or righteousness that emanates from God, given and known in the reality of faith.

But if one emphasizes the priority of the graciousness of God as the basis of faith, how is one to understand becoming a believer? Many who have been nurtured in the church imperceptibly discover that they are believers, and frequently they do not remember a time when this was not the case. Others become believers in such a dramatic way that even the time is datable and the place identifiable. Most believers are probably found between these possibilities, and they understand faith less in relation to will and growth in grace than in relation to the mystery of having found themselves believers. Hence, we can say that the gospel genuinely confronts us through its declarations, when they resonate in our being, thereby transforming us. The appropriate response of a believer is thanksgiving and praise. An attitude of thanksgiving makes it possible to encompass all attainments and frustrations, good and evil, and also to affirm new possibilities for life. Affirming mystery as the origins of faith, of course, leaves unanswered the question of why some are believers and others are not. It seems best not to speculate about that question, for it leads to affirmations about boundaries that one cannot cross, as speculations on predestination, damnation, and so forth. The most that Luther could say was that the person of faith could only confess that God has a destiny for one.

Standing in the new reality of faith, believers inevitably question what has happened to them and wonder how their experience is to be understood. Being right with God—standing in righteousness before God—can be understood (as with Luther) as having righteousness imputed or ascribed to us as a cloak that covers our sins. Others, such as Wesley, interpreted justification as an actual transformation of the self, so that, in varying degrees, one could speak of the actual righteousness of the believer. Although the first position more adequately guarantees the necessity of justification in every moment of the life of the believer, the second position stresses that faith does make a difference in one's being and how one lives. A difficulty arises, however, when any statement overstresses the righteousness of the believer and thereby threatens the sharp focus on the sole dominance of God's mercy in redemption.

In order to explicate the two sides of this problem, the terms "justification" and "sanctification" became the acceptable terminology in the Reformation period, replacing the question of righteousness. Justification referred to the foundation of the faith of the believer, and sanctification referred to the new life of the believer. Whenever these states were considered successive rather than simultaneous, sanctification became a work of righteousness, thereby creating a new bondage to that which one did. Only when justification and sanctification are affirmed simultaneously can the continued trust in the righteousness of God be held as the freedom by which the believer lives the Christian life. Only then does one's destiny have certitude in God rather than in oneself. At that time the new life in Christ is seen in its proper perspective as the first fruit of faith, not as a situation of achievement or contemplation. Because the Christian is simultaneously saint and sinner, sanctification must, at every turn, be encompassed by justification. For this reason, faith as trust remains the central concept.

The same issue is reiterated in the discussions concerning the relation of faith and works. The traditional polemic against works was not that works were irrelevant but that they could not become determinative for one's relation to God. If one must fulfill conditions prior to faith, even in the minimal sense of a sign of seriousness, one's actions still contribute to one's redemption. Then calculation inevitably enters the scene and psychological uncertainty ensues. Where works are insisted on in the area of faith in a way that indicates that the accent falls upon what is being accomplished, the result is that the gospel becomes a new law. Then false conceptions of sanctification and works coalesce, placing the Christian under the burden of justification by works, turning the Good News into bad news. It is more adequate to speak of "faith not without works" than to speak of "faith and works." The former points to faith as the encompassing reality rather than faith as that to which something else must be added.

Faith, then, is the dynamic center of one's relation to God, a relation anchored in the mysterious work of God. Faith is a center around which all other facets of life and thought revolve. John Calvin has aptly described that center: "We shall have a complete definition of faith, if we say, that it is a steady and certain knowledge of the Divine benevolence towards us, which, being founded on the truth of the gratuitous promise in Christ, is both revealed to our minds, and confirmed to our hearts, by the Holy Spirit" (*Institutes* 2.3.7).

JOHN DILLENBERGER

Bibliography

John Dillenberger, *Contours of Faith.*
Martin Luther, *The Freedom of a Christian.*
Paul Tillich, *The Dynamics of Faith.*

Cross Reference: Experience–Religious, Justification, Liberalism, Sanctification.

FALL (*See* SIN.)

FEMINIST THEOLOGY

Virginia Woolf once wrote that if she were to rewrite history, it would be from the time of the late eighteenth century when the middle-class woman began to write. Woolf's observation is a rich opening into feminist theology: It is, after all, about women writing, about how they have inserted themselves into theology, about theology based on and for women. The observation also suggests the momentousness of the endeavor: that history is changed in the sense of being constituted differently, written differently, and directed differently. But Woolf's particular formulation also reveals the limits and struggles of feminist theology in the nineteenth and twentieth centuries, for it has been, at least in large part, focused through a white, middle-class woman's lens of experience, which is now challenged and changed through the voices of poor women, women of color, ethnic women, and women who claim explicitly their lesbian identity. Even as Woolf's observation is rich in multiple meanings when it is applied to feminist theology, it also suggests that a simple definition of feminist theology is not possible. Yet it is important to identify some of the ways in which, when women write theology, the world begins to appear different.

Aspects of Feminist Theology. One prominent aspect of feminist theology is its critique of patriarchy, of the systematic valuing of men as different from and better than women. Patriarchy is the complex set of values and religious beliefs that runs through society's laws, language, cultural practices, and psychological constructs. For instance, the refusal in a denomination to ordain women (still practiced by the majority of Christians) has to do with the belief that women cannot represent God because a woman's value is not as high as a man's. This belief manifests itself in requirements for ordination and religious leadership, in limiting women to roles of support in church institutions, in psychological constructs in which women feel inferior to men and men superior to women, and in images of God as patriarch and religious belief systems that equate divinity with maleness and maleness with divinity. Feminist theology resists patriarchy as a comprehensive system of personal and political oppression, including all the specific capillaries of patriarchal power: ordination practices, linguistic practices, cultural assumptions, personal beliefs.

Yet feminist theology is not a "mere" critique of an erroneous patriarchal system. A second aspect of feminist theology is that it serves to clear a space for women writing about their experiences and especially their spirituality. In 1960 Valerie Saiving wrote "The Human Situation: A Feminine View," in which she criticized Reinhold Niebuhr and Anders Nygren for identifying sin universally with self-assertion and love with selflessness, arguing that such forms of sin were based not on human experience but on man's experience. In the space cleared by her criticism, Saiving probed the nature of woman's experience as different from man's and the need for theology to reflect upon the experience of woman. Rosemary Radford Ruether, the first feminist theologian to produce a complete systematic theology based on women's experience, lists the dimensions of women's experience as the bodily experience of women, the devaluation of the body by patriarchy (where, for example, menstruation is stain), the negation and trivialization of women in patriarchy, but also the grace-filled experiences of women affirming themselves. The focus on women's experience has opened up the resources of feminist spirituality, which, as Sally Purvis has noted, is based on feminist experience as characterized by inclusivity, connectedness, embodiment, and liberation.

A third aspect of feminist theology entails a new vision both of Christian practice and of human flourishing. Perhaps because patriarchy is so fundamental to how we experience and structure the world, feminist theology must necessarily go to the foundations of this structure and begin to transform all the implications of how it is to be human. Thus feminist theology questions how theology is undertaken and what it is undertaken for, including how the Bible is read and how it functions in Christian praxis. Indeed, feminist theology insists that Christianity is a praxis, a way of acting, of doing and being in the world. And certainly the resources in feminist theology are applied in multiple ways to the images, metaphors, structures, and possibilities of what it is to be human. Among new forms of cultural critique, feminist theology is a significant movement, offering not only the critique of various systems of sin and death but also images and visions of new forms of planetary, including human, flourishing.

These three aspects—the critique of patriarchy, the speaking of women's experience, and the transformative discourse of Christianity and culture—serve as an umbrella for the diverse and rich works and events that go under the term "feminist theology." It must be noted, at this point, that these three aspects of feminist theology not only cover the recent works (those since Saiving's article in 1960) but also include the first wave of feminist theology occurring in the suffragemovement. From 1860 to 1920, women such as Elizabeth Cady Stanton and Susan B. Anthony criticized patriarchy in relation to electoral politics, ordination of women, and divorce legislation; and they wrote of women's experience in terms of their relationships, their experiences of marriage and divorce, their spirituality, and their personal feelings and actions in relation to topics as diverse as restrictive hoop skirts, educational practices, and the ways scripture was interpreted. Like feminist theology of the present, suffrage theology struggled to be aware of its own differences in the voices of black women and in the experiences of northern and southern women.

Topics of Feminist Theology. Feminist theology has continually tried to address a wide variety of cultural, structural, and religious topics in Christianity and in American society. Indeed, the wealth of topics addressed by feminist theology suggests that feminist theology is not only a "topical" theology, and thus for women only, but a theological approach that brings a formal and material understanding of Christian praxis to bear and that offers to all a fresh expression of how God acts within the world. What follows is a brief delineation of four of the

187

basic topics that frequently appear in feminist theology: scripture and tradition, anthropology, symbols, and ethics.

Scripture and Tradition. Stanton and other early suffragists argued that scripture was key to women's oppression in Christianity and in American culture. Furthermore, Stanton contended that feminism could have no significant power in this country if it failed to address what scripture said and how scripture was used against women. In this vein, an enormous amount of scholarship has been devoted to scripture in at least three areas. First of all, feminist scholars have paid a great deal of attention to carefully reading what the scriptures say about women and how the scriptures have been used against women. The lens of feminist theology and the power of women's faith experience have provoked the careful focusing on patriarchal translations, as when Phoebe's title *diakonos* is translated "deaconess" or "servant" when it is applied to her, and "minister" or "deacon" when it is used to describe a male leader. Likewise feminist theology examines patriarchal interpretations (as when Eve is simply blamed for sin rather than noted for enabling Adam, the generic human, to become a particular man) and patriarchal oversights (as when the Samaritan woman in John 4 is not the focus of the call to mission or when the rape of a woman in Judges 19 is ignored or belittled in commentaries).

The second dimension of feminist interpretation of the Bible concentrates on forgotten or largely ignored women of the scriptures, such as Shiphar, Hagar, Nympha of Laodicea, and Prisca. One of the most exciting areas in feminist theology has focused on forgotten or ignored women, both exceptional women who were able to produce but also women who left traces, or were part of movements, whose lives of sainthood spawned testimonies for survival and hope.

The third dimension has to do with the authority of the Bible, how it comes to be used against women as a tool of oppression and how it might be used as a resource in feminist theology as a tool of emancipation. Elisabeth Schüssler Fiorenza suggests that the Bible should be understood as "prototype," engendering possibilities of creative transformation, rather than as "archetype," containing eternal or ontological truths that apply to any and all situations. For instance, biblical teachings about women keeping silence in the church should be seen as a pastoral-theological practice the church used to address a particular situation, not as an eternal rule for all Christian practice at all times everywhere. Such a turn to reading the Bible as prototype allows us to appreciate how the Bible itself was formed in practical situations in the church and models for us some ways the early Christians attempted to live their faith out in the church and in the culture.

Similar areas in the study of historical theology have arisen as feminists investigate how theology has been used to oppress women and the ways in which it might be a resource for feminist theology. What the dominant theological tradition has said about women has occasioned much work for feminist theologians, who have pointed out the discrepancies between such sayings and other theological sayings that would call into question misogynist passages and practices. Certainly the authority of tradition has also been a question for feminist theologians, with a variety of answers that range from those that re-center authority to the authority of the future and its open possibilities for women (e.g., the work of Peggy Way) to the authority of partnership between men and women (e.g., the work of Letty Russell) to those that reconstruct the authority of tradition by interpreting theology through the interests of women (e.g., the work of Elisabeth Schüssler Fiorenza). Feminist theologians have also wanted to move beyond the rigid limits of patriarchal-defined tradition and to explore traditions of goddess religion, Gnosticism, and current post-Christian movements of spirituality. Christine Downing's work explores the classical Greek myths of sisterhood and friendship and provides new sources in such new definitions of tradition.

Anthropology. Since patriarchy, at least in Western Christianity, has been constructed through the notion that men and women are fundamentally different ways or forms of being human, feminist theologians have carefully deconstructed modern anthropology. Feminist theologians have used the position of the marginality of women to examine the basic tenets of modern anthropological constructs: that man is individual, autonomous, and disembodied. In this construct, woman is seen as inferior and as "other" because she represents all the lesser values such as relationality, interdependence, and embodiment. Feminist theology considers a new anthropology built upon these "lesser" values, arguing that humans are all relational, interdependent, and embodied. The denial of these values configures sin as the oppression of others, the usurpation of power, and the dehumanization of others. Indeed, many feminist theologians contend that anyimage of human flourishing must consider what it means to be relational, embodied, and interdependent.

Symbols. Central to any theology is reflection on and construction of basic symbols such as Christology, God, sin, salvation, ecclesiology. One of the most complex symbols has been Christology, with some feminist theologians focusing on the maleness of Jesus and others insisting on the priority of Christ's power, while still others stress the relations between ecclesiology and Christology. Accordingly, new christological images have arisen such as Jacqueline Grant's black woman Jesus. Ecclesiology, perhaps because of the power of women-church, by which is meant the redemptive community of men and women seeking the transformation of patriarchy, receives a great deal of attention in feminist theology. Ecclesiology as formed through women-church has been interpreted as *ekklesia*, the community of equals, and, in the work of Rosemary Radford Ruether, is interpreted as the true church in which the Spirit of God moves. In relation to ecclesiology, the symbol of God's Word in the work of Rebecca Chopp has been reinterpreted to name women's experience of gaining the power to speak and to write their lives on their own terms. Such reconstructions, at least upon first reading, often do not seem to fit the normal reinterpretation of symbols; but that is the point for Christian feminist theologians, who contend that the traditional construction of symbols such as God, Christ, and sin have served as the legitimation of patriarchy.

Ethics. Central to almost all feminist theology is a concern for ethics, as this relates to claims of justice, the nature of ethics, and specific ethical topics. Feminists opposing the injustice and inequities of patriarchy pay specific attention to theories of justice and visions of the just community. As feminists have probed the resources and limits of modern ethical theory, they have also come to question the nature and self-imposed limits of ethical theory, especially criticizing the well-accepted separation of the public and private and of the political and the personal in modern ethical theory. In the midst of rethinking the meaning of justice and the nature of ethics itself, feminist theologians have reached out to address countless ethical topics, including violence against women, racism, anti-Semitism, environmental destruction, and abortion.

Types of Feminist Theology. Feminist theology is more appropriately termed "feminist theologies," for the concerns, issues, and topics addressed vary widely, as does the focus of attention and perspective. A typology of four approaches can help display variety, yet such a typology must be understood as only heuristically helpful, since feminists will employ various approaches on different issues or will seek to combine several features of different approaches.

1. In *liberal egalitarianism* the focus is on the equality of women, and great faith is put in Western Enlightenment claims of equality, freedom, and liberty to bring about the fully equal church or society. The assumption is that nothing is wrong, in essence, with the ideas and principles of society: in fact, better application of the ideas of equality, freedom, and liberty will bring about a just and equal social order. Feminists use this perspective to argue for the ordination of women and to correct the Christian symbol structure by including feminine symbols of God under the notion that God can be equally represented by male and female.

2. Romantic expressivist describes the second type, which concentrates on the particularity and uniqueness of women's voices, expressing what women will bring to society given women's full participation in society. This perspective assumes that women experience and speak quite differently from the way men do, and a harmonious balance will occur if men and women can each fully represent their particularities. Questions of women's particular spirituality or the unique gifts women bring to the church receive great attention.

3. Sectarian separateness focuses on the assumption that patriarchal structures are incapable of change. This type tends to concentrate on separate spaces for women, a separate feminist religion, and separate communities. Only within such separation can women live in purity, untouched by the stains of patriarchy. A profound, radical critique can be mounted against patriarchy with this position, and deep explorations into women's experiences and women's visions of their lives are offered in this position.

4. Feminist theology can take the perspective of the *radical transformist,* who tends to focus on how women's marginal opposition in society can help to criticize and transform the social order, the assumption being that only radical transformation of personal, linguistic, cultural, and political structures will allow human, let alone other planetary, flourishing. In this perspective, feminists tend to combine the resources of psychoanalysis, political theory, philosophy, linguistic theory, and theology to resist the present structures of the specific values placed on men's and women's lives. In this complex, multi-disciplinary perspective, feminists also resist the gendered limits placed on social forms, such as the limits of knowledge as identified through male values of autonomy and objectivity or through the modern ridiculing of emotion as female. Feminists who employ the perspective of the radical transformist tend to emphasize the need for forming new visions of being human and new visions of the social order.

Conclusion. Feminist theology questions the fundamental bases of modern life: the gender differential of who we are, how we act, who God is, and how we structure our lives. In the midst of this critique, feminist theology is a source of genuine renewal and hope, for the power of women writing, even beyond what Woolf indicated, is the power to change history.

REBECCA S. CHOPP

Bibliography

Rebecca S. Chopp, *The Power to Speak: Feminism, Language, God.*
Jacquelyn Grant, *White Women's Christ and Black Women's Jesus: Feminist Christology and Womanist Response.*
Sally Purvis, "Christian Feminist Spirituality," in *Christian Spirituality: Post-Reformation and Modern,* ed. Louis Dupré and Don Saliers.
Rosemary Radford Ruether, *Sexism and God-Talk: Toward a Feminist Theology.*
Elisabeth Schüssler Fiorenza, *Bread Not Stone: The Challenge of Feminist Biblical Interpretation.*

Cross Reference: Deconstructionism, Ethics–Christian, Justice, Liberation Theology, Praxis, Womanist Theology.

FORGIVENESS (*See* GRACE.)

FREEDOM

The fall of the Berlin Wall on November 9, 1989, and the collapse of Communist oppression in the countries of the so-called Eastern bloc have focused

191

attention at the end of the century on the ever-widening potential for freedom throughout the world. Whether in South Africa, Central America, or the Philippines, the advance of freedom is fundamental to becoming human. Although these events mark a great moment for political freedom, food shortages, ethnic unrest, and economic collapse remain threats against it in the newly freed countries. Where political freedom nears, new forces of captivity also draw near. So the price of freedom is still eternal vigilance.

The Western view of freedom derives from the two principal strands of our tradition—the Jewish strand, emphasizing socio-political structures, and the Greco-Roman strand, stressing personal attitudes. The notion of freedom that originated in the Greco-Roman world eventually began to overshadow the Hebrew dynamics of freedom. The struggle in the church today is over which strand will determine future understandings and expressions of freedom.

In Socrates (470–399 B.C.E.) and Plato (427–347 B.C.E.), the concern for freedom was related to fate. Later, in Aristotle (384–322 B.C.E.), freedom is seen against the foil of despotism, and the state stands out as the community of the free over against the slaves. The Stoa sublimates political freedom while simultaneously legitimating actual slavery by a perceived ontological structure. Freedom was thus located in an inner realm where persons could live out what they really wanted to be. An ideal figure like Socrates came to be seen as even triumphing over the fear of death.

In the Hebrew scriptures there is no exact equivalent to the Greek word *eleutheria* (freedom), which is so common in the New Testament. The Hebrew scriptures speak of freedom only as "liberation" for the future in an open process (Hans-Werner Bartsch). The New Testament continues this strand of thought (*see* Luke 4:18f.), but it adds the mode of liberation through Jesus Christ (John 8:36) and the more personal freedom beyond the misused covenant law (Gal. 5:1-14).

Freedom on the Bright Side of History. The recent North American Protestant debate over freedom has been strongly influenced by the way neoorthodox theologians sought to correct overly optimistic views of the social gospel. They usually crafted a finely honed balance between human history and natural history, as is illustrated in Reinhold Niebuhr's statement that "both human and natural history enter into the formation of events, in that both the free actions of men and natural necessities are involved." Arguments derived from this premise became fairly complex in a number of theologians. The bottom line was that human beings have the freedom to impose their will and their ends on nature. They can follow the flux of events and grasp basic patterns. They can also lift themselves above the immediacies of the configurations of nature and offer goals that do not appear in nature as such. This freedom, however, is ultimately hidden and will be grasped by individuals only introspectively. Scientific accounts cannot bear it out. So we end up with introspective evidence among those "who know that they make free and responsible decisions" (Niebuhr). Freedom here is grasped, as in the Stoa, from an inner sanctuary of freedom, although the social freedoms of our democracies are realistically dealt with. Unfortunately, at the end of this line of thought we often find freedom merely as freedom for unlimited consumption.

Orientation points for grasping freedom are always found between a metaphysical ground of freedom and its merely societal function as ethical choice. Some process thinkers have offered new solutions by looking at the fabric of nature itself, especially as to the coordination of the metaphysical ground of freedom and divine omnipotence. Charles Hartshorne claims, "Our having at least some freedom is not an absolute exception to an otherwise total lack of freedom in nature, but a special intensified form of a *general principle* pervasive of reality, down to the very atoms and still further." Here an ontological ground of freedom in nature itself accounts for freedom overriding fate.

All the reflections on freedom remain, however, within the Greek framework of *theoria,* a vision of the character of the human being from the inside, especially among those who enjoy the privileges of freedom on the bright side of history. All honest attempts to be biblical in conceiving of freedom notwithstanding, an important social location has usually been left out.

Freedom on the Underside of History. The North American view of freedom today cannot be grasped apart from the civil rights struggle of the 1960s. It overturned much individualistic thinking about inner freedom by championing concrete freedom. As James H. Cone has stated, "In the moment of liberation, there are no universal truths; there is only the truth of liberation itself, which the oppressed define in the struggle for freedom." Here freedom can be grasped only in the struggle against the condition of enslavement. We actually have to become one with the oppressed, "making their cause our cause by involving ourselves in the liberation struggle."

Here freedom is no longer being grasped in abstraction from the real world around us. The Greco-Roman view gives way to the predominantly Hebrew view of liberation. We are free only as we relate to the conditions of oppression and battle them. In fact, our private freedoms (e.g., economic freedom, our "right" to consume, where not even the sky, in the destruction of its ozone layer, is the limit) are largely enslavements and often contribute to the oppression of others. True freedom is thus a communal affair in which we increasingly include others in the justice of earthly welfare and of the life to come. Authentic freedom expresses itself not in private weal, but in commonweal. It is manifest not as "freedom as theory," but as "freedom as praxis" in solidarity with others. Absolute self-determination produces absolute oppression. So freedom needs to be linked to God's plan of salvation (Gustavo Gutiérrez).

Analogia liberationis. The issue of freedom finally comes down to the question of the image of God. For theological liberalism, freedom itself is often viewed as characterizing the human being as image of God *(imago Dei)*. But it is questionable whether it makes sense to talk about any likeness of God in the human being as such. The image of God so-called might lack our ability to transcend ourselves and the world, "to look at both, and to see [ourselves] in perspective as the center in which all parts of the world converge" (Paul Tillich). We need to consider the weight of sin.

True freedom is not grounded in ourselves as center, but in the process of freeing, which originates beyond ourselves and draws us into ever-widening circles of accountability. Here the women's liberation movement makes the new view of freedom irreversible (Rosemary Radford Ruether). In the end there is no freedom without justice. Freedom is not primarily grasped in introspection in terms of self-mirroring. Freedom emerges time and again in what happens *to* us, to others, and to all creation from the "outside" in an overpowering dynamics of justice. We are invited to participate in what is already going on in the freeing power of God's work of liberation, establishing justice in creation. We can freely choose justice, in analogy to God's liberating work. The character of being human is thus grasped in an *analogia liberationis*.

FREDERICK HERZOG

Bibliography

James H. Cone, *A Black Theology of Liberation.*
Gustavo Gutiérrez, *A Theology of Liberation.*
Charles Hartshorne, *Omnipotence and Other Theological Mistakes.*
Rosemary Radford Ruether, *Sexism and God-Talk.*

Cross Reference: Feminist Theology, Justice, Liberation Theology, Neoorthodoxy, Process Theology, Social Gospel.

FUNDAMENTAL THEOLOGY (*See* DOGMATIC THEOLOGY.)

FUNDAMENTALISM

In America fundamentalism is a movement within Protestantism that was organized immediately after World War I in opposition to "modernism," which included liberal theology primarily, and also Darwinism and secularism. A subgroup of evangelicalism, fundamentalism staunchly affirmed with evangelicals "fundamentals of the faith," including the deity of Christ, his virgin birth, his bodily resurrection, and his substitutionary atonement. What distinguishes fundamentalists from other evangelicals is their strident opposition to modernism. They are, to quote George Marsden, "militant anti-modernist evangelicals."

The two chief pillars of fundamentalist theology that reflect this movement's primary concern with anti-modernism are biblical inerrancy and dispensationalism. The modern doctrine of inerrancy was most thoroughly developed by Presbyterian conservatives at Princeton Theological Seminary in the late nineteenth century as an anti-modernist response to "higher criticism," a socio-historical approach to the Bible advocated by theological liberals. Central to fundamentalist theology from the movement's inception, inerrancy holds that the Bible is the Word of God, in the sense that it is the infallible product of the Holy Spirit's guidance. This infallibility, or inerrancy, applies to the entire scriptural record; there are no errors of any sort in the Bible. For fundamentalists the inerrant Bible stands alone on all matters as the final authority. Fundamentalists assert that the Bible "means what it says" and must therefore be read "literally." Strongly tied to biblical inerrancy is dispensationalism. This eschatological system was brought to America in the 1860s and 1870s by John Nelson Darby and was promoted through a series of prophecy conferences in the following decades. Out of these conferences came much of the leadership of the early fundamentalist movement, and as the years went by dispensationalism became increasingly interwoven with fundamentalism. Dispensationalism is theologically anti-modernist both in its hyperliteral approach to the Bible and in its view of history as shaped by supernatural forces, a view at odds with the tendency in liberal theology to minimize the distinction between the natural and the supernatural. Moreover, dispensationalism informs fundamentalists that the modern institutional church is increasingly untrue to the Christian faith, and that modern civilization is corrupt and growing more corrupt.

But fundamentalism is not simply or strictly an anti-modernist theology. Fundamentalism in the United States is a religious movement, and what finally distinguishes fundamentalists from their fellow evangelicals (the line here is admittedly blurred) is the active and strident militancy of their anti-modernism. From the very beginning of the movement, when the World's Christian Fundamentals Association was created in 1919, this militancy has been evident. Unhappy with what they saw as apostasy in the American church and decay in American civilization, these fundamentalists organized crusades to rid Protestant denominations of modernist theology and the public schools of evolutionist teaching. It was a monumental and well-publicized campaign, led by such worthy fundamentalist combatants as William Bell Riley and J. Gresham Machen. But the crusades failed. By the end of the 1920s, fundamentalism was in retreat. Its advocates were powerless minorities in the Northern Baptist and the Northern Presbyterian denominations, where the struggle for control had been the fiercest. Moreover, the anti-evolutionist movement, though having had some successes, sputtered and stalled.

Contrary to what many observers concluded, defeat at the national level did not mean the demise of American fundamentalism. Instead, in the 1930s and 1940s fundamentalists successfully organized at the local or congregational level. The success of grassroots fundamentalism in these years was due in great measure to a rapidly expanding network of nondenominational organizations, which included publishing houses, mission boards, and radio stations. At the center of this fundamentalist support structure were the approximately seventy Bible institutes that dotted the country. These schools, the most prominent of which was Moody Bible Institute, served as denominational surrogates, providing nearby fundamentalist churches with ministers, teaching materials, Bible conferences, church secretaries, and a host of other services.

Flourishing at the grassroots level, fundamentalism by the 1940s had reemerged on the national scene. In that decade not only did fundamentalists use radio to bring the gospel to the masses, but also they created national evangelistic organizations such as Youth for Christ, from whose ranks came Billy Graham. But this emphasis on national revival, as opposed to anti-modernist crusades, exacerbated tensions within American fundamentalism. Many fundamentalists had responded to the debacle of the 1920s by embracing the notion of "separation," adding to their doctrinal requirements a refusal to cooperate with those who did not entirely share their views. For this group of fundamentalists, militant separation was now a test of orthodoxy. But in the 1940s and 1950s a group of moderate (and often younger) fundamentalists emerged who rejected both extreme separatism and the emphasis on dispensationalism. To the militants, such compromises were anathema. When the dispute exploded into open conflict in the mid-1950s, the focal point of the fighting was Billy Graham, whose willingness to work with nonfundamentalists in organizing evangelistic crusades represented to the separatists everything that was wrong with the moderates. By the latter half of the 1950s, the fundamentalist movement had divided into (1) those who called themselves "new evangelicals," or simply "evangelicals," and who formed associations with evangelicals outside the fundamentalist tradition, and (2) militant separatists who defiantly retained the fundamentalist label.

For the next two decades separatist fundamentalists maintained a low profile, eschewing national activities for local church-building and evangelizing. But in the late 1970s and 1980s, fundamentalism made a dramatic reappearance on the national scene. Fundamentalism had always been associated with patriotism, militarism, and free-market economics; in post-Vietnam, post-Watergate America such sentiments were definitely in vogue, and politically energized fundamentalists played an important and quite visible role in the resurgence of the religious and political right. As might be expected, fundamentalists framed their political involvement in religious and moral terms. The most prominent manifestation of fundamentalist politics was the Reverend Jerry Falwell's Moral Majority. Created in 1979 with the goal of electing to public office "pro-life, pro-family, and pro-America" candidates, Moral Majority was quite active in the election and re-election of Ronald Reagan, as well as in countless congressional, state, and local races. Many fundamentalists also became involved in the 1988 presidential campaign of Pat Robertson, whose emphasis on returning America to its moral moorings permitted fundamentalists to overlook the televangelist's charismatic beliefs.

Besides electoral politics, fundamentalists became involved in an array of related issues. In response to the emergent feminist and gay and lesbian movements, fundamentalists actively worked against gay rights, the Equal Rights Amendment, and, perhaps most important, abortion rights. Remarkably, the "right to life" effort led formerly inactive fundamentalists to engage in lobbying, picketing, and on occasion, civil disobedience. Fundamentalists also became involved in what they saw as the rapid and dangerous spread of secularism in the public schools. Hence, they worked on behalf of school prayer and, returning to an old issue, equal time for "creation science" in the public schools. More in keeping with the separatist side of their heritage, fundamentalists also created thousands of alternative schools for their children, schools for which they sought tax support and freedom from government regulation.

Activist fundamentalists were attacked by some of their number for violating the principle of militant separatism by cooperating with nonfundamentalists, including Catholics and evangelicals. Working together to implement a right-wing political agenda also contributed to the narrowing of the gap between moderate fundamentalists and conservative evangelicals. One clear indication that the line between the two groups was blurring was the increased emphasis among many evangelicals on a traditional fundamentalist touchstone: the inerrancy of the Bible. In the Southern Baptist Convention (SBC), for example, conservative evangelicals and fundamentalists joined to capture the levers of denominational power; controlling these, they began to purge the leadership of SBC agencies and seminaries of non-inerrantist moderates. As in the 1920s, fundamentalists have sparked controversy and schism in a leading Protestant denomination, but in this instance they are winning the fight.

Fundamentalists will not be disappearing from the American scene any time soon. And while nonfundamentalist theologians tend to find fundamentalist theology, particularly dispensationalism and inerrancy, to be, at best, terribly problematic, fundamentalist theology must be taken seriously, if for no other reason than its obvious popular appeal. Many believers find compelling fundamentalism's high view of scripture and its emphasis on a clear distinction between the natural and the supernatural. Moreover, fundamentalism's anti-modernist impulse, though perhaps manifested in a questionable and inconsistent fashion, is a cogent challenge to theologies more enamored of modernity.

WILLIAM VANCE TROLLINGER, JR.

Bibliography

Nancy Tatom Ammerman, *Bible Believers: Fundamentalists in the Modern World.*

Kathleen C. Boone, *The Bible Tells Them So: The Discourse of Protestant Fundamentalism.*

George M. Marsden, *Fundamentalism and American Culture: The Shaping of Twentieth-Century Evangelicalism: 1870–1925.*

Ernest Sandeen, *The Roots of Fundamentalism: British and American Millenarianism, 1800–1930.*

Timothy P. Weber, *Living in the Shadow of the Second Coming: American Premillennialism, 1875–1982.*

Cross Reference: Atonement, Creation Science, Dispensationalism, Evangelicalism, Inerrancy, Liberalism, Miracles, Resurrection.

FUTURE (*See* Eschatology, Hope, Time.)

GOD

The idea of God is at once the most important and yet the most questionable of all religious doctrines or "symbols" in Western culture. This idea or symbol points to the central object of both Christian and Jewish faiths, the sole "subject" of their revelation, and the final principle of both reality and meaning throughout human existence. Nevertheless, of all concepts in modern cultural life—and in varying degrees for "believers" and "doubters" alike—the idea of God remains the most elusive, the most frequently challenged, the most persistently criticized and negated of all important convictions. Is there a God? Can such a One be experienced, known, or spoken of? Is such experience testable, such knowledge verifiable, and such speech meaningful? Or is all such experience illusory, such seeming knowledge in fact a projection, such speech empty? These issues are foundational for philosophy of religion, philosophical theology, and confessional theology alike.

Almost every dominant motif and movement in modernity—its expanding scientific inquiry, its emphasis on what is natural, experienced, and verifiable, its persistent search for the greater well-being of humans in this world, its increasing emphasis on autonomy and on present satisfactions—has progressively challenged the concept of God and unsettled both its significance and its certainty. This challenge has come on two fronts: (1) The traditional concepts of God, inherited from the premodern cultures of medieval, Renaissance, and Reformation Europe, in revealing themselves in almost every aspect to have anachronistic elements and to be unintelligible in the light of modern knowledge and modern attitudes toward reality, have in consequence had to be fundamentally reformulated. (2) More important, the very possibility of an idea of God, its knowability, its coherence, and its meaning, has been questioned; to much of modernity such an idea is on a number of grounds impossible, and as a consequence, the whole enterprise of a theistic religion appears as a futile, expensive, and even harmful activity.

Because of this second point, the main perplexity connected with the symbol of God has in modern times differed noticeably from earlier perplexities. Our fundamental questions in religious reflection are not about the *nature* of the divine and the *character* of God's activity or will toward us, which represented the main questions of an earlier time. The questions now are the *possibility* of God's existence in a seemingly naturalistic world, the *possibility* of valid knowledge of God and meaningful discourse about God, and the *possibility* of any sort of "religious" existence, style of life, or hope at all. As a result, the efforts of religious thinkers in our century have by and large been directed at these two interrelated problems: (1) a justification of the meaning and the validity of the concept of God in relation to other, apparently less questionable forms of experience—scientific, philosophical, social, political, artistic, psychological, or existentialist; and (2) a reformulation of that concept so that it can be meaningful and relevant to the modern world.

Despite the new and sharper edge to the question of God in modern times, certain continuing issues characteristic of the traditional discussion of this concept also have been present, albeit in specifically modern form. In the concept of God, as in the reality experienced in religious existence, dialectical tensions have appeared and reappeared as paradoxes and polarities at the heart of theological discussion. These perennial problems *internal* to the concept of God (whether orthodox or reformulated) also characterize modern discussions and manifest themselves with each option characteristic of modern theology and philosophy of religion.

The General Idea of God. In Western culture, dominated as it has been by the Jewish and the Christian traditions, the word or symbol "God" has generally referred to one supreme or holy being, the unity of ultimate reality and ultimate goodness. So conceived, God is believed to have created the entire universe, to rule over it, and to intend to bring it to its fulfillment or realization, to "save" it. Thus, as a functioning word in our own cultural world, "God" in the first instance refers to the central and sole object of religious existence—commitment, devotion, dependence, fear, trust, love, and belief—and to the center of worship, prayer, and religious meditation. Secondarily, "God" has been the object of religious and philosophical reflection, the supreme object of theology and of most (though not all) forms of speculative metaphysics.

So understood, God represents a puzzling and elusive notion by no means easy to define, as the traditions of Jewish, Christian, and Islamic religious thought have clearly recognized. As the supreme being or ground of being, the Creator and ruler of all, God transcends (exceeds or goes beyond) all creaturely limits and distinctions. As Creator of time and space, God is not *in* either time or space as is all else; as the source of all finite realities and their interrelations, God is transcendent to all experienced substances, causes, and ordinary relations; as that on which all depends, God is neither essentially dependent on nor a mere effect of other things. Thus, deity can hardly be spoken of as simply "a being" among other beings, changeable as is all else, dependent and vulnerable as is every creature, and mortal as is all life; otherwise, the divine would be a mere contingent creature and thus not "God." For these reasons, the concept of God inevitably tends toward that of the transcendent absolute of much speculative philosophy: necessary, impersonal, unrelated, independent, changeless, eternal.

On the other hand, God in Jewish and Christian witness, piety, and experience is also in some way personal, righteous, and caring for the individual and social welfare of all persons. The reflective problems in this concept of God, illustrated by debates throughout Western history, therefore have a dual source: in the fact that God, however described, is *unlike* ordinary things of which we can easily and clearly speak, and in the fact that inherent in the religious reality itself and in its reflected concepts are certain dialectical tensions or paradoxes—absolute-related, impersonal-personal, eternal-temporal, changeless-changing, actual yet potential, self-sufficient or necessary and yet in some manner dependent. Such dialectical tensions stretch, if they do not defy, our ordinary powers of speech, definition, and precise comprehension. Yet regardless of the way in which one may approach the divine—whether religiously or philosophically—one first encounters "mystery." This encounter also generates, among other things, special procedures and special forms or rules of speech—a characteristic as old as religion itself.

Biblical and Early Christian Concepts of God. The origins of this understanding of God lie in the Hebrew and Christian religious traditions, especially in their sacred scriptures. In the Hebrew scriptures, God or Yahweh is "undeniably" one and transcendent to all the limited and special forces and powers of our experience of nature, society, or self. Yahweh's central characteristic is a concern for and relation to history, especially to a particular people in history—Israel. Although God manifests power and glory throughout the vast scope of nature, the main arena for the divine "works" is the particular sequence of historical events related to the calling, establishment, nurture, and protection of the chosen people. In this activity in history, God is revealed as a righteous God, the source of the law, and quick to punish those, even chosen ones, who defy this law. Yahweh is, however, also a God of mercy, patience, faithfulness, and grace, since according to the prophets, despite Israel's obvious unworthiness and continued betrayal of the covenant with God, God promises to redeem Israel in the future. This God of history, covenant, judgment, and promised redemption is throughout assumed to be, and often clearly affirmed to be, the ruler of all events. Finally, by inevitable implication, this sovereign lord of history is seen to be also the creator and ruler of the entire cosmos.

These themes in the notion of God are continued and modified in the New Testament: God is one God—Creator and Redeemer—a God concerned with history, judgment, and redemption. In continuity with and contrast to the revealed Yahweh, the central manifestation of the New Testament's God shifts from the notion of God as interactive director of history's events to that of the living God of Abraham, Isaac, Jacob, and Jesus of Nazareth, through whom the divine righteous and loving will for human beings is revealed, the divine judgments made known, the divine power to save even from death effected, and in whose speedy return God's sovereignty over all creation will be fully and visibly established. The presence of God is now perceived less in the temple and in the law, becoming known primarily in the Spirit, who dwells in the minds and hearts, witness and hopes of the Christian community. Consequently, a new set of Christian symbols appears, helping to define "God" not only as Creator and Redeemer but also as Son and Logos, and supplementing the symbols of divine activity (e.g., covenant, law, and messianic promise) with newly perceived divine actions (e.g., incarnation, atonement, Holy Spirit, parousia, and, as a summation of these "new" concepts, Trinity).

During the crucial formative centuries of Christianity, the dominant intellectual inheritance through which Western life understood itself and its world was that of Greco-Roman philosophy. During this long period, the biblical notion of God was given its main conceptual shape with the help first of Platonism and Stoicism and then, during the High Middle Ages, of Aristotelianism. The transcendent and absolute aspects or implications of the biblical creator and ruler were, in the developing conception of God from 150 c.e. to 400 c.e., enlarged and extended: God became eternal in the sense of utterly nontemporal, necessary in the sense of absolute noncontingency, self-sufficient in the sense of absolute independence, changeless in the sense of participating in and relating to no change, purely spiritual instead of in any fashion material, unaffected by and thus seemingly unrelated and even unrelatable to the world. The patristic notion of God as absolute depended not only on Hellenistic philosophy, whose categories formed its expression; it also stemmed from the character of patristic piety, which emphasized (as did most Hellenistic spirituality) the victory of the incorruptible, immortal, and changeless principle of deity over the corruptible, mortal, and passing character of creaturely life.

Reformation and Modern Concepts of God. Although with the Reformation the philosophical or metaphysical definition of God as absolute, changeless, and eternal radically receded in prominence in theology, the same problems remained. The "ontological" concepts of self-sufficiency and eternity continued, but what came to determine the shape of the doctrine of God in each Reformer was the center of Reformation piety or religion—namely, the new emphasis on the priority and sole sovereignty of divine grace in redemption, on the utter unworthiness and inactivity of the recipient of grace, and finally on the absolute priority and decisiveness of divine election. In contrast to the dominant metaphysical characterization of God by patristic and medieval theologians, then, the principal Reformers (Luther, Calvin, Zwingli, et al.) conceived of God centrally through personal rather than metaphysical categories: as almighty or sovereign power, as righteous or holy will, as gracious and reconciling love.

Nonetheless, for primarily religious rather than metaphysical reasons, Reformation theologians also confronted and expressed the same paradox tending toward contradiction: an eternal, hidden, and yet all-sovereign divine electing will on the one hand, and the affirmation of the presence and activity of God in relation to a real and not sham sequence of historical events and of human decisions on the other hand. Although it was Calvin especially who drew out most clearly the implications of this new paradox based on Reformation piety rather than on traditional philosophy, this paradox is evident in and fundamental for the theologies of Luther and Zwingli as well.

At the start of the post-Reformation period, there were two dominant conceptions of God, one Catholic and the other Protestant. They differed markedly in the categories with which God was described; yet to our twentieth-century eyes they exhibited the same paradoxical (not to say contradictory) character: the Catholic conception of an absolute, purely actual, changeless being "illegitimately" (so to speak) related to the world, and the Protestant conception of an eternal, sovereign, divine will ordaining and effecting all temporal events from eternity, thus again "illegitimately" related and even responsive to historical crises and human needs. Understandably, subsequent modern reflection on the issue of God, at least since the seventeenth century, has been largely constituted by sustained philosophical and theological criticism of these two inherited conceptions, and thence characterized either by humanist and naturalist rejection of the concept entirely or by a more or less radical theological reformulation of it.

The grounds for the modern critique of the idea of God have been essentially three: (1) the new emphasis on experience as the sole relevant and dependable source for valued and meaningful concepts and the sole ground for the testing of those concepts; (2) the corresponding shift to the subject as the sole seat of legitimate authority in all matters pertaining to truth and as the sole originating source of significant moral and personal action; and finally, since the principle of authority in matters of truth and morals has moved radically inward to the subject, (3) the radical questioning of all external forms of authority, especially those coming from church traditions or scripture.

A powerful "naturalistic" viewpoint, which finds belief in God anachronistic and incredible and thus a religious relation to God either offensive or irrelevant, has arisen and spread pervasively throughout the Western and Communist worlds into almost every class. From this viewpoint, "nature," as understood by science, is the seat and source of all that is real; men and women are the source of values, and their needs and wishes are the sole criteria of values. Thus, this world and its history represent the sole locus of hope. Whether in socialistic or capitalistic form (or whether theorized by Karl Marx, Sigmund Freud, Jean-Paul Sartre, Albert Camus, or by most if not all the leaders of the scientific and philosophical communities), this naturalistic humanism has dominated the cultural scene. As a consequence, its powerful presence has posed the central intellectual issues for theologians concerned with the defense and reformulation of the concept of God. Even if God has receded from the center of Western consciousness, "the religious" dimension or concern has apparently not been displaced, for the political and social worlds of Western culture are structured ideologically, which means that its chief conflicts are still inspired by competing forms of religiosity.

Insofar as thinkers have sought to defend and retrieve a concept of God, these new emphases on the authority of experience and the human subjects of experience have slowly but effectively reshaped that concept. First, the traditional concept of the divine self existing alone, a notion essentially and necessarily quite out of relation to any human experiences of the divine, became understandably a most questionable concept: How could there be experience and knowledge of any such unrelated object? Thus, most modern "doctrines" of God remain within the parameters of possible experience and speak of the divine (as of anything else) only on the basis of our experience, in terms of either God's metaphysical relations to the world, our immediate experience of God, or God's special activities of revelation in history. Second, if all that is real for us must be within the area of our experience, then inevitably the sense of the reality and value of the changing, temporal world of process will increase, for this is the world we experience and know. Thus, however much or little the transcendence of God may be emphasized in modern doctrines, we find now that the *relatedness* of God to the world, to the events of history, and to temporality itself has become the starting point for discourse about God rather than an embarrassment to it. Most concepts of God in modern times are therefore dynamic, related, even sharing in some aspects of temporality and dependence, regardless of whatever categories (personal and biblical, or ontological and metaphysical) they may choose to use.

Modern Reformulations of the Concept of God.

Knowledge of God. The question about how God is to be known—by rational inquiry of some sort, through religious experience, or through a revelation responded to by faith—has been a traditional and recurrent question throughout Christian history. In that history there have been those who, while denying neither the efficacy nor the significance of mystical experience or of revelation, insist that the existence of God can be established by philosophical argument. They have thought that the nature of God can be known and defined, at least in part, by reason alone, that is, by "natural theology." On the other side have been those who distrust philosophical reason as "pagan" or at least as misguided; correspondingly, they have argued that the true and living God, the God of Abraham, Christ, and the church, can be known only in revelation. As a consequence, for them a valid understanding of the nature and intents of God must proceed from revelation alone and not also from philosophical reasoning. Although the developments in modern culture have not effaced this traditional issue and its contesting parties, still these developments have to some extent effected changes in the way each side argues its case.

The question of the *possibility* of a concept of God, the most radical question about God's reality, has come to the fore. The natural theologians and the revelationists find themselves increasingly concerned with the origin of this idea in philosophy or in the experience of revelation respectively. They ask, How do we come to know God? and, What do we know about God in the way we do know it?

Although the sharpness and difficulty of the question of the reality of God and of the intelligibility of that concept has made a natural theology eminently desirable if not necessary for modern believers, still the drift—not to say flood tide—of modern rationality away from metaphysical speculation has raised increasing difficulties for that enterprise in modern culture. Whereas in many epochs only orthodox members of the church might be scornful or ungrateful at the use of philosophy in theology and especially at the idea of a natural theology, now it is the philosophical community more than the theological community that raises questions about the possibility of metaphysics and of natural theology of any sort. In modernity natural theologians have had to contend with philosophical resistance to their speculative, metaphysical labors as well as with religious-theological resistance, and they face the bizarre and arduous task, not forced upon their predecessors, of presenting a reasoned defense of metaphysical reason even before they begin their quest by way of such reason for God.

The modern critique of authority—the emphatic denial of absolute authority to any document or institution—has transformed the interpretation of revelation and its cognitive meaning. With this modern critique of scriptural and dogmatic authority and of a "propositional view of revelation," theologians have come to understand that revelation comes *through* the words of scripture and tradition and is received not as an objective proposition but on the "religious" level as an experience or "feeling" (Friedrich Schleiermacher), as an "encounter" resulting in a personal acknowledgment or a decision of faith as an existential reality and activity below the conceptual and ordinary cognitive level. The obvious problem of a cognitive event (not only of certainty *that* its object is but also of knowledge of *what* it might be) taking place by way of such a prelinguistic, preconceptual, and preexperiential "experience" thus plagues current revelationists as it did not their predecessors. It should be noted that neither one of the traditional avenues to the knowledge of God, metaphysics or revelation, is in the least straight and smooth in our own day!

Despite these added difficulties, each answer has in our own time had its powerful and persuasive adherents. Those who emphasize the knowability of God by reason have offered one version or another of the classical "proofs" of God: the cosmological, from the existence of the finite world (mainly the neo-Thomists); the teleological, from the order of the finite world (note especially the brilliant use of this argument by Alfred North Whitehead as well as by a variety of evolutionists such as F. R. Tennant and Teilhard de Chardin); the ontological, from the implications of the concept of God itself as a concept of a perfect and so necessary being (the original work of Charles Hartshorne is unique at this point); and the moral argument, from the implications of moral experience. Those widely variant forms of philosophical approach have been united in arguing that any theology intellectually respectable enough to speak to modern, intelligent people must represent its religious heritage in the intellectual form of such a rationally grounded philosophical theology. Without such a philosophical base for our knowledge of God, our certainty of the divine reality and our comprehension of the relation of this concept to our other concepts will be seriously lacking. As a consequence, the idea of God will increasingly be regarded as merely subjective and idiosyncratic, a private matter of "feeling" and therefore unreal, vacant of content, and in the end "meaningless." Powerful recent examples of these arguments for a philosophical basis for our knowledge of God have been the Hegelian idealists, the new-scholastic and now the transcendental Thomists, and perhaps most notably the growing and flourishing school of process or neoclassical theologians.

On the other side have been those who have shared a more jaundiced view of culture's reasoning and of its philosophical "proofs"; on religious grounds they have emphasized the transcendence and mystery of God and the actuality and sufficiency of revelation as the source and norm for the concept of God. They are aware that most philosophy has come to regard metaphysical speculation and all proofs of a divine reality as representing a dubious and uncritical use of reason, and therefore itself devoid of certainty, objectivity, and meaning. They have also sensed the ideological and invalid character of much "modern" thinking. For them, modern thought, far from providing an objective and valid ground for our ultimate faith, represents in itself a significant aspect of the modern problem, needing new principles of illumination if it is to help our religious existence.

Most important, the main problem of the knowledge of God, they insist, is not that we cannot know God with our finite minds, but that in fact secretly we do not at all wish to know God. As Karl Barth argued, natural theology represents the persistent and systematic attempt of self-sufficient people to create a "God" of their own and so to avoid relationship with or knowledge of the real God. A philosophical God, the product of our own metaphysical thinking and the construct of our own wayward modern wisdom, may be infinitely more comfortable for us to live with; nevertheless, such a "God" is a far cry indeed from the real God who confronts us in judgment and may confront us therefore also in grace. Furthermore, the very center of Christian promise resides in the *re-creation* of what we are and of how and what we think, not in their mere extension and solidification. Thus, God—not "our own words to ourselves"—must speak to us in revelation. Such an event of revelation provides the sole basis and the sole norm for the religious existence of the Christian community from which and for which valid and legitimate theology speaks. To be sure, theology does speak to the world as well as to the church; but in its speech it must seek to represent not the wisdom of the world but the message of the gospel, not the word of humanity but the word of God. Theology may use philosophy, which it cannot avoid, in explicating this message in coherent and adequate form. Its primal obligation, however, is to be faithful to revelation and not to the pressures of public rationality as the world defines rationality. Faith, therefore, precedes and controls the use of reason in theology.

Language About God. A second issue, characteristic of the whole tradition yet vital to recent theology, is concerned with the question of the nature of the categories or concepts fundamental to or appropriate for Christian speech about God. Should these be "personal," "historical," and "ontic" in character, as they surely are in scripture, or should they be ontological, metaphysical, and therefore "impersonal" in character, as in almost every speculative philosophical system, even an idealistic or a panpsychistic one?

On both sides there are compelling reasons apparently intrinsic to the character and claims of the Christian religion. In its fundamental symbolic content, exemplified in its belief in God as creator and providential ruler, in its view of human beings as finite, temporal, and yet "real," and in its idea of history as the arena of God's activity, Christian faith cannot avoid making assertions about the character of ultimate reality and about the essential structures of natural, human, and historical existence. Inescapably, it must employ metaphysical and existential words to express its own deepest meanings. Intrinsically related to reality as the anchor of value within reality, God must therefore be expressed in categories appropriate to the discussion of the structures of reality as a whole, that is, in ontological or metaphysical categories.

On the other hand, there is little question that the center of Christian piety, its religious center, has classically been expressible only by means of anthropomorphic language. Just as a description of a human being devoid of any personal inwardness, decision, action, and responsibility would subvert all that Christianity has to say about human nature, so a description of God void of all personal categories (intents, purposes, mercy, love, and so on) can hardly express what Christians intend to say about God. While, therefore, the ontological or philosophical theologians seem (initially at least) better able to explicate conceptually the symbols of creation and providence, the biblical theologians, using personal categories, gain strength when they speak of sin, the law, and the gospel, and especially when they speak of God's "judgment" and God's "love."

The Concept of God: Agency, Temporality, and History. Although the issues of agency, temporality, and history are not completely new to Christian discussion of God, the characteristic emphases of modern culture have nevertheless intensified each of them, shifted their focus and balance, and thus reshaped these issues dramatically. As a consequence, the doctrine of God in Christian theology appears in undeniably new forms, whatever particular symbol (e.g., creation, providence, eschatology) in systematic theology is being discussed.

Recently, theologians have been less and less able or willing to say blandly that God wills, intends, or even affects whatever happens, including "evil" actions and events. Apparently, to deny human freedom and to saddle God with evil (e.g., the rise to power of Adolf Hitler) runs counter to all that we believe about ourselves, history, and God. This increasing tendency to conceive God's agency as limited has in turn led to two typical theological moves in the present far less prominent in the classical tradition. The first is the denial of the absoluteness and aseity of God in every respect: God's perfection and even God's necessity do not involve God's absoluteness, says Hartshorne; and in order that God be good and we be free, says Whitehead, God must be radically distinguished from the principle of ultimate reality, from the force and power of reality, from "creativity." Thus, the finitude of God, in the sense that God is not the *source* of finite reality in all its aspects, but rather that God is only one of a number of correlated and primal ultimate "factors" constitutive of finite actuality, is now asserted by a most important school of Christian theology. Needless to say, this is new in the tradition.

Another kind of move, occasioned by the same issues but implying a quite different theological viewpoint, emphasizes the "self-limitation" of God in the creation of a contingent, relative, and dependent creature, but a creature that within limits is genuinely autonomous. This creature is capable of and called to *self-constitution,* to becoming itself through its own commitments, decisions, and actions; as a consequence, this creature is capable of original, novel action and so is "free" to sin or to accept grace, that is, free to act in ways neither determined nor predetermined by God. Creaturely freedom or autonomy now plays a role much larger than before, qualifying the absolute sovereignty of the divine will and the divine power. Correspondingly, the goodness of God and so God's separation from evil have been much more jealously guarded by metaphysics (through the concept of the finitude of God) and by theology (through the conception of the divine self-limitation).

To the Hellenic and Hellenistic epochs, the divine was both "more real" and "more good" to the extent that it was *not* involved in change and in relatedness. In our epoch, we tend to reverse this apprehension, probably considering a changeless and unrelated God as a compensatory chimera of the imagination—unexperienced and so unknown—and as a notion void of all real content and value since such a deity would lack relatedness to the changing world where initially all reality and value reside. Thus, the most prominent characteristic of contemporary theologies of all sorts is what may be termed their "war with the Greeks." There is hardly a conception of God from Hegel onward that is not dynamic, changing, and in some manner intrinsically related to the world of change. The most influential instance of this dynamic view of God is the Whiteheadian one, in which God is conceived as an example of process rather than its negation. God, thus, shares in the metaphysical categories of process: temporality, potentiality, change, relatedness, development, and dependence or passivity.

With quite different tactics, the biblical or neoorthodox theologians have carried on *their* war with the Greeks. Although they retained erstwhile the symbols of the absoluteness and aseity of God while using personal and historical categories of biblical speech, they too produced a conception of a dynamic and related God. And, like their rivals in the process school, their main conscious opposition was to "the Greek concept of God" as changeless, unrelated, aloof. Theirs then was a "God who acts in history"; who "comes" or "is coming"; who effects "mighty deeds" of revelation and redemption, and so on. All these are clearly temporal as well as personal words expressive of actions over time and within time, of relatedness, of a relative dependence ("encounter," "judge")—words implying temporality, change, passivity, and potentiality as well as "personality" in God. The neoorthodox did not draw out explicitly the ontological implications of this their central language about God. Nevertheless, their view entailed radical changes from any recognizably "orthodox" conception of God. These changes have been even more evident in the post-neoorthodox eschatological theologies in which, for some, God is so temporal that, far from representing an eternity beyond time, the divine being is now said to be only "future."

In recent decades, a number of liberationist or political theologies have appeared, calling on Christian action and Christian theology to turn again toward the wide spectrum of social history's crises and oppressions as their main if not exclusive area of concern. The new theologies stress their identity with a given oppressed community, call for revolutionary action or praxis, and recognize only theological reflection that arises out of both. Thus, we have black theologies, feminist theologies, and Third World theologies. As a consequence of this identification with groups oppressed by Western social reality, they tend to make alliance with Marxist thought rather than with Western philosophy and social theory in general. And, finally, they see the divine action as itself adversarial to all that is the case in the sorry present; while they are also utopian, they are markedly anti-developmental in the essential themes of their thought.

Such adversarial theologies understandably wish to deny the relation of God to all that characterizes the dominant and oppressive past and present of Western history. Yet, as socially centered theologies, they wish also to identify God in some important sense with history. For them God is neither the God of the past nor the God of the present; nor is God a God beyond time, a God vertically above or below each moment, the ground and determiner of all being. Rather, God is "eschatological," the one who is coming, the "God of the future," the one who from the future will master the present and establish the divine sovereign rule in future history. The power with which this movement has redirected the concentration of theology back to history and forward into the future has been impressive and marks this as a most creative form of current theology.

The sharpest theological debates in the last decade and a half (at least outside the United States) have centered on the issues summarized here: whether theology can be carried on apart from revolutionary action; whether God has been active and sovereign in the past and the present, and will be in the future; whether the gospel is a promise of redemption for the individual soul or only for historical society; whether that promise is to be fulfilled here and in eternity or solely in a kingdom characterizing the historical, social future; and whether in Christ God's redemptive action was once and for all accomplished and manifest (even if its effects remain fragmentary), or whether in Jesus are to be found solely promises for a future social parousia of God's kingdom.

LANGDON GILKEY

Bibliography

Elisabeth Schüssler Fiorenza, *In Memory of Her.*
Charles Hartshorne, *The Divine Relativity.*
Hans Küng, *Does God Exist?*
Paul Tillich, *Systematic Theology*, vols. 1 and 3.
David Tracy and John B. Cobb, Jr., *Talking About God: Doing Theology in the Context of Modern Pluralism.*

Cross Reference: Atonement, Covenant, Creation, Grace, Holy Spirit, Incarnation, Panentheism, Providence, Revelation, Theism, Transcendence, Trinity, Ultimate Concern.

The foregoing article is abridged, from *Christian Theology*, edited by Peter C. Hodgson and Robert H. King, copyright © 1985 Fortress Press. Used by permission of Augsburg Fortress.

GOOD (See VIRTUE.)

GRACE

Although Christians may join the rest of the human race in speaking of the human quality of grace—an effortless charm—they are quite specific when they speak in regard to their Christian faith and theology. Then grace always relates to God's activity in Jesus Christ.

Grace from the Greek word *charis* most focally translates as divine "favor." But believers make much more of the concept than that which one root connection suggests. Indeed, it can serve as a condensation of or code word for the basic feature of Christian faith and life.

Thus grace expresses the character of God. God had the freedom to remain unrelated; instead God was moved to create a universe, to situate humans in it, and to move toward them. Despite the divine intent that they be "good" and remain so, the biblical writings picture men and women as fallen, removed from positive relations to God, and threatened by the dangers of destruction. As revealed in Christian scriptures and grasped in Christian faith, God is love; whatever else it means, this reality suggests that God is moved by nothing other than that love to visit humans, bring them back to God, and restore them. This love, unmotivated and spontaneous—which means that it does not need to find redeeming qualities in its object—finds expression in grace.

Grace therefore, better than any other term, exemplifies the revelation of the divine character in action and the relation of the divine to human beings. Consequently, grace is conceived as personal, a movement from the being of God to the drama of human existence. Not a mere idea or concept, grace further belongs to the "storied" character of Christian faith. That is, in the event associated with Jesus Christ and in witness to that event in the form of the Christian story, one sees and experiences grace in action. The coming of Jesus and especially the giving of himself in his birth, life, and death, along with the vindication of his death for others through the act of God raising him from the dead, makes possible the realization of grace.

Although the Hebrew scriptures include terms that approach the understanding of grace as it appears in the Christian story, grace as it enters Christian life is chiefly a New Testament term. Within the New Testament, Paul employs it on 101 occasions when he wants to stress the central feature of God's relation to fallen humans. (In non-Pauline writings it appears 51 times.) Often when the apostle uses the term, he stresses that it is the best way to express what goes on in the divine-human relationship. He speaks as easily of "the grace of God" as of "the grace of Christ," having proposed that nothing better depicts the person of God than the grace-full aspect.

In the Pauline writings, the stress is always on the "free gift of grace" (cf. Rom. 5:15). On this point, most Christians agree with one another, though over the course of time a controversy did unfold as to exactly how grace comes to humans and how they receive grace. Yet in every case, grace is seen as a needed remedy for something in the human situation, a sign of the divine favor, the agent of a restored relation.

The question eventually became, Is the entire notion of grace something that moves in one direction? Must not humans supply something to attract and sustain grace? In general, medieval Catholicism came to stress that the human actor had to do something to draw down God's favor and then had to sustain that favor by certain courses of action and expressions of will. To the Protestant Reformers in the train of Luther, this understanding led to grievous flaws and faults in Catholicism. If grace was somehow merited, was it still grace? If it demanded human cooperation and went farther than being merely received and responded to, how would the fallen human ever be sure that she or he had done enough to deserve grace? If grace was deserved, was it truly grace?

The Reformers instead said that grace was not "infused" into humans but imparted from without as a gift. Although grace was received in faith, it did not depend on sacrifices believers would make in the sense of acts of generosity or mercy done to impress God. Naturally, those who experience grace would realize that they in turn become agents of proclaiming its availability and in transmitting it to others.

Christians have argued not only over the notion of the "infusion" of grace but over whether it is irresistible, whether it can be withstood, denied, or withdrawn. There have been debates over how grace relates to human freedom and the free will. But through the years and especially in an ecumenical age some of the old hostilities over the meanings of grace have diminished. The notion of grace as pure gift is as likely to be heard proclaimed in Catholic as in Protestant circles. In an often grace-less world, more and more believers have stressed the wonderful and rare character of divine grace and have urged that it be responded to more than that it be precisely defined.

MARTIN E. MARTY

Bibliography

Leonardo Boff, *Liberating Grace.*
Roger Haight, *The Experience and Language of Grace.*
Karl Rahner, *Theological Investigations,* vol. 1.
Thomas F. Torrance, *The Doctrine of Grace in the Apostolic Fathers.*
Phillip S. Watson, *The Concept of Grace.*

Cross Reference: Christology, Law and Gospel, Love, Soteriology.

THE HARTFORD APPEAL

"An Appeal for Theological Affirmation," which quickly became known as the Hartford Appeal, issued from a three-day meeting of theologians at the Hartford Seminary Foundation in Connecticut, in January 1975. Organized at the initiative of sociologist Peter L. Berger and then Lutheran pastor Richard John

Neuhaus, who also prepared the preliminary draft for the meeting's deliberation, the meeting was thoroughly ecumenical and entirely unofficial. In its final form, the Appeal invited theological response to thirteen themes in current Christian thought that were described as "pervasive, false, and debilitating to the Church's life and work."

The essential problem, Hartford said, is "the loss of transcendence" in Christian thought and practice. The following are representative of the themes cited by the Hartford Appeal: "Religious language refers to human experience and nothing else, God being humanity's noblest creation." "Since what is human is good, evil can adequately be understood as failure to realize human potential." "The world must set the agenda for the Church. Social, political, and economic programs to improve the quality of life are ultimately normative for the Church's mission in the world." "The question of hope beyond death is irrelevant or at best marginal to the Christian understanding of human fulfillment." The twenty-four original signers of the Appeal (including Elizabeth Bettenhausen, William Sloane Coffin, Avery Dulles, George W. Forell, Stanley Hauerwas, Thomas Hopko, George A. Lindbeck, Richard J. Mouw, Carl J. Peter, Alexander Schmemann, George H. Tavard, Bruce Vawter, and Robert Wilken) reflected a broad spectrum of theological and social commitments.

The Appeal immediately sparked a very lively debate, both in the popular press and in scholarly circles. Some in the religious and general press hailed it as the portent of "a new reformation." Wolfhart Pannenberg joined other scholars in commending Hartford for pointing the way beyond both fundamentalist obscurantism and liberal secularization. At the same time, the Appeal elicited vigorous criticisms. A number of counter-statements were issued in the succeeding months, notable among them being "The Boston Affirmations." The Boston group claimed that Hartford had undercut Christian responsibility for social change. Responses to Hartford from evangelical and Catholic sources were generally favorable, but leadership sectors of the mainline Protestant churches expressed concern that they were being attacked by the Appeal.

The Hartford group met again in September of 1975 to discuss papers that had been prepared to elaborate the intent of the Appeal. A common criticism of Hartford is that it did not contain a clear or comprehensive confession of faith. George Lindbeck responded to that criticism in his paper, "A Battle for Theology: Hartford in Historical Perspective," comparing Hartford with similar events in Christian history. "The Hartford Appeal is *sui generis*," Lindbeck wrote, "because it battles for the possibility of theology rather than itself proposing a theology. It does not affirm, but rather asks for affirmation; it does not theologize, but rather calls for theology; it does not confess the faith, but rather pleads that it be confessed." The papers of the second meeting (by Berger, Lindbeck, Dulles, Forell, Peter, Mouw, Schmemann, and Neuhaus), as well as the Appeal itself, were published as *Against the World for the World:*

The Hartford Appeal and the Future of American Religion (1976). In response to the misperception that Hartford was attempting to establish a new orthodoxy, Berger and Neuhaus wrote in the preface to the book, "Hartford is not designed to exclude anyone from theological discourse or to foreclose possibilities. On the contrary, it is a wide-open invitation and, we hope, a useful referent in what must be an energetic and multifarious exchange on the future of religion in our kind of world."

Whether the "wide-open invitation" had much effect is disputed, but Hartford did establish itself as a continuing point of reference in American religious thought, and most of its original signers continued to be theologically active proponents of its arguments. The irony has been observed that Hartford's call for a recovery of "transcendence" has been seized upon by some theologians, notably by feminists, to argue that God is so thoroughly transcendent and beyond our knowing that theological language must content itself with dealing with human experience. Such misunderstandings no doubt underscore the truth of Lindbeck's observation that confessing the faith and issuing calls for the confession of the faith are perennial tasks in the life of the church.

RICHARD JOHN NEUHAUS

Bibliography

The text of the appeal is included in Edwin S. Gaustad, *A Documentary History of Religion in America, II.*

Cross Reference: Secularity, Transcendence.

HEALTH

Few words fluctuate as wildly between broad and narrow denotations as "health." At the inclusive end of its spectrum of meanings, health seems to embrace almost all of the conditions of life, as it does, for example, in the opening sentence of the 1946 charter of the World Health Organization (WHO), where health is defined as "complete physical, mental and social well-being." WHO's definition has served as the representative statement of international aspirations for health in its broadest sense.

But the word also carries more narrow, exclusive meanings. During a century that boasts unprecedented successes at raising life expectancy, eradicating killer diseases like smallpox, and intervening with high technology microsurgical techniques, we have witnessed the dismemberment of cure into specialties and subspecialties, the fragmentation of care among a variety of institutions, and the transformation of health from a self-evident quality to a complex puzzle. To the epidemiologist, for example, health becomes the defeat of a particular pathogen. To the liver transplant team, however, it means the restored functioning of a particular organ system. In marked contrast to those who champion holistic viewpoints, modern health care has manifested a pluralism of such piecemeal understandings.

Further, few words carry as many assumptive burdens as this one. Although health now functions primarily as a secular idea, it has a long religious history of linking together assumptions about the most elementary forms of life—cells, organs, individuals—and the larger cosmos. In ancient religions, shamans (ecstatic healers with special access to spiritual powers) demonstrated that illness was never simply a property of one patient or one infected limb. Instead, their healing rites attempted to restore order to a larger cosmic imbalance at the same time that it cured an individual. Although the religious overtones that once accompanied the concept are no longer heard by most, modern discourse about health still reveals larger assumptions. As we draw upon germ theories, genetic codes, and environmental factors to account for health and illness, secular cosmologies play roles analogous to those of the sacred cosmologies of earlier eras.

One result of this multivalent situation is that health increasingly becomes a private affair. As individuals make their way from specialists to therapists to case workers, they encounter a smorgasbord of understandings from which to pick and choose. Fitness consultants, folk healers, and spiritual gurus add their gospels to the mix. The ironic outcome is that despite public saturation with talk about health, the idea loses its public salience. This loss of shared public understandings of health contributes to an unhealthy national and international situation in which consumer expectations converge and contend over costly resources. Without shared understandings, individuals limp along on their own, and societies make ad hoc health policy decisions that seek to balance special interests. In both cases, life-and-death decisions are made without addressing the fundamental issues that lurk beneath the surface: the nature of health, the purposes of medicine, the justice of health care systems, and the relative value of health vis-à-vis other human goods.

Within this linguistic situation Christians are pulled in both broad and narrow directions. The Hebrew and Christian scriptures bear witness to a fundamental commitment to life and the preservation of health—a tradition that reaches back to Moses. Both the decalogue and the detailed levitical health legislation attest to a broad and deep concern for all that enhances life and well-being. At the dawn of Christian history, Jesus' radical fusion of health and salvation in his ministry of forgiving, accepting, and healing intensified the pressure to embrace a broad understanding. Together the Jewish and Christian heritages undergird centuries of commitment to care for all sorts of human brokenness while giving special attention to human illness. Over the centuries, these traditions offered explanations of illness ranging from theocentric to demonic to naturalistic causes; adherents experimented with forms of cure ranging from rites of prayer and anointing to the development of specialized institutions (hospitals) and professions (deaconesses and medical missionaries) that welcomed the insights of science and technology. They taught ways of life and spiritual disciplines that sought to enhance well being in all of its dimensions. This holistic view of health provided a foundation on which many of the narrower modern versions have been able to build since the Renaissance.

Now, however, the Christian tradition finds itself at odds with both ruling sets of definitions. Influenced by the same pluralizing and privatizing dynamics that shape modern societies, Christian interpretations of health often seem fragmented and contradictory. They range from those of Pentecostal faith healers to Christian Scientists to "mainline" believers who accept the modern division of labor that turns health over to physicians and scientists and looks to clergy and churches for spiritual needs. Yet the tradition, when responsive to its sources, bears an imaginative repertoire that challenges both the secular inclusiveness of the WHO definition and the reductionistic biomedicalism of the health care complex.

It does so by making relative the concept of health in several ways. First, it places health in a theological light by viewing it as a gift, rather than as a right, duty, or private possession. Health is perceived as an expression of God's creativity; whenever it is experienced one stands in the presence of God's creation. Second, the Christian tradition places its discussions of health within the conditions of finitude and fallenness. Health is not perceived as some pure or infinite condition. Rather, human health is experienced in relation to disease, death, and human limitation. The tradition resists temptations to seek perfect and limitless health; it works to nurture health in the midst of disease, and it seeks redemptive healing in very unhealthy circumstances. Third, health is not isolated as a solitary good or made private as only an individual concern. Health is one of many goods, more necessary than most but always related to others. It is placed in a penultimate location, subject to greater goods like love of God and neighbor. It becomes a matter of communal, ecological, and, finally, cosmic proportions.

A noteworthy theological attempt to redefine health in light of the Christian tradition and modern science was made by Paul Tillich in 1961. Synthesizing the various modern fragments of health, he proposed a complex understanding consisting of mechanical, chemical, biological, psychological, spiritual, and historical dimensions. Health is not, in this reading, a quality to be found within any one of these zones. Instead it is a "multi-dimensional unity." This proposal includes several key elements that must be a part of future attempts to reframe modern discussions of health. First, it is more inclusive than the secular models of WHO or modern medicine. It reaches into spiritual and cultural dimensions— realms sadly missing from most health care discussions. Second, it allows for specific understandings of health even as it relates them. There is room for the discoveries of the specialists within this perspective. Third, it is sufficiently

215

interactive to allow for human complexity and ambiguity. Changes in one dimension of life—even health-enhancing ones!—might have unhealthy side effects in others.

At stake in the definitional battle over the meaning of health are healthy or pathological views of humanity and its place in the universe. Ideas about those fundamental questions have enormous consequences as they shape practices and institutions that attempt to care for people. As Christians redefine health in light of their traditions, they challenge modern reductionisms (some would say idolatries) that make health the greatest concern and death the ultimate enemy. In so doing they remind humans of their location in a theological setting that puts health, humans, and their source in their proper places.

JAMES P. WIND

Bibliography

Stephen E. Lammers and Allen Verhey, eds., *On Moral Medicine: Theological Perspectives in Medical Ethics.*

Ronald L. Numbers and Darrel W. Amundsen, eds., *Caring and Curing: Health and Medicine in the Western Religious Traditions.*

Lawrence E. Sullivan, ed., *Healing and Restoring: Health and Medicine in the World's Religious Traditions.*

Paul Tillich, "The Meaning of Health," *Perspectives in Biology and Medicine* 5 (Autumn 1961).

Cross Reference: Anthropology, Ethics–Christian, Justice, Moral Theology, Soteriology.

HERESY

Heresy is a belief, held by a member of a church, that denies or seriously distorts a central teaching of that community. Heresy is therefore usually distinguished from apostasy, the complete renunciation of the community's faith.

Heresy also differs from schism; heresy is a belief judged contrary to a community's essential teachings, whereas schism is the community's critical term for any movement that divides the community. In other words, heresy is theological error, while schism is ecclesiastical division. Historically, however, heresy and schism have often gone together: The definition of a heresy may lead to schism (as in the Nestorian and Monophysite schisms following the Council of Chalcedon); or a basically schismatic movement may also include heretical teachings (as in Donatism). This interrelation of heresy and schism indicates that the social function of heresy is a threat to the truth of the community's teachings, its unity, and the authority of its teaching office.

As threats to the truth and unity of the community, heresies have often led to the development of dogmas, defined to protect that truth and unity. Indeed, typically the rise of a heresy, perhaps at first only dimly sensed to be a departure from tradition, prompts the community to define a dogma not explicitly stated before. As departures from tradition, according to J. W. C. Wand, heretical movements in the Christian church have manifested three classical marks: novelty, parochialism, and stubborn resistance.

Roman Catholic theology has thoroughly articulated distinctions between different kinds of heresy. In canon law, a central distinction must be made between formal heresy and material heresy. Formal heresy is the deliberate, persistent adherence by a baptized Catholic to a belief known by that person to be contrary to the church's essential teaching. Material heresy also is adherence to a belief contrary to essential church teaching, but it is less culpable since the belief is held without knowledge that it is heretical. Material heresy, therefore, is less serious, because it is mitigated by various degrees of ignorance.

Although confessional Protestant churches (defining themselves by creeds and confessions) often lack these precise Roman Catholic distinctions, they employ the concept of heresy to define the boundaries of acceptable belief and practice. For Protestant churches without creeds or confessions, the definition of heresy and discipline against it have been less strict.

In the West the Enlightenment changed the understanding of heresy in a way that has affected both Roman Catholics and Protestants. In earlier periods, when church and state were united, heresy was often punished by the secular arm of government in concert with the established religion; the history of heresy was also the history of religious repression in Christendom. In reaction to this, the Enlightenment produced a complex shift in sensibilities that greatly modified the concept: the rise of religious tolerance, the separation of church and state in some nations, a questioning of religious authority, doubts that traditional dogmatic formulations should definitively govern modern reformulations of essential Christian beliefs, a stress on religious individualism, and an awareness of religious pluralism (both intra-culturally and cross-culturally).

Sociologist Peter Berger, for example, notes this shift in sensibility by describing a "heretical imperative" in the modern period. People no longer regard religious commitment as determined by outside forces or religious authority; instead, they see a multitude of religious options that compel the individual to make choices. Other historians have stressed that heresy is often intertwined with social protest; the definition of a movement as heretical often reflects complex interactions between dominant and repressed social groups. For all these reasons, this shift in sensibility has diminished the practical enforcement of strictures against heresies within some religious communities, and it has raised questions about the very legitimacy of the concept of heresy.

Nonetheless, some modern theologians have attempted to defend the need for a concept of heresy that takes these developments into account. Like Berger, Roman Catholic theologian Karl Rahner argues that the bewildering "pluralism of experience" affecting all persons in the modern period, including believers, has

217

changed the form of heresy: "Latent heresy," as subtle and false emphases or exaggerations of the church's teaching, is a fact of life. This shift makes heresy more difficult to locate and also places a greater burden on the individual believer, instead of the church's teaching office, to identify heresy. In a different vein, Protestant theologian Karl Barth affirms the church's continuing need to identify heresy as a rejection of the revelation of the Word of God in Christ, yet he also argues that dogmatic theology cannot presume to declare in advance what is basic to the faith. Thus, he avers, the church must ever be open to formulations of God's Word for a new situation.

In the twentieth century, the concept of heresy in Protestant churches has become a primary means of identifying social situations fundamentally opposed to Christian faith. Such a social situation constitutes a *status confessionis,* an issue on which the church cannot allow disagreement without sacrificing its integrity and witness. Three modern instances in Protestant churches are most often cited. First, the Barmen Declaration of the Synod of the Confessing Church in Germany (1934) denounced the Nazi-controlled "German Christian" movement in the Evangelical Church as being in essential opposition to the lordship of Jesus Christ. Second, the West German "church brotherhoods" in 1958 challenged the Synod of the Evangelical Church in Germany to declare atomic war a *status confessionis,* affirming that no Christian may participate in preparations for atomic war. Third, the Lutheran World Federation meeting in Dar es Salaam (1977) pronounced South African apartheid a *status confessionis,* calling upon its churches unequivocally to reject apartheid as a denial of Lutheran confession; the World Alliance of Reformed Churches meeting in Ottawa (1982) further stated that the moral and theological justification of apartheid, as held in some of its South African member churches, was heresy.

In the 1990s, the understanding of heresy continues to be affected by complex modern forces such as the questioning of religious authority, pluralism, and increased awareness of the social witness of the church. The result is that the church is still faced with the question of how to formulate a concept of heresy that defends the integrity of the church's essential teachings without violating legitimate internal pluralism, that maintains unity without suppressing diversity, and that promotes clarity in the church's message to the surrounding pluralistic world.

DAVID J. GOUWENS

Bibliography

Karl Barth, *Church Dogmatics,* 1/2.
Peter Berger, *The Heretical Imperative: Contemporary Possibilities of Religious Affirmation.*
John DeGruchy and Charles Villa-Vicencio, eds., *Apartheid Is a Heresy.*

Karl Rahner, "What Is Heresy?" in *Theological Investigations*. Vol. 5: *Later Writings*. J. W. C. Wand, *The Four Great Heresies*.

Cross Reference: Authority, Dogmatic Theology, Tradition.

HERMENEUTICS

In its most general meaning, "hermeneutics" designates that discipline whose object is the theoretical clarification of the issues involving human understanding. More narrowly, hermeneutics deals with the understanding of written, most often historically distant texts. The discussions within the field of hermeneutics focus on a network of topics including understanding, explanation, analysis, meaning and meaningfulness, interpretation, experience, textuality, appropriation, language, and historicity. The goal of hermeneutical reflection is to present a theoretically clear and responsible account that describes, informs, and at points guides the human situation of understanding as interpretation.

Hermeneutical studies today tend to take one of two main directions: that concerned with the methods and conditions of valid interpretations (epistemological), and that concerned with understanding as a fundamental way of human being (ontological).

The first tendency has a long heritage in the association of interpretation with rhetorical studies, certain schools of literary theory, and a dominant concern with epistemology. It is strengthened by the success and clarity of natural scientific methods that serve as models for clear and responsible interpretation. The central issues for such a tendency are the problems of potential misunderstanding and the achievement of valid understanding. Clarification of an author's intent, methods of linguistic, compositional, and symbolic analysis, specification of procedural criteria, and clarification of the conditions for understanding as knowledge are suggested as means of dealing with the central issues.

The second tendency is less concerned with the epistemological issues, focusing rather on the ontological conditions for understanding. Drawing on an equally rich heritage of metaphysical and philosophical reflection, historical studies, and recent literary and phenomenological investigations, this set of explorations discloses elements fundamental to all human understanding (e.g., temporality, language, mood) and explains how these elements interact. Less concerned with method, validity, and correctness, this tendency uses discussions of historicity, the role of imagination, dialogue as a model of textual interaction, the relation of truth to textuality, and the like to bring to reflective awareness the conditions for, and possibilities of, understanding. These two tendencies are not mutually exclusive but do, in fact, designate interests and goals within the larger field of hermeneutics.

Hermeneutic scholarship has most often been associated with biblical study in modern and current Christian theology. A distinction is frequently made between exegesis and hermeneutics. The former designates the close linguistic and literary investigation of passages and whole texts, usually with the goal of explaining the range of meanings or the stages of development that the text had for its earlier audiences. The latter designates the methods and conditions that enable the text to be responsibly interpreted for a contemporary audience. Although there is an evident affinity between biblical studies and hermeneutics, hermeneutical study is not limited to biblical investigations. Particularly when theology is understood to involve some form of correlation between the interpretation of foundational Christian texts and the interpretation of later human experience, hermeneutical investigation in both its epistemological and ontological tendencies plays a significant role beyond scriptural investigation.

The activity of interpreting anew a religious tradition already long developed is evident from very early in Jewish and Christian histories. This hermeneutic action tends to become hermeneutics proper at those points where some crisis in understanding is experienced. Whether the crisis be obscure or ambiguous textual meanings, contradictions, accusations of irrelevance, historical distance, or some other breach in what was assumed to be stable meanings, hermeneutical reflection comes as a response, often occasioned by such questions as, What is the importance of tradition? or, Does this text still mean anything now? or, What does it mean to act in the light of this scripture or credal text?

The history of hermeneutical reflection in its theological setting, then, can be traced as a history of crises within and for the broad Christian tradition. Such early issues as the differentiation of emergent Christianity from its Jewish sources and the relation of Christian theological positions to Greek and Roman philosophy occasioned the development of sustained reflections on schemes of fulfillment, allegory, typology, and analogy as methods of proper interpretation. Later, as Christian culture grew more stable, the issues of obscure or unworthy meanings contributed to the development of ordered interpretative schemes that differentiated minimally between literal or grammatical and spiritual meanings (e.g., Origen), often identifying several senses including the literal, moral, allegorical, anagogical, eschatological, and typological. Within these morphologies of textual understanding, the priority of one type of understanding over another, or the identification of one guiding principle to control the levels of meaning (e.g., Augustine's guideline that one had not yet understood scripture if the interpretation did not further both love of God and love of neighbor), became a consistent focus of attention. The High Middle Ages, the Renaissance, and the Reformation were increasingly critical of allegorical methods while supporting interpretations that prized the words and constructions of the text itself. Not "literal" in a modern sense, this trend of interpretation adopted the term to designate a skepticism toward imposing dogmatic patterns on scriptural texts.

Doctrinal issues were clearly of concern (e.g., creation, natural law, redemption, grace and law, faith and works), but the claim was that the theological interpretation became misinterpretation when used to proof-text alien, often philosophical positions rather than to reflect biblical language. Enlightenment rationalism and the rise of historicism in the eighteenth and nineteenth centuries brought new crises that formed the basis for modern and current critical hermeneutics. Various tendencies can be observed, including the reduction of religious and scriptural meaning to moral and rational truths; the critical treatment of scripture texts as one might read other classical texts; the use of extra-theological, especially linguistic and historical, methods of interpretation; and the recognition of the cultural situation of the biblical writings and meanings. No longer were the hermeneutical problems those within a culture sharing a relatively appreciative view of religion, especially Christianity. The success of the natural sciences, changing European politics, and the development of linguistic and historical sophistication, among a host of other factors, led to an increasing marginalization of religious reflection and biblical interpretation. Modern and present hermeneutics begins in this set of crises and works to specify the criteria and important issues for adequate religious interpretations of historically and linguistically distant texts in today's world.

Within the discussion of modern hermeneutics, several points of relative agreement and several issues for further reflection emerge. Among the areas of broad agreement are the following.

1. All human understanding is interpretative. Understanding, ranging from the most mundane issues of everyday life to the most sophisticated textual and scientific observations, is not a matter of self-evident observation and immediate recognition. Rather, all understanding is the interpretation of experience "as" something. This structure of the "as" means that understanding, unlike reflex, is not in the realm of immediacy, but that it is always mediated by a series of factors and judgments, often not evident. This critical initial recognition separates hermeneutical endeavors from most forms of positivism and empiricism. For religious textual studies, it calls into question any "self-evident" or "literal" meaning by recognizing that a claim to understand the meaning of a text is an interpretation of the written page from a particular perspective.

2. The "hermeneutical circle" is one fitting way to describe interpretative understanding. If all understanding is interpretative, then the obvious risk is to construe all interpretation as the imperialization of meaning by the interpreter. The "hermeneutical circle" is an attempt to describe better the situation of understanding as an interactive balance or play between the object for interpretation and the interpretative intent. In such a description the preunderstanding and prejudgments of the interpreter are recognized as that point of view from which specific questions for the object of interpretation arise. Likewise, the object for interpretation puts certain limits and demands on the interpreter that

221

allow for the judgment that an interpretation is inadequate. The circular interaction of preunderstanding and the intended object for understanding best accounts for a situation in which all interpretation is interpretation from a particular viewpoint. Hermeneutical reflection attempts to explore the complexity of this circular relation in order to bring it to reflective awareness rather than to do away with the circle with the illusion of objective meaning. For religious textual studies, to recognize this circular structure of understanding is simultaneously to recognize that any interpretation is involved in the play of the specific questions and assumptions that the interpreter brings to the text as well as to the formal structures within the text. All understanding is open to critical revision through a change in the interpretative viewpoint, more enhanced textual methods, and a better awareness of the evident and not-so-evident circular play.

3. *All human understanding is historically conditioned.* Minimally, historicity enters into the hermeneutical circle with the recognition that both the object for interpretation and the interpreter exist together at a certain time. The time of interpretative encounter is most often one in which an object from the past bears on the present in a way not altogether clear. The recognition of this temporal disjunction places certain demands on the interpreter, primarily, demands for historical and linguistic information that would better delineate the origin and history of the effects of the object on a series of interpreters. But more than this, historicity is the condition of the interpreter. The temporality of interpretation includes the projective endeavor to secure a stable yet reformable grasp on the possibilities for meaning and action amidst a realm of possible interpretations. Thus the choice of interpretations in the present becomes the identification and selection of future possibility in the light of past understandings and the object already at hand. For textual studies these aspects of historicity not only call for responsible historical scholarship but also underscore the value decisions that need to be made, both in the choice of texts to be interpreted and in the seriousness of interpretations that are advanced.

4. *All human understanding is linguistically conditioned.* Language itself is interpretative in a most fundamental way. To know a language is to understand time, objects, and action in a certain way. Understanding the condition of language and its bearing on interpretation includes an understanding of the language of the text and that of the interpreter, but it also extends beyond this to include the possibilities for being that the language of the text and the text as language provide for imaginative understanding. For religious textual studies, the recognition of the linguistic conditions of understanding, like that of the historical, expands the horizons of interpretation to the limits of language itself and places demands on the interpreter to be informed of the persuasive impact of language in grammatical, literary, rhetorical, philosophical, and spiritual ways.

5. *The object of hermeneutical understanding is best described as a "text."* Although the more ontological trends within hermeneutical study recognize the

interpretative dimensions of all human experience, hermeneutics tends to focus on objects broadly understood as textual. Its first concern is with the interpretation of written texts as opposed to oral presentation, performance, or ritual action. When the understanding of textuality is extended beyond the narrow limits of inscription to include instances of purposive communication in a shared language that has a common form of composition and generic structure, then "textuality" itself becomes a larger category, such as "classic." This expanded understanding of textuality allows for the possibility of focusing attention not only on inscription, but also on art, music, actions, and even lives as objects for interpretation. Particularly in theological circles, this movement has broadened the hermeneutical endeavor by including such topics as the lives of the saints as Christian classics, ethical action as textual, and the life of Jesus as the central Christian classic.

6. *An intrinsic part of interpretation is application or appropriation.* One of the differentiating factors between methods of textual explanation and textual understanding lies in the recognition and consequent theoretical clarification of the relation between the more formal means of textual study and the contingent demands to understand the bearing of the text on a contemporary world. This process is not understood to be a linear one in which the finished results of methodologically controlled textual, social, or political study are subsequently applied to a world outside the text. Rather, the model again is one of play, a situation in which the theory directs action in light of the text while at the same time the action reflects on the text to allow for the recovery of forgotten meaning or the disclosure of new meaning. Whether clarified by considerations of praxis, reader-response theory, reception theory, theory of action, or ethics, the task of human understanding and consequently the theory of hermeneutics includes, as an inner moment, a reflection on application.

The identification of broad areas of consensus does not imply that hermeneutics is so unified as to escape tensions even at the point of consensus. Several issues demanding further consideration are currently evident.

1. *Understanding is subject to systematic distortion.* It is one thing to correct the misapplication or the mistaken use of a method of interpretation. It is another thing altogether to recognize that the method itself distorts the understanding or that the conventional criteria of truth, knowledge, or application are themselves socially, politically, sexually, or in some other way ideologically biased. This is the present work of critical theory, namely, to unveil the cultural, psychological, epistemological, and political structures that not only condition but also alter in a regular and discernible way the communication that is at the heart of understanding. At points the results of a critical theoretical investigation seem to undermine hermeneutical assumptions about the positive role of tradition and the priority of classics. Thus a significant issue in hermeneutics today is the relative importance of critical theories in the overall interpretive project.

2. *Plurality is a characteristic of today's understanding.* Premodern world

223

views were, on the whole, more comfortable with the assumption that there was a unified order to existence that could be discovered in the first principles of metaphysics or revealed religious knowledge. Today's world views are less at home with either the metaphysical or the religious sense of unity. Global awareness, the specter of systematic distortions, suspicions of academic elitism, and the recognition of significant cultural diversity displace the assumptions of unity in favor of the recognition of plural understandings. The situation of plural claims for true understanding ushers in the discussions of relativity and regenerates the discussion of true understanding, the criteria of relative adequacy in contesting interpretations, and the role of cultural diversity in the interpretation of shared objects of experience.

3. The ambiguity of interpretation places stress on the process of application. The issues of ambiguity are not the same as those of plurality, which describes a situation of alternative, sometimes seemingly exclusive, interpretations. In contrast, ambiguity describes the situation of uncertainty in the *object* and, consequently, *method* of that which is to be interpreted. One response within hermeneutical theory is to call for a more sophisticated awareness of the contexts and methods of interpretation, but this response does not do away with the seemingly intractable situation that any significant object for interpretation may be understood in several ways. More troubling is the relation between ambiguity and application. If application or appropriation is understood as an inner moment of interpretation, then it generally exhibits a point at which a decision must be made on what to do or how to act in light of the text. Most often this action is not simply one of proposing another interpretation but one of taking a stance. If the ambiguity is inherent in the intended object, then application becomes problematic both because any action is open to ambiguous interpretation and because decisive action in the face of ambiguity is realistically problematic. Thus, within today's hermeneutical reflection the topics of praxis, pragmatism, and action have increasingly become the focus of attention.

JOHN McCARTHY

Bibliography

Hans-Georg Gadamer, *Truth and Method,* 2nd ed. Trans. Joel Weinsheimer and Donald G. Marshall.

Kurt Mueller-Vollmer, ed., *The Hermeneutics Reader.*

Paul Ricoeur, "Biblical Hermeneutics," *Semeia* 4 (1975): 29-148.

Anthony Thiselton, *The Two Horizons: New Testament Hermeneutics and Philosophical Description.*

David Tracy, *Plurality and Ambiguity: Hermeneutics, Religion, Hope.*

Cross Reference: Ambiguity, Epistemology, Feminist Theology, Metaphor, Myth, Philosophical Theology, Political Theology, Postmodern Theology, Symbol, Systematic Theology, Theological Method.

HISTORICAL THEOLOGY

The term "historical theology" has two meanings. It can refer to the history of Christian thought, that is, to a historical and critical account of the development of Christian ideas, doctrines, and beliefs. In this sense historical theology is a subfield within the history of Christianity, and its methods and goals are those appropriate to historical study. It has close parallels to intellectual history, and it has been pursued in relation to the history of philosophy, history of politics and culture, and in recent years social history.

On the other hand, historical theology can refer to the theological analysis of the sources of Christian thought: the Holy Scriptures, church councils (e.g., Nicea) and confessions of faith (e.g., the Thirty-nine Articles), the writings of the theologians of the early church (e.g., Gregory of Nyssa), medieval thinkers (e.g., Thomas Aquinas), Reformers (e.g., John Calvin), early modern thinkers (e.g., Friedrich Schleiermacher), and early-twentieth-century theologians (e.g., Karl Barth). In this sense historical theology is a subdiscipline of systematic theology.

Those who practice historical theology in the first sense of the term are concerned chiefly to interpret Christian sources in their historical setting (e.g., Augustine in the setting of the later Roman Empire), while those who follow the second are interested in drawing out the implications of classical thinkers for today's life and thought (e.g., Karl Rahner's recent efforts to draw upon Thomas Aquinas). Yet neither approach excludes the other, and neither is possible without the contribution of the other.

From early times Christian thinkers have been interested in the transmission of the teachings of their predecessors. Already in the second century, Irenaeus of Lyon had defended the Christian creed against Gnostic critics by appealing to traditions that had been handed on in the principal Christian centers in the Roman Empire. Later, as a result of disputes over the doctrine of Christ in the fifth century, Christians began to collect passages from earlier authors for the purpose of supporting their views and refuting the views of their opponents. The decree of the Council of Chalcedon (451) that Christ is known "in two natures" and "one person" begins with the words, "Following then the holy fathers." In the Middle Ages theologians customarily cited "authorities" to establish what the tradition teaches and to set the terms of the discussion. During the Reformation and into the seventeenth century, Protestant and Roman Catholic thinkers supported their theological views with extensive citations from the theologians of the early church and prominent medieval thinkers.

The critical study of earlier Christian sources has long been a feature of Christian thought. In the twelfth century Peter Abelard wrote *Sic et Non*, a collection of passages from early Christian writers on moral and theological topics. He showed that there were significant differences among these authorities (some had said "sic"—"yes"—while others countered "non"). To explain these differences he offered several possibilities: Certain quotations were not genuine (i.e., they did not come from the writer to whom they were attributed); some opinions that were set forth by a particular thinker were later retracted or altered; or the same terms were sometimes used with different meanings. He also considered the possibility that in the course of time views that were once permissible were shown to have difficulties and were later forbidden. He did not, however, enlarge this focus to include the idea that the time and place in which something was written could help to explain differences between Christian teachers.

A century later Thomas Aquinas examined and compared "authorities" (e.g., John Chrysostom and Gregory the Great) in his *Summa Theologiae*. Thomas carefully and critically studied the statements of different Christian writers in light of the whole of Christian teaching, subtly showing that certain expressions were infelicitous or ambiguous and required greater theological and philosophical precision. To account for differences among "authorities" and to justify his own intellectual enterprise, he argued that new circumstances called for new formulations. Theology, he said, cannot be confined to the terminology found in the scriptures: "If it is necessary to speak of God only in those words which the Holy Scriptures hand on to us when speaking of God, it would follow that one could not speak of God in any language other than the original language of the Old or New Testament." Because of the need to "confute heretics," "it is necessary to find new words to express the ancient faith about God." Thomas, like his predecessors, however, did not argue that doctrinal change was based on historical developments. This was the task of a later generation of Christian thinkers.

Only in the seventeenth and eighteenth centuries did scholars begin to conceive of theology as having a "history." The term "historical theology" *(theologica historica)* was coined by Heinrich Alting (1583–1644), and by it he meant the presentation of Christian doctrines in chronological (i.e., historical) order in contrast to dogmatic theology, which presented them systematically. Johann Salomo Semler (1725–1791) was the first to conceive of the field as a genuinely historical enterprise. He argued that the things said about God have been expressed in language and conceptions formed by the times in which the writers lived. No thinker stands in precisely the same relation to the scriptures as another, and in the course of the church's history there have been different ways of expressing Christian belief. Although Semler understood this task to be historical (i.e., ordering these differences chronologically), it is noteworthy that the categories he used to interpret the sources were drawn from dogmatic theology (doctrine of the Trinity, Christology, soteriology, eschatology), and his book *Historical Introduction to the Dogmatic Teaching About God from Its Origin and Its Practice in the Present* was written as a preface to the "systematic theology" *(Glaubenslehre)* of Siegmund Jacob Baumgarten, published in 1764.

Early in the nineteenth century, historical theology (or history of dogma as it was often called) came to be established as a separate discipline concerned with the history of Christian thought from its beginnings up to the Reformation, and in some cases to the present. Its greatest exponents were historians (e.g., Ferdinand Christian Baur, Adolf von Harnack, and Johann Joseph Ignaz von Döllinger), although theologians were still drawn to the field (e.g., Isaac August Dorner, Albrecht Ritschl, and John Henry Newman). The line between theologians and historians cannot be drawn clearly.

In the early twentieth century, historical theology continued to be closely associated with systematic theology. But as the study of the sources accelerated, and scholars without training in theology (e.g., those whose training was in intellectual history instead) entered the field, the discipline became more self-consciously historical and the ties to theology were weakened. In time the term "historical theology" was replaced by "history of Christian thought," and the discipline was concerned with the intellectual history of Christianity. Much of the energy of the discipline went into literary study and examination of the cultural, intellectual, and social setting in which Christian ideas and beliefs were formed. This "historicizing" of the field was quickened by its growing technical requirements: the need for competence in many languages, new demands for knowledge of social and political history, and familiarity with the methods of the social sciences.

The success of "historical theology" as an independent discipline and its sophistication about the interpretation of past epochs have changed profoundly our view of the history of Christian thought (e.g., there is new appreciation of the thinking of "heretics" and greater awareness of social factors in shaping Christian ideas), yet in some ways it has also made access to the past more difficult. The easy familiarity of early generations of theologians with the classical sources of Christian theology has been lost. Historical theology is now thought to be the business of historians, and the study of Christian sources (including the scriptures) must first be filtered by historians and literary critics before the texts can be interpreted "theologically." The result has been not only a loss of perspective in Christian theology but a loss of understanding and depth. It is assumed that the Bible, the writings of early Christian thinkers, and the treatises of the scholastics belong to the past and can only have theological relevance if they are "translated" into the categories of our age.

The difficulty with this program of translation is that the scriptures and early Christian tradition have a singular place in Christian memory. These sources speak, as it were, the native language of Christian life and thought. They cannot be viewed simply as "historical," as though their chief value were to bear witness to the past. Although "translating" the language of the scriptures into the idiom of a later age is always necessary (as Thomas Aquinas and many Christian thinkers have recognized), there is another sense in which the language of scripture and tradition is irreplaceable. "When we are dealing with the divine and holy mysteries of the faith, we must not hand on anything whatsoever without recourse to the Holy Scriptures," wrote Cyril of Jerusalem in the fourth century.

At the present moment in Christian history, the task of "translating" the scriptures and tradition into the language of our time is less urgent than that of rediscovering what has been forgotten, that is, learning anew how to use the language of scriptures and tradition in speaking about God and God's ways with humankind. God's revelation is not a body of free-floating truths. The Christian theological tradition cannot be appropriated independently of the language, ideas, practices, and form of life that have been the bearer of its beliefs. Its starting point is the history of ancient Israel, the life, death, and resurrection of Jesus Christ, and the calling into being of a new community by the Holy Spirit. Christian thought rests on revelation that took place in history, and knowledge of this revelation has been handed on in a historical community extending over time.

Christianity is and has always been a religion not only of a book but of books. Whether these books are commentaries on the scriptures, theological treatises, decrees of councils, sermons, or devotional writings, they have been shaped by the time in which their authors lived. Although the doctrine of the Council of Nicea may possibly be understood as an abstract formulation of Christian doctrine, its creed was formulated in response to specific challenges to Christian faith in the language and categories that were current at the time. This point is evident in the famous term *homoousios* (of one substance), which became part of the creed. Some objected because this term could not be found in the Bible, but it was nevertheless adopted and has become part of Christian vocabulary.

Nicea illustrates a fundamental feature of Christian theology. Its concepts and terms grow out of very concrete historical settings, and without constant recourse to this history it is difficult, if not impossible, to understand what Christians believe and teach. Extracted from their place in history, the language and concepts of Christian doctrine lose particularity and hence intelligibility.

> Concepts are creatures of history: they come into being, are molded and occasionally transformed through their complex and flexible relationships to other concepts and to the particularities of human existence, and may even fade and wither. The lives of concepts are inextricably related to the lives of actual persons and communities. Therefore the concept one learns is always shaped by contingent circumstances, and its mastery requires reference to those circumstances. (Wood, 76)

Historical knowledge, however, is not the chief concern of historical theology, for the subject matter of theology is the living God. If the theological writings of the past are seen solely in the light of the time and place in which they were written, historical theology can easily lose its distinctively theological character. In his *Summa Theologiae,* Thomas Aquinas wrote, "God is the object of this science." He recognized that theology treats many things (e.g., history, human beings, and creation), but always for these things to be theological they must be seen "under the aspect of God." Even "theological" topics (in the broad sense of the term—e.g., the work of salvation, Christ, the church, and last things and signs) "we treat in this science in so far as they have reference to God."

It is not sufficient, then, for historical theology to reconstruct the meaning of texts in their historical setting, to observe changing conceptions from one generation to another, and to note the differences between those who lived in former ages and ourselves. There must be a theological point of reference, some unity among the diversity, and that can only be the triune God who binds the present generation of faith to those in the past who knew, loved, and adored this God, and sought to express the mystery of Father, Son, and Holy Spirit through their words and ideas.

The student does not come to the study of historical theology empty-handed, as though engaged in a disinterested inquiry into what Christians thought at particular moments in the past. Like all theology, historical theology is concerned with how the church *should* formulate its beliefs and teachings. As Ian Ker notes in *John Henry Newman: A Biography*, Newman himself once observed that it was unprofitable to read the theologians of the early church without some idea of what one was looking for:

Till then their writings are blank paper—controversy is like the head administered to sympathetic ink. Thus I read Justin very carefully in 1828—and made most copious notes—but I conceive most of my time was thrown away. I was like a sailor landed at Athens or Grand Cairo, who stares about—does not know what to admire, what to examine—makes random remarks, and forgets all about it when he has gone.

The path to theological maturity leads necessarily through the study of the Christian past, and this requires a kind of spiritual and intellectual apprenticeship. Before we become masters we must become disciples. From the great thinkers of Christian history, we learn how to use the language of faith, to understand the inner logic of theological ideas, to discern the relation between seemingly disparate concepts, to discover what is central and what peripheral, and to love God above all things. Before we learn to speak on our own we must allow others to form our words and guide our thoughts. Historical theology is an exercise in humility, for we discover that theology is as much a matter of receiving as it is of constructing, that it has to do with the heart as well as with the intellect, with character as well as with doctrines, with love as well as with understanding.

ROBERT L. WILKEN

Bibliography

Adolf von Harnack, *History of Dogma*.
John Henry Newman, *Essay on the Development of Christian Doctrine*.
Wolfhart Pannenberg, *Systematische Theologie*, vol. 1.
Jaroslav Pelikan, *Historical Theology: Continuity and Change in Christian Doctrine*.

Friedrich Schleiermacher, *Brief Outline on the Study of Theology*.
Charles M. Wood, *The Formation of Christian Understanding*.

Cross Reference: Biblical Theology, Dogmatic Theology, Systematic Theology, Tradition.

HISTORY (*See* ESCHATOLOGY, PROVIDENCE, TIME.)

HOLOCAUST

The Holocaust was the systematic murder during World War II, by the Nazis, of eleven million people, of whom about six million were Jews. Other victims included, but were not limited to, gypsies (of whom about one million were exterminated), homosexuals, Soviet prisoners of war, Poles, non-Soviet communists, and those who had protested against Hitler's policies. This latter group included some intellectuals, several thousand Roman Catholic priests, and some Protestant clergy and theologians of whom Dietrich Bonhoeffer is best known. "Holocaust" comes from the Greek word used in the Septuagint (the Greek translation of the Hebrew Bible) for "burnt offering"; it referred to a sacrifice completely consumed by fire. Convinced that Hitler had no intention of making an offering to God, some scholars prefer the term *Shoah* ("destruction") to "holocaust."

The Jewish victims of the attempted Nazi genocide are distinguished from all other victims of the Holocaust (except gypsies) for several reasons. First, all Jews were to be eliminated; the so-called Jewish problem was to receive a "final solution" *(Endlösung)*. Hence, even the youngest children were targeted. Second, although the Nazis made plans for final solutions for other groups, the "war against the Jews" took precedence. Elimination of the others could wait until the world war was over. The urgency to eliminate the Jews even affected Nazi military strategy. Although there was a shortage of trains for moving German troops into battle against the Allied Forces, railroad cars were pressed into service to transport Jews to the killing centers (of which Auschwitz, though the most famous, was only one). Third, with regard to killing Jews, no conflicting considerations—economic, military, or otherwise—were taken into account. The effort was carried forward to ensure that there would not be a single Jew upon planet Earth, which was to be left "clean of Jews" *(Judenrein)*.

The Holocaust has become a topic of signal theological importance since the Second Vatican Council of the Roman Catholic Church in the 1960s, because scholars, both Jewish and Christian, have come to see that the Christian tradition itself was one of the factors that made the wholesale slaughter of Jews possible. There were other factors: the power of the modern bureaucratic state; the victory of value-free, problem-solving reason in the era of modernity; the rise of racism as a "philosophy" in the nineteenth century; and the willingness of professionals (lawyers, medical doctors, scientists, engineers, clergy) to cooperate in Hitler's program of mass destruction. Nonetheless, "post-Holocaust theologians" recognize that the church's "teaching of contempt" for Jews and Judaism was a two-thousand-year-old practice that served as a necessary but insufficient condition for the occurrence of the Holocaust. To post-Holocaust theologians the Holocaust is an "orienting event," because it enables them to see how the anti-Judaism of the Christian tradition contributed to the Holocaust and how the Christian tradition must be rethought in the light of the potentialities for evil that the Holocaust has disclosed it to bear.

To speak of the "anti-Judaism" of the Christian tradition sounds extreme; but more than seventy writers throughout the early and medieval eras of church history wrote tracts entitled "Against the Jews" *(Adversus Judaeos)*. The mode of thought of these tracts found its way into many other kinds of writings such as sermons, biblical interpretations, and systematic theologies. This tradition paints Jews and Judaism as the images of everything negative and bad in religion. Jews and Judaism are on the wrong side of several dichotomies: works-righteousness vs. grace; letter vs. spirit; legalism vs. faith; law vs. gospel; old vs. new; exclusivism vs. inclusivism. The anti-Jewish reading of the Bible appropriated all the biblical promises for the church and assigned all the condemnations and denunciations to the Jews, thus projecting an unremitting parody of evil upon the Jewish people. The church, called the "new Israel" (an expression not found in the New Testament), was said to displace the Jewish people in the covenant with God. This displacement (or supersessionist) argument contended that, because Jews failed to accept Jesus as Messiah, they were cursed by God and are no longer in covenant with God; and this argument also considered the church alone as the "true" or "spiritual" Israel. All Jews should therefore convert to Christianity and cease to exist *as Jews*. The chief reason cited for God's rejection of the Jewish people is that in crucifying Jesus the Jews "killed God" (the charge of deicide). The church throughout history has often used such teachings to justify anti-Jewish acts and attitudes in the name of Jesus.

Post-Holocaust theological scholarship proceeds on a number of fronts. An explosion in our knowledge of Judaism as it was at the time of Jesus and Paul has led to significant revisions in how Jesus and Paul are understood in their respective settings. There is no unanimity on the issue of how Paul is to be understood, but there is growing agreement on how he is *not* to be interpreted: The old model depicting Paul as opposed to Judaism is being widely challenged. Similarly, the historical Jesus is being interpreted *in* rather than *against* his setting. The strong tendency of much New Testament literature (particularly that written during the latter part of the first century) to distance itself from Judaism is increasingly viewed as reflecting Jewish-Christian tensions at the time of its writing. Theologically, post-Holocaust Christians are submitting the Christian tradition to a radical ideology critique. The meaning of the Christian witness is being interpreted in such a way as to disengage it from the economic, social, political, and cultural world whose injustices it has been used to sanction. Theologians also question the kind and extent of authority that can be accorded to biblical passages that give voice to anti-Judaism, with some theologians arguing that the heart of the New Testament message—the love who is God—itself demands that no authority be given to such statements.

CLARK M. WILLIAMSON

Bibliography

John P. Gager, *The Origins of Anti-Semitism.*
Raul Hilberg, *The Destruction of the European Jews.*
Rosemary Radford Ruether, *Faith and Fratricide.*
Krister Stendahl, *Paul Among Jews and Gentiles.*
Clark M. Williamson, *When Jews and Christians Meet.*

Cross Reference: Evil, Judaism.

HOLY (*See* GOD.)

HOLY SPIRIT

To explore a theology of the Holy Spirit is to ask fundamental questions about the meaning and purpose of life. No period in history has been in greater need of God's present activity in the world and a comprehensive and integrated spiritual vision for the future and destiny of planet Earth than the present. The Christian church's theology, however, has been glaringly deficient in setting forth a detailed doctrine of the Spirit, although scripture contains a strong basis for theological reflection. An urgent need exists for a doctrine of the Holy Spirit, especially in light of the new scientific picture of the cosmos, which has evoked questions about humanity's most cherished religious and philosophical perspectives of reality.

The view of the world given by science challenges traditional understandings of the God-world relation by redefining the concept of nature. Traditional views have portrayed nature as a machine and have defined matter as possessing no intrinsic value. Basic to a redefinition of nature is the argument that vitality exists in matter. The introduction of the vital character of matter questions earlier notions of the Holy Spirit and implies an understanding of the Spirit as the God-world relation itself. Such a notion of the Spirit can be defined as a model of reality, as a picture of the way God relates to the world and the world relates to God. The idea of the Holy Spirit as the God-world relation can also be defined as an operational idea for devising concepts of transition from an earlier cultural era to an emerging new one. In this sense, the Spirit is understood as the divine purpose and intent coming to fulfillment through humans in the transformation of culture from one epoch to the next.

The notion of the Holy Spirit as the God-world relation is affirmed in the Christian doctrine of the Trinity. The idea of Spirit as the third person of the Trinity declares God to be the ground of this world and the natural life within it. This affirmation means that the Holy Spirit is central to the world and human life. As such the Spirit is the power that sustains the world and human life at the same time that it moves the world and human life to transcend themselves in concrete events.

Some basic presuppositions underlie a notion of the Spirit defined as the God-world relation. Modern science has modified eighteenth-century definitions of nature as a finite deterministic mechanism that is static and dualistic in character. This traditional definition of nature is rivaled by a dynamic holistic concept that understands nature as an infinite, ever-expanding process. In the earlier view of nature, matter is seen as fixed in character—inert, compartmental, inactive, and unresponsive. Current science perceives matter more as a living active power, restless and insurgent in character, imbued with intrinsic value, possessing depth and interiority, and inclined toward organization. The current view suggests a notion of vitality in matter that challenges understandings of spirit that deny any possibility of divine-human reciprocity and cooperation. Specifically challenged are interpretations of the Spirit as immaterial, unearthly, and wholly transcendent and the human response to the Spirit as purely subjective, passive, powerless, and submissive. Further, current views of nature support an understanding of the earth as an organic entity whose natural processes are imbued with the presence of the Holy Spirit. The contemporary scientific picture of nature therefore leads to a rethinking of the God-world and God-human relationships.

Biblical scholars have cited at least seven characteristics concerning the Holy Spirit and its relationship to the world. One characteristic is that the Spirit is an essential category for designating God's presence in the world. Throughout the Hebrew scriptures, the Spirit is the designation of divine validation of the work of the prophets, Israel's leaders, and the Israelite community itself. In the New Testament, Spirit as the validating category for God's presence in the world undergirded the messiah's appearance and the Christian community that emerged.

A second characteristic of biblical views is that the Holy Spirit is not spatially outside the created order. This means that the Spirit was present not only and essentially at Pentecost, but from the first stirrings of creation. The Spirit evolves with the destiny of the universe that God establishes for the created order itself. Therefore the Spirit is intrinsic to the fulfillment of the divine purposes.

Third, biblical understandings of the Holy Spirit provide a basis for understanding the God-world relation. God is the source and meaning of the work of the Spirit. Therefore, any speculation about the Spirit must refer to God. The world is the "location" or "arena" of the Holy Spirit. Thus, the Spirit is concretely interrelated with God and the world. In his book, *God as Spirit,*

233

W. H. Lampe emphasizes the concept of the Spirit as "the immanent creative activity of the transcendent creator." The Spirit points to the one God who is transcendent and immanent, and it makes God known in the external natural order and also within the life and faith of human beings. Lampe associates the Spirit with the power, meaning, and purpose of God in creation and especially within human life. He asserts that the life-giving presence of God as the Spirit is the real manifestation of Jesus' presence in the world. The Holy Spirit is the Spirit of truth who continues the revelation of Jesus Christ in the present.

Fourth, biblical witness about the Holy Spirit concludes that the best way to describe the Spirit's work is through God's purposes for the created order. Thus it is impossible to discern the Holy Spirit without relating the Spirit to the final consummation orchestrated by God. This eschatological interpretation of the Spirit is supported by both the biblical witness and the early Greek understandings of spirit. Further, the biblical tradition tends to relate the Hebrew and Greek words for the Spirit, *ruach* and *pneuma,* to energy in speaking of God's purposes for the world. Therefore, the Spirit as intrinsic to God's purposes is linked to understanding or intelligibility as well as to eschatology. Eduard Schweizer states that when taken as a whole the biblical witness offers a notion of the Holy Spirit as one that is linked not only to the Jesus of the New Testament but also to the future consummation of God and the eschatological meaning of Jesus' death and resurrection. He emphasizes the Hebrew scripture's testimony of the Spirit's work in affirming all of life. Further, Schweizer stresses the unity that the Holy Spirit brings to human creation, the blessedness of all of life, God's divine intent for human destiny, the fulfillment of God's future, and the promised gifts of the Spirit such as peace and justice.

Fifth, the Hebrew and Christian scriptures contain strong patterns of similarity with regard to the Holy Spirit as the basis of divine love and faithfulness. The New Testament particularly claims that Jesus provides the essential link with the Spirit that allows for the interpretation of God's will in nature and history. In relating Christ and the Holy Spirit, however, one must not neglect the Hebrew scriptures, which speak of the Spirit as active in the creation and also in the redemption of God's people (*see* Ps. 33, 104, 147; Job 27, 32, 33; Ezek. 37; and Isa. 44). If Jesus' activity is to be recognized, he must be understood as the embodiment of the Hebrew scripture's notion of Spirit as God's presence in the world.

Sixth, in the New Testament the Holy Spirit is closely connected with the resurrected Lord, thus emphasizing the saving aspect of God's work in the world. However, the biblical witness as a whole relates salvation to nature and the world as God's complete relationship with creation. Cast in this larger framework, salvation allows for its central position in theology and guards theology from simplistic notions of salvation in the understanding of God's activity in the world. God's saving work in Jesus Christ manifested in the Spirit relates to all phenomena. Therefore, by relating pneumatology and Christology the biblical witness identifies the meaning of Christ as the meaning of the Holy Spirit. The Spirit is independent within the Trinitarian framework. Christ himself is not the Spirit; rather the Holy Spirit points to God's entire work in the whole created process. The unified yet individual witness of the biblical sources reflects the wholeness yet distinctive character of the Godhead. The Trinity offers a workable model of a comprehensive ordering and understanding of the human experience of God in the world.

The seventh characteristic of the Bible's views of the Holy Spirit is that the Spirit is active in nature *and* in history and life. It is this view especially that provides the matrix of the argument that the Spirit is alive in matter and therefore in all natural processes.

Modern theologians such as Teilhard de Chardin and Wolfhart Pannenberg have contributed comprehensive notions of the Spirit and its relationship to nature that are consonant with biblical witness and the vital character of matter. From Teilhard's perspective, the Spirit and matter are fundamentally one and the same. He qualifies this relationship by stating that between the Spirit and matter is a reversal that makes them also opposed to one another. Teilhard means that the Spirit is not something that is superimposed on human beings nor is it a by product of the cosmos. Rather, the Spirit represents simply the higher state assumed in and outside of humans by what he calls "the stuff of the universe."

Pannenberg asserts that the Creative Spirit is the origin of all living matter that transcends living beings. In this sense every organism lives beyond itself. Therefore, he defines the Spirit on the basis of the self-transcending tendency of all organic life.

The traditional alienation of nature from ethical and theological reflection is a glaring mistake that can no longer be tolerated in the church's theology. This oversight is especially incommensurate with the construction of a theology of the Holy Spirit at a time in history when the consequences of unrestricted technological advancement threaten the existence of the planet itself. The modern world is in a process of an unprecedented shift in its collective consciousness. The reclaiming of nature is of paramount importance to the theological task if the cutting edge of the Christian message is to continue to have potency, relevance, or impact on the world in the present and the future.

An essential element of the theological task is to be a relevant meaning-giver to the world in the midst of the novel complexities of an emerging reality. The reformulation of the idea of the Holy Spirit provides a conceptual matrix of universal meaning and purpose for an evolving epoch struggling to take shape and form. The unrelenting nuclear threat, the ethically undirected progress of high technology, the rapid depletion of natural resources, the catastrophic ecological consequences of the gross misuse of the environment, the patriarchal domination of nature and of norms for reality, and the loss of meaning, relevance, and credibility of religious truth claims converge to form a frightening picture of the modern world. A universal notion of the Spirit that is intrinsically related to the natural process provides an essential and hitherto neglected understanding of the God-world relation. Such a concept is an interpretative principle that is capable of discerning and directing the destiny of the world in a new age.

One illustration of a reformulated theology of the Holy Spirit is found in the thought of feminist theologian Rosemary Radford Ruether, who describes with powerful accuracy the circumstances in which a new theology of the Spirit as the God-world relation itself must emerge. She calls for a radical rethinking of the Western theological tradition's understanding of the hierarchical chain of being and chain of command. The eco-feminist theology of nature that Ruether proposes challenges the tradition in four significant ways. First, she questions the hierarchy of the human over nonhuman nature as a relationship of ontological and moral value. Second, she criticizes the right of the human to treat the nonhuman as private property and material wealth to be exploited. Third, she challenges the structures of social domination—male over female, owner over worker—that mediate this domination of nonhuman nature. Fourth, she replaces the notion of the Spirit as nonmaterial and matter as nonspiritual, inferior, valueless, and dominated with the idea of "God/ness," a primal matrix who is neither stifling immanence nor rootless transcendence. Ruether's proposal rejects the bifurcation of the Spirit and matter and instead conceives them as the inside and outside of the same thing.

The science-religion interface is now the key to the theological enterprise. Theology's full participation in the dialogue with science is the starting place for a re-creating of culture that is based on understanding the Holy Spirit as the entity that evolves within the natural processes at the same time that it transcends nature and guides the world to its final destiny according to the benevolent intent of the Creator. The task of this new theology of the Holy Spirit is to function as a microcosm of an evolving macrocosm of universal spiritual consciousness that is the God-world relation itself. Such a notion of the Spirit must participate with scientific insights in forming the crucial questions of existence and offer feasible trajectories for a new synthesis of the structures of reality for an emerging era.

LORA GROSS

Bibliography

Alisdair Heron, *Holy Spirit*.
Carolyn Merchant, *The Death of Nature: Women, Ecology, and the Scientific Revolution*.
Rosemary Radford Ruether, *Sexism and God-Talk: Towards a Feminist Theology*.
H. Paul Santmire, *The Travail of Nature*.
Teilhard de Chardin, *Activation of Energy*.
———, *Human Energy*.

Cross Reference: Being/Becoming, Christology, Cosmology, God, Pentecostalism, Process Theology, Science and Christianity, Technology, Trinity.

HOMILETICS

Homiletics is the scientific study of the art of preaching. Homileticians are theologians who specialize in the teaching of preaching. Homiletics is concerned with every aspect of the preaching task: the study of the text, the preparation of the sermon, and the delivery of the message. But these matters inevitably involve many other issues: the question of hermeneutics; the language of the sermon; various methodologies of sermon structure; the relationship of the congregation or listeners to the sermon; and the sermon as one aspect of a larger service of worship. All of these questions must be seen in light of the history of preaching and the theology of preaching. In its broadest sense, then, homiletics is a study that involves the integration of every aspect of theological study into the act of preaching.

Although the prevalence of courses on homiletics in seminaries has varied over the centuries, no other subject has a longer history in theological education. Probably because preaching was largely an oral matter in the early centuries, few sermon manuscripts from that time have survived. But we know that very early preaching was a matter of intense study, because of the attention given to it in the writings of such early church fathers as Origen (185–254), Chrysostom (John of Antioch, 347–407), and Augustine (354–430). The first treatise on homiletics, so far as we know, was written by Augustine. It was by no means the last, however. During the Middle Ages no fewer than six hundred treatises on homiletics were produced. The primary intent of these works, as of those that preceded them, was to fuse Greek rhetoric with Christian theology. This approach left the sermon in bondage to classical speech structures and more often than not resulted in allegorical, highly fanciful sermons. Typical of these were the rhyming sermons of the Schoolmen, so opposed by John Wycliffe (1324–1384). His emphasis on the "naked text" helped turn the direction of preaching away from its Greek captor.

The hold of classical rhetoric, however, proved hard to break. *The Preparation and Delivery of Sermons,* by John Broadus, has been in print longer than any modern text on homiletics—since the Civil War. It has been termed "a christianized rhetoric" because of its heavy dependence on rules of classical speech. The boredom and frustration of many listeners (and preachers) with Broadus' stylized approach to preparing sermons led homileticians to seek other approaches to preaching.

The first step in the modern corrective to preaching has been a return to the biblical origins of the sermon. Instead of attempting to fit the Christian sermon into Greek speech categories, recent preaching theory has asked what the Christian faith and the biblical text demand. One answer has been renewed attention to the biblical story. Instead of finding a phrase or subject suggested by a biblical verse and creating a topical sermon around it, some homileticians have suggested a narrative approach to the text. That is, they favor sermons that take more seriously the context of the scripture, and they advocate a storylike approach to a sermon. Generally such sermons emphasize the setting of the text, both historically and biblically, and attempt to allow the text "to speak its own message." Rather than use a typical analytical or argumentative "three-point" approach, these sermons seek to develop a "plot" that follows the unfolding biblical narrative. Among that of many other homiletical writers, the work of Edmund Steimle, Morris Niedenthal, Charles Rice, and Eugene Lowry has been important in this area. They, in turn, were greatly influenced, directly or indirectly, by writers in narrative theology such as Hans Frei *(The Eclipse of Biblical Narrative)* and Brian Wicker *(Story-Shaped World)*, and by writers in hermeneutics and language such as Paul Ricoeur, Jürgen Habermas, and Walter Ong.

Narrative preaching gained widespread attention and initial acceptance as a corrective to more abstract sermon forms. Many aspects of the method have continued to find favor. (An interesting variant of this method has been developed by David Buttrick in *Homiletic,* a phenomenological approach to "how sermons happen in consciousness.") But critics of this approach find it too limiting and insist that no single approach to the sermon can adequately define the act of preaching.

Another important development in recent homiletical thought has been the emphasis on inductive preaching. Numerous critics have scored the traditional sermon for its deductive, "heavy downward" movement. They feel that the sermon takes too much on itself in its traditional form, causing the congregation to become mere passive recipients of its message. Inductive preaching seeks to present the sermon in a more open manner, withholding judgment and using implicit rather than explicit conclusions. Listeners are thereby encouraged to be active participants in "overhearing" the gospel, often through story or parable, rather than defensive avoiders of preaching. Again, this approach seems to be more useful for some subjects and audiences than others; and though its principles in the broadest sense are useful, not even its strongest advocates (e.g., Fred Craddock, *As One Without Authority* and *Overhearing the Gospel*) regard it as more than one approach among others.

These new approaches to the text and the methodology of the sermon have been joined by a new emphasis in sermon delivery. Since the invention of the printing press and the advent of popular literacy, reading a sermon manuscript has increasingly become the standard method of sermon delivery. But this was in contrast to the early Christian practice of preaching "free style"; that is, either without notes or with limited notes. Many notable Christian preachers have used the free style or oral style (including Augustine, Aquinas, Calvin, Baxter, Maclaren, Spurgeon, Liddon, Sheen, and Bonhoeffer), but increasingly the essay-style sermon demanded a manuscript for its presentation. Recently, some homileticians have moved away from both essay sermons and manuscripts. They argue that the spoken medium demands a spoken style, and that the oral style invites participation rather than passive observation. In current homiletics, this note was first sounded in *Preaching for Today* (Clyde Fant) and has been advocated recently by numerous homileticians, including Fred Craddock and Eugene Lowry.

Today's homiletics has also devoted increased attention to the theology of preaching, black preaching, Third World preaching, and the preaching of women. The theology of preaching has been examined by many, including Richard Lischer *(A Theology of Preaching)*, Joseph Sittler *(The Anguish of Preaching)*, and Karl Rahner *(The Renewal of Preaching)*. Black preaching has been increasingly influential; its homileticians include Henry H. Mitchell *(The Recovery of Preaching)*, James Earl Massey *(Designing the Sermon)*, and Howard Thurman (sermon volumes). Third World preaching has been examined by Justo González and Catherine Gunsalus González *(Liberation Preaching)*, Gustavo Gutiérrez *(The Mystical and Political Dimension of the Christian Faith)*, and others. The entire question of the preaching of women has become increasingly lively, as has the question of gender language in preaching. Prominent writers include Letty M. Russell *(The Liberating Word)*, Rosemary Radford Ruether *(Sexism and God-Talk)*, and Elisabeth Schüssler Fiorenza *(In Memory of Her)*.

CLYDE FANT

Cross Reference: Narrative Theology, Worship.

HOPE

The Western history of hope stands in the tension between the Greek and the biblical estimations of this power. According to the Greek Promethean myth, hope is an evil that comes out of Pandora's box to confuse the human spirit. Our wisdom of experience says the same: "Hoping and waiting makes many a fool." Whoever might expect something else, misses the chance of the present. Their spirits are not here but rather in the dreams of the future. "Why roam in the distance? See, the good lies so near. Learn only to achieve happiness, then happiness is always there," wrote Goethe. Similarly, through the Sisyphus myth of Albert Camus, existential philosophy proclaimed, "Think clearly and do not hope," because hopes are the playing field of political and economical deceivers, who sell illusions and destroy the real life.

Contrasted to this, the biblical texts understand hope as a positive, divine power of life. It is the expectation of a good future that is awakened through God's promise and supported by trust in God. Consequently, hope is unequivocal and unambiguous. It does not detach the human spirit from the present through delusions, but rather the opposite; it pulls the promised future into the present and places the experienced present in the dawn of God's future. Hope does not empty out one's life but rather fills it with new powers. Whoever "lives in hope" carries the future also (Leibniz). Whoever believes in God, hopes in the future; whoever loses hope, loses God. Therefore, Dante writes in the *Divine Comedy* over the entrance to hell: "Let all hope go, whoever enters here." For many people, the opposite of this sentence holds true: Those who lose all hope are in hell.

The "God of hope" (Rom. 15:13) is the God of Abraham and Sarah, Issac and Rebekah, Jacob and Rachel. Their experiences of God brought them to the exodus from their present and into the search for the fulfillment of God's promises. If Abraham is the father of the Jewish, Christian, and Islamic faiths, then these three religions are to be understood as religions of hope. They are future-oriented and historical, and in these respects, they are aggressive religions when one compares them with Eastern, African, and indigenous traditional religions of nature. The goal of Christian hope is "Christ and his universal Parousia"; the goal of Jewish hope is the "Torah and the Kingdom of God"; and the goal of Islamic hope is complete theocracy. The eternal presence of God's self in the kingdom of God's glory is implied in these different images of hope: in the new heaven and the new earth in which God lives and comes to rest; in the eternal life of all God's creatures who are brought into place through God's justice.

In the Jewish, Christian, and Islamic writings, there are many individual promises of God for health, long life, many descendants, blessing of the harvest, and a fertile earth; but already in the postexilic time of Israel these particular hopes were integrated into the greater promises of God through the major prophets of Israel: the return home of God's people out of Babylonian exile (Ezekiel 37), the birth of the messianic king (Isaiah 9), the universal peace among nations (Isaiah 2), peace between people and animals (Isaiah 11), the overcoming of death (Isaiah 24), the new creation of heaven and earth (Isaiah 65), and finally, the arrival of the eternal glory of God (Isaiah 6).

The history of Israel's promises is the history of a continually new interpretation of hope in light of the experiences of history and a growing expansion of this hope. History is experienced in the reciprocal interpretation of expectation and experience. On the basis of the expectation, one has new experiences, and on the basis of the experience, one gains new expectations. Every historical fulfillment of the promise is perceived as a security for greater hope. Every historical disappointment becomes occasion for deeper trust in God (Ps. 73:23ff.). The basis for this amazing history of hope is theological: God is the basis of the promises and of history, and the hopes of humans are directed to God's self and God's future. Therefore, the psalmist says: "God is my trust."

For the Christian faith, Christ is the "hope of the world" because the hoped-for Messiah of Israel has appeared in Jesus of Nazareth and in his gospel. In his life, death, and resurrection, the future kingdom of God has already become present, and in his spirit, hope has already become determining for the present. The believers discover that in Christ "indestructible life" in the middle of this destroyed and threatened world has appeared. This experience is the basis of their world-conquering hope, their passion for life, and their resistance against the powers of death.

This happens in two ways. First, Christian hope is based on the memory of the suffering and death of Christ. In the midst of the anonymous history of humanity's suffering, the history of Christ's suffering is found. Between the many crosses in the world stands his cross on Golgotha. In the suffering and dying of God's son, God enters the world's history of suffering. Through the solidarity of Christ with the suffering ones, God comes to them. "He has borne our griefs and carried our sorrows" (Isa. 53:4). The divine compassion (theopathy) brings hope to the hopeless. Therefore, an old Christian saying says, *"Ave crux—unica spes"* (Be greeted: Cross—our only hope).

Second, Christian hope is aroused through the resurrection of Christ from the dead. All human hopes end at death; therefore, only the overcoming of death can arouse indestructible hope. The Christian experience of God understands itself as "born anew to a living hope through the resurrection of Jesus Christ from the dead" (I Pet. 1:3). The word of hope in the "resurrection" speaks not only of individual hope but of a future for all, the living and the dead. It brings the believers into an unforgettable community with the dead because this same hope connects the living and the dead. Exactly because it speaks of a future of life for the dead, "resurrection" is a word of justice for the forgotten and a word of resistance; it is not only the redemption of humanity from death, but also the cosmic rebirth of life and the new creation of all things because the resurrecting God is the creator of the world and lover of life. Redemption is also the "restoration of all things."

In the Middle Ages a theology of *caritas* (charity) was devised, and during the Reformation, a theology of faith. Today's task is to design a universal theology of hope that directs and prepares individual believers and the church, the church and Israel, human culture and nature to the kingdom of God. We love only so far as we can hope. Only if we include all things into our hope in God will we be ready to love all things and to meet them with respect.

JÜRGEN MOLTMANN

Bibliography

Ernst Bloch, *The Principle of Hope*.
Gabriel Marcel, *The Philosophy of Hope*.
Jürgen Moltmann, *Theology of Hope*.
J. Pieper, *Über die Hoffnung*.
J. A. T. Robinson, *In the End God*.

Cross Reference: Eschatology, Resurrection, Suffering.

HUMANISM

The term "humanism" admits of so wide a variety of usage as to seem utterly drenched in ambiguity. On the one hand, those who conceive religion to involve nothing more than complete absorption in whatever is envisaged as supremely valuable and who would forswear the very idea of God as an irrelevant anachronism call themselves humanists. On the other hand, those who are scholarly practitioners of one or another of the intellectual disciplines collectively spoken of as the humanities are themselves spoken of as humanists. Or, again, a philosopher who is radically opposed to any and all positivistic accounts of experience will be spoken of as one representing a humanistic outlook. So many other perspectives and points of view of various kinds are taken to exemplify a humanistic orientation that one finds it difficult to define with any real precision what the concept of humanism embraces and what it excludes. Thus, inevitably, the fugitiveness of the term drives us to turn to the more manageable, or at least the more readily specifiable, reality brought into view by the usages of intellectual historians—namely, the great fascination with the glory that was Greece and the grandeur that was Rome that began to take hold of the European imagination in the fifteenth and sixteenth centuries.

Renaissance humanists were, of course, by no means without their medieval precursors. Already in the thirteenth century Dante, for example, was deeply steeped in the Latin classics of ancient Rome, and the *Commedia* is as reliant on pagan as on Christian symbolism. But it was not till late in the fourteenth century that university scholars began to win any real command of Attic Greek, though by the time of Ficino and Pico della Mirandola and Spenser the educated men of Europe were reveling in the legacies of Greece, which were persuading them that (as Pico phrased it) the Supreme Maker, having placed man in the center of the world, had decreed that he, being "restrained by no narrow bonds," should define his own nature for himself. By the late fifteenth century, this new spirit of autonomy was in the full tide of fashion.

In Southern Europe the idioms of this whole insurgency differed somewhat from those by which it was marked in Northern Europe, the Italian humanist tending to embrace a Greek vision of life as an art whereas the German humanist was more drawn to a kind of Roman vision of life as a stoic discipline. Yet the spirit pervading the entire European scene was one of rebellion, and the new humanists, whether in the North or in the South, knew themselves to be committed to revolt against their medieval forebears.

In his passion for learning, in the poise and urbanity of his intelligence, in his cultural conservatism, in his utter impatience with all fanaticisms whether of the medieval past or of the new Reformers of his own period, Erasmus is often rightly thought to present a quintessential case of the humanism of the Renaissance, as it emerged in the fifteenth and sixteenth centuries. He is also a characteristic exemplar of his moment in history in his failure to advance any large and impressively original systematic philosophy. In *Ideas and Men: The Story of Western Thought* (1950), Crane Brinton shrewdly noticed that "the formal metaphysical thought of the humanists is not one of their strong points." Erasmus, like Thomas More and John Colet, was deeply devoted to Platonism, but these Northern Europeans, like such Italian humanists as Ficino and Pico della Mirandola, in their evasion of what Brinton calls "the big questions," added nothing of primary significance to the Platonist tradition. So, for all his withering scorn of the old prejudices and superstitions of the medieval world, he had little more to propose in their stead than such a distrust of Scholasticism and such a respect for freedom of inquiry as would finally provide the seedbed out of which the eighteenth-century Enlightenment would grow.

There is, of course, an immense distance between the world of Erasmus and Sir Thomas More and that of Benjamin Franklin, Diderot, Holbach, Thomas Paine, and Condorcet. Perhaps the most obvious difference arises out of the fact that, whereas the Renaissance humanists were inclined toward aristocratic perspectives on the human community, the men of the Enlightenment were largely possessed by democratic enthusiasms. But the divide between these two climates of opinion was established far more decisively by the well-nigh unshakable indifference of the humanists toward scientific enterprise. Already in the fourteenth century Petrarch was asking "what does it advantage us to be familiar with the nature of animals, birds, fishes, and reptiles, while we are ignorant of the nature of the race of man to which we belong, and do not know or care whence we come or whither we go?" And the ridicule that Erasmus reserves for the "natural philosophers" in the *Praise of Folly* strikes an abiding note in the testimony of these men who did so much to brighten the early morning-time of the modern world. They seem to have felt that there is something grubby and mediocre in hard scientific labor, and they consistently accorded pride of place to the study of humanity over the study of nature.

This was, however, a valuation that was to undergo a considerable reversal in the period of the Enlightenment. Yet, in its emphasis on freedom of conscience and on freedom of the mind, the humanist tradition may be seen to have been a guardian of precisely those faculties on which scientific inquiry most essentially depends, and thus it may also be seen to have formed a kind of *praeparatio* for the Age of Reason, or at least to have found it not impossible, with its insistence on the dignity and worth of human life on this earth, to cooperate, as it were, with the new scientific emphasis on universal law and on the prevalence throughout the whole of nature of a harmonious causal order.

Moreover, the "sacred philology" (as Paul Kristeller terms it in *Renaissance Thought*, 1961) of Renaissance humanism also played a part in paving the way for late modernity. Indeed, the edition of the Greek New Testament that Erasmus published in 1516 is an enduring landmark that caused great distress in orthodox circles at the time of its appearance, since the translations of the Latin Vulgate, however erroneous many of them in fact were, had come to have the authority of revelation itself. But Erasmus in effect was saying through this enormous achievement that the New Testament is to be studied like any other ancient text, in accordance with the same philological standards and the same methods of textual analysis. And thus "the higher criticism" of the Bible in the modern period may be said to have one of its remoter precursors in him.

Although humanism, in its metaphysical aspect, was largely committed from the fifteenth century forward to some form of Christian Platonism, once it began to mingle with and be incorporated into various strands of Enlightenment ideology, it inevitably underwent to a considerable degree a process of secularization. The distinguished Neo-Thomist philosopher Jacques Maritain is surely right in declaring (in *True Humanism*) that "the springs of Western humanism . . . [are] classical and Christian," but by the advent of the nineteenth century the tradition, in so far as it retained any real coherence, had generally lost its earlier theocentric orientation, its outlook having become (as Maritain remarked) essentially "anthropocentric." So much is this the case today that it seems not at all inappropriate that the 1950 edition of the *Encyclopedia Britannica* should define the term "humanism" as denominating "any system of thought or action which assigns a predominant interest to the affairs of men as compared with the supernatural."

So it is not surprising that such a book as John Dewey's *A Common Faith,* which comprises the Terry Lectures he delivered at Yale in 1933, should be widely felt to present the definitive exposition of modern humanism in its secular mode. His whole scheme of argument in this book is calculated to liberate religion from any supernatural dimension, which he conceives the advances of modern culture and science to have thoroughly discredited: only by way of such a disjunction, he contends, can the religious phase of experience win the freedom to develop freely on its own account. "For [in] the moment we have a religion, whether that of the Sioux Indian or of Judaism or of Christianity, [in] that moment the ideal factors in experience that may be called religious take on a load that is not inherent in them, a load of current beliefs and of institutional practices that are irrelevant to them." That is to say, the various particular religions entail special bodies of belief and special practices having one or another kind of institutional organization—whereas the adjective "religious," in Dewey's view, denotes attitudes that may be taken toward the world in general and toward any and every kind of experience.

Dewey suggests that the fundamental human enterprise involves the quest for such an orientation, for such an adjustment to the world, as will yield a sense of security and peace. And he considers the term "religion" to cover that whole range of experience in which "the idealizing imagination" seizes upon those aims and purposes and ends devotion to which promises to harmonize the various impulses of the human spirit and thus to open the way to the kind of ultimate serenity and poise that will allow us to keep a loving regard for the good of others. It is, he urges, within the terms of such considerations as these that we shall find "all the elements for a religious faith that shall not be confined to sect, class, or race," the sort of faith indeed that may be thought to be something like the "common faith" of humankind. "We are," he says, "in the presence neither of ideals completely embodied in existence, nor yet of ideals that are mere rootless ideals, fantasies, utopias. For there are forces in Nature and society that generate and support the ideals. They are further unified by the action that gives them coherence and solidity. It is this *active* relation between ideal and actual to which I would give the name 'God'."

There are, in short, certain preeminently real and concrete goods—

the values of art in all its forms, of knowledge, of effort and of rest after striving, of education and fellowship, of friendship and love, of growth in mind and body. These goods are there and yet they are relatively embryonic. Many persons are shut out from generous participation in them; there are forces at work that threaten and sap existent goods as well as prevent their expansion. A clear and intense conception of a union of ideal ends with actual conditions is capable of arousing steady emotion. It may be fed by every experience, no matter what its material. In a distracted age, the need for such an idea is urgent. It can unify interests and energies now dispersed; it can direct action and generate the heat of emotion and the light of intelligence. Whether one gives the name 'God' to this union, operative in thought and action, is a matter for individual decision. But the *function* of such a working union of the ideal and actual seems to me to be identical with the force that has in fact been attached to the conception of God in all the religions that have a spiritual content; and a clear idea of that function seems to me urgently needed at the present time.

Now the kind of *via media* that Dewey sought to chart between dogmatic supernaturalism and dogmatic atheism has proved enormously attractive to modern humanists, so much so that within their party *A Common Faith* has attained a well-nigh scriptural status. One suspects that its great appeal results in part from the degree to which Dewey's "common faith" invites active engagement in the struggle to overcome the hiatus between the actual and the ideal. Certainly on the American scene it is the large place in the religious life he accords social meliorism that has given his program its great charm, and, though within the religious community the ranks of self professed humanists are today much smaller than they were in the 1920s and 1930s and 1940s (when such men as Roy Wood Sellars, E. S. Ames, A. E. Haydon, and John Haynes Holmes were influential figures), one cannot begin to understand the basic humanist creed without reference to Dewey's Terry Lectures.

NATHAN A. SCOTT, JR.

245

Bibliography

Crane Brinton, *Ideas and Men: The Story of Western Thought.*
S. Dresden, *Humanism in the Renaissance.*
Jacques Maritain, *True Humanism.*
Albert Rabil, ed., *Renaissance Humanism: Foundations, Forms, and Legacy,* vol. 3.
John Herman Randall, Jr., *The Making of the Modern Mind.*

Cross Reference: Biblical Criticism, Culture, Secularity, Virtue.

IDOLATRY

Idolatry is a basic theological and ethical concept in the Christian tradition. The term derives from the Greek *eidololatria,* meaning the "worship of images." In the biblical tradition the transcendence of God came to be symbolized negatively, by the insistence that God could be neither named nor imagined. (Indeed the correct pronunciation and meaning of the Hebrew name for God, "YHWH," remains a mystery, and any attempt to pronounce the name is forbidden by Jewish tradition.) To be able to name and image something is to have power over it, to be able to control and manipulate it. But one cannot have power over the One who is truly transcendent; thus, any god who can be named and imaged is not the true God but an idol. Idolatry is an act of substitution; one gives to that which is less than God (that which can be named and imaged) all the worship, service, and devotion that belongs to God alone.

Idolatry is at once both a religious and an ethical concept. To treat something as worthy of worship is to treat it as sacred. To say that something is sacred is to say that it is most important or most valued. Every ethic (no matter how apparently "secular") is finally grounded in some sense of the sacred, from which it derives its hierarchy of values. Paul Tillich captured this dynamic when he defined faith as "ultimate concern" and idolatry as ultimate concern about that which is less than ultimate. That which is worthy of faith or worship must truly be ultimate in value and being—all encompassing, infinite, and eternal. To surrender one's will and being, as an expression of ultimate concern, to that which is less than ultimate leads to sin and injustice.

Finite goods such as power and wealth, when made the object of ultimate concern, always create divisions between individuals, between those who have and those who do not. God is the one good, who is infinitely and completely available to all. God's availability to one does not diminish availability to another. Hence, whereas idolatry creates divisions and injustice, true faith creates unity and harmony. All humanity is one by virtue of sharing in common the life of God. This point is emphasized in the teachings of Jesus where he insists that one should love one's enemies even as God does, for the love of God rains on the just and the unjust alike (Matt. 5:43-48).

It can be argued that the fundamental ground of the human rights tradition in the West, which insists on the essential dignity of all human beings across all class, racial, ethnic, religious, and national boundaries, has its roots in the biblical insight that all human beings have an inherent transcendent dignity derived from being created in the image of a God without image. Attempts at dehumanization invariably reduce both the human and the divine to an idol, that is, an image and a name (or definition). Refusing to accept that the human reflects the transcendence of a God without image, some proceed to define others as less than human and to justify it by reducing God to a projection of their own privileged identity or self-definition. Thus "God" comes to be thought of as Aryan (e.g., the Nazis) or white or male or Christian, and so on. However, authentic biblical faith calls such self-justifications by their true name—idolatry.

Authentic faith enables us to see that all are equal by virtue of being created in the image of a God without image. Because all share an indefinable and un-imaginable human dignity, any attempt to "define the human" can only result in dehumanization. The ultimate test of authentic faith is love of neighbor. Jesus, in direct continuity with the Prophetic-Pharisaic (Rabbinic) tradition, speaks of "the greatest commandment" as love of God above all and one's neighbor as oneself (Mark 12:28-34). The neighbor, for Jesus, is precisely the alien or stranger who is not like me (e.g., the parable of the good Samaritan). The heart of biblical faith is found in the ethic of welcoming the stranger (Exod. 22:21; Deut. 10:19). For it is the stranger who is wholly other than ourselves (in race, nationality, sex, religion, etc.), who reminds us of the Wholly Otherness or transcendence of God. The alien or stranger comes bearing the image of God so as to remind us that God is truly transcendent and not merely an extension of our self-serving identity. To reject the one who is strange and alien to us is to reject the transcendence of God and to reduce God to an idol created in our own biased image and likeness (as males or females, whites or blacks, Christians or Hindus).

In sociological terms, idolatry takes the form of ideology. Marx, drawing on the prophetic biblical tradition, accused religion of being an opium used by the privileged classes to drug the working classes. For him, religions are ideologies whose only purpose is to legitimate inherently unjust social orders by promising pie in the sky to the oppressed if they will only accept their inferior lot in life now. Where Marx could only envision religion as ideology, Max Weber argued that while some forms of religion serve to legitimate the routine order or status quo of society, other forms of religion delegitimate and transform society. In theological terms one could say that while the former are prone to idolatry the latter manifest the transforming power of transcendence mediated by communities of authentic faith seeking social justice. Liberation theology takes as its central task the unmasking of the idolatries of social identity, which seek to legitimate the

247

preferential treatment of privileged groups whether of nation, class, race, sex, or religion. Authentic faith has an apocalyptic quality to it that brings to an end the psychological and social worlds constructed by the divisive power of sin and death, and it does so in order to manifest the transforming power of a new creation in which God is "all in all."

DARRELL J. FASCHING

Bibliography

Darrell J. Fasching, *The Ethical Challenge of Auschwitz and Hiroshima: Apocalypse or Utopia?*
————. *Narrative Theology After Auschwitz: From Alienation to Ethics.*
Kosuke Koyama, *Mount Fuji and Mount Sinai: A Critique of Idols.*
Juan Luis Segundo, *The Liberation of Theology.*
Paul Tillich, *The Dynamics of Faith.*

Cross Reference: God, Marxist Theology, Symbol, Ultimate Concern.

IMAGINATION

Explicit use of a concept of imagination by theologians is a modern (and postmodern) development, a consequence of the secularization of European society over the past three centuries. Although theologians have come to employ *imagination* as a technical term, it is a deeply ambiguous concept about which no consensus has been achieved. It has nevertheless proved to be a fruitful topic of theological inquiry in an age in which the supernaturalism of premodern theology has largely lost its persuasive authority. Both the explanatory power and the potential confusion of *imagination* are rooted in the ambiguity of the term, which can be applied to both real and illusory objects. Whereas the attribute *imaginary* stresses the unreality of what is imagined, other terms, such as *imaginative,* carry connotations of insight into inaccessible aspects of reality. Thus the imagination is a source of both error and truth.

This systematic ambiguity has influenced the development of the concept of religious imagination as well. The revolution in modern thought that was occasioned by the success of the new sciences in the seventeenth and eighteenth centuries reached its climax in the critical philosophy of Immanuel Kant (1724–1804). In response to his "Copernican" revolution, a number of influential modern thinkers, beginning with Kant himself, assigned science and religion to wholly different realms, called by Kant theoretical and practical. According to this dualism, science is the arena of fact, while religion belongs to a qualitatively different realm that can be called imagination. Both friends and foes of religion came to presuppose this dualism, despite their sharply opposed evaluations of its significance.

Over the course of the nineteenth century, the identification of religion with imagination was expressed in strikingly different ways. G. W. F. Hegel (1770–1831) introduced a fateful distinction between *Vorstellung* (imagination, thinking in sensuous forms)—the characteristic medium of religion—and *Begriff* (pure conceptual thought)—the definitive mode of philosophy. Although all three forms of Absolute Spirit—art, religion, and philosophy—contain the same truth, Hegel maintained that Spirit achieves its perfect form only when religious imagination is sublated into the pure conceptual truth of philosophy. Not all thinkers shared with Kant and Hegel the view that imagination is a form of truth inferior to philosophy. Samuel Taylor Coleridge (1772–1834) was the most notable figure in the Romantic apotheosis of imagination, by which it became a virtual organ of divinity. Reacting against the two most powerful strains in nineteenth-century British thought—the rationalistic theology of "evidences" of William Paley and the utilitarianism of Jeremy Bentham—Coleridge celebrated imagination as the "esemplastic power" (his coinage from the Greek meaning "to shape into one"). Operating through symbols, the imagination gives us access to the truth beyond anything that the mere understanding can grasp.

At the other extreme were the influential thinkers of the Hegelian Left, who developed the duality of concept and imagination into a powerful antireligious critique. In the hands of David Friedrich Strauss (1808–1874), Hegel's distinction was transformed into a dichotomy between history (the realm of scientifically ascertainable fact) and myth (the characteristic form of the religious imagination). Although Strauss denied that mythological interpretation undermined the truth of Christianity, his *Life of Jesus* (1835) unleashed a storm of protest that destroyed his career. The other leading left-wing Hegelians, Ludwig Feuerbach (1804–1872) and Karl Marx (1818–1883), devised more radical critiques of religion. Feuerbach interpreted religion as the projection by the imagination of ideal human traits into illusory, other-worldly objectifications. Marx gave this critique a political twist by identifying the motive of religious projection as the self-interested desire of the ruling classes to anesthetize the oppressed classes by inventing an imaginary religious world to disguise the real world of economic exploitation.

The association of imagination with atheistic interpretations of religion—reinforced in the early twentieth century by Emile Durkheim's sociological reductionism of God to socio-political powers and Sigmund Freud's psychoanalytic critique of religion—generally made theologians wary of the concept. The philosophical climate has changed radically, however, as the dominant positivism of the early twentieth century has succumbed to the critiques of existentialism, analytical philosophy, and pragmatism. Most important of all has been a radical change in the philosophy of science, which has all but dissolved the old dichotomy of science and religion. Influenced by the work of Thomas S. Kuhn and others, philosophers have come increasingly to acknowledge the essential role played by imagination in the work of the natural sciences themselves.

Theological interest in imagination has revived as a result of the new philosophical climate. Recent interpretations of imagination by theologians tend in two opposing directions. At one extreme are those who stress the productive or constructive nature of imagination as the human ability to build up meaning out of images and concepts (e.g., Gordon Kaufman). These theologians emphasize the inadequacy of all images to express fully the truths they represent. Feminist theologians of this type (e.g., Sallie McFague) argue that traditional male-centered religious imagery should be replaced or supplemented by more inclusive images and concepts. Other theologians (e.g., Garrett Green) stress the reproductive or receptive side of imagination—its function as the medium through which religious communities are shaped by scripture and tradition. For these theologians the human imagination is the point where religious truth—as well as falsehood—is disclosed. The concept of imagination thereby enables current theology to interpret and reformulate the traditional doctrine of revelation in terms that make comparison with other disciplines possible. Although most theologians agree that imagination includes both receptive and constructive aspects, the nature of their relationship remains a point of controversy. Exclusive emphasis on the productive side of imagination threatens to deny divine grace by turning religious truth into a human work; stress on the receptive nature of imagination carries the danger of an uncritical traditionalism unable to explain or accept religious change.

GARRETT GREEN

Bibliography

David J. Bryant, *Faith and the Play of Imagination: On the Role of Imagination in Religion.*
Garrett Green, *Imagining God: Theology and the Religious Imagination.*
Gordon D. Kaufman, *The Theological Imagination.*
Thomas S. Kuhn, *The Structure of Scientific Revolutions.*
Sallie McFague, *Models of God.*

Cross Reference: Aesthetics, Epistemology, Language–Religious, Postmodern Theology, Revelation, Symbol.

IMMANENCE (See TRANSCENDENCE.)

IMMORTALITY (See DEATH AND ETERNAL LIFE, RESURRECTION.)

INCARNATION

"Incarnation" (without the definite article) is the idea found in many religions that the divine is revealed in some this-worldly, embodied form, usually human, so that God's nature and will are conveyed in a way that is recognizable and intelligible to humans. Thus, in the Hindu scripture, the Bhagavad-Gita, Krishna is an incarnation of the supreme God Vishnu, who comes to teach and enable the way to liberation. Some Western philosophers, notably Hegel, also have generalized the idea of incarnation and supposed that humanity as such incarnates the divine Spirit or Absolute.

Christianity has traditionally taught, by contrast, the doctrine of the Incarnation (with the definite article). According to this doctrine, God, in one of the modes of God's triune being, was once for all made human in the person of Jesus Christ. He alone was and is God incarnate. Out of God's steadfast love for humankind, a particular human venue—the history of Israel—was prepared for the coming of the divine Savior. Jesus of Nazareth was a Jew, and it was Jewish faith alone that could express in human form God's nature and will for our salvation. The cross and resurrection of Jesus constitute God's own self-involvement with suffering, sinful humanity, and God's costly triumph over sin and death. Men and women are invited to respond in faith to what God has done for them in Christ, to accept the divine forgiveness and reconciliation, and to participate in the divine life through the indwelling spirit of the crucified and risen Christ.

The doctrine has biblical roots in the writings of John (John 1:14: "And the Word became flesh . . ."), of Paul (Col. 1:19: "For in [Christ] all the fullness of God was pleased to dwell . . ."), and of the writer to the Hebrews (Heb. 1:2: "But in these last days he has spoken to us by a Son . . ."). It was hammered out—in response to "heretical" objections—over the first five centuries of the Christian era and was formulated at the great Councils of the undivided Church, especially those of Nicea in 325 and Chalcedon in 451. It remained one of the cornerstones of Christianity despite the strong schism that split the Eastern and the Western churches, and it has been held in common by Roman Catholics and Protestants from the time of the Reformation.

This key doctrine of historical Christianity has come under repeated criticism and received radical reinterpretation within Christian theology itself in the course of the twentieth century. Three reasons in particular lie behind this more or less radical tendency to reject the divinity of Christ and to speak instead of what God did in and through the man, Jesus of Nazareth, and of Jesus' intense God-consciousness as constituting his lasting significance for the church and for the world. In the first place, it is argued that the New Testament evidence, critically sifted, does not require the strong incarnational doctrine. Second, it is questioned whether the idea of one who is both God and man makes any sense. Third, it is held that the traditional doctrine makes it impossible to do justice to the other world faiths as channels and venues of religious fulfillment and a saving knowledge of God. (These objections do not, of course, touch the wider, looser, more general sense of incarnation as God's presence and involvement in the material universe and the human world.)

Critical study of the New Testament suggests that Jesus of Nazareth was a teacher, prophet, and healer whose sense of the presence of God and the love of God for the poor and outcast was so powerful that the movement it sparked not only survived his cruel death but enabled a community of faith to grow and flourish, one in which Jesus himself was spoken of in more and more exalted ways. As the Christian movement, originally a Jewish sect, spread out into the Greek world with its more philosophical thought forms and categories, the doctrine of the Incarnation became hardened into fixed credal formulas. Of course, this process can be interpreted either as an increasingly fantastic product of the religious imagination or as deepening insight into the identity of Jesus Christ. Those who reject the development and try to get back to a purely human, Jewish Jesus have some difficulty with the resurrection narratives in the New Testament and with the evident conviction of the early Christians that they were both disciples and worshipers of a living Lord. Nor is it easy on such a view to explain the comparable experience of Christians ever since of Jesus as living and sovereign in the church. Christians do not just remember a teacher from the past. They encounter, in prayer and sacrament, the risen Christ.

It is difficult to see how this dispute could possibly be resolved by appeal to historical evidence alone. Certainly the New Testament evidence would have to be compatible with the church's developed theology of the Incarnation, but its truth would have to be shown by more than historical investigation. Only on the basis of experienced participation in the faith of the church can this truth be properly recognized.

The accusation that the Incarnation makes no sense—that it is a contradiction to assert of Jesus that he was both human and divine—assumes that we have precise and complete concepts of both humanity and divinity, so that their incompatibility is obvious. Defenders of the doctrine of the Incarnation reply that we have no such clearly defined, exhaustive concept of humanity, let alone divinity. It is not obviously impossible for the infinite creative mind behind the whole world's being and destiny to have entered God's creation in finite human form and expressed God's nature and will in a finite human mode. Created human personhood may indeed alone be capable of becoming the vehicle and expression of God's personal presence and activity here on earth. On this view the human mind and will of Jesus are included within the mind and will of the divine Word or Son as their incarnate personal instrument.

The notion of a divine "kenosis" or "self-emptying" may help to make this clear. Modern Christian theology has ceased to ascribe omniscience and omnipotence to the man Jesus. God's power and knowledge rather are held to be channeled through the limited power and mind of a first-century Jewish rabbi and prophet who goes to the cross out of love for humankind rather than remain in divine aloofness and invulnerability. Christians hold that in raising him from the dead, God revealed that this Jesus was more than a rabbi and a prophet, that he who now returned to God's side had indeed come from God and was God's very self in human form. Such a "kenotic" view helps to make more sense of the critically sifted New Testament portrait of the humanity of Jesus.

It is true that such an incarnational Christology makes it difficult to accord equal religious and salvific significance to all the world religions. But it is implausible to expect Christianity to abandon its most characteristic doctrines simply to accommodate some global pluralistic theory of all religions being equally viable paths to the same goal. On the other hand, modern Christianity is unwilling to be as absolutist and exclusivist as it was in the past. A more "inclusivist" view of the decisive significance of God's self-revelation in the Christ event will see God's dealings with the human world as reaching an unrepeatable climax in the Incarnation of the divine Word or Son in Jesus, but it will also see the same universal Word at work throughout the history of religions, wherever the experience of God and the love of God has reached something akin to Christ-like proportions. On this "inclusivist" view, the different world religions do indeed put men and women in touch with the living God, but that knowledge is provisional and destined to be complemented and enhanced by the knowledge of God in Christ, if not here, then in eternity.

The dispute between non-incarnational and incarnational versions of the Christian faith is likely to continue in the foreseeable future, as Christianity and the great world religions come increasingly into contact and dialogue. Factors favoring the non-incarnational view will include the sheer difficulty of understanding the doctrine of the Incarnation, a sense for the nature and power of religious "myth," a historical appreciation of factors shaping the development of the doctrine in the early centuries, and above all, the desire to forsake intolerant attitudes to other faiths under the circumstances of global interreligious encounter. Well-known representatives in modern church theology of the "pluralist" reinterpretation of the doctrine of the Incarnation as "myth" include John Hick on the Protestant side and Paul Knitter on the Roman Catholic side.

Factors favoring the incarnational view will include its early appearance in the scriptural record, its centrality in the centuries-old Christian mainstream traditions, East and West, and above all, the moral and religious power of the doctrine, which may be spelled out in a number of ways. In the first place it is the claim of traditional Christianity that a much more personal and intimate knowledge of God is made available to men and women through this crossing of the divine-human divide and through this personal presence of God on the human scene in Jesus Christ and the consequent gift of the spirit of Christ in the hearts and in the fellowship of Christians. In the second place, the problem of evil and suffering in God's creation is somewhat eased if it can be seen that the cross of Christ is God's cross in the world and that God is thus, in A. N. Whitehead's words, the fellow sufferer who understands. In this way God accepts responsibility for the risks and the costs of the creation of a human world. In the third place, on a traditional Christian view, the ultimate future of creation is understood to be a community of love, gathered up into the trinitarian life of God and patterned on Jesus' union with the God he called Father. This "eschatological" vision inspires all Christian action for human community here and now.

Thus in the fourth place, Christians have drawn out the ethical significance of a religion of the Incarnation. The material creation is not alien to God if the Word has become flesh. Christian spirituality takes the body seriously as the vehicle, not the enemy, of spiritual life. Christian involvement in the thoroughly earthly problems and needs of their fellow human beings is patterned on the divine "kenosis" in the Incarnation. This is bound to take on social and political dimensions. A religion of the Incarnation cannot hold aloof from the political problems of injustice and oppression. Incarnational theology is at once a sacramental theology, finding spiritual significance in the things of the earth, and a political theology, drawing on those spiritual resources for a renewal and transformation of the conditions of life on earth.

BRIAN HEBBLETHWAITE

Bibliography

Steven Davis, ed., *Encountering Jesus*.
Brian Hebblethwaite, *The Incarnation*.
John Hick and Paul Knitter, eds., *The Myth of Christian Uniqueness*.
Werner Kasper, *Jesus the Christ*.
Jürgen Moltmann, *The Way of Jesus Christ*.
Geoffrey Parrinder, *Avatar and Incarnation*.

Cross Reference: Anthropology, Christology, Pluralism, Revelation, Trinity.

INERRANCY

Inerrancy means different things to different people who affirm it. For some conservative Protestants, the term "inerrancy" is a symbol for the authority of the Bible. It dictates no particular set of beliefs about what the Bible teaches but affirms that whatever the Bible teaches should be received as true. For such conservative Christians inerrancy describes a reverent attitude toward Scripture, a posture of obedient listening to the word of God. In the classical Christian creeds and confessions this attitude is expressed by the word "infallibility."

For other conservative Protestants, inerrancy describes a particular theory about the defense and interpretation of the Bible. This theory holds that the Bible gives accurate and up-to-the-minute information, not only on religious matters, but on all other matters the Bible addresses, such as science and history. This approach encourages a literalistic reading of the Bible as a book speaking uniquely to our time.

The first recorded use of "inerrant" in English was in 1652 with reference to movement of the planets. In the eighteenth century, the rise of empirical science led some Christians to defend the Bible's accuracy on scientific grounds. The reigning philosophy of Scottish Common Sense encouraged a literal reading of Scripture by asserting that all people in all times and places think alike. This attitude, brought to America by John Witherspoon in 1768, foreshadowed resistance to biblical scholarship that stressed the uniquely ancient and New Eastern aspects of biblical literature.

The concept of inerrancy came into significant theological usage in the period of Scholastic Protestantism late in the seventeenth century. In response to threats from Counter-Reformation Roman Catholics and the rise of philosophical rationalism, theologians such as François Turretin in Geneva shifted the authority of the Bible from its infallible religious content to its inerrant literary form. The Helvetic Consensus Formula of 1675, encouraged by Turretin, claimed inspiration even for the (nonexistent) vowel points in the original Hebrew manuscripts.

Turretin's theology and Common Sense biblical interpretation were standard at Princeton and many other American theological seminaries from 1812 to the 1920s. In response to the new Higher Criticism of the Bible, A. A. Hodge and B. B. Warfield of Princeton Seminary co-authored an article on inspiration in 1881. It became the classic American definition of inerrancy. Hodge contended:

> Nevertheless the historical faith of the church has always been, that all the affirmations of Scripture of all kinds, whether of spiritual doctrine or duty, or of physical or historical fact, or of psychological or philosophical principle, are without any error, when the *ipsissima verba* of the original autographs are ascertained and interpreted in their natural and intended sense.

Warfield gave the apologetic defense of this doctrine, arguing that "No 'error' can be asserted, therefore, which cannot be proved to have been aboriginal in the text." Since none of the original manuscripts of the biblical writings existed, the Old Princeton apologists claimed to have an unassailable case.

Recent discussion of inerrancy was focused by the publication in 1976 of a book by Harold Lindsell, *The Battle for the Bible*. In the name of inerrancy, Lindsell began a campaign to purge Evangelicalism, an American movement older and broader than fundamentalism that gained public attention in the 1970s with the election to the United States presidency of Southern Baptist Sunday school teacher Jimmy Carter and with the rising popularity of persons attesting to "born again" experiences. Lindsell branded many self-identified evangelical persons, churches, and institutions as false evangelicals. Only those who adhered to Lindsell's theory of the inerrancy of Scripture could wear the evangelical label. He

255

wrote that when the Bible speaks on matters of "chemistry, astronomy, philosophy, or medicine" it contains no error judged by current standards. Thus, for Lindsell, "The Bible, if true in all its parts, cannot possibly teach that the earth is flat . . . or that events happened at times other than we know they did."

In 1978 an organization was formed called "The International Council on Biblical Inerrancy." It initiated a ten-year drive to "attempt to win back that portion of the church which has drifted away from this historic position of inerrancy." The initial position paper of the group, "The Chicago Statement on Biblical Inerrancy," manifested the influence of two kinds of inerrantists. One group, primarily biblical scholars, made significant qualifications in the theory, including denial "that inerrancy is negated by Biblical phenomena such as a lack of modern technical precision, irregularities of grammar or spelling, observational descriptions of nature . . ." Another group, composed of theologians, apologists, and philosophers of religion, asserted a theory that supported Lindsell's approach, saying that God caused each biblical writer "to use the very words that He chose." The inconsistency between a theory that asserts that God chose the very words of the biblical writers and the experience of biblical interpretation that includes irregularities of grammar and spelling has not been resolved.

The words "evangelical" and "fundamentalist" continue to be used ambiguously. Inerrancy may properly be regarded as a fundamentalist attempt to explain evangelical faith in the authority of the Bible. Inerrancy has been and probably will continue to be an ambiguous and disputed concept. For many it will remain simply a synonym for the authority of the Bible. For others, it will prescribe adherence to some form of the Hodge-Warfield apologetic defense of the Bible and commend a literalistic reading of Scripture.

JACK ROGERS

Bibliography

Norman L. Geisler, *Inerrancy.*
Robison B. James, *The Unfettered Word: Southern Baptists Confront the Authority-Inerrancy Question.*
Harold Lindsell, *The Battle for the Bible.*
Jack B. Rogers and Donald K. McKim, *The Authority and Interpretation of the Bible: An Historical Approach.*
John D. Woodbridge, *Biblical Authority: A Critique of the Rogers/McKim Proposal.*

Cross Reference: Apologetics, Authority, Fundamentalism, Inspiration.

INSIGHT

Insight refers to a critical element in the process of knowing, a mental illumination grasping a solution to a problem or an answer to a question. It is pivotal to achieving understanding and knowledge. Because of his attention to the role of insight in the knowing process, this term has come to have a special reference to the philosophy and philosophical theology of Bernard J. F. Lonergan, (1904–1984). Lonergan was the leading Anglo-American representative of the Roman Catholic theological tradition known as "transcendental Thomism," a movement that relates Thomistic philosophy and theology to the twentieth century by conversing with modern philosophy (particularly Kant) and science. Lonergan's thought has inspired and become the basis for the work of a significant number of Roman Catholic theologians in North America, Ireland, Australia, and the Philippines.

Lonergan is best known for two influential books: *Insight: A Study of Human Understanding* (1957) and *Method in Theology* (1972). These books represent two phases of Lonergan's career-long project. Taking his clue from his own original interpretation of Aquinas, Lonergan believed that philosophy and theology could respond to the challenges of modernity if they were grounded in an adequate analysis of knowing and the knowing subject. His long-range intent was to provide theology with a dependable method. But in laying the foundations for his treatment of theological method, Lonergan made original contributions to philosophy also.

In *Insight,* Lonergan begins with a detailed study of method in the mathematical and empirical sciences in order to discover the basic structure of all human knowing and to formulate the general method that guides knowing. When this method is applied to understanding objects, the result is science. But when it is applied to understanding the knowing subject, the result is a philosophy grounded in the dynamic structure of the human knower. The foundation of such a philosophy is cognitional theory, an understanding of the structure of the act of knowing and of the knowing and acting subject.

Lonergan's cognitional theory discovers four distinct levels of consciousness and intent in the act of knowing and in the knowing subject: experience (the empirical level), understanding (the intelligent level), judgment (the rational level), and decision (the responsible level). "Insight" is the key event mediating between experience and understanding and between understanding and judgment. Experience raises a question for understanding: What have I experienced? Insight is a flash of illumination grasping a possible understanding in relation to the data of experience. But once the understanding has been formulated in concepts, a new question arises: Is the understanding correct? There must be a return to the level of experience in order to judge the correctness of the understanding. Insight again mediates between abstract understanding and concrete experience. It grounds the judgment, affirming (or negating) the correctness of the understanding. Knowledge is thus the result of making a judgment concerning the correctness of the understanding of what has been experienced. This, in turn, raises a question for decision: How shall I act given my knowledge?

Cognitional theory provides an understanding of the general method of all human knowing and an example of that dynamic process. In working out cognitional theory we have *experienced* the process of knowing, we have *understood* that process, we have *judged* that this understanding of the process is in fact how knowing occurs, and we have *decided* to act in accord with this general method of knowing. Lonergan calls the conscious employment of this method in philosophy "transcendental method." He argues that it generates higher-order questions and reveals the dynamic relation between the divisions of philosophy to be grounded in the dynamic structure of the knowing subject itself. Cognitional theory corresponds to the level of experience and responds to the question, What am I doing when I am knowing? Epistemology corresponds to the level of understanding and responds to the question, Why is doing that knowing? Metaphysics corresponds to the level of judgment and responds to the question, What do I know when I am knowing? Ethics corresponds to the level of decision and responds to the question, How ought I to act given what I know? Transcendental method, in short, not only governs how any question is answered, but it also leads the knower to be self-transcending in raising ever higher-order questions. In reflecting on our knowing and acting, transcendental method finally raises the questions of God and religion.

In *Method in Theology* Lonergan shows how transcendental method can be the basis for method in theology. He suggests a division of theological labor into eight "functional specialties," which occur in two phases: a mediating phase that encounters the past and a mediated phase that confronts the future. Within each phase, the four functional specialties correspond to the four levels of the knowing and acting subject. Research, interpretation, history, and dialectic correspond respectively to experience, understanding, judgment, and decision. Foundations, doctrines, systematics, and communications correspond respectively to decision, judgment, understanding, and experience. These two phases are linked by the occurrence and objectification of "conversion," which Lonergan understands to be the intellectual, moral, and religious transformation of the human subject and its world. This understanding of theological method is solidly grounded in the dynamic structure of the knowing and acting subject and provides a framework for creative collaboration between theologians.

THOMAS E. HOSINSKI

Bibliography

Frederick E. Crowe, *The Lonergan Enterprise.*
Bernard J. F. Lonergan, *Insight: A Study of Human Understanding.*
_____, *Method in Theology,* 2nd ed.
_____, *Understanding and Being: An Introduction and Companion to Insight.*
Hugo A. Meynell, *The Theology of Bernard Lonergan.*

Cross Reference: Epistemology, Theological Method.

INSPIRATION

Inspiration, in a religious sense, generally denotes the belief that an individual has been enlightened or even overtaken by a divine power. In some religious traditions inspiration is evidenced by trances, dreams, mystical visions, frenzies, or other ecstatic experiences. The ancient Greeks, for example, spoke of poets and philosophers who were so overshadowed by the nine Muses that they were no longer in control of themselves but spoke and acted at the will of the Muses. A similar understanding of inspiration as ecstatic experience can be found in a few places in the Hebrew scriptures (e.g., Saul in I Sam. 10:5-13 is overtaken by the Spirit of God and is "turned into another man"). The Hebrew scriptures, however, usually present the Hebrew prophets as being inspired by God in a way that does not negate their normal human faculties. The prophets remain in control of their thoughts and actions as they deliver their messages to the people.

The idea of inspiration is of great importance in Christian thought in relation to biblical authority. The Christian church speaks of the scriptures as inspired, as does Judaism also. Whereas almost all theologians would agree that the Bible is in some sense "inspired," there is no agreement concerning the locus and mode of that inspiration. Explanations range from the idea that inspiration refers simply to the heightened intellectual and spiritual acumen of the biblical writers to the idea that inspiration means that God dictated every word and letter in the Bible.

Part of the disagreement over how the Bible is inspired results from the different approaches taken to the subject. A deductive approach begins with an understanding of the doctrine of inspiration and then attempts to force the Bible into that framework. Such approaches often begin with the notion that God is truth and is incapable of error. If the Bible is inspired by God, then the Bible must also partake of this nature of God, truth without error. A perfect God could not produce an imperfect scripture. According to this understanding, inspiration guarantees the inerrancy of all information—whether historical, scientific, geographical, or theological. This view of inspiration often describes God dictating every word to the biblical authors, who acted simply as scribes to record the message that came to them. Since these "authors" functioned only as conduits through which the words of God passed, the Bible is pure revelation of God, untainted by human ideas or human misunderstandings.

This plenary, verbal view of inspiration contains two significant flaws. First, as a critical reading of the Bible indicates, the Bible is not free of errors in history, geography, and science. Contradictions within the Bible itself are not uncommon. The deductive argument that a perfect God would not produce an imperfect Bible fails to deal honestly with the Bible as we now have it. Attempts to avoid this problem by claiming that inerrancy applies only to the original autographs of the scriptures are specious because no such manuscripts exist. Furthermore, if only the original autographs were inspired, and not the Bible in its present form, then the doctrine of inspiration is of no use to the modern Christian. The second flaw

259

with the plenary, verbal view of inspiration is its locus of inspiration in the biblical writer. This view holds to a model of authorship similar to the role of the Hebrew prophets in which God spoke to the prophets who then proclaimed God's message in written or oral form. Similarly, this view assumes, God spoke to the biblical writers who then transcribed that message that was later included in the Bible. Scholarly studies of the Bible, however, demonstrate that in many cases there was not a single author of a biblical book, at least in the way the term "author" is normally used. Many of the biblical writings are products of long processes involving the use of multiple sources, multiple editors, and several editions of the work. Biblical books are, in many cases, more the products of communities than the works of individual authors. The dictation, or scribal, theory of authorship fails therefore because it is not supported by the evidence of the Bible itself.

A better way to approach the question of inspiration is inductively, thus allowing the evidence of the Bible to define the contours and contents of the doctrine. The word "inspired" (*theopneustos,* "God-breathed") occurs only once in the Bible as a description of the scriptures (II Tim. 3:16). Although its usage in that text is somewhat ambiguous, the passage affirms that scripture is useful for the church in the performance of its tasks in the world. No claims are made in the passage, however, for the nature or method of inspiration of the scriptures. Divine inspiration does not guarantee the inerrancy or the efficacy of the scriptures, for scripture achieves its purpose of bringing persons into a right relationship with God and humanity only when the message of the scriptures is received and appropriated. A feasible doctrine of inspiration must include the idea that the spirit of God is at work not only in the individuals who wrote the scriptures but also in the communities that preserved, shaped, and transmitted the traditions behind the scriptures; in the selective decisions of the canonization process; and in the continuing interpretation and application of the scriptures in the church. To claim that the Bible is inspired is to affirm that through these writings people have encountered the God who revealed God's self to the people and the communities who produced the scriptures.

Inspiration is closely intertwined with revelation, canonization, and authority. Inspiration and revelation are not limited to the Bible. The writers of nonscriptural works may also be inspired—led by the spirit of God to an understanding of the revelation of God. But by canonizing certain works the church has indicated which inspired writings most clearly contain the revelation of God and are most effective in helping people to encounter that God. These writings, then, have a unique authoritative status for the church.

MITCHELL G. REDDISH

Bibliography

W. J. Abraham, *The Divine Inspiration of Holy Scripture.*
Paul Achtemeier, *The Inspiration of Scripture: Problems and Proposals.*

Dewey M. Beegle, *Scripture, Tradition, and Infallibility.*
G. C. Berkouwer, *Holy Scripture.*
Bruce Vawter, *Biblical Inspiration.*

Cross Reference: Authority, Canon, Fundamentalism, Inerrancy, Revelation.

INSTITUTIONALIZED VIOLENCE

Institutionalized violence is a description of the indirect forms of pressure that are built into the very structures of a society and hence into human relationships. Lack of educational opportunity, poor housing, racial or sexual barriers to equal employment, condescension, and so on maim and cripple human lives in apparently peaceful ways. They are structures, thus they are described as institutionalized; they destroy, thus they are termed violence.

The term "institutionalized violence" reveals the unequal distribution of power in a society, what Starhawk has called "power over." The insight that "power over" has a structure that should be termed violent has come primarily from the debates over the use of violence versus nonviolence in resistance to oppression.

At the World Council of Churches Consultation on Racism meeting at Notting Hill, England, in 1969, the center of the problem was identified as "not simply that of violence versus nonviolence, but the use of power for the powerful and the need of power for the powerless." In particular, nonwhite members of the commission opened the eyes of the world church to the fact that "the really decisive question is not the question of violence—especially since the concept of 'violence' can be widened to cover indirect forms of pressure—but the question of the justification of the power, the consequent limits of power, and the fact that power can become unjust and tyrannical" (quoted in Thistlethwaite, 44).

It is equally important to keep in mind that when the exercise of "power over" is challenged, whether by violent or by nonviolent means, the direct exercise of power in the use of force is almost always the result. An example of this frequent response can be seen in what is called the Sharpeville massacre, which occurred in South Africa in 1960. A nonviolent demonstration was organized by the African National Congress. The police opened fire on the crowd, killing 67 and wounding 186 others, including children. The majority of those shot were hit in the back. Bishop Desmond Tutu reminds us that "it was whilst blacks were protesting peacefully against the much hated pass laws that the Sharpeville massacre happened" and that "the Sharpeville paradigm has been repeated again and again."

In many parts of the world, in many religious traditions, people are grappling with new definitions of violence and nonviolence and attempting to see more clearly what Tutu describes as "the Sharpeville paradigm." The Palestinian *Intifada,* the uprising of Palestinian people forced to live under numerous restrictions in the state of Israel, has produced similar reflections. How are we to

261

understand rock-throwing by children at armed soldiers who are trained to shoot for the base of their spines, a wound that paralyzes for life? Are the children violent? And are the soldiers exercising legally sanctioned force? Or is this a situation of institutionalized violence, the denial of equal civil rights to Palestinians, that has erupted into overt violence? Dom Helder Camara has coined the well-known phrase "the spiral of violence." The spiral of violence begins with what Helder Camara calls "violence No. 1," the "legalized violence of privilege." Resistance to this established violence is met with force, which is in turn resisted further and so forth. The only way to break the spiral of violence "is to have the courage to face the injustices which constitute violence No. 1."

Similar insights have emerged from the struggle to end violence against women. The violent home, Lenore Walker argues, moves through a cycle in which a tension-building phase erupts into battering and then moves through a period of apparent calm that again degenerates into the psychological terror of the tension-building phase and so forth. Walker argues that the battering of women is the direct result of their subordinate position in the society.

Institutionalized violence is an addition to the churches' historical teachings on nonviolence and violence: pacifism, just war, and crusade. It exhibits some progress over these traditional positions because it is a reflection initiated by those who are out of power: people of color, the poor, women. Further, an understanding of institutionalized violence is an advance on the traditional positions because it reveals the interconnectedness of both overt and covert violence.

SUSAN THISTLETHWAITE

Bibliography

Dom Helder Camara, *The Spiral of Violence: Prayer and Practice.*
R. Emerson Dobash and Russell Dobash, *Violence Against Wives: A Case Against the Patriarchy.*
Starhawk, *Truth or Dare: Encounters with Power, Authority, and Mystery.*
Susan Thistlethwaite, *A Just Peace Church.*
Charles Villa-Vicencio, *Theology and Violence: The South African Debate.*

Cross Reference: Black Theology, Feminist Theology, Justice, Liberation Theology, Womanist Theology.

JUDAISM

Why is Judaism important for Christian theology? Quite simply, the New Testament, indeed Christian theology, is unintelligible without considerable knowledge of Judaism. An understanding of the Jewish origins of Christianity helps Christians contemplate the essence of Christianity. In these endeavors Christians must be alert, both to shun all forms of anti-Semitism, which is really anti-Judaism, and to avoid the excesses of philo-Semitism—the uncritical celebration of Judaism. Both extremes undermine the integrity of Christianity.

Jewish Theology. The heart of Jewish theology is the confession that there is only one God, who is infinite, all powerful, benevolent, and gracious. The classical text for this belief is the Shema (Deuteronomy 6:4): "Hear, O Israel! The Lord is our God, the Lord alone." At Sinai God revealed himself not merely as an idea but as a person to the children of Israel through Moses. God's will is disclosed in the Torah, which is both written (broadly understood as the Hebrew Scriptures = the Christian Old Testament) and oral (partly and eventually written down in the Mishnah and Tosephta and expanded in the Talmudim).

Jews do not consider the Torah a burden or the embodiment of a legal system. Its observance is a joy because it clarifies God's will and purpose, which includes the election of Israel to a special covenant relationship. The purpose involves promise. Jews viewed history as linear. God was perceived in history, and the end of human history was considered a joyful communion with God (usually after judgment).

Frequently Jesus' teachings, and Paul's stress upon salvation solely through faith by God's grace, are seen as an important contrast with Judaism. It is now clear, however, that early Jewish documents do not support the claim often heard in Christianity, that a person is saved by obeying the works of the Law. Some of the apocryphal works (viz., Psalm 155) and Dead Sea Scrolls (viz., the Hymn Scroll) contain the idea that only God can make a person righteous.

Indeed, even the basic creed of Judaism, the Shema of Deuteronomy 6:4, stresses that no one can fully obey the Ten Commandments and God's will. Jewish thinkers during the time of Jesus recognized that all Jews are sinful before God. Liturgies were composed and the cult in the Jerusalem Temple was organized so that God could be approached with confessions of sin and pleas for forgiveness (*see* Psalm 51, the Prayer of Manasseh, the earliest versions of the Kaddish, and the 18 Benedictions). Indeed, the most holy person in Judaism—the high priest—confessed his own sins on the Day of Atonement, the most sacred Sabbath of Sabbaths; he then made a sacrifice to God because of them. Subsequently he could sacrifice the appropriate animals to God and ask forgiveness for others.

Christian Origins. Christianity originated within Judaism. The proclamation that Jesus is the Christ who came at the end of time to fulfill God's promises is grounded in the Jewish conceptions that time is moving toward God's purpose and that the Hebrew Scriptures contain God's promises. Christian theologians are now affirming more clearly than before that Christianity has inherited the Jewish scriptures.

Jesus and his earliest followers were all Jews. Being dedicated to Jewish scriptures and traditions, they worshiped in the Temple and were devoted to God and the kingdom of God. Jesus held that those who hear (= obey) the word of God and keep it are blessed (Luke 11:28). Jesus' followers interpreted him in terms of the fulfillment of the promises in scripture.

During the first century Judaism was not monolithic; in fact, many Jewish groups existed, including the Essenes, Sadducees, Zealots, Pharisees, Herodians, and others (the Samaritans also claimed to be Jews). Despite their sad portrayal in popular Christianity, the Pharisees were not summarily branded as hypocrites by Jesus and his earliest followers. According to Luke, they invited him to their homes for meals, and they warned him that Herod Antipas sought to kill him (Luke 13:31). Some Pharisees followed Jesus; the best-known example is Paul, who claimed that he continued to be a faithful Jew.

Jesus was very close to many Pharisees and that is why he is often portrayed arguing with them; but he was not a Pharisee. He was also not a Zealot, Essene, or apocalyptist. He never quoted Jewish authorities revered in these groups. His direct authoritative speech dismayed some hearers and impressed others. Obviously, some of Jesus' followers came from the numerous groups within Judaism, but many did not belong to any well-defined group.

Foreground of Christianity. The foreground, and not just the background, of Christianity is constituted by Judaism. Some of the main theological concepts in Christian theology are inherited directly from Judaism, whence they originated and underwent significant development. Some of these important concepts are the Messiah, the kingdom of God, the son of man, paradise, the end of time (eschatology), and resurrection. Moreover, the concept of the cosmos with a heaven above and earth beneath, the belief in two ages (the present and future ones), and a thoroughgoing monotheism with a morality grounded in the Ten Commandments were taken over from Judaism by Christianity.

Apocalyptic theology is originally uniquely Jewish. It emphasizes that God will soon intervene in this world (either directly or through an intermediator) and triumph over evil powers, bringing to actuality the divine promise of peace, harmony, love, and everlasting life throughout the world. This perspective lies at the heart of Jesus' message and Paul's theology that stressed the centrality of God and God's coming triumph over evil.

Today scholars concur that Jesus' teaching is only intelligible within the thought world of Judaism. His essential message was the proclamation that God's kingdom is coming into the world and that nothing else matters except serving God alone and being dedicated to God's kingdom. Even Jesus' healing miracles are now understood in relation to other contemporaneous miracle workers in Galilee,

264

namely Honi and Hanina. It is also probable that the tradition that Jesus is "the son of God" is Jewish. Even the so-called Lord's Prayer is a thoroughly Jewish prayer, and many of its phrases are found in early Jewish prayers, some of which, like the Kaddish, are recited in edited forms in synagogues today.

Biblical scholars have also increasingly identified the Jewish character of biblical books that were formerly considered as written from a Greek perspective. The Gospel of John is now recognized as a very Jewish document. The dualism so prominent in John derives from Jewish theology: The stress on the world above and the world below and the portrayal of the "children of light" (John 12:36) who know "the works of God" (John 6:28), and do not "walk in darkness" but in "the light of life" (John 8:12) cumulatively indicate that the author of John was probably influenced by Essene thought. The implication in the Gospel of John that Jesus' followers were attending synagogues and being cast out of them reflects the strong link between John's community and Judaism. It also mirrors the eventual movement of institutional Christianity away from Judaism.

Jesus and his followers liberally interpreted the scriptures and traditions. Characteristic of Jews, for instance, were the veneration of the Sabbath, circumcision, the use of the lunar calendar, observance of dietary regulations (to eat and drink only what is approved in the scriptures), and obeying the rules for purification (which were being increased during the time of Jesus). Although Jesus was apparently critical of some of these rules, Paul in a more radical way urged believers to ignore them.

Two claims are unique to Christianity: the proclamation that Jesus is the Messiah (the Christ) who has come, and that God has raised him from the dead. Yet each of these cardinal beliefs derives from fundamentally Jewish conceptions—messianism and resurrection—which were developed significantly in the two centuries before the birth of Jesus. The New Testament is now being studied not only within the history of the church but also within the history of Judaism.

Permanent Indebtedness. Christian theology originated within Judaism and it is permanently indebted to Judaism. To believe that God alone saves the sinner, that God sent the son in the fullness of time to redeem the world, that Jesus' mission was to proclaim that God's kingdom was beginning to break into the present, that Jesus was crucified as a Jew by Roman soldiers, and that Jesus was resurrected by God is to think in Jewish terms and with Jewish perspectives.

Today theologians are seeking to recover the essential purity of Christianity by replacing a hatred of Jews with an appreciation of them and of Judaism.

JAMES H. CHARLESWORTH

265

Bibliography

J. Christiaan Beker, *Paul's Apocalyptic Gospel: The Coming Triumph of God.*
James H. Charlesworth, *Jesus Within Judaism.*
Jacob Neusner, *Judaism: The Evidence of the Mishnah.*
E. E. Urbach, *The Sages: Their Concepts and Beliefs,* 2 vols.

Cross Reference: Christology, Holocaust.

JUDGMENT–FINAL (*See* ESCHATOLOGY, KINGDOM OF GOD.)

JUSTICE

Justice concerns the distribution of goods, rights, and responsibilities among the members of a community. In the broadest sense, questions of justice may involve any or all of the following: (1) specific *claims* that persons make that they are entitled to goods or to freedoms on the basis of justice; (2) *theories* of justice that provide explanations and arguments for such claims; (3) institutions such as courts and legislatures set up to *adjudicate* such claims and *enforce* them; and (4) systems set up to determine and enforce appropriate *punishment* or *reparations* in cases where the claims of justice have been violated.

The earliest concepts of justice in the ancient world were linked to ideas of cosmic order. Justice then was conceived as a power that maintains right relationships, both in the world of nature and among human beings. In Greek myth and philosophy, justice *(dike)* was not usually represented as a personal being, but as an impersonal force that both human and divine beings had to respect. Even the most powerful gods and rulers dare not violate the demands of impartial justice toward their subjects. Similar ideas appear in cultures as diverse as that of ancient Egypt, where justice *(ma'at)* directs the course of heavenly bodies and human action, and that of China, where the "Mandate of Heaven" determines the prosperity and power of states and their rulers. In the Hebrew scriptures, justice or righteousness *(zedekah)* characterizes right relationships both to God and to other persons.

In Greek thought, as cities, laws, and systems of government developed, the idea of justice became more specifically associated with relationships between people. Aristotle's division of justice into questions of distribution, transactions, and punishment set the framework for many subsequent European discussions. In the Hebrew scriptures, a person's justice in relation to others can be distinguished, but never entirely separated, from righteousness toward God and the right use of the created order. Holiness encompasses the worship of God, fairness to one's neighbors, and the right use of the land (Leviticus 17–27).

Modern concepts of justice share the ancient concern with proper use and distribution of resources, but they often disagree sharply with the idea that justice is part of an order that exists apart from human choices. Since the seventeenth century, Western philosophers have usually regarded the requirements of justice as an extension through the whole society of the sort of arrangements that individuals make to exchange goods and services with one another. The American philosopher John Rawls has devised the most comprehensive current version of this "social contract" theory of justice.

A theory of justice that decides what is just on the basis of agreements between the parties obviously cannot rest on preconceived ideas about what persons need or want. As a result, modern ideas of justice tend to be formal or procedural. They stress fairness in the rules to which persons agree and impartiality in the administration of the rules once they are settled, rather than identify rights or goods to which people are entitled as a matter of justice. Basic requirements such as honesty and promise-keeping may be essential in order to arrive at any agreements at all, but most of the requirements of justice will emerge from the agreements themselves.

Along with the idea that persons create standards of justice by their own reason and by mutual consent, modern philosophical theories have often held questions of justice to be the most important, if not the only, public questions of morality. Other questions about values and behavior are then held to belong to the private sphere of individual choice and freedom.

Judaism, Christianity, and Islam have shown active concern for justice in the modern world, but there are also strong traditions in these three faiths which deny that justice is the ultimate moral issue. The justice shaped by law and administered in human institutions is usually subordinated to the will of God or to a higher law of love. God's will and the law of love are not necessarily incompatible with human justice, but their supreme importance means that agreed social standards of justice cannot have the last word in moral judgment.

In today's Christian thought, this leads to a certain tension with prevailing philosophical and legal theories of justice. Though all theologians would agree that justice under law is an important social achievement, morally better than arbitrary tyranny or the exploitation of the weak by the strong, some find individualistic, consensual systems of justice too permissive and inattentive to other important moral questions. Others believe that the standards of justice that can be achieved by mutual consent fall far short of the human care that the love of God requires. These questions about justice take different forms in the principal divisions of moral theology today.

Modern theories of "natural law" have been most extensively used in Roman Catholic moral thought, though natural law also has an important place in jurisprudence and, increasingly, in Protestant theology as well. Natural law theories are rooted in the ancient notion that human justice is inseparable from the natural order. Although the emphasis on reasoned moral judgments in the natural

267

law tradition yields a respect for conscience that is compatible with individual rights and freedoms, the idea that there is a natural order of human life that should guide individual choice and activity obviously places limits on the arrangements to which persons can mutually agree. Human life requires certain objective conditions to flourish, and laws and institutions that ignore those requirements are unjust, even if they enjoy the consent of those who live under them.

The concept of natural law as a higher law, against which the enactments of particular governments and rulers may be measured, has a variety of political implications. Social conservatives may stress the need for responsible moral and religious authorities to impose necessary and "natural" limits on behavior, regardless of what people and their representatives say they want. Natural law, however, can also provide a basis for radical social criticism. If legal and economic systems fail to provide persons with the minimal elements of a good human life, natural law suggests that these systems are unjust and should be changed, even though they may enjoy widespread approval. In American Catholic thought, the work of John A. Ryan, especially his book *A Living Wage* (1906), illustrates this use of natural law as an instrument of social criticism. John Courtney Murray, also a Roman Catholic, argued that natural law limitations on public choices, far from violating the spirit of democracy, are essential to the meaning of constitutional government. Although critics of natural law thinking often portray it as inevitably conservative and authoritarian, natural law has been invoked for a great variety of political purposes. One must inquire carefully into a specific author's ideas about human nature and human flourishing in order to determine what the political effect of natural law ideas might be.

In contrast to the reservations that natural law theorists often express about the "social contract," Christian Realism is a Protestant movement that offers a generally positive assessment of modern liberal democracy. Christian Realists insist, however, that nations and leaders must recognize the imperfections and limitations of even their finest achievements. Realism requires a certain flexibility in political and legal systems. Rather than attempt a definition of justice that suits all times and circumstances, Christian Realism seeks agreement on a just resolution of particular conflicts. Christian Realists try to formulate "middle axioms" to guide choices for the foreseeable future, rather than to conceive universal principles that will always apply.

In addition to the flexibility and responsiveness to change that this historical awareness implies, Christian Realists also stress that moral ideas are easily distorted by self-interest. Whether evaluating someone else's claims for justice or our own, it is important to acknowledge the human tendency to claim more for ourselves and to treat the claims of others less seriously than they deserve.

Reinhold Niebuhr, the foremost American proponent of Christian Realism, applied these realistic considerations to the idea of justice in modern society. Justice, he argued, is not a permanent, determinate standard, but the result of a complex equilibrium between the social forces that work toward equality and those that demand greater liberty. Persons often feel they are unjustly treated because they lack the resources and opportunities available to others, but they also complain of injustice when their freedom is restricted in order to ensure that everyone is treated equally. Concrete, historical movements for justice reflect the tension between these goals, and there is no permanent solution to the problem. Often the greatest injustices are done when a nation makes absolute a specific, historical achievement of justice and refuses to acknowledge subsequent needs for change. For Christians, attentiveness to the law of love that lies beyond justice provides an important element of flexibility and responsiveness to new conditions. More important, those who seriously consider the requirements of love for others are less apt to exploit the idea of justice in ways that turn its ambiguities into a vehicle for their own self-interest.

In recent years, liberation theology has raised questions about justice from a perspective that contrasts sharply with that of Christian Realism. If the message of the realists is a warning to established powers that the claims of justice are not always on their side, the liberation theologians proclaim to the poor the Good News that God's justice is especially concerned with their plight. Liberation theology finds in Jesus' identification with the poor people of the land the key to the mission of the church today. Biblical justice is not an impartial, uninvolved weighing of the claims of all parties. It involves what Roman Catholics in Latin America have called a "preferential option for the poor." The works of theologians Gustavo Gutiérrez and Jon Sobrino and the pronouncements of the Conference of Latin American Bishops (CELAM II) stand out as examples of this interpretation.

The idea of justice in liberation theology is closely linked to an idea of the role of the church in situations where economic power, racism, or the legacies of colonialism have created powerful forces of exploitation and oppression. Although the church has often benefited from its association with these forces, liberation theology emphasizes the eschatological proclamation of the New Testament that the present order and its values are rapidly passing away. Today's Christians, following the example of Jesus, must risk complete identification with those whose lives have been distorted by the existing powers, but who are destined to be the bearers of a new era.

It is not clear that this theological imperative for the church to act with and for the poor can, or should, be translated into a theory of justice for society as a whole. Critics sometimes argue that a "preferential option for the poor" is as unfair as the prevailing bias against them. A true concept of justice, the critics suggest, must insist on strict impartiality. The liberation theologians, however, seem less concerned to attack the ideal of impartiality than to call attention to how difficult it is to achieve. Where a long history of injustice has reduced opportunities for the poor, encouraged prejudice against them, and bred indifference to their plight, even the best intentions to be fair to particular individuals in present situations will not suffice to overcome the effects of past injustices. Only a conscious effort by the poor to assert their own claims will achieve results that begin to approximate the impartial care for all persons that marks the biblical idea of God's justice. A mere effort to be neutral is not enough.

In the end, then, liberation theology makes radical, rather than discards, the historical connection between justice and impartiality. A more serious challenge to the ideal of impartiality comes from the ethics of virtue. In recent years, both philosophers and theologians have raised serious questions about procedural theories of justice. They suggest that morality cannot be primarily a matter applying fair rules to the pursuit of individual interests. Far more important is the way that those interests and choices are shaped by communities of family, faith, or ethnic identity. Justice and impartiality may be conceptually linked in modern thought, but that only demonstrates the limitations of modern theories of justice. Impartial justice cannot tell us what sorts of virtues we ought to pursue or what images of human goodness ought to shape our lives when we face difficult choices. Relevant concepts of justice, by contrast, are rooted in particular moral and religious traditions. They shape a character that allows us to choose between competing claims with integrity, instead of attempting to see them from a neutral perspective that belongs to no one in particular.

In recent theology, this renewed interest in virtue leads also to a new emphasis on the distinctiveness of the Christian way of life. Christian virtues are based on the Gospel narratives and are shaped by the present-day influences of a Christian community. Stanley Hauerwas and James Wm. McClendon, Jr., are among those whose work reflects this turn toward a Christian ethics of virtue. Anything that this theology has to say about justice will take the form of a community shaped by the Christian values of sharing and mutual care, rather than the form of a prescription about rights or the distribution of goods in the society at large. The church does not offer a social ethics for society to adopt or reject. The church lives in ways that witness to an alternative to the individualistic, materialistic, and present-centered values that usually prevail, but it cannot translate its way of life into a set of propositions that will be clear and persuasive to everyone. Indeed, justice as a Christian virtue will not even be intelligible to those whose lives are shaped by quite different presuppositions.

Today's Christian thinking about justice, then, ranges from a critical engagement with public political ideas in natural law thought and Christian Realism, to a revolutionary critique of modern society in liberation theology, and to an emphasis on the uniqueness of Christian community in theological versions of the ethics of virtue. This wide range of Christian ideas about justice reflects not only the pluralism of theology but also a renewed interest in philosophical alternatives to consensual and procedural theories of justice. No single theory of justice dominates contemporary thought, and so it is impossible to derive a straightforward estimate of what justice requires from a simple definition of justice on which everyone agrees.

For the foreseeable future, arguments about justice will involve claims about how specific goods and duties ought to be distributed and claims about the meaning of justice itself. For Christian theology, these discussions raise the additional issue of how this most important question of social ethics is related to God as the ultimate source of all good and as the final guide of human life.

ROBIN W. LOVIN

Bibliography

Gustavo Gutiérrez, *A Theology of Liberation*.
Stanley Hauerwas, *Against the Nations: War and Survival in Liberal Society*.
David Hollenbach, *Claims in Conflict: Retrieving and Renewing the Catholic Human Rights Tradition*.
Reinhold Niebuhr, "Liberty and Equality" in Ronald Stone, ed., *Faith and Politics*.
John Rawls, *A Theory of Justice*.
Michael Sandel, *Liberalism and the Limits of Justice*.
Ronald H. Stone, *Christian Realism and Peacemaking*.

Cross Reference: CELAM II, Economics, Ethics–Christian, Institutionalized Violence, Liberation Theology, Moral Theology, Virtue.

JUSTIFICATION

Justification is a primary biblical and dogmatic concept denoting the action of God in reestablishing a proper relationship with fallen creation. This is accomplished through the cross and resurrection of Jesus Christ and its subsequent proclamation. Justification means, therefore, that through Christ sinners set against God are "set right" with God, the source of all justice and the final judge of all. The apostle Paul insisted that humans are "justified by faith apart from works of law" (Rom. 3:28), that is, set right simply by faith in Christ and his "righteousness" (justice) rather than by dependence on their own accomplishments, virtues, or holiness.

Justification is God in action: forgiving the sinner for Christ's sake and granting the righteousness of Christ so that the sinner is newly established and determined. This activity of God is the fundamental content of the gospel. Justification as the outright divine gift of righteousness for Jesus' sake reveals that the primary fault (original sin) of fallen beings is not merely persistent (habitual or inherited) moral misbehavior (actual sins) but unbelief, the inability to trust God and the divine gift of created life. To be a sinner is to be trapped by anxiety and to seek self-justification over against God (to live by the law), inherently to refuse to surrender control of one's own destiny (bondage).

271

Justification therefore always has predestination as its correlate. Justification is ultimately the carrying out of the divine predestination concretely in the present through the proclamation of the gospel. As such it is in its most nearly pure form simply a divine pronouncement made for Jesus' sake—what the Reformers called a "forensic declaration" or imputation—that can be received only by hearing and believing. The pronouncement itself stops the hearers in their tracks or renders them passive before the divine judgment. Rejection of or resistance to the pronouncement is itself the mark of unbelief. From the point of view of the doctrine of justification, therefore, just the hearing and being grasped by such proclamation is the only way to be "set right" with a God who acts. God seeks faith, love, and hope. Justification is the means to achieve it.

Following Paul, the Protestant Reformation of the sixteenth century insisted that sinners are justified by faith in the gospel alone. Since that time, justification has gained prominence as a, if not the, primary metaphor for describing the establishment of the proper relationship between God and fallen humanity. Many Protestants, particularly Lutherans, have insisted that justification is not just one article of faith among others, but the central and chief article, the "plumb line" (Luther) by which all other doctrines are to be judged and "the article by which the church stands or falls."

The concept of justification has provoked a fundamental division in Christian theology. Since its beginning, but primarily since the Protestant Reformation, Christian theology has been split between those who understand justification to mean a "repair" (in the sense of revitalizing or empowering whatever natural powers have survived the Fall) and those who understand it more radically as a new creation (II Cor. 3:6; Gal. 6:15), or death and new life in Christ (Rom. 6, 7; Eph. 2:1, 5; Col. 2:13, 20, 3:3; I Pet. 2:24). In the former instance justification is understood as a more or less continuous process of moral and spiritual transformation assisted by divine grace, enabling one to progress toward the goal of righteousness. In the latter case it is understood simply as the bestowal of the goal through the divine self-communication, and thus as the end of the old, the death of the sinner, and the gift of new life and freedom through the re-creative power of the divine pronouncement itself. The former is more characteristic of Roman Catholic views and the latter of Protestants.

Even though current ecumenical discussion has demonstrated hopeful convergences between these two ways of understanding justification, the divide and its effects persist. Those who look upon justification as a process of repair tend toward the idea that the self, in spite of the Fall, is able in some measure to cooperate with divine grace, which augments the inherent religious nature of the self. Although grace is an indispensable help, one is still not justified by grace *alone*. In contrast, those who understand justification as new creation, as death and new life, are often suspected of disrespecting creation or whatever is left of it after the Fall and what can be accomplished "in the saints" and in the church, with the help of grace. The justifying Word—the "current" of life in creation—makes the person a person under God again rather than a self-made person. Those who were dead in sin are made alive in Christ. The difficulty in putting these two contrasting positions together is patent, and in one degree or another they persist to this day.

In religious discourse today perhaps the chief question about justification language has been that of its relevance. Does it not presuppose an experience of guilt and the afflictions of an anxious conscience no longer shared by modern persons? For the most part, such a question, though important for preaching, fails to note the sweeping theological function of justification language. In the first place, justification language is not a language in search of someone who supposedly feels a "need" for it. Paul preached justification by faith precisely because it was the truth that attacked the secure—those who thought they had no need for it. Justification puts humans under question before God. True, justification does comfort the afflicted, but it also—and perhaps even primarily—afflicts the comfortable. In the second place, the question of justification decides the fundamental theological question of the nature of God. A God who justifies the ungodly for God's own namesake must be a living God who acts in the present to do a new thing: justifying not only sinners, but Godself, vindicating the divine claim to be precisely the creator-redeemer. Third, based on the foregoing points, justification language functions for the theologian and preacher to instruct and drive toward a particular kind of speech about and for God. It would be a disastrous mistake if one were to assume from what is said in this article that one is merely to talk *about* justification. Rather, what justification language proposes is precisely this: that proper language about and from God is language that does the deed; it actually justifies. The ultimate purpose of the language is to drive to an actual giving of the gift in the living present, as in the absolution: I declare unto you the forgiveness of all your sins for Jesus' sake. The point toward which it drives is simply that God is to come alive as creator and redeemer in our speech.

GERHARD O. FORDE

Bibliography

H. George Anderson, T. Austin Murphy, and Joseph Burgess, eds., "Lutherans and Catholics in Dialogue VII," in *Justification by Faith.*
Markus Barth, *Justification.*
Gerhard O. Forde, *Justification by Faith: A Matter of Death and Life.*
Alister E. McGrath, *Iustitia Dei. A History of the Christian Doctrine of Justification,* 2 vols.

John Reumann, *Righteousness in the New Testament*. With responses by Joseph A. Fitzmyer and Jerome D. Quinn.

Cross Reference: Election, Grace, Law and Gospel, Soteriology.

KINGDOM OF GOD

The kingdom of God is one of the most fruitful yet controversial concepts in Christian theology. It has been employed to uphold the status quo, and it has been a revolutionary ideal used to break social forms and customs. Although appropriated from Judaism, it was radically transformed by Jesus and so reinterpreted by the early Christian community.

In the New Testament the concept signifies the sovereignty or kingly rule of God. Its basic intent is to affirm the fact that God reigns in all aspects of personal and social life. It is not a general, but a unique, kind of rule or reign. Whereas Judaism encountered the rule of God through obedience to the Law and looked forward to the complete establishment of God's rule, the New Testament asserted that in a new and peculiar way the kingdom of God had already come.

Jesus said that if he cast out demons through the power of God, "then the kingdom of God has come upon you." The Gospel of Mark takes its departure from the assertion that the time has reached fulfillment and that the kingdom of God has come—"repent and believe the good news." This claim is not merely a statement of living under God's commandments and so living under godly rule. Rather, it is a new manifestation of God's power and sovereignty in which God's nature, power, and will are brought to bear.

The early Christian community believed that in Jesus of Nazareth the Christ (or Messiah) was encountered and that God's kingdom was made manifest. People could either repent and believe or they could reject it, but regardless of human response, the Kingdom had come. This motif is central for Mark and John and is strongly stated in Matthew and Luke. That for which Israel had hoped and prayed had come to pass in Jesus the Christ. God's freedom and rule expressed itself in a new and an amazing way in his life, death, and resurrection.

Nevertheless, the New Testament also makes references to the kingdom of God as still to come. Some references are apocalyptic visions, and others are predictions about future particular historical events. Together they provide a source to interpret the kingdom of God as still to come. At different periods in the church's history, stress has often been laid on the future dimension of the Kingdom. This point of view moved in one of two directions: It either tended to uphold the status quo under the direction of the church, or it tended to revolutionize the forces of society in the name of the coming Kingdom.

The first position was that taken by the Roman Catholic Church. It tended to identify the kingdom of God with the church as opposed to the world, which it considered the kingdom of Satan. Insofar as the world was good, however, it was under the direction of the kingdom of God through the church. This life was but preparation for a life to come that would be lived in the presence of God. Meanwhile, humanity's relation to God's rule was mediated through the church. Emphasis was not upon a fresh breaking in of the Kingdom or upon a final cataclysmic judgment of the world.

Throughout Christian history another interpretation of the kingdom of God constantly reappeared. It did not believe that the Kingdom was really present, and particularly it did not believe that the kingdom of God could be equated with the church. It stressed the Kingdom as imminent or as about to break in upon the world. The Montanist movement represented such a protest against the early Catholic church's attempt to spiritualize and indefinitely postpone the coming of the kingdom of God. During the Middle Ages various protests, those of the Franciscan Spiritualists being the most thoroughgoing, were made on behalf of an immediate return of the Christ, bringing with him God's kingdom. Wherever this interpretation of the kingdom of God appears, it bemeans the role of the church and pronounces a negative judgment against culture and society. It condemns social institutions as instruments of the kingdom of Satan. It sees little or no relation between God's rule and life as it is being lived at a given moment. The object is not to transform life within history so as to bring it into conformity with an ever-present dynamic will of God. Rather, the object is to negate history through an all-encompassing judgment, as God ushers in the divine Kingdom through a new heaven and new earth.

The very concept of kingdom of God is so dynamic that it constantly brings forth a series of options. The fact that the symbol is that of a kingdom implies a close relationship to analogous structures of life and history. Of necessity, such a concept must deal concretely with the day-to-day affairs of living men and women. Furthermore, this symbol, by its very nature, must include the personal and social aspects of life, since to be less inclusive would do violence to the symbol of "kingdom" or of "rule."

Insofar as it is the kingdom of God, the symbol stresses the freedom and the sovereignty of God the creator, sustainer, and the redeemer. It transcends the totality of this life, both personal and social, and demands that the Christian take a stand against this life. It appears as a completion of this life, as a fulfillment, as the final meaning of history; yet it is God's kingdom, God's work and not people's action. In this sense the kingdom of God is never the inevitable consequence or development of human life and history.

Thus, the concept of the kingdom of God posed a number of the central theological problems with which Christian theology still wrestles. If one affirms that the kingdom of God has already come, then one must make clear what this means. How is the kingdom of God in operation? Is it through a series of laws or commands? Are these primarily moral and personal or are they ontological? How is God's rule to be discovered in and for culture or the state? Is the kingdom of God directly operative in personal and social life, or is it mediated through the church or through other forces? Can it be mediated differently through the church on the one hand and through the structures of life on the other? Is it possible that the kingdom of God is already present as a special perspective through which humans are called to new life? If so, what is the content of this perspective, and on what is it based and how is it maintained?

If one affirms that the kingdom of God is present, but that its real meaning is hidden and the Kingdom is still to come, then one faces an additional set of creative possibilities. How is the kingdom of God to come? Is it to mean the end of all history as we now know it? If so, what is the relation of the kingdom of God to history and the partial meaning of life as one now experiences it? Is the kingdom of God related to some kind of perfection of our present social and cultural order? How is the coming of the kingdom of God to be related to the life of the church? Does the church fully embody the kingdom of God? Does it not also embody the forces of evil? Does not the church, in some sense, have to be the bearer of the kingdom of God? In doing this, does not the church have to embody the presence of the Kingdom and yet point beyond itself to God and the fulfillment of the Kingdom?

At present, theological discussion remains torn between two basic emphases. One stresses the reality of the presence of the kingdom of God transforming this life through judgment and mercy. The Kingdom is here as a new reality in life, but it is engaged in a life-and-death struggle with satanic forces and demonic powers. History is thus a great stage on which the drama of redemption is fought. However, the battle, though desperately real, has been won in the victory of Jesus the Christ. History has a positive meaning because it has a beginning, center, and fulfillment. But in and of itself history has no meaning. Only in relation to the dynamic presence of the kingdom of God can it be seen as meaningful. Thus the minor motif is the kingdom of God still to come.

The other point of view stresses the Kingdom yet to come. Though it is recognized that God rules, for God is sovereign, the demonic forces are so great that nothing but suffering can be anticipated. In theory history must be important, but in actuality one cannot expect much from it. Only a new divine manifestation of salvific power will suffice. The kingdom of God really has yet to come in any power of genuine significance; so God's judgment is expected, at any moment when the kingdom of God will be ushered in.

Both emphases recognize the dual stress of the kingdom of God: It is here; it is yet to come. Each emphasizes one point as a major motif and the other point as a minor motif. Between these two poles the present interpretation moves. No longer does the optimistic view persist that the unfolding of history itself is bringing closer the final stages of the kingdom of God. It is no longer understood as an evolutionary concept or primarily as a moral-ethical concept. That was the view of the Social Gospel in American life. Recent developments in Latin American liberation theology represent a similar concern to relate the concept of the kingdom of God to the entirety of the social situation but using a dialectical method rather than holding to an evolutionary or a progressive unfolding. Thus the concept continues to function in a creative way in current theology.

JERALD C. BRAUER

Bibliography

John Bright, *The Kingdom of God.*
Gustavo Gutiérrez, *A Theology of Liberation.*
H. Richard Niebuhr, *The Kingdom of God in America.*
Rudolph Otto, *The Kingdom of God and the Son of Man.*
H. G. Wood, et al., *The Kingdom of God and History.*

Cross Reference: Dispensationalism, Eschatology, Liberation Theology, Social Gospel.

LAITY

"Laity" comes from the Greek *laos,* which means simply "people," that is, all the people of God by virtue of baptism. This includes every member of the church—those who are clergy, laity, recipients of God's grace, and participants in Christ's ministry to the world.

Throughout the history of the church, there has been a recurring tendency to subordinate the ministry of the laity to the ministry of the clergy, as if pastors and priests were a sort of upper-crust Christian licensed to rule over the lowly laity. This tendency was condemned by the Reformers, who asserted the principle of the "priesthood of all believers."

In recent church renewal, there has been a uniform reassertion of the principle of the priesthood of all believers. The Second Vatican Council emphasized I Peter 2:9-10 as the foundational text for all thought about the place of the laity, the people of God, in the church: "But you are a chosen race, a royal priesthood, a holy nation, God's own people, that you may declare the wonderful deeds of him who called you out of darkness into his marvelous light."

Israel had been told, "You shall be to me a kingdom of priests and a holy nation" (Exod. 19:6), "a people holy to the Lord your God" (Deut. 7:6). Although priests in Israel held a special mediatorial role between the people and God, it was understood that the whole nation, as a "kingdom of priests," bore responsibility to be God's people in the world. The church further emphasized the corporate, shared priesthood of all believers that had characterized Israel's self-understanding. In the church, each baptized person shares in Christ's priesthood to the world. Nowhere in the New Testament is the word "priest" (Greek, *hieros*) used to refer to someone who holds office in the church. "Priest" is applied first to Christ and his work of self-sacrifice on the cross, his intercession in behalf of the world, and his representation of the world to God (most vividly in the Epistle to the Hebrews), and secondarily to the work of all the people of God, who share in Christ's priestly work. So Revelation begins with the acclamation, "To him who loves us and has freed us from our sins by his blood and made us a kingdom, priests to his God and Father" (Rev. 1:5).

The responsibility of the *laos* to be priests to the world was signified in the early baptismal rites when the baptized person was given symbolic instruments (a candle, a white robe) and gestures (the laying-on-of-hands and the signing of the cross) as signs of that new Christian's ministry to the world. Unfortunately, these symbols gradually became associated with the act of ordination to the priesthood rather than baptism, an indication of the growing clericalization of the church. New rites of baptism within many churches seek to recover the significance of baptism as "ordination" of all believers to the priesthood of Christ.

God's people are characterized by a wonderful diversity of baptismal gifts. "For as in one body we have many members, and all the members do not have the same function, so we, though many, are one body in Christ, and individually members one of another" (Rom. 12:4-5). At the same time, even in their diversity, they are called to unity because there is "one Lord, one faith, one baptism" (Eph. 4:5). Christians exist, not as isolated individuals, but as a people, the *laos*. The normative mode of Christian existence is as a member of a body, a people, a community in Christ. Paul never tires of comparing the church to a human body. "If one member suffers, all suffer together; if one member is honored, all rejoice together. Now you are the body of Christ and individually members of it" (I Cor. 12:26-27).

From among the *laos,* at a very early date in the life of the church, certain individuals were designated as leaders for the church. They were set apart for the special ministries of teaching, preaching, presiding at the Eucharist, and other acts "to equip the saints for the work of ministry, for building up the body of Christ" (Eph. 4:12). This is the origin of the clergy, the *clēros* arising out of the *laos*. To assert the primacy of the laity before the clergy in no way detracts from the necessity and the value of the clergy for the life of the church; rather, it emphasizes that the ministry of the laity, the baptismally bestowed ministry of the whole people of God, is the source of significance for the clergy. The church's ordained leaders, the clergy, are significant only as a means for what must occur in the ministry of the church's people, the laity.

WILLIAM H. WILLIMON

Bibliography

Austin Flannery, ed., *Vatican Council II: The Conciliar and Post Conciliar Documents*.
Hans Küng, *The Church*.
Edward Schillebeeckx, *Ministry: Leadership in the Community of Jesus Christ*.

Cross Reference: Ecclesiology, Ordination, Priesthood.

LANGUAGE–RELIGIOUS

Until the turn of the twentieth century the primary concern of philosophy had always been truth and reality, but since then the stress has moved to linguistic meaning.

Some of the roots of linguistic philosophy originated in Vienna (with a group known as the Vienna Circle), while others originated in England, primarily in the work of Bertrand Russell and the young Ludwig Wittgenstein. The Viennese group sought to explain language and meaningfulness on the basis of what they took scientific discourse to be, while the British sought to come at it from the perspective of logic and mathematics. Both root systems were most directly and influentially expressed in the book *Language, Truth and Logic* by A. J. Ayer, a young Englishman who had studied in Vienna. Shortly before World War II, many members of the Vienna Circle came to America, and after the war many American philosophers studied in England. Thus this movement came to dominate American philosophy.

The central thrust of Ayer's book and early linguistic philosophy (often termed "analytic philosophy") was the "verifiability criterion of meaningfulness." The point of this formidable phrase was really quite simple. The idea was to try to settle whether or not a statement or a theory is actually a *meaningful* one before investing a great deal of effort on the question of its truth. This idea resulted in proposing that unless a given proposition could in principle be *tested* as to its truth value, it would be set aside as cognitively meaningless. That is to say, unless a statement can be shown to be strictly redundant or self-contradictory (according to the laws of logic) on the one hand, or in some way reducible to propositions about concrete, observable experience on the other hand, it is simply devoid of any possible truth value (cognitivity).

An example should prove helpful at this point. Suppose it is asserted that the room you are now in is full of hippopotamuses. You look around and report that you do not see, hear, or smell any such animals at all. To which comes the reply, "Of course not—they are in principle inexperienceable hippopotamuses." Now, since it is affirmed that these beasts are "in principle" beyond experience, it follows that there is absolutely no way to establish whether the assertion is true or false. In short, it is a meaningless mouthing of sounds that appears to be affirming

279

something but actually is not; just as the words "Why is a mouse when it whirls?" appear to be asking a question but are not. Another way to point out the meaninglessness of the assertion is to reflect on the fact that there is no difference at all between affirming it and denying it; both acts result in the same experiences. If *nothing* counts for or against a proposition, it can hardly be said to be making a cognitive claim.

Now Ayer's concern was not with hippopotamuses, but with the claims that philosophers and theologians have been making for thousands of years about such notions as the eternal forms of truth and beauty, a spiritual reality including God and angels that entirely transcends the reality we know, our absolute duty, and the like. He proposed that we set aside all such questions as meaningless because they are in principle irresolvable, thus a waste of time and effort. All metaphysical, theological, and ethical statements are consequently classified as *cognitively meaningless,* although they well may be *emotionally meaningful* to many people. Emotional meaning, however, was said to be the business not of philosophy but rather of psychology.

The force of this fresh challenge to those who would speak religiously was, and is, considerable. Prior to linguistic analysis the main issue had been whether or not religious statements were true; now the issue became whether or not they are even asserting anything. In the words of the young Wittgenstein, taken from his highly influential book *Tractatus logico-philosophicus* (a book that powerfully informed Ayer's work): "Whatever can be said at all can be said clearly. Whereof we cannot speak, thereof we must remain silent." Talk of God was thus placed beyond the range of meaningful discourse, because there would seem to be no way to evaluate it. In a word, religious language, along with all metaphysical and ethical language, does not meet the criterion of meaningfulness.

A wide variety of responses to the challenge of early linguistic or analytic philosophy have been made by those who find speaking religiously a valuable activity. Some have welcomed this emphasis because it brings out what they take to be the central purpose of God-talk, namely to focus our emotive and moral perspectives. These thinkers have claimed that by means of the religious use of language we express our deepest commitments. Other thinkers have argued that God-talk *is,* in fact, beyond the reach of cognitive meaning, not because it is meaningless or because it is essentially emotive or moral in its nature, but rather because it is personal and mysterious. In other words, these thinkers maintain that religious discourse is unique, following criteria of its own, and thus need not answer to those of scientific or philosophic discourse.

At the same time there are those who contend that God-talk can be shown to *meet* the verifiability criterion of meaningfulness. Some thinkers maintain that there are religious or "metaphysical facts" that can be established experientially in the here and now, while others suggest that such realities must wait until the afterlife to receive confirmation. In either case the claim is that this experiential dimension of God-talk renders it cognitively meaningful. Although this perspective has a good deal to be said for it, establishing or confirming such religious facts constitutes a very difficult task that is a long way from being firmly established.

Along with those making the foregoing responses, there have always been thinkers, both religious and nonreligious, who contend that the verifiability criterion is much too narrow even for science itself, let alone for philosophy. Many specific criticisms have been raised about the "meaningfulness" of some of the terms used to state and explain the verifiability criterion itself, and serious questions have been raised about the status of the criterion according to its own specifications. To put it bluntly, does the criterion itself conform to its own requirements? Perhaps it is really a definition or a proposal for science only. This sort of question has opened up many related and increasingly more important issues concerning the various dimensions of meaningfulness within the various regions of language. Ayer and others have sought to modify their perspective as a result of this sort of critique, but in essence they have not altered the main thrust. Nonetheless, fewer and fewer philosophers and theologians now take the early analytic posture very seriously.

Undoubtedly the strongest force contributing to the broader development of linguistic philosophy was the later work of Wittgenstein. After finishing his first book, the *Tractatus,* he "retired" from philosophy (at the age of twenty-five!) because he felt that if he was correct, philosophy was now essentially complete. Some fifteen years later he returned to Cambridge University and devoted the rest of his life to pursuing an approach to philosophy that was fundamentally opposed to his early work. The pivotal point of his fresh posture, expressed most thoroughly in his book *Philosophical Investigations* was that language is an extremely complex and diverse phenomenon that cannot be reduced to a single explanation or criterion of meaning. Moreover, he continually stressed that language is essentially a social activity inextricably interwoven with other aspects of human life. It is more like the various games and shared activities we enter into than it is like logic and mathematics.

The ramifications of the later Wittgenstein's approach for those who would use language religiously are considerable. Without claiming that this approach solves all the relevant problems, it is suggested here that the exploration of God-talk grounded in the insights of more recent linguistic philosophy (often termed "ordinary language analysis") is far more fruitful than any of the postures already discussed. They all have valuable points to make, but until the very board on which the whole game is played is restructured, no real progress can be made. Philosophers such as J. L. Austin, John Wisdom, and Max Black, and theologians such as Ian Ramsey, Basil Mitchell, and David Burrell, who have followed the later Wittgenstein's lead, seem to me to make the most headway.

One of the more helpful analyses of God-talk from a Wittgensteinian perspective was offered by Ian Ramsey. He called attention to the twofold thrust of most theological and biblical language. On the one hand, such talk is nearly always grounded in human experience by the use of terms like "father," "king," "wise," "loving," and so on. On the other hand, these terms are generally joined with terms that indicate that the initial ones are not to be taken literally but analogically, such as "heavenly," "eternal," "all," or "infinitely." Thus we speak of God as "heavenly Father," "all wise," and "infinitely loving." Ramsey called the former terms "models," because they refer to aspects of experience with which we are very familiar and which encapsulate characteristics we value highly. He called the latter terms "qualifiers," because they instruct us about how to use the model terms.

In Ramsey's view, the terms "heavenly" and "infinite" are not to be taken literally as referring to physical space and time, but metaphorically, so as to point out talk of God in two directions at once: toward the tangible dimension of experience *and* toward the intangible, more comprehensive dimension it mediates. The qualifying aspect of our talk of God does not call attention to a different, higher "realm," but rather to a deeper, richer dimension within and throughout our everyday life. Far from divesting religious language of its meaning and force, this interpretation enlivens and expands it by making it both experiential, which was the valid concern of those proposing the verifiability criterion, and yet "more," which is the legitimate theological issue.

To speak of God-talk as essentially metaphorical in nature opens up a whole, and as yet mostly unexplored, territory. By its very nature, metaphorical speech is two-dimensional. That is, it signifies one aspect of reality by means of another. Analogy, paradox, and irony all participate in this general function of language, so it is not surprising that they, too, should be employed in religious speech. For in talking of God we are talking of a transcendent reality by using the only language that we have, namely that through which we speak of and interact with our everyday world. Metaphor enables us to speak of this transcendent reality, while at the same time speaking of our common, everyday life. This view of the meaning of religious language (expounded by Sallie McFague in *Metaphorical Theology*) carries with it the possibility of speech that is at once cognitively meaningful and capable of signifying the divine.

JERRY H. GILL

Bibliography

A. Flew and A. MacIntyre, *New Essays in Philosophical Theology*.
James Wm. McClendon, Jr., and James Smith, *Understanding Religious Convictions*.
Sallie McFague, *Speaking in Parables*.
Ian Ramsey, *Religious Language*.

Cross Reference: Analogy, Deconstructionism, Epistemology, Hermeneutics, Insight, Liminality, Paradigm, Paradox, Revelation, Structuralism, Symbol.

LAST THINGS (*See* ESCHATOLOGY.)

LAW AND GOSPEL

Law and gospel are two closely related terms that have played an important role in Christian theology. The concepts behind the terms "law" (God's urging, compelling, and commanding all creatures, in particular humans, and holding them accountable) and "gospel" (God's unconditional promise through Jesus Christ) are found throughout scripture.

However, theologians most apt to use this distinction are influenced by Paul, who, especially in Romans and Galatians, distinguishes justification by works of the law from justification by faith in the gospel. By the law Paul means (1) the will of God for the entire creation that is known by all persons, including Gentiles, and (2) the moral commandments and cultic rituals of ancient Israel. The law is the expression of the will of God that humans live in grateful trust in God and build a trustworthy world for their fellow creatures. However, people misuse the law to justify themselves and as a result are filled with pride or despair at their works. Paul understands the gospel as the Good News of what God has done in Jesus Christ for humanity and the entire creation. The gospel is more than information regarding the work of God in Jesus Christ; it is a means of God's liberating power to save (Rom. 1:16; I Cor. 15:2).

Augustine retained the Pauline doctrine of law and gospel, especially in his anti-Pelagian writings. In *On the Spirit and the Letter* (412 c.e.), he uses II Cor. 3:6, "letter and spirit," and Romans to distinguish between law (letter) and gospel (Spirit). Only the Holy Spirit (gospel) can give life, not the works of the law (letter).

Some Reformation theologians, especially Luther (1483–1546), made the Pauline distinction the basis for their theology. By this use Luther clarifies a central Reformation teaching—the meaning of justification by faith. In his *Commentary on Galatians,* Luther says that what makes a person a theologian is knowing how to distinguish law from gospel. The law both compels our love of creation and our neighbor and accuses and condemns us when we fail to do so. As a result of our sin, the law is death, the gospel life. The law compels and demands, the gospel unconditionally gives.

The law-gospel distinction is functional; that is, what Luther asks about the proclaimed word of God is *not* "What is it?" but "What does it *do?*" Preaching is either law or gospel, depending on how it strikes a person. A word that does not demand or accuse is not law in terms of this distinction. A proclamation that does not pardon or comfort the sinner is not gospel.

The point of making the distinction is to keep from losing the gospel, to keep the Good News good. But, according to Luther, most theology and most preaching are law because they do not see that Christ comes to end the rule of law in the hearer, but instead seeks to find ways to allow the old self to go on living under the law. A common form of such preaching is moral exhortation purporting to be the way of salvation. The gospel as the promise of final forgiveness proclaimed ahead of time means that the law-gospel distinction entails the formula *simul justus et peccator* (a Latin term that means that in this life we are simultaneously righteous because of Christ's forgiveness even though we remain sinful until death).

Other Reformers of the sixteenth and seventeenth centuries, including Melanchthon, used the law-gospel distinction as well. Calvin attended to the distinction in the *Institutes;* however, it was not as central for him as it was for Luther. Since Calvin used the term "law" to mean primarily the "rule of righteous living" that God requires of us, his emphasis differed decidedly from Luther's use.

The principal debates around the distinction, especially between Lutheran and Calvinist theologians, have been about the question of the uses of the law. Luther speaks of two uses of the law. The first, or civil use, is much like the way most of us speak of law as guidelines that preserve peace and order by compelling us to obey under threat of punishment. For Luther the Ten Commandments are a summary of the way such law is built into the created world and is known by believers and unbelievers alike.

The second use of the law (Luther calls this the "theological" or "accusing" use of the law) drives us into awareness of our sin, perhaps into despair and anger at God, and leaves us with no excuse. The law's second use can happen to us when we hear it preached or when our experience of life leaves us crushed. What we need then is not more law but unconditional words of forgiveness, love, acceptance, and hope from the only one who can speak without any conditions; what we need is the gospel of Christ. Set free by the gospel, we can then live life (with its laws) for the sake of our neighbors (the purpose of the law) and not for our own well-being—since our well-being is already established by God through Christ.

Some Lutherans distinguished a third usage: to teach the converted how to learn from the law to live and walk in the law. But even among some "third use" Lutherans, the third use is really only the first and second uses for the regenerate person insofar as he or she is still a sinner, and the good works of the regenerate are, strictly speaking, not works of the law but works and fruits of the Spirit.

The distinction between law and gospel remains the subject of considerable debate in twentieth-century thought. Perhaps the most notable debate was that between Karl Barth and Werner Elert during the years of the church struggle in Nazi Germany. Less known at the time, but increasing later on in its influence, is the Scandinavian use of the distinction, especially in the work of Gustaf Wingren. After a period of disrepute in Germany, because of its identification with the

German Christian Movement, the distinction has returned to a prominent place in current German theology and plays a smaller, though significant role, in current American theology.

PATRICK R. KEIFERT

Bibliography

Paul Althaus, *Luther's Ethics*.
Karl Barth, *God, Grace, and Gospel*.
Werner Elert, *Law and Gospel*.
Gustaf Wingren, *Creation and Law*.

Cross Reference: Biblical Theology, Grace, Justification.

LIBERALISM

Liberalism in theology is characterized by a deep respect for the authority of reason and experience in religion, an openness to culture, a willingness to adapt theological expression to cultural forms, and continuing flexibility in interpreting the sacred texts and practices of its tradition. Its antithesis is conservatism or, in its extreme form, fundamentalism, which places the authority of sacred texts or practices or both above that of reason and experience, is often antagonistic to cultural forms, and is literalistic in interpreting its texts and practices. Liberalism is found in both Protestant and Roman Catholic Christianity, as well as in Judaism, Islam, and Asian religions with well-developed theologies, such as Buddhism and Hinduism.

Liberalism in the West takes its rise from the Enlightenment of the eighteenth century, which gave reason and sense experience a prominence they had not had before. As trust in reason and observation spread from philosophy and science to historical studies, literary criticism, and morality, religions were forced either to resist the new rational and empirical conclusions or to adapt their theologies to harmonize with reason and observation. Liberalism adapts.

There are many forms of adaptation, however, and what is liberal to one group is often quite conservative to another. The German theologian Friedrich Schleiermacher (1768–1834) is often called the father of modern liberal theology because he maintained that doctrines have their bases in religious consciousness rather than in external reality and because he thereby avoided any clash with scientific world views. Yet to religion's "cultured despisers" in avant-garde Berlin, to whom Schleiermacher addressed his most famous book, he was a conservative, simply because he remained a committed Christian. Similarly, Protestant evangelicals are liberals from a fundamentalist perspective, yet they dissociate themselves in their own minds from liberalism.

Liberals demonstrate their flexibility and adaptability in four areas. Because a theologian is liberal in these areas does not necessarily mean, however, that he or she is liberal in another, although there is often carry-over from one area to another. The first area is scientific analysis of sacred texts and practices with respect to their origins, their construction in their historical settings, and their theological meanings. Liberal theologians study sacred texts and practices by applying scientific, critical methods. Karl Barth (1886–1968), the founder of Neoorthodoxy, accepted biblical criticism, and he is therefore considered a liberal by fundamentalists, who reject it. Yet Barth viewed Schleiermacher as a liberal because Schleiermacher constructed his view of human being on the basis of human experience rather than revelation. Hans Küng lost his position as an endorsed Roman Catholic theologian for questioning the practice of papal infallibility, and he is therefore considered a liberal by conservative Roman Catholic theologians, who regard the practice as undebatable; yet in other aspects of his theology, Küng is quite traditional.

The second area is the formulation of the nature of human being through humanistic and social scientific studies prior to human being's being interpreted by any religion. This is the area in which Schleiermacher pioneered and in which Paul Tillich (1886–1965) and others have persevered. Tillich conducted his analysis of human being, including the human predicament, in existential terms; then he interpreted the Bible in the same terms so that it could address the questions he thought human beings were actually asking. The so-called empirical school of theology associated with The University of Chicago and with theologians such as Charles Hartshorne, Bernard Meland, Bernard Loomer, and John Cobb, has done something similar, but with Whiteheadian instead of existential categories. Edward Schillebeeckx and David Tracy in the Roman Catholic tradition also have made use of analyses of human experience to interpret sacred texts and practices.

The third area is the understanding of the origin and continuation of the universe in scientific terms, especially those of evolution and astrophysics, and the adaptation of the doctrines of creation and providence to fit the scientific data. Some theologians, such as James Gustafson in *Ethics from a Theocentric Perspective,* have gone so far as to construct their doctrines of creation and providence largely from scientific evidence.

The final area is the acceptance of morality as essentially independent of the command of God or the commandments of sacred texts. Liberals in this area do not deny the importance of religion for morality with respect to motivation and personal dedication to the good, but they believe that the content of morality is grounded in the human situation and is knowable outside special divine revelation. Justice, for example, though it may be illuminated and enriched by the teachings of Moses or Jesus, exists as a moral principle independently of their teachings. James Gustafson's *Christ and the Moral Life* is an example of liberal Protestant thinking in this area, and several of the essays of Charles Curran in the Roman

Catholic tradition argue for grounding morality in the universal human condition.

The strength of liberalism lies in its conviction that religion must make sense in order to survive. Liberalism has shown great skill and ingenuity in interpreting theology in the light of humanistic and scientific understanding. Its weakness is the risk that such adaptation threatens of sliding past harmonization to skepticism or secularism.

JOHN P. CROSSLEY, JR.

Bibliography

Karl Barth, "Evangelical Theology in the Nineteenth Century," in *The Humanity of God.*
John B. Cobb, Jr., *A Christian Natural Theology.*
Hans Küng, *Infallible? An Inquiry.*
H. Richard Niebuhr, "The Christ of Culture," in *Christ and Culture.*
Friedrich Schleiermacher, *On Religion: Speeches to Its Cultured Despisers,* trans. John Oman.
Paul Tillich, *Dynamics of Faith.*
David Tracy, *Blessed Rage for Order: The New Pluralism in Theology.*

Cross Reference: Creation, Culture, Empirical Theology, Experience–Religious, Fundamentalism, Humanism, Providence, Secularity, Social Gospel.

LIBERATION THEOLOGY

Liberation theology or "theology of liberation" is a term that was coined in the late 1960s in Latin America, first in Spanish and later in Portuguese. The term originally referred to the type of theological reflection emerging during those years among Latin American Christian theologians, primarily Roman Catholic clergymen working in close connection with the social-political-economic struggles of poor and believing Latin Americans. The Peruvian Roman Catholic theologian Gustavo Gutiérrez, a diocesan priest with European degrees in psychology and theology, is generally held as the main founder of this theological approach. Probably the first printed use of the term, Gutiérrez's 1968 article in Spanish, "Toward a Theology of Liberation," provided the thrust for the movement. Shortly after that article, he wrote *A Theology of Liberation: Perspectives* (also in Spanish), which is usually considered the cornerstone of liberation theology. Writing about the same time as Gutiérrez, the Brazilian Presbyterian Rubem Alves and the Argentinean Lutheran José Míguez Bonino were the first Latin American Protestant liberation theologians. Besides Gutiérrez, the Brazilians Hugo Assmann and Leonardo Boff were among the very first Roman Catholic theologians to contribute to its development.

Some Premises for the Understanding of Liberation Theology. Liberation theology cannot be studied or properly understood outside its social milieu, its

287

historical transformations, or its ecclesiastical implications. In fact, one of the key traits of liberation theology is that it considers itself—and *all* other theologies—as a "second moment" in the life of a Christian community or a Christian person.

This leads to at least three different implications with important consequences. The first is that ordinary human *life*—actual daily life in community, including its spiritual dimensions—has chronological, logical, and pastoral precedence over theological reflection: Life comes first, theology comes only thereafter, striving to understand and serve *life,* including, albeit by no means being exclusively reduced to, the specific faith-life of the community. The second implication of liberation theology's conception of theology as a "second moment" is that *all* theologies, knowingly or not, are theologies of specific life-experiences, of singular praxes peculiar to historically bound societies. In other words, theologies are attempts by concrete believers to respond to their specific life-challenges in light of their faith-tradition and faith experience; all theologies, therefore, stem from and try to respond to singular, not universal experiences. The third aspect is that theology is not an exclusively individual, intellectual, or specialized task, even when it tricks itself into believing that it is. It is, instead, the fruit of life in community, of shared faith, and of multiple efforts (often invisible and unrecognized), and it should be acknowledged and encouraged as such, as a shared responsibility of all members of a believing, Spirit-filled human community.

In this sense Latin American liberation theology recognizes itself both as a theology flowing from the life-experience of Latin America's poor Christians, especially those who struggle at the end of the twentieth century to free themselves from a host of oppressions, and as a theology whose main thrust is precisely to understand and nurture that very struggle in light of the Christian faith and to illuminate and deepen the Christian faith with the challenges of that specific life-experience.

Liberation theology is one of the theologies that articulate the experience of a growing segment of Latin American oppressed Christians whose active commitment to the integral liberation of all oppressed peoples and persons is central to their experience of God and thus, as a "second moment," key to their understanding of the scriptures, the Christ, the church, salvation, the mission of Christians, the reign of God, and the Christian faith. For liberation theology, then, what is central is not the theology of liberation, but God's call for the liberation of the oppressed. Consequently, any theology of liberation is, at its best, nothing but a means for that task—unimportant in and by itself and, like all theologies, irrelevant to other experiences, as well as destined to be superseded by the historical flow of the experience that gave birth to it.

Roots of Liberation Theology. In the late 1960s, Latin America was characterized by turmoil, crises, and growing grassroots movements of protest against oppression. During that time, a number of factors increased the commitment of persons and institutions to the liberation struggles of the downtrodden against oppression and repression. Among these factors were the frustration of the economic hopes raised throughout the Americas by the presence of a Roman Catholic, John F. Kennedy, in the presidency of the United States; the overthrow of most democratic experiments by military coups usually endorsed by the United States' administration; the inroads of Protestantism and communism among the poor, thus eroding a traditional Roman Catholic stronghold; and the growing attention of clergy, lay activists, and religious (sisters and brothers in religious orders) to social and economic issues, a trend encouraged by Vatican II, by the popes since John XXIII, and by the World Council of Churches.

Many theologians, some of whom studied under Johann Baptist Metz, Jürgen Moltmann, Karl Rahner, and Joseph Ratzinger, took an active, radical role in their preferential "option for the poor" in Brazil and throughout Latin America. Several were chaplains for students or working-class Christian youth organizations. Often, their work entailed fostering the self-organization of the poor in "basic ecclesial communities"—small groups of neighbors gathering for reading the Bible and discussing solutions for their neighborhood's problems. Frequently, they animated "popular education circles"—experiments in informal adult literacy programs inspired by the Brazilian educator Paulo Freire—under the names of "conscientization" or "pedagogy for liberation."

Most of these new experiments in pastoral work among the poor elicited new forms of theological reflection—among both the formally educated religious agents and the involved Christian poor—in a continuing, complex dialogue that seems to constitute the basic ground of liberation theology.

Reception of Liberation Theology in Society and Church. An expanding number of authors, books, journals, publishing houses, educational institutions, meetings, discussions, workshops, and documents have been broadening, deepening, and transforming the thrust and scope of liberation theology. This development of liberation theology—together with the pastoral, organizational, educational, and theological innovations already mentioned—has increasingly caught the attention of political, military, ecclesiastical, and diplomatic authorities. Fears of popular rebellions, especially among military dictators, have prompted violent backlashes toward those ecclesial experiments, the first occurring in Brazil.

Between 1966 and 1991, this persecution and martyrdom of the church of the poor in at least half of the Latin American countries claimed the lives of well over a hundred clergy and religious and more than a hundred thousand laypeople. Probably more than anything else, this persecution has led to daily, unavoidable theological discussions. Those who are martyred die in the name of the same religious faith in whose name they are being martyred. Church leaders can hardly avoid taking sides; and whatever side persons choose, they feel compelled to

289

justify theologically. Nor can politicos, the mass media, and educational institutions avoid discussing these issues. Thus, liberation theology is at the center of church life throughout Latin America: condemned as a pseudo-Christian rationale for Marxist socialism and violent revolution; or pronounced as superseded and therefore irrelevant; or, finally, embraced as a source of light to tackle the burning challenges of today's Latin America.

Church authorities have in fact espoused many of the central themes of liberation theology since its inception in 1968. The second conference of Latin American Roman Catholic bishops—CELAM II, often referred to as "Medellin," after the Colombian city where it was held—was the first important event of its kind. Shortly thereafter, Pope Paul VI (e.g., in his *Evangelii Nuntiandi*) and the World Council of Churches started shaping policies and pronouncements convergent with, and at least indirectly influenced by, liberation theology.

Liberation Theology and the Social Sciences. The concern of liberation theology with the transformation of society has gone hand in hand with a deep interest in understanding how societies work and how religious institutions actually interrelate with the inner workings of human societies. In a way similar to that in which Western European theologies related to philosophy in recent centuries, liberation theology has granted the social sciences (e.g., sociology, economics, history, anthropology, social psychology) a role as key auxiliaries for the theological endeavor.

If theology is "a second moment"—emerging from and vying to respond to the concrete challenges that believers experience in their real lives in community—the understanding of the "previous moment" or the "first moment" as the pre-text and the context of theology is, therefore, critical for the task of theology. In this very direction liberation theology has adopted and adapted the old "life-revision method," so popular in Catholic Action: see, judge, act. This methodology, often called "pastoral circle," is usually abridged thus: first, life experience; then the social analysis of that experience (seeing); thereafter, a theological reflection on that experience under the light of the Scriptures (judging); and afterward, planning a praxis directed toward the transformation of the shared experience (acting), which leads to a new experience worthy of further analysis.

In the "seeing," indeed, the social sciences have been central to the development of liberation theology. Further, in a state of affairs where the critics and persecutors of liberation theology resort to religious rationales themselves, the social sciences of religion have become essential to the development of liberation theology; conversely, church history and the sociology of religions have grown in Latin America in their constant conversation with liberation theology.

The Question of Marxism and Violent Revolution. Especially among popular conservative circles outside Latin America, much has been made of a supposedly intrinsic connection between liberation theology and Marxist theories and violent revolutionary methods. Although no serious researcher has been able thus far to substantiate such claims, liberation theology has been the object of rejection, uncritical dismissal, veiled condemnation, and outright persecution on the basis of such claims.

True, a loose connection exists between liberation theology and Marxist theories—at least among some liberation theologians. First, in nations where invasion, domination, exploitation, and repression play an important part in the way society works, it is unexceptional to resort to social theories concerned with these issues and with the resources present in society for its transformation. Thus, dependency theory, as well as other revised versions of Marxist theories, such as those by the late Peruvian José Carlos Mariategui and the late Italian Antonio Gramsci, have attracted the attention of some people involved in liberation theology. Second, many of the so-called Marxist features of liberation theology—such as its emphasis on justice and peace on earth, its perception of today's Latin American capitalist societies as unjust and violent, its indictment of northern capitalist societies as deeply responsible for underdeveloping the Third World, and its call for Christians to take sides with the oppressed and their efforts toward integral liberation (all of which are among precisely what liberation theology sees as inevitable consequences of consistently following Jesus in present-day Latin America)—existed long before, far beyond, and in many ways deeply counter to Marxist views. Last, liberation theology's interest in Marxism is at the very least heterogeneous—varying from one region, period, and author to another, and ranging from complete ignorance and disinterest to serious, systematic, and sympathetic concern. Liberation theology's interest in Marxism is also more often prompted by inimical accusations than by spontaneous curiosity, and typically liberation theology is guided by pastoral and theological, Christian concerns, rather than by a Marxist logic proper.

As for liberation theology's supposed defense of violent revolution, again, there is very thin evidence to support such a claim. Certainly, some groups and individuals sympathetic to liberation theology—in times and regions experiencing state terrorism, as in several Central American countries in the 1980s—have cooperated with armed revolutionary organizations and struggles. The rule, however, has been the articulation of liberation theology to nonviolent, democratic groups and the advocation of nonviolent actions and objectives— struggling peacefully and precisely against institutionalized violence as it is manifest in economic, political, and military realms.

The Founding Perspective of Liberation Theology. What liberation theology brings to the theological conversation is not so much new themes as a new way of looking at all the ancient themes of Christian theology—God, the Christ, the Spirit, the Trinity, the reign of God, the church, sin, salvation, and the sacraments. In addition, liberation theology makes the clear claim that this new approach is, in actuality, the oldest one in Christian history: that of the first Christian communities.

This way of looking at God and theology is approached from the perspective of those who suffer injustice—persons and peoples who are subjected to an agony that they did not cause or provoke. These innocent persons and peoples suffer because powerful agents, while they pursue their selfish interests and who are able to spare the pain of the innocents but freely choose not to do so, inflict torment on them.

From this perspective of the oppressed (a view from the "underside of history"), liberation theology tackles its task. God, thus, is viewed as the God of the poor, a tender Creator moved by and caring for suffering innocent creatures. God is seen opting for the poor through the birth, passion, death, and resurrection of Jesus, and urging all of us in the Spirit to listen to the cry of the poor and thus to live in loving solidarity with the poor.

For liberation theology, the reign of God is what Jesus, the church, Christianity, Christian ethics, the sacraments, conversion, spirituality, and salvation are all about: a way of life according to the Spirit of God as revealed in Jesus; that is, a loving, tender, caring, joyful, celebrating community of sisters and brothers living in justice and peace and sharing in common the gifts that God gives us through our cooperative, compassionate laboring within mother Earth. For liberation theology, this utopian reign of God is both "already among us"—in each one of our Spirit-filled acts and relationships of love, solidarity, justice—and "not quite here yet," insofar as it is always possible and necessary to go farther, collectively and individually, in the incarnation of God's loving call. It is both to be pursued, built, deepened, and consolidated in the here-and-now of our concrete lives—pursued spiritually, ecclesially, culturally, politically, and economically—and to be fulfilled in the hereafter, in the plenitude of our communion with God.

Some Theological Implications of the Perspective of Liberation Theology. For liberation theology, it is only for God's reign that Jesus' followers are convoked in assembly—as "church"—to institute ministries (preaching, teaching, witnessing, and developing sacraments, which are signs and instruments of salvation or "God's reign"). Consequently, the reign of God becomes the ultimate criterion, out of which Christians can judge, critique, define, transform, correct, confess, convert, and repent of our ways—including the ways in which we understand, organize, and live as "church."

Sinfulness, which is another way of naming the tendency to work against the reign of God, is thus always simultaneously a deliberate breaking away from God, from the community of God's creatures, and from one's own deepest being. For liberation theology, accordingly, all sin is idolatry: turning away from God—and thus inevitably away from God's preferred poor—to worship the dominion of our own greedy selves. In this sense, liberation theology denounces the annual sacrifice of hundreds of thousands of Latin American poor—on the altars of private corporate profits, national security, and armed elites' thirst for power—as the paradigmatic sin of our times and places, a sin all the graver when God is invoked in attempting to justify it. Open to criticism, especially when coming from the oppressed themselves or from women and men committed to the liberation of the oppressed and the building of a reign of justice and peace on earth, liberation theology is undergoing significant transformations in these last years of the twentieth century. The oppression of women within and without Christianity, the future of African American and Native American communities and their cultural wealth, the ecological prospects of the earth among whose fruits we are, the global threat to life posed by the twofold nemesis of the debt crisis and the arms race, and the profound need for a consistent spirituality of life-in-community haunting the global community: These are probably the five chief centers of concern nurturing the current labors of Latin American liberation theology.

OTTO MADURO

Bibliography

Philip Berryman, *Liberation Theology*.
Leonardo and Clodovis Boff, *Introducing Liberation Theology*.
Robert McAfee Brown, *Gustavo Gutiérrez: An Introduction to Liberation Theology*.
Marc H. Ellis and Otto Maduro, eds., *Expanding the View: Gustavo Gutiérrez and the Future of Liberation Theology*.
Arthur McGovern, *Liberation Theology and Its Critics*.

Cross Reference: Basic Christian Communities, CELAM II, Death and Eternal Life, Epistemology, Institutionalized Violence, Marxist Theology, Praxis.

LIMINALITY

Liminality is the state or condition of transition or of being on the *limen,* "threshold." Persons or entities in liminal states are neither here nor there. They are, in the words of Victor Turner, "betwixt and between the positions assigned and arranged by law, culture, convention and ceremonial."

At the end of the twentieth century, liminality is used by growing numbers of theologians, particularly those influenced by sociology and anthropology of religion. The current invocation of the term is largely due to the writings of British anthropologist Victor Turner. In two of his works, *The Forest of Symbols: Aspects of Ndembu Ritual* (1967) and *The Ritual Process: Structure and Anti-Structure* (1969), Turner developed the notion of liminality from the writings of Arnold van Gennep. Van Gennep, in his *Rites de passage,* had previously identified various phases of "rites which accompany every change of place, state, social position and age."

These rites of passage have three phases. In a puberty ritual, to take one example, the first phase is that of detachment, in which the main subject of the ritual, in transition from childhood to adulthood, becomes detached from his or her mundane life. Second, usually during some form of seclusion, there is the "in limbo," suspension in a space or a time that is between all structured positions. This phase is the liminal phase proper. Third comes the phase of "re-aggregation," being returned to mundane life, though with new status, new roles, and a new position. The rite as a whole represents what Turner called movement from structure, to anti-structure, then back to structure. These three phases were charted by Turner in different kinds of rites of passage, whether these be rituals of life-crises, afflictions, or calendrical seasons.

In all these cases, the second phase, the suspension in limbo, tended to give liminality its proper character. In highly ritualistic societies, the state of liminality was often viewed as sacred time or sacred space, with the liminal person often also seen as sacred. Turner's notion of liminality, then, was frequently invoked as one way to identify religious experience. Very intense or protracted liminal experiences, what Turner termed "hyperliminal" experiences, were viewed as especially "sacred" or "religious."

This notion of religion as liminality tended to bring religion into close relation with social and cultural structures because liminality was an experience interstitial to (interacting with, though not necessarily "of" or "in") social structures. In fact, later in his career, Turner began to identify phenomena of liminality in the cultural functions of industrialized societies. In industrialized societies "liminoid phenomena" tend to be more individual than collective, thrive along social margins and in interstices, are prone to be seen as quirky or idiosyncratic, and are regularly features of social critiques or revolutionary manifestos.

Especially for theologians with interests in engaging cultural issues, Turner's notion of liminality provided a way to identify a religious dimension that was intrinsic to many types of cultural practices (politics, economics, popular culture, music, literature) but not identical to them.

Beyond using Turner's notion of liminality as one way to locate and study the role and place of religious experience in social structures, theologians' other substantive responses can be broadly presented as of two principal types: celebrations and problematic condition.

First, there are theological strategies that readily characterize Christian religious experience as "liminal" and then celebrate that liminality. Deconstructionist theologians (or a/theologians) highlight religious experience as play, for example, championing the carnival and the movements of erring, wandering—or simply suspension.

Other theologians have seen Turner's notion of liminality as a trait of Christian experience, prompted by New Testament parables, for example, such that Christian existence is described as always unsettled, working at the margins of the social order, both troubled and troubling. The "parables of the kingdom" thus give rise to living in a liminal domain. Liberation theologians (feminist, African American, gay, lesbian, Latin American), who understand their oppression as cases of marginalization, have particularly sought to value their marginal space by creating, in opposition to oppressors' devaluations, a sense of Christian practice and thought as emergent from "faith on the edge." The marginal or liminal status is reinterpreted so as to function as a valuable resource for Christian faith and theological reflection.

Still other theologians of this first type tend to graft the notion of liminality to Kantian understandings of the "limits" of knowledge and perception, or to Karl Jaspers's perspectives on "boundary situations"—all in order to speak of "limit-situations" of various sorts (finitude, fundamental trust, wonder, societal alienation), which are key loci of Christian religious practice and thought. Theological study of such "limit situations" is not usually portrayed as an appropriation of the literature on liminality; nevertheless, this approach is exploring liminal terrain and should be viewed as akin to that of religious scholars who invoke the more anthropological notions of liminality.

The second principal type is made of theological strategies that view "liminality" as a problematic condition of modern culture, such that Christian religious experience appears more as an antidote for liminal cultures and their members. The liminality (or liminoid phenomena) found in modern societies—in the form of individualism, rapid change, and religious pluralism—here are seen as leading to a "deobjectification" (Thomas Luckmann and Peter Berger) of religion and doctrine. The result is unfortunate in the view of theologians such as George Lindbeck, for example, since fewer people today know themselves to be parts of particular religious traditions or as active participants in specific religious communities. The remedy for this is not any Christian celebration of liminal experience; instead, theological strategies are employed that increase senses of tradition, explore sacred narratives, embrace ecclesial structures, and convey "competence" in learning the grammars and lexicons of religious communities and their doctrines. There is little celebration of liminality here, surely not of "anti-structure"; rather the theological strategy is to facilitate discovery of new narrative traditions and communal structures.

MARK KLINE TAYLOR

Bibliography

Leonardo Boff, *Faith on the Edge: Religion and Marginalized Existence.*
Carol Crist, *Diving Deep and Surfacing: Women Writers on Spiritual Quest.*

Hugh T. McElwain, *Theology of Limits and the Limits of Theology: Reflections on Language, Environment, and Death.*
Victor Turner, *The Ritual Process: Structure and Anti-Structure.*
————, *Dramas, Fields, and Metaphors: Symbolic Action in Human Society.*

Cross Reference: Deconstructionism, Feminist Theology, Liberation Theology.

LITURGICAL MOVEMENT

The liturgical movement refers to a historical development that has greatly altered the worship life of many churches of Western Christianity. Originating in the 1830s, it has spread during the past century and a half to reshape the worship life of the liturgically conservative and moderate churches, even affecting some parts of the least traditional churches. In general, it has meant more emphasis on "full, conscious, and active participation" of the entire congregation and greater emphasis on sacramental worship for Protestants and on the centrality of the Word of God for Roman Catholics. The Second Vatican Council (1962–1965) signified the official acceptance in Roman Catholicism of many of the movement's goals, and the last quarter of a century has seen many of these goals also become official agenda for Protestants around the world. Following is a brief survey of the impact and development of the movement in various Western traditions of worship.

In the Anglican tradition, the first signs of the movement appeared in what came to be known as the Oxford Movement (or Tractarianism or Puseyism) beginning in 1833. Early leaders such as John Keble (1792–1866), John Henry Newman (1801–1890), and Edward B. Pusey (1800–1882) stressed the sacramental aspects of Anglican worship and the authority of the church. Closely related, the Cambridge Movement, led by John Mason Neale (1818–1866) and others, emphasized the recovery of Gothic architecture and the whole panoply of medieval vestments and ceremonial. For the Victorians, it was a Catholic revival in a very Protestant environment. In the twentieth century, A. G. Hebert (1886–1963) and others led the way in relating worship to social issues, and the parish communion came to be the rallying point of the movement. In the United States, Massey H. Shepherd, Jr. (1913–1990), and the Associated Parishes (from 1947 on) undertook leadership. The most visible accomplishments were the 1979 revision of the *Book of Common Prayer* and, in England, the *Alternative Service Book, 1980,* both of which show the degree to which the objectives of the liturgical movement have been effected.

For Roman Catholics, the origins of the movement can also be traced to 1833, the year in which Prosper Guéranger (1805–1875) reestablished the monastery of Solesmes in France. For more than a century, the movement was largely led and promoted by fellow Benedictines, notably Lambert Beauduin (1873–1960) in Belgium, Odo Casel (1886–1948) in Germany, and Virgil Michel (1890–1938) in the United States. Their program led to a recovery of many lost treasures, such as Gregorian chant and the primacy of the liturgy over personal devotions. A sign of the end of this era was the papal encyclical, *Mediator Dei* of 1947. In the two decades after World War II, the movement took a quite different direction, essentially adopting a Protestant agenda in which the crusade for use of the vernacular came to predominate. Vatican II saw the triumph of the movement with the adoption of the *Constitution on the Sacred Liturgy* in 1963. As mandated by the *Constitution,* all the liturgical books were revised and translated into the various languages of the world during the next quarter century. The reading and preaching of scripture again became an important part of Sunday masses, and congregational hymn singing and prayer became widespread.

In the Lutheran tradition, stirrings were again apparent in the middle of the nineteenth century as Enlightenment rationalism began to wane. In Germany, Wilhelm Lohe (1808–1872), Theodor Kliefoth (1810–1895), and Ludwig Schoeberlein (1813–1881) pointed the way to restoration of sixteenth-century Lutheran practices. Nikolai F. S. Grundtvig (1783–1872) provided leadership in Denmark for recovery of a deeper sacramental life. In America, various leaders moved toward a gradual coalescence of the scattered Lutheran bodies to produce the "Common Service" of 1888, based on old Lutheran models, and to recover the importance of hymnody. The twentieth-century developments have been slow but steady, especially under the longtime promotion of Luther D. Reed (1873–1972). These culminated in 1978 with publication of the *Lutheran Book of Worship,* followed by the Missouri Synod's *Lutheran Worship* in 1982. The recovery of the Eucharist as the normal Sunday service is prominent in both books in the context of much congregational song.

Efforts in the Reformed tradition were somewhat more diffuse. The Mercersburg Theology in the 1840s and 1850s represents an effort by such leaders as John W. Nevin (1803–1886) and Philip Schaff (1819–1893) to shake German Reformed Christians free from the prevailing American frontier patterns of worship in order to recover sixteenth-century Reformed liturgies and the theology that undergirded them. From the Presbyterian side, Charles W. Baird (1828–1887) led the way in calling for optional forms for those services based on Reformation liturgies. In 1865, the Church Service Society was founded in Scotland to promote such activities. One consequence was the publication of the first *Book of Common Worship* in the United States in 1906 and a new *Book of Common Order* in Scotland in 1928. The influence of other churches has become most apparent in the most recent series, *Supplemental Liturgical Resources,* of which six volumes had appeared in 1990. While retaining Reformed characteristics, they show a move into the mainstream of the liturgical movement.

For the Methodist tradition, the rate of change has been somewhat faster. At first alienated by the Oxford Movement in England and then slowly attracted by it, Methodism has long had a cadre of people regarded by their peers as "high church,'' of whom Thomas O. Summers (1812–1882), patriarch of Southern Methodism, was preeminent. Although the 1905 *Hymnal* showed the legacy of revivalism, by the 1935 edition, aestheticism and liberal theology had taken over only to give way in 1965 to neoorthodox historicism. But by the 1989 edition, Methodism had moved into a distinctly ecumenical stance. This was largely the result of seventeen volumes of *Supplemental Worship Resources* published from 1972 to 1988 and the advent of liturgical scholars on the faculties of most Methodist seminaries.

Other traditions have been more or less affected: Quakers the least of all, the liberal descendants of the Puritans quite considerably, the Frontier tradition and Anabaptists only little, and the Pentecostal even less. Yet even in these groups, such things as the ecumenical lectionary and the church year (on which the lectionary is based) continue to make inroads. Thus the most important consequence of the liturgical movement may have been its ecumenical success, most graphically signified in the World Council of Churches' document, *Baptism, Eucharist, and Ministry* (1982).

JAMES F. WHITE

Bibliography

Constitution on the Sacred Liturgy.
Ernest B. Koenker, *The Liturgical Renaissance in the Roman Catholic Church.*
James F. White, *Protestant Worship: Traditions in Transition.*

Cross Reference: Ecumenism, Ritual, Vatican II, Worship.

LITURGY (*See* WORSHIP.)

LORD'S SUPPER (*See* SACRAMENTS/SACRAMENTAL THEOLOGY, WORSHIP.)

LOVE

Love is a pivotal concept in the Bible, theology, and ethics. In the New Testament, the most common words for love are *philia* and *agape*. *Philia* denotes the friendship and affectionate, mutual regard of people who are closely connected either by blood or by faith. *Agape* denotes God's unmerited love of human beings or the love that humans have for one another, which is created and motivated by God's love. *Agape* connotes a love that has not been elicited by the goodness or lovability of its object. Although the verb *agapao* appears frequently in Greek literature from the time of Homer on, the noun *agape* occurs almost exclusively in the Bible. *Agape* was apparently used by the biblical authors to underline their distinctive conception of love, which contrasts most notably with love conceived as *eros*. *Eros* is not used in the New Testament. Whereas *eros* denotes passionate desire that loves its object for the object's ability to satisfy one's own needs, *agape* specifies a love that chooses its object rationally and freely, holds to it with fidelity, and loves it for its own sake.

The archetype of *agape* is God's love, which is manifested in God's indiscriminate goodness to all creation, in divine forgiveness of repentant sinners, in the love of the persons of the Trinity for each other, and in the love of the Son for all people. Love is the very being and activity of God (I John 4:8). Except for the summary of the law to love God and one's neighbor (Mark 12:30-31 and parallels), the Synoptic Gospels refer only once (Luke 11:42) to Jesus' teaching of human love for God. In the rest of the New Testament, the "love of God" usually means God's love for humanity. The gracious and radical quality of divine love is most clearly expressed in God's loving human beings while still sinners and in God's Son laying down his life for human beings (John 15:13). God's gracious and self-giving love, however, invites and empowers a loving response to God and neighbor. Christians are called to love one another as God has loved them (John 13:34). This kind of love, according to Paul, is the greatest spiritual gift (I Corinthians 13); it is a powerful force uniting and strengthening the Christian community. More radical than the command to love the members of one's own community is the call to love one's enemies (Matt. 5:44, 46; Luke 6:27, 32). This command, which arguably derives from the historical Jesus, has constantly challenged Christians, often with little success, to love the outsider.

In the church's history, the doctrines of trinity and atonement have been rich resources for explicating the dimensions of love. The Catholic tradition, appealing to the personal relations within the Trinity, has often emphasized unity and community as love's essential features. The Protestant tradition, appealing to Christ's freely chosen death for sinners, has often stressed self-sacrifice as the distinctive essence of love. Both emphases are also found in the Orthodox tradition. Throughout the history of these traditions, questions about the compatibility of self-love with other-love, the importance of self-denial, the possibility of truly loving those other than one's own, and the possibility of disinterested love have been hotly debated.

The debate has been focused in the twentieth century by Anders Nygren's analysis of the doctrine of love in *Agape and Eros* (1954). Nygren held that *agape* disallows every kind of self-regard; Christians are to love as God loves. Since only God can love in a wholly other-regarding way, people love others without seeking personal benefit only to the extent that they are passive channels through whom God works. According to Nygren, most of Christian history until the time of Martin Luther lived out of a misguided conception of love that contaminated the evangelical concept of love as disinterested and self-sacrificial. Although Nygren's position has been partially supported by Karl Barth and others, it has also been criticized from several quarters. While maintaining other-regard as a crucial element in Christian love, Gene Outka admits that self-regarding actions may be legitimate. Robert Merrihew Adams argues that certain kinds of self-concern, which is different from narrow self-interest, are important in the Christian life. And Robert Johann asserts that the entire problem of disinterested love disappears when people recognize that they are most themselves when they are most for others, when they acknowledge that personal fulfillment is identically a matter of generous service.

The idea that other-regard, particularly self-sacrifice, ought to be the essence of love has been most recently criticized by feminist theology, which charges that defining Christian love strictly in terms of self-sacrifice has allowed men to manipulate women. Feminist theologians make the point that insofar as many women tend to neglect their own development as persons, a call to self-sacrifice may reinforce women's sin of self-denial. For this reason, Barbara Hilkert Andolsen and others have argued against the belief that self-love is always morally negative and have championed a definition of love as mutuality. According to this perspective, situations of sacrifice should be viewed not as the ideal, but as symptoms of disruption in the harmony that should exist among people. Another feminist interpretation is offered by Margaret Farley, who appeals to the Trinity, in which there exist equality, unity, and community, as warrant for this conception of love as mutuality.

The social sciences have played an important role in helping to define the political and economic ramifications of Christian love. With biblical scholarship's recovery of the social character of the gospel and the rise of theologies of liberation, stress is now placed on the social dimension of love rather than on individual relationships. In this new definition, love means seeking the kingdom of God with its social and political ramifications. Correlatively, the unity of love of God and love of neighbor is declared inseparable, and the close connection of love with justice is emphasized. In contrast to many liberation theologians, Stanley Hauerwas and others caution, however, that in the first place Christian love does not mean the removing of all injustice from the world but that it does mean the personal character to accept without regret Jesus' story as one's own and the institutional commitment to make the church the community where truth can be spoken without distortion.

The meaning of Christian love, then, continues to be an important topic of discussion. Traditional interpretations continue to be affirmed and selectively appropriated, while new interpretations are constructed in response to new situations. Current discussions particularly stress the dynamic and relational aspects of love, the wholeness and mutuality it engenders, and its socio-political implications.

WILLIAM MADGES

Bibliography

Barbara Hilkert Andolsen, "Agape in Feminist Ethics," *The Journal of Religious Ethics* 9 (1981): 69-83.

Joseph Gremillion, ed., *The Gospel of Peace and Justice: Catholic Social Teaching Since Pope John.*

Gene Outka, *Agape: An Ethical Analysis.*

Karl Rahner, "Reflections on the Unity of the Love of Neighbor and the Love of God," in *Theological Investigations* 6.

Paul Rigby and Paul O'Grady, "Agape and Altruism: Debates in Theology and Social Psychology," *Journal of the American Academy of Religion* 57 (1989): 719-37.

Cross Reference: Ethics–Christian.

MARXIST THEOLOGY

Is there such a thing as Marxist theology? Joseph Cardinal Ratzinger, prefect of the Vatican's Congregation of the Faith, apparently thinks so, and he takes a dim view of it. The "Instruction on Certain Aspects of the Theology of Liberation," issued by his Congregation (1984), warns that Latin American liberation theology tends to go beyond a Marxist analysis of social conditions to devise a new interpretation of Christianity "uncritically borrowed" from Marxist ideology. The Instruction outlines in a systematic way the essential features of this allegedly Marxist theology.

Its core consists in the acceptance of Marx's vision of the unity of theory and praxis. Marxist analysis, in other words, is inseparable from active participation in revolutionary movements for social change. Class struggle is not only the object of Marxist analysis but constitutive of it. To dedicate oneself to class struggle in solidarity with the oppressed is to align one's actions and one's critical reflections with this "fundamental law of history." The Instruction observes that Marxist analysis thus cannot be separated from the assumption that society is characterized by unjust domination and founded on violence. This assumption, in turn, justifies a revolutionary counterviolence, which embraces both the weapons of criticism and active support for those insurgencies that will intensify the class struggle and achieve its goal of a communist society.

Whatever the intrinsic merits of the Marxist ideology, the Instruction rejects it as "incompatible with the Christian vision of humanity." A theology constructed on this set of assumptions is "a perversion of the Christian message" in the sense that Marxist analysis now becomes the vehicle for "a radical politicization of faith's affirmations and . . . theological judgments." Specifically, key Christian metaphors, such as the kingdom of God, are identified with politically correct movements within the struggle. Indeed, God's own identity as communicated in the scriptures is now disclosed within these movements: Participation in them becomes the only valid sign of faithfulness to God's special love for the poor,

301

while Jesus Christ is reduced to a "symbol who sums up in himself the requirement of the struggle of the oppressed." Not surprisingly, given the way in which "this new interpretation touches the whole of the Christian mystery," the church itself becomes an important battlefield in the class struggle. Building a "church of the poor," in opposition to the traditional "sacramental and hierarchical structure of the church," becomes an important objective for the new "orthopraxis" inspired by this Marxist theology.

Although such a perspective systematically distorts traditional Christian doctrine on "the transcendence and gratuity of liberation in Jesus Christ, true God and true man; the sovereignty of grace and the true nature of the means of salvation, especially of the church and the sacraments," the Instruction does not equate it with Latin American liberation theology as such. Indeed, as the subsequent "Instruction on Christian Freedom and Liberation" (1986) underscores even more explicitly, the Vatican does not intend with these documents to disavow Catholicism's so-called preferential option for the poor, or to whitewash the glaring injustices in Latin America that provoked the development of liberation theology. Nevertheless, the Vatican insists that "we are facing . . . a real system, even if some hesitate to follow the logic to its conclusion."

This seemingly minor concession, however, has made it possible for liberation theologians to deflect the charge that theirs is, in fact, a Marxist theology. With the notable exception of Juan Luis Segundo, the leading exponents of liberation theology have categorically denied that the "caricature" presented by the first Instruction adequately describes their own theological reflections. The more positive tone of the second Instruction, moreover, has generally been interpreted by them as putting the Vatican's seal of approval on their movement and on the questions raised by their theologies. Although one may naturally sympathize with any heretic who successfully eludes the Grand Inquisitor, this artful response is of little help in determining whether Marxist theology really exists or is simply a logical construct designed to rally the dwindling defenders of orthodoxy. In either case, the first Instruction can be used as a template. If there is such a thing as Marxist theology, surely it must exhibit systematically the methodological pattern and substantive themes outlined by Cardinal Ratzinger.

It may be too tedious to demonstrate convincingly that any given theologian's perspective really conforms to this system. If one were to pursue the task further, one would have to consider the relatively neglected work of the Spaniard Alfredo Fierro, *The Militant Gospel: A Critical Introduction to Political Theologies* (1977), in which the author's formidable appreciation of the Marxist philosophy of "historical materialism" is matched by a rigorous attempt to recast the broad outlines of Christian theology in its categories. None of the principal Latin American liberation theologians has demonstrated anything approaching Fierro's awareness of the critical questions inherent in a Marxist theology or his willingness to answer them in a Marxist fashion. So, perhaps, there is at least one example of a really existing Marxist theology, if only in programmatic form.

A more useful exercise might be to track the ways in which Marxism has influenced a variety of Christian theological perspectives, especially in the United States. A generation ago, a number of Marxist philosophers and Christian theologians were promoting a "Marxist-Christian dialogue," as if it represented some radical departure from the way in which theologians ordinarily regard the cultural milieu in which they do their thinking. These enthusiasts for interfaith dialogue had apparently forgotten the extent to which the prominent figures in the development of Christian theology in the first half of this century—the Niebuhr brothers (H. Richard and Reinhold), Paul Tillich, Karl Barth and his disciples, as well as James Luther Adams and a host of others—had already participated in the conversation and, for one reason or another, had found Marxism wanting, at least in its pure form.

Reinhold Niebuhr's involvement with Marxism during the 1930s is especially illuminating, for his various attempts to fathom the scale and scope of Marxism as a religious social movement, as an apocalyptic fantasy, and finally, as a paradoxically modern mythology, decisively influenced his break with conventional Protestant liberalism and inspired his quest for a more "conservative" theological horizon in which to scrutinize the vicissitudes of Christian social activism. Although Niebuhr later came to regard Soviet Marxism as an evil more menacing than the Nazism that he had helped prepare American Protestants to resist militarily in World War II, the "Christian realism" for which he is typically remembered is inconceivable apart from his intellectual and spiritual struggle with Marxism.

On this side of the 1960s' Marxist-Christian dialogue, it may take a specialist to measure accurately Marxism's influence among theologians. The specialty in question, however, is not theological; required, instead, is a solid grasp of the diversity represented among a variety of overlapping and sometimes conflicting Marxist traditions. To understand Marxism's influence on any particular theologian, it is essential to know whether he or she is in conversation with the Marxism of, say, Louis Althusser, or Ernst Bloch, or Antonio Gramsci, or the Frankfort School, and among those of the Frankfort School, for example, whether the center of gravity rests on Tillich's engaging friends, Max Horkheimer and Theodor W. Adorno, or on the cryptic utterances of Walter Benjamin, or on the postwar generation represented by Jürgen Habermas's eclectic attempt to reconstruct the philosophy of historical materialism. Even beyond these identifiable clusters of self-avowed Marxists, there are the legions of philosophers, social theorists, and intellectuals, ranging from Heidegger to Emmanuel Mounier and Peter Berger, whose perspectives not only have emerged through struggle with various Marxist traditions but also have exercised significant influence on the development of contemporary Christian theologies.

303

Obtaining a reliable map of these discussions is indispensable, if would-be theologians are to determine whether Marxism is capable of sponsoring the kind of self-correcting, immanent criticism that will answer the obvious religious and moral objections to it outlined in Ratzinger's first Instruction.

Cornel West's groundbreaking effort, *Prophesy Deliverance! An Afro-American Revolutionary Christianity* (1982), outlines a program for constructive theology, prefaced by an informative review of the terrain featured on such a map. He lets his readers know where he is coming from not only by providing an impressive survey of an ensemble of Marxist traditions but also by evaluating their strengths and weaknesses from a perspective informed by the struggle for African American liberation. Rather than foreclosing opportunities for mutual understanding and collaboration with non-Marxists and post-Marxists, a self-consciously situated Marxist analysis, such as West's, offers reassurance that shared values and common ground can be identified, upon which to explore outstanding differences. The kind of Marxist-Christian dialogue to which West invites his readers thus does not demand an act of blind faith of those who would participate in it.

If a Marxist theology worthy of serious consideration in our times ever were to emerge, it would probably unfold along the lines West has laid out. But in light of the upheavals in Eastern Europe and the Soviet Union, remembered even now as the Revolution of 1989 and the failed coup of 1991, the odds against such a theology are increasingly heavy. What happened was a devastating blow, precisely because any Marxism worthy of serious consideration is far more than a rhetorical tradition cherished mostly by alienated intellectuals and social activists bent on marginalizing themselves. In its most challenging form, Marxism has been a robust philosophy of history, capable of generating empirically testable claims as a social science. The Revolution of 1989 ratified in the public arena of "really existing Socialism" the death by a thousand qualifications that already tended to separate Marxism from its most distinctive and substantive—and hence, falsifiable—claims. What remains is mostly fragments—at worst, some arcane dialectics reminiscent of corrupt forms of Gnosticism; at best, an epistemological breakthrough regarding the unity of theory and practice in human understanding, which remains unsurpassed by all but the most philosophically rigorous forms of pragmatism and phenomenology. Though Marxism now stands discredited as an integral world view capable of ordering really existing societies toward the common good, its prophetic insights, however partial and fragmentary, form part of the common inheritance of Western civilization. On that basis, no doubt, it will continue to be studied and critically appropriated by Christian theologians seeking to understand the world in which God is continuing to make history.

DENNIS P. McCANN

Bibliography

Richard J. Bernstein, *Praxis and Action*
Nicholas Lash, *A Matter of Hope: A Theologian's Reflections on the Thought of Karl Marx.*
Dennis P. McCann, *Christian Realism and Liberation Theology.*
Karl Marx and Friedrich Engels, *On Religion.*
Cornel West, *Prophesy Deliverance! An Afro-American Revolutionary Christianity.*

Cross Reference: Black Theology, Hope, Liberation Theology, Political Theology, Praxis.

METAPHOR

The modern theological study of metaphor necessarily draws on several disciplines simultaneously: rhetoric, literary theory, linguistics, philosophy, biblical studies, and theology proper. Like so many of the theological investigations occasioned by this turn to language, the study of metaphor in theology is important, not only for how it informs the awareness of metaphor, but also for how it reshapes the study of theology as an essentially interdependent set of disciplines.

The theological study of metaphor can be considered under four headings: metaphor as stylistic device, metaphor as judgment, metaphor as ontological, and metaphor as theological.

Metaphor As Stylistic Device. Often the study of metaphor has been determined by two basic assumptions: first, that language is extrinsic and relatively transparent to what is real, and second, that within language there is a relatively clear distinction to be made between the literal and the figurative. In this context, metaphor has been understood as a figure of speech, the use of which adds color to the composition and reveals the ability of the author. From this perspective the metaphor is a stylistic device, useful for engaging interest and emotion, but one that, when desiring transparent or exact description, can be discarded in favor of a more literal approach.

In a theological framework that has privileged conceptual understanding, metaphors have often been understood as appropriate for prayer, worship, scripture, and poetry, but ultimately as literary devices that can be displaced by more rigorous theological explanation or credal expositions. Likewise, with an increasingly sharp division between faith and science, metaphor has often been excluded from the realm of truth and reality and consigned to the realm of opinion and the literary imagination. Inasmuch as theological disciplines even considered metaphor, they tended to follow the reigning cultural assumptions, seeing religious metaphors as cultural or stylistic devices, the most adequate understanding of which frequently leading to metaphysical explanation or theological concept.

305

Metaphor As Judgment. The theory of metaphor as ornamental device has not proved to be sufficient to account for all that occurs with metaphors. The key to a more adequate account of metaphor comes with the recognition that metaphor is a predicative proposition. Metaphor occurs first as proposition, not as word. Two normally distinct propositions are conjoined in a sentence in order to bring about a different, sometimes startling, understanding. Unless a metaphor has become a cliche, it creates a semantic link between two otherwise unlike things. In doing so, the metaphor reveals its roots in the process of human knowing. The conjunction of unlike things brought about in metaphor may itself be a model of human knowing, of the attempt to understand by inventing comparisons to explain what at first seems to be beyond words.

The recognition of an epistemological dimension to metaphor has, and is having, a significant effect on the self-understanding of theology. If metaphorical speech is not simply explained as stylistic device or dismissed as preconceptual suggestion—if metaphor is a process of human knowing as judgment—then the use of metaphor in religious speech does not mark it out as distinct from other human enterprises. Within both the natural and social sciences the recognition of the roles of metaphor and model in the process of human understanding has softened the rigid distinctions between theological and scientific reflection. In light of this, the relation between science and theology is being rethought from the side of both disciplines.

Metaphor As Ontological. With the recognition that metaphor is a predicative proposition, an ontological dimension is also introduced. The metaphor proposes that something "is" something else. The "is" of the metaphor has the twin character of assertion and denial, that one thing is another and at the same time is not another. To say, for example, "the desert is a space in your mind," is to assert simultaneously that the desert is but at the same time is not "a space" and "in your mind." This tensive assertion and denial suggests both a dialectical character to metaphor and a demand for a careful consideration of the tentative claims for reference and truth. Metaphorical propositions suggest an understanding of being that is more at home with language and plurality as ontological categories than with concept and certitude.

The effect on theology is again significant. Recognition of an ontological dimension to metaphor suggests that for theology the investigation of the fundamental truth status and reference of religious language is well served by a detour through the linguistic analysis of metaphor. The tensive ontology of metaphor augments the traditional analysis of analogy as well as the current studies of symbol and sign, each of which attempts to explain how language, image, thought, and action can touch the surplus of meaning often called mystery. Like the effect of recognizing an epistemological dimension to metaphor, this ontological dimension calls into question any further marginalization of theology by explaining how a significant facet of religious speech is part of the fabric of human speech and human being as a whole.

Metaphor As Theological. A cursory review of current work in theology reveals the effect of metaphor analysis. No longer confined to the morphological, literary analysis that characterized earlier discussion in the field of scripture, the discussion of metaphor has become central to the analysis of parable and narrative as a way of explaining the world of meaning suggested by such texts. Narrative theological investigation has exceeded the confines of scriptural study to become a subfield of theology in its own right. Christological analysis and the analysis of the doctrine of God have relied extensively on metaphor study as well as the cognate analyses of models and stories. In short, the field of theology draws on the study of metaphor to enrich many of its traditional understandings.

Currently, the theological issues that are most involved with the analysis of metaphor include: (1) the continuing investigation of religious language, particularly because of the renewed interest in rhetoric occasioned by "deconstruction"; (2) the study of imagination as the creative, ordering intent of religious meaning; (3) the relation of poetics and theology as interweaving disciplines in the analysis of human understanding; (4) the awareness of "plurality" as a designation of what is most often called the "postmodern" condition of current reflection, including the theological; (5) the recognized complicity of language in the oppressive as well as liberating aspects of religious speech and theological investigation; (6) the continuing task of the interpretation of the traditional Christian doctrines carried on under the title of hermeneutics.

If the nineteenth century ushered in historical awareness to the theological enterprise, the twentieth century has done the same with linguistic awareness. The full effect of this theological advance is yet to be realized, but it is clear that metaphor analysis will play a significant role.

JOHN McCARTHY

Bibliography

Mary Gerhart and Allan Russell, *Metaphorical Process: The Creation of Scientific and Religious Understanding.*
Garrett Green, *Imagining God: Theology and Religious Imagination.*
Sallie McFague, *Models of God: Theology for an Ecological, Nuclear Age.*
Paul Ricoeur, *The Rule of Metaphor: Multi-disciplinary Studies of the Creation of Meaning in Language.*
Janet Martin Soskice, *Metaphor and Religious Language.*

Cross Reference: Hermeneutics, Imagination, Language–Religious, Narrative Theology, Symbol.

METAPHYSICS

When religious traditions based on a revelation try to formulate their understanding of the One who reveals, they find themselves in need of notions capable of articulating the world in relation to its transcendent origin. For if the God who reveals God's own self is not also the origin and source of all that is, then the revelation cannot claim a particular privilege. Thus, as the Exodus tradition of liberation needed to be grounded in the Genesis account of creation, so the religious thought of Judaism, Christianity, and Islam alike found itself borrowing from Greek philosophy the conceptual tools needed to articulate the "distinction" of God from the world (Sokolowski) as well as the world's relation to its originating source.

The portion of Hellenic philosophy dedicated to such questions was called, after Aristotle's corpus, metaphysics, and the earliest thinkers of Judaism (Philo) and of Christianity (Origen) borrowed from the hybrid philosophy of Plato and Aristotle with which they were acquainted in order to express central tenets of their faith. The Council of Nicea (325) also had recourse to the technical language of *substance* to clarify a crucial feature of Christian revelation regarding the relation of Son to Father in divinity, as the later Council of Chalcedon (451) employed the notions of *nature* and *person (hypostasis)* to explicate the relation of humanity and divinity in Jesus (Lonergan).

So the Christian tradition made use of the philosophy available to it from a relatively early date, employing key metaphysical notions to clarify its received teaching. Yet so long as the goal remained one of resolving contested points of doctrine or of providing clarification in scriptural commentary, theology would remain at a rudimentary stage. It was not, in fact, until the early Middle Ages, when a series of questions were put to people of faith by Peter Lombard, that the project of an intellectual synthesis of Christian faith, or theology as we know it, came to be elaborated. Thus Christian thinkers began systematically to appropriate metaphysics in the service of a theological synthesis. Yet while the project was Christian in origin and inspiration, cultivated by the intense scrutiny of modes of discourse in scripture (carried out in the twelfth century), it owes its impetus and its shape to earlier work by Muslim and Jewish thinkers, notably Ibn-Sina (Avicenna) and Moses Maimonides. Not surprisingly, this preparatory work focused on the crucial point of opposition between Hellenic metaphysics and these religious traditions: the origin of the universe.

Succinctly put, the Greeks took the universe to be a given, including its divine components, whereas Jews, Christians, and Muslims alike believed it to be a gift of the one God known to them through revelation. This shift of perspectives demanded that Hellenic metaphysics be pressed beyond articulating the "true joints of the world" (Plato) to specify the world's very origins. The metaphysical adaptation required was first elaborated by Avicenna in his celebrated distinction of *existing* from *essence,* and it was pressed even further by Maimonides, who countered the prevailing presumption of an everlasting universe, arguing that Aristotle had never succeeded in demonstrating anything of the sort. Both of these thinkers were made use of by Thomas Aquinas, who refined Avicenna's distinction as well as Maimonides's arguments to show that the derivation of our contingent world from a necessary source was indeed demonstrable (in the very terms of Greek metaphysics) even if the mode of origin (everlasting or temporal) was unknowable. So metaphysics was put to use to lead one to articulate a relation between the universe and its source, which would have been novel to the Greeks but which nonetheless respected and employed their modes of thought, which had become accepted as normative for human reason.

The fruitfulness of the theological synthesis founded on this appropriation of metaphysics can hardly be gainsaid; that it was accomplished by Christian thinkers with the indispensable assistance of Muslim and Jewish philosophers appears to us to be a bonus (Burrell). The crucial importance of clarifying creation allowed subsequent theologians to devise structural parallels between that doctrine and those of the incarnation and of our incorporation into the divine life by grace. On such a pattern, theology emerged as a systematic discipline, structured by metaphysics. A subsequent questioning of the power and scope of Greek metaphysics, when its natural philosophy ("physics") seemed to stand in the way of the development of natural science, and combined with the Reformers' penchant for elevating faith over reason and for preferring scripture itself to subsequent theological elaborations, challenged this synthesis explicitly and directly. Kant's strictures against human discourse pretending to comprehend God, the world, and the human soul seemed also to return Christian thinkers forcibly to a pre-philosophic era. Yet the demands for understanding a faith that spoke of such realities and the relations among them pressed theologians to recover those portions of metaphysics compatible with a new natural science and indispensable to articulating a faith as comprehensive as Christianity.

So Christian theology continues to grapple with a metaphysical legacy, whether in more or less explicit revolt against any such norm for human reason (as in certain "deconstructionist" hermeneutics), in an explicit revision of classical forms of thought (as in so-called process theology), or in various attempts to recover those classical forms in ways that can clarify Christian doctrine for today's believers. In that respect, the discipline within Christian theology that most explicitly employs metaphysics to articulate its subject—philosophical theology—is a burgeoning enterprise, showing how believers may (and indeed must) rely on philosophical argument to articulate a faith in search of understanding.

DAVID B. BURRELL

309

Bibliography

Diogenes Allen, *Philosophy for Understanding Theology.*
Delwin Brown, Ralph Jones, and Gene Reeves, eds., *Process Theology and Christian Thought.*
David B. Burrell, *Knowing the Unknowable God.*
Bernard J. F. Lonergan, *The Way to Nicea.*
Robert Sokolowski, *The God of Faith and Reason.*

Cross Reference: Being/Becoming, Epistemology, Existential Philosophy, Philosophical Theology, Process Theology.

METHOD (*See* THEOLOGICAL METHOD.)

MILLENNIUM (*See* DISPENSATIONALISM, ESCHATOLOGY.)

MIRACLES

The Christian faith was founded on the community's assertion of a miraculous act of God: Jesus was raised from the dead. From the beginning of Christianity to the present day, miracle reports have surfaced regularly in the life of the church. And late in the twentieth century they have become more prominent primarily due to the rapid growth of pentecostal and charismatic Christianity.

It is impossible to read far in any of the Gospels without encountering miracles, often designated as "signs and wonders." In the Synoptic accounts, Jesus' ministry is largely one of healing the sick and casting out demons, activities that were taken as proof of his messiahship and signs of the imminent coming of the kingdom of God. In the Gospel of John, miracles are primarily revelatory signs of the divinity of Christ. Beyond the Gospels, miracles played a crucial role in the life of the early church. In the Acts of the Apostles they accompany the proclamation of the gospel, functioning to authenticate both the message and its bearer. In the Pauline letters, the ability to perform healings and other miracles is considered a gift of the Holy Spirit.

Despite a persistent Protestant argument that miracles were intended to empower the original proclamation of the gospel in the Roman world and that they came to an end with the passing of the apostolic age, it is difficult to draw such a conclusion, because of the actual miracle claims of the church throughout Christian history. Miracles abounded in the post-apostolic age, as a reading of the church fathers and the New Testament Apocrypha will attest. In the medieval period, countless healings and even resurrections were associated with the lives of the saints. Belief in miracles became problematic with the birth of modern science, but by no means did it disappear, even in the most scientifically advanced nations.

With the burgeoning pentecostalism of the twentieth century, spiritual healings and other miracles are again part of the daily inspiration of Christian groups worldwide. Healing ministries are so numerous and individual accounts of the healing experience (often supported with medical documentation) so much a part of life that it is impossible for theology to ignore claims for the miraculous.

The modern theological interpretation of biblical miracles has shifted with the prevailing literary and philosophical assumptions of the time. Under a Newtonian description of natural law, an existentialist interpretation of truth as subjective significance, and a form critical analysis of miracle stories in scripture, theology in the early and middle twentieth century had little interest in the miraculous per se. Theologians often assumed that the stories were a result of superstition, originally told and recorded by people untrained in the methodologies of science and historical criticism. More recently, under a probabilistic paradigm of natural law, a pluralistic interpretation of truth as context-bound, and a reading of scriptural stories informed by literary studies of narrative, biblical miracles have attracted more interest.

Earlier work in this century employed insights from the social sciences, especially psychology, to interpret the miraculous, as in Rudolf Bultmann's understanding of the resurrection of Jesus not as an event in history but as the "rise" of faith in the disciples. Later work has insisted that the question of historical fact cannot be ignored, as in Pannenberg's rehabilitation of the classic Christian argument for the resurrection of Jesus. Earlier studies focused on the structural parallels between biblical accounts and miracle stories from surrounding cultures. Later studies have concentrated on the distinctiveness of the biblical accounts, as in Howard Clark Kee's arguments that New Testament miracles typically do not employ the physical strategies recurrent in the stories of the surrounding cultures and that the revelatory function of biblical miracles clearly distinguishes them from the miraculous in nonbiblical contexts.

In addition to theological attention to the biblical miracles, contemporary philosophers, both Christian and agnostic, have expressed an occasional interest in miracles, stemming usually from the arguments of David Hume in his influential *Enquiry Concerning Human Understanding*. Hume defined miracles as violations of natural law through an act of God, and argued first that such events are conceptually impossible and second that even if they were possible, it would always be more reasonable to believe that an account is false than to affirm that a miracle has actually occurred. Much of the discussion has centered on the concept of the miraculous, with Christian philosophers arguing that miracles might be coherently conceived either as unrepeatable counterinstances to natural law (e.g., Ninian Smart and Richard Swinburne) or as extraordinary coincidences occurring in accord with natural law but having unusual religious significance (e.g., R. F. Holland).

Hume's claim that miracles are impossible has been effectively refuted by numerous Christian philosophers, most of whom follow C. S. Lewis in showing that Hume's argument is circular, that in fact he defined miracles out of existence using the Newtonian assumption that natural laws are absolute and his own assumption that human experience in support of such is uniform.

Discussion of the more difficult Humean argument that belief in the miraculous is always irrational has focused on the assumptions one might bring to a miracle account. Christian philosophers and theologians have argued generally that with initial theistic assumptions and reliable eyewitness accounts, it is easily conceivable that contrary to Hume the actual occurrence of a miracle is more probable than the falsity of its account (e.g., Pannenberg, Holland, Swinburne, Keith Ward, and others). Indeed, many Christians work with the assumption that miracles are probable events within the Christian life, although improbable or impossible scientifically. Despite numerous criticisms of this position, disbelief in the miraculous is no longer inherently more rational than belief.

Recent Christian theology and philosophy have resuscitated the concept of the miraculous after a long period of neglect. The new and creative work is motivated by the changed epistemological outlook, a narratological approach to scripture, and the advent of charismatic Christianity.

DAVID McKENZIE

Bibliography

Howard Clark Kee, *Medicine, Miracle, and Magic in New Testament Times*.
James Kellenberger, "Miracles," *The International Journal for Philosophy of Religion* 10 (Autumn 1979): 145-62.
Wolfhart Pannenberg, *Jesus—God and Man*.
Richard Swinburne, *The Concept of Miracle*.
Keith Ward, "Miracles and Testimony," *Religious Studies* 21 (June 1985): 131-45.

Cross Reference: Fundamentalism, Pentecostalism, Resurrection.

MISSIOLOGY

Missiology (the science of mission) considers the missionary nature and acts of the Christian church. Indigenous to the gospel is the church's awareness of the divine mandate to preach the name of Christ to the whole world and practice what that name means (Acts 1:8). This mandate derives from the fundamental character of the biblical God, who is mission-minded and loving. The English word "mission" points to a God who "sends" God's people to proclaim the Good News (Exod. 3:14; Isa. 52:7; Rom. 10:15; and John 20:21). God's love (*hesed*, [Lam. 3:22]; *agape* [John 3:16]) is ever seeking and inviting all creation to God

(Luke 15:4; John 12:32). God's own activity in the world is mission *("missio dei")*.

The biblical foundation of missiology makes it a historically oriented discipline. An understanding of history of missions and the theological and cultural questions they posed are of fundamental importance for missiology. Such historical investigation covers the entire history of Christianity from the very early church to the present day. The attitude of Jesus and Paul toward the Gentiles is crucial to missiology (Rom. 11:13). In the modern study of missiology, the book of German Protestant scholar Gustav Warneck, *Missionslehre (Doctrine on Mission*, 1892), was considered a pioneering work. More recently, the Second Vatican Council has demonstrated an extensive interest in mission in its *Dogmatic Constitution on the Church* (1964), *Decree on Ecumenism* (1964), *Decree on the Church's Missionary Activity* (1965), and *Pastoral Constitution on the Church in the Modern World* (1965).

The stories of missionary enterprise in the great Age of Navigation beginning in the sixteenth century, which brought the Christian message to Latin America and Asia, have posed enduring missiological questions. Those questions are historically and symbolically associated with two illustrious missionary names: the Spanish missionary and historian Bartholomew de Las Casas, who arrived in the new world in 1502, and the Jesuit Matteo Ricci, who reached Beijing, China, in 1601. Missiological controversies that came to a clearer focus then were the gospel and cultural accommodation (inculturation), and the meaning of universality of the gospel.

These two issues remain relevant today. They are controversial in a world climate that has changed since the historic World Missionary Conference held in Edinburgh in 1910. Events that have changed the world include two devastating world wars, in which "Christian nations" were deeply involved; the Holocaust of the European Jewry; the attainment of political independence on the part of most of the colonized nations in Asia and Africa soon after 1945; the nuclear bombing of Hiroshima; forty years of intense global enmity between the Soviet Union and the United States; the fall of the Berlin Wall in 1989 and the expansion of democracy throughout Eastern Europe in the 1990s; the demand for full human dignity by oppressed groups; unprecedented advance in scientifically based technology and its giant-scale use and misuse; and the threat posed by Western civilization to the ecological health of our planet. Missiology must be based on the studied knowledge and experience of the condition of humanity caught in these historical realities. The loving God is at work to create a fullness of life in the concrete history of the human world (John 10:10).

The classic missiological themes of "Christ and culture" and "Christ's universality" express themselves in five central issues.

1. Mission and Humanization: Is mission identical with humanization? Mission is inseparable from evangelization. In mission, the Good News of Christ

313

must be proclaimed through human words and acts. The Christian understanding of human being rejects making a dichotomy of the physical and the spiritual (Luke 5:23, 7:50). Mission contains the concerns of humanization. Humanization means the nurture and maintenance of the dignity of the image of God in human beings. Social justice is an integral part of mission (Deut. 16:20; Amos 5:24; Mic. 6:8). Without concern for social justice (Jer. 7:6, 22:13), one cannot point to Christ and say, "Behold the Lamb of God" (John 1:29).

2. *Mission and Minority Oppressed Groups:* Has Christ come specially to the people who are on the periphery of community? A dramatic shift of the center of Christianity from the nations of the North Atlantic to Asia and Africa is taking place. This shift has occurred because Christianity is, despite various historical shortcomings, in its very nature prophetically open to the needs of the powerless racial, economic, and cultural minorities in the world. Liberation for the dignity of every human being is an important missiological theme.

3. *Mission and the People of Other Living Faiths:* Missiology deals with the theological significance of the encounter between Christians and the people of other living faiths. Is there a "radical discontinuity" (Hendrik Kraemer) between the gospel and other faiths? How do Christians bear witness to the name of Jesus Christ in interreligious circumstances? In what ways are Christians thinking of the plurality of religious truths?

4. *Mission and Culture:* Mission cannot be carried out without regard for the realities of local culture. But culture is ambiguous. Culture must be nurtured as well as criticized. Christian mission is not neutral to culture. When culture is enslaved by idolatry (e.g., the ideologies of "emperor cult" and "white skin"), mission must expose the danger of the idolatry in order to protect the welfare of the people.

5. *Mission and Ecological Crisis of the Earth:* Western Christian civilization is destroying the biosphere of our planet. What does today's ecological crisis say to our missiology?

These five issues suggest the forthcoming trends in missiology as the focus of mission shifts from an imperialistic drive to convert unbelievers to providing service in Christian love for global justice.

KOSUKE KOYAMA

Bibliography

Johannes Blauw, *The Missionary Nature of the Church.*
Kosuke Koyama, *Mount Fuji and Mount Sinai.*
Donald Senior and Carroll Stuhlmueller, *The Biblical Foundations for Mission.*
James J. Stamoolis, *Eastern Orthodox Mission Theology Today.*
J. Verkuyl, *Contemporary Missiology: An Introduction.*
Cross Reference: Ecumenism, Vatican II.

MODERNISM (*See* Liberalism.)

MORAL THEOLOGY

The Roman Catholic insistence on human mediation, the role of works together with faith, and the practice of the sacrament of reconciliation have given great importance to morality. The Catholic insistence on faith seeking understanding and understanding seeking faith has called for a reflexive, thematic, and critical understanding of the moral life, which has come to be called moral theology.

After the Reformation and the Council of Trent in the sixteenth century, a new literary genre, the *Institutiones Theologiae Moralis*, came into existence. The purpose of these books was to train confessors and penitents for absolving and confessing their sins according to number and species in the sacrament of penance. These books grew into the manuals of moral theology that became synonymous with the discipline of moral theology before the Second Vatican Council (1962–1965). These manuals employed primarily a natural law approach, insisted on the role of reason in moral analysis, and devised a casuistic method for solving moral problems and cases of conscience.

The renewal of Roman Catholicism associated with the Second Vatican Council affected the discipline and the textbooks of moral theology. The older manuals were criticized for being legalistic, act-oriented, minimalistic, based solely on neoscholastic philosophy, and unaffected by scripture and theology. The legalism of the manuals was based on making law the primary ethical category and constructing Christian morality using the Ten Commandments. More personal, relational, and historical models are now being proposed. The act-oriented approach of the older manuals, which was based on their connection to the confession of sins in the sacrament of penance, failed to give enough importance to the virtues, attitudes, and dispositions that should characterize the Christian life. In fact, these manuals had not been faithful to the insistence on the virtues in the moral theology of Thomas Aquinas, the patron of Catholic theology and philosophy. The person as both subject and agent has been emphasized in recent theological writing. Moral theologians now accentuate a life-centered, not a confessional-centered, moral theology.

The manuals of moral theology stressed the philosophical basis of the discipline, but they generally proposed a "manualistic" scholasticism as the perennial philosophy. Early efforts at renewal pointed out that such scholasticism did not truly represent the position of Thomas Aquinas. Today many different philosophical approaches and methodologies are being employed in moral theology by Catholic reformers who have underscored the need for a greater and more systematic and critical use of the scripture in moral theology. At best the older manuals employed a proof-text approach to show that the scriptures supported the conclusions of natural law. The explicitly Christian dimension of the discipline today is reflected in the importance given to Christology, pneumatology (Spirit), and eschatology.

The two most influential Catholic moral theologians in the post–Vatican II period have been Bernard Häring and Joseph Fuchs, two Germans who have done most of their teaching in Roman universities. Häring's *Law of Christ* (1954), prepared the way for many of the subsequent developments in moral theology. His later three-volume *Free and Faithful in Christ* combines biblical, theological, and sacramental dimensions with modern psychology and sociology in reflecting on a life-centered moral theology. Fuchs has never written a systematic moral theology, but in many essays he has employed a transcendental approach to the questions facing moral theology.

Moral theology has recently flourished in the United States for a number of different reasons. The ecumenical dialogue between Catholic and Protestant ethicists grew quickly after Vatican II to the point that today most Christian ethics is undertaken in an ecumenical manner. Moral theology no longer finds its home only in the seminary. Many moral theologians now teach in colleges and universities and see their discipline as an academic one on a par with other scholarly disciplines. Finally, the situation in the United States has influenced moral theology, for the country as a whole has become much more conscious of the need for ethics and values in its own public life. Questions about peace, poverty, human rights, the role of women, medical ethics, ecology, and human sexuality are discussed at length by moral theologians and others in the society.

Questions about methodology are being addressed in moral theology. The three liveliest current debates focus on the distinctive or unique aspects of Christian morality, the justification and foundation of moral norms, and the role of the teaching authority of the church.

Is there a unique Christian content in the moral order, or is the moral order the same for all human beings? In Germany the approach of autonomous ethics argues that there is a rational basis for all Christian moral teaching, whereas the faith ethics approach sees faith as calling for a unique Christian content to one's actions. The debate also has practical ramifications for Christians working with others to create a more just human society. Most admit that intent, motivation, and inspiration for the Christian are unique, but the debate centers on the content of what human beings and Christians should do.

The existence and grounding of universally binding norms continues to be a topic of great interest. An older Catholic approach insisted that certain acts were intrinsically evil and could never be permitted under any circumstances (e.g., contraception, divorce, direct killing). Today, some authors maintain that the human being can never directly go against a basic human good, and hence such actions are intrinsically wrong. "Proportionalists" maintain that certain actions in themselves are pre-moral evils that at times can be justified if there is a proportionate reason. However, certain actions are wrong because there is no proportionate reason that could justify them.

Catholic moral theology today is divided over the possibility and legitimacy of dissent from noninfallible hierarchical teaching on moral matters. The Catholic church recognizes a pastoral teaching office belonging to the pope and bishops in the church. A minority maintains that some moral teachings such as the prohibition of artificial contraception are infallible teaching and must be accepted by all. The vast majority claims there can never be an infallible church teaching on a specific moral matter. Many Catholic moral theologians recognize that in theory and in practice at times one can dissent from noninfallible church teaching precisely because such teaching might be wrong. Others, including the hierarchical teaching office, are reluctant to admit the legitimacy of dissent. Church authorities have taken disciplinary action against some Catholic moral theologians, especially because of dissenting positions in the area of sexuality.

Official Roman Catholic social teaching is intimately connected with moral theology. Modern official Catholic social teaching refers to the body of hierarchical teaching beginning with *Rerum Novarum,* the 1891 encyclical letter of Pope Leo XIII on the condition of workers. Subsequent documents were often issued on the anniversaries of *Rerum Novarum.* The most significant of these documents are: Pope Pius XI, *Quadragesimo Anno* (1931); Pope John XXIII, *Mater et Magistra* (1961), *Pacem in Terris* (1963); Vatican Council II, *Gaudium et Spes* or the Pastoral Constitution on the Church in the Modern World; Pope Paul VI, *Populorum Progressio* (1967) and *Octogesima Adveniens* (1971); International Synod of Bishops, *Justitia in Mundo* (1971); Pope John Paul II, *Laborem Exercens* (1981) and *Sollicitudo Rei Socialis* (1987).

These documents have dealt primarily with economic issues, but they have also addressed other political and social issues, especially peace and war. This body of teaching exhibits both continuities and discontinuities in its ethical methodology and in its approach to the changing issues facing society. The fundamental dignity and social nature of the human person constitute the cornerstone of this teaching.

From this anthropological perspective political society is seen as basically good, helping all human beings to achieve their destiny. This communitarian approach is opposed to the extremes of an individualism that does not give enough importance to the social aspects of the human person and of a totalitarianism that so exalts the collectivity that basic individual human rights are denied. According to the principle of subsidiarity, a limited state should seek the common good by encouraging individuals, families, neighborhoods, voluntary associations, and more local forms of government to do what they can. The central government must do those things that affect the common good and cannot be adequately dealt with by others.

In addition to commutative justice that governs personal relationships, official

317

Catholic social teaching insists on distributive and legal or social justice to direct the relationships of the individual and the society. Since 1963 this hierarchical teaching has made human rights a fundamental criterion of a just society, insisting on civil and political rights (e.g., the basic democratic freedoms) and on social and economic rights (e.g., food, clothing, shelter, and health care). Borrowing from liberation theology, recent documents have insisted on the preferential option for the poor.

In addition to these documents of the universal church teaching office, national and regional conferences of bishops have been issuing their own documents. The bishops of Latin America have proposed a liberation theology approach. In the United States the bishops have issued two widely circulated and debated pastoral letters that call for reform and change in existing structures. *The Challenge of Peace: God's Promise and Our Response* (1983) criticized United States deterrence policy but did not call for immediate unilateral nuclear disarmament. *Economic Justice for All: Pastoral Letter on Catholic Social Teaching and the U.S. Economy* (1986) criticized the individualism that too often characterizes attitudes and institutions in the United States. Some neoconservatives maintain that the bishops have not appreciated the creativity of the United States economy and the contributions of its culture. More radical critics believe that the bishops have not gone far enough.

CHARLES CURRAN

Bibliography

David M. Byers, ed., *Justice in the Marketplace: Collected Statements of the Vatican and the United States Catholic Bishops on Economic Policy, 1891–1984.*
Ronald P. Hamel and Kenneth R. Himes, eds., *Introduction to Christian Ethics: A Reader.*
Bernard Häring, *Free and Faithful in Christ*, 3 vols., 1978–1981.
Richard A. McCormick, *Notes on Moral Theology, 1965 Through 1980.*

Cross Reference: Anthropology, Dogmatic Theology, Ecology, Economics, Ethics–Christian, Justice, Philosophical Theology, Virtue.

MYSTICISM

At the end of the twentieth century mysticism is attracting a degree of interest unrivaled since the late-medieval period. Scientists are exploring parallels between mysticism and relativity physics; ecumenists are increasingly regarding it as an important locus of interreligious dialogue; and theologians are examining the relationships among mysticism, liberation, and social transformation. If these developments are to be adequately understood and appraised, the nature of mystical experience itself must be grasped.

"Mysticism" is a word notoriously difficult to define. "Intimate union with God" and "loving knowledge of the divine" are among the definitions commonly suggested. Although these provide helpful indications of the goal of the experience, they are also in their own ways limited and misleading. For, as mystics consistently point out, mystical experience exceeds the grasp of ordinary language; nothing we can think or imagine adequately describes it. As a result, mystics themselves typically employ two linguistic tactics in attempting to articulate their experience. First, they employ the language of paradox, describing mystical experience variously as a "cloud of unknowing" or a "luminous darkness." Second, they appeal to the dynamism of consciousness itself as a basis from which to specify and explain the nature of mystical experience. This essay follows this second lead.

In answering the questions, What is mystical experience? and Of what is it an experience?, we need to distinguish three terms: objects of consciousness, consciousness, and the ground of consciousness. Objects of consciousness are the things we know and to which we respond: trees, books, other people. Consciousness refers to our capacity to know and respond to these things. If we are unconscious we can do neither. The ground of consciousness refers to the source or transcendent ground of this capacity. For Christians, the source of all consciousness and all being is God, the creator. The claim made by Christian mystics is that mystical experience is an experience of this ground, of God.

The key is to recognize that mystical experience is not an experience of an object. If God is the ground of consciousness, then God cannot be an object of consciousness. To clarify this point, mystics offer an analogy from vision, pointing out that while we can see any number of objects (trees, books, people), we cannot in the same way see the power or ground of our vision itself. We can experience it; but this experience is a heightened awareness of the ground of our capacity for vision.

What then is the nature of this experience? It is helpful to distinguish two more terms: bare consciousness and mystical consciousness. Bare consciousness is a state in which all the normal operations of consciousness have been stilled. All operations of sensing, imagining, understanding, verifying, deliberating, evaluating, and the like have ceased to operate. One is conscious, alert, and aware, but not aware "of" anything. Some mystics refer to this as the "cloud of unknowing," because ordinary processes of knowing are not operative within it.

Bare consciousness is related to, but not identical with, mystical consciousness. Bare consciousness is a state of spiritual access, a necessary, but prior condition. When an explicit awareness of the transcendent ground of consciousness emerges within bare consciousness, consciousness becomes mystical. This is the "intimate union with God" and "loving knowledge of the divine" noted earlier. The mystics claim that at this point consciousness is transformed and reconfigured. The mystic's consciousness becomes conformed to the operation of the transcendent ground itself. That is to say, the normal operation of consciousness is not merely stilled in mystical consciousness; it is reconfigured so that it begins to operate in unity with the mind of God. In traditional Christian language, the mystic becomes one with the inner life of the Trinity. This is an experience that has its conditions and its causes, but it is a gift, a grace, that can neither be compelled nor controlled.

Having clarified some of the terminology and having identified several of the basic concepts associated with mysticism, we can now attempt to clarify the relevance of mysticism to three complex and fascinating issues, without trying to settle any of them. First, some thinkers suggest that mysticism offers an important avenue of interreligious dialogue. For example, when Christians speak of union with the Trinity and Buddhists speak of enlightenment through the realization of Emptiness, the question arises, Is there any basis for common understanding and disagreement? By appealing to the mystical traditions in both religions, the meaning of doctrines such as the Trinity and Emptiness can be clarified by specifying the correlative mystical experiences. The clarification of the meaning of these doctrines in turn can provide a potential basis for identifying and assessing similarities and differences.

Second, a debate has arisen concerning the relationship of mysticism to relativity physics. One of the interesting features of the modern philosophy of science is that its theorists have been unable to provide axiomatic (i.e., conceptual) foundations for either the special or the general theories of relativity. This, some suggest, is because the foundational reality of human consciousness resides in the foundations of both theories. Mysticism cultivates an awareness of the ground of human consciousness; and some physicists assert that the view of reality offered by mystics has significant parallels with the world view of relativity physics.

Third, the relationship of spirituality with social justice is receiving serious attention from political and liberation theologians. In discussions of praxis, it is increasingly recognized that in order to do what is right and just, one must be right and just. This way of being requires spiritual discipline. Mysticism involves a spiritual discipline that leads to the conformity of one's consciousness with the mind of God. If, as Christians hold, the mind of God is incarnate in Jesus of Nazareth and definitively revealed by him as committed to love and justice, then some interesting questions emerge. For example, What is the relationship of mysticism to social action? Can love and justice be fully attained without the cultivation of mystical consciousness? Can the perspective of mystical consciousness be specified in discreet public policies that promote justice and peace? If so, how?

JAMES R. PRICE III

Bibliography

Louis Bouyer, et al., *A History of Christian Spirituality*.
Georgia Harkness, *Mysticism: Its Meaning and Message*.
W. R. Inge, *Christian Mysticism*.
William James, *The Varieties of Religious Experience*.
Evelyn Underhill, *Mysticism*.

Cross Reference: Epistemology, Experience–Religious, Silence, Worship.

MYTH

A myth is a story of beginnings. Found throughout human cultures, its range is from the sacred to the secular, from the profound to the fanciful. Most anthropologists, for example, think of myths as vividly imaginary stories, indigenous to a particular culture, that give fundamental accounts of the real world as experienced and of the role and relative status human beings have within it (Doty). In religious studies, primal myths are understood as sacred when they express, often by means of gods and goddesses and characters, an ultimate reality that transcends and informs the logic of everyday reality (Eliade). Both anthropology and religious studies are interested in the referent of myths: how they persuade—by the use of symbol, metaphoric process, extraordinary characters, and images—and how they create an aura of penultimate reality for those who participate in their recitation or performance.

Myths as differentiated from history and geography are narratives about a time and space that cannot be "coordinated" with time as identified by historical-critical method or with space as denominated by geographers (Ricoeur). By suspending ordinary time and space, myths establish an extraordinary origin and destiny for human beings.

There are two common etymologies for the word "myth": (1) the root *mu,* which, in onomatopoeic linguistic theory, is a nearly universal syllable for a child's cry for the mother's breast—hence, an originating word; (2) the root *mu,* which also means "word" or words in story form, the artistic use of language in a story (in Homer), and the plot or organization of events (in Aristotle). Myth can be combined with logos (mythology) to designate words about words. Myth has also been set in opposition to logos. Separate from myth, "logos" came to designate the genres of treatise, doctrine, instruction. "Myth," separated from logos, came to designate the genres of fiction, the fable, and literature of the fantastic.

Myths are frequently divided into types: cosmogonic, theogonic, and anthropogonic; myths of paradise, of fall, and of flood; and soteriological and eschatological myths. There are advantages, however, in understanding these as varieties of the cosmogonic or as prototypical myth (Ricoeur). All of the types have to do with founding events, originating events, or acts of consciousness: origins of the world, existential phenomena, and forms of human existence (life, death, technologies, laws, initiation into society). Even eschatological myths refer to an end-time in the light of a presumed beginning or underlying order of the universe. Etiologies are best treated as marginal myths since they function primarily as explanations rather than as narratives calling for interpretation.

Several useful approaches to myth reveal it as a rich and multifaceted phenomenon. Structuralists find binary oppositions among the elements of a myth that are reconciled or transformed in its conclusion. Psychoanalysts find mythic patterns of repetition in their clients' telling of life-stories. Literary scholars discover in myths archetypal plots capable of multiple variations in modern stories as well as traditional narratives. Scientists use myth as an epistemological structure to combat the presumed self-sufficiency of theory without understanding. Genre critics use myth to reconstruct original liturgical and ritual processes.

Perhaps because it touches so many fields of inquiry, the role of myth in human understanding has been highly controversial in the history of thought. Because myth is most often associated with *originating* elements, many scholars succumb to one of two temptations: either to idealize myth at the expense of more complex and abstract thought (philosophical reflection, written texts, complex literary forms, history, scientific theory) or to reject myth in favor of other, presumably higher and more critical modes of thought. Yet the importance of myth can be seen in the vehemence with which myth is separated from other forms of inquiry: for example, myth vs. literature, myth vs. theology, myth vs. history, and myth vs. science. The efforts to polarize myth are matched only by the persistence of efforts to dissolve or to overcome the dichotomies. Philosophy and theology, two important traditional forms of Western thought, eschew myth on the one hand, as mere opinion or false belief, and on the other hand, rely on myth as a resource for thought. Philosophers, for example, readily accept Plato's seemingly contradictory practice of proscribing and then occasionally using myths to make a point in his own writing, and biblical scholars recognize myth as a literary genre, both inside and outside the religious tradition. While most philosophers, theologians, and scriptural scholars today acknowledge the need for "demythologizing" (explaining and understanding myths in current terms), they avoid "demythicizing" (eliminating, explaining away, or translating myths into other forms of expression such that every trace of the original vanishes).

The interpretation of myth is a problem for persons who live in post-Enlightenment cultures—since immediate belief in what myths express is no longer acceptable in light of scientific and historical knowledge. Yet there is reason to believe that in most cultures a range of belief, from naive to complex and sophisticated, exists. Myths and their interpretation will continue to be crucial to human beings who seek to integrate their experiences of living in the world with their understandings of its limits.

MARY GERHART

Bibliography

Wendy Doniger (O'Flaherty), *Women, Androgynes, and Other Mythical Beasts.*
William Doty, *Mythography: The Study of Myths and Rituals.*
Mircea Eliade, *Myth and Reality.*
Paul Ricoeur, "Myth and History," in *Encyclopedia of Religion,* ed. Mircea Eliade.

Cross Reference: Anthropology, Creation, Hermeneutics, Narrative Theology, Science and Christianity, Symbol.

NARRATIVE THEOLOGY

In the final decades of the twentieth century, a significant body of theological literature has made use of the category of "narrative." Some of that literature is occasionally referred to as "narrative theology." In addition, books and articles also have appeared on the narrative criticism of the Bible, narrative ethics, narrative preaching, and the role of narrative in Christian education. In other words, in practically every area of theological studies someone has attempted to use "narrative" to redescribe the nature and tasks of that discipline.

Not only does the category of narrative cross the boundaries of theological disciplines; it also crosses religious and confessional boundaries. Both Roman Catholic and Protestant theologians have made important contributions to the literature, and the topic has been much discussed also in Jewish theological scholarship.

Clearly, narrative has become a popular theme in theology. But at the same time, there is little if any agreement in the literature as to what is meant by narrative. The term is used to refer to various literary genres, everything from parables to gospels to autobiographies. Nor is there any agreement about why narrative is an important category for theology or about what role it should play in biblical interpretation and theological construction. Consequently, it is accurate to say that there has been widespread interest in the role narrative might play in theological construction, but that there is no agreement about what the program or agenda should be and about how narrative should be used in theology. Narrative theology, therefore, describes the popularity of the term "narrative" in the literature of theology today, but it would be misleading and inaccurate to suggest there is a school or movement of narrative theology that embodies a common

323

understanding of what is meant by the term and what role it should play in theology.

The Cultural Outline. Why has narrative become such a popular theme in theology? The reasons are many and varied, but at least two should be mentioned. In the first place, the cultures of North America and Western Europe in the last half of the twentieth century have witnessed an almost unparalleled assault on all forms of established tradition and authority. In the United States, one result of the civil rights struggle and the Vietnam War in the 1960s and 1970s was a pervasive disillusionment with the symbols, myths, social values, and institutions that had provided order and stability for earlier generations. Furthermore, rapidly changing social and economic patterns after World War II challenged traditional values and social institutions. Increasing numbers of people began to struggle with fundamental questions of personal and communal identity. It was no longer clear to some people what it meant to be a male or a female in society, what it meant to be a husband or a wife, or a parent.

Christians were not exempt from the crises of personal identity. The turn to narrative by Christian theologians was prompted in part by their perception that the most pressing religious and theological problem in Christian communities is deep confusion about Christian identity.

Closely related to the identity crisis, the second reason concerns the narratives that are constitutive of Christian identity, namely the biblical narratives. The turn to narrative marks the convergence of a crisis in many churches and simultaneous developments in biblical scholarship. In growing numbers, Christians in the latter half of the twentieth century have decried the biblical illiteracy that pervades the life of many churches. At the same time, some biblical scholars have raised the question whether the exclusive use of historical-critical methods in biblical interpretation have not taken the Bible out of the hands of Christians and restricted it to a new "priesthood" of professional biblical scholars. Might not other methods of interpretation, such as different forms of literary criticism, enable readers to hear the theological voice in the biblical text, a voice that seems to have fallen silent both in the life of the church and in the guild of contemporary biblical scholarship?

Early Forms of Narrative Theology. Although the literature on narrative theology did not begin to emerge until the 1970s, many resources for narrative theology were uncovered in the history of Christian theology. Most obvious were the different forms of narrative that are prevalent in the Hebrew Bible and New Testament. Israel recites its faith by remembering its history, either in the form of carefully crafted creeds or in the more extended forms of narrative such as the deuteronomistic history. So too, the New Testament Gospels, which give Jesus his identity as the Christ, are narratives that include other forms of narrative, such as parables. Narrative, of course, is by no means the only genre in the Bible, but it does appear to have a central, indispensable role.

In the history of Christian thought, several important texts either make use of narrative or devise theological categories that either presuppose or invite narrative. Perhaps the most important is Augustine's *Confessions,* which casts a long shadow in subsequent Christian theology. The first nine books of the *Confessions* are Augustine's autobiography, written in the form of a prayer to God. The last four books are Augustine's reflections on philosophical and theological topics such as the nature of memory and time.

In the sixteenth century, John Calvin began his *Institutes of the Christian Religion* by describing all true and sound wisdom as having two parts: the knowledge of God and the knowledge of self. Calvin did not insist that knowledge of God is found in narrative, but he did argue that no one could obtain "sound doctrine" unless that person became a student of scripture. One could argue that true and sound wisdom for Calvin had something to do with the relation between the narratives in the Bible that render the identity of God and the narratives people tell to others and to themselves in order to articulate their self-understanding.

In the first half of the twentieth century, H. Richard Niebuhr described revelation as the appropriation in internal history of the events of external history. When that appropriation takes place, revelation occurs as "that part of our inner history which illumines the rest of it and which is itself intelligible." In his *Church Dogmatics,* Karl Barth devised his Christology by appealing to the narratives of the Synoptic Gospels and gleaning from them what he described as Jesus' "life-act."

The Emergence of Narrative Theology. No single publication clearly marks the beginning of narrative theology. Nonetheless, the publication in 1970 of Stephen Crites's article, "The Narrative Quality of Experience," could be said to represent the opening salvo in the literature. Crites devised a distinction between what he called mundane and sacred stories, and argued that experience "is itself an incipient story." Crites's article soon became one of the most frequently cited texts in the subsequent literature on narrative theology, which can be divided into four distinct fields.

1. The Use of Narrative in Biblical Studies. A text that prompted an early interest in the genre of narrative within the Bible was Amos Wilder's *Early Christian Rhetoric.* Wilder examined different genres in the Bible and then argued that "the narrative mode is uniquely important in Christianity." Several scholars of Hebrew scripture came to a similar conclusion concerning the significance of the role of narrative in Torah. Different forms of "canonical criticism" were published in the 1970s and in slightly different ways each invited responses from theologians.

The 1960s and 1970s were also a period in which a significant amount of material on New Testament parables was published. New Testament scholars and theologians found themselves in conversations about the metaphorical character of parables and the attendant claim that Christian knowing is itself parabolic and metaphorical.

Perhaps the most important development in biblical scholarship, however, was the turn away from historical criticism to different forms of literary criticism, including structuralism, post-structuralism, deconstruction, and reader response theory in order to interpret biblical texts. The conversation about literary criticism in biblical studies led many theologians to pay careful attention to the theological significance of different biblical genres such as gospel narrative and parable.

2. *Narrative Hermeneutics.* Interest in literary criticism also marked a turn in biblical and theological hermeneutics. In 1975 Hans W. Frei published *The Eclipse of Biblical Narrative,* in which he argued that the distinction between meaning and reference is an Enlightenment development, that so-called pre-critical readers of the Bible assumed neither that the meaning of a text could be separated from the question of its referent nor that the truthfulness of a text was a matter of its historicity. Using the works of both Karl Barth and Eric Auerbach, Frei argued that biblical narrative renders a world of its own and demands that the reader understand from within that world, not from "outside" on the basis of philosophical or "general" hermeneutics.

During the same period, Paul Ricoeur was more willing than Frei to listen to contemporary forms of literary criticism and to construct a "poetics." Ricoeur undertook a careful examination first of symbol and myth, and later, of metaphor and narrative. In professional theological circles during the 1970s and 1980s, the discussion of theological hermeneutics was dominated by the debate between the "schools" of Chicago and Yale, the debate between Ricoeur and Frei on the one hand and on the other between David Tracy and George Lindbeck. In *The Nature of Doctrine* (1984), Lindbeck devised a typology of theological method and argued for a "cultural-linguistic" model, in which doctrine was understood as the product of the language and life of particular confessional communities. One could not understand the nature of a doctrine unless one understood the role of that doctrine in the life and language of the community. Tracy, in *The Analogical Imagination,* argued that Lindbeck too neatly separated his cultural-linguistic model from an experiential-expressive model and in so doing ignored the relation between language and the affective dimension of human existence.

3. *The Role of Narrative in Theological Construction.* A leading issue in the discussion of narrative by theologians was whether narrative could or should serve only as a bridge or introduction to the tasks of theology or whether it also might serve as the basis for the reconstruction of basic Christian doctrines. Thus far, significant attempts have been made in two areas to reconstruct doctrine by means of narrative.

The first is the area of Christology. In 1974 Edward Schillebeeckx published

Jesus: An Experiment in Christology, in which he announced that he would meet the need for a "post-critical, narrative history" in Christology. Unfortunately, Schillebeecckx's book turned out to be neither "post-critical" nor "narrative history." A more serious attempt was Hans Frei's *The Identity of Jesus Christ* (1967 and 1975). Other significant attempts at a narrative Christology were Walter Kasper's *Jesus the Christ* (1976), Frans Jozef van Beeck's *Christ Proclaimed* (1979), and Robert Krieg's *Story Shaped Christology* (1988).

The second area in which narrative has been used for the reconstruction of doctrine is the Trinity. Jürgen Moltmann worked briefly with the idea of the narrative history of the triune God, but the theme soon disappeared from his work. It has been more thoroughly explored in the concluding section of Eberhard Jungel's *God As the Mystery of the World.*

4. *The Role of Narrative in Ethics and Practical Theology.* Finally, narrative has been used to rethink the nature of Christian ethics and the tasks of practical theology. Stanley Hauerwas and James Wm. McClendon, Jr., have made important contributions to narrative ethics and to biographical theology, but the most important contribution has been Alasdair MacIntyre's *After Virtue* (1981). MacIntyre argued that we live out of narratives "and because we understand our own lives in terms of the narratives we live out . . . the form of a narrative is appropriate for understanding the action of others." In *Faith in History and Society* (1977), Johann Baptist Metz worked out the intriguing concept of "the dangerous memory of Jesus" for the purpose of analyzing the "narrative structure of practical and critical reason."

Unresolved Issues. Narrative theology is still in its infancy, and although the movement still appears to be full of promise and unexplored ideas, it also faces numerous unresolved critical issues: What precisely is the relation between narrative and history? What is the relation between narrative texts and other genres in the Bible? Must narrative theology respond in some way to questions about the metaphysical status of its claims? What precisely is "narrative truth" and what are the criteria for "truthfulness" in narrative theology? What role does the imagination play in narrative hermeneutics? Before significant advances can be made in narrative theology, some of these critical issues must be clarified by narrative theologians.

GEORGE W. STROUP

Bibliography

Hans W. Frei, *The Eclipse of Biblical Narrative.*
Michael Goldberg, *Theology and Narrative: A Critical Introduction.*
Stanley Hauerwas and L. Gregory Jones, eds., *Why Narrative? Readings in Narrative Theology.*

Cross Reference: Biblical Criticism, Deconstructionism, Myth, Symbol, Theological Method.

NATURAL THEOLOGY

Traditionally, Catholicism and Protestantism have defined natural theology as the branch of theology that expands the knowledge of God through reason's capacity to interpret the evidence of God's revelation as creator within the universe and in human nature. Medieval Catholic scholasticism distinguished natural knowledge of God as creator from revealed knowledge of God as redeemer in Jesus Christ leading to full salvation. Protestants and Catholics agreed that the natural knowledge of God as creator was fulfilled through revealed knowledge through faith in Jesus Christ. Twentieth-century theology often expresses this classical distinction between natural and revealed knowledge of God by distinguishing general (universal) from special (historical) revelation. Both traditional and modern advocates of natural theology appeal to God's universal revelation authenticated by experience and biblical evidence.

Various pre-Christian Greek philosophies sought to move beyond mythological thinking about the divine to more rational interpretations. Most significant for later Christian natural theology are the philosophies of Plato (427–347 B.C.E.) and Aristotle (384–322 B.C.E.). Leading Catholic theologians in the early church taught that these and certain other Greek and Roman philosophers had some true knowledge of God. The gradual equation of the God of Greek philosophy with the Hebrew-Christian idea of God as creator is traceable from the Christian Apologists (ca. 150 C.E.) to its definitive formulation in Thomas Aquinas (d. 1274 C.E.). In Vatican Council I (1869–1870), the Roman Catholic Church defined natural theology by following Aquinas and upholding the distinction between natural knowledge of God attainable by "natural reason" and knowledge of the divine "mysteries" available only to faith. The Council declared: "If anyone shall have said that the one true God, our Creator and our Lord, cannot be known with certitude by those things which have been made, by the natural light of human reason: let him be anathema."

Sixteenth-century Protestant Reformers affirmed God's universal revelation attested in the Bible. However, on account of their stress on universal human depravity, they criticized Catholic natural theology and held that true knowledge of God derived solely from faith in Jesus Christ. Seventeenth-century Protestant orthodoxy evaluated natural theology more positively. Protestant liberalism in the nineteenth century largely accepted Immanuel Kant's rejection of natural theology's "proofs" for God's existence based on universal revelation as incompatible with philosophical and scientific reasoning. Friedrich Schleier-macher and Albrecht Ritschl opposed natural theology as too abstract and metaphysical. Yet Kant and Schleiermacher led many liberals to posit a universal moral or religious consciousness in humanity in a manner reminiscent of traditional natural theology. This led to a style of natural theology that accentuated God's presence within human consciousness rather than in nature.

Karl Barth (1886–1968) was an "avowed opponent of all natural theology" because it posits a true knowledge of God as creator divorced from knowledge of God as redeemer. While conceding that the Hebrew and Christian scriptures attest God's revelation in creation and in human beings as God's creatures, he held that this testimony is comprehensible only in light of God's central covenant activity and not in isolation from it. Furthermore, Barth interpreted the Bible's dominant witness to include that of universal human sinfulness and the necessity of God's reconciling work in Jesus Christ as the basis of salvation. Hence, it is wrong to affirm a true knowledge of God, the creator, as the basis for a natural theology. Barth therefore viewed non-Christian religions as human attempts at self-salvation—a temptation to which Christianity often also succumbs.

Since 1930, both Catholics and Protestants have criticized Barth's analysis of natural theology and have attempted to reformulate it. Today it is justifiable to speak of an emerging "ecumenical consensus" in favor of natural theology. This consensus is characterized by the following emphases.

First, biblical traditions proclaim that God, the universal creator of the universe and humanity, is manifested objectively in all creation and in every human being. Hebrew scriptures affirm this (Genesis 1–2; Psalms 8, 19, 104; Job 38–39; and Isa. 40:21-23). In the New Testament, Paul underlines God's universal self-revelation to the Gentiles through creation, asserting: "Ever since the creation of the world [God's] invisible nature, namely, [God's] eternal power and deity, has been clearly perceived in the things that have been made" (Rom. 1:20; cf. Acts 14:15-17; 17:22-31). Paul also views the presence of conscience in the Gentiles as God's law "written on their hearts" (Rom. 2:15) as further evidence of God's universal revelation in creation. In addition, the Fourth Gospel teaches God's revelation in creation by means of his word through whom "all things were made" (John 1:3) and whose life "was the light" illuminating all human beings (John 1:4, 9-11). For John, the eternal word of God who "became flesh" (John 1:14) in Jesus Christ was manifesting God throughout the entire history of creation and of humanity prior to the incarnation.

Affirming this universal and objective revelation of God in creation, the ecumenical consensus opposes Barth's view. It concurs with Barth that all revelation entails God's initiative, and it maintains that God's revelation in creation is more indirect than divine self-revelation in salvation history. In contrast to the position of Vatican I, which equated saving revelation with the communication of, and acceptance of, divine truths and depiction of natural theology as though it were the product of unaided human reason separable from God's initiative, Catholic theology since Vatican II interprets both forms of God's revelation in more dynamic, historical, and personalistic categories. Now all of God's revelation is viewed from the perspective of God's saving activity fulfilled in Jesus Christ. Hence God's revelation in creation is christologically ordered; it must be viewed in light of God's saving intent permeating all divine revelatory activity in creation and in relationship to humanity.

Second, an ecumenical consensus is evident with respect to the way human persons are viewed as created with the capacity for knowing God. Here the focus shifts from God's revelation in the cosmos to the human self as a manifestation of God's universal revelation. As already noted, the human conscience is interpreted as a sign of the self's unique relationship to God. A more comprehensive biblical term indicative of the special relationship of human beings to God is found in the testimony that humans are created "in the image of God" (Gen. 1:27). Traditional Roman Catholic teaching interpreted the image in a twofold sense. In the first sense, as rational or spiritual creatures, all human beings are in God's image. Being in God's image in this sense is something indestructible. However, being in the image of God in the second sense meant to be in the "likeness" of God entailing the added gift of supernatural communion with God. The latter was lost through Adam's fall. Catholic exegetes now concur with the more traditional and prevailing Protestant exegesis that rejects as unbiblical and static this twofold interpretation of the concept of the image of God. According to the ecumenical consensus, each human being as God's creature is in the image of God as a complete self. Moreover, in spite of universal sinfulness, human beings remain in God's image. Being in God's image presupposes a relatedness to, or openness toward, God, which was given at creation and may come to fulfillment or may be thwarted through sin.

Currently, this openness toward God in creation is seen variously in terms of human longing for God, in the human question concerning God's existence, in the human quest for truth that finally is the question concerning God or transcendence (Karl Rahner, Paul Tillich, Wolfhart Pannenberg), in the longing for authentic human existence (Bultmann), in humanity's hope for the future (Moltmann), or finally, in the human longing for overcoming oppressive socio-political structures destructive of human selfhood and society (liberation theologies). This more dynamic understanding of the self's relationship to God given in and with the nature of the self in God's image leads to a more existential interpretation of the self's innate capacity for an initial awareness of God. The possibility for the knowledge of God as creator, then, is neither construable primarily in terms of reason's unaided possibility for arriving at belief in God nor in terms of rational proofs for God's existence set forth in traditional natural theology. Rather, the self's initial relationship to God as creator is a pre-reflective, or existential, experience of the whole self in relationship to God.

This emerging ecumenical natural theology seeks to do greater justice to the continuity between God's activity as creator and redeemer, and it is often more trinitarian in depicting the totality of God's self-revelation. It opposes Barth's excessively negative assessment of the possibilities for the knowledge of God based on universal revelation and therewith of natural theology. It is also critical of pre–Vatican II Catholic theology for being too rationalistic and abstract in its portrayal of the knowledge of God, the creator. At the same time, current natural theology appropriates something of Barth's christocentric understanding of revelation in a way allowing for a greater appreciation of God's grace always undergirding creation.

Third, the ecumenical consensus departs from Barth's strongly negative assessment of the possibilities for true knowledge of God as creator in the non-Christian religions. It does so by maintaining God's universal presence in creation and in the moral and religious consciousness of humanity that finds expression outside the Hebrew-Christian traditions.

DAVID L. MUELLER

Bibliography

Walter Abbott, ed., *The Documents of Vatican II.*
John Baillie, *Our Knowledge of God*
Emil Brunner and Karl Barth, *Natural Theology.*
Avery Dulles, *Models of Revelation.*
Charles Hartshorne, *A Natural Theology for Our Time.*

Cross Reference: Epistemology, Incarnation, Neoorthodoxy, Pluralism, Revelation

NATURALISM

Naturalism refers theologically to a school of American thinkers who in the first decades of this century led in transforming American culture from its Christian and Idealist suppositions to the secularism that most American intellectuals now take for granted. The apex of the school can be conveniently dated from the appearance of George Santayana's *Interpretations of Religion and Poetry* (1900) to the death of John Dewey (1952). It includes not only philosophers but figures such as Oliver Wendell Holmes and novelist James Farrell. The intellectual center of the school was the Columbia University faculty of philosophy under the leadership of Frederick Woodbridge and John Dewey, and later their student J. H. Randall, Jr. Perhaps its most brilliant and idiosyncratic proponent was Harvard's Santayana, who provided in his *Life of Reason* (1905–1906) the most affecting expression and justification of naturalist attitudes. He was the decisive influence on the naturalists' reflection on religion.

Naturalism was the philosophical expression of the practical insight that society, its public life, and its institutions were no longer in need of theological justification, that any theological justification would violate modern society's pluralist and democratic cast, and that traditional religious institutions opposed scientific inquiry into nature and human experience whenever that inquiry touched on doctrinally privileged areas. On the one hand, an emerging secularist elite needed a new public understanding, and Naturalism provided a home-grown alternative to Marxism. On the other hand, religious life was in need of critique and reinterpretation, and Naturalism supplied both.

Naturalist questions about religion were common at the time: (1) What is the status of religious knowledge in a world view dominated by scientific method? (2) How are common and public values to be saved and affirmed when their age-old underpinning in religious communities and institutions is problematic? (3) Can we find a way to speak of the undoubted transcendent dimension of human experience when it is not possible any longer to ground philosophically our religious speech about God (i.e., when theology is impossible)? The naturalist answers can be briefly stated: (1) Religion is noncognitive and so there is no conflict between religion and science. (2) Values are intrinsic to human experience and not based on religious claims to special revelation or insight. (3) Religious devotion to the supernatural is replaced by devotion to ideals and to the community's progress through scientific inquiry.

Naturalism was greatly influenced by Darwin and the growth of the life sciences in the late nineteenth and early twentieth centuries. As a child of the Enlightenment, Naturalism was convinced that all inherited understandings and practices are subject to criticism and reconstruction, and so it consistently challenged authorities. It took for granted the nineteenth-century European assessments of religion as passionate, symbolic, and noncognitive. It confronted the temptation to relativism within the increasingly widespread recognition that culture is empirical, not normative, and that even science is probable, never certain. It fit within the broad stream of Western empiricism, though mounting acute criticisms of it. It took over the nineteenth-century Idealist devotion to culture and values. It accepted with qualification the materialist devotion to science as the single way to knowledge and the materialist metaphysical position that matter takes precedence over spirit.

The philosophical positions common to naturalists are relatively few and clear-cut, at least on the surface. The term "nature" is taken to include whatever does or can fall within human experience, not as a dialectical opposite to other terms such as "convention," "art," or "the supernatural." Whatever is experienced is real, and no one thing is more real than another. Although we may value things differently for different purposes, everything within the horizon of experience is real and natural. Equally, there are many ways in which humans experience the world, among them art, politics, morality, religion, common sense, and science. No one takes precedence over others in value; no one delivers a privileged or normative experience.

Naturalism viewed itself as a philosophic expression of the intent of the sciences to explain phenomena through identification of natural causes and conditions. Naturalists viewed nature as intelligible, inquiry to be unlimited, and the understandings garnered from inquiry to be hypothetical and reformable.

The naturalist doctrines on the correlation of scientific inquiry and knowledge of the real seem to exclude theological inquiry, since God is not an object that falls within human experience, and they exclude revelation as a possibility, since the religious traditions seem to regard the content of revelation as knowledge, yet beyond question and any empirical verification. Generally speaking, traditional religious concerns, methods, and claims are outdated and obscurantist. The naturalist critique of traditional religion is presented in John Dewey's *A Common Faith* (1934).

However, there is another side to the naturalist program, one stemming from Santayana and Woodbridge and reaching its culmination in Randall and Sterling Lamprecht, among others. This other side attempts a constructive evaluation of traditional religion and recognizes a sphere of experience and existence about which religious speech seems necessary, though always noncognitive.

Naturalism, although it remains an active and productive school in American philosophy, is now overshadowed by other philosophical concerns and methods illustrated in process philosophies, phenomenology, existentialism, and linguistic philosophies such as ordinary language analysis, structuralism, and deconstruction. Much of the naturalist creative advance is now simply taken for granted by these other schools, and recent philosophy tends to be more highly technical and "professional" and less public and accessible than naturalism.

Naturalism's impact on American Christian theology through such figures as Henry Nelson Wieman and on Jewish thought through Felix Adler and Mordecai Kaplan seems a permanent legacy. Naturalist criticism and efforts at reconstruction may turn out to be of great value to the internal life of those religious communities that set a high value on intellectual life.

WILLIAM M. SHEA

Bibliography

Yervant Krikorian, ed., *Naturalism and the Human Spirit*.
Sterling P. Lamprecht, *The Metaphysics of Naturalism*.
J. H. Randall, Jr., *The Role of Knowledge in Western Religion*.
William M. Shea, *The Naturalists and the Supernatural*.
Frederick J. E. Woodbridge, *An Essay on Nature*.

Cross Reference: Agnosticism, Empirical Theology, Humanism, Science and Christianity, Secularity.

NECESSITY (*See* ELECTION, FREEDOM.)

NEOORTHODOXY

Neoorthodoxy can most easily be understood as a theological response to the developing crisis in the Western world in the first half of the twentieth century. In keeping with the nineteenth-century theology usually called "liberalism," Christianity had become increasingly wedded to the then successful and self-confident democratic, industrial, and scientific culture of the West. When, therefore, the self-confidence of that culture began to wane and its foundations seemingly began to collapse after World War I, the more sensitive Christian leaders understandably responded. Karl Barth and Emil Brunner, for example, made a passionate attempt to locate the sources of the Christian message and the grounds for its hope beyond a culture in crisis. The fear that a Christianity dominated by the thought-forms of a disintegrating culture could not survive and, even more, that a "culture religion" could offer no message of hope to a society that despaired of its powers was the driving force in this effort to reestablish Christian faith on the foundations of God's revelation in scripture rather than on the bases of Western scientific, political, or social thought. The earliest emphases of the neoorthodox movement (see the works of Barth, Brunner, Anders Nygren, Gustav Aulen, and Reinhold Niebuhr), therefore, were a radical criticism of the "liberal" union of culture and Christianity and a corresponding assertion of the discontinuity of Christianity in all its aspects from the dominant thought-forms of Western life.

The central theological motifs of the neoorthodox movement stem from this basic drive toward discontinuity and separation of religion from culture. In the place of the liberal emphasis on the immanence of God in the life of nature and human society came the vigorous affirmation of the transcendence of God—of God's unknowableness and consequent difference from all thoughts about God in cultural terms. In the place of the liberal faith in the inherent goodness of human beings appeared the categorical insistence that salvation must come to humans from beyond themselves. Thus the liberal conception of history as a gradual, progressive development of human powers toward a fulfilled good life was transformed into a view of history that is "dialectical" and "catastrophic" in character. Men and women are and remain sinners in both their personal and their social existence; thus history exists in a tension between God's judgment on human sin and God's grace, which alone can redeem this situation. The only hope for women and men, therefore, lies not so much in the liberal program of education and enlargement of human benevolent powers, but rather in the "crisis" of faith when men and women repent before God, live in a new state of forgiveness, humility, and obedience, and look to the final fulfillment of God's purposes beyond history (see especially the writings of Reinhold Niebuhr).

All across the theological spectrum, this "crisis" of human natural powers—of the discontinuity between the gospel and cultural life—was the dominant motif of neoorthodox thought. From this motif came the central themes of neoorthodox theology: the insistence on the radical disparity of religious and cultural truth (e.g., the Word of God in scripture vs. the human word in culture, and revelation vs. philosophical reason and natural theology); the new emphasis on the seriousness and universality of sin (e.g., the reappearance of the symbol of the fall as a central aspect of Christian self-understanding); the clear distinction between the religious or good person at her or his best and the Incarnate Lord (e.g., the "Jesus of history" vs. the "Christ of faith"); and finally, the insistence that even the best society is no more than an approximation to the kingdom of God (e.g., the renewed interest in the church as the unique bearer in history of God's purposes and grace, and in eschatology as the sole object of ultimate hope in history). These central themes were interpreted in a variety of ways by many diverse thinkers from the more "orthodox" Barth to the more "liberal" Bultmann and Tillich. In each case, however, one can see the desire to reinterpret Christian doctrine in terms of the transcendence of God and of God's grace and in terms of the inability of natural human powers either to achieve salvation or to avoid self-destruction.

Neoorthodox thinkers, seeking to protest the nineteenth century's "culture religion," drew their inspiration and theological materials largely from Reformation sources. This movement can, therefore, validly be called "neoorthodox" or even "neo-Reformation." We should understand, however, that these theologians returned to this "orthodox" tradition, not in order to be dogmatically orthodox, but because they found there the most compelling and relevant theological thinking. Neoorthodoxy, however, cannot be understood solely as return to an "orthodox" perspective, as its name implies; it was also genuinely "neo" in character. As it increasingly recognized, the movement was also the child of the liberalism against which it reacted, for it retained in a revised form many of the most important affirmations and principles of liberal Christianity.

First, neoorthodoxy agreed with liberalism that the whole area of spatio-temporal fact and event is the valid object of scientific inquiry, with the result that the hypotheses of science in the areas of natural and historical events were regarded as authoritative if not exhaustive. Thus, although such symbols as "creation out of nothing" and the "fall of Adam" again became important theologically, neoorthodoxy did not quarrel with scientific explanations of the origin of nature and human life. Likewise, although the Incarnation became the central theological doctrine of all neoorthodoxy, the "factual" manifestations and explanations of the Incarnation (e.g., the virgin birth, miracles, and the empty tomb) did not play such a central role in any of these theologies as they had in orthodoxy itself. In other words, to neoorthodox thinkers theological doctrines were statements containing symbolic rather than literal, factual truth; they were propositions pointing to the religious dimensions of events rather than propositions containing factual information about events (see Niebuhr's use of "myth," Tillich's use of "symbolic language," and C. H. Dodd's "fact and interpretation.") The intricate relation between the historic facts and the religious, symbolic, or "mythical" interpretations of those facts remained as an important and never quite resolved problem for neoorthodoxy.

Second, neoorthodoxy affirmed with liberalism that all the activities and products of human religious life (scriptures, creeds, laws, church statements, acts, and so forth) are historically conditioned. From these resources neoorthodox theology drew two "liberal" conclusions: (1) These scriptures and institutions must be studied historically and critically in order to be understood, and (2) none of these products of human religious life is itself infallible or a direct, unmediated result of divine activity. For the neoorthodox thinker, Christian truth was not merely relative human wisdom, because it contains the Word of God; and the church is not merely another social institution, since it is also the body of Christ, the people of God in history. Hence arose other problems peculiar to neoorthodox theology: What is the relation of the Word of God in scripture to the human words that make up the scriptures? And what is the relation of the Word and the Spirit of God, which establish and constitute the church, to the relative, even sinful historical institutions we call churches? Out of this same combination of orthodox and liberal elements, however, came also the unusual grace of neoorthodox Christianity at its best: namely, that it at once emphasized the uniqueness of Christian belief and the importance of a sound theology, without at the same time being intolerant, credal, or exclusivist in its spirit. One of the most remarkable "liberal" traits of this theology, besides its tolerance of diverse points of view, was its sometimes explicit, sometimes implicit acceptance of universalism with regard to salvation, or at least its sweeping repudiation of the doctrine of eternal damnation for those outside the faith.

Finally, the union of religion and culture in liberalism had given to liberal Christianity a passionate concern to relate the Christian gospel creatively to human social existence and to find in Christian faith the basis for work toward an improved social environment for all people. At least in its Anglo-Saxon forms (e.g., in Niebuhr, John Bennett, Tillich, and a host of others), neoorthodoxy shared and perpetuated this emphasis on the social relevance of the gospel to the problems of war and peace and to economic, political, and racial justice. Instead of referring to social reform as "the building of the kingdom of God" (as liberals did), it spoke of the call to manifest Christ's lordship over all aspects of a sinful world, and it spoke of the necessity of Christian obedience in love to one's neighbor in all the facets of life. The presupposition of this neoorthodox social concern was the important liberal idea that social institutions represent a historical human construct and so are not directly ordained in their present form by God's providential will.

Neoorthodoxy was, therefore, a genuinely new synthesis of two widely divergent interpretations of the Christian religion: that of the Reformation and that of nineteenth-century liberalism. A movement rather than a "school," neoorthodoxy influenced almost every theologian and biblical scholar from 1925 to 1960. It presented, therefore, a variety of emphases and characteristics, but its central themes of divine transcendence, the depth of the human predicament, and the complete relevance of the Christian faith were almost universally expressed. This synthesis of the old and the new was immensely creative in reestablishing a concern for the religious message of the Bible, for the unique history and traditions of the Christian churches, for the essential theological elements of the Christian faith and message, and for the relevance of that message for the totality of human life, personal and social.

Two decades after World War II, however, when the re-creation of society in Europe and the liberation of exploited and dominated peoples in the post-war world became overriding religious concerns, neoorthodoxy, with its realistic, often grim view of history and its possibilities, lost its dominance. It was replaced by the new political and eschatological theologies with their emphases on human action within history to bring about God's new and liberated future for humankind.

LANGDON GILKEY

Bibliography

Gustav Aulen, *Christus Victor.*
Karl Barth, *The Word of God and the Word of Man.*
_____, *The Humanity of God.*
Emil Brunner, *The Theology of Crisis.*
_____, *Man in Revolt.*
_____, *The Mediator.*
Rudolf Bultmann, *History and Eschatology.*
Reinhold Niebuhr, *Moral Man and Immoral Society.*
_____, *Reflections on the End of an Era.*
_____, *The Nature and Destiny of Man.*
_____, *Faith and History.*

Cross Reference: Culture, Kingdom of God, Liberalism, Revelation.

ORDINATION

Ordination is the consecration of the Christian clergy to service in and to the church. Its meaning differs among Protestant denominations and between Protestants and Catholics, but there are important similarities that connect the various Christian traditions' concerns about ordination.

337

Protestants generally recognize three marks or qualifications for ordination: an inward call, an outward call or affirmation by the congregation, and gifts (including, in many cases, education) for ministry. The ceremony or ritual of consecration usually includes exhortations, prayers, and laying on of hands. This ceremony is not regarded as conferring new rights or power, as infusing the Holy Spirit for the work of the ministry, or as maintaining historical succession with the apostles; nor is it regarded as a sacrament.

The work for which the clergy are ordained is centered in proclamation of the Word (preaching) and administration of the sacraments. As proclaimer of Word and administrator of sacrament, the ordained person is entrusted with assembling, edifying, and building up the church, and with leading it, teaching, and administering discipline. The ordained minister is expected to be a model of Christian commitment and service.

At the point of interpreting how the ordained minister models Christian service or the person of Christ, Protestant and Catholic understandings diverge most widely. Although Catholics recognize that all Christians participate in priesthood, persons ordained to the priesthood function uniquely as representatives of Christ, offering the sacrament of bread and wine and thus the sacrifice of Christ's body and blood to God on behalf of the people.

Current ecumenical debate on ordination has focused on several issues for the church. At the center of most is the fundamental question about how the life of the church is to be ordered. Protestants and Catholics are involved in dialogue on several key issues, one being the sacramentality of the ordained priesthood. What does it mean to say that the priest acts *in persona Christi* (in the person of Christ)? Catholics have suggested that this means that the priest is an *alter Christus,* an "other Christ." This view is problematical to successors of the Reformation, who affirm the priesthood of all believers.

A second concern about ordination in the dialogues of the World Council of Churches is the meaning of the Eucharist (the sacrament or celebration of the Lord's Supper)—particularly its importance and significance in relation to ordination.

A third area of dialogue and debate has to do with Tradition as opposed to traditions. Within that discussion, the subject of the maleness of the bishop, priest, or pastor as representative of Christ has received particular attention in the last decade. In addition, for some Christians the question of an ordained clergy with its implied separation from the laity is a thorny issue: Should there even be an ordained ministry? For others, ordination for ministries other than the preaching ministry seems to be needed in light of the expanded needs of churches today and the equality of ordained ministers called to meet those needs.

Apostolic succession—the notion that the clergy can be ordained only by a bishop with a pedigree stretching back to the original apostles—is a fourth point of contention among some Christians concerned with maintaining the Tradition in ordination.

The ordination of women poses a fifth subject of ecumenical debate. Approximately one-third of the member churches of the World Council of Churches (including Lutherans, Methodists, Presbyterians, Episcopalians, Disciples of Christ, and some Baptists) ordain women. The ordination of women to the office of bishop (e.g., that of Barbara Harris in the Episcopal Church of the United States) presents additional challenges to the ecumenical dialogue about ordination.

Arguments for and against women's ordination range widely for Protestants and somewhat more narrowly for Catholics, but they all focus on key points. Arguments against women's ordination include certain passages of scripture interpreted as subordinating women to men; woman's place in the orders of creation; woman's status as second in creation and first in sin; the infiltration of the church by the secular women's movement; woman's emotional and biological unsuitability; the force of Tradition, which has disallowed ordination for women; and the maleness of Christ, who, thereby, cannot be represented fully by a female.

Emphasizing these last two arguments, Roman Catholic and Eastern Orthodox churches oppose the ordination of women. In 1988, the Orthodox church concluded that priestly ordination must be denied to women "on the example of the Theotokos [Mary, the mother of God], who did not exercise the sacramental priestly function in the Church, even though she was made worthy to become the Mother of the Incarnate Son and Word of God." The Orthodox church did call, however, for the revival of the order of women deacons and expressed regret that it had fallen "into disuse." The Roman church continues to assert that the role of the priest in representing Christ precludes feminine representation of a male Christ.

Arguments in favor of women's ordination include certain passages of scripture interpreted as canceling hierarchical relationships between the sexes; women's ordination as an issue of religious liberty and freedom to respond to God's call; women's ordination as a basic human right; feminine images for divinity in scripture; the role of women as deacons and ministers in the early church and as judges in ancient Israel; the presence of qualified and gifted women claiming God's call; and the need for women's participation in the ordained ministry in order to model the full variety and diversity of the whole people of God.

A sixth challenging issue for the modern church is that of ordination of homosexual persons. The Evangelical Lutheran Church of America and the Church of England have both refused to condemn the ordination of homosexual clergy. Other churches are struggling with the difficult issues raised by those who claim that such ordination is not opposed to God's intent but rather joins in expressing the fullness of divine purpose.

Although issues about ordination prompt ecumenical discussion, ordination itself is first and last a theological issue because it reflects on the nature of God's activity by, through, and to the people of God.

ELIZABETH BARNES

Bibliography

Mark E. Chapman, "The Ordination of Women: Evangelical and Catholic," *Dialog* (Spring 1989): 133-36.

John H. Erickson, "The International Orthodox–Roman Catholic Commission's Statement on Ordination," *Ecumenical Trends* 18 (April 1989): 49-52.

Thomas G. Halbrooks, "The Meaning and Significance of Ordination Among Southern Baptists, 1848–1945," *Baptist History and Heritage* 23 (July 1988): 24-32.

Jon Nilson, "'Let Bishops Give Proof of the Church's Motherly Concern': The Prospect of Women Bishops in Light of Vatican II," *Journal of Ecumenical Studies* 25 (Fall 1988): 3-15.

Emmanuel Sullivan, "The 1988 Lambeth Conference and Ecumenism," *Ecumenical Trends* 17 (November 1988): 145-48.

Cross Reference: Priesthood, Sacraments/Sacramental Theology.

PANENTHEISM

Panentheism views God and the world in interrelationship. It contrasts with theism, which understands God to be entirely independent of the world, and pantheism, which understands God and the world to be in some sense identical. A panentheistic universe is one in which God and the world dynamically interact so that they in some respects transcend each other and in other respects are immanent within each other. God and the world are interdependent.

The transcendent aspect of God is the sense in which God is absolute with regard to qualities such as goodness, wisdom, and power—those qualities that constitute God's self-chosen character, and without which God would not be God. Panentheistic thinkers often refer to this as the "abstract" pole in God, or the "primordial nature" of God, or the eternity of God. These aspects of God are most like the traditional concepts applied to God in theism. However, panentheistic thinkers consider the abstract pole but one aspect of God: God is constituted not only by abstract qualities, but also by concrete qualities gained in interaction with the world. God is the supremely open one, alone able to receive the entirety of every element in the world, feeling each actuality as each actuality itself feels. This openness in God involves God in coexperiencing the suffering as well as the joy in the world; it is the basis of God's perfect knowledge of the world as it is and as it might be. For panentheistic thinkers (who in the twentieth century have included Alfred North Whitehead, Nicholas Berdyaev, Martin Buber, Teilhard de Chardin, Charles Hartshorne, and John B. Cobb, Jr.), this absolute openness to relativity is also necessary for God to be God. They call it the "concrete" pole in God, or the "consequent nature" of God, or the relativity of God. Thus for panentheism, God is not only supremely abstract and absolute but also supremely concrete and related: God is dipolar. God's integration of the abstract and the concrete poles constitutes the fullness of God.

The attribution of two poles to the divine reality means that God is both active and passive, giver and receiver, absolute and relative. The integration of these attributes rests with the freedom of God. What God does with the received world depends on God's own purposes, stemming from the divine character as formed through the primordial pole. Thus, although the world influences God, it cannot determine who God is or who God will be.

A God who is continuously receiving an ever-changing world into the divine life is a dynamic God who is ever in the process of becoming. Unlike theistic views that eschew change or becoming as a threat to the divine perfection, panentheism values the process of becoming, seeing it as the ultimate expression of life. God is the Supreme Becoming One—Supreme, because only God's becoming is a never-ending process; Becoming, because the very Godness of God is the divine ability continuously to receive every element constituting the universe; and One, because God unifies the world into the divine life. God, in a panentheistic universe, is an everlastingly dynamic and complex unity.

Panentheism redefines the perfection of God. Traditionally, becoming could never be ascribed to God since it involved change. Change, in turn, challenged the perfection of God, since presumably one would change for better or for worse. In a panentheistic view, change is necessary to perfection, not a challenge to it. God's perfection means that God is supremely open to the world. Since the world changes, with new actualities continuously coming into existence, God's openness to the world involves God in change as God continuously receives an ever-new world. God is continuously adding new experiences to the divine life, integrating them within the enduring divine character. The type of change involved is one of everlasting self-excelling or a dynamically increasing richness of experience.

To summarize, the panentheistic conception of God considers God eternal in respect to the divine character, or the abstract pole in God; temporal in respect to an ability to increase in experience; conscious, or possessing purposes in keeping with the divine character; omniscient, knowing all there is to be known, whether as actual or as potential; and world-inclusive, incorporating the world into the divine self. The world also transcends God in the sense that it is truly other than God, involved in its own processes of becoming. Given the interrelationship of all elements within the world, what each element becomes depends upon its temporal and spatial situation and upon its degree of freedom to become what it will within its own limitations. Its freedom measures its transcendence of all others, including God.

Immanence as well as transcendence marks a panentheistic universe. Relations are internal to existence, resulting in varying degrees of immanence for God and the world. The world is fully immanent within God, since God is supremely open to the world, receiving it into the divine life. God is partially immanent within the world, since every finite reality receives the influence of God and must integrate that influence into its own becoming. This reciprocity of influence forms the interdependence between God and the world. Panentheism can describe a system of thought that builds on dynamics similar to those outlined here (process philosophy and theology are the foremost examples) or a tendency within theology today. As a tendency, it represents a move away from traditional theism's positing of God as entirely independent of the world, immutable, and impassive. Insofar as God is seen as open to the world, and therefore open to the suffering of the world such that God, also, suffers, theism moves toward panentheism.

MARJORIE HEWITT SUCHOCKI

Bibliography

John B. Cobb, Jr., *God and the World.*
Charles Hartshorne and William L. Reese, eds., *Philosophers Speak of God.*
Alfred North Whitehead, *Process and Reality* (rev. ed., David Griffin and Donald Sherburne, eds.).
_____, *Religion in the Making.*

Cross Reference: Being/Becoming, Metaphysics, Process Theology, Theism.

PAPACY

The papacy is the office of the pope, the bishop of Rome and head of the Roman Catholic Church. In calling the papacy an "office," Catholicism suggests that it is more a task and function than a privilege.

In Roman Catholic conception, the roots of the papacy lie in Jesus' choice of twelve close associates ("apostles") during his lifetime. Simon Peter became the leader of the twelve (whose number was probably a deliberate echo of the twelve tribes of Israel). The so-called Petrine ministry is the service that Peter, and those who followed him in leading the Christian church, expended on the community. The tradition that Peter and Paul traveled to Rome to found a church at the central city of the first-century Western world helped to make the church in Rome especially significant. Later, the head of the Roman church, along with heads of the other principal churches (in Jerusalem, Antioch, and Alexandria), exercised considerable influence outside his own area. When the tradition became firm that each local church would have its own presiding officer (called a presbyter or bishop), churches instituted the practice of tracing and recording the historical lineage of their bishop back to the apostles of Jesus. In this climate, the bishop of Rome came to be considered the successor of Peter as the head of the church in Rome, and (in Roman Catholic interpretation) also as the head of the entire Christian community.

The story of the growth of papal power during the Middle Ages (beginning with Gregory I at the end of the sixth century) is fascinating, with chapters that edify and chapters that show many abuses of power. During the separation of the Western and Eastern portions of Christendom, which culminated in the mutual excommunications of 1054, the tensions between the claims of the bishop of Rome to jurisdiction over the entire church and the traditions of Eastern leaders to rule their areas collegially contributed to the final separation. The Protestant Reformers of the sixteenth century considered the papacy one of their worst enemies, not only because it opposed the changes they wanted but also because the power and mentality of the papacy struck them as out of touch with the New Testament.

Roman Catholicism made many church reforms during the Council of Trent in the middle of the sixteenth century, but thereafter the papacy continued more to oppose Protestantism and modernity than to approve them. At the First Vatican Council (1869–1870), the assembled bishops declared the infallibility of the pope (under restricted circumstances). The Second Vatican Council (1962–1965) balanced this teaching with a more thorough affirmation of how the papacy functions in concert with the bishops and, indeed, with the entire church.

Beginning with Pope John XXIII, who convened the Second Vatican Council, the papacy and Roman Catholicism have been in dialogue with the modern world. The recent popes (Paul VI and John Paul II) have become well known as travelers, taking around the globe a message of concern for the poor, both those lacking material necessities and those drowning in materialism. The Second Vatican Council also brought Roman Catholics into more extensive dialogue with other Christians concerned about the ecumenical state and future of the church. In this exchange, discussions among theologians have produced some significant breakthroughs regarding how the papacy might function for the entire Christian church.

Most ecumenical theologians now agree that Peter does represent an important early ministry in the church and that through Peter (as a symbol) Christians might express well the unity that ought to be one of their four leading marks (along with holiness, catholicity, and apostolicity). The pope, functioning in the symbolic line of Peter, could be the "place" where the entire church finds a single representative voice. Viewed in this way, some of the traditional privileges claimed for the papacy, though not without problems, are more acceptable. For example, the infallibility of the pope could be considered an extension of the preservation of the church in the truth of the gospel. Inasmuch as God has made the church the means for continuing the formal proclamation of the Good News of Christ and for celebrating the sacraments of Christian life, the church has to be authenticated by God—insured against failure. It has to be able to provide what it promises: the words and acts of salvation. The pope would participate in this divine gift to the church to the extent that the Petrine ministry is essential to the functioning of the church. Specifically, the pope could not err in formal declarations of truths of faith or morals that bore directly on the mission of the church.

Many questions, both theoretical and practical, remain about how Christians might overcome their centuries of alienation (and about how they might retain the riches of the various church traditions they have nurtured while isolated) by some ecumenical establishment of the papacy as a primary focus for the church's unity. But in principle, at least, many mainstream Christian theologians, and some mainstream denominational leaders, seem willing to discuss progress toward such unity. What is at stake is not merely the historical or theological pros and cons of the papacy as a human institution. What is at stake is a ministry in the church given for the sake of the church's unity. Not to build up this ministry might well be to fail Jesus' command (John 17) to make his followers one.

DENISE LARDNER CARMODY

Bibliography

R. E. Brown, K. P. Donfried, and J. Reumann, eds., *Peter in the New Testament.*
Heinrich Fries and Karl Rahner, *Unity of the Churches: An Actual Possibility.*
Patrick Granfield, *The Limits of the Papacy.*
J. M. R. Tillard, *The Bishop of Rome.*

Cross Reference: Authority, Roman Catholicism, Vatican II.

PARADIGM

In ordinary use, "paradigm" simply means a pattern or example. However, a new technical meaning has been attached in philosophy of science, and this latter use has come to be of interest to theologians.

"Paradigm" became an important term in philosophy of science following the publication of Thomas Kuhn's *The Structure of Scientific Revolutions* in 1962. Kuhn argued that to understand the history of science one needs to appreciate the role of paradigms—achievements so widely accepted and emulated by the scientific community that they govern the practice of science for years to come.

Such achievements are recorded in texts such as Isaac Newton's *Principia* and Charles Lyell's *Geology*.

The paradigm provides shared beliefs and standards for scientific work. It includes concepts, theories, and natural laws, and it relates them to experimental results. It involves commitments to preferred types of instrumentation and to the ways they are to be employed. It also involves higher-level, quasi-metaphysical commitments, telling scientists what are the basic entities in the universe. Finally, it commits scientists to intellectual values such as explanatory scope or precision in making predictions.

Paradigms provide comprehensive world views that greatly influence the interpretation of scientific data; consequently they are highly resistant to falsification. Kuhn claimed that the history of science alternates periods of "normal science," wherein one paradigm dominates the field, with revolutionary periods, wherein the prevailing paradigm suffers a crisis brought on by repeated failures and is eventually replaced by a new one. For instance, Aristotle's physics was replaced by the Newtonian paradigm, which was later replaced by Einstein's theory.

Kuhn's understanding of the history of science as governed by paradigms set him apart from earlier philosophers in a number of ways. He emphasized the role of the scientific community in judging when to reject one paradigm for another, and he pointed to the difficulty in providing an objective account of the rationality of such judgments, since standards for good science are themselves paradigm-dependent. He also called into question earlier ideas about progress in science. It had been assumed that scientific growth is cumulative, adding further knowledge to earlier discoveries and approximating to an accurate (true) account of reality. However, Kuhn's emphasis on the discontinuities before and after a revolution shows this to be a false picture of scientific growth.

Some observers have suggested that during the two decades following its publication *The Structure of Scientific Revolutions* has had a wider academic influence than any other book. Kuhn's views have been extended and applied by admirers and sharply criticized by others. Two main criticisms are, first, that he provides an irrationalist account of science—which he denies, saying that he shows only that scientific rationality is different from that supposed by earlier philosophers of science. Second, it is claimed that his use of "paradigm" is ambiguous, sometimes referring to the concrete achievements and other times to the complex of laws and methodological and metaphysical commitments that these achievements entail. In response, Kuhn proposes in the second edition (1970) to replace "paradigm" with two terms: "exemplar" for the achievement, and "disciplinary matrix" for the scientific world view it entails.

Scholars in assorted fields have found Kuhn's concept of a paradigm useful for describing the history or current practice of their disciplines. Ian Barbour claims that religions share many features with scientific paradigms: They provide comprehensive world views that interpret the community's experience; they are resistant to falsification, being called into question only in times of crisis; and they are based not so much on a set of rules as on an exemplary life, such as that of Jesus. Differences he notes are that a religion is a way of life, not just a set of beliefs; religions are less subject to control by experience than are paradigms; and religions lack the general laws found in science.

A second way that Kuhn's concept has been used is to apply not to entire religions (such as Christianity) but rather to schools of thought within Christian theology. Hans Küng has noted that texts such as Thomas Aquinas's *Summa Theologiae* and John Calvin's *Institutes* have served as exemplars for future work in theology, providing something akin to normal science—which itself eventually becomes disrupted by a crisis and the birth of a new paradigm.

One consequence of employing the concept of paradigm to describe theology is to take a step toward overcoming the sharp split between scientific knowledge and religion, formalized by Immanuel Kant and bequeathed to the liberal Protestant tradition. Furthermore, it provides some support for the rationality of theism: Insofar as theological systems resemble science in their structure and manner of support they share in the rational credibility of science, which has become for many the model of rationality in the modern period.

NANCEY MURPHY

Bibliography

Ian Barbour, *Myths, Models, and Paradigms.*
———, *Religion in an Age of Science.*
Thomas Kuhn, *The Structure of Scientific Revolutions,* 2nd ed.
Hans Küng and David Tracy, eds., *Paradigm Change in Theology.*

Cross Reference: Science and Christianity, Theological Method.

PARADOX

The term "paradox," etymologically derived from the Greek words *para* ("beyond") and *doxa* ("opinion"), can denote a statement that exceeds the capacity of thought and goes against common opinion, but more frequently it is used with reference to a statement that appears to be self-contradictory, unbelievable, or absurd. A paradoxical statement is distinguished from a contradiction, however, in the sense that a paradox contains two terms or propositions standing in opposition to each other, both of which are affirmed as true, while in a contradiction one term excludes the other.

The notion of paradox originates in Greek philosophy with the logical paradoxes of Zeno of Elea (c. 490 B.C.E.) and continues to be of interest to modern logicians, who have discovered a number of mathematical paradoxes requiring a reexamination of logical intuitions and theory. In Christian theology, the notion of paradox was employed in formulating the concepts of Christ and God by the early church fathers, most notably Tertullian (c. 160–220 C.E.) and Athanasius (c. 293–373 C.E.), who used it especially to affirm the dual nature of Christ as both human and divine in the doctrine of the Incarnation and the unity of God in three persons *(persona)* in the doctrine of the Trinity. On the paradox of Christ's death and resurrection, Tertullian is famous for having written, "The Son of God died: it is by all means to be believed, because it is absurd *[credo, quia absurdum]*. And He was buried, and rose again: the fact is certain, because it is impossible *[certum est quia impossible]"* *(The Flesh of Christ)*.

In the modern era, the foremost advocate of a theology of paradox has been the Danish philosopher and religious thinker Søren Kierkegaard (1813–1855), who describes the God-Man as the Absolute Paradox and emphasizes the paradox of faith that believes in God by virtue of the absurd. According to Kierkegaard, paradox is a limit concept that constitutes the passion of thought in its drive to discover that which thought cannot think. When the understanding *(Forstanden)* comes up against that which it cannot comprehend, it must either will its own downfall in recognition of an absolute difference that cannot be grasped (resulting in the happy passion of faith) or else take affront at it in offense, declaring the paradox to be foolishness. In either case, Kierkegaard claims, the Absolute Paradox is not something discovered by the understanding, but it announces itself as a paradox to the understanding. In itself, the Absolute Paradox is not absurd, nor is it absurd to the Christian believer; only from the standpoint of the understanding does the Absolute Paradox appear as the absurd so that the understanding may grasp the fact that it cannot be understood. The most that the understanding can do is to acknowledge that the Absolute Paradox is. In Kierkegaard's view, however, the Absolute Paradox does not constitute a logical contradiction but rather a qualitative contradiction based on the infinite difference between God and being an individual human person.

Kierkegaard's theology of paradox is directed specifically against Hegelian idealism, which in his view does away with the concept of paradox through mediation or the overcoming of oppositions in a higher unity of thought attainable only in philosophy. The issue of paradox thus focuses not only the problem of the relation of faith and reason or the understanding (e.g., whether faith is rational, irrational, nonrational, or suprarational) but also the broader issue of the relation of theology and philosophy.

In more recent religious thought, the influence of Kierkegaard can be seen in the early dialectical theology of Karl Barth and the philosophical theology of Paul Tillich, among others. Like Kierkegaard, Barth emphasizes the infinite qualitative distinction between God and human beings and contends that knowledge of God is given only through revelation, not through reason. Tillich views the christological paradox as the only paradox and thus the source of all paradoxical statements in Christianity, which he distinguishes from rational and irrational, absurd and nonsensical statements. Although no longer a primary term in theology, the concept of paradox still functions in current discussions of the nature of God and Christ by such thinkers as Wolfhart Pannenberg, Jürgen Moltmann, Karl Rahner, and Edward Schillebeeckx, who continue to espouse trinitarian and incarnational doctrines. In the field of philosophy of religion, the problem of fideism, or belief that religious truths are based on faith rather than on reason or empirical evidence, remains a lively issue. In the current theological state of affairs, however, there is a search for nonclassical and nonmetaphysical modes of expressing the paradoxical nature of Christianity, and more attention is given to the emotive and metaphorical nature of religious language, problems of historicity and the loss of a sense of transcendence, religious pluralism and relativism, and the social, psychological, and political implications of Christian claims about God and Christ.

SYLVIA I. WALSH

Bibliography

R. W. Hepburn, *Christianity and Paradox.*
R. T. Herbert, *Paradox and Identity in Theology.*
Søren Kierkegaard, *Fear and Trembling.*
————, *Philosophical Fragments.*
————, *Training in Christianity.*
J. Heywood Thomas, *Subjectivity and Paradox.*
John Wisdom, *Paradox and Discovery.*

Cross Reference: Existential Philosophy, Language–Religious.

PEACE/PEACEMAKING

The 1980s witnessed a resurgence of religious efforts in work for peace or peacemaking. The efforts were a worldwide response to the wars fueled by injustice and poverty and to the terror of nuclear war threatened by the superpowers. All the world's great religions searched their traditions for the resources for peace thinking and peace activity. Ideological movements from Marxism to neoconservative capitalism also sought to contribute to peace from their own traditions.

The Roman Catholic and Protestant peace initiatives in the United States strove to correct traditions that had previously focused more on just war concepts than on peace thinking. This search involved research into biblical traditions, historical analysis, and current theological-ethical formulations. The policies of the church were grounded in reflection on or were related to the biblical witness of *shalom*.

In its most frequent use in the Hebrew scriptures, *shalom* is an emphatically social concept. It has a very broad range of meanings and a certain imprecision in particular uses. Basically it means "well-being," possibly even "salvation." It points to national prosperity. As a personal greeting it is a wish for bodily health. Between peoples it implies an alliance, a relationship; as such, it has covenantal implications. Solomon and Hiram (I Kings 5:12) have *shalom* in an alliance. The covenant of God with Israel is a covenant of peace (Isa. 54:10). Religiously, *shalom* is often one of the expected elements of eschatological fulfillment (Zech. 9:10). In the prophets *shalom* refers to a real political peace for Israel. The false prophets prophesy such a peace though it is not to be realized. Jeremiah and Ezekiel plead for Israel to see that its real, immediate future is war and destruction (Ezek. 13:16).

The New Testament, through its dependence on the Greek translation of the Hebrew scriptures, brings *shalom*'s "well being" meaning into Greek, displacing the more passive Greek *eirene*, which meant being at a state of rest. Both *shalom* and *eirene* have the meaning of peace as opposed to war. In the New Testament uses, various layers of meaning can be found: (1) peace as a feeling of rest, (2) peace as reconciliation, (3) peace as salvation, and (4) peace as salvatory relations among people.

Matthew 5:9, "Blessed are the peacemakers, for they will be called children of God," is the only use of "peacemaker" in the New Testament. Those who actively intervene between two contending parties to make peace are blessed and regarded as children of God. Here, as in other Greek literature, "peace" is used as the opposite of war. Sometimes the peacemaker is the ruler who establishes peace in the world. Matthew's blessing may be eschatological, but it recommends an active role of promoting peace. It is, at least, stronger than Paul's recommendation in his list of moral teachings to the Romans: "If it is possible, so far as it depends on you, live peaceably with all (12:18)." *Shalom* or *eirene* in the sense of salvation are at the center of the Christian faith. They are more than fantastic vision: Personally and in community they may be realized. Socially and politically they are not realized, but in both the Hebrew scriptures and the New Testament the faithful are urged to live peaceably and to be peacemakers.

Finding a proliferation of the meanings of peace in scripture and church history, scholars have articulated various meanings of *shalom*. A fivefold analysis of *shalom* proposed by Dana Wilbanks is representative of current efforts: (1) The biblical vision of peace is eschatological, (2) the biblical vision of peace includes justice as integral to its meaning, (3) the biblical vision of peace encompasses both individuals and their communities, (4) the biblical vision of peace sees the realization of peace as both divine gift and human task, and (5) the biblical vision of peace requires witnesses and agents.

There is no credible way to imply that ancient writers knew anything about the possibilities of humanity ultimately destroying itself. Confronted as we are, however, with the question of whether or not humanity will survive, the meaning of peacemaking for our time involves the salvation of humanity as a species. Peacemaking and the promotion of peace may go on in the family, school, business, church, and government, but theologically speaking, peacemaking today means the existential, activist work in society to prevent the destruction of the human species. Its primary focus is on preventing world-destructive war.

In the United States, Roman Catholic, Presbyterian, United Methodist, and United Church of Christ churches have turned to ancient traditions of just war theory to show that current war is morally not justified. All have called for reducing the militaristic tendencies of the modern world and have spoken against relying on nuclear terror to deter war. They all have initiated activist peace programs based on a theory of *shalom*.

The desperation of poor people, the greed of the powerful and wealthy, the anarchy of international rulers, the failures of rulers and governments, and international military interventions continue to threaten. Peacemaking work in the churches is complex as Christians continue to confront clashes between a Christ of peace and militaristic cultures.

RONALD H. STONE

Bibliography

Roland H. Bainton, *Christian Attitudes Toward War and Peace.*
José Míguez Bonino, *Toward a Christian Political Ethics.*
Alan Geyer, *The Idea of Disarmament.*
Ronald H. Stone, *Christian Realism and Peacemaking.*
Susan Thistlethwaite, ed., *A Just Peace Church.*

Cross Reference: Eschatology, Justice.

PENANCE (*See* SACRAMENTS/SACRAMENTAL THEOLOGY.)

PENTECOSTALISM

"Pentecost" is a term derived from the feast held on the "fiftieth" day after the ceremony of the barley sheaf during Passover (Acts 2), and the term "Pentecostalism" has been used in twentieth-century Christianity in at least two primary ways: to refer to classic Pentecostalism and to designate new Pentecostalism.

Classic Pentecostalism refers generally to a grouping of several conservative, evangelical denominations including the Pentecostal Holiness Church, the Church of God, the Assemblies of God, the International Church of the Four Square Gospel, and the Church of God in Christ. These churches generally stress the centrality of ecstatic *experience* in the Christian life. For example, they hold to the necessity of all believers receiving the "Baptism of the Holy Spirit," which occurs subsequent to conversion itself. Speaking in tongues is the objective testimony to the reality of this experience in the believer's life. For Pentecostals, the tongues experience is a duplication of the events described in Acts 2. Whether these tongues are recognizable foreign languages (as Acts 2 suggests) or whether they are unintelligible speech is a matter of individual interpretation and experience. Among most Pentecostal groups, the gift of "tongues" in worship must be accompanied by the gift of interpretation.

Pentecostals also emphasize other gifts ("charismata"), such as healing and prophetic utterances. Like many other evangelical denominations, Pentecostals hold to a plenary view of the inspiration of scripture, salvation by conversion, and a literal acceptance of the miracles and the bodily resurrection of Jesus. Thus, in worship, it is the occasional utterance ("message from the Lord"), which may be in language readily understandable or in a "tongue," that distinguishes Pentecostal worshipers from their evangelistic non-Pentecostal counterparts.

The beginnings of the Pentecostal movement in the United States are usually traced to Topeka, Kansas, where, in 1901, a former Methodist minister, C. F. Parham, received the Baptism of the Holy Spirit. Many of the initial converts to the Pentecostal movement came from a splinter group within Methodism that stressed complete sanctification (holiness). The fledgling movement gained national and international prominence through the Pentecostal revival at the Azusa Street Mission in Los Angeles around 1906 to 1909, and most Pentecostal groups trace their origin to it.

Although the theological characteristics of the classic Pentecostal groups began to appear within the denominations of mainline Protestantism early in the twentieth century, the event that is regarded as the beginning of the "new" Pentecostalism did not occur until April 1960, when the Reverend Dennis Bennett confided in his upper-middle class Episcopal congregation in Van Nuys, California, that he had received the Baptism of the Holy Spirit and that for some time he had been speaking in tongues. "New Pentecostal" and "charismatic Christian" were used to refer to those non-Pentecostal Christians who had embraced a theology formerly equated only with the denominational or confessional Pentecostal traditions.

In the years following Bennett's "confession" the charismatic movement made inroads into virtually every mainline denomination, including the Catholic and Eastern Orthodox churches. The start of the charismatic movement in American Catholicism is usually identified with the faculty-student prayer study at Duquesne University in 1967. Through the work of mission and evangelistic groups such as the Full Gospel Business Men's Fellowship International (FGBMFI)—an interdenominational organization of laypeople founded in 1961 by Demos Shakarian—the spread of the charismatic movement was phenomenal. By 1988 the FGBMFI boasted chapters in eighty-seven countries.

With the charismatic movement firmly entrenched in both the United States and around the world by the 1980s, systematic and extensive reflection and critique of the movement began to take place. Some interpreters believe it is destined to be regarded as the most significant movement within Christendom in the twentieth century. Others contend that its novelty is already beginning to wear thin and that the movement must now address the social implications of the Christian life, moving beyond the realm of personal experience. On balance one certain consequence of the charismatic movement with which few would disagree is that the nature and role of the experience of the Holy Spirit will be taken more seriously throughout all segments of Christianity for years to come.

WATSON E. MILLS

Bibliography

S. M. Burgess and Gary B. McGee, eds., *Dictionary of Pentecostal and Charismatic Movements.*
Watson E. Mills, ed., *Speaking in Tongues: A Guide to Research on Glossolalia.*

Cross Reference: Evangelicalism, Fundamentalism, Holy Spirit, Popular Religion, Sanctification.

PERFECTION (*See* PROCESS THEOLOGY, SANCTIFICATION.)

PHENOMENOLOGY

In its clearest and most definite sense, phenomenology refers to a *movement* in German philosophy founded by Edmund Husserl at the beginning of the twentieth century. Its aim was to expose and finally to confirm the experiences of reality in the everyday world that serve as the foundations of all sciences. However, as a century-long movement, phenomenology has come to mean more than this. From the very beginning, Husserl's philosophical program of a "rigorously scientific philosophy" oriented toward the cognitive foundations of all the sciences was questioned, corrected, extended, and appropriated for other agendas.

Accordingly, phenomenology can best be set forth in two quite different senses: first, as a way of thinking and inquiry, more or less described in the original phase; and second, as an umbrella term for a variety of movements, most of which originated in Europe and which have some continuity with and historical dependence on the phenomenology of Husserl.

Phenomenology As a Way of Thinking. In academic philosophy, phenomenology is a certain way of constructing philosophy. However, as a "way of thinking" (reflecting), phenomenology can also occur outside philosophy in other disciplines; in theology, literary criticism, and religious studies. Expressed negatively, phenomenology is a way of thinking toward or about things that attempts to avoid as much as possible the ever-present tendency to transpose things subjectively into what we want them to be, thus, obscuring their objective features and functions. Phenomenology searches for the attitude, perspective, method, and language that would best permit something to display its distinctive, actual reality. For example, if I am persuaded in advance that all living things are "really" machines, I will conclude that human beings have no freedom, not on the basis of examining human beings but on the basis of that prejudged principle. A phenomenological approach to the question of human freedom would try to settle the matter not by a principle brought to the issue (e.g., "all living things are machines") but by attending to what human beings show themselves to be. In the original Husserlian phase of phenomenology, this "objective" side was expressed in such phrases as "to the things themselves," "the intuitive grasp of what is essential," and "philosophy as a rigorous science."

On the other hand, the only way we human beings experience anything is *as human beings.* And to experience something is not simply to have one of our senses (eyes, ears) altered by an external cause; it is to apprehend a *meaning.* An apprehended coffee cup is a different set of meanings (shape, function, appearance as a whole, grade of importance, beauty, etc.) from that of an apprehended kitten (shape, function, etc.). To grasp the comprehensive entity "nation" and the abstract entity "triangle" is to grasp not just different objects but different sets of meanings. These different sets of meanings arise with the *specific way we experience* different things. Thus, to apprehend how things display themselves (the objective side) is at the same time to apprehend how or in what way they are experienced. The phenomenological "way of thinking" then is an attempt to understand and describe *things as experienced.* This way of thinking is neither merely subjective (making things into whatever we want or project) nor merely objective (pretending we know things over and above our modes of experience). In the early phase of phenomenology, the experiential side was expressed in such phrases as "meaning-constituting acts," "intentional consciousness," and "life-world."

Anything that appears (a phenomenon) can be interrogated using this way of thinking. Hence, some theologians, philosophers, and historians of religion direct this way of thinking at such things as religion itself, belief, the community of faith, and even (in a strange way) the sacred.

Phenomenology As a Historical Movement. Theologies that formulate theological method *as* a phenomenological way of thinking are rare. That is to say, the early Husserlian phase of phenomenology has rarely been extensively and directly appropriated by theologians. Phenomenology has influenced theology, but less by way of its original "transcendental" or even "essence analysis" form as by way of the many historical turns phenomenology took beginning with Heidegger's *Being and Time* (1927). To study phenomenology is to study the many texts of a hundred-year-long and very diverse movement. This history includes at least four important "turns" or shifts onto new ground away from Husserl's original focus on problems of grounding human *knowledge*. The four developments are: the turn to human *existence* and the ontology of human being-in-the-world (M. Heidegger, J.-P. Sartre); the turn to *language* and the rise of phenomenological hermeneutics (H. G. Gadamer, P. Ricoeur); the turn to *history and the social* (A. Schütz, the Frankfort School, and E. Levinas); and the turn to philosophical postmodernism (Heidegger, M. Foucault, J. Derrida). Although the movements generated by these shifts are a great distance from the original phase and program of phenomenology, they nevertheless reflect in some way the phenomenological way of thinking; that is, they refuse to entertain any subject matter as isolated from the perspectives, circumstances, and activities of those who think.

Present-day theologies are "phenomenological" to the extent that they show the influence of the phenomenological way of thinking and participate in one or more of these historical shifts. The earliest (Husserlian) phase of the movement is present more in Catholic than in Protestant theologies, for example in Henry Duméry, Robert Sokolowski, and James Hart. Existentialist theologies (R. Bultmann) and Catholic transcendental theologies (K. Rahner) have drawn on Heidegger and the turn to existence. The turn to hermeneutics and language appears in the "new hermeneutics" (e.g., Ricoeur), structuralist, and deconstructionist theologies (e.g., M. C. Taylor). Phenomenological social theory appears in occasional ecclesiologies, theological anthropologies, and theological ethics. Feminist and liberation theologies have incorporated both the critical theory of the Frankfort School and postmodern hermeneutics and deconstruction. History and comparative religion (G. Van der Leeuw, M. Eliade) have incorporated phenomenology in analyses of religion as combining objective and experiential aspects.

The contributions, applications, and insights of these movements to theology are difficult to summarize. A few that stand out are the use of the phenomenology of personal agency to illumine faith (C. Cirne-Lima), moral agency and moral experience (J. Nabert, T. Ogletree), the dynamics of human evil (Nabert) and freedom (P. Hodgson), and the agent's openness to being as a precondition of relation to God (H. Duméry, Rahner, R. L. Hart); and, the use of phenomenology to explore the workings of myth and metaphor in theological discourse (Ricoeur), the fundamental event that generates moral experience (E. Levinas), the intersubjective dimensions of religious communities (E. Farley), and the contours of the experience of the sacred (M. Scheler, Van der Leeuw).

EDWARD FARLEY

Bibliography

Maurice Natanson, *Edmund Husserl: Philosopher of Infinite Tasks.*
Robert Solomon, ed., *Phenomenology and Existentialism.*
Herbert Spiegelberg, *The Phenomenological Movement: A Historical Introduction,* 2 vols. 3rd rev. and enlarged ed.
David Stewart and Algis Mickunas, *Exploring Phenomenology: A Guide to the Field and Its Literature.*
Richard Zaner, *Phenomenology and Social Reality: Criticism As a Philosophical Discipline.*

Cross Reference: Deconstructionism, Existential Philosophy, Experience –Religious, Hermeneutics.

PHILOSOPHICAL THEOLOGY

Although the discipline of philosophical theology is nearly as old as Christianity itself, the term has only come into wide use in the latter part of the twentieth century. Since the term covers a wide array of intellectual pursuits, four categories may serve as a useful map of the territory, despite the fact that they are neither mutually exclusive (some cases may fit into more than one category) nor exhaustive (some works in philosophical theology may not fit neatly into any of the categories).

1. Theological Foundations. This aspect of systematic or doctrinal theology deals with theological method and with the sources of authority for theology. It inquires after theology's starting points—scripture? tradition? experience?—and the proper method of developing theological positions from them. It might be described as theology's attempt to explain and substantiate itself. In Catholic circles "fundamental theology" is more often used to refer to the areas of inquiry covered here.

A wide variety of positions are included here, due in some measure to ecclesiastical differences (e.g., the Protestant emphasis on Scripture vs. the Roman Catholic focus on church teaching). Much variation, however, is due to philosophical differences. For example, heirs of Thomas Reid (such as the Princeton School) emphasized the similarities between theology and science and saw theology as a straightforward inductive generalization of the teaching (the facts) of the Bible. Heirs of Immanuel Kant, on the other hand, tend to begin with a universal religious experience and see theology's task as the expression and explication of that experience by means of Christian symbols. Hence theology is a hermeneutic rather than a scientific discipline. (A brief history of the development of this discipline is included in Francis Schüssler Fiorenza, *Foundational Theology* [1984], and fresh light is cast on some of the differences by George Lindbeck, *The Nature of Doctrine* [1984].)

To the extent that it concentrates on theological method as a method of reasoning, theological foundations relates closely to an important topic in category 3 below, namely, the question of the reasonableness of Christian belief.

A recent and important development in theological foundations is a response to the argument in epistemology (or theory of knowledge) concerning foundationalism—the view that a belief can be justified only by deriving it from some other belief that cannot itself be called into question. This philosophical position imagines knowledge to be like a building needing a foundation to support it. Since the 1950s, philosophers such as W. V. O. Quine have argued that foundationalism is a mistake, since there are no beliefs that can serve as the foundation. They imagine knowledge to be more like a net or web, where each belief is held in place by all the surrounding beliefs. Consequently, justification of a particular belief does not require finding some indubitable belief to base it on but only requires showing that it is strongly connected to other beliefs that have not been called into question.

"Post-liberal" or "postmodern" theologians claim that foundationalist epistemology led their modern predecessors to misconstrue the nature of theological reasoning, in particular by leading them to seek an indubitable starting point for theology. One option was to begin with Scripture, but this placed a greater burden on the doctrine of revelation than it could rightly bear (*see* Ronald Thiemann, *Revelation and Theology* [1985]). The second option, religious experience, has been criticized for its anthropocentrism.

One consequence of accepting a non-foundational view of knowledge is "intratextual theology," in which the coherence of the network of belief and practice is the primary criterion for justification. There is a strong affinity between narrative theology and this understanding of theological method. A second consequence may be a thorough rethinking of this part of philosophical theology. Discussions of theological method will continue, but they may not so often take the form of theological prolegomena. And of course the very name "theological foundations" will have to change if non-foundationalist theologians have their way.

2. Explication of Christian Doctrine by Means of Philosophical Concepts. Within this category it is necessary to distinguish two varieties. One is the systematic presentation of Christian theology within the framework of a philosophical world view. Thomas Aquinas's synthesis of Christianity with Aristotelian cosmology is one example, but recent existentialist theology is another. The second variety aims more at analysis than synthesis, using philosophical concepts as tools to examine and explain individual theological doctrines. An example is the application of relative identity logic to the doctrine of the Trinity. Relative identity logic is a set of formalisms designed to answer the question whether it is possible for a to be identical with b when we consider a and b under one concept (a is the same river as *b*) but not under another concept (*a* is not the same body of water as *b*).

Differences between these two varieties of philosophical theology may depend on different views of philosophy: In one view philosophy can legitimately tell us about the very nature of reality and how to live in accordance with it. In another view (for which we are indebted in some measure to Kant, but even more to British analytic philosophy in the twentieth century), the philosopher has no independent access to reality apart from science, history, and so forth. The philosopher must analyze and clarify the concepts used in other disciplines and in ordinary language. Philosophical theology of the systematic sort generally presupposes the grander view of philosophy, while the second sort presupposes the view of philosophy as conceptual clarification.

The most important recent development in this category of philosophical theology has been the waning of interest in systems and a remarkable growth in the application of analytic and other kinds of philosophy to particular theological problems.

3. Investigation of Philosophical Problems That Arise from Theological Claims. Topics considered here include proofs or evidence for the existence of God, the rationality of Christian belief or religious belief in general, the nature of God's action in the world, miracles, the problem of evil, the nature of religious experience and religious language, life after death, the role of divine law in ethics, and the problem of religious pluralism.

To distinguish this category, one could say (half seriously) that in the former category philosophers are doing theology while in this one theologians are doing philosophy. However, the important distinction to draw is between philosophical theology and philosophy of religion (a discipline that arose during the Enlightenment), since their typical areas of inquiry overlap considerably. It is sometimes said that the difference lies in the fact that while philosophical theology presupposes Christian convictions, philosophy of religion intends to examine religion from a neutral, objective standpoint. To some extent this is a useful distinction; it is common for philosophical theologians to assume various elements of the Christian tradition in their discussions. However, the modern hope that such matters could be dealt with "from the point of view of eternity" has turned out to be a false one. It is now widely recognized that all thought is historically conditioned and presupposes basic assumptions about reality (for example, that the existence of the universe is—or is not—self-explanatory). Thus it may be more accurate to distinguish the two disciplines according to their traditions and communities of reference—theological versus philosophical. The differences, in fact, are as often rhetorical as substantive; they employ different styles of discourse, and because they address different audiences they can make different assumptions. Thus Alvin Plantinga, who argues that belief in God is a proper starting point for philosophy, will never be mistaken for a theologian, and David

357

Tracy, who questions whether philosophical theology ought to be undertaken from a standpoint of faith, will never be mistaken for a philosopher.

The growing awareness, already mentioned, of the tradition-dependent character of all discourse may be the most significant recent development in this sort of philosophical theology. It has led, for example, to a change in the tone of theological discussions of world religions. It has led to a blurring of distinctions between discussions of theological method (category 1) and essays on the rationality of Christian belief; in a pluralist world one cannot talk about theological method without thinking of how one's theological formulations will stand up to scrutiny in other communities. Even discussions of the problem of evil tend to take account of the fact that there is no universal view of what constitutes blessedness or suffering.

As an illustration of the developments in the numerous topics here, a survey can be made of the problem of God's action in the world. This problem has long been understood as a question of how to reconcile the Christian view of God as the cause of all that happens with a scientific or commonsense view that events have natural causes. The problem became especially acute in the modern period when it was thought that events were determined by a system of natural laws: How could God have continuing intercourse with the world without violating the very laws that were established by divine decree at creation?

Two things have happened to alter discussion on this issue. One is that science itself has called causal determinism into question. The second shift is a new philosophical perspective on the problem. Whereas it was originally seen as a metaphysical problem—how to reconcile two kinds of causation—it is now very often treated as a problem in philosophy of action. Here inquiry begins with the question of what we mean in attributing action to an agent: What are the necessary conditions for saying that x performed act a? Then one can ask whether or how God's reported acts meet these conditions; for example, is there an analogy between a human agent acting by means of bodily movements and God acting by means of events within the universe at large? (*See,* for example, Arthur Peacocke, *Theology for a Scientific Age* [1990].)

4. Inquiry at the Interface Between Theology and Other Disciplines. As has been made clear, philosophical theology shares concerns with various branches of philosophy—most notably with philosophy of religion, but also with epistemology, ethics, philosophy of language, and philosophy of action. However, theology shares concerns with a number of other disciplines as well: anthropology and the other human sciences, history, and even the natural sciences. To call investigations of the relations between theology and these other disciplines "philosophical theology" requires some explanation. In general, whenever one steps back from a discipline and considers its very nature and the relations of that discipline to another, one is engaging in a philosophical task—philosophy *of* science, or philosophy *of* history, or philosophy *of* law. However, to do so in light of a Christian view of knowledge, history, and so on, makes it a theological task as well. For example, Wolfhart Pannenberg criticizes the standard views of historiography (theories about how to justify historical knowledge) as being too anthropocentric (rather than theocentric) and as being systematically biased against recognizing claims about the unique acts of God in history (see *Theology and the Philosophy of Science* [1976]). So here he engages in the debate about the nature of historical research (a question for the philosophy of history), and he does so from a theological standpoint. Hence, it is reasonable to describe his work on this topic as philosophical theology.

The most striking development within this category of philosophical theology is the increased interest in the relations between theology and the natural sciences. While conservative Christians, especially since Darwin, have been concerned about the relations between theology and science, Christians influenced by liberal and neoorthodox thought have been inclined to think that no relation is possible between the two disciplines, because they use distinct languages to describe different dimensions of reality. However, since the 1970s works on theology and the natural sciences by theologians with liberal or neoorthodox roots have been appearing in ever greater number. (Ian Barbour's *Issues in Science and Religion* [1966], and *Myths, Models, and Paradigms* [1974] have been two of the most influential.) These attempts to relate theology positively to the natural sciences reflect changes in views of the nature of theology, of theological method, and of theological language; they therefore relate closely to topics in other categories of philosophical theology. Furthermore, the content of science (as well as other disciplines) is sometimes seen to have an important bearing on problems in philosophical theology; for example, the change from deterministic to relativistic physics may have some bearing on the problem of God's action in the world.

So, in summary, we might say that philosophical theology deals in various ways with issues of faith and reason. As knowledge grows and conceptions of reason change, philosophical theology faces ever new challenges.

NANCEY MURPHY

Bibliography

Ian Barbour, *Issues in Science and Religion.*
————, *Myths, Models, and Paradigms.*
Francis Schüssler Fiorenza, *Foundational Theology.*
George Lindbeck, *The Nature of Doctrine.*
Wolfhart Pannenberg, *Theology and the Philosophy of Science.*
Arthur Peacocke, *Theology for a Scientific Age.*

Cross Reference: Apologetics, Epistemology, Language–Religious, Theological Method.

PLURALISM

The term "pluralism" is used in at least three senses. One use expresses the observation that there is an actual plurality of religious and other beliefs, practices, and so on in the world. For instance, one might speak of the "pluralism of Los Angeles," referring to the fact that many differing belief systems, customs, and so forth are to be found in Los Angeles. The factual pluralism or plural nature of world cultures is of course important, and this pluralism helps therefore to stimulate reflection on the truth of the Christian (or any other) faith. We could better call this pluralism "diversity."

The second meaning of the term is political: A pluralistic political system allows within it the free exercise of diverse religious practices and beliefs, as well as diverse political stances. A pluralistic society is one that does not conceive itself as enforcing a single ideology or faith. This sense of pluralism is equivalent to the word "secular" in one of its two main meanings. A secular state or a secular university is one that in theory separates religion from the state or university, and so it does not entrench some established faith or commitment. The other, quite different, meaning of "secular" is equivalent to "antireligious." Thus while Albania in the fifty years since the beginning of World War II has been a secular or antireligious state under Marxist rule, India since independence has been a secular or pluralistic state. India is highly religious and Albania (officially at least) highly antireligious. It is therefore easier to substitute the term "pluralistic" for the relevant use of "secular" and to reserve "secular" to mean antireligious, or at least nonreligious.

The third meaning of "pluralistic" is the most important. It refers to a theory of religions or, more broadly, world views, including secular world views. It is the theory, principally, that all religions ultimately point to the same truth. Naturally, it is affected both by religious diversity and by political pluralism. Let us then briefly note some historical developments both as to diversity and as to political pluralism or toleration.

Diversity was a feature of the milieu of early Christianity up to the age of Constantine (late 280s–337). With the eventual dominance of the church, diversity was discouraged, although it flourished in early medieval Spain with the symbiosis of Islam, Christianity, and Judaism. But the main period of Western Christian history was relatively monocultural, so that even in modern times Christian theology has tended, like philosophy, to be taught in a more or less exclusively Western way. Even the experience of other cultures and religions during the age of discovery was filtered through the lens of empire and colonialism, while the colossal achievements of Western culture—through the Enlightenment, the formation of capitalism, the industrial revolution, and the alarming but satisfying advances of modern science—gave the West a sense of superiority that made it easy to discount or underestimate the achievements of other religions and cultures. But during the thirty years from 1960 to 1990, something of a sea change in these attitudes came about, for three reasons: (1) the growth of indigenous Western interest in Eastern religions, especially Buddhism, Hinduism, and Chinese modes of thought and practice; (2) the resurgence of Islam, which could no longer be ignored politically, especially in the wake of the Iranian Revolution in 1979 and the Iraqi invasion of Kuwait in 1990; (3) the magnificent success of Japanese economics, followed by that of Korea, Taiwan, Hong Kong, and Singapore—all of which gave new weight to Far Eastern cultures and religions. And so a recognition of diversity stimulated Christian writings on other cultures and reinforced the impetus to dialogue. Accompanying these changes, but a less observed factor in the perception of diversity, was the growing shift of the center of gravity in Christianity southward—with the relatively greater importance demographically of Christians in Latin America, black Africa, and parts of Asia and the South Pacific.

The perception of diversity has had important effects on Christian attitudes to other religions, but also noteworthy are some changes in regard to pluralism in the sense of the separation of church (religious institutions) and state (governmental systems). In this sense of pluralism, there have been vital shifts, due to migration and other factors. The United States' and Indian constitutions legislate a pluralistic attitude, and other northern nations have moved in the same direction because of the increased presence of Muslims and other traditionally absent populations in previously Christian-dominated countries. Moreover, the political events of 1989 in Eastern Europe and the former Soviet Union have opened up a new lot of countries with a pluralistic ethos (though the Catholic church has tried to reexert dominance in Poland).

The modern realization of diversity has led to an increased Christian interest in theologies and practices that incorporate elements from other religious traditions. These are examined below. Historically, however, the churches have tended to suppress diversity, both during the hegemony of Roman Catholic and Eastern Orthodox churches up to the Reformation, and to some degree after the Reformation, when the principle of *cuius regio eius religio* ("of whom the rule, of that person the religion") came to be widely applied. Contributing to the erosion of such establishmentarianism were: (1) the emergence of the Radical Reformation, including the Anabaptists and others, which in arguing for adult baptism made faith a matter of personal response rather than governmental decree; (2) the growth of Enlightenment thinking in the second half of the eighteenth century, which called into question traditional beliefs and authoritarian practices; (3) the American Revolution with its consequence—a separation of church and state, stimulated by Enlightenment thinking and a history of settlement by non-conformists and Radical Reformers from Europe (Baptists in Rhode Island, the Pilgrim ancestors, the Society of Friends in Pennsylvania, and others); (4) the evolution of democratic thought following the French Revolution and, in Britain, the resultant emancipation of Jews and others; and (5) modern Hindu ideology (stressing a pluralist theology) and the creation of an important pluralistic state—India—in 1947. Until recently the old establishmentarian arrangement was carried on, oddly enough, through the imposition of secular Marxism as the official "religion" or ideology in the countries where it has been dominant.

Christians and others have proposed various responses to the challenge presented by alternative formulations of truth and practice. The positions are (1) absolute exclusivism, (2) absolute relativism, (3) hegemonistic inclusivism, (4) realistic pluralism, and (5) regulative pluralism.

1. The first of these positions has been common in many religions that simply see their own tradition of revelation or authority as true and that view other systems of belief as false—possibly as demonic. A sophisticated variant of this position is found in Karl Barth (1886–1968) and in Hendrik Kraemer's *The Christian Message in a Non-Christian World* (1938), which was in part founded on Barth's ideas. It had great influence because it seemed to resolve the problem many missionaries felt, preaching the Christian faith amid sometimes attractive non-Christian cultures and feeling the need for a theological basis for rejecting them. Basically, the Barthian position was that the gospel in Christ transcends religion. The Christian religion, like others, represents a human projection (this was in the tradition of Feuerbach, Marx, and Freud), though in response to the gospel. Other religions are considered *simply* projections, that is, without benefit of the gospel. What Barth and Kraemer neglected was that other faiths (e.g., Buddhism and Hinduism) could use similar arguments. Kraemer added the point that every religious system is totalitarian, by which he meant "organic," with each past borrowing part of its meaning from the whole. So even apparent similarities between religions are actually differences, because correspondingly similar items take their meanings in part from different items in each unique system. But this, though a partly valid insight, if taken too far would make comparisons between religions impossible. Every person's face may be unique, but faces can be compared. In brief, absolute exclusivism seems to fail. If every tradition insists on its own diversity and unique authority, the way is open for absolute relativism.

2. Absolute relativism relies on the complete incommensurability of differing systems, perhaps because one has to be an insider to experience the meaning of each. So every faith has no access to the truth of the others. A position of relativism was traditional in Jainism and might be deduced from positions such as that of D. Z. Phillips in his *The Concept of Prayer* (1966), itself influenced by some remarks of Ludwig Wittgenstein (1889–1951). But it is doubtful whether an absolutely relativistic position can be sustained, since it appears to destroy notions of truth and rightness.

3. Hegemonistic inclusivism sees truth in other faiths. Nevertheless, it still asserts the priority of the chosen faith. A highly tolerant variety was espoused by Nicholas of Cusa (1401–1464), who saw God's essence as unknowable and yet partially describable symbolically through conjectures. Although he held to the priority of the Christian faith, he acknowledged conjectural truth in other faiths. Some varieties may be limited in scope to particular traditions, because of the situation of the author. Thus, J. N. Farquhar (1861–1929) could allude to Christ as "the Crown of Hinduism" in his book so titled (1913): This was the statement of a liberal missionary position. There have been many writings in the second half of the twentieth century (e.g., the documents of Vatican II and the works of Karl Rahner) that deal with other religious traditions from an inclusivist point of view. This trend is reinforced, and in practice presupposed, by the rise of interreligious dialogue.

Throughout history and contemporary cultures, one can also find numerous cases of non-Christian faiths adopting a kind of inclusivist position. For instance, Islam has always given special recognition to peoples of the Book, namely Christians and Jews. This inclusivist recognition was made formal particularly during the Ottoman Empire through the *millet* system, which gave partial autonomy to these groups within the overarching fabric of an Islamic system.

4. Although it had hegemonistic overtones, the attempt by Swami Vivekenanda (1863–1902) to present a genuinely pluralistic position at the World's Parliament of Religions in Chicago in 1893, where he achieved considerable publicity and fame, was an important modern expression of "realistic pluralism." According to this position all religions are so many different paths to, and versions of, the one Truth. Vivekenanda expounded this idea in relation to the diverse levels of truth described in Advaita Vedanta (nondualism), in which the Ultimate is inexpressible and at a lower level appears as God (Allah, et al.). The differing faiths at a lower level use differing symbolism (Allah, Vishnu, Amitabha, et al.) of the One. Vivekenanda stressed the mystical path, which both in the Hindu and other traditions means that the Ultimate is ineffable. Since the God of worship is at a lower level, there were critics of his position among Christian, Hindu, and other theists not mystically inclined. In the Hindu tradition others followed the general position of Vivekenanda, notably Sarvepalli Radhakrishnan (1888–1975) and Mahatma Gandhi (1869–1948). His position was important in the framing and theory of the Indian pluralistic constitution, since it gave an intelligible place to minority religions such as Christianity, Zoroastrianism, and Islam. (Sikhism however had problems because it has been treated as a form of Hinduism.)

In the Christian setting, the best-known version of realistic pluralism is that of John Hick. In his *Interpretation of Religion* (1989) and other writings (notably *God and the Universe of Faiths*, 1973), he has outlined his "Copernican revolution," seeing religions like the planets, in orbit around the Real, rather than seeing them all revolving around Christianity. Each faith has its insights into the nature of the Real, which, however, is like a *noumenon* of which the empirical religions are so to speak *phenomena* (he uses here the well-known Kantian distinction). To the objection that one cannot "get round behind the phenomena" to see the Real, Hick responds that it is an inductive hypothesis, proceeding from the evidence of religions. It takes a religious, rather than a naturalistic or projectionist, view of religious experiences or the responses of humanity toward the Real. In brief, it infers the existence of the divine from the testimony of religious people. Naturally, absolute exclusivists committed to such slogans as *extra ecclesiam nulla salus* ("outside the church no salvation") will resist Hick's ecumenical realistic pluralism.

Not altogether different, but less extensively worked out philosophically and harder to fit into the data of world religions (notably Theravada Buddhism), is the personalistic pluralism of Wilfred Cantwell Smith, who sees all religions as striving toward a personally conceived Ultimate. An earlier kind of this realistic pluralism was that of William E. Hocking (1873–1966), for whom the Real was Absolute Mind.

5. Finally, "regulative pluralism" (where "regulative" is a term drawn from Kant) is the notion that while the differing religions have differing values and beliefs, they are undergoing historical evolution, growing toward a common truth. (There were elements of this idea in Hocking's work.) But that common truth is as yet undefined. This position was sketched by R. C. Zaehner (1913–1974) in his *Concordant Discord* (1970), and it is implicit in certain forms of religious dialogue that do not prescribe the way dialogue will end. It is found also in my own view of the evolution of religious truth (with Steven Konstantine, *A Christian Systematic Theology in World Context,* 1991).

Meanwhile, however, as a backlash against various forms of liberalism, there are numerous militant movements across the world that reaffirm a kind of absolutist exclusivism (Muslim Brotherhood, Hindu revivalism, Sinhala Buddhist nationalism, Russian Orthodox patriotism, Protestant fundamentalism, Jewish religious nationalism, and others). Nevertheless, because political pluralism is necessary for peaceful coexistence and although both realistic and regulative pluralism have attractions, hegemonistic inclusivism will remain the principal motif among theologians in the more liberal forms of the various religious traditions.

NINIAN SMART

Bibliography

John Hick, *God and the Universe of Faiths.*
———, *An Interpretation of Religion.*
Hendrik Kraemer, *The Christian Message in a Non-Christian World.*
Ninian Smart, *Beyond Ideology.*

Ninian Smart and Steven Konstantine, *A Christian Systematic Theology in World Context.*
Wilfred Cantwell Smith, *Towards a World Theology.*
R. C. Zaehner, *Concordant Discord.*

Cross Reference: Ambiguity, Apologetics, Ecumenism, Liberalism, Secularity, Silence.

POLITICAL THEOLOGY

Political theology does not intend to be a rigorous ethical theory; rather, it aims to provide a new paradigm of the character and task of theology. Political theology has worked particularly to criticize the other-worldly dimensions of Christian eschatology, to transform Christian concepts of God, to devise a political hermeneutic for engaging in Christian theology, and to outline a theory of the practice for the church in the late twentieth century. It seeks not to make politics the center of theology but rather to relate theology to the political conflict that is deciding the future of humanity and the earth.

Background. Today's political theology was initiated and shaped in Germany in the late 1960s by the Catholic theologian Johannes B. Metz and the Protestant theologian Jürgen Moltmann, with important additions by Helmut Peukert and Dorothee Soelle. Other theologians who have contributed significantly to political theology are J. Deotis Roberts, John B. Cobb, Jr., Matthew Lamb, and M. Douglas Meeks in the United States, José Míguez Bonino in Argentina, Charles Davis in Canada, Alfredo Fierro in Spain, and Alistair Kee in Great Britain. Political theology has been influential in the development of Latin American liberation theology, and black theology in Africa and North America.

In the late 1960s, Moltmann and Metz considered politics to be the "all-inclusive" horizon of humanity. Politics had become the destiny of the human race, but politics had not become truly human in a world threatened by possible nuclear holocaust. In this situation, political theology has argued that the church should join the common struggle of all humanity for a common future. Indeed the very character of Christian theology should contribute to the search for possible human cooperation to realize hopeful historical possibilities in the face of a threatening apocalyptic future.

The background of political theology lies in the theology of secularity. Both Metz (following Karl Rahner) and Moltmann (following Dietrich Bonhoeffer) began with the assumption that theology should not oppose secularity since secularity—emerging out of the hopeful Enlightenment promises of autonomy, maturity, and responsibility—is a human affirmation of God's creation and the incarnation of God. Secularization thus frees the world from theo-political control of the church and religious control of politics.

But under the influence of revisionist Marxists such as Ernst Bloch, Theodor

W. Adorno, Max Horkheimer, and Jürgen Habermas (the last three associated with the Frankfort School of Social Criticism), Metz and Moltmann devised a new theological bearing that placed the dialectic between eschatology and history at the heart of theology and thus made a qualitative step beyond the theology of secularity. Secularity had to be questioned precisely at the point of its deepest faith and most compelling promise, namely, progress. Political theology has sought to undermine the uncritical acceptance of the Enlightenment promises as if they had been realized, when in point of fact they are at best still promises and at worst distorted.

Inspired by the writings of the young Marx, political theologians have found in humanistic Marxism some of the messianic hopes that had emigrated from the church. The Marxist criticism of religion asks why society is so unhealthily religious, and the most widely known answer of Marx is that religion is an opium of the people. Religion numbs people to their suffering and makes them politically unaware of the causes of their suffering. Religion, according to Marx, decorates the chains of the slaves with flowers. But the humanist reading has discovered that Marx also recognized in religion a positive element. Religion is an expression of and protest against the real misery of humanity. Marx criticized the other-worldly eschatology that provided a merely illusory compensation for human misery and thereby helped to perpetuate the conditions that caused it.

Some parallels exist between the Marxist analysis and the political hermeneutic of the gospel devised in political theology. For one, political theology understands messianic Christian faith as a protest against real misery and simultaneously the imperative for liberation from political and economic oppression. Thus the new criterion of theology and faith is to be found in praxis, for unless theory contains initiative for transforming the world, it remains doomed to the status of a mere story of the existing world. Christian political theology as a theory-praxis must prove itself in the power to overcome the real misery of humanity.

In contrast to Marxists, however, Christians see human misery as slavery to sin and death and look to God for liberation from sin by grace and from death by resurrection. Transcendent and immanent hopes interact. Hope grounded in the Resurrection transcends all historical anticipations. And thus no revolutionary achievement can be made absolute. Hope keeps alive the will to transcend every realization of freedom, to resist resignation to failure, and to free from legalistic compulsion political work for freedom.

Transformations of the Concept of God. Following upon its Marxist analysis of the political and historical inadequacies of Christian concepts of God, political theology begins its transformation of the concept of God by using the eschatological perspective in which God is dialectically related to history from the future. Political theology's orientation to the future depends on the promises of

God that have already been given. What Metz calls the "dangerous memories" of the tradition mediate into the present the *eschatological proviso*. These memories bear the promises of God and enliven hope in midst of the irrationalities and oppression of the present. Eschatology uncovers the ambiguities of the present. The light of these promise-bearing memories discloses the present darkness of the world. History is provisional, not yet perfected. The *eschatological proviso* makes relative all present systems and makes clear the cruciality of historical activity in relation to God. Eschatology leads to a political hermeneutic that leads to a new political praxis.

Mediational in character, political theology concentrates on biblical narratives of God's involvement in the negations and suffering of history. The promise of God is uncovered in the resurrection and the crucifixion of Jesus Christ. The resurrection uncovers God as present in history and as the effective power of the coming reign of righteousness and peace. The resurrection reveals the future of God in the light of which the world's conditions of injustice are disclosed and judged. These conditions also suggest that the presence of God in the world—through resurrection—is one of suffering love. At the heart of political theology is its view of human freedom, which interprets the cross in the light of systemic sin and structural evil. The crucifixion uncovers God as present in history within the suffering of God's creatures. As such, God gives to the human being passion, the power of suffering love, the only power stronger than the power of nothingness. If the message of the cross and resurrection and of the kingdom of God announced by Jesus is the center of Christian theology, then theology must be pursued within the church's actual historical existence among the political conflicts of the world.

Political Hermeneutic. The resulting theological method is critical of other forms of theological hermeneutic. Metz argued against the Thomistic doctrine of nature and natural law because of its ahistorical character. He found transcendental Thomism, with its turn toward the subject, to be apolitical (*see* his *Theology of the World*). Moltmann similarly criticized the dualistic and static nature of an extreme Lutheran doctrine of the two kingdoms and the orders of creation and the individualistic and reclusive tendencies of various forms of modern existentialism (*see* his *On Human Dignity*). Political theology has steadfastly criticized the sequestering of religion, the narrowing down of religion to the inner life. As the mirror image of the Enlightenment's optimism about the progress of human behavior and understanding, middle-class religion strengthens the conditions of the elite's privilege over those who cannot benefit from the logic of progress and at the same time promotes the increasing subjugation of the elite itself to a life of fate without real choices. The point of theological hermeneutic can no longer be simply pure understanding. The task is not to explain the world but to transform it. As Moltmann put it, "In the past two centuries, a Christian faith in God without hope for the future of the world has called forth a secular hope for the future of the world without faith in God" (*Religion, Revolution, and the Future*, 200).

Political theology has provided a critique of the ways in which Western religion and politics have been falsely related. It has argued against political movements that use religion for their own ends and religious movements that merely legitimate political interests. Both political religions and religious politics make themselves available for human domination. But there is no simple solution to the problematic relationship of religion to politics, of altar to throne. History suggests that there have been "no states without gods and no divinities without states." Since being adopted as the state religion of Rome, Christianity has often served the raison d'être of the state by providing the cultural unity of the realm and the legitimation of power as if it were divine. From the time of the service of the early Christian theorist Eusebius to the cult of the Roman emperors, through the time of the elevation of Constantine as God's representative on earth, to the pre–World War II support given by Protestant and Catholic churches to the National Socialist depiction of Hitler as a messianic figure, to the more recent religious justification of the politics of the right and the left in North America, religion has been used for the political oppression of human beings. Politics takes over the roles and authorizing mechanism of religion. It uses religion for legitimation and stabilization of the present order.

On the other hand, the religious use of politics must be criticized. The church cannot become a political party, else it should lose its freedom to bring God's promise of the reign of righteousness to bear on all politics. But neither can theology and the church escape politics. There is no such thing as an apolitical theology or nonpolitical church. People of faith are always involved in social relationships and power relationships. The church cannot withdraw from the political realm. To do so would simply give a legitimation to the status quo. The church should exist as an institution of critical freedom, seeking in its mission to subvert the ideologies of class, race, and society. In this way the church constantly refuses to be a national, cultural, or ethnic power group.

Political theology challenges all theology to become aware of the ideologies that suffuse church and theology today and that facilitate the hardening of the status quo. The liberation of theology is at stake. All theology should begin with ideology critique through which theologian and church become aware of their actual political situation. Theology should ask the question, *Cui bono*, or, for whose good does it exist, whose benefit does it serve? Political theology's contribution to this liberation takes place in the foci of memory, future, suffering, solidarity, and praxis.

Theory for Church Practice. In its process of liberating persons and structures from political and economic oppression, political theology has sought to widen the church's view of salvation. Moltmann speaks of five interrelated spheres of oppression and liberation in which the messianic activity of the church must join all others who seek the dignity of human beings and of the ecosphere: the *political*, *economic*, *cultural*, *natural*, and *personal* spheres. To address the suffering in each of these spheres is to undermine the idols and ideologies that undergird the exploitation of some people by others and of the earth by human beings. In the *political* sphere, the idols of the ruling few must be replaced with democracy. The messianic contribution is the identification of God's power with the crucified one. In the *economic* dimension, the ideologies that, through property rules, exclude many from livelihood must be replaced with rules that put belonging to community and access to what is required for life above the accumulation of wealth as power. The messianic contribution is the identification of God as the triune community of creative righteousness. In the *cultural* dimension, the idols of racism, sexism, and ageism that define certain people as less than fully human must be replaced with the image of the triune God as the dignity of every person. In the *natural* dimension, the mechanistic denigration of nature and the body must be replaced with a symbiosis of the human being and nature. The messianic contribution is a view of God the Holy Spirit as immanent in nature. Finally, in the *personal* dimension, the despair, anxiety, and meaninglessness felt by the person must be replaced with hope and trust that open up the future. The messianic contribution is the forgiveness of guilt and the freedom from the fear of death that deliver persons from the life-destroying laws of self-justification and compulsion to immortality.

While insisting that Christian faith is inherently political, political theology has worked against a reduction of faith to political and social activity and activism. Countering the utilitarian moralism of revolutionary movements and achievement-centered values of society today, Moltmann and Metz have also devised extensive theologies of spirituality and play. Faith is not just a modality leading toward action, but it is doxology, the joy and praise of God. Likewise, theology is not just a theory of practice but pure theory, the enjoyment of God rooted in God's free love in creation and redemption.

M. DOUGLAS MEEKS

Bibliography

José Míguez Bonino, *Doing Theology in a Revolutionary Situation.*
John B. Cobb, Jr., *Process Theology As Political Theology.*
M. Douglas Meeks, *God the Economist: The Doctrine of God and Political Economy.*
Johannes B. Metz, *Theology of the World.*
_____, *Faith in History and Society.*
_____, *The Emergent Church.*
Jürgen Moltmann, *Religion, Revolution, and the Future.*
_____, *On Human Dignity: Political Theology and Ethics.*
_____, *The Crucified God.*

Cross Reference: Eschatology, Ethics–Christian, Hope, Justice, Liberation Theology, Marxist Theology, Praxis, Secularity.

POPE (See PAPACY, ROMAN CATHOLICISM, VATICAN II.)

POPULAR RELIGION

Popular religion is an ill-digested but intuitively useful category for describing a wide variety of phenomena that do not conveniently fit within a conventional descriptive framework. Like the Supreme Court in trying to define obscenity, one usually knows popular religion when one encounters it, but one may not always be able to isolate it conceptually. Perhaps the best general word for popular religion is "extra-ecclesiastical": It consists of religious expression or behavior that takes place apart from, and sometimes in conflict with, the kinds of theology taught in the seminaries, the worship conducted in the "mainline" churches, and the organizational structures promoted by denominational bureaucracies. Whether popular religion is revitalizing, destructive, trivial, or amusing depends very much on the perspective of the observer. In the following discussion, examples are drawn primarily from the United States, although the principles can be extended to the relationship between institutional religion of any sort and popular variations on its themes in any modern society. (The "folk religion" of premodern societies is a related but distinct topic.)

Another characteristic of much of what is usually called popular religion is a preoccupation with the achievement of temporal ends through supernatural means. This borders on traditional definitions of magic, as opposed to religion, and the sometimes dubious character of its manifestations has resulted in skepticism and, at times, scandal. Miracles—earthly events that seemingly defy the rules of scientific causality—abound in popular practice, and they are especially appealing when they result in healings, wealth, or other immediate personal good fortune. Other supernatural events, however, such as the imminent second coming of Jesus, are also staples of popular belief. Since many institutional churches, such as the Roman Catholic and Southern Baptist, entertain and at times even encourage belief in the miraculous, the line between "popular" and "official" religion is clearly a porous one.

Although a fascination with the supernatural is a general characteristic of popular religion, the particular forms it takes illustrate the symbiotic relationship between popular belief and specific, more formally organized religious traditions and communities. For Roman Catholics, the officially recognized cult of the saints—especially the Virgin Mary—continues to generate what the hierarchy regards as excessive, unauthorized, or otherwise suspect devotional manifestations. The appearance of the Virgin to several teenagers in Medjugorje, Yugoslavia, during the 1980s divided local clergy and bishops on the issue of authenticity. Although the official church has encouraged devotions engendered by a similar apparition at Fatima in Portugal in 1917, the work of the "Blue Army" (an organization militantly dedicated to promoting these devotions) in promoting such devotion in the United States in recent years has often annoyed American clergy through its highly conservative political overtones as well as its covert challenge to the liturgical reforms generated by Vatican II. The failure of these devotees of the miraculous to secede from the Catholic church and to create new institutional structures has kept their activities within the category of "popular" religion or piety rather than that of sectarianism, a phenomenon often rooted in popular ferment.

Popular activity within the more diverse and loosely structured world of Protestantism has been associated variously with the revivalist, fundamentalist, and pentecostal impulses in particular. Revivalism, from its beginnings in the Great Awakening of the 1740s and its scattered precedents, has been a popular phenomenon alternatively supported and resisted by the various Protestant denominations. Volatile by its very nature, revival preaching aimed at an emotional conversion has largely been domesticated since the more tumultuous days of Charles G. Finney and Billy Sunday into the milder preaching of Billy Graham, who now appears at ecumenical sites such as Notre Dame and Moscow. Graham's role as a preacher beyond denominational confines was filled as well during the 1980s by "televangelists" such as Jerry Falwell, Jimmy Swaggart, and Jim and Tammy Bakker, but the implication of Swaggart and the Bakkers in widely publicized sexual and financial scandals brought the impact of such ministries into eclipse. Revival preaching is now more likely to be used to reinvigorate local congregations under denominational auspices than to challenge institutional structures.

Fundamentalism and Pentecostalism both originated around the turn of the twentieth century as popular movements, although they eventually assumed varying degrees of institutional stability. The fundamentalist preoccupation with millennialism and the pentecostal fascination with miraculous healings—one of the "gifts of the Spirit" central to the tradition—have both resulted in considerable popular activity, as is evident in the careers of such dramatic evangelists as A. A. Allen, Oral Roberts, and, most disastrously, Jim Jones and his Peoples Temple. (Jones began his career as a faith healer in Richmond, Indiana.)

Yet another locus of popular religion is a loosely related series of movements including Mesmerism, Christian Science, New Thought, Positive Thinking, and the "New Age" enthusiasms of the later twentieth century. Although Christian Science is exceptional in its rigid institutionalization, other movements promising well-being and prosperity through correct thinking have been promoted in far less organized form through the work of "inspirational" speakers and writers such as Norman Vincent Peale and his informal successor, Robert Schuller of Garden

Grove, California's "Crystal Cathedral." A more evangelical version of the same message—transcendence of adversity through individualistic thought or devotion—flourishes in popular books by authors such as Peter and Catherine Marshall. Such works now form staple lines for leading publishers, and they are widely distributed through chain bookstores at shopping malls (which also promote "New Age" literature drawing on Native American, Asian, or occult sources) as well as "Christian" bookstores specializing in evangelical literature, Bibles, cassette tapes, and other devotional goods. Lives of Jesus, such as Bruce Barton's *The Man Nobody Knows* (1925) and Roman Catholic Fulton Oursler's *The Greatest Story Ever Told* (1949), have also been staples of mass-media-distributed popular religiosity, and have cut sharply across confessional lines in their appeal.

A variety of other religious phenomena might be classified as popular religion, including Native American revitalization movements such as the Ghost Dance, African American folk Christianity and urban "cults" (such as Father Divine's Peace Mission Movement), and civil religion. Each of these, however, has its own distinctive identity. Popular religion is a category best reserved for religious currents existing at the fringes of institutional religion and spread through the mass media rather than pulpits, Sunday schools, or seminaries. Its appeal is in its immediacy: It promises, and may sometimes deliver, results that the "mainline" churches are too prudent to endorse. Its forms change, but its basic contours endure indefinitely as a challenge to what Max Weber identified as the "routinization of charisma" and what Victor Turner called "structure" in opposition to popular religion's "anti-structure."

PETER W. WILLIAMS

Bibliography

Wayne Elzey, "Popular Culture," in C. H. Lippy and P. W. Williams, eds., *Encyclopedia of the American Religious Experience,* vol. 3.
Charles H. Lippy, ed., *Twentieth-Century Shapers of American Popular Religion.*
Peter W. Williams, *Popular Religion in America,* 2nd ed.

Cross Reference: Civil Religion, Experience–Religious, Fundamentalism, Pentecostalism, Religion.

POSTLIBERALISM (*See* DECONSTRUCTIONISM, POSTMODERN THEOLOGY.)

POSTMODERN THEOLOGY

In its most basic sense, "postmodern" obviously refers to what comes after "modern"—it suggests that an era which began with the Enlightenment in the seventeenth century, if not earlier, has now come to an end. For philosophical reasons, but also in the aftermath of the two World Wars and the Holocaust, we no longer share the Enlightenment's confidence that reason will provide a secure foundation for human progress.

Friedrich Nietzsche (1844–1900) stands as the prophet of postmodernism. When Nietzsche said, "God is dead," he challenged far more than religion. He denied that there is any single "truth" or "moral right" or "meaning of history." Martin Heidegger (1889–1976), Michel Foucault (1926–1984), and Jacques Derrida (1930–) represent further key stages of postmodern thought.

Particularly in his later work, Heidegger turned away from the tradition of Western metaphysics to a preoccupation with language. Language, in his view, makes a world, and it is in language that Being discloses itself. In a series of historical studies (of insane asylums, prisons, sexuality, and other themes), Foucault challenged the sharp lines we draw between sanity and insanity, reason and unreason. Any general philosophical attempts to make sense of the world, he argued, inevitably repress minority, non-standard points of view.

Of all these postmodern figures, Derrida is the most radical and the hardest to understand. He discusses texts in terms of themselves and other texts, raising fundamental questions about whether there is any objective reality against which the truth of a text can be measured, whether there even is a "real world" outside the text. At the same time, in "deconstructing" texts, Derrida makes wildly unlikely interpretations begin to seem plausible, challenging the idea that there is any "correct" interpretation at all.

The term "postmodernism" may be most widely used in art (especially architecture) and literature. In contrast to the sleek efficiency of twentieth-century modernist architecture, postmodernist buildings reintroduce decoration, sometimes in unexpected and even comic ways. They reject the idea that there is one correct way to design a building, and they deliberately draw our attention to their own status as architecture. Similarly, postmodernist fiction (Jorge Luis Borges, Donald Barthelme, and Umberto Eco are often-cited examples) is often playful and fragmentary. It will not let us lose ourselves in the story but keeps reminding us that we are reading a fictional text.

Writers like Mark C. Taylor (1945–) have applied Derrida and postmodernism to theological issues. Taylor would agree with Nietzsche that God is dead, but that does not lead him to an optimistic, human-centered atheism such as Feuerbach devised in the nineteenth century. Indeed, forcing a choice between theism and atheism seems to Taylor the kind of dichotomous thinking that good postmodernists should reject. Modern philosophy wanted to clear the decks of tradition, start afresh, and find truth. Postmodernism, Taylor says, is "historically allusive." There is no "objective truth"—"either God exists or God does not exist." There is simply a variety of religious texts, susceptible to a variety of interpretations—no "right answer"—and when postmodernists choose to believe in fictions, they will nevertheless remember that they *are* fictions. A/theologians (the word is Taylor's, and the typographical experimentation is characteristic) have to learn to play with texts and symbols, resisting the temptation to lay out constructive proposals.

The work of Robert Scharlemann (1929–) has elements in common with Taylor's. For Scharlemann one of the functions of theology is to overthrow our traditional questions. We should not think of God as one "being" among others, who exists or does not exist. We should not try to penetrate behind language to some other dimension of reality, but we should acknowledge that we live in a world created by language. Scharlemann's primary intellectual debts, however, are to Heidegger and Paul Tillich rather than to Derrida. Thus he at least keeps open the possibility that religious texts evoke something beyond themselves, and his style, while dense and sometimes enigmatic, is more traditional than Taylor's frequently playful and fragmentary works.

In 1984 George Lindbeck (1923–) published *The Nature of Doctrine,* which set forth a program for a "postliberal" theology. Lindbeck's position owes more to the theology of Karl Barth (and the philosophy of Ludwig Wittgenstein), particularly as Barth's work was interpreted by Lindbeck's Yale colleague Hans Frei (1922–1988), than to the tradition of postmodernism. Although some people seem to use the terms interchangeably, "postliberalism" appears to be a quite different phenomenon. But there are intriguing similarities.

Religious doctrines, Lindbeck says, do not function primarily to assert true propositions or to express religious experiences. Rather they serve as *rules* to specify the appropriate ways of speaking and acting in a given community. The doctrine of the Trinity, for instance, need not imply claims about the real nature of God. It simply specifies rules for what Christians should say or not say about God. Against those who interpret religious language as the expression of prelinguistic experience, Lindbeck insists that only language makes religious experience even possible. Therefore, Christians should not begin with our experience today, and try to fit the Bible into it, but let the Bible's language and narratives define the world, making sense of *our* lives in *its* terms.

In its resistance to efforts to "get behind" language, in its affirmation of particularity, and in its suspicion of universal standards of rationality, postliberal theology is "postmodern." It too recognizes that the Enlightenment is over, and it looks back to Barth, whose work reflects the postmodern crisis that hit Europe in the aftermath of World War I. On the other hand, in letting biblical language and the biblical world shape its view of things, it accepts traditional authority in a way many postmodernists would find anathema.

Taylor, indeed, would probably dismiss Lindbeck as retreating into premodernity rather than advancing into postmodernity. Taylor's critics, on the other hand, might wonder in what sense he is a theologian at all (and he might concede the point). Since postmodernism begins with Nietzsche's assertion that

God is dead, "postmodern theology" might seem a contradiction in terms, and we still lack clear evidence to prove that it is not. So far at least, the real theologians seem not quite postmodern, and the real postmodernists seem not quite theologians.

WILLIAM C. PLACHER

Bibliography

George A. Lindbeck, *The Nature of Doctrine.*
Allan Megill, *Prophets of Extremity.*
Robert P. Scharlemann, *Inscriptions and Reflections.*
Mark C. Taylor, *Altarity.*

Cross Reference: Deconstructionism, Imagination.

PRACTICAL THEOLOGY

Practical theology arises at the confluence of theological reflection and ecclesial action. It is critical and constructive reflection on the diverse experiences, understandings, and activities of communities of faith, leading to both phronesis and transformation. "Phronesis" denotes a practical wisdom that successfully interrelates the general and the particular. "Transformation" embraces not only individuals and their communities but also the world around them.

Some scholars contend that all theology is practical. The current discussion recognizes that perspective and hails the shift of interest in present theological inquiry from the quest for universally valid constructs, abstracted from any particular socio-historical setting, to the clarifying of situation-specific expressions of faith and faithfulness. Feminist and Latin American liberation theologians are particularly at the forefront in this reorientation. But this development does not nullify the need for reconceptualizing the category of the theological enterprise traditionally identified as practical theology per se.

The framework for most of the current reassessment was set in the early nineteenth century of Friedrich Schleiermacher, who characterized practical theology as the "crown" of an interrelated process of inquiry. Schleiermacher invoked the image of a tree to visualize the process: Philosophical theology constitutes the roots, historical theology (including biblical theology) composes the trunk, and practical theology the branches, leaves, and fruit. Schleiermacher emphasized the essential equality among these three dimensions of the theological task, and he worried that he would be mistakenly accused of subordinating the lower two activities to their more lofty partner. In fact, just the opposite occurred. Practical theology never was able to shake off the suspicion that genuine inquiry into truth went on only in the two more fundamental areas, in regard to which the "crown" came to be viewed as nothing more than the practical application of theological understandings already—and independently—obtained.

An influential renewal of focus on practical theology in the 1950s cast light on the other chief flaw in Schleiermacher's proposal, namely, its emphasis not on communities of faith but on the trained pastoral leadership within them. Seward Hiltner, for example, sought to unify the practical disciplines in American theological education around the task of Christian shepherding. He saw practical theology essentially as pastoral theology, and he sought to establish the scholarly legitimacy of the practical fields among seminary faculties. But the result was a concentration on providing professional church leaders with practical skills and techniques in ministry—what Edward Farley later called the triumph of the "clerical paradigm."

The rich ferment that characterizes current efforts to reconceptualize the nature of practical theology makes it a difficult terrain to map. The 1980s saw a widespread resurgence of interest in the subject in the United States, initiated particularly by discussions at The University of Chicago and paralleled by similar developments in Europe. The leading figures in America have included constructive theologians (such as David Tracy, John B. Cobb, Jr., and Edward Farley) and contributors from the practical disciplines (including Don Browning, James Fowler, and James Poling). From the wealth of disparate approaches, some general characteristics can be specified.

1. Practical theology focuses holistically on the entire range of dynamics that characterizes life in a community of faith. This focus is generating seminal studies in the variety and complexity of actual congregational life. It is also contributing significantly to a broadening of practical seminary education beyond the preparation of clerical professionals to embrace the pastor's equipping of the saints for their own engagement in genuine ministry.

2. Practical theology acknowledges the key role of praxis in the achievement of new understandings. "Praxis" denotes a dialectical integration of critical reasoning and creative action in a particular social setting, leading to both change and insight and calling for renewed engagement with the now-altered given situation.

3. Practical theology must necessarily devise a sufficient "hermeneutic of situations"—a "science of interpretation" that provides for today's situations what traditional hermeneutics does for the interpretation of biblical and other historical texts. This task entails discovering the categories and methods of "thick description" that will do justice to the complexity of lived experience. It also includes the critical exposing of cultural and ideological biases that participant-observers bring with them to the interpretative task.

4. Practical theologians will necessarily be open and alert dialogue partners with social scientists. This aspect is not a matter of pure receptivity on the theological side, nor does it define practical theology as one social science among others. It requires a dialectic of engagement in which the work of the various social sciences is critically appropriated. In this regard, practical theology is entirely in concurrence with developments in biblical and historical disciplines.

5. Practical theologians insist on being taken seriously as coparticipants in the construction of theological concepts. No theological activity is understood any longer to be undertaken in a vacuum. Circumstances and settings fundamentally shape theological understandings. What becomes necessary at this juncture is the effective engagement of "classical" and "practical" scholars in mutually informative and critically corrective inquiries into the very nature of what they seek to understand—what Tracy calls "mutually critical correlation."

The aim of practical theology is not only to understand the world but also to change it—and even to be changed in the process. The formation and transformation of persons-in-community, and of the environs influenced by them, are very much at the heart of practical theology's fundamental orientation.

DAVID POLK

Bibliography

Don Browning, ed., *Practical Theology*.

Don Browning, David Polk, and Ian Evison, eds., *The Education of the Practical Theologian*.

Joseph Hough and John B. Cobb, Jr., *Christian Identity and Theological Education*.

Dennis P. McCann and Charles R. Strain, *Polity and Praxis: A Program for American Practical Theology*.

Lewis Mudge and James Poling, eds., *Formation and Reflection: The Promise of Practical Theology*.

Cross Reference: Correlation, Feminist Theology, Liberation Theology, Praxis, Systematic Theology.

PRAXIS

A praxis theology is the critical reflection and action, in the light of faith commitment, that grows out of and seeks to contribute to the transformation of a social order, the creation of a new way of being the church, and the cultivation of a spirituality that is historically committed in the world. It is a form of reflection on the struggles by which the oppressed attempt to satisfy their innermost needs.

The term "praxis" describes a methodological option—a way of pursuing theology—that is based on the dialectic of theory and practice. It attempts to overcome the shortcomings of both unreflective activity and reflection that does not intend transformative action. Action is never self-explanatory; theory provides an understanding of action. Theory, in formulating the goals sought and the means to bring them about, also anticipates and predetermines action. Action, in particular political action, needs theory to be effective. And only when theory leads to the objective transformation of the world does it constitute praxis. The praxis method is not neutral. It assumes a particular content: the well-being of the oppressed—persons and peoples kept marginal from centers of decision making that affect their lives in fundamental ways.

All theologies have practical consequences, but not all constitute a praxis. Only the theologies that contribute to the enhancement of the consciousness of the oppressed and those in solidarity with them, that strive to create a more inclusive and just social structure, and that intend to establish institutions for enabling the Christian ideals of liberation, justice, and freedom can properly be called praxis theologies.

A theology of praxis is based on the tension and unity of the church's thinking (its scriptures, sacred teachings, and theological documents) and its responses to the conflict-ridden social reality in which it lives. In this setting, theological reflection helps to unveil otherwise hidden sources of Christian spirituality, the gospel, God's nature, and human nature.

Among the key motives for pursuing a theology of praxis is a renewed commitment to justice and freedom as essential elements of the evangelical message. A strong emphasis is placed on the God who is historically incarnated among the oppressed and who actively makes all human options morally and religiously significant. God not only hears the cry of the oppressed but also enables the creation of community even when it seems that community is not possible. The re-creation of society and community and the struggle for liberation are placed in relation to God's kingdom. A thoroughly religious spirituality—one that calls and nourishes the faithful to a full-hearted commitment to God's purpose and to serve the poor—is sought.

Praxis theologies contain at least five characteristics:

1. A theology of praxis is undertaken from the perspective of the oppressed and in active solidarity with their struggles. The reality of massive human suffering is the foundation of its radical critique and denunciation of society. When theory is consciously appropriated by the oppressed and sustains them in their struggles, it becomes an actual force. The oppressed themselves bridge the gap between theory and practice.

2. Theological reflection takes seriously the socio-historical situation and seeks to contribute to it. In many situations, it even achieves a revolutionary character. Theological words and pastoral deeds never disregard their socio-political content and consequences; in fact, sociological and political categories become an intrinsic part of theological reflection.

3. Theologies of praxis stress the importance of social analysis. They provide an analysis of the causes of oppression and of the ways that key institutions work. They also assist in the creation of alternative institutions and organizations, making their intent to transform the world more effective.

4. Theologies of praxis entail a particular interpretation of human nature. Humans are perceived as conscious practical beings; that is, creative praxis is determinative of our humanity. In all forms of conscious creation, humans are ultimately involved in self re-creation by transforming nature in order to satisfy basic human needs, by transforming social reality into a more inclusive and just order, by producing objects of beauty or art, and by creating theoretical systems that generate understanding of ourselves, the world, and our ground of Being.

5. The theology of praxis also implies a particular interpretation of the relationship between the individual and society and the radical nature of historicity. The theology of praxis makes the individual aware that socio-historical conditioning is not absolute. Society is not merely given; it can be changed. History is not fated; it remains open. And social development is possible, but it needs collective, deliberate, and concerted action. The choices made within history and society do not bring about the fullness of God's kingdom, but they do make a difference in the well-being of humanity. As such, they are meaningful. In this sense, then, the theology of praxis is a theology of history and a historically conscious theology. Praxis is particularly important today in the theologies of liberation (black, feminist, womanist, and third-world theologies).

ISMAEL GARCÍA

Bibliography

Richard J. Bernstein, *Praxis and Action: Contemporary Philosophies of Human Activity.*
José Míguez Bonino, *Doing Theology in a Revolutionary Situation.*
Rebecca S. Chopp, *The Praxis of Suffering: An Interpretation of Liberation and Political Theologies.*
Gustavo Gutiérrez, *A Theology of Liberation.*
Nicholas Lobkowicz, *Theory and Practice: History of a Concept from Aristotle to Marx.*
Matthew Lamb, *Solidarity with Victims.*

Cross Reference: Black Theology, Feminist Theology, Liberation Theology, Marxist Theology, Society, Womanist Theology.

PRAYER (*See* SILENCE, WORSHIP.)

PREACHING (*See* HOMILETICS.)

PREDESTINATION (*See* ELECTION, JUSTIFICATION.)

PRIESTHOOD

The nature, role, and history of priesthood within the Christian traditions are filled with questions. Christian language about priesthood ranges from rejection of its use for anyone other than Christ and the baptized community to theologies that distinguish priestly states within hierarchically structured institutions. Further, the meaning of priesthood is entangled with the notions of sacrifice in Christian worship, theology, and politics. This essay discusses the existing consensus, explores the controverted questions, and outlines a history of various responses to them.

In the New Testament, Christ is the only priest who has no successors (Heb. 4:14, 9:26). Although he is not of the priestly class or tribe, he stands as mediator between the divine and the human, having offered his own life in sacrifice. Early Christians, in interpreting the passion and death of Jesus, related the final supper and crucifixion of their prophet to the sacrifice of the Jewish passover lamb and the establishment of a new covenant (Mark 14:23-24). They understood this meal as an anticipation of the messianic banquet about which Jesus had preached in parables (Matt. 22:1-14). What was prophesied as a new covenant (Jer. 31:31) had arrived in Jesus. These New Testament images of Jesus as lamb, banquet host, and covenant-giver should be placed in the context of the speculation about the priestly and royal character of the messiah in Qumran literature and in the Gospel of Mark (12:35-37).

Around these metaphors, however, many questions swirl. What does it mean to call Christ the high priest? Is his role related to the worship in the temple? Is he a substitute for the priest in the Jewish Scriptures, his extension, or his transformation? What is the relationship between the heavenly worship described in the Letter to the Hebrews (Heb. 7:26–8:7) and the public worship and action of the Christian community?

In I Peter 2:9, the community itself is called a ''chosen race, a royal priesthood, a holy nation.'' In this phrase, Christians see their sharing in the one priesthood of Christ. All their ministries to the community flow from this proclamation. But if Christ's role is irreplaceable, then what does sharing in his priestly reality mean? Traditionally, this has meant that with the baptismal commitments of faith, all Christians become priests in the pattern of Christ—preaching, sacrificing their lives for their brothers and sisters, and becoming prayerful stewards of the universe. Their ministerial gifts are a call and a task to be performed for the sake of the reign of God.

Within later New Testament texts and in the immediate post-apostolic period, specific roles of leadership were associated with these worshiping, prophetic, and administrative functions. The presbyters (I Pet. 5:1-4; Titus 1:5; I Tim. 5:17; James 5:14), deacons (I Tim. 3:8, 6:1-7), and *episcopoi* (I Tim. 3:1) of the early church guided the community into institutional life in the second century.

The term "presbyter" (elder) became "priest" in English; the term *episcopos* (overseer) became "bishop." The differentiation of these roles, their hierarchical arrangement, and the emergence of the episcopacy as a single authority over presbyteral and diaconal assistants evolved slowly and diversely in different communities at the end of the first century. Only at the beginning of the second century do leadership roles in worship seem to be securely allotted to bishops and presbyters. According to the *Didache* (97–110 C.E.) and Ignatius of Antioch (c. 115), there was conflict about this development. The leadership of charismatic prophets (both male and female), however, eventually gave way to church polities with a single, monarchical bishop. Presbyters assisted as counselors and replacements for the bishop in rural areas; deaconesses and deacons contributed administrative services for the poor, the homeless, widows, and orphans; and they assisted the bishop at the rites of initiation. To interpret the institutionalization of the hierarchy and the monarchical bishop, scholars are probing late antiquity's understanding of civil roles, the social status of presbyters and bishops, and the nature of public religious authority and worship.

With the destruction of the Jewish Temple in Jerusalem by the Romans and the closing of the non-Christian temples, language about sacrifice in Christian circles was more widely used. Earlier, writers and preachers spoke about the "spiritual sacrifice" that was offered (I Pet. 2:4-10; cf. Rev. 5:10). Sacrifice was what took place in people's lives in imitation of Jesus' self-sacrifice. Jewish sacrifices involved the blood of animals and petitions for forgiveness; and in non-Jewish circles, sacrifices to the gods hoped for appeasement of divine wrath or apotropaic protection. Hence Christians did not appropriate language about sacrifice until they believed that it would not be misunderstood.

By the early Middle Ages, the celebration of the Eucharist became more and more narrowly focused on sacrifice, a reenactment of Christ's sacrifice of the cross. Priests and bishops were to offer this one sacrifice to God repeatedly so that its infinite merits could be given to the baptized, whose priestly status had been largely forgotten. Although theologians consistently said that Christ's one priestly sacrifice was sufficient for redemption, popular piety and clerical venality often turned the Eucharist (mass) into a sacrificial drama in which Christ was again victimized for the salvation of the world. The financial stipends received for the celebration of masses, originally meant to support the day-to-day living of the priests, became the monetary base for the considerable power of monasteries, cathedrals, and dioceses. This complex social unity of power, wealth, and religious piety was part of the scandal against which Luther and other church Reformers of the sixteenth century preached.

The controversies about what the New Testament meant by the priesthood of Christ became further embroiled in the politics of religious denominations and empires. Luther rejected any priesthood that was not that of Christ or of the baptized. Roman Catholics, Orthodox Christians, and Anglicans stressed, to varying degrees, the role of the clerical priesthood. Recent ecumenical accords have found some common understanding on the role of various ministries in the church, but they often disagree about what to entitle them or how to interrelate them. What counts as a legitimate or as an illegitimate development from the New Testament data remains a stumbling block to a common Christian understanding of priesthood.

All Christian traditions have begun to discuss fundamental issues about priesthood, often influenced by the concerns of historians and the hermeneutical suspicions of social and political theorists. (1) What kinds of authority derive from charismatic gifts in the community and from elected or appointed offices? (2) What are the relationships among prophecy, worship, administration, and community formation? (3) What is the nature of authority in civil and political communities, and what have been their effects upon the evolution of ministries and priestly or episcopal identity? (4) Can there be diverse community orders, reflecting the multiple cultures within a single church? And (5) What are the competencies appropriate for leadership and on what bases is there inclusion or exclusion of members from these ministries (gender, race, marriage or celibacy, sexual orientation, physical or mental handicaps, etc.)?

Theologians influenced by the cultural critiques of Nietzsche and Freud raise questions about the worthwhileness of priesthood and ministerial service in themselves. (1) What is the meaning of Christ's sacrifice of himself for his friends? (2) How in the postmodern world can self-sacrifice remain as generosity and not become self-victimization? (3) When is giving oneself away to another, dying for what one believes, truly authentic and when is it simply foolhardy, stupid, and self-destructive? And finally, (4) What is the relationship between the religious meaning of sacrifice and priesthood and its public, political embodiment? The debates over priesthood in the Christian communities pose foundational questions that perplex the heart and mind of the tradition itself.

STEPHEN HAPPEL

Bibliography

Raymond E. Brown, *Priest and Bishop: Biblical Reflections.*
Bernard Cooke, *Ministry of Word and Sacraments: History and Theology.*
Hans Küng, *Why Priests?*
Karl Rahner, *Servants of the Lord.*
Edward Schillebeeckx, *Ministry: Leadership in the Community of Jesus Christ.*

Cross Reference: Christology, Ordination, Worship.

PROCESS THEOLOGY

Although the term "process theology" is occasionally used more broadly, it usually refers to the theological movement based primarily on the "process philosophy" of Alfred North Whitehead (1861–1947) and Charles Hartshorne (b. 1897).

After having focused on mathematics and the philosophy of nature in his native England, Whitehead came to Harvard University at age sixty-three and quickly created the most extensive philosophical cosmology of the twentieth century. In *Science and the Modern World* (1925), he argued that our cosmology should be based on aesthetic, ethical, and religious intuitions as well as on science, and that scientific developments themselves were pointing away from a mechanistic toward an organismic world view. This new world view led Whitehead, who had earlier been agnostic, to an affirmation, on strictly philosophical grounds, of the existence of God as the "principle of limitation," which accounts for the basic order of the world. In later books, especially *Religion in the Making* (1926), *Process and Reality* (1929), and *Adventures of Ideas* (1933), Whitehead developed his idea of God far beyond this suggestion of an impersonal principle.

Hartshorne had formed his own philosophical theology considerably before coming to Harvard, from 1925–1928, where he served as an assistant to Whitehead. Although Hartshorne has had his own emphases and has even differed with Whitehead on some issues, he has adopted large portions of Whitehead's thought (*see* Lewis Ford, ed., *Two Process Philosophers: Hartshorne's Encounter with Whitehead*). He has given special attention to the idea of God and to arguments for the existence of this God, most thoroughly in *Man's Vision of God* (1941). His overall theistic metaphysics is expressed most comprehensively in *Reality as Social Process* (1953) and *Creative Synthesis and Philosophic Method* (1970).

Based on the thought of Whitehead and Hartshorne, process theology is one of the few types of theology in the twentieth century grounded in a metaphysical position in which theism is defended philosophically and science and religion are included within the same scheme of thought. The term "process" signifies that the "really real" is not something devoid of becoming, be it eternal forms, an eternal deity, bits of matter, or a substance thought to underlie changing qualities. The really real things, the actual entities, are momentary events with an internal process of becoming. This internal process, called "concrescence" (meaning becoming concrete), involves some degree of spontaneity or self-determination. It is also experiential. Actual entities are thus said to be "occasions of experience." The experience need not be conscious; consciousness is a very high level of experience, which arises only in high-grade occasions of experience. But, even though events at the level of electrons, molecules, and cells do not have consciousness, they have feelings and realize values, however trivial. The term "panexperientialism" can be used to describe this view, but it means not that all *things,* but only that all *individuals,* have experience: Things such as rocks are aggregates, which have no experiential unity, therefore no feelings or purposes.

This view provides a solution to the modern mind-body problem created by the assumption that "matter" is completely devoid of spontaneity and experience and therefore different in kind from "mind." Because the mind is different only in degree from the brain cells, not in kind, the interaction of brain and mind is not unintelligible. One can therefore avoid materialism's reductionistic treatment of mind and idealism's reductionistic treatment of matter, affirming instead the equal reality of the human mind, with its freedom, and of the rest of nature, with its integrity apart from the human perception of it. This resolution provides the basis for a theology of nature that not only reconciles science and religion (*see* Ian Barbour, *Religion in an Age of Science*) but also supports a religious ecological vision and ethic. Four features of the portrayal of nature are crucial for this ecological vision.

First, there is no dualism between humanity and nature. All individuals are said to have intrinsic value and therefore to be worthy of respect as ends in themselves. The anthropocentrism of most Christian theology, especially in the modern period, is thereby overcome. God did not create nature simply as a backdrop for the divine-human drama, and certainly not for human plunder, but cherishes individuals of each kind for their own sakes.

Second, unlike Albert Schweitzer and some forms of "deep ecology," process theology does not proclaim the idea that all individuals have the same degree of intrinsic value. A chimpanzee has more intrinsic value than a microbe, a human more than a malarial mosquito. A basis is thereby provided for discriminating value judgments.

Third, the units of which the world is composed are momentary events (not enduring substances), which constitute themselves by unifying aspects of other events in the environment into a creative synthesis. Relations to others are therefore *internal* to an individual; these relations are constitutive of what the individual is. One's welfare is therefore tied up with the welfare of one's world. This idea completely reverses the picture, pervasive especially in the modern period, of a world made up of substances whose relations to others are mainly external to them. Some have come to refer to process theology as "process-relational theology" in order to emphasize this point; it has also been called the "postmodern ecological world view." One implication for an ecological ethic of this point about internal relations is that it prevents the hierarchy of intrinsic value from leading to the conclusion that species with less intrinsic value should be eliminated to make room for increased populations of those with greater intrinsic value. The ecological as well as the intrinsic value of all things must be considered.

A fourth point is that the "others" included in each event are not simply the other finite processes in the environment but the all-inclusive process, God. God is therefore pervasive of nature, present in every individual, from electrons to amoebae to birds to humans. Each species is worthy of reverence as a unique mode of divine presence.

The point about internal relatedness can also be made in terms of perception. The idea that all individuals, including those without sensory organs, have experience means that sensory perception is not the basic form of perception. It is a special form of perception derivative from a nonsensory "prehension," which is common to all individuals and in which aspects of the prehended objects are taken into the prehending subject. This doctrine allows process theologians to speak of human religious experience as one in which God is directly experienced and thereby becomes incarnate in the experiencer. This idea provides, in turn, the basis for a Christology in which incarnation is spoken of literally. The task for Christology proper is to show not how God could have been present in Jesus, but how this presence could have been different enough from the divine presence in all people, indeed in all individuals, to justify taking Jesus as of decisive importance (*see* John B. Cobb, Jr., *Christ in a Pluralistic Age*).

Correlative with process theology's doctrines of nature and experience are its doctrines of God and the God-world relation. Process theology rejects the idea that the world is a purely contingent product, wholly external to God. Rather, God is essentially soul of the universe, so that God has always interacted with some universe, in the sense of a multiplicity of finite actual entities. Our particular world is contingent, but its creation involved not a creation *ex nihilo*, in the sense of an absolute beginning of finite things, but a bringing into dominance of new forms of order.

This position has special importance for the problem of evil. It implies that evil exists because all creatures have some degree of the twofold power to determine themselves and to affect others (for good or ill), which can be influenced but not controlled by God, and it suggests that this would have been a necessary feature of any world God had created. This position also implies that the great degree of freedom possessed by humans, which includes the power to go radically against the divine will, is a necessary concomitant of their high level of experience, which includes their language and self-consciousness. Contingency in the world in general, and freedom in humans in particular, are therefore not due to a divine self-limitation that could in principle be revoked now and then to prevent especially horrible evils. Process theologians believe that this set of ideas makes the defense of God's perfect goodness more plausible than it is in those theodicies that say that God does, or at least could, control all events (*see* Burton Z. Cooper, *Why, God?* and David Ray Griffin, *Evil Revisited*).

Implicit in this point that all creatures necessarily have the inherent power both to determine themselves (partially) and to influence others—a power that is not overridable by God—is a distinction between God, as the ultimate actuality, and creativity, as the ultimate reality. Creativity is the twofold power to exert self-determination and to influence others. As the ultimate reality it is that which is embodied in all actualities. It is thus the "material cause" of all things, except that it is not passive matter but dynamic activity, like Tillich's being itself. Unlike Tillich, however, who identified God with being itself, process theologians say that God is not creativity but the primordial *embodiment* of creativity. This distinction between God and the ultimate reality has provided the basis for a new understanding of the relation between the theistic religions, such as Christianity, and nontheistic religions, on the grounds that creativity is parallel to Buddhist Emptiness and Advaita Vedanta's Brahman (*see* Cobb, *Beyond Dialogue: Toward a Mutual Transformation of Christianity and Buddhism*).

Another distinctive feature of process theology is the doctrine of divine dipolarity. Whitehead and Hartshorne portray the dipolarity differently. Whitehead speaks of the "primordial nature" and the "consequent nature." The primordial nature is God's influence on the world in terms of an appetitive envisagement of the primordial potentialities ("eternal objects") for finite realization. This is God as the Divine Eros, who lures the world forward with a vision of novel possibilities. This is the side of God discussed earlier. The consequent nature is God as affected by and responsive to the world. Hartshorne speaks instead of God's "abstract essence" and "consequent states." The abstract essence has most of the attributes given to God as a whole by classical theism—immutability, impassibility, eternity, and independence, leading Hartshorne to refer to his doctrine as "neo-classical theism." But this pole, even more clearly than Whitehead's "primordial nature," is a mere abstraction from God. God as consequent upon the world, for Hartshorne as for Whitehead, is God as fully actual. And this pole, and therefore God, is in process and emotionally affected by the world.

Whereas classical theism, following Greek philosophy, equated perfection with completeness and therefore unchangeableness, Hartshorne argues that we must think of God in terms of two kinds of perfection. God's abstract essence exemplifies the unchanging type of perfection. For example, to say that God is omniscient is to say that God always knows everything knowable; this abstract feature of God does not change. But God's concrete knowledge does change because, given the ultimate reality of process, new things happen and therefore become knowable. God's concrete states thereby exemplify the relative type of perfection, a perfection that can be surpassed. Of course, God in one moment is surpassable by no creature but only by God in a later moment. The same distinction can be made with regard to other attributes. For example, God at every moment loves all creatures perfectly, wishing them all well and feeling their experiences sympathetically—suffering with their pains, rejoicing with their joys.

To say that God grows is not to say that God becomes wiser or more loving; it means only that, as new creatures arise and new experiences occur, the objects of the divine love have increased and therefore the divine experience has been enriched.

Process theologians have used the doctrine of the consequent nature of God to recover the biblical view that God responds to the world and in particular the view, symbolized by the crucified Christ, that God suffers with the world. This doctrine of the consequent nature has also been used to explain our sense that life has an ultimate meaning, even if there be no life after death, because all things are said to have "objective immortality" in God, who cherishes them everlastingly (see Schubert Ogden, The Reality of God).

One division within process theologians is between those who stress God's activity in the world and those who, like Hartshorne, give primary attention to the world's contribution to God. Some process theologians stress both ideas, giving equal weight to the two sides of panentheism as the doctrine that all things are in God and God is in all things.

The distinction between the creative and the responsive sides of God provides the basis for two meanings of salvation, one in which God alone provides salvation and one in which we must cooperate. On the one hand, we are taken up into God's consequent nature willy-nilly, so we are saved from ultimate meaninglessness by God alone. On the other hand, we are saved to the degree that God becomes actually effective in our lives—to the degree that we become "deified," as Eastern Orthodoxy says—so that we feel and act in harmony with the divine grace luring us forward; our salvation in this sense depends upon our free response. It depends, however, not simply on our free response in an individualistic sense, but on the response of others to whom we are internally related, because God is indirectly present in us through others insofar as they are internal to us, as well as being directly experienced by us. Furthermore, the ways in which God can be directly experienced by and present in us are largely determined by the ways in which God is present, or not present, in those around us. These reflections provide the basis for a strong doctrine of the church (see Bernard J. Lee, The Becoming of the Church) and for thinking of process theology as political theology (as in Cobb's work so titled). Although process philosophy allows for the possibility of life after death, as Whitehead recognized, neither he nor Hartshorne has affirmed it; but some process theologians do, so that the process of creative transformation through divine grace would not come to an end with bodily death.

From the 1930s until the late 1960s, process theologians devoted their attention primarily to three tasks: defending the need for a philosophical theology against analytic philosophers of religion and neoorthodox theologians; defending the "heresies" of process theology (especially regarding divine power and becoming) in conversations with neo-Thomists and other classical theists; and showing how

387

process philosophy can be employed to make sense of traditional Christian doctrines and traditional problems of philosophy of religion (such as the relation between science and religion and the problem of evil). The leading theologians of the early decades were Bernard Loomer (who is usually given credit for coining the terms "process philosophy" and "process theology," and who later came to speak of "process-relational" modes of thought), Bernard Meland (who concentrated on the theology of culture), Norman Pittenger (who has written some hundred books, many of which serve as quite readable introductions to process theology), and Daniel Day Williams (whose *The Spirit and the Forms of Love* has been hailed as the first process systematic theology). Among the next generation John Cobb and Schubert Ogden have been dominant.

Since the 1970s, process theologians have been bringing their perspective to bear on a number of issues of the times, such as liberation theology (Ogden, *Faith and Freedom;* Delwin Brown, *To Set at Liberty*), ecological theology (Cobb, *Is It Too Late? A Theology of Ecology;* Cobb and Charles Birch, *The Liberation of Life;* Jay McDaniel, *Of God and Pelicans*), feminist theology (Catherine Keller, *From a Broken Web: Separation, Sexism, and Self;* Rita Brock, *Journeys by Heart: A Christology of Erotic Power*), Christianity and Judaism (Clark Williamson, *Has God Forsaken His People?;* Bernard J. Lee, *Conversations on the Road Not Taken* [3 vols.]), Christianity and other religions (Cobb, *Beyond Dialogue*), biblical hermeneutics (Lewis Ford, *The Lure of God;* William A. Beardslee, *A House for Hope;* Beardslee et al., *Biblical Preaching on the Death of Jesus*), and postmodernism (Griffin, Beardslee, and Joe Holland, *Varieties of Postmodern Theology*).

One sign of the growing visibility of process theology in recent decades is the increasing attention, mainly but not entirely negative, given to it by evangelical theologians (Ronald Nash, ed., *Process Theology;* Royce Gruenler, *The Inexhaustible God: Biblical Faith and the Challenge of Process Theism*).

DAVID RAY GRIFFIN

Bibliography

Delwin Brown, Ralph E. James, Jr., and Gene Reeves, eds., *Process Philosophy and Christian Thought.*
Harry James Cargas and Bernard Lee, eds., *Religious Experience and Process Theology: The Pastoral Implications of a Major Modern Movement.*
John B. Cobb, Jr., and David Ray Griffin, *Process Theology: An Introductory Exposition.*
Ewert Cousins, ed., *Process Theology: Basic Writings.*
Marjorie Hewitt Suchocki, *God-Christ-Church: A Practical Guide to Process Theology.*

Cross Reference: Ecclesiology, Ecology, Economics, Evil, God, Metaphysics, Natural Theology, Panentheism, Science and Christianity, Soul/Body.

PROTESTANTISM

Protestantism is a worldwide Christian movement that took shape during the late fifteenth and early sixteenth centuries in Western Europe. Until its appearance, the Christian world was divided into the Orthodox East and the Catholic or Roman Catholic West. Protestantism produced a division in the West, leaving Roman Catholicism intact but diminished and leading to the rise of many separate non-Catholic churches. These churches and the culture they generated are together called Protestantism.

Protestantism was not immediately a global phenomenon. One philosopher described it as a family quarrel of northwest European peoples, since it had little success in establishing itself even in Mediterranean countries of Europe. It resulted from any number of efforts to reform the Roman Catholic Church, efforts that began in Central Europe—in German territories and Switzerland, spreading to the Lowlands, Scandinavia, and parts of France—and on the British Isles. In reaction, a concurrent Catholic reform came to be called the Counter-Reformation; its leadership successfully blocked the spread of Protestantism into Italy, Spain, and most of France.

In the late eighteenth and early nineteenth centuries, Protestantism's latent impulse to convert people and to spread led to a missionary undertaking. From the British Isles, numerous European continental bases, and North America, adventurous evangelizers took the gospel of Protestantism to Asia, the Pacific Islands, and Africa. They established beachheads and often gained many converts, especially under the auspices of European colonial powers, but they had little success in the Middle East and, for a time, in Latin America.

Today much Protestant growth is in those latter nations, now in their post-colonial stages. One twentieth-century form of Protestantism, a set of "Spirit-filled" fervent movements called Pentecostalism that often takes life through independent inspirations of charismatic leaders, is the most rapidly growing form of Protestantism in Latin America and Africa. This stress on the global spread of Protestantism and the presence of Pentecostalism underscores a characteristic feature of Protestantism. It is a dynamic, sprawling movement that can reform itself, take new shapes, and gain new converts without the impulse of a central authority such as the papacy is for Roman Catholicism.

Of the 350,000,000 Protestants in the world, North American Protestants number about 95,000,000. In Africa, Asia, and Europe, Protestants number around 75,000,000.

The name "Protestant" arose from the fact that those who signed a reform document in Germany in 1529 were thus labeled. Although the early leaders looked like and often were representatives of territories or nations that resented the political force of the papacy and the Italian territories, the theologians, pastors, and lay leaders defined their mission differently. They wanted to restore the pure, or at least purer, gospel that they believed was lost as the Christian movement changed from a persecuted minority in the Roman Empire to a persecuting monopoly after Christianity became the official faith of the Empire in the West following the fourth and fifth centuries.

Protests against Catholic misuses of power, Roman immorality, or, as they saw it, false doctrine and distortion of the gospel, would not have been sufficient to keep the movement going. Its preachers were convinced that the heart of Protestantism's positive thrust lay in that gospel, their interpretation of the Christian message. Almost to a person they would have agreed with Martin Luther, a German Reformer, that Catholicism had come to be an elaborate system that used its graded hierarchical government to create barriers between God and humans.

Protestantism wanted to remove these barriers. Some leaders spoke of the "priesthood of all believers" as a means by which people, still guided by ordained ministers (very few Protestants have tried to do without an ordained clergy), could have direct access to God. With that broken barrier, Protestants also stressed what became a "formal principle," that all believers should also be free to read and hear and interpret the Bible. This freedom did not necessarily mean that pure individualism reigned; Protestants read the Bible in communities of interpretation called, variously, Reformed, Anglican, Lutheran, Anabaptist, and more. But they had to assent in conscience and with reason and could not be coerced into accepting an officially interpreted scripture.

With this formal principle, which in the eyes of many made Protestantism a "Bible-movement," there was also a content or substance, often called its "material principle." Variously interpreted, this usually came down to the announcement that, though Catholicism expected that sinners had at least in part to earn or merit their salvation through observance of intricate and demanding or demeaning rites and obligations, the Holy Spirit through biblical authors instead had declared that rescue from sin and the gift of eternal salvation were free. Often picturing the sinner before the bar of God's justice, Protestants liked to say that the death and resurrection of Jesus Christ had brought a new reality to transactions between God and humans. Humans were saved by the activity of the love of a gracious God; they were "justified by grace through faith." Their good works should follow from this justifying activity and would not earn them divine favor. So Protestantism also came to be a "faith-movement."

What happened to ecclesiastical authority? This varied and varies throughout Protestantism. Some Protestant movements, such as Anglicanism in England and the Lutheran Church in Sweden, remained episcopal, keeping bishops in the line of apostolic succession, as they had known church life in Catholicism. Others kept bishops for the good order of the church, as in Germany or later in a reform movement within Anglicanism that came to be separate as Methodism. Presbyterianism, a movement of Reformed churches, was and is characterized by the authority of presbyters or elders, and, with many other Protestants, also works through synods, conventions, or other meetings of elected clergy and laity. And in Congregational, Baptist, and Disciples of Christ denominations, among others, the stated intent is that the local congregation is the expression of the church. These local churches, of course, can choose to form consociations or other means of coming and working together beyond the immediate area. In general, there is much more lay initiative and authority in Protestantism than in Catholicism.

Protestantism as a cultural movement, whatever the official teaching of its churches, turned out to be an impulse that accents what one modern scholar calls "the exalted individual." Some evangelical ("gospel"-centered) renewal movements speak of believers having found Jesus as their "personal Savior." Culturally, Protestantism also often gave rise to an individualism that, according to some economic historians, took the form of a "Protestant ethic" that was especially congenial to the independent and competitive life that went into capitalism.

The term "Protestantism," with its root in the word "protest," has always carried with it the notion that the churches and their members should engage in prophetic protest against the Christian church itself when it makes claims that Protestants regard as idolatrous. Usually this "prophetic stance" has been directed against Catholicism, but it is also advocated as a principle of self-reform for Protestants. Suspicious of accretions of power in the state or the church or the economic order, people are to be moved by the witness of the Hebrew prophets, who used the commands and promises of God, established in an ancient covenant, to measure how humans employed power and to cry out when there were abuses. In practice, of course, Protestants have not always turned this prophetic voice upon themselves and their own church governments, but the message is always there, waiting to be heard anew. Thus in modern America, Martin Luther King, Jr., was acting on Baptist and Protestant principles when he spoke up for the oppressed, against entrenched misuse of power in the state and failure to pursue justice in the churches.

Protestantism has gone through many stages, as the current growth of Pentecostalism suggests. From the viewpoint of someone looking back into world history, several stages stand out, and they can be conveniently if somewhat too neatly associated with centuries. The sixteenth century was a time of reform and protest, of ferment and eruption; Protestant movements sprang up as if by spontaneous evolution. In the seventeenth century many of these ferments settled down and congealed. Leaders constructed formulas and constitutions that picked up the scholastic and dogmatic character of medieval Catholicism. Stress was placed on doctrinal orthodoxy.

From the middle of the seventeenth through the middle of the eighteenth century, reactions took the form of the cry of the heart and a desire for more emotional expression. At that time, various Pietist, evangelical, and Methodist movements grew up under the auspices of evangelists, revivalists, or quiet nurturers of piety. Sometimes these created what they called "the little church inside the churches," but often they led to new schisms. Again, in reaction to Pietisms, some Christians in the later eighteenth century adopted the Enlightenment styles, with their accent on reason and progress at the expense of biblical revelation.

In the nineteenth century there were renewals of orthodoxy, revivals of Pietism, chastenings of rationalism, and an effervescence of new evangelizing expressions. At this time Protestants also gave some impetus to reform in the civil realm, contributing especially to the abolition of slavery in England and, in association with the Civil War, in the United States. Protestant reformist energies also went into efforts for temperance or the prohibition of the sale of alcoholic beverages. One set of Protestants concentrated on reform of vice, on anything over which individuals had control: profanity, prostitution, drunkenness, dueling, and the like. The theologically more liberal tended to reform through criticizing social structures themselves: Industrial capitalism was often singled out as a villain. The result was a group of movements called, variously, the Social Gospel, Christian Socialism, Social Christianity, and the like.

While these emphases carried over into the twentieth century, a fresh impulse sought to overcome the chaos of divided Protestantism. The result came to be called "ecumenical" (for worldwide unity). Among its products, some of them connected with Eastern Orthodoxy, were a World Council of Churches, many national councils, mergers of denominations, and federated or cooperative activity.

Protestantism predictably displays a wide variety of forms of worship. The Quakers or Society of Friends are distinctive as a very rare Protestantism that does not celebrate the sacraments. Most others, while rejecting many Catholic sacraments for being part of a system of barter with God, have kept baptism as the initiating act, often connecting it with the idea of being "born again" (in the more Baptist-minded churches) or becoming part of the covenanted church community (in most others). Protestants also celebrate the Lord's Supper or holy communion, but they attach various meanings to it. For some it is a memorial of Christ's activity; for others it means, as it does in Catholicism, that in the bread and wine of the meal believers receive the body and blood of Christ as a "real presence." For most Protestants, the proclamation of the gospel in the sermon and the congregational response in prayer and hymn-singing is the distinctive combination in worship.

The Protestant way of life finds both complex social forms and simpler personal expressions. Socially, Protestant leaders encountered the problem of how to govern not only the church but also the state, the civil authority. This problem grew out of the fact that in Catholicism church and state were somehow one. Pope and emperor, bishop and prince, priest and local official interacted, often contentiously, in a polity that united them. The question usually was, Which was the higher authority? Theologically, the church claimed to be, or at least claimed that it was on a par with the civil realm. Practically, since it was usually the bearer of arms, the state turned out to be. But Protestantism began to sunder the old ties.

In England, under the reform of Henry VIII, the church, as we have seen, retained bishops. The monarch became the head of the Church of England. In Germany the princes in effect often became the bishops, and the clergy seemed to be lower-level civil servants. Reformed churches in Switzerland, Scotland, and the Netherlands stressed lay civil authority but expected it to be responsive to churchly direction. In some cases, as in Geneva and Massachusetts Bay, the Reformed or Calvinist leadership effected a virtual theocracy, a "God-ruled" state.

From the beginning, however, there were impulses in much of Protestantism to go farther. The Anabaptists and other dissenters, often themselves persecuted by other Protestants, in many cases moved toward democratic polities and absolute rejection of the claims of the state in spiritual matters. Not until the late-eighteenth-century Enlightenment, however, did significant Protestant "establishments" move or see themselves moved toward "disestablishment." The classic case of this was the new United States, where nine of the thirteen original colonies had had an established church. The Constitution of 1787, with its Bill of Rights in 1789, effectively took the Congress out of the church-establishing business, and in the course of time the states fell into line. Thus in the United States and eventually elsewhere most Protestants adopted as a fundamental tenet of their faith "the separation of church and state." In any case, vital Protestantisms have a great interest in proclaiming and protecting religious liberty.

In personal life, Protestantism has stressed the voluntary character of response. That is, the justified sinners who make up the church, now freed of the obligation to please God and merit salvation through good works, have been expected to make "faith active in love." Protestants have been enjoined so consistently to follow their faith with good works that they are often seen by others as "do-gooders." That is, their leadership, be it in church or school (often Sunday school) or home, has combined evangelical nurture with so many strictures and incentives that it can be, often is, or is perceived to be, legalistic.

In times past, although Catholicism through its sacramental system often tolerated or encouraged the life of fiesta, siesta, and carnival, Protestantism was suspicious of secular celebration. Instead, through a doctrine of "vocation" or calling, in which each believer was, before God, on an equal plane (originally with priests and monks and nuns), they were all expected to serve God in their daily walks and ways. This meant that they were to take responsibility for the stewardship of the earth. In the economic realm they were to work hard, waste not at all, earn much, give an accounting of themselves, and—since such a way of life tended to have an economic yield—be generous in giving for church and human need. Voluntary associations, many of them existing for reform or social service, sprang up on Protestant soil and lived on in the churches as well as in secular societies resulting from Protestantism. As mentioned, to some economic historians the growth of Protestantism was concurrent with and influential in the rise of capitalism, though exactly what this connection means is controverted.

Protestants have generally been less productive in the visual arts than have Catholics, though there have been geniuses like Rembrandt, whose interpretation of the gospel was an evangelical expression. With music the ties have been more vivid; from Johann Sebastian Bach down to twentieth-century composers, there has been a tradition of formal music to match the folk music, black spirituals, and other popular expressions of hymnody. In literature giants like John Milton and John Bunyan have been seen as classical Protestants, and this Protestant expression in poetry and prose continues into the present time.

Protestants have built hospitals and encouraged health and healing while trying to provide interpretations of disease, suffering, pain, and death. By their proclamation of the resurrection of Christ and belief in life eternal, however they conceive it, they join other Christians in witnessing that the temporal order, in which they have such a great investment, does not exhaust God's purposes. They use that insight to judge a succession of temporal orders and to bring initiative to devising ever new ones or responding creatively to those that others invent—Protestantism being especially porous to the diffusion of secular societies and cultures.

MARTIN E. MARTY

Bibliography

Robert McAfee Brown, *The Spirit of Protestantism.*
John Dillenberger and Claude Welch, *Protestant Christianity Interpreted Through Its Development.*
George Forell, *The Protestant Faith.*
Martin E. Marty, *Protestantism.*

Cross Reference: Ecclesiology, Ecumenism, Pentecostalism, Roman Catholicism, Social Gospel.

PROVIDENCE

Beliefs about the divine origin, governance, and final disposition of the world are at the core of most of the world's great religions, including Christianity. "To deny providence *is* to deny religion," H. H. Farmer once wrote. Although still very much part of popular piety, belief in God's providence has, in the words of another theologian, "been in deep recession for several centuries" because of the impact of natural science, historical relativism, and the experience of radical evil in the modern world.

The doctrine of providence is closely associated with the doctrine of creation and is often considered a part of it. Paul Tillich distinguished between three modes of divine creativity: originating, sustaining, and directing. Although he identified providence with God's directing creativity, it can be construed to include sustaining creativity or divine preservation as well. The reason is that the word "providence" contains a double meaning. It comes from the Latin *providentia,* which means literally a foreseeing *(pro-videre)* or foreknowing. But a contracted form of *providentia* is *prudentia* (prudence), which means, in English as well as Latin, an exercise of sound judgment or wisdom in practical matters. Thus providence is a "fore-seeing" that is also a "seeing-for," a caring-for. Thomas Aquinas understood providence to be an aspect of God's prudence, and thus he stressed divine preservation and wisdom more than he did that of foreknowledge.

The deeply held religious conviction that God is the maker of all things and the provider for their well-being was elaborated in a set of doctrines that became increasingly problematic as they were refined. These doctrines included the claims that the cosmos is rigidly ordered into a hierarchy of being, from the material to the spiritual; that it is a closed and changeless mechanism; that history is a linear story of salvation with a beginning, middle, and end; that God exercises world governance on the political model of the rule of a monarch; that God is able to accomplish what God wills to accomplish in earthly affairs, either indirectly through the contingencies of nature and human purposes, or when necessary by exercising a direct divine causality in the form of miracles—the so-called logic of divine sovereignty or triumph; and that evil is part of God's providence and serves an educative, even salvific, function. These views, which constituted a theological consensus from Augustine to Calvin (though not without internal tensions of which the classic thinkers were well aware), began to unravel in the seventeenth and eighteenth centuries under the impact of natural science and historical consciousness. The primary theological defense was gradually to withdraw God from any direct involvement in cosmos and history, by turning either to a purely transcendent hope, or to inner religious experience, or to a special history of salvation cut off from world history. The unraveling accelerated in the twentieth century as the result of cognitive, ethical, political, historical, and ecological crises of unprecedented magnitude. Tillich goes so far as to suggest that today "fate overshadows the Christian world, as it overshadowed the ancient world two thousand years ago." It remains to be seen whether a new faith in divine providence can triumph over despair, meaninglessness, and terror.

Any reconstruction of the doctrine of providence would have to take into account the creativity, contingency, spontaneity, and freedom that seem to pervade the entire cosmos. Creativity is the fundamental characteristic not simply of God but of the world: So at least claim the process theologians, who have

395

pointed the discussion in a helpful direction. God is involved in world process in such a way as to influence, lure, persuade, empower it, but not to control, coerce, or manipulate it. John Cobb suggests that we need to rethink divine causality in terms of "real influence" rather than the necessity of a cause-effect sequence. Such an influence is often exercised in the form of a feeling, a presence, an invitation, a lure, not an overt action. Creatures may experience this lure as an eros, desire, or nisus that draws and drives them toward the realization of greater rather than lesser value; that is, toward greater intensity and richness of being. God may be thought of as the universal Eros that draws all things to godself. On this model, God transcends the world not as first cause but as final cause, as the creative power of the future. This power is not an additional factor in nature, history, and individual lives alongside finite factors, but rather is "the quality of inner directedness present in every situation" (Tillich).

How might we think afresh of God's providential presence in the three arenas just mentioned—nature, history, and individual lives? This is an enormously complex question, one of the most difficult facing theology today, and easy answers are not available. In regard to individual lives, perhaps providence is experienced at those times when persons find themselves empowered to go on, to start over afresh, after debilitating defeats, sufferings, or disappointments. This is the experience of good-coming-out-of-evil, without which it is difficult to sustain life from day to day.

As far as history is concerned, it may help to think of God's influence, persuasion, or inner directedness in terms of "shaping" specific patterns of transformative, emancipatory life. The shapes in which God appears in history are not simply individual human beings on the one hand, or a general influence or lure on the other, but rather specific structures of ethico-historical practice involving individuals, communities, and institutions. Today we must insist that there is no triumphal march of God in history, no special history of salvation, but only a plurality of partial, fragmentary, ambiguous histories of freedom. History itself remains deeply ambiguous, a tragicomic process by which fragile syntheses of values and praxis are achieved through confrontation and compromise, prevail for a while, then break down. The pattern of history is not linear but spiral, and the wholeness it achieves remains open and incomplete, analogous to the perfection of a work of art or an act of love. The goal of history, never attained but only approximated, might be described as "communicative freedom" or "boundless communication." Such communication involves a dialogical rationality that opens everything to question, dissolves all privileges, transcends all provincialisms, overcomes all distortions and concealments, builds new forms of solidarity. Expressed in a Pauline metaphor, it is the "wisdom of God," which destroys all "cleverness" and "boasting." Such wisdom is the manifestation of God's providence.

The metaphor of wisdom might be applied to the natural world as well. Here the wisdom of God manifests itself not in the form of communication, language, and freedom, but rather in the form of primal, creative energy—an energy that infuses and shapes the whole cosmos in its continual evolution and inexhaustible spontaneity. Toward what end? The enhancement of order and complexity, the anticipation of communication and freedom? Between these two forms of the wisdom of God—reason in history and in the cosmos—deep connections undoubtedly exist, but they remain largely unexplored.

PETER C. HODGSON

Bibliography

Thomas Aquinas, *Providence and Predestination.*
Langdon Gilkey, *Reaping the Whirlwind.*
Julian Hartt, "Creation and Providence," in *Christian Theology: An Introduction to Its Traditions and Tasks.*
Peter C. Hodgson, *God in History.*
John Polkinghorne, *Science and Providence.*
Owen Thomas, ed., *God's Activity in the World.*
Paul Tillich, *Systematic Theology,* 1:252-71.
Maurice Wiles, ed., *Providence.*

Cross Reference: Creation, Evil, God, Miracles, Process Theology.

REASON (See Epistemology, Natural Theology, Revelation.)

RECONCILIATION (See Atonement.)

REDEMPTION (See Atonement.)

RELIGION

Few other words and concepts have generated the breadth and depth of reflection, investigation, exploration, and disputation that "religion" has. Thinkers through the centuries have enriched the connotations that attach to it. Religion is a concept that has exercised people motivated by many different interests: Philosophers, theologians, historians, literary critics, psychologists, anthropologists, dramatists, poets, sociologists, and philologists are among those who have contributed insights regarding it.

Some who have contributed most to understanding "religion" have not characterized themselves as religious persons. Other contributors have insisted that they understand something of religion only because of their experiences of and within religion. Thus, neither "insiders" nor "outsiders" exclusively control all that must be taken into account in reflecting insightfully on religion.

Yet all agree that religion has to do with universal life experiences and the ways in which sense is made of those experiences and meaning is attached to them. These universal experiences constitute the field from which the perennial human effort to make sense of the world (or deny that sense in some instances) arises: birth, death; joy, sorrow; knowledge, ignorance; success, failure; love, hate; suffering, relief; body, spirit. This list indicates that matters of primary concern to religion are universal, because of the fact that no human anywhere past, present, or future lives without experiencing them.

The issue of universality also surfaces in another way: how humans relate to the universe. Human beings are not only social beings; they are notably capable of solitary and private experiences that challenge them to reflect upon the nature of the universe within which such experiences occur. When asked what is the most important question a person must confront, Albert Einstein is reported to have replied: "Is the universe a friendly place?" That question resonates with Alfred North Whitehead's comment that "religion is what a person does with his [or her] solitariness." Whitehead meant that it is in times of deepest disconnection, whether voluntary or not, from the immediate surroundings of which we are ordinarily conscious, that we may experience contact with something that seems permanent, valuable, and intelligible, and it is through this transformative contact that we seek to make sense of and attribute meaning to the hurly-burly of social and natural immediacy when we return to it.

Humans respond to these experiences in different ways. The differences come to expression in the sense and meaning attached to experience, and these expressions take many forms. In some cases they take the form of marvelously differentiated ritual practices. In others they become stories of foremothers and forefathers in their founding activities, which serve to socialize new members into the ethos and life patterns of the group that tells these stories. In yet other cases the expression comes in the ethical norms that are believed to be the bases upon which the good and satisfying life can and must be lived. In still other cases are creeds, to which intellectual assent is expected as a condition for participating in the group defining itself through such affirmations.

Other expressions are also used: architecture assumes importance in some traditions; music making, dance, drama, and other performative arts come to the fore in some; theories of government, education, and economics deemed most consistent with primary experiences are devised in others. When such expressions characterize and satisfy groups of people through periods of time, identification with and participation in such expressions constitute a religious tradition.

When some of these (and many other possible) constituent forms of expression configure themselves as one particular tradition, like the image one sees at a particular time through the eyepiece of a kaleidoscope, a strange but recurrent phenomenon sometimes arises. The claim is made by some participants that this and only this particular "religion" is *the* (not *a*) true religion. The occasional corollary of this claim is that all others are false religions. This exclusivistic tendency has been particularly endemic to the family of Western monotheistic religious traditions—Judaism, Christianity, and Islam.

In addition to the great variety of experiences that fall under the name "religion," the study of religion has contributed to making the subject complicated. In one respect, the recognition that many persons, whom some would call most "religious," neither think nor speak of themselves in such terms, is provocative. Characterizing such persons as "religious" is a description imposed by others who are seeking to gain a greater degree of understanding of (and, alas, all too often, to seek control over) the people being explored through the use of such an umbrella term as "religious." In such cases the investigator employs the term expecting that insight and understanding will be facilitated by looking at the lives, stories, and practices of a person or group of people through the prism of "religion."

Such methodical study expects to achieve an inclusive and comprehensive understanding of religion. Yet when the focus shifts from one person or group to another, different activities, attitudes, and beliefs come under consideration, and new or nuanced understandings result. If the first set of "findings" is brought into conversation with a second set of "findings," an incipient comparativism emerges. At the most rudimentary level such comparisons often seem insignificant; for example, some traditions encourage burial of the dead, whereas others encourage cremation. As the study becomes more sophisticated, however, the differences between burial and cremation may clearly reflect dramatically different world views and belief systems, and the differences may jar a thinker into new dimensions of understanding. In Christianity, burial has been traditional because of a particular interpretation of the hope for "the resurrection of the body." Further, there has been a close connection between concepts of the self and the particular body that is thought to be inseparable from the self. By contrast, in Hinduism cremation has been the typical means for disposing of the body in conjunction with a belief in the transmigration of the spirit that sees any body as the transient residence of something that is permanent and ultimately destined to be free of incarnation. Burial and cremation manifest profoundly differing estimates of the importance of corporeality, the meaning of selfhood, life beyond death, and so forth.

The thinker or scholar who employs the term "religion" (or some alternative that can be translated as "religion") as a lens through which to examine and reflect upon self or others may be held accountable for how narrowly or comprehensively it is applied. If, for example, one holds, as some do, that psychology and sociology adequately and exhaustively explain "religion," one will thereby dismiss all views that hold that religion has to do with the overflow and abundance within experience, the "Something More" (William James) that no psychological or sociological explanation can sufficiently comprehend. To be sure, humans are social and psychological beings, and much can be learned from and through psychological and sociological studies of religion. But when such studies are regarded as exhaustive, they participate in a particular form of rationalistic reductionism.

When religion is thought of in "nothing but . . ." terms, the view dissatisfies persons who have experienced "Something More." This tendency toward reductionism among certain scholars often leaves religious people suspicious of scholarly study of religion. Theories generated through such methods fail to cover the range of experiences of many persons who participate in religion. Further, scholars do not hold themselves accountable to the institutions through which particular religions are propounded and perpetuated. That distance and independence, so necessary in the academy, often appears to be arrogance and aloofness to persons active in and committed to the institutions of the religious tradition being studied and adds to their suspicion.

Because the recurrent testimony within religious traditions is to experiences that seem to surpass the limits imposed by certain forms of rationalism, some have moved the discussion of religion to the realm of emotion, or morality, or imagination. Such a shift implies an utter denial that rationality is the highest of human capabilities and, further, an insistence that the limitations of reason disqualify its proponents from adequately understanding religion. Pascal's aphorism, "The heart has reasons that reason knows not of," is celebrated in such moves. By acknowledging and reclaiming the role of emotion and imagination in religion, such thinkers seem to be more comprehensive in what they are willing to consider in attempting to understand religion. The challenge in such moves is to retain an adequate place for reason, even while being skeptical of its primacy. A place for reason must be retained simply because so many of the expressions that contribute to constituting a religious tradition take the form of beliefs and truth claims. Thus, if religion is to be understood comprehensively, the religious forms wherein reason is expressed must be examined using criteria appropriate to rational explanation without conceding supremacy to rationality.

Experiences interpreted as appearances of a god (hierophanies) and as revelations are special challenges in assessing the place of reason, or any other human capability, in religious experience. Certain experiences have been so powerfully transformative in the lives of some persons that they have denied any contribution of their own to the experience and have, instead, insisted that they were entirely passive in receiving a vision, a message, or the presence of Another. Upon reflecting about what conditions must pertain in order for such experiences to happen at all, they, and others moved by their testimonies, have sometimes concluded that the divine (by whatever name and in whatever guise) has both presented itself to be experienced and simultaneously created the conditions by which it could be apprehended, since no innate human capability is sufficient to accomplish such an apprehension.

From such a perspective one of the corollary conclusions is that "religion" is what occurs when humans attempt to achieve contact with the Other through the use of some or all human capabilities. In such a characterization the emphasis is on human initiative and seeking. By contrast, revelation is conceived of as the event of the presentation by the Other of Itself to humans, who are utterly incapable of making such contact through their own efforts. Such an argument has sometimes been employed by apologists of Christianity in an effort to differentiate it from "religion," based on a claim that revelation lies at the center of Christianity and that this central revelation differentiates it from all religions. Such a polemical view of religion is deficient.

Religion is concerned with ultimacy, with what matters most to people and before which they are willing to subordinate themselves, as they are unwilling to do in the face of anything else. Experiences of connection with ultimacy evoke diverse expressions, which typically aim to call attention to and recommend as desirable such experiences to others. For example, most religious traditions include initiation rites through which newcomers may come to participate in the ethos, community, and style of life of a group into which they have been admitted. Further, such groups recommend patterns of behavior implicit in the ethos into which the initiate has come. Patterned behaviors or rituals reinforce the sense of connection with the ultimate.

In some literate traditions certain texts are privileged by being regarded as expressions arising from human encounters with a reality other than and infinitely greater than humans, individually and collectively. Examples of such texts are the Q'ran (Islam), the Torah (Judaism), the Bible (Christianity), and the Book of Mormon (the Church of the Latter Day Saints). The challenge unavoidably arises to interpret the meaning of the privileged text for the new and changing situations of those doing the interpreting. Often, significant differences arise in the interpretations. However, one measure of the viability of a religious tradition is the degree of its capacity for multiple interpretations over time and even among contemporaries who differ from one another. One name for the wide range of thinking that arises in such interpretative activities is theology.

Traditional or nonliterate people preserve their collective memories through different (and very effective) means from that of venerating particular writings. Such traditions commonly require some persons to give concerted attention to preserving the inherited interests of the group. Those persons constitute one category of religious leadership the shamans, the priests, the elders.

The occasional critics, who insist upon the inadequacy of old interpretations and defend new ones, are often at odds with the established leadership. This second group may in some cases be designated reformers or prophets. Persons in leadership positions, whatever roles they occupy, profoundly affect the shape and course of every tradition. Thus, human agency at the beginning and throughout the history of every tradition is an irreducible constituent in understanding religion.

In the strictest sense, "religion," as the word that names some externally observable system of rituals, stories, beliefs, and cultural expressions, is a creation of the last three centuries. But the human impulse and yearning for and experience of "Something More," to which testimony is found from every age and every culture, presents itself with an undeniable givenness to any careful student of culture and history. Religious expressions are so diverse as to defy comprehensive systematization. Thus, simplistic and reductionistic definitions or explanations of religion are deceptive. And, however understood, "religions" are so numerous that they demand the most careful and thoughtful attention of anyone aspiring to understand human existence. Therefore, any scholar purporting to give an account of humanity without providing some account of "religion," no matter how inadequate, superficial, or unpersuasive religion is considered to be, gives rise to suspicion. By contrast, scholars making any effort to understand and include religion will bespeak a desire to be as comprehensive as possible.

JAMES B. WIGGINS

Bibliography

Emile Durkheim, *Elementary Forms of the Religious Life.*
Rudolf Otto, *The Idea of the Holy.*
J. Samuel Preus, *Explaining Religion.*
Wilfred Cantwell Smith, *The Meaning and End of Religion.*

Cross Reference: Civil Religion, Experience–Religious, Pluralism, Popular Religion, Revelation, Ritual, Society, Tradition.

REPENTANCE (*See* SOTERIOLOGY.)

RESURRECTION

The resurrection of Jesus was the heart of the early preaching of Paul, and it has been formative for Christian faith ever since. This essay examines the convergence of Judeo-Christian beliefs in the resurrection and briefly suggests its continuing significance for Christians today.

Hebrew Scriptures. Without any expectation of a reward after death, Israel's belief in God permeated its whole life, more so than in most nations of that time

(Ps. 88:5; 115:17; Isa. 38:18-19; etc.). For centuries, it experienced God's faithfulness in defeats and illness as well as in victories and health, until it recognized that even death imposed no limit for God (Ps. 73:23-26; Ezek. 37:1-10; Job 19:25-27; Dan. 12:2). Enoch and Elijah were exalted to heaven without death (Gen. 5:24; II Kings 2:11), but these were unparalleled exceptions. If ever people projected their own dreams of immortality onto a doctrine of an afterlife in paradise, this is certainly not true for Israel, early or late.

In Jesus' time most Jews believed in a resurrection either of all the dead (Dan. 12:2; IV Ezra 7:32-44) or of only the righteous ones (II Macc. 7:14; cf. Luke 14:14). The Sadducees, accepting only the Torah as Holy Scripture, denied resurrection (Mark 12:18; Acts 23:8). Some Jews thought that the soul would go directly after death to God or to some place of punishment to wait for (a reunion with the resurrected body and) the last judgment (Ethiopic Enoch 22; *Theological Dictionary of the New Testament* 9. 633-35). The soul might even ascend to heaven forever by freeing itself from all material parts, but if it were not pure enough, it would fall down again into a mortal body (Philo, *Heir* 280-83; *Dreams* 1.137-41).

Jesus. According to the first three Gospels, Jesus discusses resurrection only once (Mark 12:18-27). His answer is twofold: First, the life of resurrection is different from all our conceptions; it is inconceivable in human terms (Mark 12:25; cf. I Cor. 15:35-50). Second, when God gives Godself to a person so that God becomes "the God of Abraham, Isaac, or Jacob," death cannot limit this act; God is "God of the living" (Ps. 73:23-26). Jesus presupposes life after death and expects his own resurrection; otherwise all the sayings about his role in the last judgment would be inexplicable. Some interpreters think that he expected a Son of man other than himself (Luke 12:8-9) because he did not use a "first person" designation when using the title. However, speaking in the third person of one's experience with God was natural, as Paul also evinced: "On behalf of this man [Paul caught up to heaven] I will boast, not on my own behalf."

In the Gospel accounts Jesus never introduces his words as do the prophets, who claim "Thus says the Lord"; instead, he contrasts his authority—"*I* say to you"—to the word of God in scripture (Matt. 5:22, 28, 32). In his exorcisms, the kingdom of God has already come (12:28). What happens in his ministry is greater than that which occurs in that of all kings and prophets (11:11-14; 12:41-42). Rejecting him is worse than the worst sins of the Sodomites and Gentiles (11:21-24). Jesus forgives sins as if he were God (Mark 2:7-10). How should he expect a figure still greater than he? The predictions of his resurrection in Mark 8:31; 9:31; 10:33-34 may have been worded after Easter; otherwise the despair of the disciples would be inconceivable; but a word like Mark 14:25 ("until I drink it new in the kingdom of God") is probably an authentic saying of Jesus, and it is

403

consistent with his proclamation that the kingdom has come in his ministry and will find its completion in God's final acts.

The Proclamation of the Resurrection. The earliest formulas speak in terms of Jewish confessions to God "who gives life to the dead" (Rom. 4:17) and of God "who raised Jesus from the dead" (Acts 13:33, 34; Rom. 4:24; 8:11; 10:9; I Cor. 6:14; 15:15; II Cor. 4:14; Gal. 1:1; Heb. 13:20; etc.). Thus, his resurrection is first seen as God's act on him. Paul writes of Jesus "rising" or "coming to life" only on two occasions (Rom. 14:9 and I Thess. 4:14), and outside Paul, the designation of Jesus *rising* occurs infrequently (Mark 8:31; 9:31; 10:34; Rev. 2:8).

The significance of his resurrection to believers is mentioned in perhaps a pre-Pauline formula (I Cor. 6:14; II Cor. 4:14), in Paul's letters (I Thess. 4:14; I Cor. 15:22-23; Rom. 8:29; cf. 6:8; Col. 1:18), later (in I Pet. 1:3; Rev. 1:5), but not in the Gospels. The earliest church may have thought that Jesus' resurrection served as a sign of hope for the resurrection of all the dead (believed since Daniel [12:2]) and the end of the world. Paul still expected Jesus' second coming within his own lifetime (I Thess. 4:15, which is not really different from the allusions in I Cor. 15:51; Phil. 1:23-26), though he learned to reckon with possible martyrdom. The gospel account of the dead walking through Jerusalem after Jesus' resurrection (Matt. 27:52-53) may be a reminiscence of this first period. Some scholars even see in such apocalyptic hopes the beginning of Christian theology, while others point to theology's origin in the emphasis on present salvation by grace in the very first proclamation of the church.

The stories of the Gospels interpret the resurrection of Jesus as the beginning of new discipleship and mission, perhaps leading to prison and death (Matt. 28:19-20; Luke 24:46-48; John 20:22-23; 21:15-19). This new start under Jesus' lordship soon became the center of faith. An old Jewish-Christian confession, which Paul inserts in Romans 1:3-4, speaks of the son of David (Paul's only reference to David's son) who was "designated Son of God in power . . . by his resurrection of [i.e., from] the dead." As in Judaism (Ps. 2:7) "Son of God" designates the role of the ruler over God's people (starting on Easter Day as in Acts 13:33). "Jesus is Lord" is equivalent to "God raised him from the dead" (Rom. 10:9; cf. I Thess. 1:10). The too enthusiastic identification of baptism with resurrection to the new life (II Tim. 2:18) is refuted by Paul: In baptism we are buried with Christ, in order to *walk* in newness of life and *toward* a future resurrection (Rom. 6:4, 8; cf. Phil. 3:10-11).

Therefore, Jesus' exaltation to lordship is, in the earliest period, not really distinguished from his resurrection. Luke, perhaps afraid of false teachers boasting about their new encounters with Christ, limits his appearances to the forty-day period between his resurrection and his ascension (Acts 1:21-22). Paul is, for him, no "witness to the resurrection" (in Acts 14:4, 14 "apostle" means "missionary"), whereas Paul himself regards his encounter with the exalted

Christ as equivalent to those of the Twelve, although it was "the last of all" (I Cor. 15:5-8) and completely different from visions like that of II Corinthians 12:1-7. Early hymns describe only the exaltation of Jesus (Phil. 2:9-11; I Tim. 3:16; cf. Heb. 9:11-12 and I Pet. 3:18-22; according to the Hellenistic world view manifest in this passage in Peter's epistle, the spirits to whom Christ has preached are living between earth and heaven [cf. Eph. 2:2; 6:12]).

The Johannine Testimony. Believing in the risen Christ means also believing in the Christ who speaks after Easter in his spirit. The risen Lord shapes the Fourth Gospel and provides an understanding that the disciples did not have during the earthly ministry of Jesus (2:22; 12:16; 14:26). It mirrors "the whole truth into which the spirit guided" the church (16:13) rather than the wording of Jesus of Nazareth. Thus, the authority of this Gospel is by no means less than that of the other three.

In John 11:25 Jesus proclaims: "*I* am the resurrection and the life." In him, the life of God, which is life of another quality than human physical life, is present and enters human life wherever a person is reached by his message: "Whoever lives and believes in me shall never die," since God cannot die. John often emphasizes that the believer "*has* eternal life" (e.g., 5:24; cf. Col. 2:12; 3:1), without, however, forgetting that there will be a fulfillment beyond our death: "Though he die, yet shall he live" (11:25). Even if the references to the last day (5:28-29; 6:39, 51-58; 12:48) were added later (either by the author himself or by one of his disciples), as many think, John certainly speaks of a final perfection in the future (cf. 12:25; 17:24).

In the book of Revelation, the term "resurrection" appears only in 20:5-6. Whether this "first resurrection" to a thousand years of reigning with Christ includes only martyrs or all believers is disputed. Typically, in 20:13 the term "resurrection" is no longer used, since it designates, in the wake of Jesus' resurrection, usually the final salvation of believers.

The Easter Event. The resurrection of Jesus is described nowhere in the New Testament. The oldest report is 1 Corinthians 15:5-8, with verse 5 at least belonging to a formula that Paul received in Antioch or Jerusalem (v. 3). In view of Paul's visits in Jerusalem (Gal. 1:18-19; 2:1-10), it cannot be basically different from the tradition there, which affirmed that Peter and the Twelve had seen the risen Christ (I Cor. 15:5). Paul adds the phrases that those who saw Christ included "more than five hundred at one time," James and "all the apostles," a larger group, including Junia (a female name [Rom. 16:7; cf. Phil. 4:3, which also includes women]), and finally himself. Paul knows almost all of these witnesses personally. One cannot tone down the phrase "was seen by" (usually translated "appeared to") with reference to Genesis 12:7; 17:1; 18:1; 20:2, 24, and other

405

passages (not emphasizing the vision), since I Corinthians 9:1; Mark 16:7; John 20:18, 25, 29 (cf. Acts 26:13-16) and all the stories of the appearances show that I Corinthians 15 speaks of a real seeing of the risen Jesus. Of course, this is no "proof" of his resurrection; it could have been hallucination, though this would be difficult to believe. That which is historically demonstrable is the transformation wrought among those who had witnessed the resurrection. A small group of completely desperate disciples, who did not even dare to fulfill the highest duty of burying Jesus, became courageous, convinced of having seen Jesus alive, and proclaimed him, even going to prison and death for doing so.

The details of the appearances are not clear. Mark 16:9-20 is absent from the oldest manuscripts and is a later kind of abstract of the other Gospels. Thus, Mark ends with a reference to the creed: crucified; buried, but no longer in the tomb; risen; to be seen by Peter and the other disciples (16:6-7; I Cor. 15:3-5). Variantly, Matthew (28:9-10) tells of Jesus encountering the women. And John (20:1-18) reports a still different encounter of Jesus with Mary of Magdala. What is historically probable is that the disciples had fled to Galilee and saw him there first, then returned to Jerusalem, where others may have seen him even earlier (Matt. 28:16-17; Mark 16:7; Luke 24:13-32 [but v. 33?]). Or was the sequence of appearances reversed, as narrated in John 21:1 (but cf. Luke 24:49)? Obviously, Mark and Matthew were interested only in the (first and basic?) appearance in Galilee, Luke and John (in chap. 20) in those in or near Jerusalem.

The Basis of Our Faith. Of the witnesses to the resurrection of Jesus, none describes the personal experiences of despair and shame and conversion to new insights and courage. Without I Corinthians 9:1 (and Acts) we would not even be sure whether Paul saw Christ or only heard him. All the witnesses to the resurrection can but tell: He, Jesus, came to us as the living Lord. The mystery of God surpassing all our concepts, expectations, and experiences became true in this unique event.

That we shall rise one day is not the security of a scientifically proved fact, but the certitude of faith, just as love can never be proved, but only known by our experiencing it. It is the certitude of faith expressed, for example, in Psalm 73:23-26; Mark 12:26-27; and John 11:25-26. Either there is no communication between God and human beings (in which case nihilism is the only possible philosophy), or it is true that God speaks to us, guides us, and hears us (in which case the life of a different dimension enters our lives and will never die). That which cannot die is not an immortal soul, as given to all human beings, but the new "person" that God is building up in the believer, unique in each individual, although it remains very fragmentary during our earthly lives. For faith, resurrection means that God will bring to perfection what God has started to build in us.

Modern Discussion on Resurrection. Willi Marxsen speaks of "the living Jesus." Docs this mean that the impact made by the earthly Jesus is still going on, as his slogan suggests: "The cause of Jesus continues"? Edward Schillebeeckx insists on "new experiences after his [Jesus'] death." Would it be enough to state that they were created and given by God in the hearts of the disciples? Rudolf Bultmann identifies the Easter faith with "the faith in the word of preaching," meaning that "Christ has been raised *into* (not 'in'!) the kerygma." In a way different from Marxsen's, Bultmann specifies that it is not simply the earthly Jesus, but Jesus crucified and raised who comes to us in the preaching.

The truth of these positions is their emphasis on the resurrection of Jesus as the beginning of a reestablished and even stronger discipleship. For Marxsen this discipleship is mainly a continuation of the pre-Easter relation to Jesus; for Bultmann, it is rather the acceptance and proclamation of Jesus as the one who died on our behalf and who has been legitimated (justified) by God in the resurrection: The preaching Jesus has now become the preached Christ, the earthly Jesus has entered "the kerygma." Indeed, Jesus encounters us nowhere else than in the proclamation of him by the church. Even Paul would not have understood his experience near Damascus without knowing what the Christians preached about Jesus Christ. Since the risen Lord "has been and is still the crucified one" (Mark 16:6; I Cor. 1:23; Gal. 3:1), still bearing the wound of the slaughtered sacrifice (Rev. 5:6), discipleship now means, first of all, believing in and proclaiming him as the one who died for us and is now our Lord.

However, since the disciples pointed away from themselves to the risen one, the new discipleship is, above all, God's act. This emphasizes the "prae" (before) and "extra nos" (outside us) of God's act. On Easter Day God has installed Jesus as Lord of the church, before anyone could experience, believe, and preach his resurrection. And this lordship is certainly not limited to the hearts of pious believers (e.g., I Cor. 15:20-28; Phil 2:9-11; I Tim. 3:16; and I Pet. 3:22).

Jesus has not simply been transferred to heaven like Enoch and Elijah; rather, he has been raised from the tomb before the last day. This allows prayers to him in the church of the New Testament, although they are normally directed to God. The earliest believers—and to a lesser degree, Paul—expected the resurrection of all the dead within a very short time, and Paul linked the resurrection of the believers (see I Thess. 4:13-14 and Rom. 8:29; I Cor. 15:24 does not include unbelievers) with that of Jesus, "the first-born among many brethren." Thus, resurrection certainly includes a future beyond death without the limits of time and space—a future that must be described in terms of personal life. This is what "resurrection of the body" (or "flesh," as occurring only in Luke 24:39) means. To Paul the main point is the fact that this body, though wholly different from any earthly body (e.g., Mark 12:25 and I Cor. 15:35-50), guarantees communication (with God and one another forever).

Summary. Resurrection starts here and now. Discipleship given by and witnessing to the crucified and risen Jesus Christ, and created by God who raised Christ, is the beginning and pledge (II Cor. 1:22; 5:5; Rom. 8:23) of the coming "personal" life in which God will raise us to what God started to build up in us.

EDUARD SCHWEIZER

Bibliography

Reginald Fuller, *The Formation of Resurrection Narratives*.
Willi Marxsen, *The Resurrection of Jesus of Nazareth*.
Norman Perrin, *The Resurrection According to Matthew, Mark, and Luke*.
Eduard Schweizer, "Resurrection: Fact or Illusion?" in *Horizons in Biblical Theology*, I.
Nigel Watson, *Easter Faith and Witness*.

Cross Reference: Biblical Theology, Hope, Kingdom of God, Miracles.

REVELATION

The idea of revelation in religion and theology can be elaborated from a number of different but related perspectives; namely, philological, phenomenological, biblical, historical, and theological. This essay gives preponderant attention to the theological treatment of revelation in theology today.

1. Philological. The word "revelation" is a translation of the Greek word *apokalypto*, meaning "to uncover," "to reveal," "to disclose." The last book in the Bible is often called "The Apocalypse of John." Its very first verse states that God sent an angel to John to make known to him "the revelation of Jesus Christ." When the word appears in a religious context or in a sacred text, its core meaning is the manifestation of deity, who would otherwise remain hidden and unknown. This sense of the word is not confined to biblical religion. Other religions have ways of lifting the veil that keeps the mystery of deity concealed.

2. Phenomenological. The method called phenomenology is widely applied in the scientific study of religion to discover the meaning of things. In his *Systematic Theology* Paul Tillich captures its essence: "It is the aim of the so-called phenomenological method to describe 'meanings,' disregarding, for the time being, the question of the reality to which they refer. The significance of this methodological approach lies in its demand that the meaning of a notion must be clarified and circumscribed before its validity can be determined, before it can be approved or rejected."

The results of this method indicate decisively that revelation belongs to the self-understanding of every religion. Every theistic religion holds the conviction that it originates in divine revelation and is not a merely human product. God is the author of revelation, and for that reason it is the source of authority. This phenomenological datum refutes any claim that Christianity is essentially and exclusively a religion of revelation and that all others are founded merely on human reason or nature. All religions make exclusive claims with regard to their revelations, so the mere claim to exclusivity does not establish the truth of any particular revelation.

When revelation happens in any religion, it is possible, pursuing the phenomenological method, to ask certain leading questions in order to discover the structure of each religion, and thus also of each revelation. For religion understands itself to be the reception of revelation. The first question is: Who or what is the author of the revelation in question? We are asking here the question of identity. Who is the God, or gods? What spirit or power is represented in the sacred rites of this religion? The second question is: By what means does this revelation take place? The instrumental means are legion, including plants, trees, stones, rivers, dreams, visions, holy places, holy seasons, oracles, or word. In the Christian religion the revealing medium is the concrete life and destiny of a particular man, Jesus of Nazareth, whose living presence is communicated through the preaching of the Word and the administration of the sacraments. The third question is: What is the content of the revelation? It could be the identity or name of the deity. It could be the mind or will of the deity, or some special message. In biblical religion it is the whole economy of salvation, including Yahweh's covenant with Israel, the Ten Commandments, the sending of the messiah, the mission to the nations, and the anticipation of the final advent of the kingdom of God. The fourth question is: Who are the original recipients of the revelation? They could be mediators, soothsayers, miracle workers, healers, incarnations, prophets, apostles, and the like. Oftentimes the original mediator of revelation becomes historically significant as the founder of a religion. Outside Christianity are the striking examples of Zoroaster, Muhammad, and Gautama. The fifth question is: What are the effects of the revelation on the recipients? Something happens to which the believers bear witness in words and deeds. Every religion speaks of the life-transforming changes in different ways; all speak of some kind of salvation. They may call it inspiration, illumination, unification, regeneration, justification, sanctification, or something akin to these states of being. The answers to these five questions will yield a kind of catechism for each religion, a summary of the fundamental principles that describe each system of belief.

3. Biblical. When we turn to the Bible, we quickly discover that Israel's distinctive view of revelation lies in its relation to Yahweh, the living God of promise, who kept his word by liberating the people from bondage in Egypt. This event proved that Yahweh is the Lord of history, who directs not merely the history

409

of Israel but also the history of all the nations. Yahweh makes civilizations to rise and fall. Yahweh revealed to the Hebrews a holy and gracious character and a holy will in law and commandments, which is balanced by mercy and forgiveness. In addition to being the Lord of Israel and all the nations, Yahweh is revealed as the maker of heaven and earth. The whole world is created and governed by his almighty will and word, and nothing in creation has any being or meaning of its own apart from the Creator.

One distinctive strand of thinking about revelation in the Hebrew scriptures has to do with reference to the future. The religions of many of Israel's neighbors were concerned with the hidden mystery of life as it is, or with the origin of things. For them, what is revealed is something hidden about the past or the present. As a historical religion, founded on the word of promise, Israel, in contrast, directed its hope to the future, looking forward to that which is to come. This element is the messianic or eschatological factor in Israel's faith.

The New Testament takes over Israel's ideas of revelation but links them particularly to the eschatological concept of the coming of God in the power and glory of the approaching Kingdom. Revelation is not primarily the impartation of supernatural knowledge, but the disclosure of the coming new age that had already dawned in the personal life, death, and resurrection of Jesus as God's messiah. The entire history of revelation becomes concretely focused and concentrated on Jesus of Nazareth, from his preexistence through his earthly ministry to his coming again at the end of history. This person, Jesus of Nazareth, is pictured as the decisive self-revelation of God, the basis and content of the apostolic message and its mission to the nations.

What is revealed is God's holy and gracious will to repossess the world in thrall to idols and lost in sin and death. Biblical revelation encompasses the whole history of salvation initiated by God's covenant with Israel, made actual in the life, death, and resurrection of Jesus Christ, and at last to be consummated at the *parousia* (the final advent of Christ). Revelation thus spans the whole spectrum of time and history—past, present, and future. The book of Revelation symbolizes the role of Christ in the history of revelation by calling him the "alpha and omega," the beginning and the end.

4. Historical. When the biblical message was proclaimed on Greek soil, it became necessary to translate its basic terms into a Hellenistic system of concepts. In the course of this translation, the idea of revelation was transformed from its Hebraic framework of history and eschatology to the more intellectual model of Hellenistic philosophy, where revelation was defined as the communication of knowledge concerning divine things. It was traditionally believed that all people possess a natural knowledge of God, as in Romans 1:20, which states that God has revealed God's own invisible nature, power, and deity "in the things that have been made." But in addition to this there is a supernatural knowledge above nature that is unattainable by reason. This supernatural knowledge about God and eternal truths is revealed in the Bible and can be accepted only by faith. Consequently, the mainline tradition in ancient and medieval Christianity held to a propositional view of revelation, guaranteed by the authority of the Bible on account of its being verbally inspired and virtually dictated by the Holy Spirit. Today this view of the Bible as a compendium of revealed and infallibly true statements about God and supernatural matters is maintained mostly among conservative Christians, particularly the fundamentalists. They define revelation primarily as true doctrinal propositions supported by biblical proof passages that must be believed in order for one to be saved.

With the rise of literary and historical criticism of the Bible, the view of the Bible as a book of inspired revealed oracles, a kind of Bartlett's quotations of divine wisdom, began to break down, giving way to two radically different approaches to the Bible. One approach uses the historical critical method to support a humanistic philosophy of religion. The Bible is read primarily as a segment of the history of religions; its writings are essentially products of human religious experience. If the Bible is not divinely inspired, it may still be *inspiring*, like many other religious writings. The test of the value of scripture lies not in what it communicates concerning God's revelation, but in its effect upon the religious consciousness.

The other approach also takes seriously the historical character of the Bible but reads it as a record of God's revelatory acts in history. In this view the Bible is not primarily a report of what human beings have thought about God; it is a recital of what God has done in history for humanity and its salvation. This new view of revelation came into prominence in the early part of the twentieth century with the rise of dialectical (or neoorthodox) theology, a movement associated with the names of Karl Barth and Emil Brunner. Dialectical theology called for a recovery of Hebraic categories of thought and a return to the Reformation theology of Luther and Calvin, recapturing their strong emphasis on the priority of God's Word as revealed in Jesus Christ, attested by scripture, and preached as the gospel by the church today.

5. Theological. The new view of revelation advanced by dialectical theology moved between the traditional orthodox propositionalist concept of revelation and the modern liberal humanistic reduction of revelation to religious experience. But the new theology of revelation proposed by Barth and enshrined in his monumental *Church Dogmatics* did not achieve a lasting consensus. Every theology after Barth has felt obliged to establish itself as a theology of revelation, but many questions have continued to be disputed in theology.

Paul Althaus, a Lutheran critic of Barth's theology and former professor of theology at Erlangen University (Germany), explained the inflation of the concept of revelation in theology as an overreaction to Immanuel Kant's rejection of

411

natural theology and his metaphysical agnosticism. Kant had asked the question, How do you know? in a most radical way, and theology had retreated to the safe asylum of some alleged revelation beyond the limits of human reason. The presupposition of the inflationary development of the concept of revelation in dialectical theology was the modern agnostic philosopher whose skepticism closed all other avenues of access to the knowledge of God. Embarrassing as it may seem, the other side of the coin of radical revelationism is modern atheism with its dictum, "God is dead!" This means that the retreat to absolute revelation is the response of taking the word of the atheist at face value, thus confining all knowledge of God to a special revelation, as that is perceived in the language tradition of a particular community of faith. The new view of revelation may in the end prove to be a desperate apologetic maneuver in the face of the modern negative critics of religion such as Auguste Comte, Karl Marx, Ludwig Feuerbach, Friedrich Nietzsche, and Sigmund Freud. If revelation is so transcendentally defined as to be out of the reach of these critics and so sequestered in an invulnerable area accessible only to Christian faith and theology, it may in the end have priced itself out of the market altogether. If the only evidence for revelation is the will of theology to assert it somehow, why should anyone who does not already believe in it take its truth claim seriously?

There are serious reasons to call into question the dominant position of the idea of revelation in current theology. First, it tends to identify the basic human predicament as the lack of the knowledge of God. But what if it is not lack of knowledge but the positive rebellion of the human will against God that is the problem? Then sin and guilt come into focus. Then reconciliation—not revelation, which answers to the question of knowledge—becomes the key motif as the answer to the question of sin as estrangement. Second, when revelation becomes the focal point of theology, it relegates Jesus Christ primarily to the role of revelation. Then to devise a high Christology, in line with the New Testament witnesses of John and Paul, theology must proceed to make Jesus Christ into the *sole* revelation of God, the absolutely exclusive medium of revelation.

A number of theologians have questioned this procedure on biblical grounds (Paul Althaus, Werner Elert, Emil Brunner, Gustaf Wingren, Wolfhart Pannenberg, et al.). In biblical theology God is revealed in Jesus of Nazareth, but not first and only in him. There is a twofold revelation of God: through creation and the law and through the gospel of Christ. There is the revelation not only of God's love in Jesus Christ but also of divine law through the demands of justice. It is essential to draw a proper distinction between revelation and salvation. Jesus Christ is not the sole revelation of God; he is the sole savior. The unique thing that happens in Christ is the act of reconciliation; this is a unique event enacted in history, and something absolutely new in the world. The dramatic historical character of the Christ event tends to be diminished by the inflation of revelation as an answer to the modern question of how people attain knowledge of God. The

412

assumption that the question of reconciliation and forgiveness is no longer the central human question does not necessarily correspond either to the biblical message or to the human condition as people experience it today.

The category of revelation is undoubtedly indispensable to the understanding of how human beings enter into fellowship with God, who as the Creator is wholly other than the world as creation. And the category of history is indispensable for a theology based on the history of salvation narrated in the Bible, reaching its climax in God's reconciling activity in Jesus Christ. Yet, we have found it necessary to sound a word of caution when a single category assumes control of the whole of theology and becomes the sole explanatory principle.

CARL E. BRAATEN

Bibliography

Karl Barth, "The Christian Understanding of Revelation," in *Against the Stream.*
Carl E. Braaten, *History and Hermeneutics.*
Emil Brunner, *Revelation and Reason.*
H. Richard Niebuhr, *The Meaning of Revelation.*
Wolfhart Pannenberg, ed., *Revelation As History.*

Cross Reference: Creation, Epistemology, Incarnation, Transcendence.

RIGHTEOUSNESS (*See* JUSTICE, LAW AND GOSPEL.)

RITUAL

The word "ritual" is sometimes used in ways that make it either prejudicial or useless in scholarly discussion. In popular speech the term, like its next of kin "myth," often has a negative connotation, meaning something like "de-spirited, boring routine." Even in theological circles it is sometimes used negatively as a way of pejoratively labeling someone else's practices, in which case it suggests merely external acts without internal passion. The tacit assumption seems to be that *we* celebrate liturgies, *we* worship, but *they* engage in ritual.

The current trend in ritual studies is to avoid such uses and employ the word more descriptively and less normatively. There is also a clear movement away from making the word "ritual" refer only to religious ritual, although the term certainly includes religious ritual. When ritual is used as a general term, one then designates specific subtypes such as liturgy, rites of passage, and seasonal rites. One of the effects of this reformulation has been to broaden what is meant by "liturgy." The word now sometimes means religious ritual of any kind, from any tradition. It no longer designates only Christian ritual, or more specifically, Christian eucharistic ritual.

An example of a provocative current definition of ritual is Roland Delattre's. Ritual, he says, consists of "those carefully rehearsed symbolic motions and gestures through which we regularly go, in which we articulate the felt shape and rhythm of our own humanity and of reality as we experience it, and by means of which we negotiate the terms or conditions for our presence among and our participation in the plurality of realities through which our humanity makes its passage" (282).

A second one is that of Jonathan Z. Smith, for whom ritual is "a means of performing the way things ought to be in such a way that this ritualized perfection is recollected in the ordinary, uncontrolled, course of things" ("The Bare Facts of Ritual," 124-25).

Both definitions emphasize the function of ritual, although they also try to specify the formal qualities of ritual, which is careful, rehearsed, symbolic, performed (i.e., using motion and gesture), and regular. Stanley Tambiah's definition more extensively identifies some of the commonly accepted formal characteristics. For him ritual is "a culturally constructed system of symbolic communication. It is constituted of patterned and ordered sequences of words and acts, often expressed in multiple media, whose content and arrangement are characterized in varying degree by formality (conventionality), stereotypy (rigidity), condensation (fusion), and redundancy (repetition)" (119).

Accompanying this reformulation of the vocabulary of ritual studies is a growing recognition that ritual requires interdisciplinary study. Both the practice and the idea of ritual have become the center of collaborative research conducted by anthropologists, religiologists, psychologists, performance theorists, sociologists, theologians, and even geneticists and biologists.

Interdisciplinary research has recast the image of ritual in two significant ways. One is that ritual now appears capable of precipitating social transformation, even revolution. It has become a cultural "actor," and it is no longer merely the object of other kinds of action, or worse, an inhibitor of action. The second way the image of ritual has changed is that it now appears to be part of a "family" of related activities including drama, civil and judicial ceremony, animal ritualization, and interpersonal decorum. No longer magnificently isolated (and thus sterile), ritual is now understood to be part of a continuum that links the most mundane of habitual behavior (such as brushing teeth) with the most elevated (such as liturgical celebration). This reconceptualization does not mean that ritual is equated with habit or habit with liturgy, but it does mean that their continuities, not just their differences, are deemed to be of theoretical importance. Sometimes the term "ritualization" (as distinct from "rite" or "ritual") is used to designate the least differentiated form of ritual. Whereas we would speak of synagogue worship as ritual, we might refer to the ritual-like dimensions of watching T.V., being an adolescent, or playing football as ritualization.

A significant feature of the discussion of ritual today is its emphasis upon performance or enactment. The fact that religion is embodied and acted out, not just read about, thought about, or believed, implies that if one wants to understand it, one cannot be content merely to study texts, even ritual texts. One needs to observe the performances based on such texts. In some cases the performance of a rite deviates considerably from the text that supposedly prescribes it. A student of ritual is drawn into "the field," which is to say, into situations where one can observe or participate in ritual as a way of studying it. The effect has been to challenge the textual preoccupation of theology and religious studies and to remove texts from their privileged position in the theory and practice of studying religion. One cannot assume that either text or performance is central to religion. One has to observe and then decide. In some religious traditions, for example Zen Buddhism, there is considerable opposition between texts, words, and book knowledge, on the one hand, and deeds, performance, and embodied knowledge on the other. In other traditions, for instance the Navajo and the Jewish, there is little opposition.

RONALD L. GRIMES

Bibliography

Roland Delattre, "Ritual Resourcefulness and Cultural Pluralism," in *Soundings* 61 (Fall 1978): 281-301.
Ronald L. Grimes, *Beginnings in Ritual Studies.*
_____, *Ritual Criticism: Case Studies in Its Practice, Essays on Its Theory.*
Jonathan Z. Smith, "The Bare Facts of Ritual," in *History of Religions,* vol. 20.
_____, *To Take Place: Toward Theory in Ritual.*
Stanley J. Tambiah, "A Performative Approach to Ritual," in *Proceedings of the British Academy* 65.
Victor Turner, *The Ritual Process: Structure and Anti-Structure.*

Cross Reference: Culture, Liminality, Liturgical Movement, Myth, Sacraments/Sacramental Theology, Worship.

ROMAN CATHOLICISM

The term "Roman Catholicism" can bring myriad images to mind. Liturgically, some may think of a papal mass at the majestic basilica of St. Peter in Rome. Focusing on a great feast day such as Christmas, they may remember the kaleidoscope of color, of cardinals in their scarlet robes and ambassadors in formal attire, of African men in colorful dashikis and Asian women in graceful saris. They may also recall the mixture of languages—prayers in Italian, English, French, German, Spanish, even Polish and Arabic, as well as scripture readings in New Testament Greek and the solemn orations of the mass in Latin. Presiding over

415

all this colorful variety and linguistic diversity is the Bishop of Rome, whom Roman Catholics revere as the pope, the successor of St. Peter and visible head of the church.

Others may recall the celebration of the Eucharist in a small rural church in the American heartland, where many members of the congregation are related and all know one another as neighbors; others may think of a large urban cathedral where a dozen masses are celebrated each weekend and where thousands of people pray each Sunday; some may remember a tin-roofed shed in an Asian jungle, where the members of the congregation have walked bare-footed to mass and now sit cross-legged on mats on the floor; still others may have experienced a mass celebrated quietly by a visiting priest in the home of a Catholic family in a country where there are few Christians and no churches of any denomination.

Ecclesiastically, some may think of the papal curia with its numerous offices, a bureaucracy so extensive that some have joked that even God does not know the titles of all the officials. In contrast, others may think of a small Roman Catholic parish that is without a resident pastor and that is administered by a committee of lay volunteers.

Theologically, some may turn attention to Roman Catholic scholars who concentrate their attention on the scholastic syntheses of the Middle Ages, which used the philosophy of Aristotle as the medium for doctrinal reflection. Some may think of theologians who have used historical-critical methodologies devised during the twentieth century. And others may focus on liberation theologians, who use as their starting point the experience of the poor and oppressed.

Somehow, though not without tension and disagreement, Roman Catholicism manages to incorporate these pluralistic liturgical, ecclesiastical, and theological images into a eucharistic community centered on the Bishop of Rome.

What, then, we may ask, is Roman Catholicism? Some consider "Roman Catholicism" an anomalous term. On the one hand, "catholic" is derived from the Greek word *katholikos,* which means "general" or "universal." On the other hand, "Roman" designates a particular place, once the center of a huge empire, but now the capital of a medium-sized country. How does one legitimately unite the universal with the particular, the general with the specific within Roman Catholicism?

Roman Catholics have used a variety of images to explain the relationship between particular local churches throughout the world and the Bishop of Rome as the visible center of unity. Some have described the Roman Catholic Church as the "barque of Peter" in which the pope is at the helm of a ship sailed by the collaborative efforts of all Catholics working together as its crew. Others have compared the Roman Catholic Church to a pyramid with the pope at the summit, the clergy ranked in hierarchical order in the middle, and the laity at the base. Still others have likened Roman Catholicism to a wheel with the pope at the center, the clergy as the spokes, and the laity as the rim. All of these images indicate both structural interconnection and hierarchical subordination; however, these images are less successful in communicating the basically spiritual relationship of communion between individual Roman Catholics and the Bishop of Rome.

Complicating the usage of "Roman Catholicism" is the fact that the term has been employed not only as a means of self-definition but also as a way of differentiating those Christians who are in communion with the Bishop of Rome and those who are not. Frequently, Roman Catholicism is considered one branch of Christianity, in contrast to Protestantism and Orthodoxy. Such a contrast rightly emphasizes the differences, but it may easily obscure the fact that Roman Catholics share much in common with Orthodox and Protestant Christians. To add to the terminological confusion, other groups of Christians also describe themselves as "Catholic"; some Anglo-Catholics, for example, consider themselves a bridge between Roman Catholicism and Protestantism while some Oriental Christians see themselves as representing the Catholic church prior to the schism between East and West.

A further complication of the term stems from the fact that "Roman Catholic" has frequently been used polemically. Those who supported the Reformation came to be known as "Protestants," while those who remained in communion with Rome were known as "(Roman) Catholics." Some Protestants, of course, have been unwilling to allow a Roman monopoly of the title "Catholic"; in England, for example, derogatory terms such as "papist" and "Romish" were used to describe those in communion with the Bishop of Rome. Polemics have also obscured historical reality; one nineteenth-century polemicist characterized "Roman Catholics" as "a sect organized by the Jesuits out of the relics of the Marian party in the reign of Queen Elizabeth." Although "catholic" has sometimes been used as a term of contention, for most Christians, it is part of their credal confession; at least since the fourth century, Christians have professed their belief "in one, holy, catholic, and apostolic church." How did it happen, then, that Christians have come to use the word "catholic" in a variety of senses?

Although the word "catholic" does not appear in the New Testament, the idea of universality is repeatedly emphasized: the gospel is intended for all people, of all places and of all times, of all races and all social classes. The first known instance where the term "Catholic" was applied to the church is in a letter of Ignatius of Antioch to the Christian community at Smyrna at the beginning of the second century: "Wherever the bishop is, there let the people be, just as where Jesus Christ is, there is the Catholic Church."

In subsequent centuries, describing the church as Catholic became commonplace. During the fourth century, for example, Cyril of Jerusalem gave a four-point explanation of why the church is called "catholic" or "universal." His first reason was geographical: The church "is spread throughout the world, from end to end of the earth." His second reason was doctrinal: The church "teaches universally and completely all the doctrines which a person should know concerning things visible and invisible, heavenly and earthly.'' His third point was liturgical: The church provides the correct way of worship for all people, ''rulers and ruled, lettered and unlettered.'' Cyril's fourth reason was soteriological: The church ''treats and heals universally every sort of sin committed by soul and body, and it possesses every conceivable virtue, whether in deeds, words or in spiritual gifts of every kind'' (*Catechesis* 18:23).

Undergirding these different dimensions of ''Catholic'' is the presumption of a fundamental unity exemplified in the remark òf Clement of Alexandria in the third century: ''Both in origin and in development, the primitive and Catholic Church is the only one, agreeing as it does in the unity of one faith'' (*Stromata* 7:17). Such an emphasis on the church's unity of belief emerged very clearly during the Donatist controversy in the fifth century, when Augustine emphasized: ''Although all heretics wish to be styled Catholic, yet if any one asks where is the Catholic place of worship none of them would venture to point out his own conventicle'' (*Contra Epistolam quam vocant Fundamenti* 4).

In the early church, ''Catholic'' was used to express a number of essential characteristics of the church. First, as suggested by Ignatius of Antioch, there is a sacramental relationship between the visible eucharistic community gathered around its bishop and the heavenly Christian community assembled around Christ. Second, there is a conviction that the gospel message of redemption and reconciliation is intended for all people. Third, there is an insistence on the need for ''Catholic doctrine'' (or orthodoxy) in contrast to the divisive teachings of various heretics. Fourth, there is an emphasis on maintaining ''Catholic unity'' through the communion of each local church with its bishop and of all bishops with one another and with the Bishop of Rome in particular.

During and after the Reformation, Roman Catholic apologists frequently used such patristic writings to support the claim that the Roman Catholic Church is the ''one true Church of Christ.'' By implication, Protestant churches were in the same position as the Donatists of Augustine's day; they were not really churches in the proper sense of the term. Such a view was popular until the time of the Second Vatican Council. The post-conciliar years have seen a greater manifestation of the diversity that has always existed below the surface of Roman Catholic unity. One place where this diversity has been particularly evident is the area of theology. Certainly, prior to the Council, there existed a diversity of theological schools with their own particular orientations; however, after the Council, this diversity has been considerably amplified through the use of many different philosophical approaches and methodologies, as well as through dialogue with other Christians and with members of other faiths.

This new direction in theology owes much to the decision of Pope John XXIII to invite Orthodox and Protestant churches to send observers to Vatican II. These observers not only witnessed the discussions on the floor of the Council, they also made suggestions about the documents under consideration. As a result, Vatican II made a number of important clarifications in Roman Catholic doctrine. For example, instead of equating the church of Christ with the Roman Catholic Church as had sometimes been done in the past, the "Constitution on the Church" stated that the church of Christ "subsists in the Catholic Church." In effect, Vatican II recognized the "churchness" of other Christian communions.

Vatican II also made other ecumenically significant decisions. The "Decree on Ecumenism," which declared that "the restoration of unity among all Christians is one of the principal concerns of the Second Vatican Council," proposed a number of steps toward unity: first, a process of reconciliation to overcome the polemics and prejudices of the past; second, collaboration on civic and social projects of common Christian concern; third, prayer and scripture-reading in common; and fourth, dialogue to resolve the issues that divide Christians.

Since Vatican II, notable progress toward unity has been achieved, though in different degrees in different places. For example, with few exceptions, the polemics of the past have ended; the relations between Protestants and Catholics are much more open than at any previous time. Consequently, collaboration on social and civic projects has generally become easier, although on specific issues (such as abortion, capital punishment, and nuclear disarmament) new tensions have arisen.

Simultaneously, ecumenical prayer services have become widespread; however, these are usually held only on special occasions such as Thanksgiving and the Week of Prayer for Christian Unity; moreover, intercommunion (eucharistic sharing with non-Roman Catholics) remains a sensitive issue. Ecumenical dialogue has been initiated in many places and at different levels: local, national, and international. Officially sponsored bilateral dialogues, such as that between Lutherans and Roman Catholics, have succeeded in achieving consensus on many issues that were previously regarded as divisive. To date, however, comparatively little has been accomplished in making use of such agreements in practice.

Undoubtedly the most neuralgic issue separating Roman Catholics and other Christians is the papacy. Indeed, Pope Paul VI once acknowledged that his office was a large obstacle to Christian unity. Several ecumenical dialogues have attempted to consider the papacy in ecumenical perspective; for example, some ecumenists have come to the conclusion that there is need for an "ecumenical papacy," understood in the sense of a "petrine ministry of service."

Whatever the future of ecumenical dialogue about the papacy, the shape of Roman Catholicism has been changing under the leadership of popes John XXIII, Paul VI, and John Paul II. Rather than being "a prisoner in the Vatican," as was the case with their immediate predecessors, each of these three popes has reached out to people throughout the world. Indicative of the changes that have occurred in the past century is the contrast between the First Vatican Council (1869–70), where the overwhelming majority of the participants were from Europe or North America, and Vatican II (1962–65), where there were numerous participants from Africa, Asia, and South America. And if demographic predictions prove correct, early in the third millennium, the majority of Roman Catholics will be found in countries of the so-called Third World.

Roman Catholics in the United States find themselves in a unique situation. In contrast to European countries where Catholicism has existed for many centuries, American Catholicism is comparatively young. The experience of Catholic immigrants in America was frequently different from that of their Protestant counterparts. First of all, with the exception of the British and most Irish, Catholic immigrants had to accommodate themselves not only to a new country but also to a new language. Second, while the United States was a land of promise offering not only economic opportunity but also religious freedom, still it was a country where a Protestant ethos predominated. Moreover, many Protestants were suspicious of immigrants who worshiped in a foreign language (Latin) and were loyal to a foreign prelate (the pope). Many Catholic immigrants, even when they tried to adjust to their new country, encountered economic discrimination and social ostracism. In particular, obedience to the pope was often made the grounds for impugning the civic loyalty of Roman Catholics. It was only with World War II, when American Protestants and Catholics together fought for a common cause, that the patriotism of American Catholics was no longer easily called into question. And it was only with the election in 1960 of John F. Kennedy, a Catholic, to the presidency that American Catholics generally felt that they were fully accepted as citizens.

Nonetheless, the Roman Catholic Church in the United States is still in large measure an "immigrant church" with a membership that presently includes a high percentage of immigrants and children of immigrants. For Catholic immigrants, their church has often played a central role in the process of "Americanization." While the Catholic church has continually provided a variety of services—educational, social, charitable, medical, and so forth—for its members, there have been conflicting views about the process of Americanization itself. Some, implicitly relying on the image of the "melting pot," have advocated as rapid and as thorough an assimilation as possible; others, however, apparently favoring the image of a "stew composed of many ingredients," have advocated the preservation of their language and culture as a means of preserving their ethnic identity and their Catholic faith. In any case, Roman Catholicism in the United States retains a notable ethnic dimension. For example, in some metropolitan areas, Sunday mass is celebrated in dozens of different languages, each with its unique liturgical style and expression of popular religiosity.

On the whole, the pluralistic environment of the United States has provided a congenial soil for the cultural diversity that characterizes Roman Catholicism. Indeed the American motto, *e pluribus unum* ("one from many") resonates well with the basic meaning of Catholicism: a universality that respects diversity. Accordingly, it does not seem surprising that the United States is one place where the *aggiornomento* (or updating of the church) mandated by Vatican II has occasioned a process of both vigorous discussion and vital renewal.

JOHN T. FORD

Bibliography

Karl Adam, *The Spirit of Catholicism*.
Yves Congar, *Diversity and Communion*.
Lawrence Cunningham, *The Catholic Experience: Space, Time, Silence, Prayer, Sacraments, Story, Person, Catholicity, Community, and Expectations*.
Avery Dulles, *The Catholicity of the Church*.
James Hennesey, *American Catholics: A History of the Roman Catholic Community in the United States*.
Richard McBrien, *Catholicism*.

Cross Reference. Papacy, Priesthood, Sacraments/Sacramental Theology, Silence, Vatican II

SACRAMENTS/SACRAMENTAL THEOLOGY

From being a subordinate section in dogmatics or even a chapter in canon law, sacramental theology has in the twentieth century relocated, in its most interesting manifestations, into the blossoming new field of liturgics or the study of worship. Instead of the sacraments being fitted willy-nilly into a ready-made theological system or having the minimum conditions for their validity set down by the lawyers, the liturgical texts and the concrete performance of the liturgy are being examined for the understanding they yield of the sacramental rites; and the results are being offered as a contribution to shaping the larger theological vision and enhancing the practical celebration.

Liturgics itself being an interdisciplinary enterprise, sacramental theology has in turn benefited from and contributed to the biblical theology of the 1930s to the 1950s, the renewed interest from the 1940s to the 1960s in the patristic period and in the doctrine of the church, and the attention given to theological anthropology from the 1960s through the 1980s with the help of linguistic philosophy, hermeneutical theory, semiotics, and ritual studies. Moreover, the whole cumulative exercise has been an ecumenical one, as can be measured from the long maturation in the Faith and Order commission of the World Council of Churches of the studies on baptism, eucharist, and ministry and then the reception of the resulting "Lima text" among the constituent churches.

The Paschal Mystery. A beginning of the reconception of sacramental theology may perhaps be found in the work of Odo Casel at the Benedictine abbey of Maria Laach in the Rhineland in the 1920s and 1930s. Some of his important essays were collected in *The Mystery of Christian Worship* (1962). Casel rediscovered the importance of the "paschal mystery," that is, the death and resurrection of Jesus Christ, which lies at the heart of God's redemptive work for humankind, and in which believers are given a share through their participation in the sacraments of Baptism and the Eucharist or Lord's Supper.

In biblical language, "mystery" designates the saving purpose of God for the world, long hidden but now revealed in Jesus Christ and destined for completion in God's final kingdom (Mark 4:11; Rom. 11:25, 16:25-27; Col. 1:25-27, 2:2-3, 4:3; Eph. 1:9-10, 3:1-12, 6:19; Rev. 10:7). Christ himself can be called "the mystery of our religion" (I Tim. 3:16). The church came to spread out this single mystery into the various "mysteries" that made up Christ's life (his birth, his baptism, his transfiguration, and above all his death and resurrection), the feasts by which they were celebrated in the calendar, and the rites by which Christians gained access to the salvation which Christ had won for humankind (especially Baptism and the Lord's Supper).

All this came to its most concentrated expression in the Paschal Vigil, in the night between Holy Saturday and Easter Day, when the Old Testament scriptures foretelling Christ's death and resurrection were read, and those acts were performed that Christ himself had instituted: baptism into discipleship (Matt. 28:19), by which a person died to sin in order to walk in newness of life (Romans 6) as a member of Christ's body, the church (I Cor. 12:12-13); and the Lord's Supper (Matt. 26:26-29), by which the company of disciples was given communion in Christ (I Cor. 10:16-17) and the Lord's death was proclaimed until he comes again (I Cor. 11:26). Every Sunday is in fact special: "We all assemble together on Sunday [for worship], because it is the first day, on which God transformed darkness and matter, and made the world; and Jesus Christ our Savior rose from the dead on that day" (Justin Martyr, second century). It is an achievement of liturgical and sacramental theology in our century to have recovered an emphasis on Sunday and on Easter as the Lord's day on which the Lord's people gather to find him in their midst at the Lord's meal.

The Biblical Memorial. Casel's own work remained controversial on account of the links he made between the Christian sacraments and the mystery rites of Hellenistic religion, which he saw as a somewhat positive preparation for the gospel. In fact, however, examination of the biblical evidence was quite soon able to find sufficient rootage in the scriptures for the basically acceptable thrust of Casel's teaching on the sacraments. New Testament scholars such as C. H. Dodd and Joachim Jeremias investigated the notion of memorial ("Do this in remembrance of me''), especially the latter in his book *The Eucharistic Words of Jesus.*

Although many have jibbed at Jeremias's exegesis that considers the Eucharist as primarily intended to remind God of the Christ (and so pray for his return), investigation of the memory root (Hebrew *ZKR*) has shown that Israel had a notion of liturgical rites and prayers in which the faithful human response of obedience to the divinely commanded ceremony allowed God to realize the promise by which the blessings once given to the generations of old were extended into the present. This was eminently true of the Passover celebration, whereby each generation entered into the deliverance from Egypt (Exodus 12–13). Now if, in the Christian dispensation, ''Christ our passover has been sacrificed for us,'' then ''let us keep the feast'' (1 Cor. 5:7-8), which he instituted on the eve of his death. Through his living presence the Christ who died and rose again brings to the gathered assembly the benefits of his redeeming work. Sacramental theologians have thus helped believers to avoid the two extremes of taking the sacrament either as a bare psychological event in the minds of the participants or as a repetition of Calvary, to name the two positions Catholics and Protestants respectively have at least suspected the other of holding. A fine account of the biblical notion of dynamic memorial (or ''anamnesis'') is found in Max Thurian's *The Eucharistic Memorial* (1960).

The Pneumatological Dimension. A further feature that helps sacramental theology to give an acceptable account of the efficacy of the rites is a regained recognition of the pneumatological dimension, that is, the part played by the Holy Spirit in the sacraments. From New Testament times, a role had been recognized to the Holy Spirit in the making of Christians, whether the sacramental mediation of the Spirit was associated directly with water baptism itself or was focused rather on a related rite that would later be called chrismation (anointing) or confirmation (John 3:3-7; Acts 2:38; 8:14-17; 19:5-6; II Cor. 1:22; Eph. 1:13; 4:30; Titus 3:5-7; I John 2:20, 27). As the doctrine of the Holy Spirit became more sharply defined in the fourth century, so the Spirit's consecratory role in the Eucharist also became more openly expressed. Especially in Eastern liturgies, the Holy Spirit is asked, in a prayer of ''epiklesis'' or invocation, to make the bread and wine into the body and blood of Christ, so that communicants may receive all spiritual benefits.

In the twentieth century, the Orthodox churches have brought the theological importance of the sacramental work of the Holy Spirit to the attention of Western churches, both Catholic and Protestant. By introducing some form of ''epiklesis'' into their revised rites, they have recognized that the effectiveness of the sacraments is entirely dependent on the divine response to prayer, instead of being a ''magical'' operation on the human side.

The Trinitarian Character. By now the trinitarian character of the sacraments will have become clear. Whatever the phrase ''baptism in the name of [the Lord] Jesus

[Christ]'' may mean in the Acts of the Apostles (2:38; 8:16, 37; 10:48; 19:5), the post-biblical church consistently baptized ''in the name of the Father and of the Son and of the Holy Spirit'' in accordance with the command of the risen Lord recorded in Matthew 28:16-20. The trinitarian name may have been pronounced either in the form of questions to the candidates (''Do you believe in God the Father almighty; Jesus Christ his Son; the Holy Spirit?'') or as a formula by the officiating minister (''I baptize you in the name of the Father and of the Son and of the Holy Spirit,'' in the West; ''So-and-so is baptized in the name of the Father and of the Son and of the Holy Spirit,'' in the East) or both. As the surrounding prayers usually make clear, baptism is the sign of adoption into God's family and even of being given a share in God's life, so that the baptized, as fellow heirs with Christ the Son, may in the Holy Spirit call on God as ''Abba, Father'' (Rom. 8:14-17) and start in faith to enjoy eternal life (John 17:3; Heb. 6:4-6).

In the classical liturgies of both East and West, the eucharistic prayer at the heart of the Lord's Supper is addressed to the Father through Christ the Son in the Holy Spirit. As St. Basil pointed out in his late-fourth-century treatise ''On the Holy Spirit,'' the movement by which Christians return thanks thus corresponds to the fact that all the prior blessings from ''the Father of lights'' (James 1:17) are mediated to them by the Son in the Holy Spirit.

At times when the doctrine of the Trinity has been under challenge, the stable use of the trinitarian name in the sacramental rites has helped to conserve Christian faith in the Triune God. In the late twentieth century, this could again turn out to be a testing point in some churches. Good accounts of the essentially trinitarian character of Christian worship are found in Peter Brunner's *Worship in the Name of Jesus* (1968) and Cipriano Vagaggini's *Theological Dimensions of the Liturgy* (1976).

Church and Sacraments. Twentieth-century sacramental theology has regained an awareness of the intimate connections between the sacraments and the church as a whole, instead of seeing them almost exclusively as channels of grace to individuals. The church both celebrates the sacraments and is built up by them. As shown in the dialogue between the Lutheran Eberhard Jüngel and the Catholic Karl Rahner in their *Was ist ein Sakrament?* (1971), accents may continue to differ between the Christian confessions. Protestants tend to begin with the Word and sacraments by which God continually creates and constitutes the church, so that the church may then ''administer'' what it first receives. Catholics emphasize the church already established as the body of Christ, without which the sacraments could not be performed. There is a striking agreement between, say, Jüngel (drawing on Luther's interpretation of I Tim. 3:16 in *The Babylonian Captivity of the Church*) and the Flemish Dominican Edward Schillebeeckx (author of *Christ the Sacrament of Encounter with God*, 1963) that Christ himself is ''the primary sacrament." But Jüngel balks when the Second Vatican Council, in its dogmatic constitution *Lumen Gentium*, goes on to refer to the *church* as "a kind of sacrament, that is, the sign and *instrument* of union with God and the unity of people." According to many Protestants, that attributes too active a role to the church in the mediation of salvation.

This continuing difference should not obscure the fact that a considerable ecclesiological renewal has taken place under the rubric of the church as a baptismal and eucharistic community. This extends to the Orthodox churches, as may be seen in the works of Alexander Schmemann, *Of Water and the Spirit* (1974) and *The Eucharist: Sacrament of the Kingdom* (1988).

The Kingdom of God. Beginning with exegetical work from Johannes Weiss and Albert Schweitzer to C. H. Dodd, twentieth-century New Testament scholarship has refocused attention on the kingdom of God as a leading category in the preaching and ministry of Jesus. From Karl Barth to Wolfhart Pannenberg and Jürgen Moltmann, dogmaticians have sought to draw the theological consequences in a more eschatological account of the Christian faith. Examination of sacramental rites and of traditional commentaries on them shows, as Geoffrey Wainwright argued in *Eucharist and Eschatology* (1971), that the sacraments have often helped to maintain the vision of the last things in Christian consciousness. By their character as "promise," "pledge," "taste," "image," "prefiguration," they express the tension between what is "already now" given in virtue of the work of Christ and of the Holy Spirit and what is "not yet" attained but will "one day" be completed in the divine Kingdom sketched in Jesus' parables or the city of God envisioned in the book of Revelation.

In the interval before the final end, the sacraments pattern and enable the life that befits the community of believers. The ethical implications and consequences of the sacramental celebrations have received much attention in recent decades, as for instance in William Willimon's *The Service of God: Christian Work and Worship* (1983) or Timothy Sedgwick's *Sacramental Ethics: Paschal Identity and the Christian Life* (1987). In particular, the social and political dimensions of the Eucharist as a meal of justice and peace have been explored by such Roman Catholic writers as Gustavo Gutiérrez from Peru (*A Theology of Liberation*, 1973), Tissa Balasuriya from Sri Lanka (*The Eucharist and Human Liberation*, 1979), and Monika Hellwig from the United States (*The Eucharist and the Hunger of the World*, 1976). The ecological aspects of the sacramental use of the material creation are starting to be noticed, as presaged by Alexander Schmemann in his treatment of the human vocation to be "the priest of the world" (*The World as Sacrament*, 1966; rev. as *For the Life of the World*, 1973).

Sacramental Anthropology. In the twentieth century, the human sciences have devoted sustained attention to the complex systems of symbols—words, gestures, objects, even institutions—by which people and communities explore, describe, interpret, and fashion reality, express and form their thoughts, emotions, and values, and communicate across time and space in ways that both build and convey traditions as well as both allowing and reflecting social relations in the present. Linguistic philosophy speaks of "performative language," or "how to do things with words" (to borrow the title of J. L. Austin's book of 1962). Hermeneutical theory emphasizes the importance of a tradition in the "reading" of "texts," broadly understood. Semiotics uncovers the structures and dynamics of the processes of signification. Ritual studies examine the consecrated ways by which groups define and maintain their identity and place in the world.

Particularly since the 1960s, sacramental theologians have begun to draw on such human sciences as an aid to understanding the function of the sacraments as such and the possible dysfunction in particular performances of them. Christian theologians do not, of course, remain content with a purely humanistic account of the sacraments, since they believe that the presence and action of God in them is their God-given raison d'être. They therefore locate them in the history of creation, redemption, and salvation as recounted in the biblical narratives and envisioned in the biblical promises; and they are aware that the sacraments are a way in which God's grace comes to correct and complete the fallen nature of humankind. The sacraments can therefore in turn become instructive about the human condition and calling. Outstanding work in the anthropology of the sacraments has been done by the French Catholic L. M. Chauvet in his *Symbole et sacrement* (1987) and by the German Protestants represented in Rainer Volp's *Zeichen* (1982). An American introduction to this perspective can be found in George S. Worgul's *From Magic to Metaphor* (1980).

Number and Definition? Oddly for some, sacramental theologians have ceased to be preoccupied with fixing a number for the sacraments (nine? seven? three? two?) or with proposing a scholastic definition of the genus into which all claimants would have to fit. These historically controversial matters still affect to some degree the confessional responses to the Lima document, *Baptism, Eucharist, and Ministry;* but the greater ecumenical openness manifested by the churches allows the Faith and Order Commission of the World Council of Churches to essay the following "sacramental view of the history of salvation," which well reflects twentieth-century scholarship in our field and diminishes the importance of differences over the number of particular sacraments and a generic definition of them:

> In the incarnation, life, death and resurrection of Jesus Christ, God has communicated effectively the mystery of his saving love to the world. Through the power of the Holy Spirit, the risen Christ continues this saving action of God by being present and active in our midst. For this purpose God continues to act through

human persons, through their words, signs and actions, together with elements of creation. Thus God communicates to the faithful, and through their witness to the world, his saving promise and grace. Those who hear and receive in faith and trust this gracious action of God are thereby liberated from their captivity to sin and transformed in their lives. Those who receive this gift, respond to it in thanksgiving and praise and are brought into a koinonia [or communion] with the Holy Trinity and with each other and are sent to proclaim the gospel to the whole world. Through this sacramental action, communicated through words, signs and actions, this community, the church, is called, equipped and sent, empowered and guided by the Holy Spirit to witness to God's reconciling and recreating love in a sinful and broken world. And so all who in faith long for fullness of life in Christ may experience the first-fruits of God's kingdom—present and yet to be fully accomplished in a new heaven and earth.

Within this framework, ecumenical debate could still continue as to which particular rites are appropriately designated sacraments. But the divisive and disabling character of historical differences on this question is already being mitigated by such considerations as the following. First and most important, Baptism and the Lord's Supper are now very widely recognized as the preeminent sacraments, however many other there may or may not be. Second, Roman Catholic theologians increasingly acknowledge that confirmation belongs as closely with baptism as chrismation does for the Orthodox, and that penance or reconciliation is a renewal of baptism. Third, many Protestant churches in their responses to *Baptism, Eucharist, and Ministry* admit that there is something sacramental about ordination, with its laying on of hands and prayer for the Spirit for the sake of ministry through word and sacrament. Fourth, in a very broad range of churches, Christians have come from very different starting points to the practice of imposition of hands with prayer, and sometimes anointing, for the healing of the sick (James 5:13-16; cf. Mark 16:18 and the healings performed by Jesus).

GEOFFREY WAINWRIGHT

Bibliography

Baptism, Eucharist, and Ministry 1982–1990 (Faith and Order Paper #149).
Robert W. Jenson, *Visible Words: The Interpretation and Practice of Christian Sacraments.*
Joseph Martos, *Doors to the Sacred: A Historical Introduction to Sacraments in the Catholic Church.*
Max Thurian and Geoffrey Wainwright, *Baptism and Eucharist: Ecumenical Convergence in Celebration.*
James F. White, *Sacraments As God's Self-Giving.*

Cross Reference: Biblical Theology, Dogmatic Theology, Kingdom of God, Liturgical Movement, Ritual, Trinity.

SACRIFICE (See ATONEMENT, PRIESTHOOD.)

SALVATION (See ATONEMENT, SOTERIOLOGY.)

SANCTIFICATION

Sanctification literally means the process of becoming a saint. More generally, sanctification refers to the presence and growth of holiness in the lives of Christians. Yet the concepts of "saintliness" and "holiness" are nearly as foreign to persons today as is "sanctification." More helpful, perhaps, is the understanding that objects or persons of holiness are set apart from the ordinary world of the profane. Similarly a saint is one who has been set apart as a model of religious and moral purity. Christians have historically affirmed that God alone is truly and completely holy. Human holiness, in both its religious and moral aspects, is derivative. Still, the New Testament writers and later generations of Christian theologians expect that Christians will be set apart from others in both the spiritual and the moral qualities of their lives. Spiritually, Christians are identified by their relationship with God. Morally, there is the expectation of a life of increasing purity.

In Christian thought sanctification has typically been related to justification. Not surprisingly, many questions that apply to justification emerge in a consideration of this doctrine: When does sanctification begin? When is it completed? What is its extent? How is sanctification accomplished? Is it entirely a gift of God or in part a human achievement? In what does sanctification consist? Finally, how is sanctification related to justification? Three views of sanctification have dominated and continue to dominate Christian thinking. According to Roman Catholic theology, sanctifying grace is infused into the soul at baptism. This act cleanses the soul of sin. The new Christian is not only justified but is in fact made holy. But this sanctifying grace may be lost if the person should commit a mortal sin. The loss incurred by mortal sin may then be removed, however, by penance and other sacraments, sanctification thereby being restored.

Some evangelical Protestants, especially those in the Wesleyan tradition, and most Pentecostals understand sanctification as an instantaneous experience of grace, occurring either at the moment of conversion or, more typically, at a later time. Sanctification is viewed as a gift of the Holy Spirit, or "second blessing." This experience may issue in the state known as entire sanctification or moral purity. Alternatively, gradual growth in holiness may be climaxed by a special blessing of grace that produces entire sanctification. Few have claimed such perfection in their own lives, but the expectation and possibility of complete sinlessness remain.

Most Protestants have been less optimistic that any human can achieve perfection in this life. The power of sin remains a force to be reckoned with in the lives of all Christians; although justified, Christians remain liable to actual sin. The best that can be hoped for is a gradual increase in moral purity. Sanctification is thus held to begin with justification at baptism, but it remains incomplete until the eschatological moment when all things are brought to perfection. In the view of Protestant theology, sanctification is both gift and goal; it is given by the Holy Spirit through the Word and the sacraments, but it remains a prize to be sought in the Christian life.

In these times, statements of the Christian doctrine of sanctification often take into account the insights of developmental psychology and the riches of the Christian tradition. Recent studies of moral and intellectual development define the normal human stages in which the possibility and progress of Christian sanctification may be exemplified. These studies further indicate that any growth in holiness must be seen in light of temporal and social aspects.

In its temporal aspect, sanctification should be understood as but one movement in the divine symphony of creation, redemption, and consummation, both in human history and in individual lives. It is a gradual moral and religious growth, initiated at birth and baptism, accompanied by justifying grace, which proceeds throughout life, never to be completed until all is completed. The intensity of holiness in an individual's life may fluctuate from time to time, although it is to be expected that one will not permanently revert to a lower stage.

In its social aspect, sanctification is to be viewed as a response to the divine initiative that is mediated to the individual through family, church, and society. Individuals do not achieve holiness; holiness is a gift of God. As a gift, however, it must be received in faith and exercised in action. Although individuals may be graced with holiness, it is not received in isolation, but through the social institutions of family and church, which are responsible for inculcating holiness.

The Christian doctrine of sanctification differs from secular theories of moral development not only in its appeal to a divine source but also in its moral and spiritual content. Defined by the divine character, holiness is revealed fully in Jesus Christ. The process of sanctification, therefore, is the pursuit of ever greater Christlikeness. This growth occurs as the believer faithfully seeks to appropriate the teachings of Christ, incorporate the attitudes of Christ, and exemplify the spirit of Christ. Christlikeness includes both an intimate relationship with God and a compassionate sensitivity for all people that Jesus himself summarized as loving God and neighbor with one's whole being. The First Epistle of John reminds Christians that such love is possible only because "God first loved us," demonstrating once again that sanctification is both gift and goal; both beyond natural human capability and yet the expectation of Christian discipleship.

GLENN HEWITT

Bibliography

R. N. Flew, *The Idea of Perfection in Christian Theology.*

Stephen Happel and James J. Walter, *Conversion and Discipleship: A Christian Foundation for Ethics and Doctrine.*

Stanley Hauerwas, *A Community of Character: Toward a Constructive Christian Social Ethic.*

W. E. Hulme, *Dynamics of Sanctification.*

J. Philip Wogaman, *Christian Moral Judgment.*

Cross Reference: Justification, Pentecostalism.

SATISFACTION (*See* ATONEMENT.)

SCHISM (*See* HERESY.)

SCIENCE AND CHRISTIANITY

Physics and biology are the two principal natural sciences with which Christian theology must reckon, although there is important dialogue with other natural sciences such as chemistry and geology. Technical sciences such as medical science and computer science sometimes raise both theoretical and ethical issues. Scientists increasingly recognize that theory, models, data, and description are more entwined than once supposed. Discoveries in physics and revisions of scientific theories over time have also softened the realism in science in favor of more historical and culture-bound accounts.

The relations between physics and theology are surprisingly cordial at present; the relations between biology and theology are more difficult. Astrophysics and nuclear physics, combining quantum mechanics and relativity theory, are describing a universe "fine-tuned" for life, while evolutionary and molecular biology seems to be discovering that the history of life is a random walk with much struggle and chance, driven by selfish genes.

Physics has made dramatic discoveries in the astronomical and submicroscopic ranges, both remote from the ordinary range of human perception. The universe (this universe at least) originated twenty billion years ago in a "big bang" and has since been expanding. From the primal burst of energy, elementary particles formed, and afterward hydrogen (the simplest element), which serves as fuel for the stars. In the stellar furnaces all the heavier atoms were and are forged. Early stars subsequently exploded (becoming supernovae), from which hydrogen and the heavier elements coagulated again to form, in our case, the solar system and planet Earth.

In the last twenty years physics has discovered that startling interrelationships are required for these creative processes to work. Recent theory interrelates the two levels; astronomical phenomena such as the formation of galaxies, stars, and planets depend critically on the microphysical phenomena. In turn, the middle level, that which can be observed by the ordinary human senses, depends on the interacting microscopic and astronomical levels. If the scale of the universe had been much reduced, there would not have been enough time for elements to form. If the expansion rate of the universe had been a little faster or slower, then the universe would already have recollapsed or the galaxies and stars would not have formed.

Change slightly the strengths of any of the four forces that govern the universe (the strong nuclear force, the weak nuclear force, electromagnetism, gravitation), change critical particle masses and charges, and the stars would burn too quickly or too slowly, or atoms and molecules (including water, carbon, and oxygen) or amino acids (the building blocks of life) would not form or remain stable.

These results have been summarized as the "anthropic principle" (an unfortunately anthropocentric term), which argues that the universe has been "fine-tuned" from the start and in its fundamental construction for the subsequent construction of stars, planets, life, and mind. There are nontheological, naturalistic ways of interpreting these discoveries, but a plausible interpretation is divine design. Theologians and philosophers have often been wary of design arguments, remembering William Paley, his fine-tuned watch, and the many telling criticisms of such arguments. Nevertheless, the physical world is resembling a fine-tuned watch again, and now many quantitative calculations support the argument.

Biology is a stark contrast—at first at least. Biology also has expanded in the range of the very small and that of large scale history. In discovering DNA, molecular biologists have decoded the "secret of life" (once ascribed to the Spirit of God). Evolutionary history has located the secret of life in natural selection operating over incremental variations across enormous timespans, with the fittest selected to survive. Speciation begins with the simple and results in the complex, from microbes to persons. As with physics, the two levels have been theoretically interrelated. The genetic level supplies variations, does the coding of life in DNA, and constructs molecular proteins. Organisms cope at their levels of ordinary perception, inhabiting ecosystems, and across deep evolutionary time species are "selected" as they track changing environments, transforming from one into another.

The evolutionary process can seem both random and, within structural constraints and mutations available, optimizing of adapted fit. Natural selection is thought to be blind, both in the genetic variations bubbling up without regard to the needs of the organism, some few of which by chance are beneficial, and in the evolutionary selective forces, which select for survival, without regard to advance. Evolutionary theorists insist that nothing in natural selection theory

431

guarantees progress; many doubt that the theory predicts long-term historical innovations. Further, since individual organisms are selected for their self-interested reproductive skills, in competition with others, selection favors "selfish" organisms.

Although dominant throughout biology, evolutionary theory has proved quite problematic itself, independently of any theological agenda. The theory may be incomplete. If Darwin is biology's Newton, its Einstein may be still to come.

Theological reaction is mixed. Fundamentalist theology denies (much or all of) evolution and sometimes seeks to prevent its teaching in public schools. Other theologians construct an evolutionary theism, emphasizing the continuing vital creative processes over time, the ascent of life from the simple to the complex, the production of more out of less over long millennia.

The watchmaker-design approach to the concept of a Creator, if appropriate in physics, may not be the model for biology, where more autonomy and self-creativity is combined with the divine will for life, a divine parenting entwined with spontaneous creative process. Organisms defend their lives; their selfishness, so-called, is really self-actualizing, the defense of vitality. Reproduction is the perpetual sharing of biological value and promise. Struggle and suffering, and life renewed in the midst of its death and perishing, are central themes in Christianity, although nonmoral, natural history is "cruciform" even before humans arrive, and in all creating of life there seems to be struggling through to something higher.

In human history, where moral selfishness does emerge, superimposed on biological self-actualizing, humans fall into sin. They need creative redemption from their selfishness, and the cruciform character of life intensifies. Here too theologians have long spoken of a salvation by suffering through to something higher. Although biologists are often uncertain whether life has arrived on Earth by divine intent, they are almost unanimous in their respect for life and seek biological conservation on an endangered planet.

HOLMES ROLSTON III

Bibliography

Ian Barbour, *Religion in an Age of Science.*
Paul Davies, *God and the New Physics.*
A. R. Peacocke, *Creation and the World of Science.*
Holmes Rolston III, *Science and Religion: A Critical Survey.*

Cross Reference: Cosmology, Creation Science, Ecology, Fundamentalism.

SECOND VATICAN COUNCIL (*See* Vatican II.)

SECULARITY

The Problem. Is secularity a sin against God and humankind? Or is it the opening of a new age of human freedom and a purification of the Christian faith? Secularity appears as a complex subject that requires the unraveling of strands belonging to semantics, history, sociology, and religious studies, especially theology.

1. The first problem is lexical. The Latin root *saeculum* denotes a period of time such as a generation, a decade, or, less specifically, an age. The Latin translation of the Greek New Testament uses *saeculum* to render the Greek, *aion* (age), but it begins to confuse the issue by alternately using the Latin for "world" as a translation of *aion* and, even worse, by translating as "eternal" the biblical *aionios* (literally "ages"). Standard dictionaries identify "secular" as that which pertains to the worldly or temporal as distinct from the spiritual and eternal. The opposition of material and spiritual and temporal and eternal has pervaded and clouded the discussion of this term.

These oppositions entered the Christian faith primarily as it encountered the world of Hellenistic philosophy and religions. The *saeculum* was the temporal and material sphere of human activity wherein most Christians lived their daily lives; the *religious* belonged to a "separated" area of mediation to the "eternal," including a negation of the "world" that could be practiced only by a few in ascetic and monastic life. So pronounced was this distinction that the noun "religious" came to be applied to persons who professed poverty, chastity, and obedience. In turn, priests serving "in the world" were called "secular."

2. The complex questions about secularity, however, cannot be answered simply by clarifying vocabulary. Any discussion of secularity has to deal with the historical process of the struggle and tension between the "religious" (as the representation of transcendence in human life) and the "secular" (as representing autonomous human agency) in politics, economics, science, and culture generally.

The struggle between religious authority (mainly the pope) and civil authority (the kings and princes of the emerging nations) persisted in Europe after the eleventh century and led to a growing autonomy of the civil realm. The takeover by civil power of property in the hands of the church, the elimination of ecclesiastical control over areas of human life (cemeteries, matrimony, education), the suppression of ecclesiastical privileges (a special jurisdiction for the clergy, exemption from duties and taxes) and in some cases the suppression of certain religious orders, marks successive stages of "secularization" in the sixteenth through the eighteenth centuries. Following the Enlightenment and the French Revolution, the issue took a clear ideological slant, claiming that secularity implied complete autonomy for human life.

3. This latest development has dominated the discussions in the nineteenth and twentieth centuries. The Bossey Ecumenical Institute defined it in 1959 as "the withdrawal of areas of life and thought from religious—and finally also from metaphysical—control and the attempt to understand and live in these areas in the terms which they alone offer.'' No longer is secularity merely a matter of struggle over structures and powers; it has become a way of perceiving reality and a method of thought and understanding. Sociological interpretations of secularization mark this stage. Since then it has been increasingly difficult to distinguish the historical process from its sociological and philosophical interpretations.

Theological Interpretations. 1. Theological interpretations have accompanied the entire process. Theories of the preeminence of religious over civil authorities in the thirteenth and fourteenth centuries (the prime example being the papal bull *Unam sanctam* in 1302), or of areas of human life in the seventeenth and eighteenth centuries (marriage, family, education) where religious authority should have a particular competence, and attempts to understand in a positive way the relation between the Christian faith and the process of secularization (since the mid–nineteenth century) have been successive movements in the theological interpretation that need examination.

Both the historical process of secularization with its concrete effects on the life of the churches and the ideological and sociological interpretations of that process prompted reflection on the part of the churches. Initially, the reflection was a defensive reaction and, later, an attempt to interpret and critically appropriate this new phenomenon.

2. The classical opposition can be best illustrated, on the Roman Catholic side, by Pius IX's condemnation of all and sundry forms of civil appropriation of what are considered fields of competence of the church, particularly modern liberalisms, culminating with the rejection of the thesis that the ''Roman Pontiff can and ought to reconcile himself with progress, liberalism and modern civilization'' (*Syllabus errorum,* 1864). Confessional Protestant theology was less coherent in its opposition but no less alarmed at the process. It would be enough to remember that Kant's famous article, ''What is the Enlightenment?,'' defending the human right to thinking free from all tutelage as ''man coming of age,'' was written in response to the protest of a high dignitary of the Lutheran Church against the secularization of marriage. In the United States (and later in Britain and other places) fundamentalism arose as a claim of absolute authority for scripture in relation to religion and *all* truth. Recent manifestations of fundamentalism in the New Religious Right have revived this claim of religion to shape law and institutions of civil society, which have supposedly fallen prey to ''secular humanism.''

3. More interesting and fruitful, however, are the ways in which theology has tried to evaluate, interpret, and appropriate secularity. These attempts marked theological discussion in Europe and North America after World War II. In this enormous theological production, four theologians represent different positions

but share a common acceptance of secularity, because, as Thomas J. J. Altizer put it, "Faith cannot speak to the world if it is not affected by the world to which it speaks."

With Karl Barth and Rudolf Bultmann, the German theologian Friedrich Gogarten began a movement to return God's revelation to its primacy as a unique theological source and authority. For Gogarten, however, God's intervention in human history cannot be reduced to a single point in Jesus Christ. If God enters history, God does it in our real existence. Consequently, the process of secularization has to be understood as a place where we can hear the word of God. "It has become necessary," he says, "to pose the question of the Christian faith in a totally new way, that is, taking into account the secularization which practically embraces the whole of human life." This movement, which acknowledges the non-sacred nature of the world, is a "product" of the biblical faith. Gods and demons have lost their dominion over human life. The cosmos is emptied of its "divinity." If "human reason" is seen as an object of reverence and adoration rather than an instrument for responsible action, we fall into "secularism" and a new "religious" relation to the world. Christianity, therefore, has the task of vigilance to ensure that a consequent secularity does not fall prey to new "enchantments," the idolization of the world or of human reason.

Dietrich Bonhoeffer (1906–1945) makes some tantalizing references to the problem of secularity in his *Letters and Papers from Prison*. Bonhoeffer organizes his insights around two poles: the disappearance of religion in our world and the particularity of God's presence in Jesus Christ. This "religion" that has no more place in our modern world, is basically the bourgeois religion with its subjectivism and individualism, its irresponsibility for the world and society, and its obsession with individual salvation and security. It is a crutch for an immature, weak creature unable to cope with reality. The modern person has overcome that stage and is no longer interested in this god that has to be found at the edges of human possibility, in the gaps still unoccupied by science and technology. But this is not the God of Jesus Christ. "The God who makes us live in this world without using him as a working hypothesis is the God before whom we are ever standing. Before God and with him we live without God. . . . God is weak and powerless in the world, and that is exactly the way, the only way, in which he can be with us and help us." To be "conformed" to this God (which is to be conformed to Jesus Christ, the man for others) is what faith really is. "Our relation to God [is] not a religious relationship to a supreme Being of God."

Harvey Cox, in *The Secular City* (1965), attempts to relate Bonhoeffer's insights to the American situation. Rather than defending the faith, he celebrates the advent of the secular city. Following Gogarten and Bonhoeffer, he sees secularity as a consequence of the biblical faith: The story of creation is a disenchantment of the world, the exodus is the desacralization of politics, and the covenant is the deconsecration of values (the prohibition to worship any "image"

435

of God—material, doctrinal, or ethical). He distances himself from the "death of God theology" and presents an understanding of God as one who preserves transcendence within the "historical language" of our time—in the secular city, with its anonymity, its mobility, its pragmatism. Technology and pragmatism are the concrete forms of the desacralizing of the world; mobility represents the end of "a tribal society," the present possibility of an exodus; anonymity represents the freedom from the law, where relations with an "other" are a voluntary decision and not a socially preordained destiny. Cox conceives the mission of the church as liberating human beings from the weight of a sacred history and an unmovable order and moving them toward social change, reconciliation, the elimination of the racial, national, confessional, sexist, generational, and class frontiers.

For Thomas J. J. Altizer, in *The Gospel of Christian Atheism* (1966), the present crisis affects all aspects of Christianity: theology, piety, and institutions. The basic "historical event" that precipitated this crisis was announced by Nietzsche almost a century ago: "God is dead." But this is not merely a cultural fact, a subjective reality. It is God's own decision. Altizer understands God's self-emptying in the incarnation as a sort of "suicide," God's refusal to have any other existence than the everyday self-emptying into human life. This leads to a rejection of the objectifiable presence of God: Jesus is God, not as a point in time that can be later recollected, but as God's resignation of any form of presence other than human life itself. "To know that God is Jesus, is to know that God has become flesh: hence God does not exist as transcendent Spirit or sovereign Lord, now God is love" (67).

Some Open Questions. First, is the positive understanding of the process of secularization as "human emancipation" an adequate characterization of the complex reality of the economic, political, social, scientific-technological, and cultural developments of the last two hundred fifty years? How can that "coming of age" of humankind be reconciled with the growing poverty and marginalization of two-thirds of the human race, the anomie of the great urban conglomerates, and the lack of participation by large sections of the population of the advanced countries in political decisions?

Second, religion, meanwhile, has not disappeared. Is it possible that our diagnosis was not deep enough? In *Our Idea of God*, Juan Luis Segundo suggests that the "death of God" is the result of a "death of the human": Our culture has made human life so mechanistic (primarily by defining it in economic terms) that it has amputated questions of meaning and purpose. Are we not seeing in the present rebirth of old religions and above all in the obsession with magic, the occult, mystical experience, and the "new religious movements" a protest, however misguided, against this reduction of human life?

Third, if the hypothesis suggested in the last question is at least possible, should we not ask whether the opposition of faith to religion needs to be rethought as a

436

question of how the religious dimension of human life can be addressed from the biblical insights about the desacralizing of the world, politics, and ethics that we have gained in reflection about secularity? Secularization has changed the location—the form of operation and the institutional expressions—of politics, economics, and culture. Why should it "eliminate" religion? Is religion necessarily the elimination of human freedom, the sacralization of the world as it is, the idolization of established values?

Fourth, have we not confused desacralization with the reduction of human life, and so brought on tragic consequences in our relation to nature? Could not Christians at the same time accept the desacralization of the world (both human and natural) that seems to be implied in the transcendence of God but commit themselves to the sanctification of the world as God's meaningful creation and as the sign and anticipation of God's new eschatological world? When Christians in Latin America, Asia, or Africa speak of "a new militant spirituality" that does not separate material and spiritual or temporal and eternal, but incorporates the world, its tasks, and its promises into the life of prayer, celebration, and devotion, are we not redefining religion within the "secular" world, not "at the periphery but at the center of existence," as Bonhoeffer demanded?

Fifth, the theologies of secularization seem to have confused their terms of reference by interpreting secularity as a "historical event" in a certain ideological way (very much related to the modern bourgeois tradition) and as the criterion for a reinterpretation of the Christian faith. Then, when they rightly discovered and highlighted the liberating biblical tradition about the worldliness of the world and the freedom of humankind, they mistakenly identified it with that accepted criterion instead of subjecting the process and the ideology to the critical control of the biblical tradition.

These questions should not be understood as a denial of or a desire to reverse the process of secularity, nor as a refusal of the significant theological insights that were gained in the theological engagement with this process. Rather, the suggestions continue that reflection in the light of the historical experience of the Christian praxis of the last decades.

JOSÉ MÍGUEZ BONINO

Bibliography

Thomas J. J. Altizer, *The Gospel of Christian Atheism.*
Thomas J. J. Altizer and William Hamilton, *Radical Theology and the Death of God.*
Jacques Ellul, *The New Demons.*
Friedrich Gogarten, *Despair and Hope for Our Time.*
R. G. Smith, *Secular Christianity.*

Cross Reference: Death of God Theology, Society, Technology.

SEXUALITY

Christian theologians now share a general awareness that Christianity has been dominated for most of its history by anti-sexual bias often attributed to the enduring influence of Gnostic and other world-denying religions and philosophies dominant in the first centuries after Christ. The fear and rejection of sexuality in the Christian tradition led to fear and rejection of both women, who represented sexuality to the men who constructed the Christian theological tradition, and, by extension, femininity itself.

Traditional Christian treatment of sexuality occurred within a framework of soul-body dualism: The self was identified with the soul-mind-will, and the body was understood to represent a lower animal nature that was to be possessed and controlled by the rational, spiritual will. This will was understood to predominate over the body in men; in women, the body and its appetites were understood to be largely unchecked. Thus in traditional theology, and for some Christian theologians still, sexuality was and is an area of applied ethics, a category of acts requiring Christians to make moral judgments.

Christian thought today tends to speak of sexuality primarily in terms of a theology of sexuality, not as applied ethics. It treats sexuality as an integral aspect of the human person and increasingly as a dimension of human life through which revelation of God and divinely willed human nature are expressed. This is an integration of earlier opposing Catholic and Protestant views. Catholics had insisted on the sacramentality of marriage, with sexual intercourse as sacramental sign, and maintained that sacramentality was bestowed by the church. Protestantism understood marriage as a natural institution, neither under the control of the church nor sacramental. Presently emerging is an understanding of marriage as both natural (recognized, but not controlled by the church) and a sacramental (grace-giving, revelatory) institution, with marital sex at its core. Thus we now find accounts that view giving birth and sexual intercourse as avenues for experiencing the divine in human life.

Until the twentieth century procreation was understood as a primary, for Roman Catholicism *the* primary, purpose of sexuality, although some Protestant groups, such as the American Puritans, stressed the importance of sexual cherishing of the spouse. Beginning with the Anglican Lambeth Conference of 1930, artificial contraception was approved in one Protestant denomination after another, thus moving spousal intimacy to the fore. Roman Catholicism officially forbids artificial contraception, although a large majority of American Catholics use it.

Sexuality is often treated today within the understanding of human embodiment. If our bodies are not possessions of our selves but are our selves, then the sexed nature of human bodies makes us sexual persons, whether or not we engage in specific sexual acts. The implications of sex and gender for human life and activity are not clear; research is incomplete and even conflicting at points.

Among ethicists, there is great interest in continuing male-female differences in left and right brain development and use, in hormone levels and their influence on behavior, and in the implications of sexual physiology for spirituality and behavior. Whether female potential for childbearing or the externality of male genitalia affect our relationships, our concepts of self, and our activity is a question with tremendous implications for evaluating human behavior.

The understanding of humans as embodied has generated a tendency to explore sexuality not in terms of isolated acts done by humans but as expressions of, and influences on, relationships between embodied persons. Thus the evaluation of sexual acts has come to involve extended attention to the circumstances of sexual acts, and, among some, it has come to involve a focus on evaluating sexual relationships rather than sexual acts. This shift is *also* a shift from a largely *rule-based* approach to sexual acts, one dependent on scripture and, in Roman Catholicism, on natural law tradition, to a *consequentialist* approach to sexual relationships. For example, instead of evaluating genital activity in terms of whether the partners were heterosexual, married to each other, and open to procreation, the questions become whether the relationship in which the act occurred was caring, mutual, consensual, and responsible. The application of scripture to a sexual teaching productive of liberated, fully human persons, then, becomes less based on particular scriptural references to sexual acts and more focused on the implications for sexual relationships of the announcement of God's Reign, with the understanding that these implications are continually unfolding in history.

Sexuality has moved to the forefront of theological thinking today largely as a result of the women's movement and the consequent explosion of feminist research in all fields, including religion. Feminist historians and theologians exposed the link between anti-sexual and misogynist attitudes in the Christian tradition beginning with the New Testament through the Patristic, medieval, and Reformation periods to the present, forcing Christian churches, theologians, and ethicists to reconsider this aspect of the tradition. It is therefore not surprising that gender issues—the similarities, differences, and relationship of the sexes—are central issues in treatment of sexuality today. From being almost exclusively treated under applied ethics, sexuality has come to be an issue in ecclesiology (the role of women in the church, especially in ministry); theology of marriage (roles of the spouses, headship of the male, and traditional teachings on marital sex); liturgy (the use of sexist language for God and for humans); spirituality (the gender and characteristics of God); scripture (everything from Eve's role in the Fall to the household codes of the New Testament); the study of all the periods of church history (historical treatment of women, sex, marriage, and the feminine); religious anthropology (shifting from the story of human nature to the analysis of patriarchal structures which control humans); and ethical method (shifting our ethical method toward a liberationist end), where it is an important concern.

Another influence on treatment of sexuality is the inclusion in the dialogue of theologians who criticize the universalization of white Western Christian customs and concepts regarding sexuality. They defend varying Asian, African, and, to a lesser extent, Latin American sexual concepts and practices, charging that white Western imperialism in the churches is at the root of such issues as the exclusion of polygamy; the refusal of divorce; exclusion of trial marriage; disapproval of female circumcision; clitoridectomy, genital infibulation, and other traditional rites of passage; an overemphasis on virginity and celibacy; and a highly romanticized, individualistic understanding of marriage.

Despite these more or less clear trends among Christian theologians on sexuality, no consensus about the issues and their resolution exists. Strong divisions exist among Catholic, liberal Protestant, and evangelical-fundamentalist Protestant denominations on abortion, sexist language, nonmarital sex, and the role of women in church and society.

CHRISTINE GUDORF

Bibliography

Elizabeth Clark and Herbert Richardson, *Women and Religion: A Feminist Sourcebook of Christian Thought.*
Charles A. Gallagher, et al., *Embodied in Love: Sacramental Spirituality and Sexual Intimacy.*
Vincent J. Genovesi, *In Pursuit of Love: Catholic Morality and Human Sexuality.*
James B. Nelson, *Embodiment: An Approach to Sexuality and Christian Theology.*
John Shelby Spong, *Living in Sin? A Bishop Rethinks Human Sexuality.*

Cross Reference: Anthropology, Feminist Theology, Soul/Body.

SILENCE

A fundamental irony underlies all discourse about the character and significance of silence, which is the absence of sound, particularly the human voice. The very act of discussing silence annuls it, and even writing about silence shapes a voice that can break it.

Throughout Christian practice and thought, the character, function, and interpretation of silence have varied greatly. The religious functions and theological significance of silence can be classified in six distinct categories: a medium for divine inspiration or revelation, a basis for dialogue between Christians and Buddhists, a means of discipline, evidence of oppression, a constitutive element in the hermeneutics of deconstructionism, and perception of the absence of God.

The ritual use of silence as the medium through which revelation and inspiration are received has been associated with monastic communities (e.g., the Cistercians) that adopt various degrees of silence in their pursuit of discipline and worship and with the style of worship practiced by Quakers, who regard silence as a form of communion both with the divine and with the assembled group of believers. According to Thomas Merton (1915–1968), the Trappist monk who prompted much late-twentieth-century Christian fascination with silence, the connection between theology and mystical silence is that theology inspires and commends persons toward a silent life that is open to revelation. In contrast to the appreciation of silence by these groups, some Protestants consider the silent life devoid of sacramental experience and mission, for they understand that God is encountered in the proclamation of the Word.

The Christian mystic's quest for silence as "perfect emptiness" provides a common point of contact with Buddhist mystics. In this sense, silence is "a ground of openness" from and toward the divine spirit that communicates itself to all that is. And in the spirit of openness to the Other through the experience of silence, Christians and Buddhists have focused their interfaith dialogue.

A third function of silence in Christian practice has been its use as a means of religious discipline. Deriving authority from the story of the Jewish priest Zachariah, who was dumbstruck with silence as a penalty for having doubted the miraculous conception of John the Baptist by his elderly wife Elizabeth (Luke 1:5-20), Christians have used silence as a method of punitive discipline: It can be demanded of a person, as with the Vatican's temporary silencing of Leonardo Boff and Matthew Fox in order to reprimand them for taking radical dogmatic positions and to prompt them to contemplate the perceived error of their ways. Similarly, some monastic Christians subscribe to the Rule of Saint Benedict, which indicates that silence is the form of discipline to be imposed on an individual who has committed grave offenses. A different disciplinary use of silence is the one exercised by a community, as with the Old Order Amish's shunning of persons who have strayed from the norms of the community.

A fourth kind of silence is that experienced by oppressed groups whose voices have been muted by their oppressors. The theological significance of this experience of silence is manifest in the emergence of various theologies of liberation that now voice the ideas, experiences, anger, and hope of oppressed groups, for example, ethnic groups (especially blacks, Hispanics, and Asians), feminists, gays and lesbians, the homeless, and the poor.

The significance of silence for theologians is also connected to the hermeneutical method of deconstructionism, whose focus on the interstices or spaces between words—the silence between sounds—provides an orientation to examine the unwritten assumptions behind the text, the unspoken presuppositions that direct the discourse, and perhaps the oppressive forces that inhibit articulation.

441

Finally, silence can be understood as the absence of God. As a modern philosophical concept, the silence of God gained specific articulation by Friedrich Nietzsche in *Thus Spoke Zarathustra,* and the concept has become an important theme in twentieth-century literary imagination (e.g., Albert Camus's *The Stranger,* Samuel Beckett's *Waiting for Godot,* and Ingmar Bergman's *The Seventh Seal*). The theme of divine silence has also claimed theologians' attention in the brief life of the death of God theology and in their struggle to understand the horror of the Holocaust. In *Night* Elie Wiesel poignantly portrays the silence of God in the Holocaust, recalling the incident of the Nazis' hanging of a child. As the boy's frail body—silent and struggling—dangled from the gallows for more than half an hour before succumbing to death, Wiesel heard a voice behind him agonize, "Where is God now?" In silence, Wiesel thought: "Where is He? Here He is—He is hanging here on the gallows."

Although silence itself is not intrinsically religious, it undergirds and expresses a variety of religious rituals and theological perspectives that potentially signify the presence or absence of God and the oppression or communion of persons.

JOSEPH L. PRICE

Bibliography

Mary Field Belenky, et al., *Women's Ways of Knowing: The Development of Self, Voice, and Mind.*
T. Edmund Harvey, *Silence and Worship: A Study in Quaker Experience.*
Thomas Merton, *Thoughts in Solitude.*
Max Picard, *The World of Silence.*
Ambrose G. Wathan, *Silence: The Meaning of Silence in the Rule of St. Benedict.*

Cross Reference: Death of God Theology, Deconstructionism, Holocaust, Inspiration, Mysticism, Revelation.

SIN

"Sin," in Christian understanding, is whatever act, attitude, or course of life betrays the divine intent for created being. Sin alienates from God, divides the sinner from God's community, disorders the life of the sinner, and in that measure disorders creation itself. "Against thee, thee only, have I sinned" (Ps. 51:4) expresses the psalmist's awareness of sin as at heart a religious corruption of one's existence. If we understand immorality to be at root anti-social and crime to be against the state, sin is directly against God. Yet as the most profound of these disorders, sin impinges on the other two as well.

This article will (1) consider sin against the backdrop of a wider human awareness of disease and disorder in human existence, but it will do so only (2) to distinguish this backdrop sharply from the Christian understanding. Here sin is betrayal of the covenant God made with Israel and renewed in Christ Jesus, so that any breach in the full faithfulness to which Jesus Christ summons his followers is sin for them. The article will then (3) consider the special problem created for faith by the rise and apparent decay of the doctrine of "original" sin. In this connection it will indicate some of the substitute understandings of sin (legalist, subjectivist, voluntarist, physicalist) that have more recently flourished. Finally, (4) the article will assess the prospects for a strong, biblically based doctrine of sin in present-day theology.

1. Sin is not a Christian invention. Despite the suspicions of latter-day pagans, the guilty awareness of something amiss in human life is not owed primarily to fundamentalists, Puritans, or medieval Catholics, but is discovered throughout the world among widely separated peoples; the concepts of tabu and dread are witnesses to this human disquiet and serve to relate it to the displeasure of a god or of the gods. The contents of these widespread phenomena are echoed in certain common terms for sin in Hebrew scripture: *awon,* crookedness or self-abuse; *chethah,* the anti-social breaking of boundaries of conduct; *peshah,* rebellion against the Most High. All three of these recurring terms are translated in the Greek Septuagint by *hamartia,* missing the mark or veering off the road, and in its turn *hamartia* became the generic New Testament term we translate "sin." These facts suggest that the Christian concept was perceived to correspond broadly to the wider, multicultural phenomena just mentioned.

2. Broad correspondence is not simple equivalence, however, and in fact the biblical and Christian concept of sin cannot simply be equated with the wider range of phenomena reflecting guilt and disquiet—phenomena that in many cases may better be explored with the concepts provided by Sigmund Freud. The Christian concept can be grasped only through an understanding of the approach of God to humankind spelled out in the Hebrew scriptures as covenant and in the New Testament as salvation through Jesus Christ. In other words, sin can be seen through Christian eyes as sinful only in light of the new understanding that Jesus Christ gives his followers: a new sense of self (cf. "Christ in you [plural], the hope of glory," Col. 1:27 [this and all subsequent quotations Revised English Bible unless noted otherwise]); a new form of community (cf. "I am the vine; you are the branches," John 15:5); and a new awareness of God and of divine things ("The Father and I are one," John 10:30). Thereby disciples are provided with a new knowledge of what the lack of these things must entail (cf. John 3:19: "This is the judgment: the light has come into the world, but people preferred darkness to light . . ."). In a word, the Christian concept of sin is inseparable from the Christian awareness of salvation, even as the Jewish concept is inseparable from the covenant and the law that that covenant ushered into the life of the world. There can thus be no self-standing, that is, purely empirical or theoretically independent, Christian doctrine of sin: Strictly speaking, Christian awareness of sin is dependent upon salvation, the new life, new vision, new creation that come in Christ, and reversing this order distorts both the doctrine of Christ and the doctrine of sin.

Thus the measure of the believer's sin and sinfulness (or of the conquest of these) can be found neither in an objective, self-evident moral law (Kant), nor in a (conceivably neurotic) self-scrutiny; its objective measure is found in the full faithfulness Christians recognize in their incarnate, crucified, and risen Lord Jesus, who is said on account of this faithfulness to be "without sin" (Heb. 4:15). Subjectively, the believer's sin and sinfulness is to be measured against Christ's re-embodiment in the believing community ("the body of Christ") and in the life of each disciple ("for to me life is Christ," Phil. 1:21).

The topic of Jesus' full or unqualified faithfulness is crucial in our understanding here; theologies that base the doctrine of sin upon a concept of original sin (see below) are hard pressed to give any account of Christ's sinlessness save a negative one: Jesus must have been spared some genetic or racial blight that all others endure (in which case he can hardly be the model for believers not so protected); or alternatively Jesus must have shared in original sin with all others (Karl Barth) while committing no "actual" sin (in which case original sin is not the deterrent to faithful living that it is reputed to be). If on the other hand the approach favored here is taken, Jesus' "sinlessness" (more appropriately, his unqualified faithfulness) simply indicates his lasting adherence to the covenant God provided for Israel, a covenant foreshadowed in the patriarchs, fully tendered at Exodus and Sinai, rehearsed by the prophets, and now renewed in the Messiah. In this case, Jesus is not (as "sinless" might suggest) humanly defective; rather he is the truly and fully human One, the Son of man, and his faithfulness exposes any and all of our unfaithfulnesses as defects in the humanity he realized. In that case, when we sin, we show ourselves coming short of the humanity he achieved. Our sins (our failures in faithfulness, for "whatever does not proceed from faith is sin," Rom. 14:23 RSV) are not spicy additions to an otherwise bland existence; they are instead flaws, disqualifiers, subtractions from the humanity Jesus exemplifies. Thereby we are deprived of the divine glory as well, that is, the glory of Godhood fully embodied in human being (Rom. 3:23).

This way of construing the matter, in which all sin is "actual" sin and none is born guilty of inherited sin, has some powerful advantages. This way is closely tied to seeing Christ as the long expected image of God (cf. Gen. 1:27; Heb. 1:3), who fulfills God's age-long plan to be present in human life, a plan often frustrated by Adam and his kind. This way is tied, too, to the truth that Pelagius sensed but so unsuccessfully expressed, the truth that obedient Christian living is not an "impossible ideal" (thus Reinhold Niebuhr) or only reserved for (plaster) saints, but is a live option for all whom Christ graciously calls to be his. Yet this way has

444

some theoretical liabilities as well, and these can only be met in light of a closer examination of the concept of original sin.

3. If sin was precisely unfaithfulness to Jesus and the covenant, no general account of its origin or sway was either required or provided in earliest Christianity: Genesis 3 was not a causal account; Adam's sin was simply his own: "death pervaded the whole human race, inasmuch as all have sinned" (Rom. 5:12). But certain North African theologians eventually produced a new, more grandiose understanding: For Origen, the Adam and Eve story mirrors the story of each of us; Tertullian thought sin was linked with every procreative act; Augustine went beyond these to teach that sin and guilt were seminally inherited from Adam, basing his theory on a misreading of Romans 5:12 (a misreading perpetuated as recently as the King James Version). This inheritance constituted a genetic disorder in the human race, making all of us sinners from conception and birth onward apart from any sinful deeds. Thus the doctrine of original (i.e., inherited) sin was held to account for actual sins. Pelagius's (graceless) protest was condemned, yet covertly endorsed, by medieval theologians; Luther and Calvin and their sort (though not the Anabaptists) reaffirmed the Augustinian doctrine in the interest of the primacy of grace; and the theory of original sin remains, at least on paper, as the teaching of all the principal Western churches. It provided a sort of explanation for the widespread human malaise mentioned earlier, but also served as a palliative for the lethargy and guilt that characterized so much post-Reformation Christianity, Catholic and Protestant. "In Adam's Fall/We Sinned all" said The New England Primer, and that seemed to account for the human condition well enough.

Yet the difficulties of the official doctrine were immense: inherited guilt (expressed in Lamarckian terms—the inheritance of acquired characteristics—at that!), dissonance with the human nature of Christ, a naive historiography, and bad exegesis (e.g., of Romans 5) among others. In reaction, infant baptism was early invoked to remove the guilt that the theory imputed to infants, and from the Reformation onward alternative rationalizing accounts of sin often effectively replaced the official theory.

Among these rationalizing accounts, four may be singled out. Legalist theories defined sin as the breaking of the divine moral law (thus Calvin), but these fell too easily into the depersonalization of divine-human relations that the term "legalism" reproaches. Subjectivist theories made the believing subject the only measure of his or her sin, thus introducing a severe relativism into Christian morality and piety. Voluntarist theories limited sin to willful wrongdoing (Kant); these seemed inadequate to Christian awareness of the divine holiness, and to a complex human nature not easily separated into will and other segments. Physicalist theories strictly limited sin (especially in some versions of Catholic moral theology) to particular describable physical states and bodily acts, again missing the religious concept of sin itself. Each of these four shed some light on the nature of sin, but none fully captured its wide sweep or its distinctively Christian slant.

Eventually, especially in Anglo-American Christianity, the theory of original sin came under heavy attack. F. R. Tennant and N. P. Williams, both Anglicans, wrote early in the twentieth century exposing the logical and theological inconsistencies of the church doctrine. Meanwhile in America, Social Gospel advocates, deeply concerned about corporate and national evils, provided an account of sin linked not to Adam and inheritance but to sinful social structures blighting human life. Baptist Walter Rauschenbusch wrote and lectured extensively on these themes: More chapters of his *Theology for the Social Gospel* were devoted to sin than to any other topic. He invoked the biblical concept of principalities and powers to structure his critique. For such prophetic voices, Satan was real enough but was to be identified with oppressive (yet not all-powerful) collective agents in society. Yet Rauschenbusch's putative successor on the American scene, Reinhold Niebuhr, reverted to the doctrine of original sin (for him, a myth), thus somewhat obscuring the genuine advances earlier in the century.

4. The Christian doctrine of sin is clearly one on which much work is needed at present. The received church doctrine of original sin has positive values: It recognizes the widespread human malaise and attempts to explain it and relate it to the biblical account of actual sin; it seeks also to maintain the primacy of grace by insisting upon the hopelessness of the human situation considered within itself; thus it acknowledges, even as it despairs at, the ubiquity and depth of human evil. Yet as noted earlier, it has turned out to have insuperable problems both in itself and in relation to other Christian doctrines such as the humanity of Christ and the holiness of authentic Christian discipleship. Moreover, one of its claims—to explain the presence of evil in a world created by a good God—has seemed particularly weak in recent thought.

If the positive features of the received church doctrine of sin are to be maintained while its dubious features are either reformed or discarded, it will be necessary to make a starting point, not in Adam's (or Eve's!) alleged act of sin on behalf of innocent babes and faithful believers born an aeon later, but rather in the full faithfulness of Jesus of Nazareth, who resisted the temptation that confronted him all the way to his cross, who overcame the principalities and powers of his day even at the price of his life, and who, risen from the dead, summoned followers to abandon every sin and to follow in good faith the pioneer of their salvation.

A doctrine of sin linked to this central narrative can readily acknowledge the truth in legalist, subjectivist, voluntarist, and physicalist accounts: There are divine commands, sometimes in the form of law, and sinners do transgress them; in doing so, their own selfhood is distorted and denied; sin sometimes rises to outrageous willful perversity; we are embodied selves, whose acts of sin as well as of righteousness are flesh and blood acts. Yet such a doctrine will not be limited to these partial accounts in its attempt to delineate God's faithfulness in Israel, Christ, and church by showing in their light the dark shadow sin casts. It must instead hold up this divine faithfulness as the measure of every life, and it must confess that whatever falls short of, denies, or contradicts Christ's faithfulness is sin.

JAMES WM. McCLENDON, JR.

Bibliography

On the multicultural phenomena, *see* the articles gathered under "Sin" in James Hastings, *Encyclopedia of Religion and Ethics.* F. R. Tennant, *The Origin and Propagation of Sin,* argues forcefully against the doctrine of inherited sin, and (less successfully) proposes an "evolutionary" account of sin and evil. Walter Rauschenbusch, *A Theology for the Social Gospel,* treats the social transmission of sin and the "super-personal forces of evil." Reinhold Niebuhr, *Nature and Destiny of Man,* argues the neoorthodox view of original sin. For a constructive account in line with this article, *see* James Wm. McClendon, Jr., *Doctrine: Systematic Theology, Volume II.*

Cross Reference: Atonement, Evil, Social Gospel, Soteriology.

SOCIAL GOSPEL

The Social Gospel was a largely Protestant movement that attempted to respond to changed conditions in the United States during the late nineteenth and early twentieth centuries. Among the circumstances to be addressed were a cycle of depressions and violent labor disputes, as well as rapid growth in industrial cities and towns—all of which were associated with the arrival of immigrant labor. A wide-ranging socialist movement became increasingly prominent, and progressive candidates ran significant campaigns for public office. New economic theories and the study of sociology challenged the reigning laissez faire individualism and social Darwinism of America's Gilded Age.

Proponents of the Social Gospel focused attention on the growing sense that society is a web of mutually interdependent relations and interests. The movement included interdenominational organizers and spokespersons such as Josiah Strong (1847–1916), reform-minded sociologists such as Albion Small (1854–1926), moderate theological ethicists such as Francis Greenwood Peabody (1847–1936), and radicals such as George D. Herron (1862–1926), who once expounded "The Political Economy of the Lord's Prayer." The characteristic concerns and methods of the Social Gospel movement can be seen in the work of two of its leading figures, Richard T. Ely (1854–1943), an economist with theological interests, and Walter Rauschenbusch (1861–1918), a pastor near the Hell's Kitchen area in New York City and later professor of church history at Rochester Seminary.

Ely devised an idea of "social solidarity" or the notion that we are not isolated individuals but participants in a vast matrix of interconnected interests, possibilities, and responsibilities. This idea, he said, was now beginning to be glimpsed by social philosophy and the sciences, although its heritage included biblical understandings of the disobedience of all people in Adam, the redemption of all in Christ, and the organic unity of the church and the body of Christ. Combining social solidarity with the prescription to love God and neighbor, Ely concluded that extreme individualism is immoral and that social health requires persons willing to engage in works of service. He also favored the socialization of natural monopolies, the extension of public education, public libraries, building and loan associations, disability insurance, and so on. He regarded these attitudes and policies as elements of a progressive stance that would seize opportunities for reform without embracing the weaknesses of socialism.

Walter Rauschenbusch is widely regarded as the Social Gospel's most important thinker. He, too, understood current circumstances in light of the basic apprehension that human life, though plagued by inordinate egoism, is inherently social. For this, he found essential support in a prophetic theology centered on Jesus' message of the kingdom of God, as well as in Darwinian biology, the emerging discipline of sociology, new economic theories, and contemporary socialists and reformers.

Rauschenbusch, who identified himself as a "practical socialist," maintained that people are endowed with a social instinct that stands in need of appropriate formation and intensification. He argued that the Kingdom is a social reality that involves the entire life of humanity. Like the prophets, he said, Jesus connected the Kingdom with justice, mercy, and a nonhierarchical polity of mutual service and solidarity, whereas the power of sin creates "a private kingdom of self-service" that is opposed to God's kingdom of mutual love and cooperation. "Organized around Jesus as its impelling power," and upheld by the Spirit as the Kingdom's emissary, the church should therefore pursue a prophetic mission to the whole of society by encouraging human impulses toward greater solidarity. This it could do, said Rauschenbusch, by attending to how it orders its internal life; by challenging the philosophy of competitive individualism; by promoting humane customs and attitudes toward children, women, and the poor; by supporting useful institutions, such as public education, public parks, profit sharing, and agencies of international cooperation; and by calling for a spate of legal reforms concerning taxes, child labor, a minimum wage, and so on.

In sum, the Social Gospel pointed out that modern Protestantism could no longer accurately claim that true religion is entirely a matter of personal conversion and individual salvation. Ely, Rauschenbusch, and others insisted that the age of industry presented Christian faith with the distinctive challenges and responsibilities of an intensified and expanded matrix of social relations. They found their changed situation helpfully illumined by the emerging social sciences and reformist political movements. And they concluded that it called for an interpretation of Christian ethics sufficiently bold, broad, and practically engaged to take the wider socio-economic and political realm into account. That conclusion has found institutional embodiment in many of the American churches, and it remains an important source of insight and renewal for those who continue to be concerned about Christian faith and social justice.

DOUGLAS F. OTTATI

Bibliography

Aaron I. Abell, *American Catholicism and Social Action: A Search for Social Justice.*
Richard T. Ely, *Socialism: An Examination of Its Nature, Its Strengths, and Its Weaknesses, with Suggestions for Social Reform.*
Robert T. Handy, ed., *The Social Gospel in America 1870–1920: Gladden, Ely, Rauschenbusch.*
Howard C. Hopkins, *The Rise of the Social Gospel in American Protestantism 1865–1915.*
Walter Rauschenbusch, *A Theology for the Social Gospel.*
_____, *Christianity and the Social Crisis.*

Cross Reference: Economics, Justice, Kingdom of God, Liberalism, Liberation Theology.

SOCIETY

In Christian theology the question of society concerns the relation of human communities and institutions to God and Christian faith. Social issues have always concerned theologians, but they have become especially important in the twentieth century. Technology raises problems of the social good and human control over life. Warfare, totalitarian political systems, and economic inequality pose questions of justice. The struggles for emancipation from political, cultural, and religious oppression assert the importance of human rights. These developments have demanded theological reflection and response.

Some theologians, like Paul Tillich and Langdon Gilkey, have devised theologies of culture to analyze existential questions as they take form in cultural life. Christian faith, they argue, answers these questions of ultimate concern. Other theologians address social and political issues. Early-twentieth-century Social Gospel theologians like Walter Rauschenbusch sought to "Christianize" the social order to relieve the suffering found in industrial society. The optimism of this liberal project was shattered by World War II. Thus Christian realists Reinhold Niebuhr and Paul Ramsey analyzed issues of power and justice under the ideal of Christian love never to be realized in history. Recently, Johann Baptist Metz, Beverly Wildung Harrison, and others have begun to explore political and economic life from the perspective of the oppressed. In sum, theologians construe

449

society either as the arena of power and justice in which Christians act on behalf of the poor and oppressed, as the domain of conflicts over justice and the common good to which faith must contribute, or as the medium for existential questions and Christian answers.

Four basic questions regarding society can be examined in the history and development of theology. First, there is the interpretative question about the meaning of society and Christian faith that determines the very task of theology. Interpretations of society shape the church's relation to it. In his *Social Teachings of the Christian Churches,* Ernst Troeltsch provided a typology of options regarding church and society. The "church-type" of medieval Catholicism and Calvinistic Protestantism attempted a synthesis between faith and society. The warrants for this synthesis were belief in the sovereignty of God over all life and belief in the redemptive action of Christ. The "sect-type" sought to preserve the distinctiveness of Christian community apart from society. Drawing on biblical warrants, thinkers distinguished the "world," as the domain of sin, from the community of believers. H. Richard Niebuhr, in *Christ and Culture,* expanded and refined Troeltsch's typology. Recently, John Howard Yoder has challenged the typologies of both Troeltsch and Niebuhr as being biased toward "church-type" theology. Yoder calls for Christians to be a community of Jesus' disciples in a world of conflict. These differences aside, theologians agree that modernity is concerned with individual experience, thus making organized religion difficult to sustain. This individualism has been challenged by theologians because Christian faith is essentially social in character.

Second, there are normative questions about how social life *ought* to be conducted and structured. Following Augustine, traditional theology held that a community is constituted by a historical purpose or love and that the legitimation of social structures and political authority is found in their coherence with that purpose. For Augustine secular politics was defined by the sinful love of ruling rooted in pride. Yet God assigned to the state the task of restraining evil and promoting peace. Christian theologians also used Romans 13:1-7 to assert God's institution of political authority and the need for compliance with it. And they often defined social differentiation through the idea of orders of creation (church, society, and family).

In our times, social theorists like Jürgen Habermas note that modern society is composed of different spheres of life (economic, political, private), each with unique purposes, claims, and authorities. Modern Western culture has rejected the belief that the order and unity of society is created by God and is therefore unchangeable. The spheres of life are to be judged by their distinctive claims and democratic purposes and not by religious ideals. This is often specified in the idea of the separation of church and state. Traditional theological ideas of social purpose, legitimation, and orders of creation seem inadequate for addressing social life.

Mindful of the differentiation of modern society, theologians today contribute to normative reflection on the social good. Roman Catholic theology has drawn on the idea of the human as the "image of God" and the dictates of natural law to affirm basic human rights grounding and limiting political and economic authority. Liberation theologian Gustavo Gutiérrez and feminists also have elaborated the biblical theme of liberation to address this issue. The good of society is judged by the treatment of marginal people, and the church's mission is their liberation. Still other theologians argue for the common good regarding just distribution of social benefits. The good of society is the flourishing of the social whole. In each case, a religious idea (image of God, liberation, divine sovereignty) is related to ethical norms (human rights, basic needs, common good) to specify the good of social structures and authorities.

Third, the question of society raises practical issues. In this century practical questions surround warfare and violence (nuclear war, revolution, and nonviolent resistance), economic justice, racial and sexual oppression, and technology. The United States Catholic Bishops, for instance, have drawn on just war theory and Christian pacifism to condemn nuclear war and to call for limits on the use of nuclear deterrence. Proposals for practical action thus cohere with considerations of the meaning, nature, and good of society and a vision of Christian faith.

Fourth, practical, normative, and interpretive questions about society interrelate with conceptions of the nature of human community. Many theologians, like Karl Barth, have seen the church as a locus of theological reflection, forming Christian identity and exercising institutional power. Biblical symbols have again informed thought, whether in the image of the church as the "Body of Christ" (an organic image) or in institutional notions of church. These images of the nature of the church inform how a theologian addresses social questions.

In characterizing human associations, social theorists distinguish community (Gemeinschaft) marked by personal relations, and institutional society (Gesellschaft) with specified structures. These entail different kinds of leadership, authority, and meaning structures. Thought about the church employs such social analysis and yet relates it to beliefs about God, Christ, redemption, and eschatology. If the church is examined as a human community, as James M. Gustafson does in Treasure in Earthen Vessels, then an assessment of its relation to society and the divine is different from seeing the church, as the Second Vatican Council did, as a servant and sacramental reality. In contrast, theologians like Stanley Hauerwas and Latin American "base communities" place emphasis on the identity of the gathered community of believers rather than on institutional structure and purposes. Ideas about the nature of the church cohere then with claims about human association and different visions of God's relation to the religious and political communities.

The question of society touches every aspect of Christian thought. Insisting on the social character of Christian faith, theologians recognize that religious experience is mediated by different cultures and church communities. A pluralism in Christian thought and faith grows out of this social mediation. The danger in this pluralism is identifying the values of any one society as determinative of the good. The possibility it presents is that of understanding the meaning and truth of Christian faith for our highly differentiated and pluralistic modern social life.

WILLIAM SCHWEIKER

Bibliography

Gustavo Gutiérrez, *A Theology of Liberation.*
Beverly Wildung Harrison, *Making the Connections.*
H. Richard Niebuhr, *Christ and Culture.*
John Howard Yoder, *The Politics of Jesus.*

Cross Reference: Basic Christian Communities, Culture, Economics, Ethics–Christian, Experience–Religious, Justice, Moral Theology, Political Theology, Social Gospel.

SOTERIOLOGY

Soteriology, from the Greek word *soter* (savior, deliverer), is that focus in Christian theology that seeks to interpret the *saving work* of Jesus Christ, that is, what God has done for us in Jesus Christ. Traditionally it has been distinguished from Christology, which is concerned with clarifying Jesus' "person," that is, who and what Jesus Christ was and is. Most theologians agree that the "person" and the "work" of Jesus Christ must be understood in relation to each other. Serious disputes in the early church led to the decision at Chalcedon (451 C.E.) that Jesus Christ is to be understood as "true God and true man," two natures in one person. This christological decision served for centuries as the presupposition for any understanding of his "person." More recently there has been a growing tendency to give prior attention to the saving work.

The church has never officially sanctioned a particular understanding of the saving work of Jesus Christ. Rather, several different interpretative themes have had power in the thought and worship life of the church. Most of these motifs find a basis among the many titles and terms of the New Testament that suggest but do not develop interpretations of Jesus Christ's saving work.

Prominent among these themes in the early church was the idea of *sacrifice*. Because of the long history of the role of sacrifice in the worship of the Hebrew people, this imagery was a natural one for expressing the experience of having been reconciled to God by the death of Jesus Christ. In its earlier uses among Christians, the sacrifice was understood to proclaim an act of God in which human defilement is wiped clean, sin is "expiated" by God's gracious act. At various times in Christian history the emphasis has shifted to the idea that God is "propitiated" by this sacrificial death, for example, by God's anger being assuaged. In this unfortunate shift, God is acted upon and changed rather than humans.

The images that dominated the church's soteriological thought and worship from the second through the eleventh century were those of "victory" and "ransom." Jesus Christ was understood to have won victory over the powers that held humankind in bondage, and the means of gaining this victory was usually understood to be by "ransom." In some versions Jesus Christ is the *victor* who has defeated the devil in combat. In others the devil, who is understood to hold the souls of humankind captive, is paid, and Christ is the *ransom*. In yet others Jesus Christ is the means by which the devil is tricked. For example, it was affirmed that the divinity of God the Son was hidden in the flesh of Jesus Christ. At his death, the devil, assuming that Jesus was but another fallen human being, took possession of his soul. However, because of Jesus' divinity and his sinlessness, the devil had no right to take him. Thus, having overstepped the boundary of his authority, the devil lost his right to hold other human souls. These images were powerful expressions of the experience of persons living in cultures very different from ours, and they effectively portrayed the idea of salvation being wrought by God through Jesus Christ.

Anselm of Canterbury (1033–1109) argued against these views that the root problem was that humankind, in the disobedience of Adam and Eve, had offended God's *honor*. In Anselm's time, "honor" was a vital concern, and the seriousness of an offense was understood in relation to the relative status of the offending and offended parties. For example, it was far more serious for a serf to offend a noble person than vice versa. When applied to the situation of a human being offending God, this meant that any offense is infinite. No human being could make *satisfaction* for an offense against the honor of God. Only a divine being could do that. But since humanity is the offender, humanity must make satisfaction. The only possible solution would be for the satisfaction to be made by one who is "true God and true human," and that is what the merciful God provided in the Incarnation of the Son. Jesus Christ's life of perfect obedience and sinless death "satisfied" God's honor, making it possible for God to accept some humans into the Kingdom without any violation of God's honor or justice.

Although "satisfaction" is not a biblical word or motif, in that time and place this interpretation of Jesus Christ's saving work made obvious sense and effectively displaced the emphases on victory and ransom. Peter Abelard (1079–1142) stood as its foremost critic when he argued that Anselm's theory allowed for no forgiveness. If one owes a debt, he claimed, and the debt is paid, it would not be reasonable to say that it has been forgiven. From Abelard's standpoint, Anselm missed the central point that God has mercifully provided a way for undeserving humankind to be reconciled. Abelard's criticism went farther, however, when he argued that Anselm had also misinterpreted the basic problem as something in God that needs to be changed (as in satisfying God's honor so that God may be justly merciful), whereas it is human beings themselves who must be changed. Humankind's alienation from God includes a morbid fear of God, and the problem is how we might come to trust God's love. In the life, suffering, and death of Jesus Christ, God's suffering love has been lived out among us in a way that has power to grasp both our minds and hearts. This emphasis, often unfairly called the "moral influence" theory of the atonement, was not well received in Abelard's time, but it has found favorable responses in the nineteenth and twentieth centuries.

No one soteriological motif dominates today's theologies; various reinterpretative proposals are being offered. Some continue to emphasize the traditional soteriological themes already sketched. Although every Christian theologian recognizes an indebtedness to the teachings of Christian tradition, at least six factors distinguish the current theological scene from earlier situations.

First, theologians recognize today that all doctrinal formulations must be understood in relation to their historical and cultural settings, because the use of language from the Bible or from other eras of church history may convey meanings differing from those originally intended. Thus, even where we believe that doctrinal formulations were conceptually correct, we must struggle with reinterpretations. The most that theologians can reasonably hope is to offer formulations that will be relatively more helpful to some people in a particular time and place.

Second, many theologians are convinced that profound misunderstandings of God have been implied in some of the historical soteriological teachings. They insist, for example, that the problem is not in God, for God is not like human rulers, whose anger must be appeased or whose offended honor needs to be satisfied. Such views are seen as quite incompatible with the God made known in the life and death of Jesus Christ.

Third, the origin of the human problem is understood differently. The human species evolved very slowly, with consciousness and self-consciousness emerging out of animal conditions dominated by instinct and motivated by an anxious self-protectiveness. That we must struggle to find reconciliation with God, self, and neighbor is not the result of some willful disobedience that destroyed a primeval paradisal state. It is rather the result of evolutionary developments that are not properly understood in legalistic or moralistic terms. Because of this shift, a rethinking of the cause and character of humanity's problem has occurred.

Fourth, theologians today place greater emphasis on the genuine humanness of Jesus of Nazareth. The Chalcedonian Creed affirmed the full humanity of Jesus, but it did so in a way that left it in great doubt. Some interpreters in our time affirm that formula by holding that Jesus Christ was "true human," but that we are not.

This is saying not simply that we have not yet arrived at the human wholeness which is to be seen in Jesus, but also that Jesus never had to struggle with the alienation from God, self, and neighbor that is at the heart of our lives. In other words, though "true man," Jesus was not really like us. Jesus' life then becomes an act of divine deception that is irrelevant to our lives. Therefore, while theologians insist that our salvation comes from God through Jesus Christ, they more and more insist as well that Jesus was fully like us, sharing our struggles and temptations and human limitations and showing the reality of God for us precisely in that utter humanness.

A fifth characteristic of the current circumstances of soteriological reflection is the pluralism of our "shrunken" and interdependent world. Increasingly, but with much disagreement and debate, Christian theologians are rejecting the traditional claim that "there is salvation *only* in Jesus Christ and his church." Instead, they affirm that in Jesus Christ we are shown the living presence of a gracious God who is reaching out in a noncoercive love to all creatures everywhere and always. As we learn more of other peoples and their religions, we recognize that "the fruits of the spirit" are to be found among them as well, sometimes more clearly than in a great many of the persons and groups who call themselves "Christian."

A sixth general factor emerges from the demand of the worlds' disadvantaged and exploited peoples for freedom from oppression. Most Christian theologies, and certainly liberation theologies formulated by the oppressed themselves, recognize that traditional doctrines have been formulated by the privileged and used to maintain their privileges. One of the powerful themes in current soteriology is the affirmation of Jesus Christ as *liberator* of every dimension of life. Liberation cannot be restricted to a narrow definition of the "spiritual," but, motivated by God's love, it seeks to overcome the poverty, disease, ignorance, prejudice, and political, social, and familial oppressions that prevent or inhibit growth in grace of all persons.

This emphasis may also be seen in current uses of the image of Jesus as *representative,* a term that provides contrast with the idea of Jesus as our *substitute.* While the motif of representation calls us to participate, the symbol of substitute leaves us as bystanders. Sometimes the motif of representation is joined with a *relational* understanding of persons that holds that we are largely constituted by our primary relationships and that Jesus' selfhood, rooted in his openness to God's grace, was "co-constituted" by God, fulfilling, not negating, his humanness. In this way of thinking, Jesus became "transparent" to the reality of God-for-us; indeed, he was a decisive presence of God among us. The relational model also urges that we can be ever more like Jesus Christ, our lives rooted in and reflective of the grace of God, carrying forward his liberating ministry.

In light of such factors in the present theological situation, it is hardly surprising that there is no consensus in soteriology. Theologians of varying perspectives urge

455

the use of many models and metaphors to supplement one another and to remind us of the inadequacies of any one way of affirming God's saving activity in Jesus Christ.

JEFFERY HOPPER

Bibliography

Marcus J. Borg, *Jesus: A New Vision: The Spirit, Society, and the Life of Discipleship.*
Paul S. Fiddes, *Past Event and Present Salvation: A Study in the Christian Doctrine of the Atonement.*
Jaroslav Pelikan, *Jesus Through the Centuries: His Place in the History of Culture.*

Cross Reference: Atonement, Christology, Liberation Theology.

SOUL/BODY

The very juxtaposition of "soul" with "body" indicates the problems involved in defining either word. Christian thought, standing as the inheritor of both Greek and Hebraic traditions, has lived from earliest times with an ambiguity resulting from the fact that, broadly speaking, in Greek thought "soul" is defined in dualistic opposition to "body," while in Hebraic thought no such dualism is present and the ideas that the two words convey cannot be clearly distinguished from one another.

In Greek thought, particularly as it comes from Orphism and is expressed in the earlier Platonic dialogues, there is a marked dualism between the soul and the body. The soul belongs to a divine, eternal realm, and is the undying, indestructible part of a human being, which is unfortunately confined to the body during life on earth. The body is thus nothing but a hindrance to the soul. Consequently, salvation involves the extrication of the soul from the body, the immortal part of the human being finding release from the confines of the mortal body. An old Greek proverb sums up the belief: "The body is the prison-house of the soul."

This way of thinking is so deeply imbedded in Western culture that it is often difficult to see how sharply differentiated from it is the biblical understanding. The word "soul," in particular, has a very different meaning for the biblical writers from the understanding that modern Christians usually assign to it. The Hebrew scripture's word *nephesh* basically means "breath," and the term is often used simply to designate "a living being" (not always a human, sometimes an animal); the word, along with the New Testament equivalent, *psyche,* can mean "life," and even "person" or "self." The term is much broader in biblical usage than is commonly supposed, and it can be taken to stand for the *unity* of personality, since

Hebraic thought conceives of the human being as a unity, rather than as a duality of body and soul.

This meaning can be further clarified by noting its relationship to the word "body." In Pauline thought, for example, body *(soma)* is an inclusive word for the psycho-physical unity of the flesh *(sarx)* and soul *(psyche)*. No hard and fast distinction between the two can be established. The body is the whole person, not a detachable part of that person to be distinguished in dualistic fashion from the soul. J. A. T. Robinson in *The Body* concludes that we do not *have* bodies, but we *are* bodies—that we are "flesh-animated-by-soul, the whole conceived as a psychophysical unity."

This is not just a Pauline idiosyncrasy; it concurs with the results of scholarship on the Hebrew Bible also. H. Wheeler Robinson, in *Religious Ideas of the Old Testament,* notes that the same idea of unity pervades the Hebrew scriptures: "The idea of human nature [in the Hebrew scriptures] implies a unity, not a dualism. There is no contrast between the body and the soul, such as the terms instinctively suggest to us." Again, "The Hebrew idea of personality is an animated body and not an incarnated soul." J. Pederson, in *Israel,* goes so far as to say, "The body is the soul in its outward form." There is, in fact, no distinctive word for "body" in Hebrew; such a word is not needed because there is no separate part of a human being, distinct from that person's "soul," that needs to be so distinguished.

This ancient sense of the interrelatedness and unity of the human personality is being substantiated by modern research in psychosomatic medicine, the very name of which (*psyche-soma,* or "soul-body") shows the impossibility of a cleavage between the body and the soul. Relating and reflecting on his own experience of illness and recovery, Norman Cousins, in *The Anatomy of an Illness,* has shown how much the attitude of the patient correlates with the ravages of disease.

The issue of "soul(body)" is very much alive in theology today, particularly as represented by "liberation" movements in Third World churches. There has been firm resistance to perpetuating a dualism by dividing life into "political" activity, on the one hand, and "spiritual" nurture on the other, as though either "outer" or "inner" life could be understood in isolation from the other. Gustavo Gutiérrez, Jon Sobrino, and others write about and live what they call a "spirituality of liberation," insisting that the two realities are inseparable in Christian living. All dualisms are disavowed, from a perspective that clearly exemplifies the recovery of the biblical understanding.

ROBERT McAFEE BROWN

Bibliography

Gustavo Gutiérrez, *We Drink from Our Own Wells: The Spiritual Journey of a People.*
D. R. G. Owen, *Body and Soul.*

H. Wheeler Robinson, *The Christian Doctrine of Man.*
_____, *The Religious Ideas of the Old Testament,* chap. 4.
J. A. T. Robinson, *The Body.*
Jon Sobrino, *Spirituality of Liberation.*

Cross Reference: Anthropology, Liberation Theology.

SPACE

The relation of theology to categories of space is gaining increasing attention among many theologians. For the most part, however, twentieth-century theology has been characterized by a preoccupation with temporal concerns, making spatial aspects of theological expression secondary. The influence of existentialist interpretative models on biblical studies (Bultmann) and systematic theology (Heidegger) has particularly directed theological formulations toward temporal, individual interpretations at the expense of spatial concerns. With the emerging impact of socio-political concerns in theology, and a rising interest in environmental issues, questions about the relation between theology and space are becoming more central. As this happens, at least three interrelated areas appear ripe for profitable theological inquiry: created space, lived space, and ecclesial space.

That the universe has been created is a theological affirmation. Theology must also take account of scientific findings about the nature of space and the implications for theology's understanding of *created space*. This discussion has historical roots in the attempts of Isaac Newton to come to grips with his scientific discoveries in view of his belief in an absolute, transcendent God. Jürgen Moltmann has recently provided a reappraisal of the debates about God and space that followed Newton's claims and has rightly suggested that further theological work is needed. Is matter to be distinguished from space, or is space merely the infinite extension of matter (a debate philosophically rooted in Plato and Aristotle)? Theologically, the modern problem of space lies at the heart of the controversies among theism, pantheism, and panentheism. Moltmann observes that only the concept of creation distinguishes the "space of God" from the space of the created world. The theological affirmation of created space must reject therefore equating space with the extension of objects. Although space is infinite, immovable, homogeneous, indivisible, and unique, the things in this space are not. Discussions on created space have direct implications for theological concepts about the nature of God. As early as 1440 Nicholas of Cusa provided a provocative spatial expression describing God as "an infinite sphere whose center is everywhere and circumference is nowhere." Likewise, more thought needs to be given to spatial interpretations of transcendence, omnipresence, infinity, and incarnation.

458

No less important than created space is the challenge of giving theological formulation to what may be designated *lived space,* which focuses attention on the responsibility of providing theological interpretation of the space of *this* world. Whereas classical formulations have revolved around time, liberation and political theologies have taken spatial realities more thoroughly into account, especially with regard to basic concepts such as kingdom of God, sin, and salvation. Rosemary Ruether in *Sexism and God-Talk* devises a theology of creation and eschatology that explores links between the body and nature. Kosuke Koyama's recent theological formulations *(Waterbuffalo Theology* and *Mount Fuji and Mount Sinai)* exhibit awareness not only of the necessity of rooting theological thinking within its surroundings but also of the implications this has for spatial expressions of faith. Similarly, Leonardo Boff *(Trinity and Society)* has integrated the doctrine of the Trinity into a critique of spatial societal structures.

For theology to speak of lived space, it must recognize that our epoch is shaped by what Paul Ricoeur calls "a planetary consciousness." By this he means that ours is the first historical epoch to view its destiny from a global perspective. Theology must therefore transcend its classical provincialism and speak globally, not only against the nuclear horizon but also against a technological one. Short of complete self-annihilation of lived space, technology is probably the most serious concern. It takes up space and to a large degree determines how we live spatially in relation to the rest of creation. It affects how we perceive fundamental interspatial relations. Theology faces the challenge of discerning the meaning of Christian faith in a technological world characterized by "spatial economics." When the category of space is made central to theological reflection, ecological concerns are seen not as "special interest theology" but as part of theology's intrinsic nature, a part devoted to providing continuing expression to Christianity's belief in God as Creator and the universe as God's creation.

Ecclesial space is a third area of reflection. Edward Farley argues that the existence of Christian community has spatial qualities. Theological categories such as judgment and redemption must therefore be thought of spatially as well as temporally. For example, sin has the character of making space provincial, that is, exclusively valid for oneself. Plurality of spaces is thus rejected, making all space that is outside one's own alien. *My* family, neighborhood, race, nation, religion are accepted as absolute. Such absolute, provincial space becomes the source of idolatry. On the other hand, redemptive existence disestablishes absolute, provincial space by the acceptance of a plurality of spaces. Other spaces are recognized as valid alongside one's own. Paradoxically, ecclesial space abolishes sacred spaces as indispensable and conditional for the presence of the sacred. The temple, cathedral, church building, or Bible does not capture *the* space of *ecclesia.* Discussions concerning spatial aspects of what it means to speak of the church as "body of Christ" in the world acquire new impetus. Questions about the meaning of the Eucharist, interpretations of the Holy Spirit, and inspiration of scripture also gain new dimensions in light of the analysis of ecclesial space.

A theology of space provides a foundation on which a holistic and ecumenical theology can be built. It allows classical formulations of Christian faith to be reshaped in circumstantially relevant ways, and provides structures conducive to giving Christian voice to matters of cosmology, ecology, sociology, politics, and dialogue with other religions.

D. DIXON SUTHERLAND

Bibliography

Samuel Alexander, *Space, Time, and Deity*, 2 vols.
Gaston Bachelard, *The Poetics of Space.*
John Dillenberger, *Protestant Thought and Natural Science.*
Edward Farley, *Ecclesial Reflection.*
Jürgen Moltmann, *God in Creation.*
T. F. Torrance, *Space, Time, and Incarnation.*

Cross Reference: Creation, Ecology, Panentheism, Technology, Theism, Time.

SPIRIT (*See* HOLY SPIRIT.)

SPIRITUALITY

"Spirituality" is a relatively modern term in the Christian vocabulary, having emerged in the seventeenth century and only recently having come into popular Protestant usage. Encompassing the subject matters of the traditional Roman Catholic ascetical and mystical divisions of theology, and also earlier Protestant conceptions of piety, we have now come to speak of multiple spiritualities.

A distinctive Christian spirituality focuses on the reality of God's self-giving in Christ, animated by the Holy Spirit. Spirituality refers to a *lived* experience and a disciplined life of prayer and action, but it cannot be conceived apart from the specific theological beliefs that are ingredient in the forms of life that manifest authentic Christian faith. Love of God and neighbor is at the heart of the life of prayer and action. Identifying love as the ground of spirituality, Hans Urs von Balthasar claims that, although many historical spiritualities exist, there is for Christianity an underlying single spirituality "whose one, concrete norm is Jesus Christ who endows each of these forms with its own particular meaning derived from the unity of God's triune love."

Despite their common foundation in Christ's loving example, various particular types and "schools" of Christian spirituality have emerged throughout the centuries, constructing their own distinctive patterns and focal points. So it is necessary to emphasize the differences in historical-cultural ethos as we move from the early church in its patristic sources, through the monastic movements, into the medieval spirituality of the mystics and mendicants and the *devotio moderna* (a movement of mystical piety stressing the affection and virtues in common life) of the later Middle Ages. In addition to these historical differences, there are traditional differences between Protestant and Counter-Reformation forms of the Christian life and among particular cultural types such as African American, Latin American, and Asian American. The long continuity of the Eastern Orthodox traditions, along with the hesychast revivals in more modern times, are also coming to be known in the West through the twentieth-century ecumenical movement.

Christian spiritualities may also be distinguished by broad theological and thematic styles, such as the "apophatic" (the way of negation and unknowing) and "kataphatic" (the use of images and senses as a path to God) types. Such streams of spirituality are commonly associated with the more strenuous forms of mysticism. Following Louis Dupré, mysticism may be understood as "some passively infused experience," belonging "to the core of all religious faith, whether communal or private." Christian mysticism may be contrasted with the moral-ethical way of "the life of piety" characteristic of those traditions that emphasize Christian moral holiness or responsibility in the world or both, rather than interiority.

The twentieth-century ecumenical and liturgical movements have brought forward a new awareness of the spiritual literature belonging to all the historical periods and schools. Consequently, we can discern how rich and mutually interactive the practices and the theological reflection appropriate to these practices can be. Current thinking, reflected in the publishing of the forty-volume Classics of Western Spirituality and the twenty-five-volume World Spirituality series, points in challenging new directions. Specifically, the question of Christian spirituality is discerned in the light of the encounter with non-Christian traditions of the spiritual life. But even within Christianity, a new confluence of what once was exclusively Roman Catholic, Orthodox, or Protestant is emerging. The mutual influence among forms of Christian life and prayer that have focused solely on the "interior life of prayer" with those focusing on the moral life of action in the world is producing a new literature. In his *Introduction to Spirituality*, Louis Bouyer distinguishes the "religious life" and the "interior life" from the "spiritual life." By this he intends to show that one may practice a religious life, and even possess a rich life of interior consciousness (whether religious, moral, or aesthetic), yet not cultivate awareness of spiritual reality. Christian spirituality is a form of spiritual life that deliberately cultivates a relationship with God involving the whole of existence, both in the inmost being of the soul and in one's concrete social relatedness in the world. Persons as diverse as Thomas Merton, Dorothy

461

Day, Mother Teresa, Martin Luther King, Jr., and Anthony Bloom show a commingling of contemplation and action in the whole life lived before God.

At the same time, the late twentieth century has witnessed a convergence of more sacramental and liturgical orientations with what were previously Protestant and evangelical sensibilities. Various charismatic and pentecostal movements cut across historically separated ecclesial lines, and the emergence of new forms of Christian common life such as the base Christian communities and the widespread "house churches" over the world are generating new social and cultural embodiments of Christian spirituality.

The practice of Christian spirituality includes both personal inwardness and its attendant disciplines and communal (liturgical and ethical) life. For the Christian community, all spiritual life is rooted and grounded in baptism into Christ and oriented toward living in response to the continuing presence and activity of the triune God in the whole created order. With such a grounding in the self-giving of God, authentic Christian spirituality must always take place in the ordinary circumstances of human life. We are challenged today to move from the notion of spirituality as an esoteric or elitist self-preoccupation to the praxis of inwardness before God *and* the communal and societal work of the Holy Spirit. Only then can Christian spirituality both gain its true identity and maintain its relevance in the face of human forgetfulness of God and the emptiness and confusion in contemporary culture.

DON E. SALIERS

Bibliography

Louis Dupré and Don E. Saliers, eds., in collaboration with John Meyendorff, *Christian Spirituality: Post-Reformation and Modern.* Vol. 18 of *World Spirituality: An Encyclopedic History of the Religious Quest.*

Cheslyn Jones, Geoffrey Wainwright, and Edward Yarnold, *The Study of Spirituality.*

Bernard McGinn, John Meyendorff, and Jean Leclercq, eds., *Christian Spirituality: Origins to the Twelfth Century.* Vol. 16 of *World Spirituality,* cited above.

Jill Raitt, ed., with Bernard McGinn and John Meyendorff, *Christian Spirituality: High Middle Ages and Reformation.* Vol. 17 of *World Spirituality,* cited above.

Frank C. Senn, ed., *Protestant Spiritual Traditions.*

Cross Reference: Basic Christian Communities, Holy Spirit, Pentecostalism.

STRUCTURALISM

Structuralism is a method of analysis that seeks to identify and describe the deep or invisible structures that underlie the surface of an observable reality, whether that reality be a natural language, a specific text, a society, or the human mind. Here the analysis is limited to texts. A deep structure is a system or network of abstract units, relatively empty of meaning, that exist in a logical relationship to one another. This hidden system is thought to have generated the surface structure, the text as we see it, and to account for its meaning in some way.

A comparison of structuralism with other interpretative approaches will help clarify its nature. Whereas the New Criticism, which dominated literary interpretation from about 1930 to 1960, found meaning in the forms and patterns that shaped the content of the surface structure, structuralism, which came to full bloom in Paris in the 1960s, located meaning in the relationship between surface and deep structure or in the deep structure itself. The more recent reader-response approaches to interpretation attribute the meaning of a text in varying degrees to the creativity of the reader. Deconstructionism, on the other hand, stresses the slippery nature of language, the tendency of a text always to defer meaning, to undercut itself, and to produce multiple interpretations; and deconstructionism denies that there is any such thing as a deep structure serving as a foundation for generating meaning.

From the standpoint of the needs of the theological interpretation of texts, structuralism has received certain criticisms: (1) Defining or using it apart from a great deal of highly technical vocabulary seems impossible. (2) Among literary critical theorists it has been superseded by deconstructionism. (3) Structuralism moves from the text back to the abstract deep structure; therefore, it is opposed to the intent of the theological interpretation of the Bible, which moves from the text out to the reader and relates the meaning of the text to the reader so as to promote a new way of being in the world. Despite these problems, structuralism may still be fruitful for theological interpretation, for the deep structures can be used to interpret and to organize the surface content of biblical texts in such a way that the latter can be employed to answer questions about God, Christ, faith, ethics, and the project of human existence.

An example of the theological application of structuralism can be provided by an analysis of the christological dimensions of Matthew's account of the baptism and temptation of Jesus (Matt. 3:13–4:11). An appropriate system for analyzing the passage is one provided by A. J. Greimas. In his system of "test sequences," the structure is deep in that the functions have been abstracted from the particularities of narratives in general. A function is a constant, abstract class to which the variable actions or occurrences of a particular kind belong. Greimas identified three different kinds of tests, based on distinctions regarding what is attributed or communicated to the hero.

In a plot or surface structure, as distinguished from the deep structure or test sequence, the deep structure is manifested in particular concrete events. But the order of events need not follow the order of the deep structure, for the order of the plot depends on the choices of the author.

According to the gospel story, Jesus came from Galilee to be baptized by John. But why? No reason is expressed at this point in the text. Matthew believes,

463

however, that Jesus' mission as a whole has been destined by scripture (cf. 1:22-23; 16:21; 26:24, 54); therefore, the implication is that scripture has mandated him to be baptized. His coming to John, then, is his acceptance of the mandate. A confrontation occurs when John resists Jesus' intent to be baptized. But Jesus wins in this struggle when John consents and baptizes him. The consequence of Jesus' victory is that the Spirit descends upon him. The imparting of divine power is the consequence of a qualifying test. A voice from heaven then announces that Jesus is God's son with whom God is well pleased. This declaration both mandates Jesus to be the Son of God and recognizes him for who he is. The attribution of recognition is the consequence of a glorifying test. In the temptation scene there is another confrontation—this one more hostile and serious—with the devil. But Jesus, quoting scripture, withstands the devil and maintains his faithfulness to God. In this action three different functions are manifested. Jesus wins success in the conflict with the devil; he accepts the mandate to be God's son; he secures a value—obedience—as the consequence of a main test.

We sense intuitively that this text is overcharged with christological meaning, but we may not be sure why. Structural analysis provides critical categories to explain the reason for our intuitive awareness. Ideally the qualifying, main, and glorifying tests belong to the beginning, middle, and end of an elaborated narrative. This text manifests elements from all three of the tests. It is supercharged with meaning because this brief stretch of the plot brings to concentrated, express manifestation the deep structure—beginning (qualifying test), middle (main test), and end (glorifying test)—of a fully developed narrative.

Using structuralism, theologians can analyze the depths of christological concerns in texts like Matthew's, and they can discern therein the underlying presence of the whole gospel within a condensed narrative.

DAN O. VIA

Bibliography

Jean Calloud, *Structural Analysis of Narrative*.
Jonathan Culler, *Structuralist Poetics*.
Elizabeth Struthers Malbon, *Narrative Space and Mythic Meaning in Mark*.
Daniel Patte, *Structural Exegesis for New Testament Critics*.
Dan O. Via, *The Ethics of Mark's Gospel*.

Cross Reference: Biblical Criticism, Deconstructionism.

SUFFERING

Human suffering is a religious theme par excellence: All religions and even nonreligious ideologies respond to the challenge that unremovable suffering of innocent people presents. Basic religious and theological questions arise regarding suffering: Is suffering God's will or not? Is God the source of evil as well as of good? Does God permit suffering that comes from other sources?

The Jewish and Christian traditions do not emphasize the tragic, unsolvable depth of suffering that is caused by natural defects or events. They place suffering instead in its historical framework and remarkably "ethicize" the question about why humans have to suffer. From the very first Jewish mythical narratives of origin, suffering has been seen as going against the goodness of creation. Patriarchal domination, meaningless labor, and hostility between humans and nature are "curses" in a fallen world, and do not accord with God's will.

Suffering is the result of being separated by force or separating oneself from God's life-giving love. Cain's answer to God's question, "Where is your brother?" (Gen. 4:9) is "Am I my brother's keeper?" It signals a rejection of our connectedness to one another and our separation from the giver of life. Life is to be shared, and even brutal natural sufferings, such as earthquakes, challenge the community of bystanders and ask them to become the keepers of their siblings. Even more, brutal historical man-made sufferings point to the reality of sin. The two-thirds of today's human family who lack food, water, shelter, health care, education, and work suffer as the victims of a sinful economic world order of injustice. The concept of sin is a key to helping us understand human suffering in the light of human responsibility. It is misused, though, when seen as punishment for those who suffer (see John 9:2). Blaming the victim is the easiest and most superficial way to explain suffering; on the contrary, compassion and cosuffering characterize the way of Christ.

The specific contribution of Jewish and Christian spirituality to the problem of suffering lingers inside the tension between outrage and acceptance, both voiced most clearly in the book of Job. The power of anger in the work of love necessitates outrage, protest, and resistance, but there are also patience, independence, and inner freedom in those who bear the unbearable burden. Church history shows that either outrage or acceptance prevails in a given historical situation. But if one part of the dialectical tension between outrage and acceptance is completely lost, the other will degenerate also. A church, for example, that preaches submissiveness and acceptance of God-given sufferings to women has betrayed God's active and passionate work for freeing and redeeming all of God's children.

God is not the source of evil nor does God "permit" other powers to punish or "educate" human beings. God does not make us suffer but suffers with us. Not the one who causes suffering but only the one who suffers with can answer Job and our despair. The God of the Bible is not the demonic power who sent Hitler and ordered him to murder millions of innocent Jewish people. In wake of the holocausts of Auschwitz and Hiroshima, Jewish theologians (e.g., Abraham Heschel, Hans Jonas, and Harold Kushner) and Christian theologians (e.g., James

Cone and most feminists) have shifted the enlightened question of theodicy (How can God Almighty permit evil happening to good people?) back toward ourselves into anthropodicy (How long will we permit evil happening to the poor? How can God Cosufferer abide with those under suffering?). The question—Why did God allow Auschwitz to happen?—then becomes, "Why did we allow it to happen?"

The cross of Christ symbolizes an understanding of human suffering in which humans may participate in God's pain that is love's pain. The cross used as a torture instrument by an imperial power is the ultimate response of "this world" to those who fulfill the will of the Father. Christ fulfilled God's lifegiving will to bring life in abundance (John 10:10), and for that Christ was sentenced to torture and death. To share life, to make justice come true, and to feed the hungry necessarily leads into conflicts with authorities of both church and state. It promotes breaks from friends and family, losses in career, wealth, and health, to name just the mild forms of the cross.

Persecution for the sake of truth has been a criterion of the church and is in today's liberation struggles also. Christians give their lives, risk torture and dying, and suffer with Christ "in order that we may also be glorified with him" (Rom. 8:17). Martyrs (e.g., Steve Biko, Martin Luther King, Jr., Ita Ford, and Oscar Romero) touch the deepest meaning of human suffering, which is to become "heirs of God and fellow heirs with Christ" (Rom. 8:17; *and see* II Tim. 3:12). Whenever we avoid the suffering with Christ, we will have to be "the devil's martyrs" (Thomas Müntzer). Love has its price. The "willingness to suffer" is the utmost expression of human freedom: In Christ we leave the technocratic illusion of a life free from suffering and join the option for justice, peace, and the integrity of creation.

The pastoral task is to throw the light of Christ's suffering on those seemingly meaningless pains we have to endure in order to integrate our losses into God's pain over the world. Outrage and endurance, then, come together. We hand them over into the hands of the Cosufferer and wait with Christ for the radical transformation of heaven and earth. We understand God's annunciation only when we hear the tears in God's voice. The God who "will wipe away every tear from their eyes" (Rev. 21:4) weeps in us.

DOROTHEE SOELLE

Bibliography

Alan Boesak, *Comfort and Protest: The Apocalypse from a South African Perspective.*
John Bowker, *The Problem of Suffering in the Religions of the World.*
Gustavo Gutiérrez, *On Job: God-Talk and the Suffering of the Innocent.*
Kazoh Kitamori, *Theology and the Pain of God.*
Dorothee Soelle, *Suffering.*

Cross Reference: Evil, Institutionalized Violence, Justice.

SYMBOL

A symbol is a term, idea, phrase, or object that stands for another insight, concept, or constellation of ideas. The word comes from the Greek *symballein*, which means to throw or put things together. It originally referred to a coin cut in half, of which two parties carried one half each. The value of the coin lay in its being united with its other part.

Symbols may be linguistic or nonlinguistic. In the realm of speech, a symbol unites the meaning of one thing to another. Nonlinguistic symbols may be emblems, like the flag of a country or the cross in Christianity, or gestures, like kneeling or bowing one's head. Whatever their mode of expression (word, emblem, or gesture), symbols derive their meaning from conventions recognized by a given community. Symbols are significant to the human community because of their relation to language and meaning. It is doubtful that there is meaning for the human community apart from linguisticality—the expression of the self through symbols.

The modern discussion of symbols has ranged through philosophical, literary, psychological, and theological works. Immanuel Kant saw symbols as a kind of intuitive representation. Goethe described a symbol as a particular representing a general insight or truth. By symbolism Schiller felt that inanimate nature was humanized—that it was brought into meaning for humans. These lines of thinking led from the Romantic philosophies and aesthetics to the nineteenth-century literary movement called symbolism (including, among others, Blake, Emerson, Hawthorne, Crane, and Melville), which reached its apogee in the twentieth century in the theoretical works of Northrop Frye (*The Anatomy of Criticism* and *The Rule of Metaphor*), for whom reality consists in a system of verbal relationships.

The recent science of semiotics—the study of signs and symbol sets—is an attempt to determine the use of signifiers in the human community. C. S. Peirce, with his designation of symbols, indices, and icons as subsets of signs, gave impetus to the rise of modern philosophical concerns about signs and symbols. The current philosophical discussion of symbols deals primarily with the exchange between linguistics and semiotics.

A discussion of symbolism in religion is important because of the literary nature of sacred texts, because of the use of nonlinguistic symbols in worship, because of religion's quest for meaning, and because of the hermeneutical task of fusing the horizons of religious and secular concerns. Scholars expressing the theological significance of symbols include Paul Tillich and Paul Ricoeur.

Both Tillich and Ricoeur insist that symbols, or symbolic discourse, provide the only way in which we can speak about God. Tillich declared that all language about God is symbolic except the statement that "all language about God is symbolic." Religious symbolism is, in Tillich's thought, the exclusive tool for describing the religious dimension of human existence. For him, a symbol participates in the reality it represents, but the symbol cannot exhaust such reality. To take symbolic language literally is to reduce the description of the divine reality to absurdity and, possibly, to idolatry. For God is "ecstatically transcendent," and every expression about God, the Ground of Being, is symbolic. To speak of God, we must do so by "ecstatic rationality," which involves both rational and suprarational elements. For Tillich, this paradox of being unable to speak of God literally points up the existential dilemma of human existence: A religious symbol uses the categories of ordinary experience, but in such a way that ordinary experiences are both affirmed and denied. Tillich built his entire theological system on this use of symbols to convey the knowledge of God by analogy.

Ricoeur builds his concept of symbols on his perspective of metaphor, because he feels that symbols have a broader and more diffuse usage than metaphors. Thus, he moves from the narrower to the broader realm of discourse. Symbols may apply to many fields: math, logic, psychoanalysis, poetics, and history of religions. Ricoeur seeks to find semantic meaning by using insights from the narrower literary field of metaphor to apply to the broader field of symbols. Ricoeur suggests that a symbol has two dimensions or universes of discourse: the linguistic and the nonlinguistic. Every symbol has a semantic kernel that can be discerned by a metaphorical twist that helps us to see the extension of meaning resident in all symbols.

To assimilate the meaning of a symbol, we must move through its literal meaning to its secondary signification. The nonlinguistic character of symbols is bound to humans' prelinguistic experience, which opens up the sacred dimensions of existence.

At this point, Tillich and Ricoeur agree that all religious discourse must be symbolic. Symbols are bound to reality itself instead of being free inventions of language as metaphors are. Symbolic discourse with its law of correspondence, seeing similarities between different aspects of reality, enables us to enter the realm of the sacred, where we experience God or where we can speak of God.

WILLIAM L. HENDRICKS

Bibliography

F. Ernest Johnson, ed., *Religious Symbolism.*
Paul Ricoeur, *The Symbolism of Evil.*
_____, *Interpretation Theory: Discourse and the Surplus of Meaning.*
Paul Tillich, *The Dynamics of Faith.*
_____, "The Nature of Religious Language" in *Theology of Culture.*

Cross Reference: Language–Religious, Myth, Paradox.

SYSTEMATIC THEOLOGY

Systematic theology is the intellectual discipline that seeks to express the content of a religious faith as a coherent body of propositions. In Christianity, faith is the response of the whole human person to the gospel of Jesus Christ, a response including will, emotions, and belief. Theology is narrower than faith and is concerned with belief as the intellectual and propositional element in faith.

At the present time, when many people have doubts about the truth of Christianity, there is general agreement about the importance of theology in its attempt to set forth Christian belief in the clearest possible language. But there is less agreement about the need to make theology "systematic." Some, like Kierkegaard, have believed that only God can grasp truth as a system and that for our finite minds it is glimpsed only in fragments. Others, like Barth, have thought that the attempt to construct a system goes wrong in trying to force the biblical material into a human framework. Barth preferred to speak of "dogmatics" rather than "systematic theology," although it could be argued that his *Church Dogmatics* is one of the greatest systematic theologies ever written. In defense of systematic theology, one could say that in all branches of study we make progress by relating items that had thitherto seemed unconnected. If behind Christian faith there lies the one great revelatory act of God in Christ, then all the several doctrines of Christianity belong together and receive mutual support and illumination from one another.

The biblical witness comes in many forms—narrative, prophecy, poetry, wisdom literature, and so on—and comes also from many different periods. It is surely a worthwhile activity to try to draw the many threads into a consistent statement and to find a language that will help to make it all intelligible. Certainly we must heed Kierkegaard's warning against any arrogant attempt to package the Word of God in some allegedly complete and final system. But the best systematic theologians have believed, like Schleiermacher, that what they produced was the product of a particular time and particular circumstances and that the task would have to be done anew by future generations.

One could also argue that the Bible itself gives its sanction to something like systematic theology. Mark's Gospel and Paul's Epistle to the Romans claim in their opening verses to be statements of the gospel of Jesus Christ. But they proclaim this gospel in very different ways. Mark tells the story of Jesus from the beginning of his ministry onward and makes the narrative the vehicle for the theology. Paul, on the other hand, expounds the same gospel but orders it under a sequence of theological topics, with the narrative of Christ's career only implicit in the background. In Paul we read of the fallen state of the human race and the consequent perversion of creation, of human impotence to achieve righteousness, of God's justification of the human race through the saving work of Christ, of dying and rising with Christ, of life in the Spirit, and of the vision of final universal salvation in Christ. It is worth remembering that Romans antedates Mark, the earliest Gospel, by about twenty years. Yet it would be absurd to argue that one of these types of exposition is superior to the other. An adequate statement of Christianity called for both. Romans without Mark would have been too abstract, too rabbinic. Mark without Romans might easily have failed to convey an adequate understanding of the breadth and comprehensiveness of the gospel in relation to human need. At any rate, the New Testament itself shows us that at a very early stage in Christian history, believers felt the need for an ordered statement of the main points of belief.

As time went on, this need increased, for Christianity entered into dialogue with Hellenistic learning. Systematic theology, in the broadest sense of the expression, was now fairly launched; and during the patristic age many theologians, such as Origen, Athanasius, and Augustine, worked on such fundamental Christian doctrines as the person of Christ and the triune God. In these centuries all the main topics of Christian belief received the shape that they would bear for many generations.

Theological Language. Theology is language, and in recent times much attention has been paid to the nature of its language. Theology is a relatively sophisticated language that eventually coins a wide range of technical terms; but its ultimate origins lie in faith, which itself is a response of the whole person and therefore more than simply language. In Christianity, the beginnings of faith are found in the encounter between Jesus Christ and the first disciples. So far as this was expressed in words, the language was confessional and even emotional, and it lacked the reflection, analysis, and criticism that must be present before one can properly speak of theology. For example, John's Gospel tells us that in a moment of intense feeling, Thomas says to Jesus, "My Lord and my God." This is a *confession* of faith and contains, as it were, the raw material of theology; but several centuries elapsed before the *classic* theological statements about the person of Christ were formulated, after long reflection and sometimes sharp controversy. By then the language was very different—the enthusiastic utterance of Thomas had given way to a descriptive conceptual language in which the church spoke of Christ as "consubstantial" with the Father and as one person in whom there concur two "natures." The conceptual element in this language was derived from Greek thought; but theology was never able to dispense with the more concrete historical images derived from biblical sources.

The gradual rise of what we may call the "classic" theological language was an important step in systematizing Christian belief by bringing the various elements in that belief into a unitary conceptual scheme. But even today most systematic theologies, however refined their concepts, still reflect in their structures the original pattern of the events that gave rise to faith; they begin with the doctrine of creation, go on to the historical events associated with Jesus Christ, and end with eschatological expectations. If we had unlimited understanding, we could grasp the significance of Christian faith all at once. But in fact we need to take it doctrine by doctrine.

The Articulation of Systematic Theology. Although the usual order for systematic theology has begun with the doctrine of God and moved through creation and the historical manifestation of Jesus Christ to its conclusion in eschatology, this particular order does not seem to be necessary. It is true that Barth claims that the order of reality should dictate the order of presentation, but if indeed all the doctrines constitute a unity and are coinherent in the sense that each reaches into the others, then it should be possible to enter the system at any point and move from there through the whole. This was recognized by Calvin, who began his *Institutes of the Christian Religion* by saying that two topics are of prime importance to us—the knowledge of God and the knowledge of ourselves—and that these two are so closely interlinked that we might begin with either. In fact, Calvin begins with the knowledge of God, but many theologians in the modern period (e.g., Schleiermacher and Bultmann) have begun with the study of the human being and have found in humanity pointers to God.

This anthropological starting point may be a concession to the modern secular mentality, for people who are not accustomed to thinking of God may need some introduction before they come to a theological or God-oriented way of looking at things. Even in the Middle Ages, Thomas Aquinas began his great *Summa theologiae* by discussing some of the traditional proofs for the existence of God. The type of *natural* theology that we find there has fallen out of favor, and probably very few books of theology written nowadays would begin with natural theology before going on to the theology that claims to be based on revelation. But they might nevertheless provide some kind of introduction (perhaps a part of the book devoted to a study of the human being and the openness of such a being toward God) or even a preliminary volume, like Karl Rahner's *Hearers of the Word*, which argues that our humanity is so constituted that we are already attuned to the possibility of revelation, listening, as it were, for a possible Word from God. So while all systematic theologies treat of God, Christ, the Holy Spirit, the human condition, salvation, the last things, there is no single order that is definitive.

Sources of Theology. Revelation. We have seen that the roots of Christian theology lie in the event of Jesus Christ, which was for the first disciples a "revelation," a new vision of God and of their own relation to God. But that revelatory happening, although it included language, was something more: It was an actual historical event, or series of events.

Scripture: The original revelatory event now lies far in the past, but it is mediated to us by scripture, especially by the New Testament, which contains the earliest testimonies to Christ, most of them written in a fifty-year period from roughly twenty years after the crucifixion to the end of the first century. These scriptures, as our primary witness to Christ himself, are the primary source for Christian theology. But the intense critical study of the New Testament since the eighteenth century has called into question the credibility of some of its accounts, and it can no longer be quoted indiscriminately as "proof texts" to substantiate theological assertions, as had been done by many theologians in Reformation times.

Tradition: Theology needs prolonged reflection (including critical reflection) on the words of scripture, and in the course of that reflection, certain agreed interpretations have come about. For example, the doctrine that God is Trinity in Unity is not explicitly taught in the New Testament, but from early times it has been accepted as the normative interpretation of the New Testament teaching about God. Roman Catholic theologians in particular have laid great stress on tradition, but Protestants too are influenced by tradition. Doctrines that originated in the patristic period, when matters were argued out in many famous controversies, have come to have a high degree of authority for later theologians. But even formulations once universally accepted can hardly remain unchanged forever. The classic theological language that emerged in the early centuries had, as we have seen, a unifying influence, but today it is no longer readily intelligible. Tradition is not an unchanging legacy but a process of transmission, and in recent times much attention has been paid to the development of doctrine and the factors operating in it.

Culture: Theology is studied within a cultural framework, and at any given time is in dialogue with the beliefs and intellectual movements that are influential at that time. Even if theologians resolve to exclude cultural influences from their thinking and to rely entirely on the Bible or tradition for their theological work, they will not succeed in isolating themselves, and if they did, they would surely become irrelevant. Some theologians (e.g., Paul Tillich) have frankly allowed the role of culture in their theology. Tillich's method of "correlation" looks to contemporary culture for the questions that are agitating the spirit of the time, and it seeks to find answers to them in the Christian faith. This would seem almost to give to culture the formative role in his theology.

Experience: Closely related to culture is another factor, experience, which means both the experience of the individual theologian and the experience of his or her generation. One could hardly get very far in theology simply on the testimony of others, especially if they had lived in the distant past. The matters of which they speak must find some verification in the theologian's own experience. Words like "sin" and "miracle," for instance, will be meaningful and important only if there is something corresponding to them in the theologian's experience. This may help to explain the changing moods of theology and its changing emphases. The break-up of Europe at the end of World War I is clearly reflected in Barth's early theology with its stress on human sin, finitude, and the imminence of crisis. But in the latter part of the twentieth century, these emphases have become muted. Whether justifiably or not, the experience of theologians seems more hopeful and humanistic. Karl Rahner, for instance, says bluntly, "Let it be admitted that in my theology the topic of sin and the forgiveness of sins stands somewhat in the background." In the foreground we meet the idea of the transcendence of the human being.

Types of Theology and Theological Pluralism. We have seen that the classic language of theology, built up in the patristic period from mainly Greek sources, was in its own time an influence contributing both to clarity and to systematic unity. But it has long since ceased to perform these functions. Some of its terms (e.g., *anhypostasia*) have become senseless even to theologians. Scripture too has lost much of its prestige and authority in the past two or three centuries. Karl Barth strove valiantly to build a theology on the Word of God, incorporating also the main teachings of the patristic age while going against the mainstream of modern theology. That mainstream looks instead to Schleiermacher, who at the beginning of the nineteenth century made human experience, rather than scripture or tradition, the main formative factor in theology. Since his time a plurality of theologies have been systematized on different principles, not contradicting one another but certainly emphasizing different aspects of Christianity and not easily harmonized. This is the situation of theological pluralism in which we find ourselves today.

In each of these different types of theology, there are usually two factors that serve to unify or systematize the whole. One is a central theme from the Christian tradition that serves as a doctrinal center to which all the other doctrines are related; the other is some sympathetic philosophy that provides a unifying conceptuality. For instance, in the later nineteenth century, the doctrine of the kingdom of God was made central by Albrecht Ritschl and secured by means of "value-judgments" as understood in the neo-Kantian philosophy of the time. A modern equivalent is the liberation theology of South America, though here neo-Kantianism has been superseded by Marxist analysis. Another example is Tillich's systematic theology, in which the central idea is human existence in contemporary culture and the philosophical concepts are derived from existentialism. Still another example is the theology of Jürgen Moltmann. Although in many respects he is more biblical than Tillich and so closer to Barth, he makes eschatology and the future his central theme around which Christian theology is to be expounded, and he finds the neo-Marxist philosophy of Ernst Bloch an appropriate philosophical framework.

As far as one can see, pluralism is likely to continue in systematic theology, but it may turn out to be a source of creativity and liveliness. Far from being

473

destructive or divisive, it is more likely to help in opening up the still undisclosed possibilities in Christianity.

JOHN MACQUARRIE

Bibliography

Karl Barth, *Church Dogmatics.*
Bernard Lonergan, *Method in Theology.*
John Macquarrie, *Principles of Christian Theology.*
Karl Rahner, *Foundations of Christian Faith.*
Paul Tillich, *Systematic Theology,* 3 vols.

Cross Reference: Anthropology, Biblical Theology, Correlation, Culture, Dogmatic Theology, Experience–Religious, Language–Religious, Revelation, Theological Method, Tradition.

TECHNOLOGY

Anthropologists identify the appearance of humans in the history of evolution through the presence of technological artifacts; that is, through the presence of tools. Humans are those beings who have the ability to take something from nature, such as a stone, and turn it into a tool for the transformation of nature. We call this rearrangement of nature through human intent and action "culture." Technology is more than tools and machines, it is essentially technique—a set of methods or procedures for transforming the natural world into a human world. Technology has its roots in the human ability to imagine goals or ends and then to devise the means to realize them. The essence of technology lies not in the stone tools the first humans used but in the techniques they invented to transform natural stones into cultural tools.

In premodern societies technologies preceded the development of science. Techniques were unsystematically discovered and passed on from generation to generation as inherited custom through apprenticeship. One did things a certain way because that was the way it was traditionally done. One learned how something was done rather than why it worked the way it did. Modern scientific technology differs in that it is a rational activity. One seeks to understand theoretically how a procedure works so that one can rationally break it down into its component activities and reconstruct the process so as to make it more efficient, that is, to produce the greatest effect with the least cost and energy. In traditional societies efficiency is subservient to other values. Such societies accept technical innovations very slowly—only as they are able to be integrated with the prevailing norms of society. Modern scientific societies differ in that they make technological efficiency the primary value and expect that society will adjust all other values to the requirements of technical efficiency introduced by each new innovation.

From the very beginning of the human adventure, technology has been a deeply religious phenomenon. Every technical act in a primordial tribal culture, Mircea Eliade tells us, is embedded in a mythic retelling and ritual reenactment of the story of creation—how "in the beginning" the gods and the sacred ancestors transformed chaos into cosmos, an ordered world in which humans could dwell. Throughout most of human history the myths of origin that were told tended to obscure the role of human inventiveness because of the content of myth and ritual, which made it seem as if the human world had been created once and for all in the beginning by gods and divine ancestors as part of a sacred natural order.

Our modern scientific-technological civilization represents a radical break with such views. For we now understand our human world to be created not so much by the gods and sacred ancestors as by the storytellers, who, by telling their stories, transformed chaos into cosmos—that is, into culture, the humanly created world in which we dwell. As the root meaning for the Greek *poeisis* (i.e., to make or do) suggests, the imaginative act of the poet precedes and provides the context for the more strictly "technical" acts of the craftsman. The creation of a culture or a symbolic universe that interprets the world as real and rational (i.e., the product of an incarnate divine "Logos") is necessary for the emergence of a rational scientific-technological approach to reality.

What makes a culture self-consciously technological, however, is not just the presence of science but the application of scientific consciousness to the human world—an activity that demythologizes and de-naturalizes it. Until the emergence of the social sciences in the nineteenth century, no clear consciousness of society as a realm distinct from nature existed. With the rise of historical and comparative studies of diverse cultures, human beings became aware that society is not an extension of the "natural order." Continuing this process of intellectual development, modern technological society gives rise to an existential understanding of self and a managerial understanding of society. We are aware that both the self and society are not givens, fixed with the order of nature, but are humanly made and therefore capable of being humanly transformed.

This consciousness of self and society as open to human transformation alters our understanding of theology in at least three distinct yet interrelated ways: (1) natural theology is being replaced by theology of culture, (2) the task of theology is assumed to include the liberation of human beings and the utopian transformation of society, and (3) theologians are becoming methodologically self-conscious as they engage in the tasks of theology.

Theology of Culture. If technology is about the invention of techniques—the imagining of means for the realization of ends, then we should understand that through language human beings become technological creatures, for only through language do we imagine ends and the means to realize them. Our capacity for language, for culture, and for technology are one and the same—that is, culture is the sum totality of the means and ends whereby we transform the "natural world" into the human world through our capacity for language. Culture is our artificial (i.e., humanly created), linguistically mediated "second nature." To be human is to be a technological creature by virtue of our capacity for language.

In a technological civilization, once we come to recognize that even our understanding of nature is mediated by language, natural theology has to be replaced by what Paul Tillich called "theology of culture." Theology of culture looks for signs of transcendence, not so much in nature as in the realm of culture, the realm of the word. Its task is not to conform human culture to "natural law" and the "natural order" but rather to transform culture through prophetic critique, in order to keep it perpetually open to the theonomous, eschatological power of the Word that makes all things possible and all things new.

Human Liberation and Utopian Transformation. If modern technological civilization understands itself as being created and transformed through the power of the word, the biblical tradition, above all, has made this technological consciousness possible and has given it its uniquely utopian direction. Unlike medieval civilization, whose imagination was still held captive by the classical pre-Christian mythologies of "nature" and "human nature," modern technological civilization is shaped to the core by the biblical eschatological-utopian tradition of the Word. The biblical tradition of the Word insists that humans are created in the image of a God known only in and through the Word. When we dwell in the Word we are neither male nor female, slave nor free, but all are new creatures, the first fruits of a new creation. Indeed, as Gabriel Vahanian insists, our capacities for God, for technology, and for culture (i.e., the distinctively human) converge in our capacity for the Word through which we transcend nature to participate in a new creation.

The secularization of this eschatological-utopian mode of consciousness underlies the emphasis on human liberation, which is unique to modern technological society. Although modern technology carries a considerable potential for dehumanizing life, technological consciousness also serves to humanize life by debunking the myths of "human nature" such as, "women are *by nature* inferior to men" or "blacks are *by nature* inferior to whites." In a technologically self-conscious civilization such myths appear for what they are—ideologically biased human creations. They are no longer consonant with our experience of the human and so provoke movements of human liberation that call for a utopian transformation of society.

Methodological Self-Consciousness. Finally, as Bernard Lonergan's work amply demonstrates, once theologians become historically and sociologically self-

476

conscious, they come to understand their task as a technical one, namely, that of mediating the meaning of the gospel to radically diverse linguistic-cultural universes in different times and places. Theologians no longer understand their task as uncritically passing on the revealed wisdom of the past in its "classical forms." Rather, they understand that theology must be a methodologically self-conscious (sociologically and historically critical) mediation of meaning. Theologians participate in modern technological consciousness whenever they cooperate with other scholars in the coordinated application of a host of methodologies that draw upon historical, social-scientific, linguistic, philosophical, and communications techniques, in order to identify and refine the most efficient and effective means for understanding and communicating the transformative and liberating meaning of the gospel to diverse historical cultures and subcultures.

DARRELL J. FASCHING

Bibliography

Darrell J. Fasching, *The Thought of Jacques Ellul.*
Bernard Lonergan, *Method in Theology.*
Paul Tillich, "On the Idea of a Theology of Culture," in *What Is Religion?*
Gabriel Vahanian, *God and Utopia: The Church in a Technological Civilization.*

Cross Reference: Culture, Secularity, Society.

THEISM

The English term "theism" is derived from the Greek word *theos*, meaning "God," while its opposite "atheism" is derived from *atheos*, meaning "without God." Theists believe that there is a God who created the cosmos, preserves it, is in existence, and has an active role in human history. Customarily, theism is equated with monotheism rather than polytheism, the belief in a single deity rather than in many. Theism is sometimes contrasted with deism, which understands God to have created the cosmos but not to be involved with its subsequent life through revelation, special miraculous events, or incarnation. Emphasizing the distinction between God and the cosmos, theism differs from pantheism, the view that God and the cosmos are a single reality, and panentheism, the view that the cosmos is a part of God.

Christian theism is shaped by biblical revelation, religious experience, and theological and philosophical reflection. The core of Christian theism views God as an imperishable, ultimate reality who is not derived from other beings. God is omniscient (all knowing), omnipotent (all powerful), completely good, and the source of all existence. As a spiritual being, God is nonphysical and yet everywhere present in the cosmos by virtue of God's knowledge and power, including God's creatively conserving in existence each part of the cosmos. Christian theists also believe that God has revealed Godself in human history, including the incarnation of God in Christ.

Beyond this core set of convictions, Christian theists have differed in their understanding of God in several areas. For example, some hold that God is eternal in the sense that God is outside time, whereas others hold that God is eternal only in the sense that God has no beginning or end. This second view allows that God is in time—there is a past, present, and future even for God—whereas the first view does not. Other areas of dispute involve the beliefs that God is immutable (without change), impeccable (incapable of doing evil), and simple (without parts). Some of the disputes arise from the quandary over the intelligibility of supposing that God or anything at all can be outside time, whereas others arise from conflicting intuitions about values. If one thinks immutability is more excellent than mutability, then one has reason to think that God who is the ultimate, valued reality is immutable rather than mutable. Biblically oriented theists and those who are principally informed by philosophical reflection have sometimes taken decidedly opposite positions in their theology of God. Philosophical theists like Anselm and Aquinas, for example, have held that God is not subject to passion and the defects of suffering pain. This view is dubbed impassibility after the Latin *impassibilis,* literally meaning "without passion." Theists whose theology is chiefly shaped by biblical sources have often thought otherwise, believing God to be a passionate reality subject to compassionate sorrow, even suffering, over the world's evils. Many Christian theists now endeavor to take seriously both the scriptural and philosophical resources for thinking of God. Hence, a number of Anselmian philosophers have tended to revise their view of impassibilism, insisting that although God as a perfect being is not subject to defect, God's suffering compassionately for others is not a defect but a function of God's supremely great nature. Just as philosophical theists have gained from biblically based theism, philosophical theists have also provided analyses of and arguments over biblical portrayals of God such as the concept of miracles, divine goodness, and the character of evil; the relation between divine power and human free will; and the conceivable limits (if any) of divine knowledge and activity, the incarnation, and Trinity.

The reasons for accepting theism that have received currency in the philosophical and theological literature are varied and have involved appeals to religious experience, miraculous events, and different features of the cosmos such as its contingency and purposive character, including the emergence of conscious life. The existence of moral and aesthetic values, and the development of reliable ways of knowing about ourselves and the world also have been taken to provide evidence of God. The ontological argument for God's existence has been powerfully argued in recent years and is grounded on certain conceptual truths about necessity and possibility. Each of these arguments has a long history of discussion and refinement in the face of criticism. Some of the more recent theistic arguments that stem from contemporary science, such as the "big bang" theory of the origin of the cosmos and the second law of thermodynamics, can be viewed as particular versions (sometimes less rigorous) of these other, classic arguments. Less popular today are theistic arguments that appeal to the existence of truth, motion, gaps in the evolutionary account of human evolution from nonhuman animals, and the fact that the values we grasp are ranked serially. Prudential arguments are advanced for accepting theism; these arguments do not so much seek to provide evidence for God's existence as to identify practical reasons for believing in God.

Not all theists have prized the search for intellectual arguments to provide a foundation for their beliefs. Some have contended that theism requires no rational foundation to be responsibly accepted. Some theologians have held that theism can be accepted solely on the grounds of faith or that theistic beliefs can themselves be as basic as many other well-grounded, unargued beliefs such as that we are conscious, we see colors, or we hear sounds. These theists may grant a modest role for a kind of negative apologetic in which there is argument that theism is not refuted by any objections against it such as objections that stem from the problem of evil. That being secured, they maintain there is no need for a further, positive apologetic.

Christians have differed in estimating the precision and scope of the concept of God that one can attain in this life. Some have insisted that with respect to certain basic, pivotal matters one may justifiably speak univocally of God, applying the same terms to God and human life without alteration of meaning. Thus, to say God knows something and I know something, involves using the term "knowledge" in the same sense in both contexts, even if the way God knows things and the way I do are vastly different. Other theists have assumed that the best we may attain is analogical reference to God in that terms taken from their human contexts can be employed to speak of God only indirectly, positing a certain likeness between God and humans. In part, the position one adopts will be a function of how strongly one views the evidential weight of the arguments just cited, including the authority of religious experience. But it is important to appreciate that for Christian theism the language and pictorial images used of God are thought to be governed not just by narrow intellectual constraints but also by moral ones. If God is all good, but portrayed as a racist, then not simply an intellectual error has been made but a moral and religious one also.

The current significance of theism can also be measured by the number and kind of modifications and alternatives that it has stimulated. Recently process theologians have argued for a panentheistic understanding of God; others have argued that God is a corporeal being or is finite in power and knowledge. These

479

approaches attempt to preserve important aspects of theism but represent departures from the classical tradition.

CHARLES TALIAFERRO

Bibliography

C. Stephen Evans, *Philosophy of Religion.*
Thomas V. Morris, *Our Idea of God.*
Richard Swinburne, *The Coherence of Theism.*
_____, *The Existence of God.*

Cross Reference: Agnosticism, Apologetics, Atheism, Panentheism, Process Theology.

THEOCRACY (See CIVIL RELIGION, KINGDOM OF GOD.)

THEODICY (See EVIL.)

THEOLOGICAL METHOD

The Need for Theological Reflection. Every theologian consciously or unconsciously follows a certain approach in his or her thinking and writing. In the past it has been a custom to reflect explicitly on questions of theological method whenever transformations in the wider culture or in philosophical thinking forced theologians to modify their approach to their subject matter. Examples of such developments are the so-called process of Hellenization in early Christianity, that is, the encounter between Jewish-Christian thinking and Greco-Roman ways of thinking; the rediscovery of Aristotle in the High Middle Ages, which gave rise to the scholastic method in theology; and the different reactions to the emerging scientific world view and radical challenges to Christian faith by Enlightenment thinking that led to the formation of so-called orthodox theologies on the one hand and liberal theologies on the other hand.

In the twentieth century theological method has moved to the forefront of theological attention and debate. Theology has been provoked to review its methods by the rapidly changing methodological awareness in all other fields of modern thinking (not only in the natural sciences, but also in philosophy, sociology, psychology, etc.), and by changes in its own self-understanding. Moreover, the transformation of the wider context of religious discourse under the influence of more recent developments such as the feminist movement, the emergence of liberation theologies, the ecumenical movement within Christianity, and the interfaith dialogue in which Christian theologians have been active participants, has suggested the need to attend afresh to questions of method.

Generally speaking, in recent years the circumstances of and approaches to theological thinking have been changing so rapidly that often the only undisputed constant between the different approaches to theology has been the shared concentration on method. Both a continuing consideration of what may count as an adequate approach to the subject matter of theology and the examination of the impact of its cultural and intellectual surroundings on theological thinking itself have been perceived as essential aspects of any critical theology.

Since there does not seem to be a consensus even with regard to a proper naming of the various methods used in Christian theology today, this article introduces some crucial questions raised in recent discussions of theological method and then outlines some of the chief contributors to the debate and the particular concerns of their respective agenda.

Important Concerns in the Current Debate on Theological Method. Although all Christian theologians would agree that their primary subject matter is the reflection first on God and God's possible and actual self-disclosure in human history in general and in the ministry, death, and resurrection of Jesus Christ in particular, and second on the actual and possible human response to God's presence, there is no consensus as to how to approach this twofold task. Is the theological investigation limited to a particular reading of the Bible as the record of God's revelation in human history, or does theology also include an examination of the multifaceted circumstances of Christian existence in the modern world? In other words, what are the sources of theology: the Bible or tradition or the world at large or a combination of these?

Any reading of biblical and any other texts involves the theologian in questions of understanding and interpretation, which means that he or she has to think about his or her hermeneutics, that is, the theory of interpretation. Which reading can claim to be appropriate to the texts and traditions under review? Does the decision in favor of a particular hermeneutical model tie theologians also to a particular philosophical option and make them therefore dependent on external criteria of adequacy?

This question raises the wider concern about the relationship between theology and other branches of knowledge. Should theological thinking as an interpretation of faith relate to them or distance itself from them? What is faith and how does it differ from human knowledge in general?

Another question of importance for the self-understanding of the theologian concerns the people or publics for which he or she works. Three possible publics to which the theologian may be related can be distinguished, though not always separated: academy, society, and church (David Tracy). The question about whether or not the theologian can do his or her work adequately only from within the perimeters of a believing community has been answered differently in this century. Some theologians see their work predominantly or even exclusively

481

related to the church (Karl Barth), while others wish to address a wider public (such as Rudolf Bultmann, Paul Tillich, Langdon Gilkey, John Macquarrie, Hans Küng, and David Tracy). As a result, the boundaries between the traditional concerns of Christian theology and the broader analysis of the general phenomenon of religion by religious studies are clouded.

The aim of any particular theological method will also influence the division of theological labor, especially the relationship between historical study (i.e., the understanding of the Christian tradition) and systematic reflection (i.e., the analogical appropriation of that tradition in the circumstances of the interpreter). Whether or not these circumstances have a constitutive role to play in systematic theology is discussed in the current debate on theory and praxis in theology: Is theology merely a theoretical exercise accomplished on the basis of a given set of theoretical presuppositions, or should the very approach to its subject matter be necessarily rooted in concrete human experience? This question in turn leads to the reflection on the nature of any theological statement. Can any theological statement claim to be of universal significance for all humankind? Or should theologians limit themselves to producing insights into faith and knowledge valid only for a very particular time, space, and language?

All the theological methods mentioned in the following section deal with these concerns.

The Spectrum of Current Theological Methods. In the following attempt to identify a series of distinct methodological approaches to theology, it is not suggested that the theologians mentioned would necessarily defend a purist application of any method. Rather, because of the continuing debate on theological methodology, many theologians have seen a need to amend their original approaches to theology. Only methods that are of continuing significance for Christian theology in the twentieth century are discussed here.

Orthodox Theologies. Under this rubric one normally lists all those approaches to theology that accept as their ultimate criterion of adequacy a complete faithfulness and correspondence to a particular set of sacred authorities (not to be confused with Eastern Orthodox theology). Either the Bible (or any particular part of it) is understood as the one and only criterion (Biblicism), or any post-apostolic aspect of tradition is declared absolute, such as the Magisterium (teaching office) in the Roman Catholic Church. "Orthodox" theologians find their basic orientation in the history of the Christian tradition, and they tend to evaluate any modern development accordingly with great suspicion.

Liberal Theologies. These approaches to theology, stemming mainly from within the Protestant tradition and having emerged in response to Enlightenment thinking and nineteenth-century German philosophy, are characterized by a generally optimistic view of the relationship between culture and faith. Christian thinking does not stand in conflict with modern cognitive developments in the sciences and other dimensions of Western culture. Liberal theologians do not accept a radical opposition between God and world. Instead, human experience becomes the only adequate source for any understanding of God (Friedrich Schleiermacher). Jesus of Nazareth, approached predominantly as a historical phenomenon, is appreciated as the most adequate paradigm of human response to God's loving presence (Albrecht Ritschl). The essence of Christianity thus can be seen to consist in God's kingdom as the infinite value of the human soul (Adolf von Harnack). Hence that kingdom is now located in the inner awareness of the individual believer rather than in any socio-political state of affairs. Sin is understood as the lack of proper insight into divine and human nature. Liberal theologies became increasingly suspect as soon as their happy synthesis between faith and human ethos was questioned in the aftermath of the horrors of World War I, although in principle their affirmation of human experience as the connecting point between God and the world continues to be shared by many theologians today.

Neoorthodox Theologies. There is a considerable divergence in what counts as a neoorthodox theology. Generally theologians count as neoorthodox if they have opposed both the liberal and the ''orthodox'' approach to theology, and if they have insisted on God's radical transcendence and the qualified value of human knowledge and culture. At one end of this spectrum we find Karl Barth, who during most of his theological career emphasized the radical otherness of God and the supremacy of the Word of God over any human word. At the other end of this spectrum we find Karl Rahner, whose transcendental approach to theology sees the human journey toward God as already inspired by God's universal grace. Thus, he links God and the human person more intimately than does Barth. Neoorthodox theologians do not share the optimistic starting point of their liberal colleagues. Instead, they have developed a strong sense of suspicion of notions of human progress. Their insight into the horrors committed in the twentieth century (e.g., the Holocaust and global warfare) has sharpened their awareness both of God's otherness and of human brokenness or sinfulness. A broken world needs to be healed by God's gracious intervention in Jesus Christ. The Word of God transmitted through a faithful attention to the biblical evidence requires of each individual believer a radical existential decision for or against God and divine forgiveness. Thus, human experience is taken seriously, but it is understood as either ambiguous (Reinhold and H. Richard Niebuhr, and Karl Rahner) or simply negative (Karl Barth).

Hermeneutical Theologies. The insight into the hermeneutical condition of human thinking that has been growing since Schleiermacher's time mainly among philosophers such as Dilthey, Heidegger, Gadamer, Ricoeur, and Habermas has had a significant influence on a number of theologians. The theological response to hermeneutical theory so far has happened in three moves. The first theologian this century to reflect explicitly on the nature of theological text-interpretation was

Rudolf Bultmann. For him no theology was ever free of presuppositions. Therefore he saw it as important for theologians to become aware, on the one hand, of their starting points and approaches to the scriptural sources of their thoughts and, on the other, of their existential and philosophical concerns. Bultmann's hermeneutical attention focused in particular on the nature of biblical interpretation. Since he felt that the mythological content of the Bible stood in the way of an adequate existential reading of these ancient texts by a modern enlightened reader, he devised a method of demythologizing the New Testament to enable the modern reader to grasp the true existential meaning of these texts.

The second stage of reception of hermeneutical thinking is usually referred to as "the New Hermeneutic" and includes, among others, Gerhard Ebeling, Ernst Fuchs, and John Robinson. Influenced by the later Heidegger's understanding of the (ontological) primacy of language, these theologians have aimed to retrieve the Word of God by concentrating on the power of the Word that makes itself heard through the mediation of human language and which therefore calls for adequate interpretation. Yet they insist that only a faithful interpretation can reveal the power of the Word. This "hermeneutics of agreement" can be described as a hermeneutically refined version of the traditional Reformation theology of the Word.

The third phase in the reception of hermeneutics is characterized by an active participation of theologians in the hermeneutical discussion itself. Theologians such as David Tracy affirm the need for theologians to participate in the worldwide conversation about adequate models of text-interpretation and human self-understanding.

Correlational Theologies. We need to distinguish between a number of different understandings of the possible correlation between faith and culture in theological thinking. Paul Tillich's "method of correlation" meant that philosophical analysis determined the existential quest of modern men and women whereas theological thought provided the answer in terms of affirming the "new being" offered in Christ. This understanding of correlation does not yet include a call for a mutual critique of the two ways of thinking. In David Tracy's method such a "mutually critical correlation" is called for; and likewise in the methods adopted by Hans Küng and Edward Schillebeeckx both the interpretation of the Jewish-Christian tradition and the interpretation of common human experience can challenge each other. Truth is understood as a process of disclosure, always demanding a critical commitment to further revision of one's positions. These theologians have defended the intelligibility and publicness of theological thinking for anybody both inside and outside the Jewish and Christian traditions.

Narrative Theologies. Some propagators of a narrative theology have labeled the correlational theologians "foundationalist" in order to point to their attempt to ground theological thinking in a framework of rational and publicly accessible, philosophical criteria. Over against this foundationalist approach, they hold a non-foundationalist method, based not on a particular rational argument, but on an effort to provide a "thick description" of the particular Christian tradition. No effort is made by narrative thinkers to offer any universally intelligible truth claims on behalf of Christian faith. Rather, a new attention to the biblical stories is demanded (Hans Frei) and a concentration on the particular cultural-linguistic community in which alone Christian truth claims can be sustained and defended (George Lindbeck).

A number of narrative approaches to theology have emerged recently, some of them in the general line of a newly qualified Barthian theology (Eberhard Jüngel and David Ford) and some in an effort to retrieve the original liberating power of the Jewish and Christian stories in specific social and political situations (Johann B. Metz and some of the liberation theologians).

Liberation Theologies. The general insights into various structures of oppression and into the liberating power of the Christian understanding of God and Christ are common to all the different forms of liberation theology in spite of their different accentuation of this insight. Thus, they too have adopted a correlational model in which the praxis of liberation is seen to be co-constitutive of adequate Christian theology.

Feminist theologies such as those developed by Anne Carr, Elisabeth Schüssler Fiorenza, Rosemary Radford Ruether, and Dorothee Soelle have led to the demand for a revision of the traditional understanding of God as male and of Christian faith as patriarchal in view of their nonsexist reconstructions of the Christian tradition, and they have called for a much closer attention to women's experience in theological discourse.

The political theologies of the 1960s (Jürgen Moltmann and Johann B. Metz), which had emerged partly in response to Dietrich Bonhoeffer's theological insights into God's love for and presence in the world and the related call for resistance to the Nazi regime in Germany, have in turn encouraged the formation of Latin American theologies of liberation. Theologians such as Leonardo Boff, Gustavo Gutiérrez, and Jon Sobrino have attempted to appropriate the liberating message of the Christian gospel in their particular situations of widespread oppression and deprivation. They have emphasized that the option for the poor must become the primary concern of any truly Christian understanding of a loving God. Theologians in Africa, Asia, and many other parts of the world have been developing their own versions of liberation theology out of their particular experiences of poverty and systems of cultural and political oppression.

Open Questions. Our brief and incomplete survey has demonstrated at least to what extent the different methods in theology are dependent on their prior assessment of human nature and language and of the nature of the world. Moreover, all methods are characterized by some form of correlation between faith and human experience. Either all or much of human thinking and experience

485

is bad and therefore calls for God's act of redemptive intervention (orthodox and neoorthodox theologies), or some degree of a constitutive dimension is attributed to human experience in theological reflection (liberal, hermeneutical, correlational, and liberation theologies). Clear distinctions are visible, most of all with regard to the universality of theological statements. Can theologians refer to a framework of discourse accessible in principle to every human being, or is such a framework mere ideology? Any answer to this question will have to come to terms with the intricacies of human communication. Is it possible by analogy to understand the thinking of others, or can one understand in whatever limited way a different culture? In response to this question Bernard Lonergan tried to offer such a universal method in theology by concentrating on what he conceived to be the working of the human mind. David Tracy's answer has been more cautious by pointing to the need for a global conversation on the religious classics and on the methods for their interpretation. George Lindbeck has stressed the degree to which all human experience is dependent on particular forms of cultural and linguistic expression and therefore always predetermined by existing systems of symbols that cannot be made universal. Lindbeck's method aims to give "a normative explication of the meaning a religion has only for its adherents."

The question of universal intelligibility in all discourse has received yet another kind of critical attention in the light of questions raised by so-called postmodern thinkers such as Jacques Derrida and Michel Foucault. Is our entire concept of the autonomous subject as thinking agent not flawed in itself? Is our, or indeed any, concept of truth and of God not merely a therapeutic escape from the uncertainty of the plurality of linguistic processes of signification (Mark C. Taylor)? Can there be any claim to unity when there is no unified framework of communication?

WERNER G. JEANROND

Bibliography

Werner G. Jeanrond, *Theological Hermeneutics: Development and Significance.*
Gordon Kaufman, *An Essay on Theological Method.*
George A. Lindbeck, *The Nature of Doctrine: Religion and Theology in a Postliberal Age.*
Bernard Lonergan, *Method in Theology.*
David Tracy, *Plurality and Ambiguity: Hermeneutics, Religion, Hope.*

Cross Reference: Aesthetics, Black Theology, Correlation, Deconstructionism, Empirical Theology, Epistemology, Feminist Theology, Hermeneutics, Liberation Theology, Philosophical Theology, Political Theology, Postmodern Theology, Process Theology, Systematic Theology.

THEOLOGY (*See* BIBLICAL THEOLOGY, BLACK THEOLOGY, CONFESSIONAL THEOLOGY, DEATH OF GOD THEOLOGY, DOGMATIC THEOLOGY, EMPIRICAL THEOLOGY, FEMINIST THEOLOGY, HISTORICAL THEOLOGY, LIBERATION THEOLOGY, NARRATIVE

THEOLOGY, NATURAL THEOLOGY, PHILOSOPHICAL THEOLOGY, POLITICAL THEOLOGY, POSTMODERN THEOLOGY, PRACTICAL THEOLOGY, PROCESS THEOLOGY, SACRAMENTS/SACRAMENTAL THEOLOGY, SYSTEMATIC THEOLOGY, THEOLOGICAL METHOD, WOMANIST THEOLOGY.)

TIME

Temporality is a central and irreducible feature of the finite world. Organic and inorganic forms take shape and change within time, revealing their finitude, contingency, and relativity. We exist within time, growing, aging, and facing death. Similarly, cultures are rooted in historical time, deriving a sense both of tradition and of potentiality from this historicality.

Because of the manifold and inescapable temporality of the world, questions about time are significant for theological considerations of the relation of God and the world. Since God has traditionally been understood as eternal, the relation of eternity to the temporal world raises a number of questions. Does the eternal nature of God exclude involvement in temporal processes? Can God be active in or affected by the temporal world? Are there aspects of temporal experience as we know it that reveal some form of divine participation or order? That is, does time have religious significance?

The nature of time has always puzzled philosophers and theologians. Detailed analyses of the nature of time can be found in Plato, Aristotle, Augustine, and other classical thinkers. Also, the Jewish and Christian traditions are historically oriented, seeing revelation as emerging within temporal events. However, the problem of temporal and historical process has become increasingly central in the Western understanding of reality at least since the Enlightenment. The traditional notion of a world unchanged since creation was overturned by advances in science and historiography. It became difficult to incorporate the flux of change into the explanatory system of a fixed theological framework. Most notably, science devised temporal explanations for the order evidenced in the world—order that had previously been explained by direct divine intervention. One important development was Darwin's theory of natural selection. This theory explained that the adaptation of living organisms to a changing environment took place by gradual random genetic changes occurring through time. Indications of design (such as the structure and functions of the human eye) that had been considered to prove the existence of God could now be accounted for by a natural and temporal process. For many Darwinian evolutionists, the order of the natural world, of which human beings are a part, is explainable without reference to design, order, meaning, or purpose. Obviously, such discoveries and theories conflict with Christian notions of a God who is directly responsible for the perfection evident in organic and inorganic structures. Another challenge to theology in the twentieth century has arisen with the discovery by physics of the relativity of time, which displaces any notion of an "absolute time" connected with God. Yet, the challenges to traditional thinking that come with modernity's focus on temporality have stimulated many creative developments in twentieth-century religious thought.

If the world is characterized by an irreducible temporality, then we are pressed to consider how an eternal God stands in relation to the temporal world. Several problems arise if we consider God's eternity to mean timelessness, as have some influential figures in the history of Christian theology (e.g., Anselm and Friedrich Schleiermacher). Nelson Pike has argued that the concept of a timeless God conflicts with the Christian idea of God as a person. A timeless God is unable to display personality traits involving a sense of time and change; for example, remembering, anticipating, or being affected by events. Moreover, a timeless God would be incapable of acting in time, and hence could not be construed as omniscient. Arguments like these indicate that notions of an eternal God as timeless raise serious conceptual problems, and they conflict with Christian doctrines concerning God as a person.

Concerned about the relation of an eternal God to a temporal world, some theologians have devised approaches that do not link eternity to timelessness. For example, Paul Tillich argued that eternity is misconstrued if we interpret it either as timelessness or as the endlessness of linear time. Tillich held that eternity appears within time as a transforming category, a transcendent unity of moments. That is, eternity is not simply an infinite extension of ordinary mundane time; rather, it is a religious opening within temporal experience. This opening is found in the creative freedom of spiritual experience and in the attainment of new moral and religious understanding. For Tillich, and other existentialist thinkers, time is a factor in the capacity of human beings for transcending their immediate surroundings, not trapped in the present, both remembering the past and anticipating the future. This capacity for transcendence opens human experience to higher levels of meaning and value that can be incorporated into our temporal activity. The eternal does not remain outside our lives, but it appears within temporal experience.

If we accept that God has some relation to the world of time, we are still faced with the task of understanding temporal processes as revealing meaning, order, purpose, or other indications of divine presence. As noted, this task has become more difficult in the face of several scientific advances. However, most sophisticated recent theological approaches accept the findings of science, but they reject the reductionistic world views extrapolated from those findings. Not all aspects of temporality can be explained in purely naturalistic terms but call for broader forms of understanding that intersect with the realm of religious concern.

Several formulations of a full-scale metaphysics or theology that account for the temporal and evolutionary nature of the world and that include levels of religious significance displayed through time have appeared. One such metaphysical approach derives from the process thought of Alfred North Whitehead. Here, temporal becoming replaces unchanging being as the expression of the divine nature and order. Whitehead sought to show that evolutionary processes revealed an intelligible scheme that pointed to a guiding Being. God's involvement in the world is manifested not in the evidence of static design but in the movement toward greater consciousness, freedom, and ethical awareness in human interaction with a world designed to stimulate these faculties. Religious meaning is not confined to the faculties and potentialities characterizing humanity in isolation. Instead, those faculties associated with religious meaning occur within a world that fosters their development. For example, aesthetic experience of natural beauty stimulates the sense of order and meaning in the world. In such theological models, temporality is essential to the expression and manifestation of religious meaning.

Arguments today that consider time as religiously meaningful usually avoid asserting that everything is preplanned or teleologically determined. Rather, they characterize temporal structures of the world by freedom, chance, order, and meaning. Religious thinking need not conflict with the findings of science (e.g., quantum physics, Darwinian evolution) that reveal chance and indeterminacy as an important part of reality, or with the human sense of self as involving freedom of choice and original creativity. As John Polkinghorne has argued, a degree of open-endedness or possibility is part of a religiously meaningful process of developing self-conscious, ethical beings.

It is unlikely that religious thought will fully resolve the many complex problems related to time. Yet, while theology faces profound challenges in addressing the changes and developments of the temporal world, these processes do not necessarily reveal a world that is incommensurable with religious orientations. Reflection on time thus offers a stimulus to the growth of religious understanding. This reflection can help religious thought to address human experience in a world of transformation.

JAMES J. DICENSO

Bibliography

Nelson Pike, *God and Timelessness*.
John Polkinghorne, *One World: The Interaction Between Science and Theology*.
Paul Tillich, *The Eternal Now*.
Alfred North Whitehead, *Religion in the Making*.

Cross Reference: Eschatology, Panentheism, Process Theology, Providence.

TRADITION

Tradition refers both (1) to the body of beliefs shared with past generations and handed on to succeeding ones and (2) to the process by which those beliefs are transmitted. In the past, different religious groups have understood and used tradition in the first sense in a variety of ways and have expressed different attitudes toward it. Today, as a consequence of ecumenical discussion, there is a convergence of interpretations and increased appreciation for tradition among religious groups frequently hostile to it.

Roman Catholic. Tradition plays a leading role in Roman Catholic thought and practice. At the Second Vatican Council the bishops rejected a proposed schema that spoke of two sources of revelation (scripture and tradition) and affirmed a one-source theory—revelation itself communicated through both scripture and tradition. Tradition is a comprehensive concept embracing both oral and written communication by the church itself of Christian truth. It is found in scripture, and yet it witnesses to the canon of scripture. Both tradition and scripture, however, require interpretation by the teaching office of the church.

What still distinguishes the Roman Catholic from Protestant and Eastern Orthodox concepts of tradition is a ready acceptance of development that provides a basis for late dogmas such as the Immaculate Conception of Mary (1854), Papal Infallibility (1870), and the Assumption of Mary (1950). According to the *Dogmatic Constitution on Divine Revelation,* "This tradition which comes from the apostles develops in the Church with the help of the Holy Spirit. For there is a growth in the understanding of the realities and the words which have been handed down."

Mainline Protestant. The Protestant Reformers—Luther, Calvin, and others—seized on the principle of "scripture alone," accentuating it more and more in consolidating their position against the Council of Trent's veneration of traditions "with an equal affection of piety and reverence." In actual practice, however, tradition did play a role in Protestant theology and practice. Both Luther and Calvin, for instance, accepted the first seven ecumenical councils, cited the church fathers, and invoked tradition to document their interpretation of the Bible.

Free Church Protestant. Among Reformers the group classified as "radicals," especially Anabaptists, took the most critical stance toward tradition. Anabaptists insisted not only on the principle of scripture alone but also on the New Testament alone as the final criterion of truth. The Schleitheim Confession of 1527 urgently insisted on separation from "all popish and anti-popish works and church services." Most free church groups have viewed tradition as opposed to scripture and constrictive of the operation of the Spirit in the life of the church.

Anglican. Anglican Reformers accepted the mainline Reformers' emphasis on scripture, judging that it "containeth all things necessary to salvation" and that "whatsoever is not read therein, nor may be proved thereby, is not to be required of any man" (art. 6, Thirty-nine Articles). At the same time, however, they affirmed tradition, particularly the first four ecumenical councils and the writings of the church fathers, much more self-consciously than Luther or Calvin did. Anglicans consider episcopal succession—the tradition of priestly continuity—essential to the preservation of the church and its ministry.

Eastern Orthodox. Eastern Orthodox churches place conspicuous emphasis on tradition but in a quite different sense from that of Western churches. Tradition signifies, above all, the continuing presence in the life of the church of the Holy Spirit, which guides it toward more thorough understanding of divine truth. There is no thought of separating scripture and tradition, therefore, for the same revelation that appears in scripture is recognized ever anew in the tradition communicated by the Holy Spirit to members of the body of Christ.

Ecumenical. The growth of modern biblical criticism and the ecumenical movement have cast tradition in a new light. Recognition that scripture contains the traditions of the early communities of believers has generated a more positive appreciation of tradition by Protestants. Simultaneously, nearly all groups have come to recognize that tradition (at least tacitly) influences the interpretation of scripture. Ecumenical openness encouraged by Pope John XXIII (1958–1963) and Vatican II (1962–1965) has further eroded the antipathy of Protestants to tradition and evoked an ecumenical methodology in dealing with points of theology and practice.

Bilateral dialogues between different religious groups have necessitated sensitivity to the role of tradition in the framing of theology and practice. Protestants with a pronounced emphasis on scripture remain somewhat uncomfortable with citation of other sources as authoritative, but most have learned to appreciate the one-source theory of Vatican II and to understand better why Roman Catholics, Eastern Orthodox, and Anglicans invoke tradition. Many, however, still entertain serious reservations regarding doctrines that are not fairly plain in scripture.

Multilateral dialogues, those involving more than two religious groups such as those in ecumenical councils, face more formidable challenges in methodology because of the breadth of diversity of attitudes toward tradition. The convergence statement, *Baptism, Eucharist, and Ministry,* adopted by the World Council of Churches deals with this challenge by citing as authority only scripture in the text while noting various traditions in commentary. Some churches, nevertheless, have complained that the document favors certain traditions over others. Although much progress has been made, differences are not likely to be smoothed over in the foreseeable future and will require continuing discussion.

E. GLENN HINSON

491

Bibliography

A. M. Allchin, *The Living Presence of the Past: The Dynamic of Christian Tradition.*
Yves Congar, *Tradition and Traditions.*
George V. Florovsky, *Bible, Church, and Tradition: An Eastern Orthodox View.*
Karl Rahner and Joseph Ratzinger, *Revelation and Tradition.*
James B. Torrance, "Authority, Scripture and Tradition," *Evangelical Quarterly* 87 (1987): 245-51.

Cross Reference: Eastern Orthodox Christianity, Ecumenism, Papacy, Protestantism, Revelation, Roman Catholicism, Vatican II.

TRAGEDY

Tragedy is the literary genre that, more than any other, explores human experiences of evil. By all definitions, tragedy ends badly: in the protagonist's extreme suffering and usually in his or her destruction. Tragedy raises a number of theological issues related to the meaning of evil.

The original tragedies, the Greek plays by Aeschylus, Sophocles, and Euripides, reflect ethical and religious assumptions in many ways antithetical to fundamental Christian beliefs. In particular, Greek tragedy reflects a polytheistic world view in which different gods may conflict, impose incompatible demands, and—most significantly—destroy human beings for a variety of reasons that cannot be reduced simply to the punishment of sin. According to Paul Ricoeur, the hidden and "unavowable" claim implicit in tragedy is the "scandalous theology of predestination to evil." Thus crucial differences prevent any easy reconciliation between the world view of tragedy—the "tragic vision"—and the basic Christian affirmation that a just and loving God has created a world whose basic unity is not fractured and whose goodness is not in doubt. Furthermore, tragedy sees nobility as well as hubris in the tragic hero's defiance of ordinary human limitations. Though the chorus may so advise, a tragic play as a whole does not counsel resignation to the conditions of finitude or simply condemn a character's excess, but rather it arouses admiration for the hero's striving and suffering, even when this contributes to the evil the play explores. In contrast, the virtues and aspirations of many tragic protagonists would be judged sins by most of the Christian tradition.

Nonetheless, Christian thinkers have appropriated insights into the human condition that they have seen expressed most powerfully in tragic works, including those by writers influenced by Christian culture such as Shakespeare, Melville, Dostoevski, and Faulkner. For instance, Reinhold Niebuhr appreciated tragedy's insights into the nature of human sin: its discernment of how evil can grow out of the noblest and most valuable human aspirations and passions. Christian theologians skeptical of the possibility or value of theodicy have advocated reflection on tragedy as a more appropriate response to evil than theoretical explanation or justification of God's ways. The tragic vision may be said to call for a Job-like faith in God's ultimate justice despite all the evidence, as well as to encourage compassion for the victims of suffering. Ethical thinkers have seen in tragedy valuable insights into conflicts among the virtues, or the nature of moral dilemmas, or the psychology of remorse or despair.

Most Christian thinkers have wanted to affirm that, although there are elements in tragedy that may illuminate a particular task of theology, Christian faith goes "beyond tragedy," as Niebuhr put it, in affirming that death and destruction are not the last word about human destiny. Moral evil is finally the responsibility of human agents, and natural evils are conditions of finitude; neither form of evil ought to provide grounds for accusation of God or for lament or criticism of the nature of human existence. If the Christian believes that God works in the midst of suffering to save us from evil, then even the worst adversity or the despairing death of a person cannot be taken as final, as placing him or her beyond redemption. Belief in the immortality of the soul is said to deprive any earthly suffering of its finality. Therefore, it is usually argued, if the final effect of tragedy is a sense of the inexorable waste and doom of human goodness, this tragic vision is finally incompatible with the Christian affirmation that God supports us through all things and saves us from the worst evils and that "neither death, nor life, . . . nor height, nor depth, nor anything else in all creation, will be able to separate us from the love of God in Christ Jesus our Lord" (Rom. 8:38-39). The eschatological hope that is a part of Christian faith makes impossible a tragic vision that asserts the unredeemable destruction and the ultimate failure and waste of the good.

If tragedy is defined in terms of the dramatization of ultimate failure and waste, then Christianity and tragedy are indeed irreconcilable. However, so stark an antithesis between tragic wisdom and Christian faith oversimplifies both. Such a view ignores the affirmative dimensions of most tragedies, which depict not only catastrophe but also a cathartic restoration of order. This view overlooks, as well, the need of any adequate Christian ethics for realistic discernment of the forms of evil, as well as theology's apprehension of the fearful and mysterious aspects of God's relationship to human history. The stark antithesis between tragedy and Christianity makes faith seem blithely optimistic, preventing the believer from fully recognizing suffering. It is not a vivid awareness of evil that disqualifies a view as Christian, but failure to discern possibilities of goodness and grace at work in all human experiences. Some tragic works—the greatest ones, it is submitted—offer insight into both the negativities and the affirmative dimensions of existence. To see Christian faith and tragedy as wholly incompatible or to assert that faith can only be "comic" in its literary emplotment would be to ignore the religious significance of such classic works as *Hamlet* and *King Lear*, *The Brothers Karamazov* and *Moby Dick*.

The dialogue between the interpreter of tragedy and the Christian apologist facilitates vital theological and ethical reflection on such issues as theodicy, the sources of evil, the meaning of providence, the nature of eschatological hope, and divine and human accountability. Although Christian belief imposes constraints on the construction of a "tragic theology," there are many ways in which elements of tragedy may enrich Christian faith and serve as an incentive for theological and ethical reflection.

JOHN D. BARBOUR

Bibliography

Larry D. Bouchard, *Tragic Method and Tragic Theology: Evil in Contemporary Drama and Religious Thought.*
Reinhold Niebuhr, *Beyond Tragedy.*
Paul Ricoeur, *The Symbolism of Evil.*
Nathan Scott, Jr., ed., *The Tragic Vision and the Christian Faith.*

Cross Reference: Comedy.

TRANSCENDENCE

Transcendence is significant in the theory of knowledge as something that is contrasted with immanence. Everything that cannot be the object of experience belongs to transcendence, including everything that cannot enter consciousness through sense experience. Immanuel Kant reasoned about transcendentals (primarily the notions of God, freedom, and immortality) and showed that no scientifically and universally valid claims can be made about their existence.

History of the Issue. The concepts of transcendence and immanence are especially important in determining God's relationship to the world and cosmos. Although in English the distinction is made between the theological term "heaven" and the cosmological term "sky," the Bible does not distinguish between the two. God's habitation was thought to be above the firmament. Often, corresponding to the oriental idea of a mountain of the gods, Yahweh is understood as living on a high mountain from which he comes—a mountain in the far North (Isa. 14:13), or perhaps Mount Sinai or Horeb.

Yahweh was not considered a local god who resided in a certain temple, thus confined to a particular space. "God does not live in a temple made with hands" (Acts 7:48, 17:24). God fills heaven though "heaven and the highest heaven cannot contain [God]" (I Kings 8:27). The earth is God's footstool and the heavens are God's throne (Matt. 5:34-35). Although God's presence could be asserted, there was no actual interest in making local God's habitation. God's transcendence was thought of in terms of God's mighty power and of not being confined to our earthly limitations. Jesus talks without hesitation about his "Father in heaven," and he himself is "taken up" into heaven. And one Pauline epistle refers to the dwelling place of God in the "third heaven" (II Cor. 12:2).

Although the issue of transcendence is as old as the transcendentals associated with it, the term itself is of more recent vintage, and it most likely emerged with the growing dissociation of God from the world, or the tangible from the ideal, at the beginning of modernity. As more and more events were considered without immediate reference to God, a bifurcation emerged between the natural and the supernatural and between the immanent and the transcendent.

The big challenge came with the Copernican-Brunoic shock. Giordano Bruno (1548–1600) was deeply influenced by Copernicus's heliocentric theory. The Copernican theory of the earth moving around the sun led Bruno to reject entirely a geocentric and an anthropocentric conception of the universe. According to Bruno the space of the universe is infinite; neither reason nor nature can assign to it a limit. He reasoned that the universe is filled with an infinity of worlds similar to our own. The once familiar notion of a three-tiered universe with the netherworld below and the heavens above had collapsed. Therefore, it became extremely difficult to assign a certain place to God even in the beyond. Bruno no longer drew a definite line between God and the world, nor did he want to identify the infinite "worlds" with God. Yet in considering God as completely infinite, since God can be associated with no boundary and since God's every attribute is one and infinite, Bruno came dangerously close to abandoning the distinction between God and the world.

In a similar way, Baruch Spinoza (1632–1677) asserted that God is the immanent cause of all things but not a supernatural cause. Even more than Bruno, Spinoza moved in the direction of collapsing the distinction between the creator and the created, since he allowed for only two attributes of God—thought and extension. When he stated, "By God I understand a being absolutely infinite, that is to say, substance consisting of infinite attributes, each one of which expresses eternal and infinite essence," he conferred upon God such a determinative naturalistic characteristic that the identification of God with nature became inevitable. A pantheistic position evolved, identifying God with nature and the transcendent with the immanent. Yet pantheism always harbors the danger of changing into atheism, especially when the close relationship between God and nature is resolved in favor of a unilateral equation. Moving against this materialistic trend was nineteenth-century idealism, represented by the work of Kant and Hegel.

The term "transcendentalism" was coined by Kant to denote that which is beyond sense experience while yet knowable to the mind. He considered the use of the concepts of reason as immanent, insofar as reason stays within the limit of possible experience, while ideas of such concepts of objects are transcendent. For Hegel the Absolute Spirit becomes another entity over against itself: It enters existence and creates the world. This dialectical movement makes it possible to maintain both the immanence of the world and God's transcendence. Since the Spirit, however, merely posits the ''other,'' this kind of reasoning becomes vulnerable to a projectionistic attack against anything transcendent, such as that brought forth by Ludwig Feuerbach and Karl Marx later in the nineteenth century.

In contrast to Hegel's reasoning and its emerging critique, Søren Kierkegaard emphasized the ''infinite qualitative difference between God and humanity.'' Christian faith expresses the paradoxical truth that the eternal has entered our finite world. This paradox can be accepted only by faith and cannot be verified by reason. Following Kierkegaard, Karl Barth asserted that there is no given point of contact between the human and the divine; God establishes God's own point of contact. God touches the immanent in the same way a tangent touches a circle without becoming part of it. Any human attempt to go beyond the immanent ends up in idolatry. In Jesus as the Christ, another world has entered our world and by touching it Jesus ceases to be a historical, time-bound, and directly accessible figure. In contrast to this disjunctive talk about God's transcendence, Paul Tillich used ontological terminology and characterized God as ''being itself,'' for whom any relation can only be of symbolic character. God can never become the object of human knowing or acting. Instead of viewing God as touching our sphere ''vertically from above'' (Barth), Tillich referred to God as the ''ground of being,'' employing therewith the category of depth and psychoanalytic terminology.

Since it became no longer acceptable to assert the transcendence of God in relation to a world beyond, Dietrich Bonhoeffer and others devised the notion of an *immanent transcendence,* meaning that ''God is beyond in the midst of our life. . . . The God who lets us live in the world without the working hypothesis of God is the God before whom we stand continually'' (Bonhoeffer). There could even emerge a death of God theology that attempted to talk about God in nontheistic or even atheistic terms. Thomas J. J. Altizer, for instance, claimed that the Christian notion of God is obviously a product of the fusion of the Bible with Greek ontology. The death of God as a historical event pertains not only to the God of religion, as understood by Barth, but also to the God of Christianity. We do not just feel somewhat abandoned by God, as William Hamilton had claimed, but the resurrection and dominion of Christ no longer have any precise meaning. Through the incarnational process God has so completely merged with the world that God can no longer be distinguished from it. For death of God theologians transcendence has been merged into immanence.

Today's critical philosophers who observe theology from the sideline hear theologians saying all kinds of things about God that make absolutely no sense in everyday language. For instance, they hear that Christ has been resurrected into the kerygma (e.g., Rudolf Bultmann), that God is the origin of one's restlessness (e.g., Herbert Braun), and that God is the mythological expression for the ultimacy of personal responsibility (e.g., Fritz Buri). These assertions reflect not only the accurate insight that God cannot be objectified, but also the implicit and unreflective admission that theologians have dislocated God from a cosmological reference point.

Once theology and the Christian faith became cosmologically neutral, two immediate consequences began to emerge: (1) The world we see, live in, and move in is implicitly or explicitly declared void of God; it has become atheistic. (2) Once God has become detached from the cosmological reference point, God becomes a strictly personal God. Since God is deprived of God's own sphere, God can no longer make the demands of a cosmological God. Of course, we can still say that God challenges and comforts, that one can relate to God, and that God answers our prayers. But when asked where the God who does such things is, then, as Antony Flew said, God dies the death of a thousand qualifications. God is reduced to invisibility, intangibility, and elusiveness and hardly differs logically and linguistically from being no God at all.

Basic Positions. Since history is an intrinsic part of our space-time continuum, any reference to a history-making God, a God of promise, or a God of the future implies the cosmological question where such a God can be located, and touches on the issue of immanence and transcendence. Even the pantheistic position that largely identifies God with the whole of the universe cannot avoid the issue of the ontological or existential difference between God and the world to justify its continuance of any God talk. On the other end of the spectrum, classical theism assumes a God who is transcendent from the universe. Yet any transcendence, unless it assumes a *deus otiosus* (meaning that a complacent God is no longer involved in the affairs of the world), must again deal with the relation between God and the world.

Process theology and empirical theology especially have addressed God's relationship to the world. Bernard M. Loomer, a representative of empirical theology, claims that if the experienced world, with its possibilities, is the only reality accessible to us, then one conclusion seems inevitable: God is to be identified either with a part or with the entirety of the concrete, actual world. Therefore God should be identified with the entirety of the world, with whatever unity that entirety possesses. Process representatives, such as John B. Cobb, Jr., find that in such an identification of God with the world there is no longer possible a creative advance of the world toward perfection. According to Alfred North Whitehead, the founder of process thought, the groundwork for every possible world is given through God's primordial nature, while God's subsequent nature provides through a kind of feedback the weaning of physical feelings from primordial concepts.

497

Cobb uses the intriguing metaphor of an *energy event* to allow for God's transcending interaction with the world. God as the supreme energy event is related to us in such a way that God is all-inclusive of the space-time continuum and thus that we are in this way parts of God. We are not parts of God if we understand that God is the sum total of the parts. Nor should we infer that the parts are lacking in independence and self-determination.

> God and the creatures interact as separate entities, while God includes the standpoint of all of them in his omnispatial standpoint. In this sense God is everywhere, but God is not everything. The world does not exist outside God or apart from God, but the world is not God or simply part of God. The character of the world is influenced by God, but it is not determined by him, and the world in its turn contributes novelty and richness to the divine experience. [Cobb]

This process model of a feedback relationship between God and the world Cobb labels "panentheism." It advocates neither a theism in which God occupies another, transcendent sphere nor a pantheism in which God and the world are ultimately identical.

Wolfhart Pannenberg applies the field theories of modern physics to both the relationship of the Godhead to the world and the relationship of the trinitarian persons in the Godhead. The Godhead is considered a field through which the three trinitarian persons can equally appear in relation to the world. For instance, the notion of the British physicist Michael Faraday (1791–1867) of a universal field of power in which all material corpuscular entities are considered secondary manifestations allows not only a modern interpretation of God as Spirit but also of the world as a manifestation of the Godhead. Pannenberg himself raises the important issue, however, that once the Spirit is considered a field, the Spirit becomes impersonal.

An effective answer to the challenge posed by the Copernican world model, which seems to rule out a transcendent God, should not borrow from physics or biology but should challenge this model on its own cosmological turf. The most promising notion is that of God being related to the world in a dimensional way. Within the space-time continuum, God cannot be present as an additional object. Panentheism advocates that God is like an envelope for the world. "The world is regarded as being, as it were 'within' God, but the being of God is regarded as not exhausted by, or subsumed within the world" (Peacocke). This panentheistic model also seems to be preferred by many process theologians, who occasionally talk about the world as God's body.

The metaphor of a dimensional relationship between God and the world seems to clarify the issues of spatial contiguity and spatial interaction. If we assume that God is related to us in a dimensional way, being present in a way in which God is dimensionally higher than we are, God would embrace all our available possibilities in space and time as well as possibilities that are not available to us in our present dimension or dimensions. But both elements, God's presence or immanence in our space-time continuum and God's superiority or transcendence to it, could be maintained. Yet, it would be futile for us, being confined to our space-time continuum, to look in it for traces of divine transcendence. Everything we perceive in our world is perceived as being exclusively a part of this world. The higher dimension is in principle inaccessible to us. It can be disclosed to us only by someone from that dimension telling or showing us that what we perceive as belonging exclusively to our dimension is at the same time part of another and entirely different dimension.

This twofold nature of reality, both being immanently and transcendentally caused, is contained, for instance, in the conviction that a "purely natural event" (e.g., the instantaneous healing of a sick person) is at the same time wholly God-wrought. Similarly, the assertion that Jesus Christ is fully human and divine, could be understood by assuming such a multilayered structure of reality. The limitations of this kind of reality are shown by modern science (e.g., the duality of wave and corpuscle in physics and freedom and necessity in biology).

Since a higher dimension does not simply add a vertical or horizontal story (i.e., another space), the issue of a "heavenly topography" becomes obsolete and the transition from a pre-Copernican world view to a Copernican or Einsteinian one would no longer pose a threat to God's "habitat." God would be present in our dimension (i.e., our four-dimensional space-time continuum) without being contained by it, and God would transcend it without being absent. Since, however, any intimation about this other dimension would have to be given to us in our space-time continuum, there is no empirical proof (or disproof) possible that such a dimension or transcendence does indeed exist.

HANS SCHWARZ

Bibliography

Ray Sherman Anderson, *Historical Transcendence and the Reality of God: A Christological Critique.*
Gordon Kaufman, *God the Problem.*
Robert H. King, *The Meaning of God.*
Arthur R. Peacocke, *Creation and the World of Science.*

Cross Reference: Death of God Theology, Panentheism.

TRINITY

The doctrine of the Trinity (or triunity of God) refers to the one being of God as Father, Son, and Holy Spirit. Since the early centuries of the church, it has been considered the primary statement of the Christian conception of God, distinguishing Christianity from the monotheism of Judaism and Islam, and even as the central mystery of Christian faith, both as enshrining the deepest truth of Christianity and as being the most difficult to state adequately.

The concept as such is nowhere explicitly expressed in the scriptures, though such passages as Matthew 28:19 and II Corinthians 13:14 are suggestive. (A traditional favorite proof text, I John 5:7, is now almost universally recognized as a very late addition and is omitted in most current translations of the epistle.) The doctrine was thus formulated in the church as the community sought to explicate the meaning of the revelation in Jesus Christ.

The terminology that became standard in the Latin West (God is *una substantia,* one being or nature, and *tres Personae,* three persons), as well as the application of the term ''Trinity'' to the three personae, goes back to Tertullian at the beginning of the third century. In the East the Greek formula was one *ousia* or essence and three *hypostases,* which came to be distinguished as three individuations of *ousia.*

The crucial steps in establishing the doctrine as official teaching of the church were taken at the first two general councils (at Nicea in 325 and Constantinople in 381) as a result of the conflict with Arianism. They affirmed that both Jesus Christ as the Son of God and the Holy Spirit are unqualifiedly of the same being as God the Father, that is, fully God, yet without contradicting the oneness of God. Further elaborations and debate in both East and West built on this foundation. Although the doctrine was from time to time attacked as unscriptural or irrational (for example, by the Socinians in the Reformation period), it was accepted as a staple doctrine in East and West.

In nineteenth-century Protestantism, partly because of Schleiermacher's relegating it to an appendix in his influential *The Christian Faith* and partly as a result of the massive development of biblical criticism, the doctrine was neglected as not important. Some then suggested that Trinity means essentially only a threefold viewing of God, that God is seen by the believer under three aspects, or that the doctrine refers to the activity of God as Creator, Redeemer, and Sanctifier.

In recent years, however, especially since Karl Barth's long discussion in the first volume of his *Church Dogmatics,* an extensive discussion and appreciation of the meaning of Trinity has ensued. The present discussion is generally less concerned with traditional points of debate (e.g., the acceptance in the West of the *Filioque,* affirming that the Spirit proceeds from the Son as well as from the Father, which became an ostensible reason for the division of the Eastern and Western churches) than with the basic intent and import of the doctrine.

The concept of Trinity is thus widely seen again as an essential and distinctive description of the fullness of God as revealed in Christ. That revelation involves a fundamental threefoldness, signified by the terms Father, Son, and Holy Spirit. God confronts us in Jesus Christ; God is truly present as the Son or eternal Word. But God is also apprehended as the Father, who sends the Son and to whom the

Son points. And God is known as the Holy Spirit, opening the hearts and minds of humans in faith. Yet it is the same God who is present throughout. The words Father, Son, and Holy Spirit refer to one and the same God, but the Christian cannot say who God is without pointing to the distinctive form and content of self-giving in Christ and the illumination of the Holy Spirit. The doctrine of the Trinity is thus a summing up of the gospel.

The present areas of debate focus especially (1) on the basis of the doctrine (whether it lies in the structure of the divine act of reconciliation in Christ or in the personal relation of Jesus Christ to the Father) and (2) on the proper modern meaning of the traditional terminology, especially the translation of the terms *persona* and *hypostasis* as "person." For some, like the Protestant Karl Barth and the Roman Catholic Karl Rahner, the modern conception of personality is so different from the older meaning of *persona* that to speak of three persons in common parlance suggests three consciousnesses or subjectivities (hence three personal divine entities in God, which seems to be tritheism). But the doctrine of Trinity is intended to affirm, not deny, the unity of God. It refers to an inner richness or complexity, not dividing God into parts, but describing the nature of the oneness as a living and full unity. Therefore, God should be described as one in personality or real consciousness and three in modes of being (Barth), or in distinct manners of subsisting (Rahner), that is, ways of being God. (This seems to be more in accord with the dominant Western tradition of psychological analogies for the Trinity, at least since Augustine). Both Rahner and Barth hold that God is a single divine subject, though they both are also able to use language suggesting personal relationships within God.

The contrary view is that the modern conception of person is consistent with the intent of the traditional language and that God is indeed to be described as three persons or subjects of activity and consciousness that can yet be described as one because personality is as such a social reality, personhood being constituted by intersubjective relationship. This view tends to ground the doctrine in the personal relation of Jesus Christ as the incarnate Son to the Father. So the threeness has priority. Such conceptions are argued by Wolfhart Pannenberg and in extreme form by Jürgen Moltmann, who wants to make a sharp distinction between trinitarianism and monotheism (which for him is inherently monarchical).

CLAUDE WELCH

Bibliography

Karl Barth, *Church Dogmatics*, 1/1.
Robert W. Jenson, *The Triune Identity*.
Jürgen Moltmann, *Trinity and Kingdom*.
Wolfhart Pannenberg, *Systematische Theologie*, vol. 1.

Karl Rahner, *The Trinity.*

Claude Welch, *In This Name: The Doctrine of the Trinity in Contemporary Theology.*

Cross Reference: Christology, Dogmatic Theology, Holy Spirit.

TRUTH (*See* AUTHORITY, JUSTICE, VIRTUE.)

ULTIMATE CONCERN

The theological significance of the concept of "ultimate concern" is closely associated with the thought of Paul Tillich. In his *Systematic Theology,* volume 1, he formulated the concept:

> Ultimate concern is the abstract translation of the great commandment: "The Lord, our God, the Lord is one; and you shall love the Lord your God with all your heart, and with all your soul, and with all your mind, and with all your strength." . . . The ultimate concern is unconditional, independent of any conditions of character, desire, or circumstance.

This characterization of ultimate concern as unconditional command has a distinctively Kantian sound to it; and if this were the only sense in which Tillich used the expression, one might well think that Tillich was appealing to a summons to unconditional duty. But Tillich uses ultimate concern in additional senses, and these make difficult a single understanding of this expression. For example, in his sermon "Our Ultimate Concern," Tillich identifies "concern" with "anxiety" (as Heidegger does in *Being and Time*), and with "infinite concern" for "the one thing needed" (as Kierkegaard does in *Purity of Heart Is to Will One Thing*). But in *Dynamics of Faith,* ultimate concern defines "what faith is"; and "faith as ultimate concern" is the theme of the entire book. Additionally, Tillich says,

> The term "ultimate concern" . . . is intentionally ambiguous. It indicates, on the one hand, *our* being ultimately concerned—the subjective side—and on the other hand, the *object* of our ultimate concern, for which of course there is no other word than "ultimate." Now in this relationship, the history of religion can be described as the attempt to find what can with justification be called this object.

These various senses of ultimate concern can be enumerated: (1) the summons to the unconditional, (2) anxiety toward willing one thing, (3) faith, and (4) the manifest history of religion.

In the first sense of ultimate concern, ultimacy is opposed to all that is *finite.* It is not that ultimate concern is the "highest" among someone's various "concerns" or "priorities"; rather, one's finite interests derive their purpose or meaning from one's ultimate concern. Thus ultimate concern is fundamental to one's "concern-ful" existence; particular purposes or goals will define one's ways of living out one's ultimate concern in practical ways. Moreover, ultimate concern is the response to a calling, a summons; it does not originate within the human subject.

Ultimate concern as anxiety toward willing one thing emphasizes Tillich's contention that ultimate concern entails risk: the risk involved in one's refusing to rest content in the finite securities of everyday life, the willingness to give up hope in idols and to become open toward the Infinite—toward the God above the god of conventional theistic belief. Hence ultimate concern involves risk-taking and calls for courage.

Tillich presents "faith" as ultimate concern in the sense that faith does not originate in the subject; rather, the human subject is "grasped by" an ultimate concern. For Tillich, faith entails a courageous response on the part of the person of faith; faith is not essentially the content of belief. Tillich is suspicious of authoritarian claims to truth and finality and to the "intellectualist" (as well as the "emotionalist" and "voluntarist") distortions of faith. Among other possible consequences, this determination keeps the Tillichean "faith" open to dialogue between and among faiths. Furthermore, in Tillich's view, all persons have faith, since all persons exist in the condition of ultimate concern. Ultimate concern produces praxis, but ultimate concern is not itself a body of "beliefs": As one's faith is, so will one believe and do.

Ultimate concern also bears the sense of the manifest history of religion: the human quest for ultimacy, for "salvation." Religion is the phenomenon of ultimate concern (faith) seeking fulfillment (salvation). In this sense, religion is an inherent element in being human.

The several senses of ultimate concern show Tillich's emphasis on the religious life as quest, as courage and risk, as willingness to be open toward the Ultimate in a world grown dangerously comfortable with the political, economic, and social structures of a desacralized cosmos, a world grown proud of itself, yet remaining restless in its anxiety.

ARTHUR H. JENTZ, JR.

Bibliography

Gordon D. Kaufman, *Theology for a Nuclear Age.*
Paul Tillich, *Dynamics of Faith.*
_____ , *Christianity and the Encounter of the World Religions.*
_____ , *The Future of Religions.*

Paul Tillich, *The New Being* (chap. 20).
David Tracy, *Plurality and Ambiguity: Hermeneutics, Religion, Hope.*

Cross Reference: God, Idolatry.

VATICAN II

In the Roman Catholic Church a formal gathering of the bishops of the world in solemn assembly is called an ecumenical council. Catholics recognize twenty-one councils in the history of Christianity as being ecumenical, although Orthodox Christians and some Protestants accept only the first seven councils (the last being Nicea II in 787) as being truly ecumenical, of which the first four (Nicea I, Constantinople, Ephesus, and Chalcedon) are considered especially crucial for the formulation of orthodox Christian doctrine.

According to Roman Catholic church law the pope alone can call a council, only bishops have a deliberative vote in the council, and the decrees of the council only have validity if they have been officially promulgated by the pope and the body of bishops who are in council.

The agenda for conciliar discussion varies according to the needs of the time. Thus, for example, Lateran V (1512–17) attempted internal church reform on the eve of the Reformation while Trent (1545–64) was a direct response of the Catholic bishops to the Protestant Reformation. No other church council was convened until 1869–70 when Vatican I discussed the office and powers of the papacy. That council, cut short by the Franco-Prussian war in Europe, defined the doctrine of papal infallibility.

Although there had been some discussion in the twentieth century about reconvening Vatican I to continue its work, Pope John XXIII surprised the world on January 25, 1959, by calling for an ecumenical council. The decision was made to have a new council devoted to updating the church (*aggiornomento* was the Italian word used) and to seek greater Christian unity. Between 1959 and the first session of the council in October of 1962, there was an intense period of preparation. Requests were made from a wide spectrum of Catholic institutions (the episcopacy, Catholic universities, religious orders, the Roman curia, etc.) for suggestions for the agenda. Nearly ten thousand proposals were sent to ten different preparatory commissions for drafting into working documents. These documents went to a central commission for further refinement. A few were then selected as working drafts to be sent to the bishops of the world for discussion in the conciliar sessions.

When the council met it was clear that there was intense dissatisfaction with the working drafts and an equally intense desire for documents that would be pastoral in tone, truly oriented toward reform, and sensitive to non-Catholic Christians. It was also clear that the majority of the council members wanted a theology that would take full account of the liturgical, biblical, and patristic renewal that had been going on in the church for nearly a century.

Pope John XXIII died in June, 1963, but the work of the council continued under his successor, Pope Paul VI. The council met in session four times with the end coming in December 1965 with the solemn promulgation of the conciliar documents. The council was clearly a watershed event in the history of Catholicism both because of the innovations at the council sessions themselves and, second, because of the fundamental change effected by the council in both the theology and the pastoral practice of the church.

Innovations in the Council. Vatican II was the first ecumenical council in which laypersons were invited to participate as experts *(periti)* in an advisory capacity to the bishops. It was also the first council to ask non-Roman Catholics to attend the council as invited observers in order to benefit from their expertise and to signal the conciliar desire for religious unity. Additionally the council addressed its deliberations in a formal and non-polemical manner to people outside the Roman Catholic communion. Thus, to quote a conspicuous example, the pastoral constitution *On the Church in the Modern World (Gaudium et Spes;* Vatican documents are often named for their opening words in Latin) addresses itself "not only to the children of the Church and to all who invoke the name of Christ, but to the whole of humanity." Furthermore, it offers the "honest assistance of the Church in fostering that brotherhood of all people which corresponds to this destiny of theirs." Again, the council was innovative in the sense that, following the express wish of Pope John XXIII, it declined to use the traditional forms of condemnation (the "anathemas") of errors. The council wished to frame its deliberations in an irenic and non-judgmental fashion. Finally, the "style" of many of the conciliar decrees was cast in a discursively pastoral fashion instead of the restricted dogmatic or disciplinary language which had been a feature of earlier conciliar language.

Innovations of the Council. Catholicism in the period after the great religious convulsions of the Reformation period was in a state of reaction against the growth of modernity. It resisted the implications of the scientific revolution; it reacted strongly against the modernism it saw deriving from everything from the rise of critical biblical criticism to the liberal impulses in political theory. Catholicism saw itself as a bulwark against modernity and, as a church, under siege by secularity.

Its program to combat such forces emphasized doctrinal orthodoxy, rigid uniformity of church practice, separation from other religious bodies, a strong affirmation of the church as an institutional reality with the pope at the apex of a structured hierarchy, and a theological orientation that emphasized the transcendental and other-worldly. What Vatican II did, in essence, was to shift those emphases in order for the church to enter into dialogue with the modern world. As one wit put it, Vatican II dragged the church, kicking and screaming, into the nineteenth century.

What were the tactics used to energize this shift? A few central themes deserve emphasis, many of which are identified by Avery Dulles, who has been a preeminent American scholar of the council.

1. Reformability. While there has always been a reform impulse in Catholicism, Catholicism after the Reformation period was suspicious of reform tendencies as unnecessarily innovative and also destructive of church unity. That the church is always in a state of reformability suggests both the need for reform and freedom from always defending the past.

2. Emphasis on the Word of God. In reaction to the Reformers, Catholicism at the Council of Trent put much emphasis on law and sacrament. Energized by the renewal of biblical scholarship, Vatican II highlighted the centrality of the Word of God as a counterbalance to that earlier emphasis.

3. Collegiality. To counteract the overemphasis on papal power, doubly underscored by the definition of papal infallibility at Vatican Council I, the documents at Vatican II emphasized the collegial role of bishops in the Catholic church.

4. Religious Freedom. Vatican II made an important breakthrough in its desire to move away from its older understanding of church-state relationships and the old notion that "error has no rights" to a nuanced acceptance of modern pluralism and the central place of human rights. The council declaration on human freedom *(Dignitatis Humanae)* was inspired mainly by the pioneering theological work of the late American theologian, John Courtney Murray.

5. The Laity in the Church. A notorious conservative of the last century said that it was the duty of the Catholic laity to "pray, pay, and obey." By contrast Vatican II emphasized the doctrine of the priesthood of the laity as a direct consequence of the dignity each Christian enjoys through baptism. The council took a big step toward the "declericalization" of Catholicism.

6. Unity but not Uniformity. The council formally recognized the cultural diversity of the people and their consequent need for a Christian life that honors that diversity. Issues ranging from the shift of the liturgy to the vernacular to the need to inculturate Christian teaching in non-European settings are a direct result of the conciliar desire to maintain basic unity while permitting the utmost flexibility of cultural forms.

7. Ecumenism. This term can be understood in three senses in relation to the council. First, the council fostered cooperation and dialogue with non-Roman Catholic Christians, which has blossomed, in the last generation, into serious bilateral conversations with many denominations. Second, the council encouraged dialogue with non-Christian religions of the West, especially Judaism and Islam. With respect to the Jews, there was a formal attempt to disavow any kind of theology from which anti-Semitism could arise. Third, there was a formal recognition of the religious wealth of the great Asian traditions like Hinduism and Buddhism with the hope that mutual exchange and cooperation could develop with these ancient religious traditions. The declaration on non-Christian religions (*Nostra Aetate*) states explicitly that the council wished to give primary consideration to that which "human beings have in common and to what promotes fellowship among them."

8. *The Social Mission of the Church.* Although Catholicism has a proud tradition of charity and care-giving that extends back to its origins, it has often emphasized its religious mission as an instrument of salvation in an other-worldly sense. Vatican II, with a much more incarnational sensitivity, wished to assume a role in testifying to the kingdom of Christ as already present in the world. It underscored the role of the church as servant and the need to think of salvation-redemption as not exclusively belonging to the end time (*eschaton*).

One other large theme needs emphasis. In a widely reprinted essay Karl Rahner argued that Vatican II was a watershed event that brought the church into an entirely new era. He pointed out that in the period of persecutions, before Constantine's edict of toleration in the early fourth century, the church was both countercultural and sectarian in that it resisted the civil majority and was persecuted by it. When Christianity finally became the state religion of Rome in the late fourth century, it began a process by which it absorbed, over its long history, the language, law, philosophical outlook, and general culture of the Greco-Roman tradition. It became, in short, a European-centered church.

At Vatican II, Rahner submitted, there were representative bishops from all over the world and, more important, there was a strongly worded conviction that the gospel needs to be inculturated in forms adaptable to cultures that are not heirs to the classical heritage of the West. Coupled with that shift is the obvious demographic trend showing an ever-increasing number of Catholics in both the Far East, Africa, and other parts of the non-European world. What Vatican II symbolized (even though it has only been partially realized) is the dawn of a new age in which we are seeing the slow birth pangs of a "world church," which is going to look very different from the church of the past.

Change and innovation characterized the council. Yet a close reading of the conciliar documents reveals that they sometimes contain an unresolved tension between traditional theological formulations and new insights. This tension reflects necessary compromises made between the views of the more traditional and more innovative streams within a church that, wrongly, from the outside has seemed unitary and monolithic.

In the constitution on the church (*Lumen Gentium*), for example, the church is described in both a vertical fashion as a hierarchical institution and horizontally as

507

the People of God. A generation of reflection on that document has shown that the actual policy of church governance cannot always easily do justice to both of those notions. Disagreements between local churches and the Vatican, construed too often as struggles between reactionaries and progressives, in fact reflect divergent theological views that appeal to the same documents for support.

The great task of post–Vatican II theologians has been to think of fruitful ways to be faithful to the inherited tradition of Catholic theological witness without being trapped in a mindless conservatism or, conversely, giving way to a temptation to lose a sense of the continuity of that tradition.

One precious clue to achieve this end was given by the council itself. In its decree on ecumenism *(Unitatis Redintegratio)*, the council spoke of a "hierarchy of truths" in Christianity, which vary "in their relationship to the foundations of Christian faith." For Catholics, as for all Christians, the Christian foundation is Jesus the Christ. All other theological truths flow from that center. The great task of the theologian today is to explain this or that doctrine not as an isolated fact but in its relationship to the core of faith. Such an approach not only makes great ecumenical sense but it also aids in ordering priorities. What the council taught, in essence, was that we need to re-view our faith with a sense of its firm foundation in the proclamation of the Good News. In doing that, we may fulfill an ancient piece of wisdom that demands that in essential matters there is to be unity; in incidental matters, liberty; but in all things, charity.

LAWRENCE S. CUNNINGHAM

Bibliography

Walter Abbott and J. Gallagher, eds., *The Documents of Vatican II.*
Avery Dulles, *The Reshaping of Catholicism.*
J. Komonchak, ed., *The Reception of Vatican II.*
Karl Rahner, "Towards a Fundamental Theological Interpretation of Vatican II," *Theological Studies* 40 (1979): 716-27.
Lucien Richard, et al., eds., *Vatican II: The Unfinished Agenda.*
H. Vorgrimler, ed., *Commentary on the Documents of Vatican II.* 5 vols.

Cross Reference: Liberation Theology, Roman Catholicism, Tradition.

VIRTUE

Virtues are those qualities that people in a definable community think reflect admirable human characteristics. These qualities must, however, reflect the presence of reason and will to count as virtues; perfect pitch, for example, is an admirable characteristic but not a virtue. A virtue, then, is a disposition to act, desire, and feel that involves the exercise of judgment and leads to a recognizable human excellence, an instance of human flourishing. Virtuous activity must also involve choosing action primarily because it manifests a good way of life. But virtuous people are not guided by the goal of possessing virtues. Rather they attend to the situations they face, letting their virtue guide their perception. I act benevolently because the situation I face fits a description that elicits my benevolence; for example, I aid a suffering person who confronts me because such action characterizes my idea of good living.

Virtues, at their core, correct difficulties that are natural to human beings, temptations that need to be resisted, or motivations that need to be strengthened. In this regard benevolence is needed because humans have selfish impulses; courage because humans allow fear to stop them from doing what they should. Ideas about virtues rest, then, on a picture of human weakness and need. Moreover, conflicts will appear in a person's character if virtue's correction is imperfect.

An especially revealing kind of conflict is that between virtues and semblances of virtue. A semblance of virtue occurs if a person chooses a virtuous action for consequences, such as an enhanced reputation, that a non-virtuous person would desire. A semblance of courage exists if I challenge the sexist behavior of my boss, despite the possible loss of my job, in order to win the regard of coworkers. Focusing on the relationships between virtues and their semblances is productive. It allows people to devise subtle ways to evaluate behavior and character and to criticize prevailing but erroneous ideas of virtue, such as pictures of courage that highlight raw aggressiveness.

In Christian theology, Roman Catholic and Protestant thinkers have often, in the past, disagreed about the way to understand the significance of virtues. For many Catholic theologians the concept of virtue was of central importance, and they distinguished between acquired natural virtues that guide people's normal life and infused virtues that are produced by God, aim toward God, and guide people's religious life. The most important natural virtues, called cardinal or hinge *(cardo)* virtues, are practical wisdom, justice, courage, and moderation. The most important infused virtues, called theological virtues, are faith, hope, and charity.

Protestant thinkers have often used versions of the idea of virtue to characterize the action of a sanctifying spirit, but usually they have also expressed misgivings about aspects of the Catholic analysis. For example, they criticized the apparent separation between people's normal and religious life, questioned the seeming lack of emphasis on the role of obligation or revealed law, and rejected any connection between virtue and the notion that personal merit can somehow be earned and stored.

Theologians continue to treat issues such as the role of transcendent forces and the best way to devise faithfully traditional notions. But they have also shifted attention to general problems about virtue and thereby become a part of discussions about virtue in both the philosophical community and the culture at large. These discussions often focus on exploring the formation and influence of character, justifying the idea that particular qualities are admirable, and dealing with problems generated by earlier, culturally bound interpretations of virtue.

In the discussions today, several vexing kinds of problems surround the understanding of virtue. One arises from the need to consider both how character is best understood and evaluated and how character affects action. How best to depict the human self then becomes an important issue; for example, what is the nature and relationship of practical judgments, emotions, and dispositions?

A second problem arises from the historical fact that traditional notions of virtue reflected and reinforced social systems that most today think treated many people in manifestly unfair ways. Can ideas of virtue be reformulated, it is asked, in a way that both maintains their distinctive power and yet does not produce such unacceptable results?

This difficulty informs the significant but narrower problem of how to relate ideas of virtue to those dominant modern theories of morality that stress people's obligation to follow universal duties. Do notions of virtue provide a needed supplement to these theories or can they replace them?

A fourth problem is whether all notions of virtue are invalid because they are intimately connected with ideas about the invariant characteristics of human nature, a notion that scientific and cultural studies have discredited. Is it possible to give a textured account of human nature that meets such legitimate modern criticisms and yet resembles the accounts that have, and seemingly must, underlie virtue theory?

A final problem concerns our inadequate understanding of those new virtues that can enable us to deal appropriately with people who manifest integral schemes of virtue that differ from our own. What new virtues are needed to live successfully in a world where different, densely constituted cultures impinge on each other?

LEE YEARLEY

Bibliography

Stanley Hauerwas, *A Community of Character: Toward a Constructive Social Ethics.*
Alasdair MacIntyre, *After Virtue,* 2nd ed.
Bernard Williams, *Ethics and the Limits of Philosophy.*
Lee Yearley, *Mencius and Aquinas: Theories of Virtue and Conceptions of Courage*
———, "Recent Work on Virtue," *Religious Studies Review* 16 (1990): 1-9.

Cross Reference: Ethics–Christian, Moral Theology, Sanctification.

WOMANIST THEOLOGY

In the preface to her collection of womanist prose entitled *In Search of Our Mothers' Gardens*, Alice Walker defines a "womanist" as a black feminist or feminist of color who, among other things, is willful, serious, loving, and "committed to survival and wholeness of entire people, male and female." Walker's literary use of this folk expression common in African American communities has become the foundational source for identifying womanist theology. This concept has generated attention from theologians and ethicists because its inherent claims seem to resonate in the plurality of life and faith experiences of black women that are clearly in contradistinction to white feminist cultural, social, and theological perspectives.

At issue in the appropriation of the term "womanist" as a descriptive genre for theology is the power of self-definition or self-naming. Womanist theology is a signification for a theology that permits African American women to define themselves, to embrace and consciously affirm their cultural and religious traditions, and their own embodiment. Thus, womanist theology directly taps into the roots of the historical liberation capability of black women, according to the derivation of Walker's definition.

Informed by biblical, theological, historical, and economic bases, womanist theology searches in particular for the voices, actions, opinions, struggles, and faith of African American women in order to shape a distinctive perspective that takes seriously their experiences and traditions in response to the liberating activity of God. Womanist theology, as a disciplined commentary about the nature of God, intimates a critical posture toward sexism, misogyny, and the objectification and abuse of black women, both within African American communities and within the dominant patriarchal culture. Womanist theology agrees with black theology in its critique of white racism and the need for black unity, and it agrees with feminist theology in its criticism of sexism and the need for the unity of women. Womanist theology moves beyond both by providing its own critique of racism in feminist theology and of sexism in black theology. It also emphasizes the dimension of class analysis since historically most African American women have been poor or are negatively affected by the unequal distribution of capital and gainful employment as a direct consequence of the economic system operative in the United States. Consequently womanist theology must be based on a tridimensional analysis of racism, sexism, and classism.

Furthermore, womanist theology is a particular consequence of the black nationalism inherent in black theology that focuses on womanist concerns. However, materials that convey black women's traditions—narratives, novels, and prayers—only recently have become a primary resource for black theology.

In addition to the social and ecclesial experiences and activities of African American women as points of departure for womanist theology, a distinctive use of the Bible and the role and significance of Jesus uniquely characterizes the womanist tradition. On the one hand those in power have most consistently and effectively used the Bible to restrict and censure the behavior of African American women. On the other hand, the Bible has significantly captured the imagination of African American women because extensive portions of it speak to the deepest aspirations of oppressed people for freedom, dignity, justice, and vindication.

Womanist theology relies on the Bible as a principal resource because of its vision and promise of a world where the humanity of everyone will be fully valued. Womanist theology engages in a liberationist hermeneutical interpretation of the Bible in spite of numerous voices from within and without the Christian tradition that have tried to equivocate on the biblical vision and promises made to oppressed and marginal persons and communities.

The prominence given to Christology by womanist theology discloses a perspective that is congruent with and flows from its liberationist interpretation of biblical revelation. For womanist theology, the humanity, the wholeness of Christ, is paramount, not the maleness of the historical person, Jesus.

This particularly "egalitarian" Christology evokes a womanist commitment to struggle not only with oppressive symptoms that are abundantly extant for African American women within church and society, but also with the causes of pervasive inequality and disenfranchisement. This egalitarian womanist revision yields deeper theological and christological questions related to images and symbolism. Such a Christology challenges womanist theology to forge a distinctively different genre as required by the particular constraints and circumstances in which it finds a locus.

TOINETTE M. EUGENE

Bibliography

Katie G. Cannon, *Black Womanist Ethics.*

Toinette M. Eugene, "Sometimes I Feel Like a Motherless Child: The Call and Response for a Liberational Ethic of Care by Black Feminists," in Mary Brabeck, ed., *Who Cares: Theory, Research, and Educational Implications of the Ethic of Care.*

_____, "Moral Values and Black Womanists," *Journal of Religious Thought* 44, no. 2 (1988): 23-34.

Jacquelyn Grant, *White Women's Christ and Black Women's Jesus: Feminist Christology and Womanist Response.*

Renita J. Weems, *Just a Sister Away: A Womanist Vision of Women's Relationships in the Bible.*

Delores S. Williams, "Womanist Theology" in Judith Plaskow and Carol P. Christ, eds., *Weaving the Visions: New Patterns in Feminist Spirituality,* 179-86.

Cross Reference: Black Theology, Christology, Feminist Theology, Liberation Theology.

WORKS (*See* LAW AND GOSPEL.)

WORSHIP

For Christians, worship is both the praise that people owe God and the means by which God's grace strengthens and guides people. Christians believe that they praise God through Christ and that God's grace has been given them in Christ. Although prayer and devotion may be individual, worship is the work of the church community.

Earliest Christian worship was influenced by worship in the synagogue, but very soon Christian worship began to take on its own distinctive shape. In I Corinthians, Paul describes the nature of worship in a predominantly Gentile congregation. He talks of the practice of the Lord's Supper (I Corinthians 11), indicating that for some, at least, it includes a communal meal, and insisting that for all it should include taking of bread and wine "in remembrance" of Christ's death. Paul also says that the assembly of Christians includes hymns, lessons, speaking in tongues, and interpretation of tongues (I Corinthians 14).

Very early on, the central worship of the congregations took place on Sunday in celebration of Christ's resurrection on the first day of the week. Almost from the beginning, Sunday worship included both the Lord's Supper and some kind of prophecy or proclamation.

As a development in Roman Catholicism, the sacrament of Communion (i.e., the Lord's Supper) was central to worship, with the sermon apparently diminishing in importance. For the Protestant Reformers of the sixteenth century, however, the church was the worshiping community that celebrated the sacraments of baptism and the Lord's Supper and that heard the Word read in scripture and proclaimed in the sermon. Although the developments in worship from the sixteenth century to today have been complicated and somewhat controversial, most Christians—both Catholic and Protestant—would now hold that normative Sunday Christian worship includes Word and sacrament.

The division between more liturgical and less liturgical churches has been in part the division between those communities where the sacrament of the Lord's Supper is stressed as central to worship and those communities where preaching is more central. Since the 1960s the Catholic church has turned from celebrating the mass in Latin to celebrating it in the language of the people, and with that shift Catholic liturgy has often placed increasing stress on scripture and sermon. Many "freer" or less liturgical Protestant churches (e.g., American Baptists, Disciples of Christ, and the United Church of Christ) have deepened their appreciation of the Lord's Supper as central to worship, and Christians concerned for the historical meaning of worship have urged more regular observance of the Supper.

Although most Christian churches agree that there are at least two sacraments (and Catholic and Orthodox Christians affirm more), there remains considerable diversity in understanding the meaning of the sacraments and considerable diversity in sacramental practice. Most Christians hold to the sacrament of baptism

513

as that rite which brings people into the church. Some churches immerse the new Christian in water; others sprinkle or pour water over the candidate's head. Drawing on biblical sources, Christians believe that baptism represents the believer's repentance, as he or she dies to sin and rises again to new life. Most Christians, seeing baptism as a sign of God's grace, are willing to baptize infants. Other Christians (including Baptists and Disciples of Christ), seeing baptism primarily as a sign of the believer's faith, reserve baptism for those who are old enough to choose baptism for themselves. For all Christians, however, baptism involves both God's initiative and the response of faith, but the emphasis is different in different communities.

As part of the worship of churches, baptism is celebrated at various times in the church year, but traditionally churches have encouraged baptism at Easter time. And in the sacrament of baptism worshipers reaffirm their own baptismal promises, and they pledge to nurture the newly baptized Christians as they grow in faith.

In celebrating the Lord's Supper, the biblical words of institution (where Jesus says of the bread and wine, "This is my body, . . . this is my blood") are interpreted very differently among Christians and among churches. Some Christians believe that the bread and wine become Christ's body and blood in the sacrament, without ceasing to be bread and wine. Some believe that bread and wine are symbols to help Christians remember the Last Supper and Christ's death. Some believe that Christ is present at the table, but not "in" the bread and wine. For most Christians, however, the Lord's Supper is a time of "eucharist," or thanksgiving, for God's gifts. It is a time of "communion," when Christians are joined to one another and to God. The sacrament looks forward to the full coming of God's reign, which scripture imagines as a banquet of all faithful people.

Preaching the Word, which together with the sacrament of the Lord's Supper constitutes most Christian worship, is usually the interpretation of scripture for the congregation and its members.

Although other elements of worship have not been recognized theologically in the same way that sacrament and word have, they are often nearly as central to the worship of Christians. Music provides the opportunity to praise God, often drawing on the great biblical tradition of the psalms. In many churches, choirs, organs, and instruments are part of the worship. In almost all churches the congregation voices its praise and faith through hymns.

Both baptism and the Lord's Supper traditionally include prayer as part of the celebration, but other prayers also are typical of Christian worship. In recent years there has been some tendency to find ways to make these prayers "of the people" rather than prayers "for the people," but a variety of styles and forms remains alive and lively.

Although the service of Word and sacraments is the heart of worship for many

Christians, other Christians worship in quite different ways. For many members of the Society of Friends, worship is a quiet waiting on the Spirit's leading, without sacrament or official sermon. For Pentecostal Christians, speaking in tongues is a sign of God's presence and a means of praise. Christians in the various Eastern Orthodox communions often include processionals in their worship, and they use icons—holy pictures and images—as visual signs of God's goodness.

For many Christians worship is further shaped by the church year, which begins at Advent (as Christians await the season of Christ's birth) and moves through the great times of preparation and festival. Worship is also celebrated at crucial moments in the life of a believer or community, especially in wedding and funeral services.

In many Christian churches, other weekly services besides the Sunday gathering of the congregation provide opportunities for worship that praises God and edifies the faithful.

DAVID L. BARTLETT

Bibliography

J. G. Davies, ed., *The New Westminster Dictionary of Liturgy and Worship*.
Cheslyn Jones, Geoffrey Wainwright, and Edward Yarnold, eds., *The Study of Liturgy*.
Frank C. Senn, *Christian Worship and Its Cultural Setting*.
James F. White, *Introduction to Christian Worship*.

Cross Reference: Homiletics, Liturgical Movement, Sacraments/Sacramental Theology, Silence, Vatican II.

NOTES ON THE CONTRIBUTORS

John D. Barbour teaches at St. Olaf College, Northfield, Minnesota. *Tragedy*

Elizabeth Barnes teaches at Baptist Theological Seminary, Richmond, Virginia. *Ordination*

David L. Bartlett teaches at Yale Divinity School, Yale University, New Haven, Connecticut. *Worship*

William A. Beardslee teaches at the School of Theology, Claremont University, Claremont, California. *Biblical Criticism*

Philip Berryman is an independent scholar in Philadelphia, Pennsylvania. *CELAM II*

Leonard J. Biallas teaches at Quincy College, Quincy, Illinois. *Dogmatic Theology*

Donald G. Bloesch teaches at Dubuque Theological Seminary, University of Dubuque, Dubuque, Iowa. *Evangelicalism*

José Míguez Bonino teaches at the Facultad Evangelica de Teologia, Buenos Aires, Argentina. *Secularity*

Larry D. Bouchard teaches at the University of Virginia, Charlottesville, Virginia. *Culture*

Carl E. Braaten teaches at the Lutheran School of Theology at Chicago, Chicago, Illinois. *Revelation*

Jerald C. Brauer previously taught at The Divinity School, The University of Chicago, Chicago, Illinois. *Kingdom of God*

Frank Burch Brown teaches at Virginia Polytechnic Institute and State University, Blacksburg, Virginia. *Aesthetics*

Robert McAfee Brown previously taught at Stanford University, Palo Alto, California. *Soul/Body*

David B. Burrell teaches at the University of Notre Dame, Notre Dame, Indiana. *Metaphysics*

Denise Lardner Carmody teaches at the University of Tulsa, Tulsa, Oklahoma. *Papacy*

James H. Charlesworth teaches at Princeton Theological Seminary, Princeton, New Jersey. *Judaism*

Rebecca S. Chopp teaches at the Candler School of Theology, Emory University, Atlanta, Georgia. *Feminist Theology*

John Clayton teaches at Lancaster University, Lancaster, United Kingdom. *Correlation*

John B. Cobb, Jr., teaches at the School of Theology, Claremont University, Claremont, California. *Economics*

Martin L. Cook teaches at Santa Clara University, Santa Clara, California. *Confessional Theology*

John P. Crossley, Jr., teaches at the University of Southern California, Los Angeles, California. *Liberalism*

Lawrence S. Cunningham teaches at the University of Notre Dame, Notre Dame, Indiana. *Vatican II*

Charles Curran teaches at Southern Methodist University, Dallas, Texas. *Moral Theology*

Lois K. Daly teaches at Siena College, Loudonville, New York. *Ecology*

William Dean teaches at Gustavus Adolphus College, St. Peter, Minnesota. *Being/Becoming, Empirical Theology*

James J. DiCenso teaches in the Department of Religious Studies, University of Toronto, Toronto, Canada. *Time*

John Dillenberger teaches at the Graduate Theological Union, Berkeley, California. *Faith*

Toinette M. Eugene teaches at Chicago Theological Seminary, Chicago, Illinois. *Womanist Theology*

James H. Evans, Jr., is President of Colgate Rochester/Crozier/Bexley Hall Seminaries, Rochester, New York. *Black Theology*

Clyde Fant teaches at Stetson University, DeLand, Florida. *Homiletics*

Edward Farley teaches at Vanderbilt University, Nashville, Tennessee. *Phenomenology*

Darrell J. Fasching teaches at the University of South Florida, Tampa, Florida. *Idolatry, Technology*

Frederick Ferré teaches at the University of Georgia, Athens, Georgia. *Atheism*

John T. Ford teaches at The Catholic University of America, Washington, D.C. *Roman Catholicism*

Gerhard O. Forde teaches at Luther Northwestern Theological Seminary, St. Paul, Minnesota. *Justification*

Ismael García teaches at Austin Theological Seminary, Austin, Texas. *Praxis*

Donald L. Gelpi teaches at the Jesuit School of Theology, Berkeley, California. *Celibacy*

Mary Gerhart teaches at Hobart and William Smith Colleges, Geneva, New York. *Myth*

Langdon Gilkey previously taught at The Divinity School, The University of Chicago, Chicago, Illinois. *Creation, God, Neoorthodoxy*

Jerry H. Gill teaches at The College of St. Rose, Albany, New York. *Language–Religious*

David J. Gouwens teaches at the Brite Divinity School, Texas Christian University, Fort Worth, Texas. *Heresy*

Garrett Green teaches at Connecticut College, New London, Connecticut. *Imagination*

David Ray Griffin teaches at the School of Theology, Claremont University, Claremont, California. *Process Theology*

Ronald L. Grimes teaches at Wilfrid Laurier University, Waterloo, Ontario. *Ritual*

Lora Gross teaches at Pacific Lutheran University, Seattle, Washington. *Holy Spirit*

Christine Gudorf teaches at Xavier University, Cincinnati, Ohio. *Sexuality*

William Hamilton previously taught at Portland State University, Portland, Oregon. *Death of God Theology*

Stephen Happel teaches at The Catholic University of America, Washington, D.C. *Priesthood*

Stanley Hauerwas teaches at The Divinity School, Duke University, Durham, North Carolina. *Ethics–Christian*

Brian Hebblethwaite teaches at Cambridge University, Cambridge, England. *Incarnation*

Monika K. Hellwig teaches at Georgetown University, Washington, D.C. *Christology*

William L. Hendricks teaches at The Southern Baptist Theological Seminary, Louisville, Kentucky. *Symbol*

Frederick Herzog teaches at The Divinity School, Duke University, Durham, North Carolina. *Freedom*

Glenn Hewitt teaches at Maryville College, Maryville, Tennessee. *Sanctification*

Harold Hewitt, Jr., is Vice-President of Finance at Whittier College, Whittier, California. *Death and Eternal Life*

E. Glenn Hinson teaches at The Southern Baptist Theological Seminary, Louisville, Kentucky. *Tradition*

Peter C. Hodgson teaches at The Divinity School, Vanderbilt University, Nashville, Tennessee. *Providence*

Jeffery Hopper teaches at the Methodist Theological School in Ohio, Delaware, Ohio. *Soteriology*

Thomas E. Hosinski teaches at the University of Portland, Portland, Oregon. *Epistemology, Insight*

Conrad Hyers teaches at Gustavus Adolphus College, St. Peter, Minnesota. *Comedy*

Thomas A. Idinopulos teaches at Miami University, Miami, Ohio. *Eastern Orthodox Christianity*

Werner G. Jeanrond teaches at the University of Dublin, Dublin, Ireland. *Theological Method*

Arthur H. Jentz, Jr., teaches at Hope College, Holland, Michigan. *Ultimate Concern*

Patrick R. Keifert teaches at Luther Northwestern Theological Seminary, St. Paul, Minnesota. *Law and Gospel*

Michael Kinnamon is Academic Dean at Lexington Theological Seminary, Lexington, Kentucky. *Ecumenism*

Lonnie D. Kliever teaches at Perkins School of Theology, Southern Methodist University, Dallas, Texas. *Experience–Religious*

Kosuke Koyama teaches at Union Theological Seminary, New York City. *Missiology*

John H. Leith teaches at Union Theological Seminary, Richmond, Virginia. *Ecclesiology*

D. Stephen Long is Director of Continuing Education at The Divinity School, Duke University, Durham, North Carolina. *Ethics–Christian*

Robin W. Lovin is Dean at Drew Theological Seminary, Madison, New Jersey. *Justice*

Dennis P. McCann teaches at DePaul University, Chicago, Illinois. *Marxist Theology*

John McCarthy teaches at Loyola University, Chicago, Illinois. *Hermeneutics, Metaphor*

James Wm. McClendon, Jr., is Distinguished Scholar-in-Residence, Fuller Theological Seminary, Pasadena, California. *Sin*

David McKenzie teaches at Berry College, Rome, Georgia. *Miracles*

Donald K. McKim previously taught at Dubuque Theological Seminary, University of Dubuque, Dubuque, Iowa. *Authority*

John Macquarrie previously taught at Oxford University, Oxford, England. *Systematic Theology*

William Madges teaches at Xavier University, Cincinnati, Ohio. *Love*

Otto Maduro teaches at Maryknoll School of Theology, Maryknoll, New York. *Liberation Theology*

Martin E. Marty teaches at The Divinity School, The University of Chicago, Chicago, Illinois. *Grace, Protestantism*

James A. Mathisen teaches at Wheaton College, Wheaton, Illinois. *Civil Religion*

M. Douglas Meeks is Dean at Wesley Theological Seminary, Washington, D.C. *Political Theology*

Patrick D. Miller teaches at Princeton Theological Seminary, Princeton, New Jersey. *Biblical Theology*

Watson E. Mills teaches at Mercer University, Macon, Georgia. *Pentecostalism*

Jürgen Moltmann teaches at the University of Tübingen, Tübingen, Germany. *Hope*

David L. Mueller teaches at The Southern Baptist Theological Seminary, Louisville, Kentucky. *Natural Theology*

Nancey Murphy teaches at Fuller Theological Seminary, Pasadena, California. *Paradigm, Philosophical Theology*

Donald W. Musser teaches at Stetson University, DeLand, Florida. *Creation Science*

Richard John Neuhaus directs The Institute on Religion and Public Life, New York, New York. *The Hartford Appeal*

Douglas F. Ottati teaches at Union Theological Seminary, Richmond, Virginia. *Social Gospel*

521

Ruth Page is Associate Dean at the University of Edinburgh, Edinburgh, Scotland. *Ambiguity*

Thomas D. Parker teaches at McCormick Theological Seminary, Chicago, Illinois. *Covenant*

Garrett E. Paul teaches at Gustavus Adolphus College, St. Peter, Minnesota. *Basic Christian Communities*

William C. Placher teaches at Wabash College, Crawfordsville, Indiana. *Postmodern Theology*

David Polk is Editor of Chalice Press, St. Louis, Missouri. *Practical Theology*

Mary Potter Engel teaches at United Theological Seminary, New Brighton, Minnesota. *Election*

James R. Price III teaches at The Catholic University of America, Washington, D.C. *Mysticism*

Joseph L. Price teaches at Whittier College, Whittier, California. *Silence*

Carl Raschke teaches at the University of Denver, Denver, Colorado. *Deconstructionism*

F. William Ratliff teaches at Midwestern Baptist Theological Seminary, Kansas City, Missouri. *Apologetics*

Mitchell G. Reddish teaches at Stetson University, DeLand, Florida. *Inspiration*

Jack Rogers is Vice-President and Professor of Theology at San Francisco Theological Seminary. *Inerrancy*

Holmes Rolston III teaches at Colorado State University, Fort Collins, Colorado. *Science and Christianity*

Robert John Russell teaches at The Graduate Theological Union, Berkeley, California. *Cosmology*

Don E. Saliers teaches at the Candler School of Theology, Emory University, Atlanta, Georgia. *Spirituality*

Robert P. Scharlemann teaches at the University of Virginia, Charlottesville, Virginia. *Autonomy*

Hans Schwarz teaches at the University of Regensburg, Regensburg, Germany. *Eschatology, Transcendence*

William Schweiker teaches at The Divinity School, The University of Chicago, Chicago, Illinois. *Society*

Eduard Schweizer teaches at the University of Zürich, Zürich, Switzerland. *Resurrection*

Nathan A. Scott, Jr., previously taught at the University of Virginia, Charlottesville, Virginia. *Humanism*

William M. Shea is Professor and Chairman, Dept. of Theological Studies, St. Louis University, St. Louis, Missouri. *Naturalism*

John C. Shelley teaches at Furman University, Greenville, South Carolina. *Existential Philosophy*

Ninian Smart teaches at the University of California, Santa Barbara, California. *Pluralism*

Dorothee Soelle previously taught at Union Theological Seminary, New York, New York. *Suffering*

Frank Anthony Spina teaches at The School of Religion, Seattle Pacific University, Seattle, Washington. *Canon*

Ronald H. Stone teaches at Pittsburgh Theological Seminary, Pittsburgh, Pennsylvania. *Peace/Peacemaking*

Charles R. Strain teaches at DePaul University, Chicago, Illinois. *Alienation*

George W. Stroup teaches at Columbia Theological Seminary, Decatur, Georgia. *Narrative Theology*

Marjorie Hewitt Suchocki teaches at the School of Theology, Claremont University, Claremont, California. *Panentheism*

D. Dixon Sutherland teaches at Stetson University, DeLand, Florida. *Space*

Charles Taliaferro teaches at St. Olaf College, Northfield, Minnesota. *Theism*

Mark Kline Taylor teaches at Princeton Theological Seminary, Princeton, New Jersey. *Anthropology, Liminality*

Eugene Teselle teaches at The Divinity School, Vanderbilt University, Nashville, Tennessee. *Atonement*

Susan Thistlethwaite teaches at Chicago Theological Seminary, Chicago, Illinois. *Institutionalized Violence*

William Vance Trollinger, Jr., teaches at Messiah College, Grantham, Pennsylvania. *Fundamentalism*

Peter Van Ness teaches at Union Theological Seminary, New York, New York. *Agnosticism*

Dan O. Via teaches at The Divinity School, Duke University, Durham, North Carolina. *Structuralism*

Geoffrey Wainwright teaches at The Divinity School, Duke University, Durham, North Carolina. *Sacraments/Sacramental Theology*

Sylvia I. Walsh teaches at Stetson University, DeLand, Florida. *Paradox*

Timothy P. Weber teaches at Denver Conservative Baptist Seminary, Denver, Colorado. *Dispensationalism*

Claude Welch teaches at The Graduate Theological Union, Berkeley, California. *Trinity*

James F. White teaches at the University of Notre Dame, Notre Dame, Indiana. *Liturgical Movement*

James B. Wiggins teaches at Syracuse University, Syracuse, New York. *Religion*

Robert L. Wilken teaches at the University of Virginia, Charlottesville, Virginia. *Historical Theology*

Peter W. Williams teaches at Miami University, Miami, Ohio. *Popular Religion*

Clark M. Williamson teaches at Christian Theological Seminary, Indianapolis, Indiana. *Holocaust*

William H. Willimon is Dean of the Chapel and teaches at Duke University, Durham, North Carolina. *Laity*

James P. Wind is Program Director for Religion at the Lilly Endowment, Indianapolis, Indiana. *Health*

Patricia L. Wismer teaches at Seattle University, Seattle, Washington. *Evil*

Lee Yearley teaches at Stanford University, Palo Alto, California. *Virtue*